Dimensions of Irish Terrorism

The International Library of Terrorism

Series Editors:
Yonah Alexander and Alan O'Day

Titles in the Series:

Terrorism: British Perspectives
Paul Wilkinson

Dimensions of Irish Terrorism
Alan O'Day

European Terrorism
Edward Moxon-Browne

Terrorism in Africa
Martha Crenshaw

Middle East Terrorism: Current Threats and Future Prospects
Yonah Alexander

Dimensions of Irish Terrorism

Edited by
Alan O'Day
University of North London and Concordia University, Montreal

G.K. Hall & Co.
An Imprint of Macmillan Publishing Company
New York

Maxwell Macmillan Canada
Toronto

This American edition published in 1994 by G.K. Hall & Co.
An Imprint of Macmillan Publishing Company

G.K. Hall & Co.
An Imprint of Macmillan Publishing Company
866 Third Avenue
New York, NY 10022

Maxwell Macmillan Canada, Inc.
1200 Eglinton Avenue East, Suite 200
Don Mills, Ontario M3C 3N1

First published in Great Britain by
Dartmouth Publishing Company Limited
Gower House
Croft Road
Aldershot
Hampshire GU11 3HR
England

Macmillan Publishing Company is part of the Maxwell Communication Group of Companies.

Library of Congress Catalog Card Number: 93-38372

PRINTED IN GREAT BRITAIN

printing number
1 2 3 4 5 6 7 8 9 10

Library of Congress Cataloging-in-Publication Data
Dimensions of Irish terrorism / edited by Alan O'Day.
    p.   cm. -- (International library of terrorism : 2)
    Includes index.
    ISBN 0-8161-7338-9 (alk. paper)
    1. Terrorism-- Northern Ireland. 2. Northern Ireland--Social
conditions. 3. Northern Ireland---Politics and government. 4. Great
Britain--Politics and government. I. O'Day, Alan. II. Series.
HV6431.I546 1994 vol. 2
[HV6433.G7]   93-38372
303.6'25'09416--dc20   CIP

The paper used in this publication meets the minimum requirements of American National Standard
for Information Sciences—Permanence of Paper for Printed Library Materials.
ANSI Z39.48—194.∞™
ISBN 0-8161-7338-9

Contents

PART IV   RESPONSES TO TERRORISM

The Question of Individual and Public Rights

Official and Public Reaction to Terrorism

Acknowledgements

The Editor and publishers wish to thank the following for permission to use copyright material.

The Army Quarterly and Defence Journal for the essay: Major K.O. Fox (1976), 'Capital Punishment and Terrorist Murder: The Continuing Debate', *Army Quarterly and Defence Journal*, **106**, pp. 189–93. Army Quarterly and Defence Journal is published at 1 West Street, Tavistock, Devon, PL19 8DS.

Blackwell Publishers for essays: Charles Carlton (1981), 'Judging Without Consensus: The Diplock Courts in Northern Ireland', *Law and Policy Quarterly*, **3**, pp. 225–42, and Birthe Jorgensen (1982), 'Defending the Terrorists: Queen's Counsel before the Courts of Northern Ireland', *Journal of Law & Society*, **9**, pp. 115–26.

Conflict Quarterly for essays: Arthur Aughey (1985), 'Between Exclusion and Recognition: The Politics of the Ulster Defence Association', *Conflict Quarterly*, **1**, pp. 40–52; Colin J. McIlheney (1985), 'Arbiters of Ulster's Destiny? The Military Role of the Protestant Paramilitaries in Northern Ireland', *Conflict Quarterly*, **5**, pp. 33–40, and Bruce Warner (1987), 'Extradition Law and Practice in the Crucible of Ulster, Ireland and Great Britain: A Metamorphosis?', *Conflict Quarterly*, **7**, pp. 57–92. Copyright © Centre for Conflict Studies, University of New Brunswick.

FBI Law Enforcement Bulletin for the essay: J.L. Stone Jr. (1987), 'Irish Terrorism Investigations', *FBI Law Enforcement Bulletin*, pp. 18–23.

Frank Cass & Co. Ltd for the essay: Jeffrey Archer (1984), 'Constitutionalism and Violence: The Case of Ireland', *Journal of Commonwealth and Comparative Politics*, **22**, pp. 111–27. Reprinted by permission from the twenty-second issue of the Journal of Commonwealth and Comparative Politics published by Frank Cass & Co. Ltd, 11 Gainsborough Road, London E11, England. Copyright © Frank Cass & Co. Ltd.

History of Childhood Quarterly for the essay: Rona M. Fields (1975), 'Psychological Genocide: The Children of Northern Ireland', *History of Childhood Quarterly*, **3**, pp. 201–24.

Journal of International Affairs for the essay: Paul Bew and Henry Patterson (1982), 'The Protestant-Catholic Conflict in Ulster', *Journal of International Affairs*, **36**, pp. 223–34.

Journal of Political Science for the essay: Edward P. Moxon-Browne (1986), 'Alienation: The Case of the Catholics in Northern Ireland', *Journal of Political Science*, **14**, pp. 74–88.

Medico–Legal Journal for the essay: R.A. Hall (1975), 'Violence and its Effects on the Community', *Medico–Legal Journal*, **43**, pp. 89–100.

Notre Dame Law Review for the essay: David R. Lowry (1977), 'Terrorism and Human Rights: Counter-Insurgency and Necessity at Common Law', *Notre Dame Lawyer*, **53**, pp. 49–89. Volume 53, Issue 1, *Notre Dame Lawyer* (October 1977) 49–89. Reprinted with permission. Copyright © by Notre Dame Law Review, University of Notre Dame.

Oxford University Press for the essay: Robert J. Spjut (1983), 'Criminal Statistics and Statistics on Security in Northern Ireland', *British Journal of Criminology*, **23**, pp. 358–80.

Plenum Publishing Corporation for the essay: William Ascher (1986), 'The Moralism of Attitudes Supporting Intergroup Violence', *Political Psychology*, **7**, pp. 403–25.

Royal United Services Institute for Defence Studies for the essay: David A. Charters (1977), 'Intelligence and Psychological Warfare Operations in Northern Ireland', *Journal of the Royal Services Institute for Defence Studies*, **122**, pp. 22–7.

Sociological Focus for the essay: James A. Schellenberg (1977), 'Area Variations of Violence in Northern Ireland', *Sociological Focus*, **10**, pp. 69–78.

The Yale Journal of World Public Order for the essay: Thomas P. Foley (1987), 'Public Security and Individual Freedom: The Dilemma of Northern Ireland', *The Yale Journal of World Public Order*, **8**, pp. 284–324.

Every effort has been made to trace all the copyright holders, but if any have been inadvertently overlooked the publishers will be pleased to make the necessary arrangement at the first opportunity.

Series Preface

The International Library of Terrorism puts into book form a wide range of important and influential academic articles on contemporary terrorist political violence. The articles were initially published in English-language journals or have previously appeared in English. Each volume in the Library is devoted to a specific geographical region which has been afflicted by political terrorism during the past two decades.

Political terrorism has been a concern of national policy in numerous states and received the attention of international bodies including the United Nations. At the same time it has gripped public imagination, on occasion causing disruption in patterns of transnational tourism or influenced international investment decisions. Not surprisingly political terrorism has found a place in the academic programmes of universities and other educational establishments. In the present series no line of inquiry or ideological outlook is deliberately favoured or excluded - the aim of the Library is to constitute a useful and representative sampling of quality work on terrorism. As the contributions are drawn from previously published studies in periodicals this imposes perimeters on the sorts of material included. All volumes then have an incompleteness resulting from lacuna in the literature. Nevertheless, the series aims to bring into wider accessibility materials scattered through many periodicals, some having only limited circulations. Indeed, in no volume can all of the articles selected be located in a single repository including even the great national and famous university libraries of Great Britain and North America.

Each volume's articles have been chosen by a recognized authority on the political terrorism of the region. In no instance does the omission of a specific article or category of material imply a value judgement for the selection process has been governed by relevance to a theme, space and similar considerations. The general editors are grateful to the individuals who compiled each book and prepared the introductions. Their efforts and scholarly judgement are the cornerstone of the series. We wish to express our thanks to John Irwin of Dartmouth Publishing Company, from whom the idea of the Library originally sprang, and who brought the project through some dark hours to fruition. Also, we appreciate the kindly efforts of Sonia Hubbard and at the development stage of the project the assistance of Christoph Mühlberg and Geneviève Schauinger.

YONAH ALEXANDER
The George Washington University
Washington DC

ALAN O'DAY
University of North London, England
and Concordia University, Montreal, Canada

Introduction

For more than two decades terrorism emanating from Northern Ireland's status as a part of the United Kingdom has been a constant feature of everyday life. Northern Ireland unquestionably belongs to the list of places where two or more ethnic or religious groups lay claim to the same territorial or social space. What is unusual about the situation is neither the violence nor ethnic rivalry but the location of the troubles. It is situated in Western Europe where such troubles if not unknown are not normally so extended or vicious in the post-1945 era. Moreover, Northern Ireland is part of a great economically advanced liberal-democratic state. In Northern Ireland as well democratic norms, albeit with some modifications, have functioned throughout the period of violence. Since August 1969 when the British military was dispatched to the province to aid in the maintenance of order the state has been in a stage of semi-seige, the police operating as a para-military force. The violence is exceptional in another, often overlooked respect. There is simply no precedent for the intensity or time span of the present-day difficulty.

Over the years the Irish problem has attracted the attention of the media and roused public feeling both in Northern Ireland and elsewhere. It has been subjected to vigorous investigation from academics drawn from many specialisms including, for instance, political scientists, historians, economists, sociologists, social anthropologists and psychologists to name but some of the more obvious. The province has served as a remarkable laboratory for academics seeking to explore the causation and management of terrorism. Despite the intra-communal animosity, all parties there have been welcoming to outsiders seeking to see the situation at first hand. Northern Ireland is geographically accessible and allows those who wish for a whiff of danger to satisfy their curiosity in relative comfort and safety. Moreover, the people speak English and there are few impediments to securing open access to information. Northern Ireland, then, has been one of the, if not the, most written about trouble-spots in the contemporary world. Some of that writing is polemical but the crisis has spawned a richly varied literature, much being of impressive quality reaching a remarkable level of impartiality. The current volume, part of a larger series with a common objective, seeks to bring a range of important work on dimensions of terrorism and political violence to a wider audience. Obviously the material available is so extensive that only a small selection can be included though it is intended that the sample be representative in terms of topics and interpretations. The articles break down into broad categories including the causation of violence, participants in terrorist activity, the impact of terrorism, and responses to the crisis. Both republican and loyalist terrorism are considered, though the latter receives more attention than sometimes has been the case.

All of the contributions display evidence of being informed by Ireland's past and by the relationship of the island with Great Britain. That history, that continued sense of subjugation of one section of the peoples of Ireland, helps account for the alienation of a portion of the population and also why terrorists have been able to win a measure of public support. But Irish problems are understood not through one collective memory but through several contradictory ones. Where historical knowledge has been of limited utility is in providing satisfactory reasons for the intensity of the current phase of violence. Grievances and tensions between communities does not inevitably lead to combat. Indeed, the history of Ireland's internal relations and of the country's linkage to Great Britain suggests that rhetoric and peaceful agitation rather than ferocious terrorism were the more regular mode of disputation. Inkshed has played a far more important role than bloodshed in Irish disputes.

In a well-understood way, though, the past, one with an unfinished revolution, has influenced the present. During the nineteenth and early twentieth centuries the majority of the island's people, mainly Catholics, sought to reorder their disadvantaged status at home while at the same time to win as much autonomy as possible for the nation. Most Protestants saw things differently; they viewed autonomy as a danger which must be thwarted. In nearly all parts of the island Catholics constituted an overwhelming majority; Protestants in the southern provinces formed only very localized pluralities. The North-east, however, proved exceptional in several ways. It was more industrialized, more thriving and certainly more Protestant. In that region, particularly in the territory now comprising Northern Ireland, they were in a majority. Gradually, even haltingly, these north-east Protestants asserted a claim to distinct identity and separation from the rest of Ireland should a self-government regime ever be established in Dublin. Their assertion was always contentious. Nationalists rejected it out of hand as Charles Stewart Parnell did in 1886; British leaders frequently showed little sympathy for Ulster. Ulster separatists had a case to prove for neither they nor the province had ever been distinguished from the rest of Ireland except in minor details. By 1914 it was apparent that the country would receive self-government and that part of Ulster at least would be exempted from its authority. Then the Great War interrupted the Irish debate. In the aftermath of the conflict Ireland joined the many new states of Europe which rose from the disintegration of empires. But, it was not one, but two new Ireland's which came into existence between 1920 and 1922. In 1920 the state of Northern Ireland, still part of the United Kingdom, received a Parliament located at Stormont for its own local affairs. In 1922 a second, and larger, Irish regime was established in Dublin.

Both new states were born in controversy. Existence of two states was a formative aspect of that controversy. The northern regime was particularly vulnerable. It lacked legitimacy or even assured boundaries. Moreover, it contained a very substantial bloc of Catholics amounting to approximately one-third of the whole population who mostly declined to give their allegiance to the new avowedly Protestant and Unionist regime. The rulers of Northern Ireland perceived this minority to be a hostile element and took steps to insure its exclusion from power and influence. In the 1960s a new generation of Unionists sought to moderate the face of discrimination in Northern Ireland and a Civil Rights Movement arose to seek the dismantling of the barriers to equality altogether. The Civil Rights campaign, Unionist acts to repel it, and the rise of a revived I.R.A. to defend Catholics have been examined from numerous angles. There is nothing in the Civil Rights platform or movement which suggested two decades of terrorism would succeed it. In fact, the protests of the late 1960s were consistent with the long history of Irish agitations and like many before it, this one swiftly advanced the objective of equal treatment. Similarly, the Unionist response to the Civil Rights campaign was something of a nasty knee-jerk, in tune with short-lived violence in the past. Again there was little hint of longer-term terrorism. The third player in the drama, British government, too acted as it had in the past, as a regulator of communal relations. It was not extraordinarily brutal, wicked or negligent, if at times unwise, during the unfolding of the conflict between 1968 and 1972.

Violence, in order to be perpetuated in Northern Ireland, requires compelling grievances, acceptance to some degree of its legitimacy and utility, mechanisms for recruiting and maintaining its agents, and a network of responses from proponents of peace which fail to undermine the authority of terrorists. Employing an array of perspectives, the bulk of the articles assess why the violence once begun has continued, who takes up arms as a terrorist in both communities, the means of sustaining support for the struggle, the implications of violence on society and how different groups in Northern Ireland and in the outside world have responded to the crisis.

It is clear that the troubles originated from the widely held sense of injustice in the Catholic community. This undoubted sense of grievance arose from an inferior status reinforced by informal and formal practices. Catholics were discriminated against in employment, housing, electoral rights, recognition of their own symbols while the policing and judicial apparatus was seen as directed towards keeping them down. Public opinion outside Northern Ireland and governmental reports and commissions endorsed the essence of Catholic claims. Since the 1960s the fabric of legal discrimination has been overhauled and abolished; informal barriers have proved more resistant to change. Locational factors along with skill levels still affect the sectarian pattern of employment; residential preferences have insured more segregated housing than existed in 1968 and Catholics have shown little disposition to join the police which remains a largely Protestant force. Despite evidence of fairer play, Catholics retain their profound disillusionment with the northern state and continue to seek eventual incorporation into an all-island nation.

With so much water for the fish, it is imperative to discover who joins terrorist organizations and how many in the community are routinely exposed to violence. Clearly, widespread disapproval of the Northern Ireland regime in the Catholic community has not led to a general insurrection. Only a small number of those in the minority community have ever joined organizations prepared to use violence. Most members have been young males, frequently from working class orgins. Those inclined towards terrorism usually are drawn from families and associational groups with a history of involvement in the Republican movement. Absence of a completed social base has had significant implications for nationalist terrorists. Although opinion surveys have indicated a broader support for some Republican activism, respectable Catholics, the natural leaders of their community, have distanced themselves from the advocates of violence. Terrorists have not at any point been able to establish a claim to be the genuine voice of the Catholic people. Electoral results in Northern Ireland have upheld the authority of moderate nationalism. Likewise, Loyalist groups resorting to violence have never appealed to more than a tiny segment of the Protestants of the north. Because most Protestants view themselves as constitutionalists and as upholders of the existing state, few have been ready to sanction a counter terror. Loyalist terrorists, though able to kill and maim, have not often attempted to extend their operations.

Since the beginning of the terrorist offensive the actual level of incidents has ebbed and flowed. A high point in the numerical toll of terrorism was reached in the mid-1970s though unsurges in the early 1980s and again late in that decade and at the beginning of the

1990s stand as pertinent reminders of the ever-present nature of the virus. Just as certain moments have seen very high levels of terrorism, some districts receive numerous attacks, others very few. On the whole people residing in Belfast and the areas close to the border with the Republic of Ireland are several times more likely to be victims than people in quiet places. Members of the security forces also bear an unusual burden of risk. Part-time former and present special police have proved to be vulnerable. Catholics living in north Belfast have been favoured as targets of Loyalist terrorists. To the outside world Northern Ireland has appeared as a society at war but the reality is that terrorism is much more confined in terms of place, time and people at risk. Property rather than people has been particularly threatened. Some articles give attention to which people are most likely to experience the effects of violence. Northern Ireland's people have displayed higher than normal psychological disorders as a consequence of the atmosphere of fear. Children in the province have shown a tendency to deviate from conventional psychological profiles, to display symptoms of disorder. While the longer-term ramifications of violence are not fully evident, there must be an expectation that a society where terrorism is endemic over many years will also have high levels of mental illness. Yet, excepting political violence, Northern Ireland has retained its place as among the communities least prone to ordinary criminality in the developed world. In this instance political violence has not spurred a general breakdown of society in its day-to-day activities.

As many of the articles note, terrorism in Northern Ireland has been mainly about gaining psychological and propaganda advantages rather than injuring or killing people. In most ethnic or religious trouble-spots one side usually aims to physically displace its rival. Although all sides in Northern Ireland pursue approaches likely to result in segregation of communities, none has assumed that in the end one side or the other will be physically removed from the province. Instead what is at stake is the future of the present political state and the relationships of peoples when that regime is altered or ceases to exist. The assumption of the continuation of a society with two different communities necessarily means that violence is a tactical instrument not a solution. Persuasion, if of an unpleasant kind, rather than genocide is the main intention, at least for all but the fanatical fringe of Republican or Loyalist militants. However, neither Republicans nor Loyalist groups employing terrorism believe they are waging a campaign which is apt to be successful in convincing the other side in Northern Ireland itself – the main thrust is to influence British Government of the hopelessness of continued involvement in the case of Republicans or outside opinion in the instance of both camps. By winning the propaganda war or neutralizing the efforts of the opposition both sides believe they can attain their objects. Terrorism, then, can be said to be propaganda by the deed in the Irish circumstance.

Terrorism studies have taken a special interest in the forms of resistance which both the State and individuals have thrown up to ward off its impact. Those techniques have included the improved mechanisms of making public opinion heard, development of fresh tactics, changes in legal procedures and innovations in traditional forms of information gathering or intelligence. Several articles consider the differing responses to terrorism over time and look at how political violence has induced new thinking. Liberal-democratic regimes have had to be sensitive to violations to human rights – when these have been transgressed otherside bodies have not been slow to react. Thus, the State has had to conform to guidelines of its own making and of others expectations for it. Overall Great

Britain has been adaptive and managed the conflict with increasing skill. But it has never been able to meet the challenge of terrorism without constant criticism, a luxury available to authoritarian regimes. Through conducting an open and justifiable campaign against terrorism British Governments have hoped to convince the world-at-large of the legitimacy of its case. This is another reminder that neither terrorism nor states seeking to thwart political violence have been able to treat the problem in isolation. Great Britain's quest to quell disorder in Northern Ireland has been undertaken within a framework of wider and more important national interests. Britain's attempts to assert the legitimacy of its response and of Northern Ireland's existence, has encouraged efforts to gain cooperation from other country's in detaining terrorist suspects, in extradition proceedings, limiting the flow of arms, funds and propaganda and in securing access to intelligence on Irish groups working abroad. In all areas it has enjoyed some success, notably during the 1980s and 90s.

Although Great Britain has been marvellously inventive in forging its way in the Irish thicket, it also has achieved no more than a stalemate in Northern Ireland. Terrorism remains a continuing problem on the ground there and no breakthrough in community relations seems likely to end the bloodletting during the current decade. British governments, though still ready to encourage political initiatives, have settled into a pattern of acceptance of a certain level of terrorism. The main thrust of policy has been directed to containing the volume and restraining its application to the territory of Northern Ireland. Though substantially successful, incidents on the British mainland reveal that the stalemate in Northern Ireland is not the same thing as a static position in the location or intensity of terrorism.

This volume illustrates and amplifies several aspects of terrorism in the Irish theatre but, of course, it does not cover all issues. The international dimension receives less attention, the use of terrorism outside Northern Ireland, the effect of some recent developments such as greater Anglo-Irish cooperation are touched upon but not investigated rigorously here. Also, the impact of the collapse of East-West Cold War polarization is not examined though the Irish problem was never a major bone of contention in super-power relations. Perhaps one of the features of the low velocity of the Irish conflict was its absence of central importance in world affairs. Additionally, the book offers little on the future of the situation in Northern Ireland – its focus is on causation and responses.

For those who have witnessed the rapid disintegration of the Soviet Bloc, political change in South Africa and developments in the middle east it is tempting to think that an end to violence is possible in Northern Ireland. Yet, on the basis of current evidence, it is difficult to be overly optimistic that terrorism will simply fade away. So long as elements are ready to resort to arms to destroy the separate status for all or part of its present territory, the future of Northern Ireland is likely to remain problematic. It is a situation that does not admit easily to the devices of liberal-democracy. Clearly, the majority in the province wish to remain a part of the United Kingdom but a substantial minority rejects that status. Democratic procedures do not afford an assured formula for reconciling conflicting ethnic aspirations. In such an impasse advocates of the bullet and bomb have a ready justification and audience for the use of violence.

Part I
Causations of Political Violence

[1]

Alienation: The Case of the Catholics in Northern Ireland

EDWARD P. MOXON-BROWNE
Queen's University of Belfast

Introduction

The word 'alienation' carries a number of intrinsic connotations that are useful when examining a case of political alienation. For Marx, the estrangement of the individual from himself was to be remedied by abolition of private property so that the plight of the individual worker, forced to be simply the means to an economic end, might be shortcircuited. Freud saw the individual estranged from himself by living up to the expectations of others so that (as Marcuse was later to point out) the individual was no longer the originator of his own acts; he was no longer his true self. He lost interest in life because it was not he who was living it.

Clearly, when we are talking about alienation of the Catholic community in Northern Ireland, we are using the term at a more superficial level. However, the historical and socio-psychological antecedents of the term are valuable adjuncts to the specifically political analysis. The alienated citizen is often apathetic because he is not recognized for what he is; and his identity may, at best, be ignored or, at worst, be denigrated. Political lassitude follows logically from a political identity being ghettoised into a backwater far removed from mainstream political life. A dictionary definition of 'alienation' will mention being 'estranged,' 'foreign in nature,' and 'belonging to another place, person or family, especially to a foreign nation or allegiance.'[1] Such a definition usefully bridges the gap between the psychological ('estranged') aspect of the term and the political ('Belonging to a foreign nation or allegiance') dimension. This coupling of two aspects of alienation are especially pertinent when we consider the Catholic minority in Northern Ireland.

In a political context the term alienation denotes the sense of being or feeling, foreign. The alienated group is one that feels foreign although it resides within the state; it feels that it does not fully belong to the wider society and often withdraws into itself and becomes increasingly aware of its separate identity. Such a group is often a numerical minority but it need not be so. The crucial attributes are that it sees itself as being subordinate or marginal to the dominant political culture. Thus Blacks in South Africa, although numerically a majority, are best analyzed as a minority, and an alienated minority within the South African state. Most alienated groups, however, are, numerically speaking, minority groups in a larger society, e.g. the Tamils of Sri Lanka, the Jews of the Soviet Union, or the Sikhs in India.

The word 'alienation' has recently become a prominent weapon in the battle of words between politicians in Britain and Ireland when referring to the position of the Catholic community in Northern Ireland. The New Ireland Forum Report[2] ascribed the impasse in Northern Ireland to the 'alienation of nationalists in Northern Ireland from political and civil institutions, from the security forces and from the manner of application of the law.' The theme seemed to have struck a sympathetic chord when the Secretary of State for Northern Ireland, in a speech in July 1984, stressed the importance of finding mechanisms through which the distinct national identity of Catholics could be expressed. More recently, after the Anglo-Irish summit, the communique spoke of the need to cater for the separate identity and aspirations of the minority. However, more recently still, (November 1984) both the British Prime Minister (Mrs. Thatcher) and the new Northern Ireland Secretary (Mr. Hurd) publicly deplored the use of the word alienation implying that it was both an exaggeration and inaccurate. In response to those statements there has been no shortage of spokesmen for the Catholic community indicating the extent of the alienation they perceive among their coreligionists. For example, the Bishop of Down and Connor, whose diocese includes Belfast, wrote in late November of 1984:

> It has been claimed this week, even at Prime Ministerial and Secretary of State level, that the degree of alienation has been exaggerated, perhaps even that the term itself if inappropriate. Living in day to day contact with the situation as I do, I have to assert quite categorically that the alienation in the nationalist community is real, it is profound, it is increasing, it is spreading to more and more sectors of that community.[1]

Since there appears to be wide disagreement between leading actors in the Northern Ireland situation as to whether and, if so how much, alienation is experienced by the Catholic community, it is timely for some kind of analysis to be carried out. Otherwise, there is a danger that the word alienation will simply become a rhetorical device for political point scoring. Already, in fact, some spokesmen for the majority Protestant community have pointed to the alienation that they feel, for example, at policemen being gunned down in the streets. This sort of counter charge, based as it undoubtedly is on a real sense of grievance, risks devaluing the intrinsic worth of 'alienation' as a political concept. The experience of alienation, claimed by the Catholic community has important policy implications. The state must, presumably, react to alienation if it perceives it as being widespread. To ignore alienation, or to wish it away by pretending it is not there, could lead to policies that are not simply unhelpful, but actually counter-productive.

In this paper, the term alienation will be operationalized along a continuum ranging from abstentionism at one extreme to support for violence against the state, at the other. The actual components of alienation that are being examined here are (in ascending order of gravity):

(a) identification with a national ethos distinct from the national ethos of the majority

(b) support for policies involving another state in policy-making; and, at the same time, abstentionism from the political process within the state

(c) lack of support for, and hostility to, the judicial system, the forces of law and order, and the penal system of the state

(d) support for political parties that condone violence as a means of effecting political change; support for paramilitary groups; support for violence to overthrow the state.

Fortunately for the social scientist, there are numerous mass opinion surveys in Northern Ireland that can be used to facilitate a reasonably accurate measurement of the four components of alienation outlined above. Mass opinion surveys can be buttressed by election results and the policy programmes of political parties. From such measurement, a number of hypotheses suggest themselves:

(a) the Catholic community experiences alienation to a greater or lesser degree in terms of the above components

(b) alienation is, however, experienced in varying degrees of severity; and socioeconomic status, age and political party affiliation will be variables strongly associated with experience of alienation

(c) tensions within the Catholic community are attributable not so much to the differential experience of alienation, but to the means of overcoming it.

Our analysis will proceed in three steps. First, we will place the Catholic community in its demographic context. Second, in the main body of the paper, we will analyse each of the four components of alienation in terms of mass opinion survey evidence. Thirdly, we will reappraise each of our hypotheses in the light of the evidence that has been adduced, and conclude with an assessment of the extent to which they can be confirmed or rejected.

The Catholic community

The national population census in the United Kingdom is conducted once every ten years. The most recent census (1981) is not a completely reliable statement of the religious complexion of the Northern Ireland population because there was a considerable resistance (especially among Catholics) to the question on the religion of the respondent and, to a lesser extent, to filling out the census form at all. It has been estimated that 22% of the total population in Northern Ireland failed to state their religion either because they refused to answer the relevant question or because they refused to fill in a form. This short-fall is reckoned to be about twice as great as that of the previous census in 1971.[4] This resistance to the census can itself be regarded as a symptom of alienation in the Catholic community: census forms were burnt in public on the streets, and a female census enumerator was shot dead.

As part of its task of ensuring that employment patterns reflect the local denominational structure of the population, the Fair Employment Agency in Northern Ireland undertook a study to ascertain, more accurately than the 1981 census, the size of the Catholic community.[5] This Report made use of school registers, parochial records, and government-sponsored household surveys. The Report, published in 1985, concluded that the

Catholic share of the total population (1,562,200) was 39.1% in 1981, compared with 34% as reported in the 1981 census (and 31% in the 1971 census). The Catholic community is relatively youthful: 46% of the under-15's in the Province were Catholic, and 36% of the adults. Moreover, the fertility rate remains higher among Catholics than Protestants (the ratio of children to married women for Catholics and Protestants is 2.57 and 1.6 respectively). Of the 26 local government districts in Northern Ireland, eight have a majority of Catholic adults, but twelve have a majority of Catholic schoolchildren. Given the age profile of the Catholic community, and its relatively higher fertility rate, it has been suggested that the minority in Northern Ireland could become a majority early in the next century. If we extrapolate present reproductive differentials between the two communities, and assume no emigration, it is possible to foresee the Catholic community becoming a majority of the voting-age population by the year 2025.[6]

The purpose of the foregoing remarks is to emphasize that the Catholic minority in Northern Ireland is (a) a very large minority and (b) increasing in size both relatively and absolutely. This has important repercussions for our discussion of alienation among Catholics. It is easier for a group that constitutes, say, 5% of the total population (e.g. Protestants in the Republic of Ireland), to accept that its political leverage or access to economic resources may be marginal in terms of the national total. It is much more difficult for a minority constituting 40% of the population to accept inferior treatment in economic, political or judicial domains. As the relative size of the Catholic community increases, the pressure on the national government in London to accommodate these increased demands (especially when expectations are higher) will increase *pari passu*.

On this 'bedrock of alienation' lies a substructure of perceived relative deprivation vis-a-vis the chosen reference group i.e. the Protestant majority. In the political sphere, a high degree of overlap[7] between religious affiliation and party identification means that the Catholic minority parties have been effectively excluded from policy-making since 1922. The refusal of the Protestant majority parties to countenance any form of 'partnership' or 'consociationalism'[8] as a formula for giving Catholics access to real political power, has alienated the two main Catholic parties from the political process. This marginality of the Catholic community to the political process is compounded by its marginality in other key state agencies e.g. the police (where Catholic participation is about 10%); the Civil Service (where a recent report[9] showed that 'Roman Catholics are not adequately represented at the key policy-making levels'); and in the judiciary where only three out of twenty judges are Catholics.

More immediate, perhaps, is the marginality of the Catholic community to the region's economic life. Aunger[10] has shown that 'there is a marked tendency for Protestants to dominate the upper occupational classes while Catholics are found predominantly in the lower classes.' Aunger also found that Catholics are two and a half times more likely to be unemployed than Protestants. In his 1978 mass opinion survey, Moxon-Browne found 7% of his Protestant respondents and 14% of his Catholic respondents without jobs.[11] Catholic males are particularly badly affected. They constitute less than 21% of the economically active population, but 44% of the unemployed. Within work contexts, Protestants are more likely to be found in supervisory roles or high status positions than are Catholics. Thus in the medical sector, for example, 21% of doctors are Catholic, but 43% of nurses. In education, Catholics have 15% of the administrative positions but 39% of those in teaching. The rather high proportion of Catholics in non-manual occupations is attributed by Aunger to the need of the Catholic community to 'service' itself. Thus teachers and clergymen account for one-third of Catholic non-manual occupations while the equivalent figure for the Protestant community is 19%. In a highly segregated society, the existence of a Catholic middle class, whose primary role is to cater to the needs of its own community, does little to mitigate the marginality of Catholics in the economy generally.

The components of 'alienation'

We turn now to consider the four components of Catholic alienation mentioned earlier. The first of these was 'identification with a national ethos distinct from the national ethos of the majority.' The birth of Northern Ireland as a political entity was destined to guarantee a bifurcated sense of national identity within its boundaries. Ireland had never been absorbed politically or culturally into the United Kingdom as effectively as Scotland or Wales. In 1920, Northern Ireland might have left the United Kingdom had it not been for the determination of a majority of its inhabitants to remain part of a British state. The resulting constitutional formula was a messy compromise (a devolved government) that pleased no-one. Catholics felt aggrieved that they were now 'trapped' in a 'Protestant state;' the Protestants felt aggrieved that their region was now to be governed at one remove from London; and the British government was less than pleased at being unable to offload responsibility for the region onto a government in Dublin.

The legacy of this settlement was that national identity became a divisive concept. Broadly speaking, Catholics tended to look south to the government in Dublin as the appropriate focus for their Irish national identity. Protestants continued to look towards London as the focus for their British identity. Politics within the region became rooted in the constitutional question: most Catholics persisted in feeling that their identity could not be given true expression except in an all-Ireland state (and this aspiration was given some legitimacy by the Constitutional claim to the territory of Northern Ireland by the Republic of Ireland). Most Protestants persisted in their fear that their British identity would be in jeopardy if Irish unity was ever achieved, and in their belief that their economic, political and cultural interests could only be safeguarded within a British state.

Opinion survey evidence suggests that Catholics are surer of their national identity than are Protestants. When asked to indicate their national 'label,' Catholics will overwhelmingly reply 'Irish' while Protestants may say 'Ulster' or 'British.' Rose argues that Protestants national identity is partly based on a negative reaction to being thought of as 'Irish:' they may be vague about what they are, but they are sure about what they are not. This is confirmed in Rose's finding that most Irish people attribute their nationality to being 'born and bred' (93% of the group) while 53% of those who see themselves as British attribute this to being 'under British rule' (an inherently less secure basis for national allegiance).[12]

In Table 1, we can see the extent to which national identity follows religious lines in Northern Ireland. We can also see that, in the ten-year period (1968-78), being British (and not being Irish) has become more important for Protestants.

Table 1
Northern identity in Northern Ireland:
Comparisons between 1968 and 1978

Question: Which of these terms best describes the way you usually think of yourself? British, Irish, Ulster, Sometimes British, Sometimes Irish, Anglo-Irish, Other?

	Catholics %		Protestants %	
	1968	1978	1968	1978
British	15	15	39	67
Irish	76	69	20	8
Ulster	5	6	32	20

N.B. Percentages are rounded to the nearest digit. Responses for 'British' 'Irish' and 'Ulster' only are shown. N = 1291 (1968) 1277 (1978).

Source: E. Moxon-Browne, *Nation, Class and Creed in Northern Ireland.* Aldershot: Gower (1983), p. 6.

In addition to this clear evidence that Catholic identify with the national ethos of the inhabitants of the Republic of Ireland, there is also evidence that they have more contact with them. In answer to the question 'Have you ever travelled to the Republic?' 64% of Catholics but only 37% of Protestants replied that they visited on 'many occasions' or 'regularly.'[13]

Next, we consider the second component of alienation: 'support for policies involving another state in policy-making; and, at the same time abstentionism from the political process within the state.' The largest party in the Catholic community is the Social Democratic and Labour Party (SDLP). It was founded in 1970 as the heir to the Nationalist Party that had carried the banner for Catholic opposition to the regime in Northern Ireland ever since its inception. The aim of the SDLP was, and still is, to act as the party of 'constitutional nationalism' playing the role of 'legitimate opposition' to the majority-dominated political system in the Province. Throughout, the party has been hampered by its inbuilt numerical inferiority and this has caused the party leadership (especially under John Hume) to attempt a broadening of the political debate to include (or involve) at one time or another various external actors e.g. the Dublin government, the British government, the EEC, and the United States.

The latest phase in this broadening process was the establishment of the New Ireland Forum in 1982. This was a conference of four political parties (three from the Republic, and the SDLP from Northern Ireland) whose task it was to map out a blueprint for a 'new Ireland' in which Catholic and Protestant, north and south, would peacefully coexist. The Report from the Forum mapped out three possible scenarios for the future of Ireland but each was eventually ruled out by the British government as being impractical at this time.

For our purposes, the importance of the New Ireland Forum was that it represented an attempt by the SDLP to enlist the involvement of political parties in another state; and thus reflected the alienation of the party from the *status quo* in Northern Ireland. The idea that the government of the Republic should be involved in any political settlement in Northern Ireland is one that is very attractive to Catholics (but distasteful to Protestants who see such involvement as the 'meddling' of a 'foreign power' in the internal affairs of the United Kingdom). Successive opinion surveys show how important the involvement of the Republic is for Catholics. In 1978 78% of Catholics agreed that 'in any political settlement in Northern Ireland the Irish government would have to be consulted' (30% of Protestants). Two years later, in response to the suggestion that the Republic's government 'should be involved in discussions about the future form of government in Northern Ireland' 58% of Catholics (14% of Protestants) agreed.[14] In 1984, when asked if the government of the Republic of Ireland should 'have any say in constitutional changes affecting Northern Ireland, or not' 61% of Catholics said Yes (10% of Protestants).[15]

The two principal political parties, in the Catholic community, the SDLP and Provisional Sinn Fein (PSF), have followed an abstentionist policy with regard to some aspects of the political process in Northern Ireland. Both parties now participate in elections at four different levels of representation: local government; the regional assembly (in Belfast); the national parliament (in London); and the European Parliament (in Strasbourg, France). However, a distinction can be made between the two parties' policy regarding taking up seats after an election. PSF takes its seats in the local government elections but not in the regional assembly or the national parliament, whereas the SDLP takes its seats in the local government elections, in the national and European Parliament, but not in the regional Assembly. The objection of PSF to taking its seats in the regional and national forum is that it does not wish to accord them legitimacy, whereas the local government councils are seen as valuable channels of influence to and from grass-roots opinion. The SDLP takes its seats in all cases except the regional Assembly because it regards the Assembly, established in 1982, as being inadequate since it has no 'Irish dimension' (i.e. no link with the Republic of Ireland). This policy of abstentionism, followed in different degrees by the two Catholic parties means that the Catholic community has virtually no representation in the regional Assembly[16] and only one representative in the Westminster Parliament (out of 17 MP's from Northern Ireland). Abstentionism is clearly a popular policy in the Catholic community since both parties have, between them, held on to their share of the vote in the last three elections. Participation in elections is a way of receiving a mandate for abstentionism. Abstentionism is a clear symptom of political alienation.

Our third component of alienation was 'lack of support for, and hostility to, the judicial system, the forces of law and order, and the penal system.' For the Catholic community, the way the law is applied and enforced is a litmus test of the state's declared intention of providing impartial justice for all its citizens. Consequently, any dissatisfaction must be a major contribution to alienation.

The legitimacy of the state is inextricably tied up with the legal measures required to maintain law and order e.g. the Emergency Provisions Act 1978 and the Prevention of Terrorism Act 1984. Both Acts shift the onus of proof on to the accused in some circumstances e.g. possession of firearms or explosives found on premises in the case of the EPA, and in the case of the PTA, an individual can be required to live in a part of the United Kingdom for reasons which are unspecified and against which it is therefore difficult to construct a defence.[17] A range of offences in both Acts are tried in special courts without a jury. The EPA still contains within it a provision for internment without trial although this is currently in abeyance. However, a source of considerable grievance is that suspects are being remanded without trial for periods of one or two years awaiting their cases to come to court. In March 1984 the House of Commons was told that 108 people had spent more than a year in custody awaiting trial.

Another issue that has become a source of grievance and controversy is the use of 'supergrasses' i.e. the convicting of a number of accused persons on the evidence of one person who is himself accused of a serious crime. There are a number of objections that have been raised to the use of 'supergrasses': an individual may settle old scores by implicating a person he dislikes; the police may be tempted to construct false evidence for the supergrass to use in his 'story;' the payment of money and the granting of immunity from prosecution to the supergrass means that a terrorist may escape trial and punishment. In general, the system of supergrasses has tended to discredit the judicial system and is partly to blame for the alienation of the Catholic community from it.

In the last two years the apparent adoption of a 'shoot to kill' policy on the part of the security forces has further alienated the Catholic community. The members of the police and army are almost exclusively Protestant, the victims of the shootings invariably Catholic. During 1983, seventeen people were killed by either the British Army or the Royal Ulster Constabulary (RUC). Thirteen members of the security forces were charged in connection with seven of these killings. In all cases there were long delays in bringing the cases to court; and in all cases the soldiers and police were acquitted. Even moderate Catholic opinion has been alienated by these apparent travesties of justice. In a recent policy document, the SDLP says:

> The fact that these trials were heard in non-jury courts
> with the repeated appearances of the same judges in
> almost every case gave rise to a serious questioning of
> the impartiality of the judiciary and whether it was now
> legal for British soldiers or the RUC to kill civilians with
> impunity. The situation unfortunately remains un-
> changed with no solider or policeman being convicted of
> a killing of a civilian while on duty in the streets of

Northern Ireland. Such a position has, must and continues to lead, to great alienation from the judicial process.[18]

The use of plastic bullets by the security forces, as a riot control
weapon, has been condemned by the European Parliament and avoided in
all parts of the United Kingdom except Northern Ireland. By the beginning
of 1985 fifteen people had been killed by plastic bullets, some of the victims
being children under 15. The use of plastic bullets has been condemned by
the SDLP since they sometimes kill innocent bystanders; they represent an
excessively dangerous weapon in circumstances where 'minimum force' is
the legal maxim governing riot control; and the rules governing their use are
often broken by the security forces.[19] The failure to prosecute, let alone
convict, those who have killed civilians with plastic bullets has 'contributed
and continues to contribute to the alienation of a substantial and increasing
section of the nationalist population from the judicial system as a whole.'[20]

In sum, the panoply of special laws in Northern Ireland gives the RUC
and Army the legal back-up for stopping, searching, detaining, arresting
and questioning individuals (mainly young unemployed Catholics) and this
constant surveillance by the forces of law and order can itself breed resentment, and a sense of alienation which, in turn, only makes the task of these
forces harder in the future. In a society where national identity is divided, it
would be more conducive to gaining the support of 'Irish' Catholics for the
judicial system if flags, crests, emblems and other symbols of 'British' identity were erased from the court buildings. The alienation of many Catholics
from the judicial system is emphasized when they feel that they are receiving
'British' or 'Protestant' justice in the courts.

In Table 2, we set out some opinion survey evidence that indicates the
extent to which Catholics are unsupportive of the law and order being
dispensed in Northern Ireland.

Table 2

Question		Catholics %	Protestants %
How fair do you think the	Very fair	4	37
RUC is in the discharge of	Fair	43	59
its duties in Northern Ireland?			
Question			
Do you think that in the main	Very fairly	4	25
the legal system in Northern	Fairly	32	64
Ireland dispenses justice	Unfairly	37	7
very fairly, fairly, unfairly,	Very unfairly	20	2
or very unfairly?			
Question			
Do you approve or disapprove	Approve	9	86
of the use of plastic bullets	Disapprove	87	8
by the security forces as a			
weapon during riots?			
Question			
Do you think that the evidence	Should be	10	35
of supergrasses should be or	Should not be	81	46
should not be admissible			
without corroboration in the			
trials of those charged with			
terrorist-type offences in			
Northern Ireland?			

Belfast Telegraph-Price Waterhouse Survey   N = 955
January 1985

Source: Belfast Telegraph 6 February 1985, p. 7

The fourth and final component of alienation consists of 'support for political parties that condone violence as a means of effecting political change; support for paramilitary groups; support for violence to overthrow the state.' This component reflects alienation at its most intense: a desire to reject the system by force rather than reform it from within. This dichotomy within the Catholic community - evolution versus revolution - is matched, respectively, by the struggle between SDLP and PSF. These two parties have been competing for the soul of the Catholic community. In the last three elections, for the regional Assembly in 1982, for the Westminster Parliament in 1983, and for the European Parliament in 1984, PSF won 35%, 43% and 38% respectively of the Catholic vote.

The policies of the PSF party, and the extent of the support for the party, embody the more extreme forms of alienation found in the Catholic community. The party sees itself, and is widely perceived to be, the 'political wing' of the IRA. Its principal goal is to expel British influence from Ireland and unite the country. In the meantime, it takes part in all elections, but only takes its seats in the local government councils. It condones the violence of the IRA on the grounds that this violence is a justified response to the presence of British troops on Irish soil.

The rapid emergence of the PSF as an electoral force dates back to the hunger strikes of 1981. These hunger strikes, staged by IRA prisoners claiming recognition of their 'political status,' resulted in ten deaths. The British government resolutely refused to make any concessions, and this obduracy led to the politicisation of a dormant republican (i.e. extreme nationalist) vote in the Catholic community. The demonstrations of popular support for the hunger strikers led to a new awareness of the political leverage that might be derived from participating in elections. These voters had previously stayed at home: now this dormant alienation was transformed into votes for an anti-system party, a party that not only fought elections but also condoned violence as a means of political change. As the party conference heard that November (1981) it was the 'ballot paper in this hand and an Armalite in this hand.' Although the popular support for the hunger strikers never really engulfed the entire Catholic community, the response (or lack of response) from the British Government to the strike went a long way to crystallize hitherto ill-defined alienation on the part of even moderate Catholics who had become frustrated at the lack of political progress within Northern Ireland. Thus the hunger strikes acted as a catalyst: PSF was able to take the tide of opportunity at its flood, and even the SDLP was forced to adopt a more militant posture. Long simmering frustration, and a feeling that even the non-violent constitutionalism of the SDLP was failing to get a response from the British government, served to benefit PSF whose ambivalent attitude towards violence, and more forthright condemnations of Britain, seemed appropriate responses to those who had nothing to lose, and possibly something to gain, by rejecting the *status quo*.

The attitude of the PSF towards violence is undoubtedly part of its electoral appeal. It is also one of the principal features that distinguishes it from SDLP supporters. It is sometimes alleged that a vote for PSF is a 'vote for violence' but this is not wholly true as the figures in Table 3 demonstrate. There is a widespread view within PSF that violence is sometimes justifiable if only because of the lack of any alternative paths towards political change. However, there are other facets of the PSF 'image' that attract voters' support. There are shown in the subsequent table (Table 4).

Table 3

Question: How strongly do you agree or disagree that the use of violence can sometimes be justified to bring about political change?

	Sinn Fein %	SDLP %
Agree	70	7
Neither	7	8
Disagree	22	81
D.K./No opinion	1	4

Source: MORI Poll (unpublished) June 1984   N = 1639

Table 4

Statement which fit respondents' ideas and impressions of Sinn Fein.

	Sinn Fein Voters %		Sinn Fein Voters %
'Extreme'	10	'Has good leaders'	41
'Makes the British take notice of the nationalists'	84	'I've always supported the party's views'	42
'Tough'	34	'Out of touch'	2
'Active in the local community'	56	'Behind the times'	2
'Evil'	2	'Trustworthy'	21
'Has good policies'	58	'Caring'	16
'Offers most hope of a solution to the troubles'	51	'Moderate'	9
'Represents people like me'	58	'Too cooperative with Britain'	1

Source: MORI Poll (unpublished) June 1984   N = 562

We have already established that there is considerable support among PSF voters for the use of violence to bring about political change. We have also seen (in Table 4) that the appeal of the party is broader than a mere mandate for the gunman. Clearly, PSF voters perceive their party as being well-led, active in local communities, representative of its grass-roots and, above all, (cited by 84% of PSF voters) able to make the British government take notice of nationalist demands. As the PSF is the 'political wing' of the IRA it is worth considering the views taken by PSF supporters towards the IRA. Does the link between the party and the paramilitary organization constitute a life-support system for the party? The answer appears to be 'yes.' Whereas 39% of SDLP voters agree that the 'IRA are basically patriots and idealists,' this figure rises to 77% for PSF voters.[21] On the more specific policy question of whether PSF should 'renounce the armed campaign of the IRA' only 22% of PSF voters agree (exactly the same percentage that is against violence for political change in Table 3).

The support for the violence of the IRA among four out of five of PSF voters represents the extreme point on the continuum of 'alienation' ranging across our four 'components:' at one extreme, a desire to work within the system, but at the other a marked inclination to overthrow the system by force. An investigation of the principal demographic features of the PSF support shows it to be young, from the lower socioeconomic strata, often unemployed, and more likely to be male than female. Some of these

features of PSF support can be seen in Table 5, while comparisons with the
SDLP can be made.

Table 5

Some comparisons between the SDLP and PSF.
Base: Catholic voters in European election 1984 (June)

Age	PSF	SDLP
18-34	38%	46%
35-54	22%	58%
55 +	16%	65%
Gender	**PSF**	**SDLP**
Male	34%	54%
Female	24%	64%
Socioeconomic status	**PSF**	**SDLP**
A B C 1	20%	66%	
C2DE	33%	57%

Source: MORI Poll (unpublished) June 1984   N = 457

Comparisons with the 'constitutional' SDLP are instructive, PSF is a
young party and is firmly based in the lower socioeconomic echelons of the
Catholic community. About 50% of PSF voters are under 34 (compared
with 29% of SDLP voters). One-fifth of PSF support comes from non-
manual socioeconomic groups, while one-third of SDLP support does. 31%
of PSF supporters are unemployed; but only 13% of SDLP supporters.
Asked what the cause of the Northern Ireland problem is, PSF supporters
are more likely to see it as a clash of national identity, and less likely to see it
as a problem of 'terrorism' than SDLP supporters. Both Catholic parties
evince strong dissatisfaction with the British Government's handling of the
situation in the Province, but this dissatisfaction is much stronger in PSF
than it is in the SDLP. The crucial difference between the two parties is their
attitudes towards violence. As we have seen (see Table 3) PSF supporters
are much more likely to condone violence than SDLP supporters and while
29% of PSF voters say they 'strongly' agree that violence is sometimes
justified, only 1% of SDLP voters fall into this extreme category.[22]

Conclusion: policy implications

Faced with widespread alienation within the Catholic community,
ranging from those who accept the status quo and are willing to make it
work, through to those who see violent change as the only hope of reform,
the British government is forced to steer a middle course between the men of
violence and the 'constitutional' politicians. But, unfortunately, concessions made to the latter are often seen, and claimed, as concessions to the
former.

Since 1969, when the present spate of civil unrest erupted, the British
government has responded to the crisis along three avenues: security,
economics, politics. In the political field, there have been several attempts
to construct a framework of devolved government within which the two
communities could cooperate to their mutual benefit. So far, this has not
been achieved. The brief power-sharing experiment of 1974 lasted five
months but was eventually wrecked by Loyalist (i.e. extreme Protestant)

reactions to the proposed North-South Council of Ireland which was perceived as the thin end of a wedge that would lead to a united Ireland. The present 78-man Assembly in Belfast is the latest experiment. Its role is purely advisory and consultative although the intention is that legislative powers could be devolved to it if there was sufficient cross-community consensus to warrant it. At the moment this seems unlikely as the two Catholic parties, PSF and the SDLP, are boycotting the Assembly because it excludes both an 'Irish dimension' (i.e. with the Republic) and any real recognition of Irish identity among Catholics in Northern Ireland. Since 1973, proportional representation has been introduced into local and regional elections in Northern Ireland (a novelty in the United Kingdom) with the aim of enhancing the influence of the Catholic minority in political affairs. While this has undoubtedly happened, it has also led to the splitting of the confessional 'blocs,' into two parties each, so that extremists on both sides now have parties to themselves (PSF for the Catholics, DUP for the Protestants). The prospects for reconciliation between moderates in each community is now more remote because the 'moderate' parties (OUP for Protestants, SDLP for Catholics) have to look over their shoulders at the more militant policies of the parties on their flanks.

Security policy has made progress in its primary aim: the reduction in the number of fatalities in the Province. In 1972 over four hundred people died in the region; now the annual total is less than one hundred. The cost has been high in terms of alienating the Catholic community. Special legislation giving the police wide powers of arrest, detention, and interrogation; long periods of remand; the abolition of juries for many trials; the use of supergrasses; the apparent immunity from conviction of policemen or soldiers who murder civilians; and the overwhelming Protestant composition of the security forces: all these facets of the security policy of the Government combine to minimize the legitimacy of the state in the eyes of the Catholic community. The policy of 'Ulsterisation' - the policy of transferring the burden of security to locally recruited personnel - has done little to kindle hope in the Catholic community that law and order will be impartially administered.

Economic policy has consisted of building up the infrastructure of the Province - roads, houses, harbours, energy supplies - so that foreign investment will stimulate greater employment opportunities. Per capita expenditure is higher in the Province than in the rest of the United Kingdom: and so is the dependence on welfare handouts.

The Government's policy towards PSF consists of a 'twin-track' approach: encouraging constitutional nationalism (as expressed in the SDLP) and ostracising PSF representatives at Ministerial level. However, PSF is a legal party and both civil servants and local councillors are expected to deal with them in the normal way. This partial boycott of PSF representatives is defended on the grounds that PSF refuses to condemn violence, and as a way of bolstering the 'parliamentary' tactics of the SDLP.

Faced by an alienated minority, a central government has, in theory, a range of options extending from total suppression of the minority to a full recognition of its separate identity *via* the creation of a separate state. Neither of these extreme policies is relevant to Northern Ireland since suppression of a minority consisting of 40% of the population is unthinkable, and territorial separateness is ruled out by the intermingling of the two communities. In between these extremes there lies a variety of options including consociationalism, cantonisation, total absorption, pluralism and relocation. So far, the Government has been attempting a policy of 'integration' or 'homogenisation' - a policy of treating the Catholic community as equal citizens of the United Kingdom: and much progress has been made in legislating away discriminatory practices and providing adequate economic resources. But it looks as if even this policy, even if successful, will have to make way for a new policy of pluralism (or more strictly 'binationalism') in order to satisfy the aspirations of the militant elements in the Catholic community. Already there have been straws in the wind: talk of the 'Irish identity' in Government circles, the financing of an Irish speaking school in Belfast, the refusal to proscribe PSF, and most recently the banning of provocative Protestant marches through Catholic residential areas. Otherwise, very little has been done officially to grant the Irish identity of Catholics its legitimate place in Northern Ireland, or to give Catholics access to policy-making in a meaningful sense, or to ensure that law, order and justice apply to all without fear or favour. If alienation means 'feeling a stranger in one's own country' then there is scope for making the Catholic community feel that they have a stake in the society they inhabit: if one is treated like an outsider, it is likely that one will behave like an outsider.

Attempts by the Government to promote 'binationalism' run into the problem of Protestant opposition. Lately, one has heard the phrase 'Protestant alienation' - a term loosely referring to the reactions of IRA violence, and 'reforms' by the Government to enhance Catholic political and economic participation. The situation is not a bi-polar one with the Protestants and British ranged against the Catholic community. On the contrary the situation is triangular: both communities are to some extent alienated from British rule,[23] albeit for different reasons and to different degrees. Thus the strategy of the Government, or any government faced by a multi-ethnic society, has to be that of 'balancing' interests and seeking the issues that bind rather than those that divide. Given the demographic trends in Northern Ireland, it seems advisable for the 'majority' of today to negotiate the terms for survival of tomorrow's minority.

NOTES

¹*The Shorter Oxford English Dictionary*, Oxford: Clarendon (1973).

²Published in the summer of 1984.

³Bishop Cahal Daly, *Communities Without Consensus*. Dublin: Irish Messenger Publications (1984), p. 5.

⁴See D. Eversley and V. Herr, *The Roman Catholic Population of Northern Ireland in 1981: A Revised Estimate*. Belfast: Fair Employment Agency (1985), p. 1.

⁵*Ibid*.

⁶D. Watt (ed), *The Constitution of Northern Ireland: Problems and Prospects*. London: Heinemann (1981), p. 88.

⁷See E. Moxon-Browne, *Nation, Class and Creed in Northern Ireland*. Aldershot: Gower (1983), p. 84.

⁸See A. Lijphart, 'Review Article: The Northern Ireland Problem: Case Theories and Solutions' in *British Journal of Political Science*, vol. 5.

⁹Fair Employment Agency, *Report of an Investigation by the FEA for Northern Ireland into the non-industrial Civil Service*. Belfast: FEA (1983), p. 65.

¹⁰R.J. Cormack and R.D. Osborne (eds), *Religion, Education and Employment: Aspects of Equal Opportunity in Northern Ireland*. Belfast: Appletree Press (1983), pp. 25-41.

¹¹E. Moxon-Browne, *op.cit.*, p. 83.

¹²R. Rose, *Government Without Consensus*. London: Faber (1971), p. 209.

¹³E. Moxon-Browne, *op.cit.*, p. 30.

¹⁴*Ibid.*, p. 20.

¹⁵LWT/MORI Poll (May 1984) N = 1028 (Quota sample).

¹⁶There are, however, five Catholics in the transectarian Alliance Party which has ten seats in the Assembly.

¹⁷C. Scorer and P. Hewitt, *The Prevention of Terrorism Act*. London: NCCL (1981).

¹⁸SDLP, *'Justice' in Northern Ireland*. Belfast: SDLP (January 1983) mimeo pp. 11-12.

¹⁹*Ibid.*

²⁰*Ibid.*

²¹MORI Poll (unpublished) June 1984.

²²*Ibid.*

²³See E. Moxon-Browne, *op.cit.*, p. 56.

[2]

THE PROTESTANT-CATHOLIC CONFLICT IN ULSTER
Paul Bew and Henry Patterson

The existence of a religious component in the Northern Ireland conflict has been clear to most commentators. There is little agreement, however, on how its significance should be evaluated. A decade ago in his influential textbook, *Ireland since the Famine*, F.S.L. Lyons commented:

At the present moment, with the entrails of Ulster bigotry laid bare to the world as never before, it is perhaps easier to understand the reality of this religious tension, though it is still difficult to explain it.[1]

In fact, the chapter in which this statement appears was begun in February 1969, on the day of a decisive general election which was to weaken substantially the position of Terence O'Neill, the Unionist prime minister who has been viewed by most writers on Ulster as a liberal reformer.[2] In his own constituency, O'Neill was faced with the opposition of Ian Paisley, the fundamentalist Protestant leader who had been waging a campaign combining populist attacks on the Unionist "Establishment" with allegations of a sellout to Dublin. Lyons referred to it as

... the most important general election in its (Ulster's) history, the paramount issue being whether or not Ulster men would at last turn their backs on the sectarianism which had poisoned the history of their province for so many generations.[3]

0022-197x/82/1314-0001$01.50/0

Since then O'Neill, like other Unionist prime ministers, has been caught between British pressure for reform and the intransigence of much of his support base. The deepening crisis in Northern Ireland after 1969 eventually led Britain to assume direct responsibility for the government of the province in March 1972. The subsequent period has witnessed the disintegration of the Unionist party and the rise of Paisleyism in its party form as the Democratic Unionist party. The DUP now rivals the Official Unionist party, the direct descendant of the party which controlled the local state for fifty years, for the role of dominant political force in the Protestant community.

On the Catholic side, the development of the Civil Rights movement in the mid-sixties appeared to presage a movement of Catholic politics away from nationalist concern with the legitimacy of the state itself towards a social democratic reformism aimed at improving the position of the Catholic population inside Northern Ireland. The emergence in 1970 of the Social Democratic and Labour party (SDLP) as a party combining the ultimate aspiration to a united Ireland with a predominant reformist stance, was seen by many as a sign of a clear break with the politics of the ghetto. Since then the SDLP has moved towards a noticeably more traditional position on the primacy of the national question and has shed some of its most articulate modernizers including Gerry Fitt and Paddy Devlin. During last year's hunger strikes, its decision not to contest the

---

1. F.S.L. Lyons, *Ireland since the Famine*, (London, 1971), p. 287.
2. For a critique of this view see Paul Bew, Peter Gibbon and Henry Patterson, *The State in Northern Ireland 1921-72*, (Manchester and New York, 1979).
3. Lyons, p. 287.

Journal of International Affairs

Fermanagh-South Tyrone by-election against the IRA hunger striker Bobby Sands undoubtedly reflected an upsurge among Catholics of religious fervor with traditional nationalist overtones.

The main Catholic daily paper, the *Irish News*, was full of obituary notices on the lines of "God's curse on you, England, you cruel-hearted monster" and invocations of "Mary, Queen of Ireland". The remarkable wall murals that began to cover gable ends in many Catholic areas of Belfast displayed religious feeling in many ways, the hunger striker as Christ with rosary beads being frequently portrayed. Paradoxically, at this moment, observers claim to perceive a youthful, radical, or even "Marxist" takeover of the Provisional IRA. It can only be said that if such a tendency did make advances, its supporters—including very notably Mrs. Bernadette (Devlin) McAliskey—paid considerable obeisance to the new mood of Catholic emotionalism. A typical report of the hunger strike campaign ran as follows:

> Now when you all kneel down to say your Rosary tonight, as I know you will do, you'll be praying for Bobby Sands, so we'll say a decade now. And the young man who a minute earlier led the H-Block chant reverently dealt out a decade of the Rosary.
>
> A moment before they had been shouting: "One, two, three, four, open up the H-Block door." Now on the steps of the Enniskillen Town Hall, the Rosary was said, rythmic, flowing, automatic and passing Catholic housewives joined in. Prayer and protest are easy companions in Fermanagh.[4]

Although the Provisionals have clearly exaggerated the degree to which the hunger strikes would enable them to challenge the SDLP directly for the political leadership of the Catholic community, there is no doubt that in Catholic, as in Protestant politics, the last dec-

ade has confounded hopes that a moderate center would emerge in local politics.

However, in evaluating these depressing tendencies it is necessary to avoid adopting an overly historicist perspective, as have so many commentators on Irish politics. It is all too easy to interpret Irish history in terms of a fundamental continuity. Historical cards of identity were handed out, it seems, sometime in the seventeenth century at the time of the Plantation of Ulster. Latter-day actors have had no choice but to act out the roles assigned them by history. In this way, for example, Paisleyism has been seen as quintessential Protestant recidivism: the return to a bigoted past. Robert Kee has described Paisley as a "historical throwback to the Presbyterian dissenting radicals of the nineteenth and even eighteenth century."[5] This ignores certain important *discontinuities* in the history of the Protestant population. Most obviously, it ignores the fact that the nationalist uprising of the United Irishmen in 1798 had substantial Presbyterian support. In the nineteenth century, Presbyterian radicals stood for something which is anathema to Paisleyism—not national independence, but the construction of a democratic and reformist alliance with Catholics.[6]

Paisleyism is not a manifestation of old political tendencies of the Protestant population, but a creation of political factors which have come into existence since 1968. It is too easy and convenient for policymakers concerned with Northern Ireland to attribute malevo-

---

4. *Irish Times*, 4 May 1981.
5. Robert Kee, *Ireland* (London, 1981), p. 8.
6. Paul Bew and Frank Wright, "Agrarian Opposition in Ulster 1848-1887" in *Irish Peasants*, ed., Sam Clark and James Donnelly, Wisconsin University Press, 1982.

lent tendencies in local politics to the strength of communal sectarian traditions. It will be the argument of this analysis that British policy, especially since the imposition of Direct Rule in 1972, has done much to bring such traditions to the forefront of politics. An explanation of these developments must examine:

1. The nature of the Unionist state and the reasons for its disintegration.
2. British government policy towards Northern Ireland, particularly since the intensification of the crisis in 1969.
3. The effects of this policy on internal political forces.

We will argue that the *unintentional* effects of British policy have been to exacerbate sectarian conflict between Catholics and Protestants.

The State and Sectarianism

It must be stressed that the Unionist mobilization against Home Rule at the end of the nineteenth and the first two decades of this century was not predominantly an Orange Order affair.[7] Despite its importance, the Order was never a force that could have provided an integrating ideology for Unionism as a mass movement. There were simply too many Protestants who not only were not members of it, but were in fact quite hostile toward it. The original unity of the Unionist movement was based on much more than the sectarianism of the Order.

Ideologically it was based on the representation of the uneven development which was such a stark reality in Ireland at the beginning of this century. Unionism was built round the contrast between "bustling", "pro-gressive" industrial Ulster and "backward", "stagnant" peasant southern Ireland.[8] The political argument was that rule from Dublin would be economically and socially retrogressive; this was of particular importance in integrating the Protestant working class into the Unionist movement.[9] The clear divergence of economic and social structures between north and south is sufficient to account for the emergence of two states and the fact that Protestants, especially those of the working class, have always been militantly antinationalist. The role of sectarianism was not to *found* the state, but rather to influence the *form* that it took. Similarly, in analyzing the politics of the Protestant community in any particular period, one must certainly count sectarianism as a factor. Still, its importance will be determined by specific circumstances; it should be accorded no predetermined significance.

The state was born in circumstances of intense political instability. By 1920 it was clear that the IRA had broken British rule throughout the south of Ireland. In the north, the Unionist political leadership was acutely apprehensive of the threat from republicanism. It was becoming clear that the British government was prepared to treat the Unionists as expendable in an attempt to consolidate the more moderate wing of the nationalist movement in power in Dublin.[10] This made necessary the maximum possible degree of Unionist unity

7. See Peter Gibbon, *The Origins of Ulster Unionism,* (Manchester, 1975). The Orange Order was founded in the 1790s as an organization appealing mostly to the lower classes advocating Protestant supremacy.
8. Ibid.
9. Henry Patterson, *Class Conflict and Sectarianism: The Protestant Working Class and the Belfast Labour Movement,* (Belfast, 1980).
10. Bew *et al.,* chapter 2.

Journal of International Affairs

and, given the lack of trust in Britain's long term intentions towards the new state, it meant an increasing reliance on a police force and a special constabulary under local control and responsive to local Protestant pressures. The adoption of a more stridently anti-Catholic position by Unionist politicians was part of the same strategy for maximizing Protestant unity.

The continued existence of the IRA (although during most of the state's history it had been too feeble to be considered a real threat) and the almost total consensus in the south that partition should be ended gave some external and internal basis for the Unionist "siege mentality". But it was the functioning of the Unionist state itself—the infamous "Protestant Parliament for a Protestant People"—which was largely responsible for that mentality. By openly demonstrating its distrust of Catholics, by excluding them from all but the most menial types of government employment, and by maintaining a form of exceptional legislation (the Special Powers Act) and an often openly partisan judicial system, it demonstrated to the Protestant population just how seriously it took the threat of Catholic subversion.

When the Civil Rights movement emerged, O'Neill and later Unionist leaders who, under British pressure, attempted to reform the state, soon came up against the basic problem that it was this very state and its method of operation that had provided the basis for Unionist unity. The fact that the reforms had been instituted by Britain made the process even more explosive, for the original form of the state had been greatly influenced by Unionist distrust of the British government. It was clear, even by 1921, that Northern Ireland would remain in the United Kingdom, more because of the immense difficulties involved in engineering a united

Ireland than from any substantial British interest in maintaining partition. In 1966 at the start of the present "Troubles", British subsidies to Northern Ireland were approximately £245 per capita (at 1975 prices); by 1978, they had risen to £480.[11] British politicians' reminders of the extent to which the province remains dependent on British support, most notoriously in Harold Wilson's use of the term "spongers" in his television broadcast during the Ulster Workers' Council strike, have served to accentuate the Protestant fear that any British government will be eager to extricate itself from such a costly commitment.

Those Unionist leaders who have cooperated with British initiatives since 1968 have laid themselves open to the charge of dividing the Protestant community precisely when it most needed to be united. The fact that these reforms concerned, among other things, just those instruments (police and the special constabulary) that had been traditionally defined as essential to the very existence of the state only intensified the opposition. The street violence which erupted in August 1969 and in which members of the special constabulary were involved precipitated the sending of British troops and created the conditions for the final crisis of the Unionist state.

British Policy

Edward Heath's abolition of the local parliament in March 1972 was a direct response to the sudden withdrawal of Catholic support for the existing state after internment and "Bloody Sunday" (the killing of thir-

---

11. Bob Rowthorn, "Northern Ireland: an Economy in Crisis", *Cambridge Journal of Economics* 5 (1981), p. 23.

teen Catholics by British troops in Derry). There was a belief that the Provisional IRA could only be defeated by isolating them politically from the Catholic masses. It was calculated that for this to occur, a major restructuring of the government of the province would be necessary. But it was chiefly in its effects on Protestant politics that Direct Rule was to have the most decisive long-term results. Direct Rule accomplished the breakup of the Unionist monolith. It was hoped that out of a period of intra-Unionist division would emerge the basis for a new kind of unity to underlie the state, that of the moderate center: the Alliance party, the Northern Ireland Labour party, the SDLP, and liberal Unionists freed from the suffocating embrace of the old party.

Yet not all the elements set free by this strategy were of a moderate disposition. The previous history of the Unionist state had had as one of its most enduring ideological effects among the Protestant population the identification of stability and security with a particular type of political control of the state's repressive apparatus.[12] At the center of the problems facing William Whitelaw, the first and most active secretary of state for Northern Ireland, was the need to transform the ideological relationship of the Protestant population to the key questions of security and stability. The Union, which had for fifty years been indissolubly linked with the form of organization of the state apparatus, was not to be guaranteed by the much less substantial reality of bargaining and compromise between "reasonable men" on both sides.[13]

But some of Whitelaw's attempted compromises only served to consolidate those forces in Protestant politics opposed to any reforms. Thus it is unknown to what extent his reputation suffered when the Provisionals divulged that he had had six of their leaders flown to London to meet with him secretly in July 1972. Similar in effect was the decision, under pressure from the SDLP and the government in the republic, to make an "Irish Dimension" a central part of any settlement in the north. This was crucial in undermining support for those sections of the Unionist party, led by Brian Faulkner, which were prepared to share power with the SDLP.

The question of the ultimate direction of British policy, and in particular, whether it was attempting to extricate the British state from Northern Ireland, has been raised frequently during the decade since Direct Rule. It was raised with particular intensity in the period between the publication of the Green Paper on the future government of Northern Ireland in the autumn of 1972 until the Sunningdale conference between the London and Dublin governments and the new northern power-sharing executive in December 1973.[14] It would re-emerge in 1975 during the truce with the Provisionals[15]; and since the talks between British Prime

---

12. Bew *et al.*, chapters 2 and 3.
13. One of Whitelaw's junior ministers retrospectively described the policy as aimed "to build up, by every means available, a band of moderate opinion drawn from both sides." *The Times*, 19 February 1975.
14. The details of these developments are sketched in Martin Wallace, *British Government in Northern Ireland from Devolution to Direct Rule*, (London, 1982).
15. In the middle of 1975 John Whale gave clear expression to the intense speculation about British policy then wracking the province, "An epic change is being accomplished in Britain's relationship with Northern Ireland. Unacknowledged as yet...British withdrawal is becoming a fact." *Sunday Times*, 22 June 1975. In fact it now appears that such speculations were deliberately encouraged to persuade the Provisionals to maintain their cease fire begun at the beginning of the year.

Dimensions of Irish Terrorism

Journal of International Affairs

Minister Margaret Thatcher and Irish Premier Charles Haughey in 1980, there has been much Unionist talk of "Foreign Office conspiracies" to hand over the north to its enemies.

The problem of discerning the intentions of successive British governments is not due to a lack of access to cabinet and other official papers or an inability to trust politicians.[16] Rather, it lies in a dislocation at the heart of British strategy. This concerns the differences between the various strategies adopted to manage, diffuse, and mitigate the violence of political and military conflict in Northern Ireland, and the overall direction of policy under successive governments, both Conservative and Labour. The latter was aimed at cutting down the powers and pretensions of any possible regime that would emerge in Northern Ireland and thus prevent the development of the kind of autonomy that had existed under the Stormont regime. In effect this was an integrationist policy. To argue this is, of course, to contest the seriousness of the various British government statements since 1972, which explicitly rule out integration and insist on the importance of an Irish dimension to any settlement.

The seriousness of such declarations has, of course, been challenged by republicans and some Trotskyists.[17] But these analyses, while rightly detecting an essential weakness in the whole Irish dimension policy, fail to deal adequately with the reasons for the dissociation of public pronouncements from the real direction of policy. For them the essence of the problem is the "national question": the aspiration of northern Catholics and their co-religionists in the Republic for an end to partition. The argument is that in response to mass nationalist militancy, the British made certain gestures towards these aspirations, sufficient to allow the reformist SDLP to deflect the "anti-imperialist" struggle from its true course.

The problem is, however, more complex than that. It will be argued that British policy, rather than being developed to deflect the aspiration for national liberation, *unintentionally* assured that nationalist issues would tend to become predominant in Catholic politics. The weakness of the Sunningdale policy came not from the necessity of deflecting nationalist aspirations into harmless channels, but rather from the attempt to manipulate political forces in ways appropriate to the creation of forms of political management which would allow a return to "normality".

James Leavy, commentator, in an analysis which claims that the 1973 White Paper on the future government of the province was a watershed in Britain's Northern Ireland policy, argued that its greatest merit was the end of attempts "to resolve the Irish Question through the establishment of a given structure of government."[18] He saw the vagueness of official pronouncements concerning the Irish dimension as the real index of its importance: "There is no attempt to fix a structure for North-South relations. Instead there is a

---

16. A large part of what follows is based on interviews with politicians and civil servants involved in the formation and implementation of Northern Ireland policy since 1972. This was part of the research into the politics of Direct Rule financed by the Social Science Research Council in which we and colleagues at the Ulster Polytechnic are involved.

17. Paul F. Power, "Sunningdale Strategy and the Northern Majority Consent Doctrine in Anglo-Irish Relations" in *Eire Ireland* XII:1. For the Trotskyist version see Terry Marlowe and Stephen Palmer, "Ireland: Imperialism in Crisis", *Revolutionary Communist* (July 1978).

18. James Leavy, "Structure or Process? New Approaches to the Problem of Northern Ireland", *Studies* 62 (Summer 1973).

commitment to a process of development which is not delimited by any given structural factors . . ." It was this supposed open-endedness which the *London Times* would refer to in explaining the policy's inevitable collapse:

. . . when the matter at issue is as fundamental as divided allegiance, the promotion of ambiguity and of a sense of impermanence is of no service from those in whose hands constitutional responsibility lies.[19]

These very different evaluations of the policy share the mistaken assessment that the intention was to alter the relationships between the three states. In fact, the whole exercise was intended to be far less innovative. It was aimed at defusing a crisis, a presumed strength of the British state.

The essence of British strategy that culminated in the Sunningdale Conference of 1973 (which brought Irish and British politicians together to discuss power-sharing) was to lay the foundation for negotiations between enough of the political forces to create the necessary conditions for restabilization. Reform of the system of government was only a secondary aim. The primary goal was to get a sufficiently broad spectrum of politicians and their support bases involved in "legitimate" politics. This would entail reforms, determined not by economic or social needs, but by the requirements of attracting the various parties (particularly the SDLP) into a manageable system of local politics. This put a clear limit on the kinds of changes that would be introduced. Viewing issues simply as they were articulated by political groups was to preclude a program of thoroughgoing reforms which would have made it more difficult for the Provisionals to appeal to the issue of nationalism.

The argument can be brought into focus by considering relations between the SDLP and the Northern Ireland Office in the period leading up to Sunningdale.[20] The 1973 White Paper's section on the Irish dimension was vague about its nature and means for implementation. Yet by the autumn of 1973 it was made clear by the SDLP and the coalition government in the republic that there had to be simultaneous progress on the demand for a Council of Ireland[21] and power-sharing or the SDLP would withdraw from the negotiations. Concentration on the Irish dimension in no way represented the SDLP's articulation of a pressing demand from the Catholic population. Rather, it reflected the fact that this was an area in which it was easy for both sides to give the impression that substantial movement was taking place. However it was certainly not the only area in which the SDLP attempted to promote reform.

There was much private discussion with the British on police reform and on putting an end to internment. The degree to which the central state apparatus should be reformed was called into question. There was also the need for a program of economic and social reconstruction.[22] The SDLP had drawn up policy papers on

---

19. *The Times*, 11 August 1975.
20. The authors are grateful to Mr. Paddy Devlin, a leading member of the SDLP, for information he has provided on many aspects of this period.
21. The members of the SDLP who were elected to the Assembly in 1973 held regular meetings to discuss the progress of their negotiations with the NIO. Much of what follows is based on minutes of these meetings.
22. In an NIO document drawn up on the state of the Inter-Party discussions (19 November 1973), it was stated "...it is the firm intention of HMG to afford significant assistance to Northern Ireland in its economic and social rehabilitation."

Journal of International Affairs

all these issues. On none of them did it see any significant movement by the Northern Ireland Office. In part
this was an effect of the nationalist inflection of the
SDLP's demands.

Thus much time was spent on trying to get the word
"royal" removed from the name of the police force.[23]
John Hume and others were even in favor of the effective reconstruction of the force through schemes of
"community policing".[24] As a result, there was a failure
to pursue less grandiose but still substantial demands,
such as an independent complaints procedure.

Similarly, as some SDLP members complained, too
much time was spent on discussing the distribution of
ministerial responsibility in the proposed executive and
on the Irish dimension, allowing the question of internment to be pushed aside. Another example of a substantive issue being sacrificed to the pursuit of the Irish
dimension issue was the question of the virtually un-
changed composition of the central state structure. The
top levels of the Northern Ireland Civil Service remained
much the same after Direct Rule as before. As a brief
SDLP internal document on the Civil Service put it:

> The problem is the lack of balance in administrative grades—in
> particular at Permanent Secretary, Deputy Secretary and
> Assistant Secretary levels .... There are few Catholics in the
> most senior posts in the Civil Service (Assistant Secretary and
> above). The present position is aggravated, however, by the
> complete absence of Catholics in senior posts in certain stra-
> tegic sections—particularly Stormont Castle and the Ministry
> of Finance.[25]

Although the document suggested various remedies
for this situation, including "a few strategic appointments", nothing more was heard of them once government office was obtained.

More important than the absence of Catholics in top
posts was the failure to confront the role of a relatively
conservative bureaucracy in the area of policy formation. Thus when the power-sharing executive was set
up, one of the first reports it considered was one on
economic and physical planning drawn up by the Ministry of Finance in consultation with the heads of the
other departments.[26] Its purpose was to explain how
that section of the 1973 White Paper on reconstruction
and development was to be implemented. It consistently down played the major structural problems of
the economy: "... our economic situation showed prom-
ising signs", while at the same time over-emphasizing
the problem that "instability" posed to dealing with the
north's economic and social problems.[27]

Our argument is that the Protestant "backlash"—the
Ulster Workers' Council strike—which destroyed the
whole power-sharing experiment, had more to do with
the inadequacies of British policy than with the ingrained
bigotry of the Protestant masses. Interviews with two
senior British civil servants involved in the negotiations
culminating at Sunningdale have led to the admission
that "with the benefit of hindsight", it was a mistake to
push the Irish dimension too much; while a majority of

---

23. We owe this point to a senior civil servant who was in the NIO at
the time.
24. The civil servant concerned referred to the schemes as "hare-
brained", a point of view shared at the time by Paddy Devlin.
25. The one-page document is unsigned and undated, but we have
no reason to doubt its source.
26. "Social, Economic and Physical Planning—Report to the Northern Ireland Executive", *Department of Finance* (Stormont, January
1974), p. 3.
27. *Ibid*, pp. 5-6.

Protestants might have been prepared to share power with the SDLP, the linking of power-sharing with the Council of Ireland proposals almost inevitably doomed them both. At the same time, one civil servant evinced surprise at the Protestants' failure to see that the actual provisions of the Sunningdale agreement on the Council of Ireland gave the Unionist members an effective vote.[28] This view of the largely symbolic nature of the proposals echoed that of the leader of the Unionists at the time: "If this nonsense was necessary to bring their (SDLP) supporters along I did not see why we should be difficult."[29]

What both ignored was the wider conjuncture of political forces which determined how these negotiations would be perceived by the Protestant masses. First there was a basic asymmetry in the effects of British policy on the Protestant and Catholic blocs since Direct Rule. British policy contributed powerfully to an increase in the self-confidence and morale of the SDLP[30] at the same time that it divided and demoralized the Unionists. Second was the process of secret bargaining and horsetrading that went on between the Northern Ireland Office and political groups in the summer and autumn of 1973. Just because the NIO was not able to move substantially on issues like internment, police reform, and a major program of economic and social reconstruction, attention was inevitably focussed on the sort of "constitutional" issue that was most likely to generate Protestant fears. Because the SDLP had so little to offer its supporters on issues like internment and policing, it had a vested interest in pushing the Irish dimension to the center of the political debate.

Mervyn Pauley, one of Ulster's most experienced political journalists, observed in February 1974, some months before the collapse of the power-sharing executive which he supported:

> Recent public statements by leading Unionist and SDLP spokesmen have certainly been contradictory when it comes to their conception of the Council of Ireland. Mr. Faulkner and his supporters contend that the body is definitely not a half-way house to a united Ireland; that Sunningdale is a political bargain which will take years rather than months to prove itself and that it will strengthen rather than weaken the Union. And anyway, they stress, there is always the Unionist veto, the periodic referenda, and the commitment to national togetherness only by consent.
>
> But the fact remains that there is a strong school of thought in the SDLP ranks which sees a Council of Ireland as the road to Irish unity—at least two Assembly men have said so publicly. Another Ulster Assembly man, Patrick Duffy, the party's treasurer said frankly at a Co. Tyrone meeting that the party and its followers were committed to getting Britain out of Northern Ireland on a satisfactory financial basis. A new independent Ireland was the party's ultimate goal he told his audience. And he expressed the view that if the SDLP reexamined its course in the light of recent developments no

---

28. At the time of interview (early 1982) both men were still in senior positions in the Civil Service and did not wish their remarks to be attributed.

29. Brian Faulkner, *Memories of a Statesman*, (London, 1978) p. 229.

30. That the SDLP's expectations of a radical solution were high is evident in much discussion among their Assembly members; from the early symbolic demand that the Assembly should meet at Armagh instead of Stormont, to the disquiet expressed at a speech by the leader of the new Coalition government in the republic, which appeared to accept that re-unification was not on—at least in the medium term: "Equivocation similar to that emanating from Coalition government spokesmen could be damaging to us at a time when we appear to be on the verge of a breakthrough". (Minutes of first meeting of Assembly Party held at Dungannon on 6 July 1973.)

Journal of International Affairs

better body can be devised for development into a Federal Irish government than a Council of Ireland as agreed at Sunningdale. As Mr. Duffy was the SDLP's adviser at Sunningdale one can only assume that he was reflecting the party's thinking at the highest levels . . . . What is puzzling many people is how two of the partners in power-sharing can express such seemingly irreconcilable views of such a crucial aspect of an otherwise sensible and patently necessary deal.[31]

Pauley's remarks highlight the ambiguities and strains of the power-sharing executive. Within a few days of his article, anti-power-sharing Unionists performed very well in the general election of 1974. Within a few months, power-sharing collapsed in the face of the Ulster worker's strike.

We have dealt at some length with this period in British policy-making because there has been little sign of any fundamental re-assessment of strategy since the collapse brought about by the UWC strike. There have, of course, been changes of emphasis, for example, during the period when the Labour Secretary of State, Merlyn Rees, was at Stormont Caste, and a constitutional convention was called, ostensibly to allow "Ulstermen" a greater say in evolving new political structures. In fact, as was frequently said at the time, the convention was seen by the NIO as a holding operation which might allow the emergence of new political forces on both sides.[32] The frustration of these hopes led to a relatively apolitical regime under Rees's successor, Roy Mason, where the emphasis shifted to securing a period of "purposive" Direct Rule, which might improve the economic and social conditions of the north. However, despite Mason's own bluff dismissal of the value of more "constitution-making", there was never any question among policy-makers that Direct Rule could not continue indefinitely and that a lasting settlement would

have to involve some form of partnership government including the SDLP. Thus the latest "rolling devolution" scheme of the Tory Secretary of State James Prior, although it purposely avoids the use of the term, "power-sharing" depends for its success on a government being formed which would have "cross-community support". Just as in the 1973 attempt to get SDLP support, there has been an Irish dimension, although a rather effete one even compared with Sunningdale. Both the SDLP and the government of Charles Haughey in the Irish Republic have declared the scheme "unworkable". If this in fact turns out to be the case, a re-assessment of British policy may well begin. A good point of departure for any such re-assessment would be the realization that the Irish dimension as an aspect of policy (not simply as a response to some popular desire for it but, at least partly, as a policy the British *chose* over issues of democratic reform and socio-economic reconstruction) should come to dominate political discussion. The long-term effects of this approach have been to strengthen the intransigent elements on the Protestant side while bringing to the fore in the SDLP some of the more militant nationalists. Softening the increasingly confrontationist tone of Northern Ireland politics would require some radical initiatives on the part of the British government in bringing about a transformation in the terms of political debate. Unfortunately, the unwillingness of successive governments to move in two crucial areas — the provision of legal protection for minority rights and a much

31. *Belfast News Letter*, 1 February 1974.
32. For a time it was hoped that the new "Ulster Nationalism" which Merlyn Rees claimed to detect in the UWC strike would lead the Protestant working class away from traditional Unionism.

more substantial rate of public investment in the province—does not bode well for any such transformation.

Protestant and Catholic Responses

The effect of British policy together with the Provisional campaign has been to create the conditions for an upsurge of Protestant populism. This has been articulated in various forms. The paramilitary Ulster Defence Association, despite its origins as an assemblage of vigilante groups in working class districts of Belfast, was soon articulating the populist view that the Protestant masses had been betrayed by the "fur-coat brigade"— middle class Unionists. Its politicization was hastened by the UWC strike where it provided much of the muscle which made it effective. Its leadership was soon to complain that all it had achieved was the replacement of one group of useless politicians by another. Out of these experiences came the adoption of an "Independent Ulster" as its solution to the conflict.[33] While its leadership has shifted its attention from military questions to politics, it has so far failed to attract the support of any substantial section of the Protestant working class. For although the core sections of that class have shrunk because of a combination of the general crisis of the UK economy, a weaker regional policy, and the deterrent effects of violence on inward investment,[34] the tendency so pronounced in that class to see the "British Link" as the basic guarantee of its economic well-being still exists.

The Paisleyite variety of populism has been most successful at the polls. The essence of his appeal was summed up in his telegram to Thatcher after the 1979 general election demanding a meeting to let her know that "the Protestant people of Ulster have had enough of violence and the Provisional IRA." The continuation

of Provisional violence would not, in itself, have guaranteed Paisley his success. This came as a result of the effects of the abolition of Stormont on the official Unionists. Possession of the state apparatus had served to produce Protestant unity in support of the old Unionist party. Loss of control of the state was to produce a profound disorientation. No unified strategy has replaced it. Instead, the predominant characteristic of the official Unionist party has been its equivocal position.

While formally committed to pressing the British government for the return of an elected legislature with substantial powers, an important section of its leadership, including its leader, James Molyneux, and the former Tory maverick, Enoch Powell, have been prepared to accept much less than this. The party has been openly divided between "integrationists" and "devolutionists" and it is this split that has provided the basis for Paisley's contention that traditional Unionism must be re-created with the DUP as its core. DUP strength therefore results from its apparent possession of a coherent strategy in comparison with the fumblings of the official Unionists. This extends to the area of economic policy, where at least some of the official Unionist leaders are supporters of monetarism, while the DUP is publicly adopting a rhetoric of anti-Thatcherism and opposition to the spending cuts. Are there any limits to the expansion of the DUP's electoral support among Protestants? Clearly, the continuation of the Provisionals' terrorist campaign will ensure a substantial place in Protestant politics for the DUP. Similarly, Paisley's surge in the 1981 local elections (the DUP

33. See Paul Arthur's essay "Independence" in Des Rea ed., *Political Co-operation in Divided Societies* (Dublin 1982).
34. Rowthorn, p. 11.

Journal of International Affairs

received just over 50% of the Unionist vote[35]) reflected not only the extreme communal polarization brought about by the hunger strikes, but also the grandiose claims which the Fianna Fail prime minister, Charles Haughey, was making for the Anglo-Irish talks he and Prime Minister Thatcher had begun in 1980. These were presented as a means of outflanking Unionist opposition in moving toward unity. The support of this type of strident nationalism by Fianna Fail governments only serves to consolidate the most irreconcilable elements in Protestant politics.[36]

Nonetheless, Paisley's belligerent, sometimes obscene demagogy and his penchant for stunts like the "Carson Trail" and the "Third Force" alienates many Protes-

tants who fear that it can only lead to a confrontation with Britain. Similarly, if British ministers were finally to break with the policy of trying to secure Catholic support by holding out hopes of an Irish dimension with no substance to it, they would not only help to clarify the issues in a positive way, but also remove the uncertainty on which the DUP—and the IRA—thrive.

35. Henry Patterson, "Paisley and Protestant Politics," *Marxism Today* (January 1982), p. 27.
36. Fianna Fail irredentism on the north has been of varying significance in its political strategy, see Bew and Patterson, *Sean Lemass and the Making of Modern Ireland 1945-66* (Dublin, 1982).

[3]

TOWARD UNDERSTANDING GROUP CONFLICT
IN NORTHERN IRELAND

JOSEPH O'DONOGHUE
Mercy College
Dobbs Ferry, N.Y.

MARY ANN O'DONOGHUE
Molloy College
Rockville Centre, N.Y.

In conventional attempts to analyze group conflict in Northern Ireland it is customary to focus on four groups. Two of these are outlawed, extremist groups, viz., the Provisional IRA (Irish Republican Army) and the Ulster Volunteer Force. The other two groups are the larger populations from which the relatively small numbers of extremists are drawn, viz., a Catholic minority of approximately half a million and a Protestant majority of slightly over one million.

Major differences among the four groups can readily be defined in terms of goals and means (Merton, 1957). Opinion polls and election returns have consistently indicated that the Catholic minority, experiencing an unemployment rate of over 40 percent in many Catholic wards in Northern Ireland, prefers some form of political unification with the Irish Republic to the south, rather than the current political situation in which Northern Ireland is a component of the United Kingdom (Boyle et al, 1980). The same indicators reveal that the majority of Protestants favor a continued separation of Northern and Southern Ireland. Extremists drawn from these two larger groups use violent means in pursuit of group goals, means which are routinely repudiated by the bulk of the Catholic and Protestant population.

The persistence of civil conflict in Northern Ireland has resulted in the involvement of additional groups whose goals, and the means selected to achieve these goals, should be included in an expanded framework of analysis. If one accepts "extensive cooperation between north and south" as a middle position between the two goals cited in Figure 1, and if one accepts "legalized force" as a middle position between violent and non-violent means, it is possible to locate five additional groups directly involved in a conflict situation.

Some of the new groups have members from outside the original area of contention. Units of the British Army were sent to Northern Ireland

International Journal of Group Tensions, 1981, Volume 11, Numbers 1-4. pp. 119-125. ©1981 International Organization for the Study of Group Tensions.

120 INTERNATIONAL JOURNAL OF GROUP TENSIONS

GOALS

		Unification of North and South Ireland	Separation of North and South Ireland continued
M			
E	*Violent*	Irish Republican Army (IRA) outlawed Catholic extremists	Ulster Volunteer Force (UVF) outlawed Protestant extremists
A			
N	*Non-*		
S	*Violent*	Catholic minority	Protestant majority

Figure 1. A basic typology for the analysis of the conflict in Northern Ireland.

GOALS

		Unification of North and South	Cooperation between North and South	Separation of North and South
	Violent	Irish Republican Army (IRA) outlawed Catholic extremists	Sinn Fein (political party in Northern Ireland)	Ulster Volunteer Force (UVF) outlawed Protestant extremists
M				
E	*Legalized*	Fianna Fail	British Army	Ulster Defense
A	*Force*	(political party	in	Association (UDA)
N		in	Northern Ireland	Northern Ireland's
S		Southern Ireland)		paramilitary group
	Non-	Catholic minority in	Business community in	Protestant majority in
	Violent	Northern Ireland	North and South	Northern Ireland

Figure 2. An expanded typology for the analysis of the conflict in Northern Ireland.

Conflict in Northern Ireland, J. O'Donoghue, et al. 121

in 1972 when the British Parliament decided that local authorities were losing the power to maintain civil order. Their continued presence has stimulated new support on behalf of eventual unification with Southern Ireland. Fianna Fail, the political party most closely associated with the unification goal, grew steadily in Southern Ireland during the 1970's, finally ousting from parliamentary control Fine Gael, the party regarded as less enthusiastic toward political involvement in Northern Ireland (Rush, 1977).

Two other groups in the expanded framework of analysis have also been experiencing an increase in power. Sinn Fein, the political wing of the IRA, has increased recently in membership and support among the Catholic minority, who realize from history that a vote for Sinn Fein is a vote for the ballot and bullet together. Other political parties competing for the Catholic vote have repeatedly repudiated violence and IRA tactics (Power, 1976).

The Ulster Defense Association, a voluntary organization of Protestants with self provided military training, has the support of the Protestant majority. Reverend Ian Paisley, the clerical fundamentalist most closely identified with Protestant paramilitaries, supports military action to eliminate suspected staging areas for IRA forces. With its promise to use its own military to preserve the status quo in job distribution, the Ulster Defense Association has a strong appeal to blue collar Protestants in a shaky economy. A reversal of religious discrimination in employment would mean a wholesale loss of jobs in now Protestant dominated work areas (Lee, 1981).

Least powerful of the five new groups in the framework is an alliance of leaders in the business community from both the North and the South. Protracted conflict in the North, combined with a loss of crossborder trade, has weakened both economies. The overall unemployment rate of almost twenty percent in the North provides a constant source of out of work recruits for both the IRA and the Protestant extremists, while road blocks and trade uncertainties have impeded the traditional business links between the two nations. Business leaders on both sides of the border would gain immense benefits from closer ties involving the heavily industrialized North and the advancing industrial movement in the South (Boyle et al, 1980).

British Army units were originally sent to Northern Ireland in the belief that their training and the expertise of their officers would serve as a neutral, stabilizing force at a time of group conflict. After ten years it is clear that the army has not been effective in its role of preventing violence by extremists. The IRA and its counterpart, the Ulster Volunteer Force, regularly engage in a trade-off of assasinations, a scenario in which the British Army, the local police, and the public are passive spectators.

Standard operating procedure of the IRA is the bombing of buildings and execution of soldiers in the British Army's Ulster Regiment. Murders are followed by the now customary phone call to the local newspaper, informing the press of the time and circumstances of each act of retaliation. Targeted cars have been planted with bombs by Irish nationalists. The explosions are followed by Protestant sectarian attacks on Catholics which in turn evoke further retaliatory action. Other incidents include cars stolen by youngsters resulting in army and police patrols opening fire (Boyle et al, 1980).

British Army units have been similarly unsuccessful in efforts to confine violence to Northern Ireland. In recent years the IRA has been able to expand its operation to include targets in England, acting on its assumption that one bombing in London has a world press impact equivalent to ten bombings in Northern Ireland. IRA spokesmen immediately claimed the execution of Lord Mountbatten in 1979 and foretold continued assasinations of prestige targets (Coogan, 1980).

The British Army's failure to achieve cooperation through legalized force can be traced to its relationship with the various groups in the conflict network. The army has a predictable, adversarial relationship with two of the three groups using violent means; (1) IRA terrorists regularly attack British units, while (2) Sinn Fein, the political arm of the IRA, conducts campaigns in which there is a clear implication that force will be necessary to expel the British troops from Northern Ireland. The Ulster Volunteer Force does not attack the British units, and its spokesmen announce retaliatory murders in response to the killing of soldiers by the IRA. The army's attempted role as peace keeper is compromised by the perception, held by both Catholics and Protestants, that it will not vigorously pursue terrorists who are not hostile to soldiers (Coogan, 1980).

This double standard has complicated the relationship of the army with the dominant Fianna Fail political party in the South. Fianna Fail leaders have chosen to given only token support to British intelligence efforts, thereby making the nation's northern tier, particularly County Donegal, a safe haven for IRA squads who know that they cannot be pursued across the the border into the Irish Republic. Police in Southern Ireland will seize weapons and explosives destined for the North in response to tips on suspected depots. In only a handful of cases, however, have they arrested or detained known members of the IRA (Coogan, 1980).

Charles J. Haughey, Fianna Fail leader in the South, voices his party's goal of unification of North and South, a position which puts him on a collision course with the policies of England's Prime Minister Margaret Thatcher and the majority of the British Parliament. In various ways Fianna Fail

Conflict in Northern Ireland, J. O'Donoghue, et al. 123

politicians have indicated that any intrusion into the South by British units or Protestant paramilitaries, as suggested by the North's Reverend Ian Paisley, will be countered by the Southern version of legalized force.

The British Army has a mixed record among the three other groups to which it must relate. The Ulster Defense Association, and the Protestant majority of the North, are beneficiaries of a system in which discrimination in hiring, documented in official British government reports, is the major factor responsible for keeping the Catholic unemployment rate 20 to 30 percent higher than the Prostestant rate. In this context the army is perceived by these two groups as supportive, providing protection against a possible uprising of the unemployed. The Catholic minority perceives the army as an adversarial preserver of an unjust status quo (Lee, 1981).

In considering long term solutions to the conflict in Northern Ireland it may be helpful to compare the inter-group relationships of the British Army, as discussed above, with those of the business community.

GROUP	RELATIONSHIP	
	with British Army	with Business Community
Irish Republican Army (IRA)	adversarial	adversarial
Sinn Fein political party	adversarial	adversarial
Ulster Volunteer Force (UVF)	neutral	adversarial
Fianna Fail political party	adversarial	supportive
Ulster Defense Association (UDA)	supportive	supportive
Catholic minority	adversarial	adversarial
Protestant majority	supportive	supportive

Figure 3. Relationships of the conflict groups with the British Army and the business community.

It should be noted that the business community differs from the army in that the business community is opposed to all three groups using violent means to achieve goals. This adversarial relationship is not based on ideology; the bombing of any business, for whatever reason, has a disastrous impact on all business in that area. Soldiers continue to be paid when explosives are used, but businessmen go bankrupt.

In contrast to the army with its search and capture objectives, goals which intrude upon the national prerogatives of politicians, the business community has an affinity toward developing a mutually beneficial relationship with the dominant Fianna Fail party in the South, since that relationship brings the promise of profits through trading across the border. Within Northern Ireland the British Army and the business community share similar supportive relationships with Protestant workers and adversarial realtionships with Catholic workers. However, the relationship between the business community and the Catholic workers, half of whom are currently unemployed, could undergo radical change if additional jobs could be created over time, steadily reducing the Catholic rate of unemployment.

CONCLUSION

Most analysts of the current tension in Northern Ireland would be skeptical of any peace plan which would replace soldiers with business leaders. Nevertheless, research on crime rates in American cities indicates a correlation between the unemployment rate and crimes of violence. When unemployment rises, violent crime increases; conversely, a drop in a city's unemployment rate is followed by a drop in the rate of violent crime (Harris, 1981).

Up to now the majority of proposals to end violence in Northern Ireland have tended to take two forms; (1) moral persuasion directed toward terrorists and the larger population to repudiate violence as degenerate, ineffective, and counterproductive, and (2) legislative action to end the job discrimination which leaders of all persuasions identify as the fuel which energizes constant civil disorder. Neither approach has been particularly effective over a ten year period. A reapportionment of currently available jobs, even if it could be politically achieved, would result in adding a Protestant to the unemployed list for every formerly unemployed Catholic who received a job. Within a matter of months, or possibly weeks, unemployed Protestants could be expected to follow the behavior pattern now associated with Catholic radicals.

In this context an alternative would be to gradually shift the military budget into a fund designated to create new jobs in Northern Ireland, with the provision that (1) the principles of equal opportunity be followed, and that (2) the results be subject to monthly audit. In its early stages

Conflict in Northern Ireland, J. O'Donoghue, et al. 125

the fund would benefit by international loans, payable when the economy of Northern Ireland achieved the production level which civil disorder now blocks. The military presence would be reduced in stages, with business and civic leaders reassuming pivotal relationships in group interactions.

REFERENCES

BOYLE, K., HADDEN, T., & HILLYARD, P. *Ten years in Northern Ireland.* Nottingham: The Cobden Trust, 1980.

COOGAN, T.P. *The I.R.A.* Glasgow: Fontana Books, 1980.

HARRIS, M. Why it's not the same old America. *Psychology Today*, 1981, *15*, 22-51.

IRISH GOVERNMENT REPORT. *Investment and national development 1979-1983.* Dublin: Government Publications, 1980.

LEE, A.M. The dynamics of terrorism in Northern Ireland: 1968-1980. *Social Research*, 1981, *48*, 100-134,

McALISTER, I. The legitimacy of opposition: the collapse of the 1974 Northern Ireland executive. *Eire-Ireland*, 1977, *12*, 25-42.

MERTON, R.K. *Social theory and social structure.* Glencoe, Ill.: Free Press, 1968.

POWER, P. Violence, consent, and the Northern Ireland problem. *The Journal of Commonwealth and Comparative Politics*, 1976, *14*, 119-140.

RUSHE, D. Pounds and sense. *Eire-Ireland*, 1977, *12*, 76-80.

[4]

Political Psychology, Vol. 7, No. 3, 1986

The Moralism of Attitudes Supporting
Intergroup Violence[1]

William Ascher[2]

Q-Sort analysis of belief structures helps to understand why some supporters of Armenian and Northern Irish Catholic independence movements condone violence. Relatively coherent moral (indeed, moralistic) beliefs, accompanied by consistent affects and expectations, are typically found for these long-standing intergroup confrontations. The importance of this consistency suggests a pivotal role for conflict-mitigating policies that can reduce either moral indignation or expectations of success, since these factors are often essential components of moralistic pro-violence perspectives.

KEY WORDS: attitudes toward violence; intergroup violence; belief structures; Armenians; Northern Ireland; Q-methodology.

INTRODUCTION

In the modern world, universalistic norms requiring moral behavior toward all human beings are highly prominent, if not consistently followed. Intergroup violence invariably defies or at least is challenged by these norms.[3] This clash between universalistic norms and the support of intergroup violence gives rise to two distinct interpretations of the etiology of such violence, implying quite different prescriptions for managing this chronic problem.

One interpretation views intergroup violence as the outgrowth of a disintegration of the belief system, and particularly of the principles of morali-

---

[1] Research by Harris Leviton, Jean Preston, and Alouette Kluge was essential to this article.
[2] Institute of Policy Sciences and Public Affairs, Duke University, Durham, North Carolina 27706.
[3] This is not true for all cultures and eras; such strong buttressing for proviolence attitudes is required only where they are attacked by general societal mores. The anthropologist William Graham Sumner (1906) was able to point out innumerable instances of intergroup violence in need of no moral or even pragmatic justification.

0162-895X/86/0900-0403$05.00/1 © 1986 International Society of Political Psychology

ty. Such violence is either an explosion of primitive impulses, such as anger or fear, that overwhelms otherwise binding moral prohibitions (Berkowitz, 1962; Kelman, 1973; Rochlin, 1973; Strachey, 1957; Yates, 1962), or it is the callous manifestation of one group's interest in exploiting another (Ball-Rokeach, 1972; Hallie, 1971; Opton and Duckless, 1970). Moral principles, if articulated at all by those engaging in or supporting intergroup violence, are conceived of as merely rationalizations for basically unprincipled actions. The generally acute conditions that lead to a flight from responsibility (danger, stress, indignity, and other factors that "dehumanize the aggressor") are the root causes.

The other interpretation views intergroup violence as the manifestation of internally consistent beliefs, including moral principles. Rather than representing the suspension or absence of moral standards, the violence is justified by legitimating beliefs that, from the individual's point of view, are as "moral" as any held by those of us who abhor violence. Articulated positions are justifications rather than rationalizations. The beliefs are thus a relatively coherent set of attitudes arising from the confrontation among groups.[4]

The question of whether belief systems associated with support for violence have any coherence is of more than academic interest; it addresses the feasibility of any tactics to control intergroup violence. Without any coherence, there would be no way to shape other belief system components (such as appeals to other normative principles or demonstrations of the futility of expecting success) so as to undermine the appeal of violence. But, as is common with conflicting plausible generalizations, both of these interpretations can be valid, depending on the circumstances. Therefore, we must first ask, "Under what circumstances might we expect that support for intergroup violence is part of a coherent, moralistic belief system?" Second, to the degree that there is consistency or coherence of beliefs, how are moral principles integrated with the other major components of belief systems? Following Lasswell, we stipulate these to be the remaining "appeal" components of affects and instrumental motivations, and the "perspective" components of identifications, demands, and expectations.[5] Third, which of these elements is useful for managing intergroup conflict?

---

[4]Rare indeed is the author who makes this argument explicitly, perhaps because of the uneasiness with taking a position that could be interpreted as endorsing violence. Nonetheless, analyses of the logic and structure of proviolence attitudes presume that a relatively coherent structure exists (for example, Burton, 1978; J. Davies, 1976; Dugard, 1982; Louch, 1982; Martic, 1975; and Pottenger, 1982).

[5]Lasswell (1932) applied the Freudian division of id, ego, and superego to explain the appeal of "any social object." The meaning of a social object to any person depends on its appeal to one *or more* of these divisions. Because attitudes and acts are social objects, the logic of this "triple appeal principle" can be applied to interpret attitudes and actions of intergroup

These questions address the *structure* of beliefs, which requires intensive rather than extensive study. Therefore we focused on small numbers from groups engaged in intergroup confrontations, but we selected two groups rather than just one, in order to distinguish idiosyncratic from general aspects. One group consists of U.S.-based members of Northern Irish Aid, an organization that aids imprisoned IRA fighters and their families; it is widely (but not unanimously) recognized that such aid encorages IRA fighters to continue to engage in violent acts. The other group is a U.S.-based Armenian organization dedicated to Armenian culture and welfare, but which also supports the political objectives of securing an independent Armenian Republic and an official Turkish government admission of the 1915 genocide. These organizations are not engaged in violence, and only some of their members support armed struggle. While this focus does not permit us to observe the behavior of "violent groups," it does permit us to contrast the attitude structures of members who condone violence with those of members who reject violence. A group of Lebanese Christian university students was also administered the same basic protocol as the Armenians, in order to examine differences in consistency between long-standing and novel confrontations. However, the Lebanese subjects were not a central focus for this study, and hence the analysis of their responses is abbreviated.[6]

Initial, largely unstructured meetings with each of these groups were designed to draw out their views on the intergroup confrontation. These rather

---

violence. In Lasswell's own applications of the principle, he assumed that a social object's appeal to a given individual could rest primarily (but probably not exclusively) on just one component (emotion, conscience, or reason). However, "no institutional pattern falls into any pigeonhole with any more than an approximate fit" (p. 534). This tripartite distinction remains prominent in the fields of social and political psychology, but it is often expressed in different terms; e.g., emotion, morality, and instrumentalism; passions, principles, and pragmatism, and so on.

[6]More precise identification of these groups would be inappropriate for political and security reasons. Each of the three initial meetings drew 12 to 20 individuals; six to nine respondents eventually completed the Q-sort protocols for each group. The Lebanese respondents were all Lebanese citizens of college age; all were Maronites or Greek Orthodox. The Irish Catholics were all American citizens (though two were born in Ulster), ranging in age from 30 to 55. Four of the nine Armenians completing the Q-sorts were raised outside of the United States (but only one in Turkish territory), the rest were American-born. The Armenians, ranging in age from 20 to 50, were all members of the Armenian Church. The reliance on subjects living in the United States might seem to reduce the "typicality" of their views. However, for the particular groups under examination, this is far less of a problem than it might seem at first glance. Few Armenians are left in Turkish Armenia, and most of the violence against Turkish officials is undertaken by Armenians abroad, some in the United States. Similarly, some of the most strident support for the IRA comes from Irish Americans. The Lebanese students had all been back to Lebanon 6 months prior to the Q-sort. Finally, it should be recalled that the Q-sort is not designed to determine whether a given distribution of attitudes is typical or representative of the population as a whole, but rather to explore whether and how attitudes are integrated into coherent viewpoints.

free-for-all discussions provided discourse for Q-sort analyses, along with additional statements reflecting the principles of justice (such as reciprocity and transgenerational responsibility) cited in the literature on intergroup violence. These 80 to 90 statements were divided into three separate Q-sorts concerning *general principles* of justice and violence, *specific principles* regarding the group's confrontation, and *expectations* of the motives, strategies, and outcomes of the confrontation. Since many of these statements pertain to the particular issues of each confrontation, the result was a somewhat different set of three Q-sorts for each of the three groups. Several statements embedded within these Q-sorts also gauged the degree of *identification* with the in-group, although variation along this dimension was limited due to the selection of subjects. (The appendix provides greater detail on the methodology.)

COHERENCE

The consistency of belief systems emerging from *long-standing* confrontations (e.g., Northern Ireland and Armenia) can be contrasted with belief systems in more novel confrontations to give us a glimpse at the results of self-selection, recruitment, and the many-labeled mechanisms of cognitive consistency or dissonance reduction (Abelson *et al.,* 1968) that tend to act over time. Individuals with attitudes consistent with support for intergroup violence would be expected to find it easier to embrace and maintain proviolence attitudes; others would be less likely to join or support the militants, or would suffer stress that prompts them eventually to drop out of proviolence activities or to realign their attitudes.

Our comparison focuses on responses of Armenian and Lebanese respondents, the latter chosen because Lebanon became the site of novel confrontation inasmuch as the relations among Lebanese Christians, Lebanese Moslems, Palestinians, Syrians and Israelis changed dramatically after the PLO began to use Lebanon as a base and even more so after the 1982 Israeli invasion. Nine pairs of general and specific statements included in the Q-sorts given to the Armenian respondents were virtually identical to statement pairs ranked by the Lebanese.[7] The "inconsistency" scores, i.e., the ac-

---

[7]Differences between the Irish Catholic Q-sort, both in format (30-statement rather than 20-statement) and content, precluded direct comparisons of levels of consistency with the Lebanese or Armenian results. The statements ranked by the Armenians and Lebanese were:

　　a.　General: "Self-defense is the only legitimate reason for using violence."
　　Armenian specific: "Violence against the Turks is justified only if our lives are in danger."
　　Lebanese specific: "Violence against the Palestinians or others is justified only if our lives are in danger."
　　b.　General: "People are responsible for the crimes committed by their fathers."
　　Armenian specific: "All Turks bear some responsibility for what some of them have done to the Armenians."

cumulated differences in the ranking of each general statement with its respective specific statement, are displayed in Table I.

In addition to the greater consistency among the participants of the long-standing confrontation (statistically significant despite the small samples), we see that among individuals *within* the Armenian sample there is no greater

---

Lebanese specific: "All Palestinians bear some responsibility for what some of them have done to the Lebanese."

   c.   General: "Independence is more important than the lives that may have to be sacrificed to achieve it."

Armenian specific: "If Armenian independence requires bloodshed, then bloodshed is necessary."

Lebanese specific: "If Lebanon's independence requires bloodshed, then bloodshed is necessary."

   d.   General: "You should treat others as they treat you."

Armenian specific: "We should respond to the Turks the same ways that they treat us."

Lebanese specific: "We should respond to Palestinians, Syrians or Israelis the same ways that they treat us."

   e.   General: "Someone who gives me no respect deserves the same from me."

Armenian specific: "If a Turk treats me like dirt, then he deserves the same treatment from me."

Lebanese specific: "If a Palestinian, Syrian or Israeli treats me like dirt, then he deserves the same treatment from me."

   f.   General: "Taking away a man's honor is as bad as taking his life."

Armenian specific: "Denying an Armenian his honor is as bad as depriving him of his life."

Lebanese specific: "Denying a Lebanese his honor is as bad as depriving him of his life."

   g.   General: "A people can stand only so much abuse before they must lash out against those who caused it."

Armenian specific: "Armenians can only take so much abuse – then it is psychologically impossible not to retaliate."

Lebanese specific: "The Lebanese can only take so much abuse – then it is psychologically impossible not to retaliate."

   h.   General: "Violence is simply an aspect of human nature."

Armenian specific: "The Armenian-Turkish struggle is the normal result of man's nature as a creature of conflict."

Lebanese specific: "The violence in Labanon is the normal result of man's nature as a creature of conflict."

   i.   General: "Under extreme circumstances, humanitarian considerations have to be suspended."

Armenian specific: "The Armenian situation is so extreme that the actions of Armenians cannot be judged as if things were normal."

Lebanese specific: "The Lebanese situation is so extreme that the actions of Lebanese Christians cannot be judged as if things were normal."

Note that sufficient time was given between the general and specific Q-sorts for the general statement rankings (these 9 were imbedded among 11 others) to be "copied" directly into the rankings of specific statements. Nevertheless, to reduce the possibility of individuals imposing consistency by remembering their responses from the general-statement Q-sort, the working of the specific statements was altered as long as the substance of the statement could be preserved. Yet, some of the individuals who agree most strongly with the last two statements are more pacifistic than anyone else among our respondents, as judged by their strong disagreement with the first two statements and their views on specific proposals for resolving the conflicts in their countries. It may be that the individuals who regard violence to be morally repugnant, but who must also find reasons why their own people are engaging in such violence, would find attitudes c and d both reasonable and comforting. Whatever the reason, these seemingly additive beliefs are not additive at all.

Table I. Inconsistency between General and Specific Statement Rankings, Armenian and Lebanese Respondents[a]

Lebanese Respondents ($N = 6$)	Armenian Respondents ($N = 9$)	
10	4	(antiviolence)
11	5	
12	6	(proviolence)
13	7	
15	8	
15	9	(proviolence)
	9	
	11	
	18	(antiviolence)
Mean 12.7	8.6	

[a]$t = 2.23$ for the difference-of-means test; significant
beyond the 0.025 level for a one-tailed test.

inconsistency among the violence-prone. The four most extremely proviolence
and antiviolence Armenian respondents are so designated in Table I. Indeed,
the most pacifistic Armenian had the *least* consistency; his general principles
were so extraordinarily pacifistic that his specific responses, although antiviolence compared to his countrymen's attitudes, were still discrepant with
his "general principles." In contrast, the second most pacifistic Armenian,
who did not express such rigidly antiviolence general views, was the most
consistent. The two most proviolence Armenians had only moderate levels
of inconsistency. This is at least preliminary evidence that consistency is not
the exclusive domain of the pacifist; that in long-standing confrontations
even proviolence individuals can select or develop relatively coherent belief
structures. This attribution of relative consistency is, however, obviously tentative. Consistency is more clearly demonstrated by showing that a coherent
attitude structure can be revealed to the outside observer.

BASIC ARMENIAN AND IRISH OUTLOOKS

Upon analyzing the Armenian and Irish views in some detail through
factor analysis of the Q-sorts, we have concluded that coherent structures
of moral principles, emotions, motives, and perspectives can be found. Before
drawing conclusions about the broad interrelations among these components,
it is useful to outline the dominant viewpoints.

The Armenian respondents held two fundamental outlooks toward
violence. Rather than reflecting out-and-out disagreement, however, the differences represent different priorities of concern. The outlooks do not completely distinguish between pro- and antiviolence attitudes, but rather provide

frameworks for situating support or opposition toward violence in the specific context. Table II summarizes some of the statement rankings.[8]

The first outlook, which can be labeled "dispassionate instrumentalism," accepts the legitimacy of violence to achieve ends beyond personal self-defense: independence and the preservation of group identity — but not revenge. When peaceful alternatives fail, violence becomes necessary. In these extreme circumstances, humanitarian concerns must be suspended, and engaging in violence does not reduce the moral standing of the individual struggling for these legitimate ends.

But if the ends justify the means, the moral standing of any action depends on the morality of the ends. Why should the Armenians' ends be considered worthier than those of the Turks? The respondents invoke the ancient historical claim to the region of East Anatolia, bolstered by the short-lived Armenian Republic of 1918. Whether these historical antecedents constitute a legitimate right to the territory is, of course, debatable. Also, Armenians supporting independence (whether instrumentalists or not) believe that the genocide, like the Holocaust of the Jews, makes the victims and survivors worthy of compensation: i.e., Turkish admission of the genocide, a homeland for the survivors, and restitution of land and wealth stripped from the Armenians.

However, the propriety of an individual's actions to achieve these ends also depends on whether the individual is self-serving in his or her support of independence and restitution. The importance of avoiding selfishness is highlighted by the fact that the most pervasive difference between the Armenians' views of the Turks and themselves was the attribution of selfishness to the Turks. Yet, although no Armenian (or Irish Catholic) could deny that success of the group is "self-serving" in the sense of benefiting the group with which the individual very strongly identifies, the individual can reduce the implied *personal* selfishness by rejecting personal material gain (while at the same time maintaining loyalty to the cause by expressing a strong commitment to resettle in an independent Armenia) and by minimizing personal *emotional* satisfaction. Thus the Armenian respondent with the most consistently instrumental attitudes nonetheless had the most negative reaction to the idea that he should receive material compensation.

The instrumentalists are also strikingly detached in their expressed affective orientation. They deny being motivated by vengeance, fear, affronts to their group's pride, or contempt for the outgroup. Although it would seem tempting to hold a highly negative image of the outgroup in order to justify violence against it, the instrumentalists instead maintain the purity of their objectives by eschewing emotional or personal motives. Armenians should

---

[8]The following table reports only one of several Q-sort result sets for the Armenians. Other results, excluded out of considerations of space, are available upon request from the author.

Table II. Armenians: Ranking of Specific Principle Statements

Statement	Factor 1	Factor 2
The world will not do anything to bring justice for the Armenian people unless we do so first.	+3	0
If after sixty years of peaceful protest we have not achieved justice, it is time to try something less peaceful.	+2	0
Armenians can only take so much abuse — then it is psychologically impossible not to retaliate.	+2	0
The Armenian situation is so extreme that the actions of Armenians cannot be judged as if things were normal.	+2	+1
Armenians will not be able to survive as a people unless we are strong.	+1	−1
If Armenian independence requires bloodshed, then bloodshed is necessary.	+1	+2
History weeds out the nations that cannot survive.	+1	−2
It was bad enough that the Turks committed the genocide — but for then to deny it now is equally bad.	+1	+3
Turks tend to lack the moral status that we have come to expect from ourselves.	0	−1
Denying an Armenian his honor is as bad as depriving his of his life.	0	+1
The Turkish officials who go along with the denial of the genocide should personally bear the punishment for this.	0	+2
The criticisms of Armenian extremists come from people who are trying to maintain their own comfort and security	0	+1
If a Turk treats me like dirt, then he deserve the same treatment from me.	−1	−3
We should respond to Turks the same ways they treat us.	+1	0
The only way for Armenians to regain our pride is to avenge the injustices we have suffered.	−1	−2
No matter how important it is for us to regain our homeland, it is extremely important to remember that Turks are people too.	−1	−2
Violence against the Turks is justified only if our own lives in danger.	−2	−1
All Turks bear some responsibility for what some of them have done to the Armenians.	−2	+2
Armenians lose some of their moral stature by engaging in violence, even if it is against Turks.	−2	0
The Armenian-Turkish struggle is the normal result of man's nature as a creature of conflict	−3	−1

not retaliate against disrespectful treatment by Turks; Armenian honor and pride are not at issue; nor are the Turks of lesser moral stature than Armenians. Yet, if the goal of Armenian independence requires bloodshed, then so be it. The legitimacy of instrumental violence is compatible with the view of the confrontation as *war,* wherein both sides, fighting for political ends, are permitted their violence. If the Turkish violence is taken by Armenians in the vein of "war is war," rather than as immorality, then the Armenians' violence is legitimized the same way. It is noteworthy that this outlook shows no hint of "dehumanization" of the outgroup.

We see here a critical distinction between instrumental views of violence and instrumental motives for supporting violence. Viewing violence as means to ends does not imply that the ends are pragmatic rather than moralistic or emotional; they may be any of these. The dispassionate instrumentalist supports the struggle for largely noninstrumental reasons, particularly when it comes to anticipated personal benefit, but this detachment permits contemplating violence as a means, without evoking feelings of selfishness, hypocrisy, or guilt.

The second outlook found among Armenian interviewees may be termed "aggrieved moralism." This perspective has two seemingly unrelated or even contradictory elements that in fact are mutually reinforcing. The first is the priority given to humanitarian concerns. There is no endorsement of the importance of independence over the sacrifice of lives, nor of the assertion that violence is necessary when peaceful alternatives fail. Like the instrumentalists, the moralists reject the eye-for-an-eye mentality of vengeance or of meeting disrespect with disrespect. Even under extreme circumstances, humanitarian concerns cannot be abandoned. While the moralists do not strongly agree that Armenians lose their moral stature by engaging in violence, they do not reject the idea either. The moral dilemma of responding to violence with violence is not lost on the moralists, but their ambivalence does not amount to a rejection of violence on this ground.

The second component of this outlook is moralistic opprobrium against *both* violence and the Turks. In the abstract, violence is legitimate only for self-defense. Consequently the genocide, and its cover-up, place enormous culpability upon the Turkish governments and people. The Armenians' own high moral standards, and their usual abhorrence of violence, make the Turkish record all the more condemnable and punishable. At the same time, Turkish treatment of Armenians, and especially the arrogant refusal of the Turkish government to acknowledge the genocide, is so heinous that some Armenians find it psychologically impossible to resist retaliating. Thus, although this outlook rejects any idea that humanitarian concerns can be suspended or that reciprocally cruel or disrespectful behavior is justifiable, it provides a basis for understanding and absolving Armenian reprisals against Turkish targets.

The Armenian respondents who hold this moralistic outlook are not much less disposed to support or to legitimize violence against the Turks; in a way, they are more antagonistic toward Turks than are the instrumentalists, who do not capitalize on the view that all Turks are culpable and thus deserve punishment. The moralists accept the general proposition that people are responsible for the crimes of their fathers, whereas the instrumentalists reject this proposition in both its general form and the specific belief that all Turks are responsible for the atrocities against Armenians. Because moral standards *can* be upheld, the injuries to the Armenian people are more serious to the moralist than to the instrumentalist, who holds Realpolitik premises. According to the moralistic outlook, Armenians are the morally superior, aggrieved party; they reject that "war is war." The moralistic outlook also accepts, while the instrumental perspective does not, that Turkish officials are personally responsible for the policies and crimes of their government.

There are two possible explanations for the apparently harsher condemnation held within what might be expected to be a "gentler," more pacifistic view. First, perhaps these views are extreme extensions of the opposition to violence; i.e., violence is so heinous that it even taints future generations and everyone connected with a government of violence. Yet, the fact that the moralists do not condemn violence by everyone (Armenians) leads to another interpretation. Armenians who regard violence as unacceptable in principle may feel compelled to justify both the violence of their countrymen and their own sympathy for this violence. Therefore, despite their unwillingness to agree with direct statements that violence is justifiable, they agree with statements that make their compatriots less culpable for falling prey to the appeals of violence. They strongly agree that "A people can stand only so much abuse before they must lash out against those who caused it." In contrast, the instrumental view that violence can be straightforwardly condoned gives its adherents relative serenity, with no need to find mitigating circumstances to excuse fellow Armenians for commiting violent acts.

Supporters of the Irish struggle for reunification have outlooks with considerable similarities to those of the Armenians. Table III summarizes the dominant factor scores for their outlooks on the specific situation of Northern Ireland. Three outlooks can be identified within our small set of Northern Irish Aid supporters. Again, these are variations in priorities and preoccupations more than direct disagreement. The first two outlooks bear similarities to dispassionate instrumentalism. The third is unique, in that it is moralistic without being condemnatory.

For the first Irish perspective, the normative issues of the morality of violence per se are secondary to the preoccupation with the substantive issues of the Irish-English confrontation. Strongest sentiments are reserved for propositions about the justice of the cause, not the means for achieving justice.[9] This outlook rests on the basic premise that current conditions in Northern Ireland are intolerable, with the discrimination against the Catholic minori-

---

[9]It is difficult to establish whether the lack of strong positions on the legitimacy of the violence per se are due to the low priority of the issue in their minds, ambivalence (possibly resulting from recognition of the problematical nature of the violence), or a failure to think through the issues.

ty constituting a form of violence. This equivalence of discrimination with violence is, not surprisingly, a key element in the argument that the violence of the IRA is neither different in kind from the treatment of Irish Catholics by Protestants and their English allies, nor disproportionate to the injustices suffered by the Catholics. Both the soldiers of the British army and the representatives of the British government must bear responsibility for provoking violence and for aiding in the Irish Protestants' continued repression of the Catholics. This is war, even if the British and the Ulster Protestants pretend it is not.

As culpable as these enemies may be, however, the issue is emphatically *not* a matter of vengeance, retaliation, or pride. Vengeance is petty; and Irish Catholic pride and honor are firm regardless of the evolution of the Ulster issue. The conflict is strictly political one, fought with respect for the opponent even if calculated attacks on the lives of specific targets are necessary. In fact, two of the three Irish Catholic respondents who share this outlook did not reject the proposition that a moral argument could be made on both sides of the Ulster issue! This outlook shares with the Armenians' dispassionate instrumentalism the rejection of emotionality, as either motive or rationalization. It rejects the idea that the Irish people lash out because of the psychological effects of the abuse they have suffered.

The second Irish perspective is held by the two strongest supporters of IRA violence. It shows intense and emotional commitment to the ultimate objectives of honor and reunification, but a coldly rational, dispassionate attitude toward the means. It vehemently rejects the proposition that the British and the Orangemen have a defensible moral position. Polarization and violence in Ulster do not justify or excuse violence (if so, violence against the Catholics would be justified as well), but the accumulated offenses against the Catholics do. These conditions force Irish Catholics into violence. Unlike the first outlook, Irish honor *is* at stake. And, if the Irish Catholics do not struggle to the utmost, no one else will accomplish their objectives for them. Thus, given that the Irish Catholic ends are both righteous and compelling, its adherents can endorse their own group's violence as purely instrumental without qualms about its moral implications, defending its morality without blurring the distinction between physical violence and socioeconomic discrimination. Violence by the long-persecuted Catholics is a means to such an imperative end that it is in an altogether different category than the condemnable violence of the Irish protestants and the British.

The final Irish outlook emphasizes the human, personal side of the Northern Irish situation, expressing sympathy and concern for both sides while still maintaining the justice and urgency of reunification. The Northern Irish situation is a tragedy of history, exacerbated by ill-conceived but not necessarily malevolent British policy, not the fault of individuals or groups. The

Table III. Irish Catholics: Rankings of Specific Principle Statements

Statement	Factor		
	1	2	3
The laws imposed on Northern Ireland by the British have no basis for being considered legitimate.	+4	+3	+4
The Protestant "Majority" in Northern Ireland is an artificial trick imposed by the British.	+4	+3	-3
The world will not do anything to bring justice in Northern Ireland unless we do so first.	+3	+2	-2
The Northern Irish have been so disoriented by the violence that "law" has little meaning.	+3	-4	-2
The discrimination against Catholics in Northern Ireland has actually been a form of violence	+3	+1	+4
If reunification requires bloodshed, then bloodshed is necessary.	+2	+2	+1
The British officials who serve under a government that oppresses Northern Ireland should bear the responsibility and risk the punishment.	+2	+2	-1
The suffering of the Northern Irish is sufficient justification for punishing the representatives of the British government.	+2	-2	-3
People who bemoan the violence of the IRA usually have a vested interest in maintaining the status quo.	+2	-1	+1
The conflict in Northern Ireland is more than a power struggle for self-respect.	+1	+1	+1
The criticisms against the IRA come from people who are trying to maintain their own comfort and security.	+1	-3	+3
The situation in Northern Ireland is so extreme that the action of Irish Catholics cannot be judged as if things were normal.	+1	-3	+3
Political violence is simply a means to an end—a way to gain reunification that we might otherwise not achieve.	+1	+4	0

The Moralism of Attitudes Supporting Intergroup Violence

Statement			
The Irish will not be able to prosper as a people unless we are strong.	0	+1	−1
History weeds out the nations that cannot survive.	0	+4	−2
Since many years of peaceful protest did not achieve justice, it is time to try something less peaceful.	0	+4	−2
No matter how important it is to reunite Ireland, we must remember that the English are human too.	0	0	+3
Supporting violence against the British and the Unionists in Northern Ireland is justified only if one's life is in danger.	−1	−3	+2
All Englishmen bear responsibility for what some of them have done to the Irish.	−1	−1	−4
Even if we could not achieve the reunification of Ireland, it would still be important to fight against British rule.	−1	0	+2
Emotions should not play a part in determining the outcome of the situation in Northern Ireland.	−2	0	−4
We should respond to the English and the Unionists as they treat us.	−2	−4	0
The English tend to lack the moral status that we expect from ourselves.	−2	0	−1
Denying an Irishman his honor is as bad as denying him his life.	−2	+2	+2
It is sad but true that both sides to the conflict in Northern Ireland can make a moral argument for their position.	−2	−1	−3
If an Englishman treats me like dirt, he deserves the same from me.	−3	+1	0
The Irish can only take so much abuse—then it is psychologically impossible not to retaliate.,	−3	+3	+2
The struggle in Northern Ireland is the normal result of man's nature as a creature of conflict.	−3	−1	−1
The Irish lose some of their moral status by engaging in violence, even if it is against the British government.	−4	−2	−2

culpability of the English people or even British officials is rejected. Northern Irish Protestants are also victims of this tragedy.

This is the only Northern Irish outlook with a pacifistic strain: Violence is justified only for personal self defense; it is important to keep in mind that the English are human too. Yet, as with the first Irish outlook, discrimination against the Northern Irish Catholic is itself a form of violence. This equation of discrimination with violence as a basis for excusing the ingroup's violence is reinforced by the belief that Irish Catholic violence is psychological unavoidable under existing conditions. In pursuit of the only just solution — reunification with the Republic of Ireland in order to rid Ulster of anti-Catholic discrimination — the IRA must be supported despite its unfortunate but psychologically unavoidable reliance on violence.

AFFECTS AND INSTRUMENTAL MOTIVES

The proposition that the belief systems of individuals who support violence are likely to be consistent rests on the idea that any individual who values rectitude and respect in the modern world, where there are pervasive norms against violence, is unlikely to hold proviolence attitudes "lightly"; that is, without comprehensive support from and consistency with other beliefs and emotions. Here we examine those emotions, and indeed find that they not only provide the impulse for involvement but also cement the relationship between moral principles and the advocacy of violence. We have noted that, in our Armenian and Irish respondents, the most highly charged affects are channeled to the consideration of ends rather than means. What affects are these, and how do they relate to the principles of justice and violence expressed in the outlooks just reviewed?

Moral indignation is highly visible among those who defend violence. It pervades the Armenians' emphasis of the Turkish cover-up, their outrage at the Turkish press campaign to discredit Armenian claims, and their condemnation of the insensitivity of the rest of the world to the plight of Armenians. The Irish Catholics similarly emphasize the indignities imposed upon IRA prisoners, the hypocrisy of the British government in both its Machiavellian manipulations of Ulster and its press campaign, and the immorality of continued anti-Catholic discrimination.

Moral indignation is prominent despite the availability of so many other emotions that conceivably could underly intergroup hostility (fear, contempt, resentment, desire for revenge, complete indifference, unalloyed hatred, etc.), all of which could be detected by examining individuals' attitudes in any depth. It is perhaps even more surprising in light of the widespread presumption that intergroup violence is motivated by amoral or immoral desires. Obviously, moral indignation of those who condone or engage in violence does not mean that the acts become moral for the observer, but it does undermine the utility of interpreting such violence as a lapse of moral judgment.

The fact that intergroup violence is under moral attack goes a long way toward explaining why moral indignation is felt by those who support the violence. The response is parallel to the attack; moral opprobrium is met with moral opprobrium. The individual who reacts to moral censure by arguing "Yes, but . . .", seems to acknowledge the validity of the criticism rather than his own rectitude. It is more compelling to counter with, "On the contrary, it is they who have sinned against us."

Related to the feelings of moral indignation is a widespread belief that the enemy holds the ingroup in contempt. A significant chunk of organizational meeting time is devoted to reporting how the Turks deride and defame Armenians, or how the English cling to anti-Irish prejudices and delight in anti-Irish jokes. If Armenians and Irish Catholics seem to get a perverse satisfaction out of evidence that they are despised by Turks and Englishmen, it is perhaps because it vindicates their struggle.

The belief that the enemy is actively engaged in attacks against the ingroup is an even more straightforward vindication, allowing the most fundamental defense of violence — personal self-defense. There is widespread agreement among the Armenian respondents that the Turks are attacking Armenians, and among the Irish Catholics that the British army and the Irish Protestants have deliberately fomented trouble and have attacked Irish Catholics unconnected with the IRA, although many of these incidents do not get reported in the British-dominated news media. The feeling of persecution is, however, a particularly complicated phenomenon, in that the personal danger to the individual depends on the level of activism that the individual undertakes in reaction to perceived persecution. The Armenians and Irish Catholics would have to admit it is most unlikely that a totally apolitical Armenian-American or Irish-American would be exposed to any danger at all from Turkish or British machination. Yet the Armenian or Irish Catholic who does care, and identifies strongly with whoever is targeted for Turkish or British actions, becomes a potential target. The occasional bombings of Armenian targets, and the British government's pressures on the U.S. government to punish Northern Irish Aid, reinforce the sense of persecution. The feeling of persecution also reinforces identification with the ingroup. For Armenian- and Irish-Americans, who might otherwise identify more strictly as Americans, persecution makes them distinctive, even more so because other Americans seem to turn a deaf ear to the Armenian and Irish Catholic appeals for support.

What impact does strong moral indignation have on the pragmatic considerations concerning an intergroup confrontation? Moral indignation seems to coincide with the *absence or rejection* of instrumental motives for the conflict. Recall that the strongest, least ambivalent advocates of violence were the least involved in terms of acknowledged personal gain or emotional satisfaction from defeating or humiliating the opponent. A.F. Davies argues that moral indignation can be distinguished from ordinary indignation or anger by its link to disinterestedness. "The individual's feeling of *righteousness*, and his sense of his claim to be listened to, is augmented by his personal 'distance' to which he can point with pride." (Davies, 1980: 321) When personal gain is at issue, the individual is more likely to question his own sincerity in taking a "righteous" stand.

Consequently, moral indignation can be stronger when one has not personally been the victim of deprivations to one's own group. Strawson defines moral indigation as "resentment on behalf of another."[10] It is significant that Armenian activists born after 1915 put considerable stress on the fact that there still are survivors of Turkish attacks. Pity for these survivors, still denied even the modest vindication of official Turkish acknowledgment of what they suffered, is a more potent source of moral indigation than is the personal situation of the younger Armenian. Similarly, the great vehemence of IRA support among Irish-Americans may be partly explained by the fact that they typically have less personal stake in Irish reunification.

The "inverse" relationship between the presence of personal instrumental motives, and moralistic principles and affects, has both theoretical and practical importance. Theoretically, it could have been otherwise; it is conceivable that all three appeals (to passion, conscience, and expediency) could exist, with the motive of personal gain simply reinforcing the others. Instead, we find a more complex balance in which expediency is rejected in order to sustain the emotional and moral stances. This is a rather impressive degree of structure and coherence.

Practically, the fact that moral indignation can be strengthened rather than diluted by the distance between the individual and the outgroup's actions helps to account for the durability and scope of intergroup hostility. While distance diminished the instrumental motives, it purifies the morality of the struggle. The immanence of the Armenian genocide to Armenians today, so astonishing to most non-Armenians, reflects the fact that Armenians feel that they are acting not just for themselves, but also for the previous generations whose economic hardships (attributed to forced emigration from Armenia) prevented them from seeking their own revenge. As long as the empathy with those who suffered is sufficiently strong, moral indignation can bridge generations and oceans. However, it is interesting to speculate on whether an emphasis on the personal benefits of participation in the conflict (ranging from the emotional satisfactions of socializing with countrymen to material gains) could erode the moralistic basis of violence by tarnishing the image of selflessness and sacrifice.

---

[10]Cited in Davies (1980: 321).

EXPECTATIONS

In the structure of belief systems that we are positing, the role of expectations becomes pivotal precisely because the commitment to violence is so ends-oriented. The justification for violence rests on both the necessity *and sufficiency* of violence to achieve the desired objectives. This bears a striking, and perhaps not altogether surprising, resemblance to the concept of the "just war" in Roman Catholic theology (Dugard, 1982; Pottenger, 1982). The concept naturally has evolved over the centuries, but one version useful for our interpretation posits that there are four criteria for the legitimate use of violence: the existence of grave injustice, the exhaustion of nonviolent means, the restraint of violence to proportionality to the gravity of the injustices, and the high likelihood that the violence will indeed eliminate the injustices. Hence the morality of violence is regarded as contingent upon expectations of how the conflict would turn out under the scenarios of high and low violence.

Our subjects' responses on the Q sorts covering expectations of motives, strategies and outcomes indicate the importance of success as a requisite for supporting violence. The two Irish Catholics giving unambivalent support to violence for their cause (who hold the second basic outlook) had the strongest expectation of Ireland's reunification by the turn of the century. The only other Irish respondent with equal optimism was the *least* comfortable with Irish Catholic violence, but this woman is unique among the respondents in her optimism that help from the Republic of Ireland and the non-Irish world would bring reunification through peaceful action. For her, the sufficiency of violence is irrelevant because it is not necessary.

The expectation of success on the part of the two strongest supporters of violence saves them from supporting futile or gratuitous violence — from relegating violence to the status of vengeance. One of these individuals dismisses the feasibility of all peaceful options; even the fairest conceivable British government would never voluntarily agree to cede Northern Ireland; the Irish Republic cannot be counted on to help; the non-Irish world is basically not interested. The other sees enlisting the support of others as more feasible, but joins with the first as the only respondents who believe that success is contingent upon first bringing the violence to the otherwise complacent lives of the British population. These expectations are completely consistent with the requirements for the just war.

The consistency between Armenian principles and expectations is more problematic, perhaps because of the objective weakness of the Armenian independence movement. The dominant perspective is characterized by what most outside observers would probably consider an inconsistency between the expectation of ultimate success and pessimistic expectations concerning developments regarded as essential for this success. Getting any help or lucky

breaks in achieving their goals is unlikely; American pressure on the Turks
would be of little use; and, in fact, it is in the perceived interest of the U.S.
government to protect Turkey. They cannot say with confidence that the
Turks will ever willingly come to terms with Armenians, nor that the Armenians will ever be able to force the Turks into an agreement. Yet they refuse
to regard the struggle as lost, or to settle for less than complete victory. For
example, they disagree strongly that they would be satisfied if the Turkish
government simply admitted that the Armenian genocide had occurred —
their goal is an independent Armenia.[11]

Some of the adherents of this outlook are relatively violence prone;
others are not. The only consistent difference between those who support
and oppose the current violence is in the proviolence individuals' belief that
action is necessary now just to keep the movement alive. Without some
dramatic action by Armenians, time is on the side of the Turks; if Turkish
recognition of the Armenian genocide is not forthcoming in the foreseeable
future, the memory and urgency of the Armenian demands might erode. Since
there is little hope that the Turks would give in to the Armenians without
being forced to, violence is left as the only action that would have any impact, even if it would not achieve Armenian independence in the near future.
Yet if violence can keep the movement alive, the movement *may* eventually
succeed; who can say what the world will be like in 20 or 30 years?

A distinctive if less common perspective prevails among the Armenian
respondents who oppose violence in the present circumstances. They are far
more optimistic about reestablishing an independent Armenian Republic
through nonviolent means. Ultimately the U.S. government will be willing
and able to help. They do not reject the idea of focusing, for now, on Armenia
culture and welfare, because regaining Armenia depends on galvanizing
Armenian identity and awareness.[12] Their optimism on this leads directly
to their optimism that an Armenian Republic will follow.

According to the first perspective, Armenians will eventually win
because they will fight doggedly against the odds. According to this perspective, Armenians will win because the long-term development of a highly
aware, world-wide Armenian community will ultimately produce irrepressi-
ble demands for a homeland, heeded by powerful allies such as the United

[11]Reinforced by a strong identification with Armenia (as evidenced by the uniformly high agreement that they would settle in an independent Armenia), they reject the idea of concentrating
on preserving Armenian culture and improving Armenian welfare as an alternative to pursuing the struggle with the Turks.

[12]According to this outlook, recognition of the genocide and an independent homeland are means
to the end of preserving the unity and well-being of the Armenian people as much as they
are ends in themselves. For these respondents, reparations for the victims of the genocide and
their descendants are an important consideration in pursuing the effort to gain a Turkish admission.

States. Thus, among some Armenians violence is unnecessary; among others it is perceived as being of limited utility. For those most supportive of Armenian violence, though, it is viewed as necessary and possibly effective in the long term, and it would be a fatal betrayal of Armenians' justice to allow the moment to pass. When an expectation of "success' is required to legitimize violence, it can be achieved by looking to the long term, which by its very nature cannot close off possibilities that seem implausible in the short term.

CONCLUSIONS

We do not find individuals whose emotions override their principles. Emotions and principles are generally mutually reinforcing. The presumption that support for intergroup violence serves psychological needs *rather* than expressing moral positions is, at least for long-standing confrontations, misguided. There are enough moral arguments of sufficient coherence to support many different positions, adopted (consciously or unconsciously) in order to conform to emotional stances, or because the support for violence simply fits with preexisting moral positions. Where there is ambivalence about the morality of violence, the actions of the outgroup, whether socioeconomic discrimination or the coverup of historical atrocities, are seen as equivalent to violence. Wherever there is coherence among affects, principles, and other beliefs, the question of whether attitudes are rationalizations or justifications is moot. Psychological needs and other needs dovetail.

None of our findings can reject the possibility that "psychological needs" are relevant, nor the operation of Lasswell's hypothesis of private motives displaced onto public objects. (Lasswell, 1930). The findings do, however, point to the insufficiency of psychological needs and rationalization as an explanatory framework, a point very much in keeping with Lasswell's triple-appeal principle: passions *and* expediency *and* principles must be taken into account (Lasswell, 1933).

It might seem that the coherence of a belief system makes it unassailable. On the contrary, coherence is a constraint: A change in one element may force changes in the others. It is important to distinguish between the versatility and the variability of elements that can go into a coherent belief system, and the flexibility of an individual's already-established belief system when confronted with evidence or arguments that undermine elements of his or her structure. We have seen that moral principles can depend on expectations that could be changed; that affects (such as moral indignation) are linked to empirical issues such as who benefits or who has admitted culpability. Although some self-delusion to bolster existing beliefs is expected, it is not infinite. Changes in the broad context (e.g., a Turkish admission that Armenians did indeed suffer a lamentable tragedy) could not be totally ignored.

The more proximate, organizational context also becomes important if we view the participant as striving to maintain rectitude and respect among peers. For example, participation in the ethnic organization contributes to the expectations of success that underpin the "just war" concept, inasmuch as participation of other individuals may seem to signal their confidence as well, even if other motives (such as sociability and the ease of being with one's own kind) may have been more important attractions.

In terms of principles, interaction with other organization members with *presumably* similar moral stances serves the same reinforcement function, even when in fact there are major but unarticulated differences in principles. In terms of affects, the organizations serve as foci for mobilizing the feelings of indignation and persecution. At Northern Irish Aid meetings members bring in "Irish Rubik cubes" made in England, with all the sides the same color. Armenian groups gather oral histories of survivors of the atrocities.

The critical point is that the multiplicity of functions served by these organizations allows a spillover of unity and mutual reinforcement from the sociocultural to the political. However, if and when attitudes *condemning* intergroup violence are articulated in the organizational setting, they may have great impact on the members. The potential for using the group dynamics to *resolve* intergroup conflicts has barely been explored.[13]. None of these potential levers would be of use if the support of violence were simply an unrooted impulse.

APPENDIX ON METHODOLOGY

Q methodology, which has undergone a renaissance in its social science applications in recent years (Brown, 1980), can systematically explore attitude structures. Each respondent orders a large number of statements or objects according to his or her preference, identification, or other criterion requested by the researcher. The forced ordering (e.g., a 30-statement Q-sort might permit two statements rated at +4 "most agree"; three each at +3 and +2; four each at +1, 0, and -2 and -3; and two at -4 "most disagree") requires the respondent to reveal which statements are of greatest salience insofar as they receive either highly positive rankings or highly negative rankings. Factors analysis is then applied for the *factoring of viewpoints:* individuals or subsets of individuals are identified as having distinctive response patterns.

[13]A notable exception is Doob and Foltz (1973).

In helping to identify distinctive attitude configurations, Q methodology enables the researchers to identify dimensions that show how beliefs are interrelated, rather than reducing each dimension to a single metric. By distinguishing different factors and indicating how each subject's responses are reflected by that factor, the analysis reveals different "types" of attitude structures and identifies which individuals are good "specimens" of each type. Further intensive probing of such specimens can then be pursued.

The methodology permits intensive exploration of attitude sets, but does not aspire to estimate their quantitative prevalence in the broader population. This contrasts with the more typical aggregate approach of gathering large samples and then examining scaled indicators of presumably proviolence attitudes. For example, the huge Institute for Social Research study of American males' attitudes toward violence (Blumenthal, 1972) correlated a host of socioeconomic indicators with only two measures of predispositions to violence: approval of violence for social control and approval of violence for social change. Whereas the construction of these measures entailed many survey questions gauging approval or disapproval of violence in specific types of circumstances, the measures themselves and their correlations with socioeconomic variables bypassed any analysis of the interrelations among attitudes. This runs a serious risk of measurement error even in gauging the true extent of proviolence orientation. A striking example is provided by responses to four statements that would seem to reflect a predisposition to violence among people involved in an independence struggle:

    a.   "Self-defense is the only legitimate reason for violence."

    b.   "Independence is more important than the lives that may have to be sacrificed to achieve it."

    c.   "A people can stand only so much abuse before they must lash out against those who caused it."

    d.   "War and killing make it impossible for people to recognize and obey the law."

Some of the respondents who agree most strongly with the last two statements are more pacifist than anyone else among our respondents, as judged by their strong disagreement with the first two statements and their views on specific proposals for resolving the conflicts in their countries. Perhaps the individuals who regard violence as morally repugnant, but also find reasons why their own people engage in such violence, would find statements c and d both reasonable and comforting.

Finally, the meaningfulness of the Q-sort results comes from the combinations of rankings of a host of statements, rather than from scores on single questions or cumulative measures established *a priori* by the researcher. Q-Sort statements typically come from the discourse (written or verbal) of the individuals or groups under examination, so as to avoid imposing the researcher's categories and preconceptions where they are not appropriate. Indeed, we found that some views not anticipated by the research team prove to be key attitudes; for example, the psychological explanation of in-group violence as generated by frustration—which we had anticipated might be *our* explanation—is a central belief in the repertoire of many respondents.

The analysis is based on the objectively isolated Q-sort factors. The interpretations of what these factors signify, and what logic may underly the connections among attitudes, are, of course, subjective. However, the idiosyncratic biases that subjectivity can introduce have been mitigated by having at least two members of the research team make independent analyses of each group's responses.

REFERENCES

Abelson, R. P., Aronson, E., McGuire, W., Newcomb, T., Rosenberg, M., and Tannenbaum, P. (eds.) (1968). *Theories of Cognitive Consistency: A Sourcebook,* Rand-McNally, Chicago.

Adorno, T. W., Frenkel-Brunswick, E., Levinson, D. J., and Sanford, R. N. (1950). *The Authoritarian Personality,* Harper, New York.

Ball-Rokeach, S. (1972). The legitimation of violence. In Short, J. F., and Wolfgang, M. E. (eds.), *Collective Violence,* Aldine-Atherton, Chicago.

Berkowitz, L. (1962). *Aggression: A Social Psychological Analysis,* McGraw-Hill, New York.

Blumenthal, M. D., Kahn, R. L., Andrews, F. M., and Head, K. B. (1972). *Justifying Violence: Attitudes of American Men,* Institute for Social Research, Ann Arbor, Michigan.

Brown, S. R. (1980). *Political Subjectivity: Applications of Q Methodology in Political Science,* Yale University Press, New Haven.

Burton, A. M. (1978). *Revolutionary Violence: The Theories,* Crane, Russack, New York.

Davies, J. G., (1976). *Christians, Politics and Violent Revolutions,* Orbis Books, Maryknoll, New York.

Davies, A. F. (1981). *Skills, Outlooks, Passions: A Psychoanalytic Contribution to the Study of Politics,* Cambridge, University Press, Cambridge.

Doob, L. W., and Foltz, W. J. (1973). The Belfast Workshop, and Application of Group Techniques to a Destructive Conflict, *J. Conflict Res.* 17: 489-512.

Dugard, J. (1982). International terrorism and the just war. In Rapoport, D. C., and Alexander, Y. (eds.), *The Morality of Terrorism,* Pergamon, New York.

Eckhardt, W. (1965). War, Propaganda, Welfare Values, and Political Ideologies. *J. Conflict Res.* 9: 345-358.

Finlay, D. J., Holsti, O. R., and Fagen, R. R. (1967). *Enemies in Politics,* Rand-McNally, Chicago.

Hallie, P. (1971). Justification and rebellion. In Sanford, N., and Comstock. C. (Eds.), *Sanctions for Evil: Sources of Social Destructiveness,* Jossey-Bass, San Francisco.

Kaplan, A. (1958). American ethics and public policy. In Morison, E. E. (ed.), *The American Style,* Harper, New York.

Kelman, H. (1973). Violence without moral restraint. *J. Social Issues* 29(4): 25-61.

Lasswell, H. D. (1930). *Psychopathology and Politics,* University of Chicago Press, Chicago.

Lasswell, H. D. (1933). The triple-appeal principle: A contribution of psychoanalysis to political and social science. *Am. J. Sociol.* 37: 523-538.

Louch, A. (1982). Terrorism: The immorality of belief. In Rapoport, D. C., and Alexander, Y. (eds.), *The Morality of Terrorism,* Pergamon, New York.

Martic, M. (1975). *Insurrection: Five Schools of Revolutionary Thought,* Dunellen, New York.

The Moralism of Attitudes Supporting Intergroup Violence

Opton, E., and Duckless, R. (1970). Mental gymnastics on Mylai. *New Republic* 162: 14-16.
Pottenger, J. R. (1982). Liberation theology: Its methodological foundations for violence. In Rapoport, D. C., and Alexander, Y. (eds.), *The Morality of Terrorism,* Pergamon, New York.
Rochlin, S. (1973). *Man's Aggression: The Defense of the Self,* Gambit, Boston.
Strachey, A. (1957). *The Unconscious Motives of War,* George Allen and Unwin, London.
Sumner, A. G. (1906). *Folkways,* Ginn, New York.
Yates, A. (1962). *Frustration and Conflict,* Wiley, New York.

[5]

Constitutionalism and Violence: The Case of Ireland

by

Jeffrey Archer
University of New England

British writers have often stressed the dominant place of violence in Irish life. The Irish were seen as barbarians by Tudor adventurers, for example, to whom the rules of civilised conduct did not apply.[1] In the mid-nineteenth century *The Times* loudly complained that

> The Irish have no feeling for law and order. If someone is killed or injured their sympathies are for the perpetrator of the deed and not the one who suffers. And if the deed should be proved and punished, they howl as if an innocent man had been convicted.[2]

Irish violence was not just the creation of English and Unionist minds, however. John Redmond, a Nationalist parliamentarian, could use a similar argument in favour of Irish Home Rule:

> As it happened in Canada so it will happen in Ireland – when you throw responsibility on the shoulders of the people, and not till then. Then respect for law will arise in Ireland; then confidence in the administration of justice will arise; and when that day comes, I am perfectly convinced that Ireland will become the most peaceable and most law-abiding, as she is today the most crimeless, part of your Empire.[3]

This assumption, or stereotype, of the lawless Irish has been transformed by some Irish writers into an idealisation of political violence when, for example, 'a flood of adulatory hagiography'[4] marked the fiftieth anniversary of the 1916 Rising. It has been very common to depict nineteenth and early twentieth-century Irish history as a struggle between violent and parliamentary modes of nationalism.

> Physical force and constitutionalism usually followed each other in cycles of failure and disillusionment. Lines of demarcation were frequently fluid.[5]

A debate has arisen over the rival claims of the violent separatists of 1916 or the constitutional Parliamentary Nationalists to have had the greater share in winning Irish independence.[6] The concepts of constitutionalism and violence have therefore been used to explain aspects of Irish political history, but they have not often been used together in an analytical or reflective manner. My intention is to use these concepts in a way that might reveal some important aspects of the Irish political tradition. The relationship between constitutionalism and violence will be examined, at least in overview, before the partition of Ireland in 1921, in the southern state now known as the Republic of Ireland, and in Northern Ireland. Some general conclusions on these concepts in Irish politics will follow. First, however, I intend to discuss briefly some aspects of constitutionalism and violence relevant to my argument.

*   *   *

Ridley has argued that the study of constitutions links political ideas with political institutions because constitutions reflect the political ideas which establish principles and shape the system of government.[7] According to Sartori, for the century and a half before World War Two, constitutionalism was widely understood as:

> a fundamental law, or a fundamental set of principles, and correlative institutional arrangements, which would restrict arbitrary power and ensure a 'limited government'.[8]

In this way constitutionalism assumes both political order and political freedom as prescriptive values. Sartori points out that political scientists today tend to stress social and political pluralistic checks, rather than constitutional checks, on arbitrary rule, but he urges us not to forget the importance of constitutional checks. If constitutional law is left to pure jurists they may be taken advantage of by unscrupulous politicians. On the other hand, Berger is concerned that in the USA an unelected judiciary can dictate to an elected government,[9] and enters into a dispute with Schram where both cite the authority of McIlwain's *Constitutionalism, Ancient and Modern*.[10] Schram refuses to accept that constitutionalism is concerned with the democratic balance of interests and cites McIlwain on constitutionalism as a legal limitation on government, evident from medieval times. Berger replies by emphasising McIlwain's second correlative element of constitutionalism: a complete responsibility of the government to the governed. Constitutionalism has become linked with various liberal-democratic ideas, as Vile asserts:

> For the functional categories of the doctrine of the separation of powers with their intimate relation to the rule of law, the concept of balance which was the essential element of theories of limited government, and the central ideas of representation and responsibility underlying theories of parliamentary government – all these continue to be important parts of our intellectual apparatus.[11]

If one is to ask the question, does constitutionalism exist in a particular state, then one must realise that there can never be a perfect match between an abstract prescriptive concept and the messy and fragmented real world.

CONSTITUTIONALISM AND VIOLENCE IN IRELAND 113

To the extent, however, that the concept is widely advocated, generally respected, and seen as a guide to political action, then one must make judgments about the degree to which politics in that state can be depicted as constitutional. One can examine the constitutional documents, if any, and ask questions about their basic principles and the extent to which genuine attempts are made to put those principles into practice. Does the government manage to maintain order without arbitrary power; are the courts free of political control; are individual rights and minority rights guaranteed; is political diversity accepted; do the government and other political leaders act peacefully, make compromises, rely on argument in a spirit of toleration of opponents; are the rules of the political game, legal and conventional, known and accepted by the leading political players? One could add to these questions the questions concerning representative government, such as: are there regular free elections; do peaceful transferences of power normally occur, and are the wishes of the electorate generally reflected in government policy? Finally, one could ask questions about the extent of economic equality and social justice. These questions are in accord with three major developments in modern constitutional theory, where the constitutional legitimacy of governments is seen first in maintaining order without arbitrary rule; secondly as combining this with representative institutions, most typically parliaments; and, thirdly, further limiting the legitimate base of governmental authority to include positive freedoms in welfare and economic equality. How does this view of constitutionalism relate to the concept of violence?

* * *

The first point to emphasise here is that violence is not the opposite of constitutionalism. Whereas constitutionalism is essentially prescriptive, violence is usually a descriptive concept, although often used in a perjorative connotation. There are some exceptions here as in the theories of St Just and Sorel, and in the Irish case the arguments for the cleansing and purifying effects of the blood sacrifice in the writings of Pearse. The relationship between constitutionalism and violence is seen most clearly in the origins of the modern nation state where rulers made some attempt to establish a monopoly over the institutions of violence. As Wolin argues:

> The theory and practice of constitutional democracy have signified a concerted effort to restrict the application of violence by setting defined limits to power, by insisting on the observance of regularized procedures and by establishing strict methods for rendering those in power accountable for their actions. The paraphernalia of constitutionalism – the rule of law, due process, the separation of powers and the system of individual rights – have not eliminated power, but they have contributed to its regularization, to eradicating that unpredictable, sheerly destructive quality that epitomizes all violence.[12]

Indeed, state violence or institutionalised violence is often not recognised as violence at all, and euphemisms such as 'legal force' are substituted for it.[13] Nardin, however, argues that the existence (or description) of violence as 'physical harm' should not be confused with its justification, and state force should be called violence if physical harm results from it.[14] It is possible to put the argument for state violence in even stronger terms. For Williams

> . . . violence is an institution as well as an act; that a social system can be a form of systematic violence and disorder, and, while it lasts, can seem, paradoxically, settled and innocent, so that protest against it seems to be the source of disturbance and violence.[15]

Of course, in both these arguments the relationship between constitutionalism and violence is implied. Nardin's physical harm by the state may be justified if the state is considered legitimate by recourse to some definition of constitutionalism. Williams' example is clearly one of an unconstitutional state which has no legitimacy. This demonstrates the ambiguity of the relationship between constitutionalism and violence. A violent revolution against an illegitimate, unconstitutional state may or may not have the intention to set up a new legitimate constitutional state but all successful revolutionaries claim to have removed injustices and founded a new legitimacy. One is therefore compelled to make judgments about the constitutionalism of both governing elites and rebels in deciding if violence can be justified.

There is also a link between constitutionalism and violence when limited constitutional rights are won through a struggle which stops short of revolution. Wilkes' battle against censorship in eighteenth-century London, or violent demonstrations against war or poverty or lack of civil rights in the USA during the 1960s and 1970s, may be seen as violence for constitutional ends.[16] In this regard the justification of violence must be proportionate to the circumstances to which it is a response; both violence and the circumstances it seeks to change are matters of degree.[17] The problem this raises is that, if unconstitutional acts of violence may serve a constitutional end for insurgents, can the same be said for the incumbents of state power? Can unconstitutional means be used to defend a constitutional state, without the state itself becoming unconstitutional? Constitutionalism and violence have an ambiguous relationship here. Both exist in varying degrees and the levels perceived in some circumstances will be a question of intense ideological disagreement. An isolated act may be one of constitutionalism or one of violence, but when we examine a complex historical movement like Irish nationalism, or an institution existing over many years like the Republic of Ireland, it becomes a question of judging how much constitutionalism and how much violence exists. More than this, if violence occurs to win or safeguard constitutionalism, then it has to be classified as simultaneously constitutional and violent. This problem is clearly demonstrated when both constitutionalism and violence are examined in Irish political history. I will start with a brief discussion of Ireland before partition.

* * *

There is a two-fold problem in examining the state in relation to Irish politics. The first part of the problem is that several legal entities, sometimes with unclear boundaries, have constituted the Irish state. From the start of the eighteenth century until partition Ireland was part of the United Kingdom, and has to be considered as part of that state. After partition a southern state, the Irish Free State, was set up which at first remained in the British Commonwealth. That state became a republic in all but name under the 1937 constitution, when known as Eire, it claimed some jurisdiction over the entire island. In 1949 it became the Republic of Ireland. After partition Northern Ireland remained part of the United Kingdom, but with its own devolved government. British neglect, apart from economic support, meant that Northern Ireland from the early 1920s can be practically treated as an independent state. In 1972 the suspension of the Northern Ireland Parliament led to a system of direct rule from Britain, similar to the nineteenth-century position for the whole of Ireland. The second part of the problem is the ambiguous nature of the British state itself. Apart from the peculiar relationships between Westminster and both the Ireland of pre-partition days and post-partition Northern Ireland, the British state has not usually been seen as society in legal dress in the continental manner. More commonly the British state has been understood as a collection of discrete instrumentalities which are only loosely linked at the level of central government. For the purposes of this paper, however, it is not too much of a distortion to examine pre-partition Ireland, the South and the North, as if they were or are separate states.

The nationalist claim that nineteenth-century Ireland was unconstitutionally and violently ruled by the British is supported by a mass of evidence: discriminatory anti-Catholic legislation; the paramilitary nature of the Royal Irish Constabulary; coercive legislation; the ill-treatment of nationalist prisoners; the failure to agree to the break-up of the United Kingdom once Home Rule was clearly the wish of the majority of the Irish electorate; and failure to attend to the poverty and miseries of Irish peasant life, most notably in the great famine of the 1840s. Many of these features were reflected, in a much milder mannner, in the way the British state treated its non-Irish subjects, and it must also be remembered that there was no real military occupation before 1916; most of the servants of the British state in Ireland were Irishmen. A great deal of Irish dissatisfaction was not with alien British rule but with poor administration and the resident Protestant Anglo-Irish Ascendancy. The nineteenth century also saw many serious attempts to solve Irish problems by the British state: Catholic emancipation; land reform; and the acceptance of Home Rule by one of the two major British political parties. In many ways Ireland was not ruled by Britain but was part of the British state, contributing to Imperial expansion, helping to form the British system of government at Westminster, and drawing on a legal and parliamentary tradition which the Irish nationalist, Thomas Davis, claimed to go back as far as 48 BC when Ollamh Fodhla, the Irish Solomon, instituted the great Fheis at Tara.[18] The demands for Home Rule itself were often demands for self-government, where residual powers would remain at Westminster, and Ireland would remain within the Empire. Thus, although one would have an impossible task to maintain that the state in Ireland was constitutional in the way that I have characterised the concept above (and one could certainly argue that the British state in England was not fully constitutional either) it is an exaggeration to assert, as O'Farrell does, that

> Violence can produce desired results. Between 1800 and 1921 England maintained its dominance of Ireland by violence and the threat of violence: this domination was terminated (or at least qualified) as a consequence of violence.[19]

O'Farrell is right, however, when he argues that the violent separatist tradition of revolt and rebellion in Ireland did not express political violence in total.

> To see Irish violence in terms of explicit challenges made by Irish nationalists to English rule – 1798, 1848, 1867, 1916 – is to gravely underestimate its extent, and to grossly overestimate the degree to which English rule, and English concepts of law and order prevailed in Ireland.[20]

These revolts were explicitly supported only by a small minority of the Irish, although then, as now, there was an ambiguity about condemning 'patriot' violence, and a tradition of violence stretching back to antiquity.[21] The most important aspect of violence missing from the list of heroic failures that fuelled the violent republican imagination was local agrarian violence.

Agrarian violence, from at least the time of the local Whiteboy movements of the early 1760s, had characteristic traits: the use of arms, violent acts, intimidation of opponents or non-supporters, a command structure on quasi-military lines, oathbound, conspiratorial, and relying on mass support, or at least mass neutrality.[22] This became the typical form of paramilitary activity for both Protestants and Catholics. As MacDonagh points out

> In many regards, the Orangemen were the natural successors to the Protestant Whiteboys. Both were concerned with social and economic dislocation – albeit from a single, simple source. It was the same sudden exorbitance, and the same vision, or rather nightmare, of role reversal which brought both into and kept both in being. *Plus ça change* ....[23]

MacDonagh sees this local denial of state legitimacy to be far from lawlessness.[24] It set up a tradition of alternative government in Ireland where both North and South in the nineteenth century could be seen as 'a multilegal' society; an aspect which was condemned and yet assimilated by both the Parliamentary Nationalists and the violent separatists. The republicans were aiming at a 'moral polity' which mirrored the peasant's 'moral economy' closely.[25] The tradition of alternative government was seen most clearly in the 1916 Declaration, in the 1919 First Dail, and in the refusal of certain republican groups to accept the legitimacy of the Southern state. The case of the First Dail between 1919 and 1921 is particularly interesting. Made up of parliamentarians elected in the 1918 United Kingdom election, the Dail rejected the legitimacy of the British state. Not only did the provisional government wage a military campaign against the British Army (including the notorious state terror of the Black and Tans) but they set up an effective government which enjoyed widespread legitimacy. Although the Dail met only twelve times, it set up an efficient system of courts and local government.[26]

Advocates of physical-force republicanism were not always careful to distance themselves from parliamentary agitation by the so-called constitutionalists. Many IRB leaders joined Issac Butt's campaign seeking amnesty for prisoners jailed in 1867, and in 1873 the IRB convention voted to delay the war with England until they had the clear support '. . . of the Irish nation as expressed by a majority of the Irish people . . .'.[27] And the revolutionary Davitt argued fiercely that all methods, 'including "constitutional" if no others be opportune', be used to fight landlordism.[28]

Just as there was a hint of constitutionalism in local agrarian alternative law and in republican alternative governments, however there was a hint of violence in Parliamentary Nationalism. Not only did the supporters of Parnell fail to play the rules of the Westminster parliamentary game (and thus transformed the rules), they also were identified by British politicians with agrarian violence, and could use this identification for their own constitutional objectives. Sorel, despite his view of English pacifism, makes this point:

> . . . Parnell's authority did not rest only on the number of votes at his disposal, but mainly on the terror which every Englishman felt at the bare announcement of agrarian troubles in Ireland. A few acts of violence . . . were exceedingly useful to the Parnellian policy . . . a Parliamentary group *sells peace of mind to the Conservatives,* who dare not use the force they command.[29]

Thus the apparent constitutional agitation for Home Rule had an implication of violence. A spell in prison has often done no harm to the votes cast for Irish politicians and many, like Davis or Duffy, are claimed by advocates of both violence and constitutionalism. Lyons has ridiculed such a hard and fast distinction between constitutionalism and violence:

It is dangerously simple because it assumes that peaceful agitation

and violent agitation are two opposing poles with no resting-place in
between. . . . Perhaps the most lethal over-simplification of this kind
to have occurred in our own day has been the tendency to assert that
constitutional agitation 'failed' and then to build upon that glib
assertion the even more disastrous proposition that violence will
therefore always hold the key to success.[30]

Easter 1916, to take the most important example, involved both a dramatic
act of violent rebellion and a theatrical declaration of a new constitutional
order.[31] Such ambiguities in Irish nationalism, linked closely with the need
to simplify and distort differences within the nationalist movement to
maximise support, have been documented recently by MacDonagh, Boyce,
and Garvin.[32] My point is that, not only are there many positions on the
continuum between constitutionalism and violence, but that these
positions depend on particular views of the legitimacy of the state. The
same action may be seen as both violent and constitutional. Whether the
violence is justified and whether the constitutionalism is real or apparent
depends on one's views of the legitimacy of the state and the alternative or
aspirant state. This argument will be developed in the next section on the
independent state that is now the Republic of Ireland.

*   *   *

The Southern state was born in the turbulence of the Anglo-Irish war
and was immediately plunged into a civil war between those nationalists
who accepted the treaty with Britain (and who therefore accepted the
legitimacy of the Free State) and the anti-treaty republican nationalists
who rejected the legitimacy of the new state. Both sides drew their authority
from the tradition of Irish separatist revolt and the 1918 UK elections
where, as fellow members of Sinn Fein, they had effectively removed the
old Irish Parliamentary party. The experience of civil war created the two
major political parties in the Republic when, in 1926, the bulk of the anti-
treaty forces followed de Valera into the new Fianna Fail party. Some
republicans remained in a small Sinn Fein party which refused (and some
of its various splintered off-spring still do) to accept the legitimacy of the
state.

Fianna Fail has been in power in the Southern state for most of the years
since 1932. In that year there was some question about the possibility of a
peaceful transference of power from the winning to the losing side in the
Civil War, from the losing to the winning side in the election. These fears
were not, however, realised and since that time there has been remarkable
stability in government, despite the bitternesses engendered by the Civil
War.[33] Both the 1922 and the 1937 Constitutions included declarations of
individual rights such as freedom of worship, due process, free speech, and
pointers to wider social rights such as education for all. The 1922
Constitution both confirmed Irish sovereignty, making it subject to the

treaty with Britain, and kept the place of the Crown. The 1937 document removed the Crown, but combined elements of Catholic social teaching and the special position of the Catholic church (since removed) with an all-Ireland sovereignty. Pending the reintegration of the national territory, however, legislation would apply only in the southern twenty-six counties. There were elements of a 'theocratic state'[34] in the constitution. Divorce was prohibited, censorship was enshrined, and (by the 1935 Criminal Law Amendment Act) the sale and import of contraceptives were banned. These points raise an interesting dilemma in constitutionalism. Before the 1970s there was little questioning or debate in the Republic about these prohibitions. This was not surprising given the enormous influence and authority of the Catholic church in an overwhelmingly Catholic state. This does, however, reveal a tension in constitutional theory between government by consent and protection of individual rights. If the great majority of the population do not want to exercise certain rights or consider them morally wrong, then to grant them is to reject government by consent. The question of majoritarian democracy is also raised here, but I intend to discuss this below in connection with Northern Ireland.

The protection of individual rights in the southern state can also be raised in connection with violence when the treatment of those labelled subversives, or those who reject the legitimacy of the state, is examined. Civil libertarians like Asmal have been concerned that such people have not been entitled to the full rights of the law.[35] IRA men, for example, do not recognise the southern state. They claim that the Second Dail of 1922 was the last all-Irish legitimate body and when, in 1938, some representatives of that Dail vested their quasi-mystical authority in the IRA Army Council, that body became the only lawful government in Ireland. The response of the state has been to pass draconian legislation. The Free State passed four Public Safety Acts between 1923 and 1927 which gave wide powers of search to the police, introduced special courts for subversives, and introduced internment without trial. The provisions which most endangered individual liberties were seen as short-run emergency responses. In 1939, 1957, and again in 1972, Fianna Fail used such legislation against the IRA.[36] In 1976 it was used again by the heirs of the Free State, the Fine Gael party. The impact of a growing international concern for human rights can be seen by the Republic being taken to the European Court in 1957. All these responses can be seen as attempts to crush violent IRA activity which was perceived as a threat to the state. The Civil War continued in miniature in gang warfare during the early 1930s; the IRA launched a campaign and were seen as a threat to Irish neutrality in World War Two, and they were again on the 'offensive' in the border area between 1956 and 1962. The current round of violence in Northern Ireland resulted in a split in IRA ranks and it is now the Provisional IRA which is dedicated to the use of violence to reunite Ireland in a new, for them, fully legitimate state. Although most of the anti-state violence in the current 'troubles' has been north of the border, there have been bombings in Dublin, attributed to loyalist Protestants, many robberies attributed to the IRA, property damage, kidnappings, and some dramatic assassinations like those of the British Ambassador to Dublin in 1976, and of Lord Mountbatten in 1979.

Whereas the Republic has attempted constitutionalism in the sense of limited government, despite the abuse of some individual rights, it has been determinedly constitutional in its representative institutions. Irish parliamentary democracy runs deep; it has some unique characteristics such as a heavy emphasis on localism and personalism.[37] But there is a paradox here, in that the great practitioners of constitutionalism have legitimised the very violence they have so violently suppressed. O'Brien, who refuses to see any legitimacy in the current IRA position because they have had little electoral support, has touched on this ambiguity which has led to doubts about the legitimacy of the state itself. He cites the famous speech made by Lemass in 1928 when Fianna Fail first entered the Dail:

> Fianna Fail is a slightly constitutional party. We are perhaps open to the definition of a constitutional party, but before anything we are a Republican party. We have adopted the method of political agitation to achieve our end . . . Five years ago the methods we adopted were not the methods we have adopted now . . . Our object is to establish a Republican Government in Ireland. If that can be done by the present methods we have, we will be very pleased, but, if not, we would not confine ourselves to them.[38]

Lemass, who was later to be a conciliatory and conservative custodian of the state, was expressing the mystique of republicanism which led a small minority to insurrection in 1916, and a larger minority to civil war in 1921. Here the right to speak for Ireland is not confined to democratically elected leaders, for they represent only the present generation; republicans claim to represent the dead and the yet to be born; they *know* their cause is right. Fianna Fail rhetoric, argues O'Brien, thus accepts the legitimacy of IRA violence, and encourages its base of support, even though it can be ruthless in suppressing the IRA itself. The gap between rhetoric and action was bridged briefly in 1970 when two Fianna Fail ministers (one of whom, Charles Haughey, was later to be Taoiseach) were dismissed for suspected gun-running to the North. O'Brien stresses the common roots of Fianna Fail and the IRA, but he neglects to mention the common roots of his party, the Irish Labour Party, and Fine Gael with the men of 1916. To a great extent the ambivalence about representative democracy is a part of a shared assumption which crosses the entire political spectrum of the Republic.

Ambivalance towards violence is widespread in Irish political culture. Rebel songs including heroic violence are extremely popular. Yeats, O'Casey, and Behan have made violence, the bomb, and the sniper an important aspect of their art. Several surveys have reflected this ambivalence. One held in 1978, found that 51 per cent had no time for the IRA, 32 per cent admired their idealism but rejected their violence, 22 per cent approved of their violence, and a disquieting 15 per cent were 'don't knows'.[39] I will now look at constitutionalism and violence in Northern Ireland.

*   *   *

The six northern counties of Ireland have had a particularly violent history, and the city of Belfast has a long tradition of sectarian riots.[40] Northern Ireland came into legal existence following Protestant rejection of Home Rule by the threat of violence, and constituted the maximum area with a 'safe' Protestant majority. The state was born amid violent chaos, with Protestant fears of the irredentism to the south and mass non-recognition of the new institutions by Catholics. The political and legal institutions set up under the 1920 Government of Ireland Act were apparently based on the 'Westminster model' and were held by Unionists, who accepted the legitimacy, if not the desirability, of the new state, as perfectly constitutional. As in the South, draconian legislation was prepared to deal with those who did not accept the legitimacy of the state. The Civil Authorities (Special Powers) Act of 1922 was at first envisaged as temporary, emergency legislation, but it became permanent in 1933. The Act included 'powers of internment and arrest on suspicion both of having committed an act prejudicial to law and order and of being about to do so'.[41] Harsh sentences including floggings were widely used at first, and were justified by Cabinet members as the law taking its course without executive interference. The execution of the Special Powers Act involved the denial of human rights but, more than this, it was used in a discriminatory way against Catholic and nationalist offenders. One permanent secretary to the Ministry of Home Affairs believed that 'exceptional legislation should apply only to "disloyal and disaffected persons", not those "loyal to the Crown"'.[42]

A largely Protestant police force backed up by a Protestant parliamentary special constabulary carried out the Act in a way that considered the Catholic third of the population 'disloyal', as indeed many of them were. Elections in Northern Ireland centred on the so-called 'constitutional' issue of maintaining partition, and sectarian cleavages resulted in a permanent Unionist majority. Certain local government constituencies were also gerrymandered in favour of Protestants, and local authorities discriminated in favour of their co-religionists in housing and employment.[43] To some extent this was merely patronage and localism, common throughout Ireland, but it also hit Catholics in a discriminatory way. But, whatever local abuse took place, the permanent Protestant majority was seen by many nationalists as a giant gerrymander. Civil rights were a major issue in the early 1970s in Northern Ireland but, as the security situation deteriorated, the old religious cleavages about the border took over.[44]

The Northern Ireland state not only neglected individual rights, it permanently excluded a large section of the population from representative government. For the forty years before 1969 it achieved a limited stability, but this depended on a majoritarian, rather than a pluralistic view of democracy. Lijphart's advocacy of consociational democracy, in which elites from divided sub-cultures join together in government, is an important argument against this unconstitutional brand of democracy.[45] State violence in Northern Ireland, and in the rest of Ireland, has usually been legal if not constitutional, but, on many occasions, the police or the police reserve used illegal violence, as when a police riot broke through the Bogside in 1969.

Loyalist violence in Northern Ireland has been a reaction to republican violence; it overlaps with illegal state violence in breaking the law to defend a state perceived as legitimate. It is ironical that the first policeman to die in the current 'troubles' was killed by a loyalist gunman protesting against the emasculation of the forces of law and order.[46] The loyalist paramilitary groups, like the Ulster Defence Association, see themselves as preserving Protestant Ulster. Not only do they see their violence as constitutional but some have also discussed plans for a new independent Ulster.[47] Constitutionalism and violence coexist. Loyalist violence and threats of violence, in reaction to the Home Rule campaign, are part of Protestant mythology about the origins of their state, in the same way that 1916 has a mythical role in the origins of the Southern state. This has tended to legitimise loyalist violence for some Protestants, just as, for some Catholics, 1916 legitimises republican violence. Certainly, leading Protestant politicians are ambivalent about loyalist violence, and some of them have identified themselves closely with Protestant paramilitary groups. Leading Catholic politicians in Northern Ireland are in a similar position to politicians in the South; they condemn the IRA, while supporting the IRA objective of Irish unity. Whereas loyalist violence has been selective for the most part, concentrating on sectarian assassinations or removing individual rivals or opponents,[48] the violence of the Provisional IRA and other republican paramilitary groups has tended to be general and aiming at destroying the 'fabric' of Ulster society. The use of indiscriminate and random terror marks a new tactic for the IRA;[49] it makes the men of 1916 appear almost medieval in their view of the rules of war.

In 1969 the British army arrived to safeguard Catholics from Protestant anger, but the power of republican ideology soon resulted in the British army fighting republicans. A great increase in violence after internment without trial was introduced in 1971, and belated recognition of crisis by the British government, led to the suspension of the Northern Ireland government and parliament in 1972. The British state was now in control of state violence in Northern Ireland. Attempts were made to set up a consociational democracy in the Northern Ireland Constitution Act of 1973; there was to be an Assembly elected on proportional representation, and a power-sharing Executive. This fell after a loyalist general strike in 1974. Since then the British Secretary of State for Northern Ireland has failed to convince Unionist politicians of the need for consociational democracy. There have been many reforms in policing, housing, local government, and anti-discrimination legislation, and one could argue that, as a result of these, the Northern Ireland state is now more constitutional.

CONSTITUTIONALISM AND VIOLENCE IN IRELAND 123

On the other hand, the security offensive against the IRA has involved more denial of individual rights, and has antagonised large sections of the Catholic population. In 1974 the European Commission on Human Rights found that violence leading to intense suffering and physical injury was inflicted on suspected insurgents in police custody in 1971.[50] Earlier, the British enquiry into physical brutality by the security forces in 1971 (the Compton Report) gave such a narrow definition of brutality that the police were exonerated. The ending of internment without trial and the replacement of the Special Powers Act with the Northern Ireland (Emergency Provisions) Act of 1973 led to a special system of courts for terrorist offences with special rules on the admissability of confessions and no juries. Claims by republicans and others that confessions were obtained by torture led to the 1979 Bennett Report which, while not accepting that torture of prisoners in police custody took place, found that many prisoners were injured in a way that could not have been self-inflicted while in detention.[51] This, together with the greatly increased size of the police and the local army reserve (both largely Protestant), has led Tomlinson to depict direct rule in Northern Ireland as reform *and* repression.[52] Other writers have concluded that the special courts and interrogation procedures have severely damaged the legitimising force of law in Northern Ireland.[53]

International attention on constitutionalism in Northern Ireland was maintained in 1980 when protesting prisoners in the H-blocks at the Maze prison took their case to the European Commission on Human Rights.[54] This can also be seen as an attempt by the IRA to gain legitimacy by depicting themselves as political prisoners. The violence in Northern Ireland has attracted widespread interest in the international news media, and this affects the violent struggle between state and insurgent where both attempt to gain publicity by stressing their own constitutional legitimacy and the unjustified violence of their opponent. This can be seen most clearly in the 1980 and 1981 hunger strikes by republican prisoners in Northern Ireland. Idealism and the selfless resolve to sacrifice one's life for the cause of Irish freedom are part of the republican mythology, where failure is converted into success, where the sufferers are the moral victors over the oppressors. Within the separatist tradition in Ireland, and also in generating international sympathy and support, the hunger strike can be seen as a non-violent tactic which attempts to give legitimacy to violence.

Attitudes to violence in Northern Ireland reveal that it is widely accepted. Rose's 1968 survey showed that 52 per cent of Protestants would support any measure to keep Northern Ireland Protestant, and 13 per cent of Catholics would support any measure to end partition.[55] A 1978 survey found that 40 per cent of the population had personally experienced political violence, and it is likely that differences between Protestants and Catholics had intensified over the turbulent decade.[56]

* * *

Compared with the massive political violence of modern warfare, or civil conflict in a state like Iran today, Irish political violence has been a modest affair. Only a handful died in the nineteenth-century insurrections, although agrarian violence counted for more. If one counts the Famine, however, and the halving of Ireland's population in these years, a case could be made for massive institutionalised violence. Belfast and northern riots between 1813 and 1907 resulted in 68 deaths, half of them in 1886.[57] In 1916 there were 500 casualties;[58] the Anglo-Irish war killed rather more than 1200;[59] the Civil War another 700;[60] and the current 'troubles' in Northern Ireland had resulted in over 2000 victims by January 1980.[61] But to this grim picture has to be added the injuries, the intimidations, and the fears of violence which, to give only two examples, embittered Irish politics after the Civil War, and forced 12 per cent of the Belfast population to leave their homes between 1969 and 1972.[62] Also the state violence of prisons, official threats and rough interrogations has to be taken into account.

The tradition of violence in Ireland goes beyond specific acts of violence; it includes an ambivalence towards violence, an acceptance of the mystique of violence, and a belief that violence can lead to great political change. But there is also a long tradition of parliamentary government, and attachment to varieties of constitutionalism. In this article I have briefly reviewed constitutionalism and violence in three different contexts. Before partition the state maintained order to a degree, was sometimes arbitrary in its actions, and frustrated the peaceful desire for Home Rule. Until 1918 violent separatists had little popular support although they did have constitutional plans. The Southern state after the Civil War maintained order although sometimes acting arbitrarily against its opponents; it enjoyed massive popular support, despite its partial claim to legitimacy through the violent separatist tradition. The internal enemies of the Southern state relied on this tradition for their sustenance and, while constitutional plans were in their programmes, they enjoyed little popular support. Northern Ireland before 1972 had some stability and a facade of constitutionalism which denied a significant minority a voice in government. It was highly repressive and discriminatory. After 1972 the repression continued but the discrimination abated. The 'men of violence' in Northern Ireland have not depended on electoral support,[63] but elected politicians have often supported violent acts. Northern Ireland presents a case of an unconstitutional state challenged by unconstitutional opponents, although it is challenged by constitutional opponents too. These judgments take into account my first two categories of constitutionalism described above. If the third category, concern for equality and social justice, is taken into account, then one can seriously question whether there has ever been constitutionalism in Ireland. The complex relationship between constitutionalism and violence has been explored: the legitimacy of the state and those who reject the state may depend on constitutionalism; violence must be justified in terms of legitimacy of the state *and* legitimacy of the insurgent; constitutionalism can involve a self-denying tension between its components of consent and rights; constitutionalism may sometimes be

CONSTITUTIONALISM AND VIOLENCE IN IRELAND 125

protected against violence only by threatening its own nature; constitutionalism may be established by a denial of its own nature; the same act may be seen as constitutional or violent, or constitutional *and* violent, according to one's view of the legitimacy of the state.

NOTES

1. See D.G. Boyce. *Nationalism in Ireland* (London, 1982), 56.
2. *The Times*, 1845, quoted in R.N. Lebow, *White Britain and Black Ireland: The Influence of Stereotypes on Colonial Policy* (Philadelphia, 1976), 48.
3. Quoted by T.F. Moloney, 'The Judiciary, the Police, and the Maintenance of Law and Order' in J.H. Morgan (ed), *The New Irish Constitution: An Exposition and Some Arguments* (first published 1912) (Port Washington, New York, 1971), 157-65.
4. F.S.L. Lyons, quoted in T.P. O'Mahoney, *The Politics of Dishonour: Ireland 1916–1977* (Dublin, 1977), 27. Lyons goes on to argue that the reputation of Pearse has been questioned by some historians, and that serious students had placed more emphasis on constitutional than on revolutionary nationalism.
5. R. Davis, *Arthur Griffith and Non-violent Sinn Fein* (Dublin, 1974), xv.
6. See O'Mahoney, *op. cit.*, 21.
7. F. Ridley, 'The Importance of Constitutions', *Parliamentary Affairs* 19 (1966), 312-23.
8. G. Sartori, 'Constitutionalism: A Preliminary Discussion', *American Political Science Review*, 61 (1962), 853-64.
9. R. Berger, 'Constitutionalism and the Limits on Judicial Power', *Comparative Politics*, 11 (1979), 483-92.
10. G. Schram, 'A Critique of Contemporary Constitutionalism', *Comparative Politics*, 11 (1979), 445-66.
11. M.J.C. Vile, *Constitutionalism and the Separation of Powers* (Oxford, 1967), 315.
12. S. Wolin, 'Violence and the Western Political Tradition', in R. Hartogs and E. Artzt (eds), *Violence: Causes and Solutions* (New York, 1973), 23-43.
13. At its strongest this argument characterises *all* opposition to the settled order as violence. For example see R. Clutterbuck, *Britain in Agony: The Growth of Political Violence* (Middlesex, 1980), where IRA violence is lumped together with industrial disputes and political demonstrations.
14. T. Nardin, 'Violence and the State: A Critique of Empirical Political Theory'. *Sage Professional Papers in Comparative Politics*, 2 (1971), 11.
15. R. Williams, 'Violence Defined', *Guardian Weekly*, 4 July 1970, 18.
16. See A. Carter, *Direct Action and Liberal Democracy* (London, 1973), 30, 31, 41, 77.
17. R. Wollheim, 'On Democracy and Violence', *The Listener*, 17 February 1972, 199-200.
18. B. Farrell (ed), *The Irish Parliamentary Tradition* (Dublin, 1973), 20.
19. P. O'Farrell, *England and Ireland since 1800* (London, 1975), 174-5.
20. *Ibid.*, 161.
21. A.T.Q. Stewart, *The Narrow Ground: Aspects of Ulster, 1609–1969* (London, 1977), 113-14.
22. O. MacDonagh, *Ireland: The Union and Its Aftermath* (revised and enlarged edition, London, 1977) 144.
23. *Ibid.*, 146.
24. Tom Garvin has argued that the influence was much more than local, and the motivation much more than economic in 'Underground Political Networks in Pre-Famine Ireland', *Past and Present*, 96 (1982), 133-55. See also the analysis of agrarian violence in terms of secret societies, religious societies and local factions, and the claim that violence existed at a higher level than the rest of western Europe, in G. Broekner, *Rural Disorder and Police Reform in Ireland, 1812–36* (London and Toronto, 1970), 7 and 239.
25. MacDonagh, *op. cit.*, 148.

26. P. Mair, 'The Break-up of the United-Kingdom: The Irish Experience of Regime-Change, 1918–49', *Studies in Public Policy,* 13 (1978), 4-5.

27. T.W. Moody, *Davitt and Irish Revolution, 1846–82* (Oxford, 1981), 122, 123.

28. *Op. cit.,* 257. By 1914 the IRB wished to take advantage of the war's opportunity, regardless of their provision for popular mandate. The intrigues within the Irish Volunteers are documented in R.D. Edwards, *Patrick Pearse: The Triumph of Failure* (London 1977), chapter 6.

29. G. Sorel, *Reflections on Violence,* translated by T.E. Hulme and J. Roth (New York, 1972), 82.

30. F.S.L. Lyons, 'The Meaning of Independence', in Farrell, *op. cit.,* 224.

31. See Edwards, *op. cit.,* chapter 7; on some of the implications of 1916 see F.X. Martin, 'The Evolution of a Myth – The Easter Rising, Dublin 1916' in E. Kamenka (ed), *Nationalism: The Nature and Evolution of an Idea* (Canberra, 1973), 56-80.

32. O. MacDonagh, 'Ambiguity in Nationalism: The Case of Ireland', *Historical Studies,* 19 (1981), 337-52; Boyce, *op. cit.;* T. Garvin, *The Evolution of Irish Nationalist Politics* (Dublin, 1981); and see also the present author's review of Boyce in *American Political Science Review* (in the press) and 'Nationalism and Myth in Ireland', paper presented to the 1982 APSA Conference, Perth.

33. F. Munger, 'The Legitimacy of Opposition: The Change of Government in Ireland in 1932', *Sage Professional Papers in Contemporary Political Sociology,* 1 (1974).

34. Mansergh, quoted in F.S.L. Lyons, *Ireland Since the Famine* (revised edition, London, 1973), 538.

35. O'Mahoney, *op. cit.,* 81.

36. In the 1957 election Sinn Fein, the political wing of the IRA, while still denying the legitimacy of state, received 3 per cent of the vote and had four abstentionist candidates elected. Two IRA men on the H-Blocks ticket, both prisoners in Northern Ireland, were elected in 1981.

37. See D. Schmitt, *The Irony of Irish Democracy* (Lexington, Massachusetts, 1973).

38. C.C. O'Brien, *Herod: Reflections on Political Violence* (London, 1978, 32, 129-39.

39. See K. Kyle, 'The *Panorama* Survey of Irish Opinion', *Political Quarterly,* 40 (1979), 24-35.

40. See I. Budge and C. O'Leary, *Belfast: Approach to Crisis* (London, 1973).

41. P. Buckland, *A History of Northern Ireland* (Dublin, 1981), 65.

42. P. Buckland, *The Factory of Grievances: Devolved Government in Northern Ireland 1921–39* (Dublin, 1979), 216.

43. See *Disturbances in Northern Ireland,* Report of the Cameron Commission, Cmnd 532 (Belfast, 1969).

44. See J. Darby, *Conflict in Northern Ireland: The Development of a Polarised Community* (Dublin, 1976). The literature of the current troubles is huge. Darby contains a useful, but now dated, bibliography.

45. A. Lijphart, 'Review Article: the Northern Ireland Problem', *British Journal of Political Science,* 5 (1975), 83-106.

46. P. Arthur, *Government and Politics of Northern Ireland* (Harlow, 1980), 121.

47. *Ibid.,* 140.

48. See M. Dillon and D. Lehane, *Political Murder in Northern Ireland* (Middlesex, 1973).

49. T. Bowden, 'The IRA and the Changing tactics of Terrorism'. *Political Quarterly,* 4 (1976), 425-37.

50. P. Taylor, *Beating the Terrorists? Interrogation in Omagh, Gough and Castlereagh* (Middlesex, 1980), 25.

51. *Op. cit.,* 328-31. Incidentally, Callaghan's Labour Government in Britain would have survived its 1979 vote of confidence in the House of Commons if Gerry Fitt had not seen Bennett as a cover-up.

52. M. Tomlinson, 'Reforming Repression' in L. O'Dowd, B. Ralston, M. Tomlinson, *Northern Ireland: Between Civil Rights and Civil War* (London, 1980), 192-3.

53. K. Boyle, T. Hadden, P. Hillyard, *Ten Years on in Northern Ireland: the Legal Control of Political Violence* (London, 1980), 107-9.

54. *Guardian Weekly,* 29 June 1980, 4.

CONSTITUTIONALISM AND VIOLENCE IN IRELAND 127

55. R. Rose, *Governing Without Consensus: An Irish Perspective* (London, 1971), 480-3.
56. R. Rose, I. McAllister, P. Mair, 'Is There a Concurring Majority about Northern Ireland'. *Studies in Public Policy,* 22 (1978), 9 and 21.
57. Stewart, *op. cit.,* 153.
58. G.A. Hayes-McCoy, 'A Military History of the 1916 Rising' in K.B. Nowlan (ed), *The Making of 1916: Studies in the History of the Rising* (Dublin, 1969), 303.
59. R. Kee, *Ourselves Alone* (London, 1976), 125.
60. J. Murphy, *Ireland in the Twentieth Century* (Dublin, 1975), 58.
61. Arthur, *op. cit.,* 140.
62. O'Farrell, *op. cit.,* 159.
63. Bobby Sands, IRA man and H-Block hunger striker, was elected to the Westminster parliament in 1981, but not on a IRA ticket. The H-Blocks issue, however, probably increased IRA support, and five Sinn Fein candidates were elected in the 1982 Northern Ireland Assembly elections.

Part II
Participants
in
Terrorism

[6]

Winter 1985

Between Exclusion and Recognition: The Politics of the Ulster Defence Association

by
Arthur Aughey

INTRODUCTION

Over the past decade there has been a notable increase in the literature devoted to Protestant paramilitarism in Northern Ireland. It has been of variable quality and sometimes distinctly *parti pris*. Of the serious academic works there would appear to be a consensus on one distinctive aspect of paramilitarism. Militant loyalism has been explored and described in terms of its ambiguity, its contradictions and its confusions of aims. The governing word appears to be "uncertainty" and the implication is, that since the collapse of the "beautiful unity" of Unionism, ideologically and institutionally, the present Ulster crisis has brought loyalists face to face with the precarious instability of their whole system of values.[1] Though this "beautiful unity" is a myth, it is a myth that exercises a powerful attraction for the Ulster Protestant. Such a situation is bound to provoke inconsistency if not schizophrenia. The simplest way to express this contradiction is to divide loyalists in paramilitary organizations into "politicos" and "militarists" or soft-liners and hard-liners. This has been the general division used to categorize members of the Ulster Defense Association from the mid-1970s onwards. For instance, O'Malley in *The Uncivil War* defines his understanding of the UDA's strategic uncertainty as being rooted in the division "between those who think purely in paramilitary terms and those who want to move in a political direction."[2] This is a valuable distinction, and a necessary one, but is not in itself sufficient to explain the complexity of argument within the UDA. As a tool of analysis or conceptual framework it is aware of division. In short, it is asking the right question but giving a somewhat distorted answer. A more subtle approach is necessary to ferret out a clearer perspective regarding militant loyalism.

While it is evident that in terms of personality and disposition some members of the UDA would be more aggressive than others, the simple physical division or counting of heads does not get to the heart of the present dilemma. Arguably, the significant split is not between persons of choleric or pacific humor but is within the paramilitary mind itself. The UDA has travelled some way from the heyday of massed ranks loyalism in the early seventies. Its leadership has been seeking a role beyond mere organizational survival and the process of reflection has been a painful one in a community known for its inarticulateness. The purpose of this article is to suggest one framework within which to conceptualize the alternatives faced by the UDA and the difficult uncertainties posed by present circumstances. The politics of the UDA are considered within the framework of a debate between the ideas of *exclusion* and of *recognition*. Further, there are three appropriate levels or dimensions of this political dichotomy. The first concerns relations with the Catholic community in Northern Ireland. The second involves the relationship with the British Government and the third encompasses the broader context of the internationalization of the Ulster problem, although particular emphasis is given to relations with the Republic of Ireland. While there are clear and obvious overlaps with the military-political division, analysis in terms of exclusion and recognition set new boundaries and suggests a more complex interpenetration. The main weakness of the existing understanding is the implication that one "line" or one "side" may win out against the other. Use of the above criteria seems to indicate that the contradictions shown by the UDA are really different sides of the same coin. Literally, each is stuck with the other. Together, they form the reality of the political life to which Protestants in general have had to accommodate since 1972.

ULSTER CATHOLICS: EXCLUSION OR RECOGNITION?

The historic voice of militant loyalism has been unequivocally exclusionist. The thrust of the cry of "No surrender" has meant no compromise whatever to meet demands emanating from sources outside the Ulster Protestant "family." It was a watchword of the majoritarian democracy institutionalized on the basis of a Protestant parliament for a Protestant people. Hence the significance of the slogan "We are the people!" implying a political and social non-identity for Catholics and the illegitimacy of the goals of Catholic politics. This was certainly not a "liberal" style of politics though it was understandable as a feature of Irish history. It was also understandable when the alternative presented by both Unionist and Nationalist leaders appeared to be one which was unacceptable to a "free" and "British" people. It was and is a position that excludes all distinction between the constitutional and the unconstitutional. All activity is swept into the same category of political threat. It helped perpetuate the idea of separateness which the present crisis has only served to exacerbate — the social and political polarization of Protestant and Catholic communities.

Conducting their survey on the problems of Northern Ireland in the late 1950s and early 1960s Barritt and Carter found "racial, religious, political, economic and social conflicts all rolled into one; ... two communities which live apart, even to the extent of playing different games."[3] In this period, however, mutual exclusion was ritualized and indeed stylized to such an extent that, Barritt and Carter argued, Protestant and Catholic could live side by side "generally at peace." Arend Lijphart defined the society as "one of majority dictatorship dealing firmly with a minority claiming both democratic rights and a different political framework."[4] The concept of majority is firmly embedded in a definition of Protestantism in Northern Ireland and in Ulster politics. The UDA inherited this concept. The campaign of the Irish Republican Army and the Catholic political challenge to simple majoritarianism generated further self-reliance and exclusionist tendencies. As *Loyalist News* put it: "Ulster is ours, not Westminster's, not Dublin's, but OURS."[5]

Following the logic of the political mentality defined by Lijphart, the UDA stated early on that those responsible for violence against Protestants would have the answer to the law — more precisely, to the "Majority Law." Only those Catholics who wished to remain *under* the majority would be welcome to stay. There was to be no idea of equality or of political partnership. Catholics were to be excluded from any positive contribution to the content of the majority law. This idea of justice is not a participatory, inclusive one. What is ultimately just is what is conducive to the maintenance of Protestant hegemony with Catholics being treated justly only on sufferance.[6]

The exclusion option has a paramilitary appeal because it pays homage to the myth that were the majority given its head then it could "clear out" Republican areas and return Northern Ireland to "peace." Such a disposition is encapsulated in the following doggerel of a Protestant drinking song:

The RC should be pressed from this part of the North
And foolish he would be to return,
To the land of the Prod where we will vow to God,
His friendship of evil to spurn.

Behind such pure bravado, the exclusionist spirit is strong though it is more frequently expressed in rage and frustration within the Protestant community than in violence against Catholics. Despite the conciliatory posture evident latterly, this spirit remains a sturdy bulwark of the UDA leadership.

In the recent interview in the local journal *Fortnight*, Andy Tyrie, the long-serving Chairman of the UDA, took care to express his own and his organization's optimism with regard to a peaceful resolution of the present crisis. Yet it was clear that he had difficulty in distancing himself from the exclusionist tendency in thought and in word. Tyrie admitted that he saw little on which loyalists could compromise without betraying the very being of their community. He also sought to establish a distinction between the Catholic community as such and the Republican threats to Protestants and their way of life. The word "Ulster" appeared to have defeated him. "Ulster" can be used as inclusive of Catholics, or may refer to the common territory inhabited by Catholics and Protestants. Alternatively, it can be interpreted as the living spirit and symbol of Protestant resistance to all things Catholic. Tyrie's own use of "Ulster" seems to be exclusionist. Commenting on recent events, he noted that, at present,

...the bulk of the nationalist groups [say] there is no future for the Ulster Protestant community and their job is to destroy it. If you're talking about the warring groups, the groups that are involved in the war — and you must see the SDLP in that, and after Cardinal Tomas O'Fiaich's recent statement, you must see him as part of the war effort against the whole Protestant community — then there's a big build-up of everything that's opposing Ulster survival.[8]

In his statement Tyrie clearly views "Ulster" as Protestant and at war with any and every Catholic and Catholic institution. It is not a matter of semantics but a matter of political realities. Yet, he retreats quickly into vagueness and equivocation. His choice to be less than clear on most other points is perhaps understandable. As a spokesman frequently quoted in the media, Tyrie, of necessity, is sensitive to the conflicts within his own organization. The UDA has chosen to respond to the growing opposition to Ulster's survival in more than words. It claims to be in the process of developing an Ulster Defence Force from within its ranks in preparation for a "doomsday situation."[9]

The notion of the Ulster Defence Force is neither a totally sinister nor exclusionist one. Rather, it can be contended that, at present, the currents within the UDA actually make it impossible to establish absolute exclusionism at the top level. The proposal for the UDF is fraught with qualifications concerning the need for a political approach *as well as* military preparations. It is the use of language again that tends to betray the confusion or uncertainty in the minds of the leadership over the purpose of political and military activity. Political activity suggests compromise, cooperation and recognition. However, the UDA document on reorganization speaks of losing ground and of combatting the forces which would "oppose the development of a strong Ulster Protestant society."[10] Such phraseology leads one to believe, first, that the UDA wants to void whatever positive gains Catholics have made since 1969, and second, that the idea of a strong Ulster Protestant society *by definition* should totally exclude Catholics from political influence. If this is not the intention of the UDA, more care and precision is needed in its statements. If such statements can be taken at face value, then the UDF may be a device to give expression (whether simply on paper or in men with arms remains to be seen) to the exclusionist tendency while the "war" is pursued by other means. If massed ranks loyalism is a thing of the past, then elite corps loyalism may be the next best thing. Circumstances often dictate policy and organization. In this case, though, the circumstances come not only from external exigencies but also from internal debate.

The other voice in this internal debate appeals less to emotion or aggression and more to political reason. The trauma of the troubles and the intractability of "zero-sum partisanship" (exclusion) has led elements of the UDA to accept, perhaps reluctantly, the emptiness and negativity of the old simplicities. There has emerged, in a limited fashion, an understanding of the common experience of Protestant and Catholic, indeed, that the very definition of Protestantism itself is closely bound up with Ulster Catholicism. Or, to paraphrase that mysterious Hegelian phrase, the common identity of identity and non-identity. The idea of exclusion sees this relationship purely in terms of master and slave. The concept of recognition embodied in some of the arguments and ideas of the UDA leadership is a disposition to view the relationship as one of equality in adversity. Recognition was a political theory expressed clearly in the New Ulster Political Research Group's (the original political wing of the UDA) document *Beyond The Religious Divide*. Published in 1979, it represented a distillation of some years of debate and reflection and it argued for an independent Ulster as a "no-loss" outcome for both communities.[11]

Under the inspiration of Glen Barr, the NUPRG proposed a form of political identity that recognized the rights of both communities but attempted to overcome the conflicting national aspirations of Protestant British and Catholic Irish. It would be an identity-in-difference. The common experience of sectarian strife, it was argued or implied, had forged a certain respect for each community's uniqueness and that this was the basis upon which commonly acceptable institutions could be built — on an Ulster basis alone. There would be a classic constitutional trade-off: Protestants would sever the British link and Catholics would sever their allegiance to a United Ireland. Both would admit the impossibility of domination, but would recognize that between themselves they could build a harmonious society. Difference would contribute to political stability rather than destroying it. As far as the NUPRG was concerned, these proposals were the best way to return Ulster to "proper politics," which meant not an exclusionist struggle but a recognition of genuine issues of socio-economic importance. The language of *Beyond The Religious Divide* is forthright, concluding that it is not designed to achieve "the creation of a Protestant dominated State, nor is it the stepping stone to a United Ireland." It does, however, provide "an opportunity for peace and stability. It is an opportunity for the Ulster people to get back their dignity."[12] Clearly "Ulster people" meant something very different here than the exclusive term traditionally used.

The transformation of the NUPRG into the Ulster Loyalist Democratic Party and the change in political spokesmen from Barr to John McMichael has not altered the open advocacy of independence. However, since the Hunger Strike of 1981 and the subsequent political successes of Provisional Strike of 1981 and the subsequent political successes of Provisional Sinn Fein (the political wing of the IRA) there has been a distinct change in the substance and spirit of the message. As far as formal policy documents are concerned, the ULDP appears to have carried the NUPRG's standard forward. In the statements "Peace With Dignity" and "The Way Ahead," it was clearly argued that recognition and involvement of both communities in Ulster's political process is a prerequisite of any way forward. Democracy must triumph, and "the imposition of partisan values, creeds and philosophies should be replaced by the accepted recognition that we are a pluralist society." Though two distinct traditions are involved, the ULDP's desire and aim is to establish constructive co-existence.[13] This is the benign model of political activity generally embraced by McMichael in public. Putting his case to Padraig O'Malley, McMichael was clear that no political party in Northern Ireland should endeavor to create a monolith (thus placing the blame with the old Protestant identity of the Unionist Party). Further, he acknowledged that there could never be any recognized settlement "if you have circumstances where there is one majority and one minority."[14] These are views to which Tyrie would also subscribe, without in the least feeling he had contradicted his previously cited opinions.

Since the Hunger Strikes of 1981, which proved such a propaganda and political success for the Provisional IRA, there has developed a sharper edge to this message of conciliation. The recognitionists openly condemn indiscriminate shootings of Catholics. This is no longer acceptable as necessary policy. But, whereas the Barr strategy was one of open-handed peaceful intent at a time when sectarian tensions were low, such a course cannot be universally accepted within the UDA while the Provisional campaign, political and military, continues. Between Catholicism and violent Republicanism a distinction must be made if the idea of recognition is to hold any ground as a political force in the organization. The elements of IRA terror have to be isolated and destroyed. They are legitimate targets for UDA "Soldiers" so long as the forces of the state are incapable of dealing with the enemies of Ulster. Both Tyrie and McMichael are quite plain about this. While the UDA ought not to "come into conflict with the Catholic community" the campaign against the IRA and INLA "cannot be shelved," serving as it does as an "ongoing crusade" through which "only the guilty suffer." To the UDA, "That's the way any war should be fought."[15]

Despite their political commitment to recognition, the UDLP/UDA's idea of what is to be recognized remains selective. Recognition is only on the basis of an Ulster community, not on the basis of an Irish Republic. Voting for Sinn Fein is seen as illegitimate, an expression of non-recognition of Protestantism, and it takes two to make recognition meaningful. The weakness of the recognitionist position within the UDA, its dependence on circumstances beyond its control, are summed up in McMichael's classically coded message after the Provisional Sinn Fein garnered ten percent of the vote in the Northern Ireland Assembly elections of October 1982:

> Where does this situation leave Ulster Protestants? If we are to survive must we adopt a simple "us-or-them" attitude and fight for what we want? And if we do, will we again be branded as small-minded bigots? What have we got to lose?[16]

That he left all these questions in their simple rhetorical form is an indication of the mental struggle between exclusion and recognition.

The uncertainty of the UDA's present attitude towards Ulster Catholics has led some commentators to question their political sincerity. For instance, O'Malley gives the distinct impression that he believes that it is a cleverly calculated maneuver. The UDA leadership may contain political amateurs, may stumble about in the fog of its rhetoric, but it has given itself a good cover, a mantle of earnest good intentions. Through this, O'Malley contends that it has gained "a measure of respectability which pays a handsome dividend: its past transgressions, if not forgotten, are for the most part largely forgiven: and its current lapses, if not forgiven, are for the most part largely excused."[17] That the UDA is now a different creature only reluctantly provoked into action and retaliation is, says O'Malley, "a conclusion the UDA itself carefully cultivates." This is perhaps too harsh and cynical a judgement. Certainly good intentions are never enough, but at least there has been some attempt at political movement. That circumstances have not been favorable is not entirely of the UDA's making. It has no independent control over its resolution and, when even small steps can lead to disaster, it is unrealistic to expect too much soon.

RELATIONS WITH THE BRITISH GOVERNMENT

Relations with the British Government present the same degree of complexity, the ironies and subtleties of which have been explored historically by David Miller in his book *Queen's Rebels*. The UDA exhibits the modern configuration of the same complexity, and in its deliberations and posturings encapsulates the tension between Britishness and Ulster Protestantism. While both are features of the same identity, they may call forth conflicting loyalties to the sovereign political authority on the one hand and to communal loyalty on the other. In the flux of the present crisis, they also involve a conceptual, ideological struggle between exclusion and recognition. Indeed in this case the two are even more confusingly intertwined and convoluted. There appear to be two significant aspects to recognition by the British Government that motivate the UDA. First, there is a negative factor, the recognition that the UDA is able, by massed-ranks loyalism, to exercise an effective veto over the plans of any administration in London. It is a possibility that must be constantly restated, otherwise it may not be believed and it gains force by being kept in the public mind. Second, there is a positive aspect which claims for the UDA the right to some sort of involvement in mapping out the constitutional future of Ulster. It is a claim to be taken seriously, particularly as a political force with ideas to contribute to the current debate. Similarly, exclusion has two aspects. The UDA may be ignored altogether as a political or military force and not be accorded any hearing by those in authority. It could also be banned altogether as an organization.

The negative dimension of recognition has been the UDA's historical experience. The price of Ulster's integrity is held to be eternal vigilance and a refusal to go along with the honeyed words from Westminster. With the fall of the Stormont administration, the inception of direct rule and then, later, with the establishment of the power-sharing Executive as an instrument of British policy, militant loyalists felt that their normal channels of communication (the Stormont "system") had been bypassed to facilitate a "sell-out" to the Irish Republic. The loyalist response, the Ulster Worker's Council strike of 1974, was what A.O. Hirschman would have termed a "boycott," that is "a weapon of customers who do not have, at least at the time of the boycott, an alternative."[1] Hirschman's economic analysis is rather an appropriate description of the political circumstances encountered by the UDA in 1974. Its action was a classic one of political negativity for there was no consensus within the Protestant community regarding an alternative. No one was prepared to seize the moment of governmental paralysis to impose one, not least the UDA.

Thus the UDA had proved that an effective "boycott" could

prevent solutions from being imposed by the British Government without the whole-hearted consent of Ulster Protestants and in a fashion that upstaged the rhetoric of Unionist politicians. It also served to show that, in the face of Westminster priorities, militant loyalists could not enforce their own solutions. As the failure of the subsequent 1977 strike showed, boycott without effective alternatives is subject to diminishing returns. Its over-employment may fragment that Protestant unity it is designed to foster. Therefore the present circumstances of the Ulster crisis place severe limitations on the purely negative power of loyalist paramilitarism. In the words of David Miller, it is useful as a means to "keep Britain up to the mark in honouring her imputed obligations," or, in other words, to recognize her duty to defend and protect Ulster from all Republican threats in order to maintain the Protestant identity.[19] The fact that the British Government certainly recognizes a duty to Northern Ireland does not mean that it recognizes it in the manner posed by the UDA. British perspectives are not those of the militant loyalist no matter how strong the professions of fidelity on both sides. Thus the negative idea of recognition, while a powerful one, was seen to be ultimately undignified by sections of the UDA leadership. The need for an alternative, to avoid the Hirschman dilemma and to get beyond the sterility of boycott, helped to stimulate thinking on the idea of Ulster independence. Here was an historical claim for a positive contribution and a recognition by British politicians that the UDA was not just the strong arm of local politicians but a legitimate party to discussions in its own right.

The central thrust behind the proposals for a negotiated independence for Northern Ireland has already been mentioned. The question remains regarding how far this was recognized as legitimate by the British Government. For here was a curious phenomenon, a loyalist organization, whose roots lay deep in the sacrifices of Ulster troops in both world wars for Empire, Queen and Country, whose Protestant community is suffused with all the symbolism of Britishness, being prepared to put forward as a *first* option breaking the link with Great Britain. In other words, on principle, the UDA was proposing to exclude the British Government from the affairs of Northern Ireland, internally if not externally. As a recent policy document argues, the outcome, though not the intention of a "London based government for Northern Ireland is by nature a repressive one." Even if this is the result of ignorance and not malice, it is time for "self-determination."[20]

The British Government's response has been, understandably, equivocal. While it professes to be open to all political suggestions for a way forward in Northern Ireland, obviously there are certain options that any Government will not accept for both domestic and international reasons. The pattern of British policy has been to encourage the UDA in its political activities, to keep it talking, and, thus, to keep it off the streets. Leaders like Tyrie and McMichael have been transformed from representatives of the sinister, hooded "thugs" to quasi-respectable political spokesmen. They both make good journalistic copy. Since the late 1970s the leadership has coveted the kudos of formal and informal links with the Northern Ireland Office. There is a nice irony in this.

Many UDA statements have attacked the middle class Unionist leadership for their historic role of "duping" the Protestant working class, of embroiling them in "border" politics rather than "proper politics." Now the paramilitaries' own working class leaders are, in fact, doing what the Unionist leadership did in the 1920s — acting as a disciplining and restraining influence to attain their own political goals.

However, the NIO has never given any visible credence to the independence option either because it fears that it would lead to Protestant hegemony or because it fears the diplomatic response of the Republic of Ireland, or both. For instance, the constitutional talks initiated in 1980 by Humphrey Atkins, then Secretary of State for Northern Ireland, specifically excluded independence from the constitutional agenda. It was not recognized as an option at all. Similarly, it has never appeared on any subsequent governmental agenda. Indeed, since the creation of the Assembly in 1982 on the initiative of the present Secretary of State, James Prior, the UDA's aggressively independent tones have been muted. Since neither of the political parties representing Catholics — the Social Democratic and Labour Party (SDLP) and PSF — participate in the Assembly, it has, in practice, become a Protestant Parliament for a Protestant People. It could well be that many in the UDA are happy with this despite all the fine words about accommodation with the "other side." It could also be that the existence of the Assembly is held to be a step in the right direction, not only towards greater local control but also, eventually, to independence. In this way, at least, the UDA might feel "passively" involved in political deliberations about a new Northern Ireland.[21]

The UDA is the largest paramilitary organization in Northern Ireland and the only one not proscribed under Schedule 2 of the Emergency Provisions Act. Exclusion through proscription has always hung over its head. Calls for proscription have been frequent and tend to follow terrorist incidents where known UDA members have been involved or implicated. The fact that most of these members have been convicted under a *nom de guerre* such as the Ulster Freedom Fighters has not fooled anyone. However, it is clear that it is neither in the interest of the Government nor the UDA for the Association to be proscribed. An open, legal UDA is also open to penetration by security forces. A legal UDA allows the organization to continue its lucrative business operations — taxis, social clubs, bars — from which members and loyalist prisoners profit. When Secretary of State for Northern Ireland, Humphrey Atkins, declared that the "test of proscription is whether an organization is actively supporting, encouraging or engaged in terrorist activities,"[22] it was obvious the Government diplomatically deemed the UDA to be innocent of such charges. To exclude the UDA might only drive it underground to something worse. Better to have it above ground where the *threat* of proscription will act as a further agent of political discipline, even though UDA leaders may claim to ignore such threats. As an established element in Ulster Protestant life, the UDA as an organization has too much to lose by rash behavior. Since 1974, the British Government too has become more sensitive in its management of opinion. Both appear to recognize the limits of the possible and have tacitly agreed to play within the "rules."

INTERNATIONAL PERSPECTIVE

Ulster Protestantism in general, and militant loyalism in particular, has traditionally been noted for its inarticulateness and self-reliance. It has usually spoken and acted in terms of the integrity of the Ulster problem and savagely denounced all outside interference. This being so, it has never really made much effort to justify its cause, preferring to rely upon God and the strength of the community. However, the modern internationalization of the Ulster problem by mainstream political nationalists and extreme Republicans has forced a reconsideration of Protestant insularity. There has been an increasing tendency to modify exclusion by a recognition of the importance of outside links and the need to engage forthrightly in the battle of ideas. This development is slow, hesitant and fitful yet increasingly salient. Two examples illustrate this new concern of the UDA.

It is no longer possible to ignore the international successes of the IRA's propaganda war, even though Protestants would tend to be united regarding the illegitimacy of any external involvement, verbal or material (except, of course, support for Protestantism). For instance, statements on Ulster by American Presidential candidates are received with hostility as are any actions deemed to lend support to the ideal of Republicanism. However, the UDA recognizes that any counterpropaganda is difficult to formulate. As Tyrie argues, Ulster has become established as a colonial problem and the IRA as an anti-colonial freedom force.[23] The UDA has not the resources to combat such a world view. Nevertheless, it has recognized the need to manufacture a counter-myth that may be of some future use. It has thus commissioned historical research by local author Ian Adamson into the curious, mysterious origins and development of the "Cruthin." The Cruthin are claimed to be the "original" Ulster tribe that colonized Scotland and the north-east of Ireland *before* the Celts. The return of the Protestant Scottish settlers during the Plantation of Ulster in the seventeenth century and the driving out of the Catholic Celts (the struggle of Planter and Gael) is viewed therefore as repatriation, not an occupation. Indeed, this is quite a reversal of historical perspective, and it establishes, so the UDA contends, the inalienable and unshakable right of Ulster Protestants to retain their true "homeland." Although most Ulster Protestants feel no need for this historical interpretation, at least it provides a useful counterpoint to the Republican interpretation of history.[24]

The important international perspective is more tangible and closer to home. It concerns relations with the Republic of Ireland. Exclusionist feeling is undoubtedly the most powerful of emotions and deeply rooted in communal experience. O'Malley provides an expression of this feeling in the UDA's journal *Ulster*, claiming "Southern Ireland is a foreign state with whom we can find nothing of importance in common. Our heritage, history and culture are separate and different."[25] Indeed, none of the political parties receiving substantial support from within the

Protestant electorate, not even the bi-confessional Alliance Party, can accept any positive role for the Irish Republic in Ulster affairs, except in the suppression of terrorism on *its own* side of the border. The main difference is simply that the UDA is usually prepared to use stronger language in its condemnation.

Recently the UDA political wing has been more concerned with stressing recognition as the positive dimension to the Protestant case. In the document "The Way Ahead" an open-handed, softer line is taken. It recognizes two distinct traditions in the island of Ireland and indicates the UDA wishes "to co-exist in peace, harmony and in mutual respect." This is much more conciliatory than the denunciations of misty, historical Celtic twilights. Significantly, "The Way Ahead" argues that the ULDP needs help and advice, and that the leadership would welcome not only the advice of the British Government but of the Irish as well, always provided that such aid is "motivated by the desire to encourage reconciliation of Ulster People" and not "self-interest or imperialist design."[26] Such pronouncements have been welcomed by the Irish Government in Dublin. On occasion party and government leaders from the Republic have engaged in dialogue with the UDA. It is clear, however, that the perspective is different on both sides. For the Dublin Government, the aim is to build support for some kind of eventual Irish unity and the recognition of the legitimacy of that ideal. For the UDA, recognition of a separate Ulster identity legitimately having its own political institutions is the goal about which there can be no compromise.

Yet, even such a predictable view of the Irish Republic is difficult to sell to the UDA rank and file. Just the acceptance of a Dublin Government showing concern over Northern Ireland goes deeply against the grain of militant loyalism. Dublin is the "enemy without." McMichael had been working on a submission for the Dublin sponsored New Ireland Forum which had invited proposals from all concerned parties regarding Ireland's constitutional development. He admitted that in the wake of the Darkley murders and the assassination of Unionist Assemblyman Edgar Graham it had been impossible to go forward. To recognize that the proceedings in Dublin had any significance for loyal Ulster people in such circumstances would have "split the movement."[27] While some may deem it a necessity of life, a part of Realpolitik, to recognize that the Republic must at least be involved in the ratification of an Ulster "solution," most do not. Lloyd George was perceptive in his view that borders, once made on a map, become indelible in the minds of an insecure people. The border between Northern Ireland and the Republic of Ireland has for too long been the symbol of Protestant fidelity. It is felt to be the cordon sanitaire for a distinctive way of life. As such, exclusion must remain the main disposition of militant loyalists towards the Dublin Government.

CONCLUSION

It is not the purpose of this paper to suggest some transcendental synthesis between these two poles of paramilitary thinking. To play around with such concepts as "exclusive recognition" or "recognized exclusion'' would really not fill any need and would be mere academic posturing. It is hard to imagine to what they might apply, although the UDA leadership might find either an "exclusive recognition" of loyalism by Britain or a "recognized exclusion" of an independent Northern Ireland from interference by the Irish Republic a congenial conclusion. Nor indeed would any simplistic moralization be appropriate. That may be left up to archbishops. The wide gulf between exclusion and recognition, the extreme difficulty of compromise, illustrate the clear intractability of the Northern Ireland "problem." As interviews with the UDA leaders show, both conceptions can exist consciously or unconsciously within the same argument.

It would be unfair to attribute such schizophrenia to the UDA leadership alone. It exists in every Protestant consciousness and every Catholic consciousness in Ulster's divided society. At least Tyrie and McMichael, whatever their shortcomings, conduct their mental wrestling in public. As Michael Oakeshott once wrote somewhere, men sometimes unexpectedly achieve great things in the fog of the unknown and uncertain. Perhaps in the struggle with the uncertainty of their own priorities, the UDA may achieve something worthwhile, a positive contribution to the politics of conflict resolution. To which one may add, but, on the other hand ....

Winter 1985

Author's Note

* The author would like to acknowledge the helpful comments made on this paper by Philip Boskett.

Footnotes

1. See for instance S. Nelson, *Ulster's Uncertain Defenders* (Appletree Press, 1984); P. O'Malley, *The Uncivil Wars* (Blackstaff Press, 1983); B. Probert, *Beyond Orange and Green* (Zed Press, 1978); G. Bell, *The Protestants of Ulster* (Pluto Press, 1976); D. Miller, *Queen's Rebels* (Gill and Macmillan, 1978); J. Darby (ed.), *Northern Ireland: The Background to the Conflict* (Appletree Press, 1983).

2. O'Malley, p. 341.

3. D.P. Barritt and C.F. Carter, *The Northern Ireland Problem* (OUP, 1962), p. 3.

4. A. Lijphart, "The Northern Ireland Problem: Cases, Theories and Solutions," *British Journal of Political Science*, 5 (1975), p. 83.

5. *Loyalist News*, 7 October, 1972.

6. *Ibid.*, 9 September, 1972.

7. Anon., "Home, Home in Belfast," in *Love Orange, Love Green: Poems of Loving, Living and Dying in Working Class Ulster* (Whitcor Publications, 1973).

8. *Fortnight*, May 1984.

9. *Ibid.*

10. Ulster Defence Association, "Reorganisation," mimeo, 1984.

11. New Ulster Political Research Group, *Beyond the Religious Divide*, March 1979.

12. *Ibid.*, p. 2.

13. Ulster Loyalist Democratic Party, *Peace with Dignity* (1983).

14. O'Malley, p. 337.

15. *Ulster*, April 1982.

16. *Ibid.*, December 1982.

17. O'Malley, p. 355.

18. A.O. Hirschman, *Exit, Voice and Loyalty* (Harvard University Press, 1970), p. 86.

19. Miller, p. 157.

20. ULDP, *The Way Ahead* (1983).

21. See *Ulster*, June 1984.

22. Speech to the House of Commons, 13 February 1981. Reported in *Belfast Telegraph*, 14 February 1981.

23. Cited in N. Frankel, "Conservations in Ulster," *Conflict Quarterly*, 3 (Fall 1982), p. 32.

24. See I. Adamson, *The Cruthin* (Donaldson Press, 1978).

25. Cited in O'Malley, p. 344.

26. *The Way Ahead*.

27. J. McMichael, Interview with P. Boskett, 19 December 1983. Once circumstances were propitious again, once the emotional wave had passed, the ULDP sent their submission to the Prime Minister of the Irish Republic. This may be deemed some form of recognition.

[7]

Conflict Quarterly

Arbiters of Ulster's Destiny?
The Military Role of the
Protestant Paramilitaries in Northern Ireland

by
Colin J. McIlheney

INTRODUCTION

May 1974 was a watershed for the influence of the Protestant paramilitaries in Northern Ireland. In association with key workers in the power stations and the manufacturing sector under the umbrella of the Ulster Workers Council, they brought about the collapse of the power-sharing executive which had been set up in the wake of the Sunningdale conference.[1] Paramilitary muscle was in evidence on the streets; formerly clandestine individuals emerged as media celebrities informing the public about the progress of the general strike; effective political power was theirs. The often talked about loyalist backlash had materialized. There was much talk of forming a provisional government and declaring independence. yet the paramilitaries failed to capitalize on their success. Riven by internal disagreement about what to do next, political control soon reverted to Westminster and the campaign by the Provisional Irish Republican Army (IRA) continued unabated.

In 1984, the Protestant paramilitaries were still in operation but the intervening decade had been a very difficult one for them. From being recognized as the arbiters of Ulster's destiny, they appear to have gone for a long walk in the wilderness. Their command structure has been ravaged by evidence from informers at major 'supergrass' trials.[2] Their candidates have been spurned at elections.[3] Their ranks have been split by violent faction feuds. Many of their active service units now languish in the Maze prison. They have been criticized for their inability to eradicate the IRA and condemned for widespread extortion and racketeering. Their external support network, based in expatriate communities in Scotland and Ontario, has been infiltrated by security forces. Whereas the IRA has confidently asserted that it goes forward with an armalite in one hand and a ballot box in the other, the Protestant paramilitaries have seemed confused over whether to concentrate on military matters or go further down the political path. This article concentrates on the Protestant paramilitaries' changing military strategies and assesses the viability of their continuation as a potent paramilitary threat.

LIQUIDATING THE ENEMY

The Protestant paramilitaries' main spell of concerted sectarian warfare was 1972-73.[4] The local parliament at Stormont was soon to be dissolved; the IRA was bombing commercial targets at will and had established no-go areas under their control; and, the British Army did not appear as if it would control events. Many individuals in the Protestant population felt that their existence and that of Northern Ireland was threatened. Militant loyalists rallied to William Craig and the Vanguard movement which organized a series of mass rallies. At one of these in Belfast's Ormeau Park, Craig declared, "We must liquidate the enemy," though there is no evidence that any of the politicians or paramilitary leadership orchestrated the terror campaign. Indeed, relations were often strained between the two. Many convicted paramilitaries complained about the lack of interest and support given to them by elected representatives. Tommy Herron, then leader of the Ulster Defence Association (UDA), viewed his organization as "being asked to lead the March on Rome," while Mussolini, in the guise of William Craig, took the train.

The sectarian attacks were of the most difficult kind to analyse. No one group was responsible, although attention to court convictions shows that elements in the UDA were involved as were fringe organizations such as the fanatical Red Hand Commandos. Sometimes the incidents were purely random killings — hooded bodies were regularly discovered — sometimes they were attacks on known Republican supporters. On some chilling occasions, attacks involved obvious psychopathic elements indicated by long hours of torture. Over these people, the recognized leaders of the paramilitaries had no control. In 1972-73 the Protestant paramilitaries terrorized Belfast, producing an atmosphere of fear which has not been recreated since and showing a feature of their character which they have retained to the present day. That is, they demonstrated the capacity to respond to political events and the campaign of the IRA in a violent manner. The hallmark of their activity was the terrorism of the reflex action, dependent for its level of support on how keenly the Protestant community felt under seige. While there has been a lot of attention focused on the way the two main Protestant paramilitary groups, the UDA and Ulster Volunteer Force, have dabbled to varying degrees with political ideas, it must be stressed that there remains in both a hard core of gunmen, ready to strike back at the IRA and Irish National Liberation Army in a 'tit for tat' fashion. Into this category fall both the Ulster Freedom Fighters and the sinister Protestant Action Force. Though their views are unclouded by any political subtleties, they have strong links with the two main organizations.

THE UDA: AVOIDING PROSCRIPTION

> Recruits join the U.D.A. to get guns,
> not for political guidance.[5]

The UDA remains the largest paramilitary organizations in Northern Ireland and the only one not proscribed under Schedule 2 of the Emergency Provisions Act (1978). The major alteration in its military tactics has been from indiscriminate attacks on Roman Catholics to selective elimination of prominent Republican activists. Even after such atrocities as the bombing of the La Mon House Hotel in 1978 when twelve civilians died and the more recent massacre of church worshippers at Darkley Pentecostal Hall in South Armagh, the reaction of the UDA was very muted. A similar pattern occurred during the high tension produced by the IRA hunger strike. The UDA, apart from a few mobilization exercises, stayed in the wings. Although the hawks within the organization have been increasing the pressure on the leadership for an upsurge in military action, there is still a taboo on pub bombings or doorstep sectarian assassinations. As Alan Murray has written, "the UDA recognized the futility, politically and militarily, of consigning innocent Catholics to their graves" and this feeling has prevailed.[6] It would be wrong to interpret this as evidence that the organization has gone soft or lacks the will to do any more. Rather, this mood reflects the views of the leadership. A change of direction was expedient both to avoid being banned and also to tie in with the new politico image.[7] Crucially, it also acknowledges that the Ulster Freedom Fighters (UFF) have retained the capacity to strike back at the IRA. Thus has come about an arrangement whereby the UDA could establish a purely terrorist wing, the UFF, which could then claim responsibility for murders and bombings, while the UDA could distance itself from such events. The UFF first appeared in 1973, organized on a cellular structure to minimize the likelihood of penetration by the security forces and claimed responsibility for attacks under the pseudonyms of Captain Black or Captain White. The population at large did not take long to realize that the UFF was merely a flag of convenience or 'nom de guerre' for elements in the UDA. Press statements from the UFF were even issued through UDA headquarters. One example, the 1980 murder in Carnlough of John Turnley, the Irish Independence Party politician, highlights the interplay between the UDA and the UFF. During the trial in 1982 of four men from Larne, later convicted of the murder, the prosecuting counsel actually stated that one of the defendents was, in fact, the "officer commanding the general wing of the UDA in Larne which assisted the military wing, sometimes referred to as the Ulster Freedom Fighters."[8] The UDA has refused to acknowledge any duality of membership. Sammy Duddy, their publicity officer, has insisted that

> Reports in the media have tied these recent sectarian attacks with the UFF and ultimately with ourselves. This is completely wrong. They are being carried out by a gang of cowboys with no allegiance to any organisation. Spokesmen have given wrong code-names, they do not belong to any recognised force.[9]

More recently, the attempted assassination of Gerry Adams, the Sinn Fein M.P. for West Belfast, was claimed by the UFF but those charged in connection with the incident also have known links with the South Antrim brigade of the UDA. There is seemingly no problem in this case with reconciling this sort of attack with the attempts of the leadership to politicize the organization. Indeed, Andy Tyrie, Supreme Commander of the UDA, positively endorsed the UFF campaign. "So long as they do bomb and shoot only active Republicans, no way would the UDA disapprove of it. We would have no objection to it whatsover."[10] The UDA has thus maintained a lower military profile while becoming more selective in its conception of what constitutes a legitimate target. This has been most important tactically because the UDA has been concerned to maximize support among constitutional politicians for the

Spring 1985

campaign to segregate loyalist prisoners in the Magilligan prison, near Londonderry. This campaign peaked during 1984 with the UDA mimicking the IRA through the use of a hunger strike and by the arrangement of street demonstrations and rallies in support of their demand.

THE UVF — FOR GOD AND ULSTER

The second main Protestant paramilitary organization is the Ulster Volunteer Force (UVF). The original UVF played a prominent part in the opposition to the Home Rule proposals of the British government in the early years of the century. They re-emerged, using the same initials but in a very different guise, in the 1960s as a group centred in the loyalist heartland of the Shankill Road in Belfast and opposed to the reformist tendencies of the Unionist Prime Minister Terence O'Neill.[11] As early as 1966 the UVF laid down the gauntlet in a statement to Belfast newspapers, by declaring war "on the IRA and its splinter groups," describing themselves as "heavily armed Protestants dedicated to this cause."[12] Their motto was the clarion call "For God and Ulster."

Membership of the UVF has been illegal for most of the period since 1966 to the present day, although it did flirt with the political option through the formation of the Volunteer Political Party. The UVF has had sporadic bursts of enthusiasm for socialist ideas and ideological *tête à têtes* with the official IRA. Throughout the troubles, its support has been concentrated in Belfast, East Antrim and North Armagh. It has been characterized by its openness to the influence of charismatic personalities. The most important of these were Gusty Spence, who shaped UVF philosophy throughout the early 1970s, even after his life imprisonment for murder, and Lennie Murphy, the alleged mastermind behind the notorious 'Shankill Butcher' gang, responsible, during their reign of terror, for twenty assassinations in North and West Belfast.[13]

The UVF has regularly tried to increase its level of foreign support and funding. Since they are seen as defenders of the *status quo*, they do not hold any appeal for the international left-wing terrorist network. As a result, the UVF has ended up with some strange bedfellows, ranging from a neo-Nazi group in Belgium to the racist National Front in mainland Britain and even including a bizarre 'Arabian Nights' expedition to Libya. The only concrete development was the growth of what could be called the Belfast-Glasgow-Toronto axis. In 1971 leading loyalists, worried at the surge in contributions to the IRA by American-based groups such as NORAID, visited Toronto. Since then, attempts have been made to utilize this Canadian 'window' with weapons being purchased in the United States, posted to Glasgow (where the UVF has had two active units in Maryhill and Bridgton) for safe keeping and then eventually sent to Belfast by one of the ferry routes where police surveillance was low. The UVF have often been derided for their lack of sophisticated military hardware and their reliance on home-made or very old guns but, through this expatriate connection, they are believed to have received a consignment of Ingram sub-machine-guns and the new 'Saturday Night Special' .22 handguns. However, the connection was severed in 1981 when a delivery of "car spare parts" from the Old Mill,

Pontiac Buick Company, Toronto, was intercepted in a post office in Glasgow, resulting in the conviction of key members who had been organizing the transactions.

This was not the only factor which reduced the ability of the UVF to undertake retaliation. In April 1983 on the evidence of Joe Bennett, a "converted terrorist" to use the government euphemism, fourteen of the top ranking members in Belfast were given long prison sentences. An atmosphere of paranoia has prevailed within the organization since. There has been almost a continuous shuffling of personnel among the brigade staff and the UVF is currently in a period of reorganization. Consequently, military activities have been curtailed and energy directed into campaigning for the welfare of members in prison.

Two controversial aspects of the UVF's activities must be considered. First, there has been an increasing number of cases where duality of membership has been discovered, that is, membership in both the UVF and the regular forces of the state, namely, the Royal Ulster Constabulary (RUC) and the Ulster Defence Regiment (UDR).[14] The Chief Constable of the RUC, Sir John Herman, stated baldly that there were bad apples in every barrel and pledged to deal with them. Nonetheless, infamous cases, such as the shooting of members of the Miami Showband near Banbridge by members of the UVF who were also serving in the UDR, adds grist to the mill for Republicans who argue there is little difference between the official arm of the state and the unofficial. It has not helped in the battle for the hearts and minds of the Roman Catholic population. Many have become alienated from the UDR, viewing it essentially as a Protestant militia.

The second matter of contention is the way, almost identical to the UDA, that the UVF has established a sister organization, known as the Protestant Action Force (PAF). This group is the naked face of loyalist terror; their purely military approach makes no concessions to, or has no pretensions toward, a political role. In 1974 they issued the grim warning that they would not cease murdering Roman Catholics until every Provisional IRA member was eradicated from Ulster. They certainly could not be accused of making hollow threats. In 1975 after murdering nineteen Catholics in less than a year it was announced that they had become a battalion of the UVF with their militants operating in the Tiger Bay area of Belfast, the large public housing estates of Newtownabbey and in what became known as the "murder triangle" encompassed by Dungannon, Armagh and Portadown.

The PAF appeared back in the headlines in 1982-83 when they claimed responsibility for a series of attacks in County Armagh. A police spokesman cast doubt on their identity when he claimed "Protestant Action Force is a blanket convenience for whatever section of the loyalist paramilitaries ... [is] doing the killings."[15] He was proven right in the most dramatic of circumstances, and in the most embarrassing way possible for the government, when seven serving members of the Ulster Defence Regiment in Armagh were charged in 1984 with commission of the murders.

Spring 1985

PAISLEY AND THE THIRD FORCE

One of the main problems experienced by the UVF and its fellow travellers is lack of acceptance within the Protestant community. At times the terrorist fish has had a very small reservoir of support in which to swim. The Protestant paramilitaries often claim they are only turned to in times of crisis and are viewed as a last resort in the event of a doomsday situation, that is, if the British government announced an intention to withdraw from the province. It would be very easy then for the paramilitaries to pose as the saviours of Ulster. In reality, however, their attempts to establish themselves as a credible political alternative have failed and an analysis of their relationship with the elected representatives of the Protestant community and in particular the Reverend Ian Paisley and his Democratic Unionist Party,[16] proves informative in this regard.

Paisley, as have most other leaders, has found it advantageous to court the paramilitaries when he thought it expedient but has disassociated himself from their excesses. A favourite complaint of the paramilitaries is that these armchair generals make inflammatory remarks about the need to wipe out the IRA and then ignore those volunteers who set about the task. The UDA has bitter memories of its embarrassing liaison with Paisley when trying to enforce the 1977 strike which singularly failed to recreate the halycon days of May 1974. Relations were further strained by Paisley's creation, in 1981, of the Third Force, which appeared in a series of nocturnal rallies on remote hilltops in Ulster, culminating in a mass demonstration in the Protestant stronghold of Newtownards. Speaking for the UDA, Andy Tyrie derided the force as the 'Third Farce' and labelled Paisley the Grand Old Duke of York, marching and marching to no effect at all. Paisley was seen as trying to take over the paramilitary domain while lacking the will to mobilize his members in any of the main combat zones. All the area commanders were leading figures in the Democratic Unionist Party and they could not be classified as an active paramilitary force. The only conviction, related to such activities, which was incurred involved three men in the border town of Enniskillen being charged with intimidation during the loyalist day of action which was called after the assassination of Unionist M.P. Robert Bradford.

On certain occasions there seems to have been a consensus between Paisley and the paramilitaries. In the village of Sixmilecross in 1981 Paisley stated "We have a choice to make, shall we allow ourselves to be murdered by the IRA, or shall we go out and kill the killers?"[17] This is very much the same tenor as Andy Tyrie's celebrated remark on BBC radio that "We must terrorise the terrorists."[18] The unresolved question was who would do the job? The Third Force proved that Protestant militancy was not a monolith. As an almost exclusively rural body, the Force, or at least many of its adherents, regarded the UDA/UVF as a group of urban gangsters, while, for their part, the established organizations saw these intruders as 'cocktail' terrorists looking for some cheap excitement.

CONCLUSION

Frank Wright has written "Loyalism today implies determination not so much to defend the U.K. link, as to prevent any move which hastens the day that Ulster is included in the Republic."[19] This has been the *leitmotiv* of the Protestant paramilitaries throughout the present conflict. They are prepared to be the last-ditch troops. For all the attention paid to political manifestos and community workers, most of their members feel more at home in the combat jacket than at the conference table. Disillusioned by the number of "housing activities and social workers," the more hawkish paramilitary members may decry the lack of "hit-men." Since they do not form a credible political force, they must retain a credible military stance; otherwise, they would play no role at all and might sink into obscurity. Only when the paramilitaries have exercised their power of veto over initiatives, as in 1974, or when they have shown they were not mere paper tigers, has the British government or the IRA paid attention. The UVF campaign of 1975, for example, forced the Provisionals to agree to a truce regarding the bombing of civilian targets.

The Roman Catholic population is most critical of the activities of the IRA precisely at those times when the Protestant paramilitaries have shown they are not bluffing and will make retaliatory strikes. John McMichael, a leading spokesman for the UDA, commented "The UDA has a million faces, not all of them violent,"[20] and yet, as this brief article has indicated, those violent faces are the very ones which have counted in the past and which will really count in the future. For the Protestant paramilitaries the political road has proved a disappointing blind alley.[21] The IRA will not be challenged at the ballot-box but in a terrorist war of attrition. Andy Tyrie presents the final say regarding why the Protestant paramilitaries will continue as a military rather than as a political force:

> It's all right talking about compromise, but we can't compromise. We have nothing to compromise with because every move we make in the sense of compromise is a step nearer a united Ireland. We won't be bought by anyone. We feel that it's going to be necessary to have our army so we can say to the British government — 'Don't forget about us.'[22]

Footnotes

1. For a full account of the events in May 1974, see Robert Fisk, *The Point of No Return: The Strike which broke the British in Ulster* (London, 1974).

2. James Robbins, "Supergrasses in Northern Ireland," *The Listener*, 11 August 1983; Eamonn McCann, "Tainted Witnesses," *The New Statesman*, 23 July 1982; and, for the background to the government's decision to shift toward this policy, David Simpson, "The Informers in Northern Ireland," *New Zealand Herald*, June 1982.

3. For a detailed analysis of their performance see Arthur Aughey and Colin McIlheney, "The Ulster Defence Association: Paramilitaries and Politics," *Conflict Quarterly*, 2 (Fall 1981), pp. 32-45.

4. A graphic description of the period of sectarian assassinations is Martin Dillon and Dennis Lehane, *Political Murder in Northern Ireland* (Harmondsworth, 1973).

5. David McKitterick, "The Class Structure of Unionism," *Crane Bag*, vol. 4, 2 (1980), p. 31.

6. Alan Murray, "Little Loyalist Counter Terror," *Fortnight*, December 1983.

7. Demands for the banning of the UDA are made regularly by the Catholic Social Democratic and Labour Party and by the non-sectarian Alliance Party, but the most recent survey, conducted by Sir George Baker, of legislative provision in the province urged that they not be declared illegal.

8. Report of Proceedings in Belfast Crown Court, *Belfast Telegraph*, 5 February 1982.

9. *Belfast News Letter*, 17 October 1982.

10. Cited in Adrian Guelke, "Loyalist and Republican Perceptions of Northern Ireland Conflict," paper presented to the IPSA Conference, Rio de Janeiro, August 1982, p. 16.

11. David Boulton, *The UVF 1966-73* (Dublin, 1973).

12. Cited in Sarah Nelson, *Ulster's Uncertain Defenders — Loyalists and the Northern Ireland Conflict* (Belfast: Appletree Press, 1984), p. 61.

13. David McKitterick, "Murphy said to be prime mover in butcher death," *Irish Times*, 17 November 1982.

14. On this topic, see Martin O'Hagan, "Loyalist-Military Link in North Armagh," *Fortnight*, March 1984, pp. 5-6; Duncan Campbell, "Victims of the Dirty War," *New Statesman*, May 1984, pp. 8-10, which includes allegations of collusion between the Special Air Services and the UVF made by Captain Fred Holroyd, a former intelligence officer in Northern Ireland. The most controversial claims are made by Nick Mulcachy in "Sodom and Kincora," *The Phoenix*, vol. 1, no. 1, January 1983, where he concludes that the British M16, influenced by Frank Kitson's work on counter-insurgency, was operating pseudo-gangs under names such as the Red Hand Commandos and also blackmailing leading members of the extremist Protestant group, Tara.

15. "The PAF returns to murder," *Belfast Telegraph*, 26 October 1982, p. 4.

16. On the changing strategies of the UVF see the chapter "The UVF, From Soldiers to Politicians and Back" in Sarah Nelson, *Ulster's Uncertain Defenders* . . . .

17. *Belfast Telegraph*, 3 July 1981.

18. *The World This Weekend*, 1 February 1981.

19. Frank Wright, "Protestant Ideology and Politics in Ulster," *European Journal of Sociology*, 14 (1973), p. 235.

20. Speaking on BBC "Spotlight" programme during the height of the 1981 IRA hunger strike.

21. One indication of changing perceptions among the established groups is the announcement by Andy Tyrie of the existence of the Ulster Defence Force. This organization intends to have "eyes and ears" in every important industry and government department and has a very different structure from the large-scale Protestant mobs which appeared in the 1970s.

22. His most recent interview with Andy Pollak in *Fortnight*, May 1984, p. 5.

[8]

Killings of Local Security Forces in Northern Ireland 1969–1981

Russell Murray

Fife, Scotland

Abstract   Governments faced with insurgency often prefer
to deploy local security units rather than regular troops; they in
turn may become the primary targets of guerrillas or terrorists.
This paper examines the circumstances in which police officers
and Ulster Defence Regiment personnel have been killed by the
Provisional IRA and similar groups since 1969. Significant differences are found between the victims from the two forces; police officers are most likely to be killed on duty and in urban
areas; nearly all UDR members are killed off-duty in rural areas.
These are related to the different threats that the police and UDR
present to the IRA's operations and objectives. In carrying on
with their ordinary duties the police undermine the IRA's attempts to render the country ungovernable. The UDR personnel
who live in rural areas represent an invaluable source of intelligence for the government.

Introduction

Although governments may be forced to deploy regular troops
against terrorist or guerrilla movements, they usually prefer to rely
as far as possible on the police forces and on locally-recruited paramilitary forces. This strategy has a number of factors to rec-
ommend it to governments. For example: troops are rarely trained
for such work and may overreact, generating anti-government

TERRORISM: An International Journal, Volume 7, Number 1
0149-0389/84/010011-00$02.00/0

feeling; the use of the police signals to the public that the terrorists are to be seen as ordinary criminals, without legitimate political aspirations; and such forces are usually more familiar with the population and the areas in which the guerrillas operate and are hence more useful in the intelligence gathering that is essential for success.

At the same time, this approach can have disadvantages. Conventional police forces are rarely organized or trained for such a role and may have problems in adapting to it while maintaining their primary role. If they concentrate too much on combatting social violence to the detriment of their normal police duties, they risk losing the very contact with and support of the public on which may depend the success of their antiterrorist operations.

Particular problems can arise when the violence stems from ethnic conflicts rather than being based on class or ideological differences. This will be especially true if the local security forces are closely or exclusively identified with one ethnic group. They are then at risk of being seen, and indeed may sometimes act, as parties to the conflict, as agents of one group, and not as potential resolvers of such conflict. This perception may not be confined to the outgroup. Members of the group from which the forces are recruited may regard an attack on the security forces as a sectarian attack and retaliate.

Writers concerned with the role of local security forces in societies that are experiencing ethnic or anticolonial violence have concentrated on the active role of such forces: their recruitment, deployment, tactics, and so on.[1] The usual conclusion is that in order to be accepted or be effective in the maintenance of order, the police and paramilitary forces require to be representative of the various ethnic groups in their society. What is not considered, presumably because it is regarded as unproblematic, is the nature of the violence that is directed against these forces. It is simply accepted that they will come under attack as the insurgents pursue their campaign. The forms that such attacks may take are not examined, merely the number of deaths that occur.

It is the contention of this paper that such violence may not be straightforward in form and that its study, especially in a situation of ethnic violence, can prove illuminating. One of the features that distinguishes organized social or political violence from most other forms of violence is the degree of planning and goal-directedness involved. Attacks are usually carefully plotted and the choice of targets and tactics reflects the objectives of the organization, mediated by its resources and by the actions of its opponents. This study examines the killings of members of the local security forces in Northern Ireland by the Irish Republican Army (IRA) and similar republican groups in the period 1969–1981.[2]

Local Security Forces in Northern Ireland

When the present disturbances began in 1969 the maintenance of order in Northern Ireland was undertaken by the police: the Royal Ulster Constabulary (RUC) and its reserve force, the Ulster Special Constabulary (USC). Both had been formed during the violent disorder that accompanied the partition of Ireland in the years after World War I and had been organized primarily to protect the new Protestant-based province of Northern Ireland. Although the RUC was responsible for normal policing, the model on which it was based was not the conventional British one, unarmed and decentralized, but its predecessor, the Royal Irish Constabulary (RIC), a centrally-controlled and armed force.[3] A high proportion of the original RUC strength consisted of ex-RIC men, and thus Catholics, but the RUC soon became identified with the Protestant community and was seen by many Catholics as a sectarian tool of the Protestant government, used to stifle moves toward political change in the North. By 1969 only 11 percent of the force were Catholics, although, surprisingly, they constituted about a third of the senior officers.[4]

The USC began in 1920 as a collection of vigilante groups formed by Protestants in the rural areas to protect their homes against IRA attack and to resist the takeover of their districts.[5] When it was established on a legal basis it comprised three classes of constables— A, B, and C —but after 1925 only the B Specials remained. They were organized along paramilitary lines and were equipped with rifles and automatic weapons to enable them to carry out their role of supporting the RUC in internal security operations. The members of the USC, all part-timers only mo-

14   *Russell Murray*

bilized as required, were, by 1969, all Protestants and recruitment was especially strong in rural areas near the border with the Irish Republic.

Following criticism of the conduct of the RUC and USC during the protests and ricts of 1968–1969, the Northern Ireland government set up an Advisory Committee (usually known as the Hunt Committee after its chairman) to make recommendations on the future organization and role of the police service. The committee advised that the RUC should cease to have any paramilitary role and should be disarmed, and that the USC should be disbanded. In place of the USC two new forces should be formed, a part-time police reserve, the Royal Ulster Constabulary Reserve (RUCR), whose members would assist the RUC in normal police duties as required, and a part-time paramilitary unit that would come under the direct command of the British army. The RUC and RUCR would no longer be directed by a government minister but would be supervised by a new Police Authority. The maintenance of order and the conduct of internal security operations would become the responsibility of the army. With some reluctance the government of Northern Ireland accepted these recommendations, despite intense opposition from some Protestants who saw the disbandment of the USC as removing the bulwark of their defense against republicanism.[6]

The RUC and RUCR increased rapidly in size during the 1970s as violence continued. The former, which had only 3,044 officers in 1969, had over twice that number by 1981. The RUCR began in 1970 with an establishment of 1,500 and reached 4,900 members by 1981. However, the hopes of the Hunt Committee that the new RUC and RUCR would function as an ordinary unarmed police force with widespread support from Catholics as well as Protestants, were not realized. A general rise in violence in 1971, including more attacks on the police, led to firearms being reissued, first for the protection of police stations and then for patrolling. Subsequently, police vehicles were armored and officers were equipped with bullet-proof vests. In addition many officers were authorized to acquire their own pistols for protection while off duty.

More importantly in some eyes, the intention to increase the proportion of Catholics in the force from the 11 percent that obtained in 1969 proved a failure. Indeed, although official figures are not available, the generally accepted view is that the proportion has actually fallen to around 8 percent. This is despite the fact that over two-thirds of the present RUC officers have joined since 1969. There are a number of reasons for this outcome, including continued hostility from Catholic politicians who have tended to use support of the RUC as a bargaining counter, but the main one seems to be that the IRA and its supporters have intimidated potential recruits and murdered Catholic officers.

The new paramilitary force, the Ulster Defence Regiment (UDR), was set up in 1970 as a regiment of the British army. The original establishment was seven battalions (one for each of the six counties that make up Northern Ireland and one in Belfast) but it now comprises 11 battalions. Its strength peaked in 1972 at around 9,000 members and is presently about 7,000, of whom 700 are women. The regiment is commanded by a brigadier and staff from the regular army but the battalion officers and other ranks are locally recruited. Although the original plan envisaged a wholly part-time force, about one-third of the members now serve on a full-time basis; others have civilian jobs with the UDR during the day and carry out their military duties at night. The basic equipment of the UDR is the same as that of regular army units serving in the internal security role except that the regiment is specifically not equipped, or trained, or deployed for riot control duties. Because of the UDR's image it is felt by the government that their use in riot control would be politically unwise.

As with the reformed RUC it was hoped that the UDR would recruit a high proportion of Catholics. In 1970, many Catholic politicians and community leaders actively encouraged their enlistment and initially they constituted 18 percent of the regiment. However, here too there was a campaign of intimidation and this, coupled with the reaction of the Catholic community to the introduction of internment in 1971, brought about a fall to 4 percent by mid-1972; the present level is about 2 percent. Moreover, although a screening procedure was set up from the beginning to exclude extremists from either side, many ex-B Specials joined the new force. Of the applicants in the first two months of recruiting, 55 percent were USC men and in the border counties of Fermanagh and Tyrone over three-quarters of applicants were USC men. All the original UDR battalion commanders had previously been senior officers in the USC.

During the 1970s there were persistent allegations from Catholics that UDR members, particularly in the counties of Armagh and Fermanagh, collaborated with Protestant paramilitary groups in sectarian murders, either by supplying official weapons or intelligence data or by actually taking part in operations, sometimes in uniform in order to lull the victims' suspicions.[7] One of the main tasks for which UDR members were officially deployed was to set up vehicle checkpoints (VCPs), and it was claimed that on occasion UDR men in uniform set up unofficial VCPs to trap possible victims. A number of current and former members of the regiment have been convicted of participation in murders and other crimes, although UDR spokesmen point out that these men number less than 1 percent of the total who have been or are members.

For most of the 1970s both the police and the UDR played very much of a subordinate role to the British army in internal security matters. The police concentrated on normal police duties in Protestant and peaceful Catholic areas and assisted the army only at the latter's request. The main role of the UDR was guarding potential stationary targets and undertaking VCP duties in rural areas; the aim was to release regular troops for active operations in the major IRA areas. From 1976 onward, however, the British government instituted a policy of "Ulsterization" in the internal security field. This was adopted for various reasons, including the wider effects on the army of a continued internal security role; the desire of the government to appear less involved with Northern Ireland affairs; an attempt to portray the IRA as common criminals with no political basis for their actions.

Under the new policy the RUC has resumed primary responsibility for internal security; the policy is sometimes referred to as "restoring the primacy of the police." Now the army acts in support of, and at the request of, the local police commander rather than the reverse. Furthermore, today in about two-thirds of Northern Ireland (those areas with the lowest levels of IRA activity) this military support is provided by the local UDR units, not by regular army units. This has enabled army levels to be reduced and those troops remaining to adopt a lower and politically more acceptable profile. However, UDR members are still excluded from riot control duties; in the first instance these are undertaken by the police who only call on the army if their own resources are inadequate.

Deaths in Northern Ireland 1969–1981

Some indication of the level of violence that has marked the current disturbances in Northern Ireland is given in Table 1. If the same level of violence were reproduced in a population the size of the United States, there would have been about 340,000 deaths over the same period. To give another comparison, the police average annual death rate is approximately 140 deaths per 100,000 officers, with a peak in 1976 of 213 per 100,000; the U.S. death rate from homicide for police officers in 1977 was 16.2 per 100,000 officers.

Within the Northern Ireland figures, members of the police (RUC/RUCR) and UDR constitute 7.4 percent and 5.5 percent respectively of the total deaths and together account for 44.8 percent of the deaths suffered by the security forces. However, as Table 2 shows, these figures conceal significant annual variations. The months after the arrival of British troops in August 1969 were relatively peaceful. The only policeman killed in 1969 was shot by Protestant rioters and both officers killed in 1970 died in the same explosion. When the level of violence accelerated after 1970, with the intensification of the IRA campaign and of sectarian murders by Protestants, the brunt of attacks on the security forces was borne by the army. Until 1974 only about a quarter of security personnel casualties were from the police or UDR. After 1974, but before the policy of "Ulsterization" was introduced, it was the local security forces who suffered most fatalities. (The figures for 1979 are distorted by the deaths of 18 soldiers in a single incident and of five in another). Roughly paralleling this shift, although

Table 1

Deaths of social violence in Northern Ireland 1969–19 81 by category of victim. (Source: British army statistics)

Year	Army	RUC/RUCR	Category		Total
			UDR	Civilians	
1969	–	1	–	12	13
1970	–	2	–	23	25
1971	43	11	5	115	174
1972	103	17	26	321	467
1973	58	13	8	170	249
1974	28	15	7	166	216
1975	14	11	6	216	247
1976	14	23	15	245	297
1977	15	14	14	69	112
1978	14	10	7	50	81
1979	38	14	10	51	113
1980	8	9	8	50	75
1981	10	21	13	55	99
Total	345	161	119	1543	2168

Killings in Northern Ireland 1969–1981 19

Table 2
RUC/R and UDR deaths
as percentage of all deaths and of security forces death

Year	RUC/R as % of all	UDR as % of all	RUC/R + UDR as % of security forces	All security forces as % of all deaths
1969	7.7	–	100.0	7.7
1970	8.0	–	100.0	8.0
1971	6.3	2.9	27.1	33.9
1972	3.6	5.6	29.5	31.3
1973	5.2	3.2	26.6	31.7
1974	6.9	3.2	44.0	23.1
1975	4.5	2.4	54.8	12.6
1976	7.7	5.1	73.1	17.5
1977	12.5	12.5	65.1	38.4
1978	12.3	8.6	54.8	38.3
1979	12.4	8.8	38.7	54.9
1980	12.0	10.7	68.0	33.3
1981	21.2	13.1	77.3	44.4
Total	7.4	5.5	44.8	28.8

not noticeable until after 1976, is an increase in the proportion of security forces deaths in the overall total.

However, as the numbers in Table 1 show, these changes in the proportions involving the police and UDR do not, in general, reflect any consistent rise in attacks on them. Although the numbers of RUC/RUCR and UDR killed show some fluctuations from year to year, the levels are fairly consistent over the period as a whole, especially after 1972. There is certainly no sign of any stepping-up of attacks on the local security forces after 1976 in response to the more active role they were adopting. Rather, what has happened is that there has been a marked decrease in the killings of soldiers and civilians. It is this factor that has produced the current situation where the police and UDR figure so prominently. In the remainder of this paper we will concentrate on those police and UDR deaths that are attributable to republican groups such as the IRA and examine their circumstances in some detail.

Police and UDR Killings 1970–1981

Not all of those police officers and UDR personnel who have died since 1969 have been killed by republicans, and of those who were some died because they were in the vicinity of a bomb that was aimed at the populace in general. The analysis that follows deals only with the 114 UDR members and 149 police officers who were deliberately killed by attackers who were definitely or very probably members of the IRA or a similar group.

The most significant finding is contained in Table 3 which shows whether the victims were on or off duty when they were attacked. There is a very marked difference between the RUC and UDR, with the RUCR occupying an intermediate position. It is clear from the circumstances that attacks on on-duty personnel are of a different nature from those involving off-duty members. The key difference is the degree of selectivity in the choice of victims. In the on-duty attacks, with a very few exceptions (all of them RUC detectives), there does not seem to be any attempt to target a particular person. The attack is made against whoever is convenient, usually whichever patrol happens to enter an ambush. For example, a tactic widely used in attacks on the police in rural

Table 3
Deaths of local security forces
by duty status of personnel

	Force					
	RUC		RUCR		UDR	
Status	N	%	N	%	N	%
On duty	84	86	26	51	20	17
Off duty	14	14	25	49	94	83
Total	98	100	51	100	114	100

areas is to lay a mine under a stretch of road and then to stage a minor crime or to make a hoax telephone call that will lure a patrol past that location. The identity of the officers who happen to respond to the call is not only unknowable but also irrelevant; it is sufficient that they are policemen.

Where the victim is attacked while off duty, however, and in most cases it is at his home, the attackers have obviously singled out a specific individual as their target. They have picked a particular time and place where they will find that individual and not one of the thousands of other police officers or UDR members. This exercise of choice means that in these cases there must be more involved in the selection of a victim than simply his membership of the security forces.

Clearly, one factor that plays a part in this selection process is whether the individual is a member of the RUC or the RUCR or the UDR. RUC officers are relatively safe while off duty while the reverse is true for UDR members. This cannot be due to RUC members being relatively better protected while off duty than the latter. The police no longer live in military-style protected barracks but in private houses throughout the country, as do members of the RUCR and UDR. It is true that most RUCR and UDR personnel have regular jobs and hence are off duty more than the RUC but few of them are killed at work. In any case, the IRA members shown that they have sufficient opportunities to kill RUC officers while they are off duty if they so wish.

One possibility is that the IRA members, for whatever reasons, would prefer to attack both groups while they are on duty but are less successful in their attacks on UDR patrols or are constrained from attacking them by some factor that does not apply in the case of RUC/RUCR patrols. In the absence of data on the number of attacks on police and UDR patrols neither alternative can be evaluated directly. However, both seem unlikely. While on duty, the UDR operate with basically the same equipment and tactics as the regular army; if anything they are probably "softer" targets. The IRA has certainly shown little hesitation or lack of success in tackling army patrols.

It is true that RUC officers are more likely to patrol in pairs, whereas the basic UDR unit is the four-man "brick," and is less likely to operate with their weapons "at the ready." There is the possibility that attacks on police patrols may be used as training exercises for IRA personnel who will graduate to attacking military units; in at least one case the killer of a policeman was aged only 14 when he shot the officer in the back. Nevertheless, it is clear from the circumstances of the attacks on the army that the IRA does not concentrate on RUC patrols because they present easier targets. The IRA has the capabilities to launch successful attacks on almost any type of target with minimum risk to the perpetrators. If risk were the major factor influencing the IRA's decisions, nearly all its attacks would be against the virtually defenseless off-duty personnel.

One factor that may well play a part in the pattern observed in Table 3 is the differential deployment of police and UDR patrols. In general, UDR units are not deployed in or near the main urban centers of IRA strength in Belfast or Londonderry, whereas this is not the case with the police, especially in recent years. If the IRA is reluctant to strike too far from its safe areas, its members will be more likely to encounter police than UDR patrols. However, this cannot be the main reason for the difference as the IRA is also strong and active in the rural areas, particularly near the border, where there is a high level of patrolling and other operations by the UDR.

The most likely explanation for the pattern is that it reflects the objectives of the IRA. The organization chooses to attack the RUC mainly while officers are on duty, mostly engaged in routine patrolling, but to kill members of the UDR, and to a lesser extent the RUCR, mainly while they are off duty. Some degree of constraint undoubtedly exists but on the whole the IRA could generate a different pattern if found suitable. A more detailed examination of the characteristics of those police officers and UDR members who have been killed and of the circumstances of their deaths may help to elucidate the IRA's choices.

Personal Characteristics of Victims

The next table (Table 4) shows, for selected groups of police officers, the numbers killed on and off duty. We have already seen that RUCR members were more than three times as likely as their RUC counterparts to be killed while off duty. The new figures show that two other categories of officers are particularly at risk of being singled out in the same way: detectives and Catholic officers (although in both cases the actual numbers involved are small).

This is supported by newspaper reports of nonfatal attacks on off-duty officers. When such attacks began in 1971, nearly all the incidents reported involved either Catholics or detectives, especially members of the Special Branch, the section of the RUC responsible for antiterrorist intelligence. The targeting of police intelligence personnel is a traditional IRA tactic.[8] What is perhaps remarkable is the IRA's apparent lack of success against the Special Branch. Only four Branch officers have been killed and one of these was engaged in riot control duties when hit by a burst of fire aimed at a group of officers; two other policemen have been killed while on plainclothes surveillance duties.

The quality of RUC intelligence was much criticised by the army in the early 1970s, especially in connection with the arrest operation that accompanied the introduction of internment. This was a major factor in the army's development of its own intelligence network. Moreover, it is probable that the Special Branch poses less of a direct threat to the IRA than do informers in their own

Table 4

Characteristics of RUC officers by duty status

Characteristic	On duty		Off duty		Total	
	N	%	N	%	N	%
a. Rank						
Constable	64	83	13	17	77	100
Sergeant	12	92	1	8	13	100
Inspector or above	8	100	–	–	8	100
b. Branch						
Uniform	75	89	9	11	84	100
Detective	9	64	5	36	14	100
b. Religion						
Protestant	75	88	10	12	85	100
Catholic	6	67	3	33	9	100
Don't Know	3	75	1	25	4	100

Killings in Northern Ireland 1969–1981 25

ranks. Nevertheless, it seems unlikely that these few deaths represent the limit of the IRA's objectives but may instead reflect problems in identifying and attacking such officers who are likely to be more security-conscious than their uniformed colleagues.

Table 4 contains one other interesting and possibly unexpected feature, and that is the absence of any senior officers killed off duty. There have been some attempts, and two civilians have been killed in their homes by the IRA apparently in the mistaken belief that they were police inspectors.[9] However, there is no evidence of any campaign by the IRA to weaken or intimidate the police by the selective assassination of senior officers. Again, this may well be due to problems of identification; the incidents involving the civilians lend support to this view.

Of course, as Table 3 showed, the group of police officers most likely to be attacked while off duty are members of the Reserve: they account for nearly two-thirds of policemen killed in such circumstances. There are indications that RUCR members are more likely to live in rural areas, and many work there, than RUC officers and this difference is especially pronounced among the off-duty deaths. They may be most at risk, therefore, because they are most vulnerable. Also, the IRA depicts the RUCR, together with the UDR, as the successors to the hated B Specials and this in itself may be sufficient grounds for the attacks to concentrate on them.

When we turn to the characteristics of the UDR victims, the singling out of Catholic members is again apparent. The first newspaper report of an attack on an off-duty UDR man, in May 1970 (the only one reported that year), concerned the only Catholic in his village to join the regiment; shots were fired into his home. Of the five UDR men who were identified as Catholics in newspaper reports and were killed while off duty, four died in 1971–1972 when maximum pressure was being put on Catholics to leave the regiment. This represents 19 percent of the off-duty UDR men killed during this period, a figure in excess of their proportion in the force.

In contrast with the police pattern, the IRA does appear to have singled out UDR officers for assassination, as Table 5 shows. (The proportion of officers among the UDR fatalities is about twice

Table 5
Rank of UDR members by duty status

		Status				
	On duty		Off duty		Total	
Rank	N	%	N	%	N	%
Private	13	31	29	69	42	100
N.C.O	6	13	40	87	46	100
Officer	-	-	11	100	11	100
Don't Know	1	7	14	93	15	100

that among the army deaths.) As there are probably not many more than about 200 officers serving in the UDR at any one time, this figure of 11 killed (and there are signs that two or three of the "Don't Knows" were officers) suggests that these men have been more at risk than any other group within the police or the UDR.

Another group particularly prone to attack among UDR members consists of men employed in rural areas. At least a quarter of the dead UDR men were farmers or farm workers or those holding jobs (such as milk collectors, delivery men, postmen) which required them to travel alone around the countryside. In many cases the job involved following a regular route, thus facilitating the IRA's choice of ambush time and place. Several of the RUCR men killed while off duty had similar jobs.

Although discussions of IRA tactics [10] usually stress its members' lack of constraint, one group is conspicuously underrepresented among the police and UDR casualties, namely women. Women are also relatively rare among the civilian deaths.[11] Only one policewoman has been killed in a deliberate attack on a patrol, in addition to three UDR women. One of the latter was singled out for a particularly vicious attack while at home sleeping, but the others were killed while on duty in circumstances where the attackers could not have known that women were present.

Circumstances of Attacks

With the exception of four police officers killed while trying to detain suspects, all of the police officers and UDR members killed by republicans, both on and off duty, died in ambushes or other sudden unprovoked attacks or were victims of boobytraps. Even when the victims were armed at the time it does not appear that any of them had a chance to use their weapons before they were killed. Most of the police officers ambushed while on foot patrol were shot at from behind. Conversely, only a single member of the IRA or any other group has been killed by either the police or UDR while taking part in an attack on a patrol.

This is because the initiative in these incidents has always been taken by the attackers. They have been able to select the combination of time, place, and tactics that will afford them the maximum chance of success with the minimum of risk. As far as the choice of time and place is concerned, they often take advantage of predictable regularities in their targets' behavior. This applies especially to attacks on off-duty personnel, most of which take place at the victims' homes, or their work, or on the journeys between them. On several occasions the victims have been deliberately set up. For example, a PIRA unit once mailed a letter to a remote farmhouse, then they took over the farm and killed the postman, a UDR man, when he delivered it.

As pointed out earlier, the police and the UDR played a secondary role to the army until 1977. Nevertheless, it is striking that apparently only a quarter of the police officers killed on duty were engaged directly on internal security duties; Table 6 indicates what policemen were doing when they were attacked. The majority of officers who died on duty were killed while carrying out normal police duties, such as routine patrolling or investigating minor crimes. Many of these crimes were in fact staged by the IRA to lure the police into an ambush. Although it is impossible to draw a clear line between normal policing and internal security duties in a situation like Northern Ireland, it is clear that at the time they were attacked the majority of on-duty officers—and all those who were off duty —were not engaged in any activity that at that time directly threatened IRA operations or members.

Russell Murray

Table 6
Circumstances of deaths of Police officers
(RUC + RUCR) killed on duty

Circumstances	N	%
a. Internal security duties		
Riot control	5	5
Security checkpoints	6	5
Checking bomb warning	5	5
Surveillance	4	4
Pursuing terrorists	2	2
b. Routine police duties		
Investigating crime or report	27	25
Patrolling	48	44
Other	13	12
Total	110	100

Most of the police officers and UDR members who have been killed were shot. Apart from a few cases where the killers used pistols, and the occasional sniping incident, most attacks have been with automatic weapons, giving the ambushers greater firepower than their victims. This has been the pattern even when the target was off duty and alone and armed, if at all, with only a pistol. The favored tactic against mobile patrols in rural areas has been the command-detonated mine, usually concealed in a culvert under the road. Although most police and UDR vehicles are armored against small-arms fire, such mines often contain several hundreds of pounds of explosives, enough to blow the vehicles and their occupants into pieces. In Belfast, where mines cannot be laid so easily, two police officers were killed in separate incidents in 1981 when their vehicles were hit by antitank rockets.

Several policemen and UDR men have been killed by boobytrap bombs of various kinds. Such devices are attractive to an attacker as they enable him to be safely distant at the moment the trap is sprung. All of the off-duty victims killed by bombs suffered death through devices concealed in their private cars, usually while they were parked outside their homes. One feature of these devices is that they are nonselective; other people, mainly friends or relative of the presumed targets, have been killed in these attacks.

Locations of Attacks

O'Day, in a general discussion of the IRA and its tactics, remarked that, "Part-time reserve personnel living in remote or comparatively defenseless areas have been unusually vulnerable to attack."[12] The media, spurred on by Protestant politicians, have stressed the dangers in the southern parts of Counties Fermanagh and Armagh, along the border with the Irish Republic; southern Armagh has acquired the label of "bandit country."[13] Mitchell, on the other hand, picks out the area to the west of Lough Neagh, mainly in County Tyrone, which lies in the heart of Northern Ireland.[14]

Table 7 gives a breakdown by location of the different categories of killings in the two main cities of Northern Ireland and in the six counties of Antrim, Armagh, Down, Londonderry (minus the city), Fermanagh, and Tyrone. Three victims (one each from the RUC, RUCR, and UDR) have been omitted from this table (and from Table 8) because they were killed in the Irish Republic while off duty. At least three other UDR men may have been killed in the Republic after being kidnapped there while off duty but their deaths have been included in these tables as their bodies were found north of the border.

If we are concerned with a single type of killing, for instance UDR members killed off duty, and wish to know where it is most likely to occur, then we need to examine the column percentages in Table 7. We will concentrate on the two main groups—police officers on duty and UDR members off duty—as the small numbers in the other groups render them more likely to chance variations. (For example, the figure for County Down under "UDR on duty" is attributable to three men, of the total of five, being killed in a single explosion.) For both categories, and indeed for the total of deaths, the same three areas stand out as the locations for a high proportion of deaths. They are the urban area of Belfast and the Counties of Armagh and Tyrone. (For the off-duty UDR deaths the distribution is not as sharply differentiated as it is for

Table 7

Location of deaths by county or city
and category of victim

Area	Police on duty		RUC off duty		RUCR off duty		UDR on duty		UDR off duty		Total	
	N	%	N	%	N	%	N	%	N	%	N	%
Belfast	33	30	4	31	5	21	1	5	15	16	58	22
%		57		7		9		2		26		100
Londonderry city	8	7	1	8	2	8	1	5	7	8	19	7
%		42		5		11		5		37		100
County Antrim	2	2	1	8	2	8	-	-	-	-	5	2
%		40		20		40		-		-		100
County Armagh	28	25	2	15	2	8	3	15	19	20	54	21
%		52		4		4		6		35		100
County Down	3	3	4	31	-	-	5	25	4	4	16	6
%		19		25		-		31		25		100
County Fermanagh	9	8	-	-	3	13	4	20	12	13	28	11
%		32		-		11		14		43		100
County Londonderry	7	6	-	-	3	13	1	5	14	15	25	10
%		28		-		12		4		56		100
County Tyrone	20	18	1	8	7	29	5	25	22	25	55	21
%		36		2		13		9		40		100
Total	110	100	13	100	24	100	20	100	93	100	260	100
%		42		5		9		8		36		100

the police. However, a tabulation of all the newspaper reports of nonfatal attacks on off-duty UDR members over the same period does yield a more clear-cut emphasis on these three areas.)

Contrary to popular impression, Fermanagh does not figure prominently in this table, not even for the deaths of off-duty RUCR or UDR members. This picture shows little change if we look instead at the row percentages in Table 7; these tell us the relative proportions of the various categories in a given area. It is true that off-duty UDR deaths are overrepresented in Fermanagh (they constitute 43 percent of deaths there as against 36 percent of the total of RUC/R and UDR deaths in Northern Ireland) but they are almost as overrepresented in County Tyrone and make up a much higher proportion of deaths in the city of Londonderry. A similar mismatch with the media image occurs when we examine the location of the County Armagh deaths in more detail. Of the 54 deaths in the table, 28 occurred in the northern half of the county and this ratio was approximately true for all categories.

Protestant politicians have emphasized the deaths of RUCR and UDR members in Fermanagh and southern Armagh because of the border factor. It is their contention that the Irish government is unable or unwilling (they generally favor the latter alternative) to take effective action against the IRA in the Republic. As a result, the Republic provides the IRA with a sanctuary from which they can launch attacks across the border and return to safety before the security forces in the North can respond.

There is no doubt that in practical terms the border cannot provide much hindrance to movement. It was never designed as the international boundary it has become but simply follows the original county boundaries.[15] As a result the border is rarely clearly demarcated by natural features such as rivers that might act as barriers but rambles in tortuous fashion across country; on a number of occasions security forces from both sides have inadvertently crossed it. Several villages and many farms, and even a few individual dwellings actually straddle the border; one of the off-duty UDR men who was kidnapped in the South was in fact tending cattle in fields of his that lay in the Republic. Although it is only 412 kilometers in length it is crossed by at least 180 roads and numerous footpaths.

Since 1970 the security forces in Northern Ireland, and increasingly in recent years those in the South also, have been concerned to impede the movement of men and matériel across the border from the South.[16] At first the main policy was to restrict traffic to a few approved roads that could easily be monitored. Other roads would be sealed off by the demolition of bridges, cratering of roads, and construction of barriers. These measures met with considerable hostility and active resistance from local Catholics, not least because of the considerable inconvenience they caused, and they effectively reversed most of the army's efforts. The tendency today is to supplement this approach with increasing use of passive and active surveillance operations.

Although these tactics have undoubtedly proved useful, they have not been completely successful in preventing or detecting cross-border movement. With the level of resources realistically available for this task it is unlikely that the security forces on either side of the border can effectively seal the border; the best they can probably hope for is to significantly inconvenience the terrorists. The nature of the terrain, coupled with the need to allow the normal cross-border traffic, much of it vital to both economies, to continue as freely as possible, is against them. Moreover, a number of possible targets, such as customs posts, the homes of security personnel, and police stations are situated within easy range of positions within the Republic. Several members of the security forces and civilians have been killed by attackers shooting or triggering mines from across the border.

The first section of Table 8 is an attempt to evaluate the contribution of this factor in respect of the deaths of local security personnel. The electoral wards in which these deaths took place were classified according to whether they were situated in the "border" area or elsewhere.[17] From an examination of those deaths (including civilians) where newspapers reported that the killers came or went over the border, it appeared that such attacks mostly took place within less than ten kilometers of the border. Barzilay, based on discussions with soldiers, makes the same point.[18] Therefore, only those wards which are actually contiguous with the border have been classified as "border" for the purposes of this table.

Killings in Northern Ireland 1969–1981   33

Table 8
Type of area where death occurred
by category of victim

Type of area	Police on duty N	%	RUC off duty N	%	RUCR off duty N	%	UDR on duty N	%	UDR off duty N	%	Total N	%
a. "Border"	13	12	-	-	4	17	5	25	28	30	50	19
%	26				8		10		56		100	
Rest of N. I.	97	88	13	100	20	83	15	75	65	70	210	81
%	46		6		10		7		31		100	
b. Rural	30	27	1	8	8	33	12	60	39	42	90	35
%	33		1		9		13		43		100	
Nonrural	80	73	12	92	16	67	8	40	54	58	170	65
%	47		7		9		5		32		100	
c. Catholic	79	72	4	31	14	58	17	85	65	70	179	69
%	44		2		8		9		36		100	
Protestant	31	28	9	69	10	42	3	15	28	30	81	31
%	38		11		12		4		35		100	
Total	110	100	13	100	24	100	20	100	93	100	260	100
%	42		5		9		8		36		100	

The results show that UDR members, especially those off duty, are more likely than policemen to be killed in the "border" area. Although that region as defined here constitutes only about ten percent of the area of Northern Ireland, between a quarter and a third of all UDR deaths have occurred in it. Put another way, more than half the local security personnel killed in the "border" area have been off-duty UDR members. It seems, therefore, that they are a prime target for cross-border IRA raiders. Nevertheless, the table also shows clearly that overall the police and UDR deaths in this "border" area only comprise a fifth of the total. This is certainly a high-risk area for these types of personnel, given its relative size and population, but in absolute terms the violence located there contributes less to the total than that in other areas, such as Belfast or the area around Lough Neagh, both of which are distant from the border.

Before passing on to the next section of the table, it should be noted that this "border effect" also pertains, although much less markedly, to on-duty UDR members. This is almost certainly a reflection of the UDR deployment patterns noted above. However, it does not hold for the deaths of off-duty RUCR officers. The numbers concerned are small but there is no noticeable overrepresentation of these deaths in the "border" area.

Another feature of attacks on off-duty UDR members that has been remarked upon by other writers is that they are more prevalent in isolated rural settings.[19] This aspect is examined in the second section of Table 8. The sites of the deaths have been categorized as "non-rural" if other people (except the victim's family) were living or working in the vicinity; thus the "non-rural" category includes villages as well as towns and cities. The typical killing in the "rural" category took place on a farm or isolated house or on a country road.

The figures in Table 8 demonstrate clearly that UDR members are indeed more likely than police officers to be killed in isolated rural settings. However, the off-duty UDR deaths do not show any marked divergence from the overall distribution, whether we look at the column or row percentages. Moreover, less than half of these deaths occurred in the "rural" settings as defined here. Although the numbers are small, the majority of UDR members

Killings in Northern Ireland 1969–1981   35

killed on duty also died in "rural" locations; again, this reflects their deployment. As in the previous section about the border, we again observe that the other part-timers, the RUCR, do not differ from the overall pattern as do the UDR men. There is no evidence of a rural bias in the distribution of fatal attacks on RUCR men. The most biased distribution in this section of Table 8 is actually that for off-duty RUC officers. Its overwhelmingly non-rural bias probably reflects the residential patterns of these officers.

It is customary in discussions of guerrilla warfare to employ Mao Tse-tung's analogy of the fish (guerrillas) and the water (local populace). The former must live and operate among the latter and their support, or at least their acquiescence, is essential for the guerrillas' survival and success. In Northern Ireland, the division between Catholics and Protestants and the identification of the IRA with the former and of the local security forces with the latter is not absolute. We have already noted that about 8 percent of RUC officers are Catholics and a few IRA members have Protestant backgrounds. Furthermore, as various surveys have shown, a significant minority of Catholics reject the IRA's political aims; even more reject their methods.[20] Nevertheless, for the IRA the water is Catholic. It is from the Catholic population that it draws its support and it is in Catholic areas that it will enjoy the greatest support and security for its operations.

For the final section of Table 8 the electoral wards in which the killings took place have been classified as Catholic if 45 percent or more of the population in them were Catholic in 1971.[21] In Northern Ireland as a whole, Catholics form just over a third of the population. However, they are in a majority in many rural areas, particularly in the western counties, in southern Armagh and southern Down, and in the city of Londonderry and parts of Belfast. Out of the 435 wards included in this system[22] 118, or 27 percent, were Catholic according to this definition.

Table 8 shows, however, that although such Catholic wards constitute less than a third of the total, over two-thirds of the deaths of police and UDR personnel have occurred in them. Interestingly, this holds true for off-duty UDR members, despite the fact that nearly all of them were Protestants who were killed in or near their homes. When we compare this section of Table 8 with the other two, it seems that for members of the UDR it is the "Catholicness" of the area where they live that constitutes the greatest danger, rather than its isolation or proximity to the border. After the killing of an off-duty man his friends often allege that the IRA must have been supplied with intelligence about his habits and movements by his Catholic neighbors.[23] In this section, again, we see a contrast between the off-duty deaths of RUCR and UDR members; the former were almost as likely to be killed in Protestant wards as in Catholic wards.

Discussion

Although a number of points of interest have emerged from this analysis, for example the relative lack of attacks on members of the RUC detective branch, we will concentrate in this discussion on what appear to be the two most significant features. One is the low level of fatalities incurred by the local security forces relative to those of the regular army. The other is the contrast between the circumstances of the fatal attacks on the RUC, on one hand, and on the UDR, on the other, with the RUCR in an intermediate position in some respects.

The low level of police and UDR casualties relative to those suffered by the regular army is in sharp contrast to IRA tactics in previous campaigns. In the South and North of Ireland after World War I, and in Northern Ireland during World War II and between 1956 and 1962 (although both outbreaks were on a small scale), it was the police who were the IRA's prime targets among the security forces. This was particularly true in the North where only three soldiers were killed by the IRA during 1920–1922 (all three in a single explosion) and no more until 1971. This was not because of a shortage of army targets during these periods. Between 1919 and 1921 there were about twice as many soldiers as police in Ireland but nearly three times as many of the latter were killed.[24] In 1921–1922 and again in 1956–1962 British troops in Northern Ireland regularly participated in internal security operations in large numbers.

The most clearly argued explanation for the concentration on the police in the period 1919–1921 is that put forward by Bow-

Killings in Northern Ireland 1969–1981   *37*

den.[25] RIC members were attacked because, as a "political police" whose primary role was the maintenance of order, they were not only the most obvious symbolic representatives of the colonial administration, they were also the main agents, rather than the army, by whom the state exercised control. In particular, they were the primary collectors of intelligence on potential or actual dissidents. Thus by attacking the police and isolating them from the community, physically and socially, through various sanctions and destroying their morale so that they ceased to function effectively, the IRA was able to achieve two objectives. First, it wrested control of many areas of the country from the government and established in them its own governmental infrastructure. Second, it deprived the government forces of the intelligence they required in order to mount effective countermeasures.

In what is now the Republic of Ireland the campaign against the police was undoubtedly successful. Resignations increased, local recruitment dropped, and even where the police maintained a presence the officers were largely confined to their barracks. The RIC was forced to recruit large numbers of British ex-soldiers— the notorious "Black and Tans" and Auxiliaries. These were almost useless in an intelligence role and their behavior in the internal security role served mainly to increase public alienation (not least in Britain where their excesses led to widespread questioning of government policy and aroused sympathy for the Irish).

The RIC in 1919 was very vulnerable. Although the policy was to station officers in areas other than their home districts (to foster their sense of identification with the state rather than the people), the great majority of the rank and file were Catholics from rural areas who had little in common with the ruling regime, much more with the insurgents. Morale in the force was already low because of problems regarding pay and working conditions. Although the officers were armed, the force was deployed mostly throughout the countryside in small barracks that could be isolated easily and overrun. Finally, the British parliament had already passed an act in 1914 granting Home Rule to Ireland (albeit in a form that was unacceptable to the IRA) and was thus committed to withdrawing from the country within a few years. In the circumstances the RIC officers, regardless of their personal courage, rarely found themselves with an ideal for which they were prepared to die.

In the absence of any detailed study of police deaths in this period it cannot be determined whether the pattern of attacks in the North was the same as in the rest of the island. However, an examination of the 74 police deaths attributable to the IRA in the six counties of Northern Ireland in the years 1920–1922 reveals the same processes described in accounts of violence in the South.[26] The circumstances of those deaths are shown in Table 9; USC members have been tabulated separately from RIC/RUC officers.

Here, in microcosm, we see for the most part the pattern of violence that was directed at the police throughout Ireland. Police stations were attacked, patrols, both mobile and foot, were ambushed in rural and urban areas, and selected officers were assassinated on and off duty. The characteristics of the RIC/RUC officers in the latter category indicate the IRA's priorities. Five were members of the hated Auxiliaries or "Black and Tans" temporarily visiting Belfast; with a few exceptions these groups were not deployed in the North. Two were men from Dublin in Belfast on some undercover mission and at least one other victim was apparently assigned to intelligence duties. Finally, the most dramatic of these deaths was that of District Inspector Swanzy. Originally stationed in Cork, he was one of two policemen named by an inquest jury as responsible for the murder of the city's Lord Mayor. Posted to Lisburn, near Belfast, for his safety, he was shot as he left church.

Table 9
Circumstances of police deaths
in Northern Ireland 1920–22

	Force			
	RIC/RUC		USC	
Circumstances	N	%	N	%
Ambush of patrol	17	49	26	67
Attack of police post	6	17	2	5
During rioting	1	3	4	10
Off duty	11	31	7	18
Total	35	100	39	100

Killings in Northern Ireland 1969–1981   *39*

Already, however, there are signs of the development of a different pattern in the killings of the off-duty USC men. The assassinated RIC/RUC officers had specific attributes and at least two were selected as individuals. In general, there does not seem to have been, either in the North or the South, attacks on off-duty RIC men simply because they were policemen. This is not the case with the USC members where, as far as one can tell from contemporary newspaper reports, their membership of the force was a sufficient ground for attack. In the winter of 1921–1922 in particular the IRA carried out numerous attacks on the homes of B Specials in rural reas.

During the same period we can also see in events in Northern Ireland the assumption of a secondary role by the IRA, one that is almost invariably ignored in discussions of their tactics. Even when writers are concerned with current events in Northern Ireland they deal only with the IRA's traditional role of trying to force the British to leave Ireland by violent means. The behavior of the IRA is assessed in relation to that end alone. This offensive role is an appropriate one for a movement representing the wishes of an ethnic majority in a colonial situation. The small Protestant minority in southern Ireland posed no effective threat to the IRA (although several were killed by the IRA for assisting the Crown forces and for providing information) and the security forces were perceived as British, not Protestant.

In the North, however, the IRA was faced with a very different situation. The Catholics were, and still are, in a minority in the six counties that formed Northern Ireland, amidst a Protestant population implacably opposed to Irish nationalism and prepared to resist it with maximum force. Moreover, there was a long history, stretching back to the seventeenth century, of sectarian violence initiated, in most recent outbreaks, by Protestants. This was especially true in Belfast.

Thus the IRA in Northern Ireland was forced to adopt a secondary role, one that often took priority over the struggle for national liberation, namely that of protector of the Catholic population. In addition to defending Catholic areas when they were attacked by the security forces or Protestant mobs, this role has two facets which tend to guide and constrain IRA tactics. One is that the IRA should refrain from actions that will result in Protestant reprisals against Catholics.[27] The other is that the IRA should respond to acts of sectarian violence with retaliatory violence of its own, partly as a deterrent against further attacks, partly as an example of the principle of "an eye for an eye."

The clearest example of this during the present disturbances occurred in southern Armagh on January 5, 1976. After a series of murders of Catholics in this area an IRA squad lined up ten Protestants being driven home after work and machine-gunned them. Coogan quotes the reply of an IRA spokesman whom he asked why this was done: "Why not? It stopped the sectarian killings in the area, didn't it?"[28]

Of the security forces involved in Northern Ireland in the 1920s it was the Protestant B Specials, rather than the RUC or the army, who were seen by the Catholic population as most responsible for attacks on innocent civilians. Although supporters of the B Specials have stressed that they were a disciplined force, it is difficult to read contemporary newspaper reports without concluding that in several incidents USC men fired indiscriminately at bystanders. Furthermore, there were a number of assassinations of Catholics that were probably carried out by USC men or with their connivance. Whatever the truth, the upshot was a legacy of Catholic hatred of the Specials.

The IRA also had more practical grounds for treating the B Specials in a different fashion, especially in rural areas. Unlike the RIC/RUC who mostly lived in or near their police posts, the USC members lived throughout the countryside, many in areas where the majority of the population were Catholics inclined to join or at least assist the IRA. This gave the USC an unrivaled knowledge of the country, for example, likely ambush sites, hiding places, or escape routes, and, more importantly, of the populace. USC men would notice the presence of strangers, of local people who were inexplicably absent at certain times, would know who were most likely to hide IRA men or matériel. They constituted a resource probably unequaled in antiguerrilla operations elsewhere. As Coogan observed: "The B Specials were—then as now—the rock on which any mass movement by the IRA in the north has inevitably foundered."[29]

Killings in Northern Ireland 1969–1981   *41*

When the Provisional IRA commenced operations in 1970 it adopted a three-pronged strategy:[30]

1. The defense of Catholics and their homes, particularly in Belfast, against attacks by the security forces as well as Protestant civilians.
2. Retaliation for attacks on Catholic civilians.
3. Offensive operations against "the British occupation system."

By contrast with earlier IRA campaigns in the North and South this strategy did not envisage the establishment of any "liberated areas" which would expand and coalesce until the IRA exercised effective control over most of the country. With the lessons of earlier failures in mind the emphasis now was to be on hit-and-run tactics.

Nor does the new strategy entail the systematic assault on the governmental infrastructure that characterized the successful IRA campaign of 1919–1921. During that period, not only police officers, but also magistrates, tax officials, and other civil servants on whom the exercise of state control and administration depended, were systematically killed or intimidated into giving up their work. Although this element has not been entirely absent since 1969 it has been insignificant in the total IRA strategy. The emphasis of the offensive prong of the PIRA strategy has been on influencing British public and government opinion through the killing of British soldiers and the destruction of business properties. The assumption was that as military casualties and the costs of compensation for bomb damage mounted the British government would come under irresistible pressure to cut its losses and accede to the Provisionals' demands. The bombings in England also reflect this belief that only attacks which hurt the British directly would be effective.

Within such a strategy attacks on the local security forces initially had a low priority. Sean MacStiofain, who was the PIRA Chief of Staff at this time, has stated that RUC and UDR members were not regarded by them as combatants, and hence as legitimate targets, until after the introduction of internment in

August 1971.[31] Indeed, he says that before then PIRA members were forbidden to make deliberate attacks on UDR patrols. Moreover, the Provisionals were concerned to project a nonsectarian image that might be tarnished by attacks on the predominantly Protestant local forces.

It is true that in recent years police and UDR casualties together have usually exceeded those of the army. However, there has not been any marked increase in attacks on these groups during this latter period. The change has come about because of a marked decrease in attacks on the army. This may reflect not only the shift in deployment patterns embodied in the policy of "Ulsterization" but also a reduced capability on the part of the IRA to undertake offensive operations. Over the same period there has been a considerable reduction in the number of bomb attacks; there were 766 explosions in 1976, only 398 in 1981.

The IRA is far from defeated; earlier claims to that effect by British politicians have invariably led to dramatic demonstrations of their ability to carry on. Nevertheless, it does appear that they are no longer able to sustain a high level of attacks against the increasingly skilled and sophisticated security forces. Even with these constraints, though, the level of operations against the police and UDR does seem to be well below the possible level. For example, according to Barzilay: " . . . many military commanders find it hard to understand why more attacks are not made on out-of-the-way country police stations which have little in the way of Army support."[32]

The second significant feature that emerges from the analysis is the difference between the RUC, on the one hand, and the UDR, on the other, concerning the circumstances of the fatal attacks on them. The key difference is that the former are generally killed while on duty, the latter while off duty leading their ordinary civilian lives. A further difference that we shall consider is that UDR members are more likely to be killed in border and rural areas, RUC men in towns and cities.

On the face of it there seems to be no obvious reasons that might lead one to expect such contrasts between apparently similar groups. Unlike the army at present, and the RIC/RUC in the past, neither the police nor members of the UDR live in fortified barracks; all live similarly in dispersed private houses. All, then, are equally vulnerable while off duty in this respect. The isolated location of many UDR dwellings may increase their risk but successful IRA assassinations of off-duty security personnel and other people at their homes in the cities have shown that such targets can be hit with little risk. No group seems more likely than the other to have personal firearms for their own protection.

While the two groups are on duty the UDR members are apparently better able to cope with an attack than are police officers. Most police patrols comprise only two officers, usually armed only with pistols. UDR patrols, however, have a minimum of four members armed with rifles or SMGs. As we argued above, though, IRA men have had considerable success attacking army patrols and thus have the capability to ambush UDR patrols as often and with as little risk as they do policemen. Alternatively, with even less trouble they could kill far more off-duty police officers. Any attempt to account for the difference must consider other factors.

The argument that will be advanced here is that the differences between the RUC and the UDR regarding when and where their personnel are most likely to be killed are due, in the main, to a combination of two factors. One is the nature of the threat that these groups represent to the IRA. The other is the extent to which killing their members in different circumstances might further IRA strategy. It must be conceded, however, that no direct evidence can be adduced to support the propositions. Nevertheless, this proactive–reactive model does appear to be consistent with what is known.

The UDR, as a force, does not appear to represent such a direct threat to the IRA and its operations as that posed by the army. In part this can be inferred from the relatively few occasions on which UDR detachments have made contact with IRA units on active service. It also follows from the type of area in which UDR patrols are mostly deployed and the tasks they undertake. There is no doubt that their extensive involvement in search duties of various kinds has inhibited the IRA's freedom of movement and action throughout much of the countryside. They have made a major indirect contribution through the provision of guards for static features, thus freeing regular troops for other duties. Nevertheless, in the areas where the IRA was most active it was the army that provided the main security presence. It is the army that has inflicted nearly all of the IRA's casualties at the hands of the security forces.

The major threat to the IRA from the UDR has come, as it came from the old USC, from individual members of the regiment, especially those living or working in the predominantly Catholic rural areas in which support for the IRA is high. Being in such areas does not necessarily render the UDR members more vulnerable; given the nature of the IRA's hit-and-run, ambush tactics, personnel living in mainly Protestant areas of the country may well be just as defenseless. Such members pose more of a threat to the IRA, however, because as they go about their daily lives they are much more likely to discover useful intelligence about IRA men and operations. For example, many arms caches have been found by off-duty UDR men in these areas. Their very presence acts as a constraint on overt IRA actions because they are spread more widely and are more unobtrusive than army patrols.

Protestants in the border areas of Fermanagh and Armagh see a further motive in the attacks on off-duty UDR members in these areas. They claim that they are a key element in an IRA plan to intimidate Protestant households into moving out so that their property, in particular farm holdings, can be taken into Catholic ownership.[33] According to these reports, the IRA tries to pick out those men who are only sons, and thus the usual heirs.[34] The killings that constitute this campaign include Protestant civilians, especially ex-members of the RUCR and UDR, and are linked to bombings of Protestant-owned businesses in the same areas.

A further factor may be at work here. The IRA wishes to maintain an image of being non-sectarian in its operations. The members claim that their targets are selected because they belong to "the British war machine" and not on the basis of their religion. Nevertheless, there are circumstances, apart from simple hatred, in which they may wish to deliberately kill Protestants. Two possible examples have already been mentioned: in reprisal for attacks on Catholics, and to bring about population shifts. Such killings can also serve to inflame Protestant public opinion and thus undermine any political initiatives that might foster Protestant–Catholic cooperation within the present political framework.

Killings in Northern Ireland 1969–1981   **45**

Attacks on UDR and RUCR members enable the IRA to kill Protestants while insisting that their religion was not a factor, only their involvement with the security forces. This claim is even extended to the killings of those Protestants who are former members of the security forces, although they may have left several years before. This factor applies especially to the UDR which is seen within both communities as the more Protestant of the two reserve forces, and is more hated by Catholics because of the involvement of past and present UDR men in sectarian crimes. Killing a UDR or RUCR member while he is off duty, particularly in his own home, has far more shock value in this respect, and carries a more potent message than the ambush of a patrol.

However, this tactic can easily backfire and lead to reprisal killings of Catholics. Very few Protestants accept the IRA claim that these attacks on the UDR and RUCR, especially when they are off duty, have no sectarian basis; they tend to regard them as attacks on the Protestant community. This in turn can lead to pressures on the IRA from its supporters to desist. In January 1974 PIRA announced that it was to cease UDR killings and expressed the hope that this would end the assassinations of Catholics. The main Protestant paramilitary group, the Ulster Volunteer Force, responded as hoped (at least in public) but attacks on off-duty UDR members resumed within two months.

It is through individual members of the regiment that the UDR most threatens the IRA. Police officers belonging to certain subgroups may also represent individual threats to the IRA because their duties or their off-duty activities give them a particular intelligence-gathering capability. The chief examples would be members of the Special Branch, Catholic officers who retain family and friendship ties in the Catholic community, and RUCR men who live or work in Catholic rural areas. However, very few RUC or RUCR officers will fall into these or similar categories; the great majority of police officers are Protestants who live in Protestant areas. In contrast to the position with the UDR, therefore, the major threat to the IRA from the police does not come from individual officers.

It is as an organized, functioning force that the RUC poses the greatest challenge to the objectives of the IRA. It does so primarily not through its involvement in the internal security role, although in that aspect it has become a far more potent threat in recent years, but simply through performing its ordinary police role. An essential step in rendering any country ungovernable—and the IRA has frequently stated that its short-term objective is to render Northern Ireland ungovernable—is to destroy the routine functioning of its police forces. If the police cease to carry out their normal duties, which are far from confined to combatting crime of whatever kind, not only will the public lose confidence in the government's ability to govern, but they may also turn elsewhere for the services usually provided by the police. This vacuum can be filled by groups like the IRA who thereby gain additional support, security, and legitimacy within their community.

Attacks on off-duty members would have little effect on preventing the RUC from performing its duties. Nor would they be likely to demoralize police officers and intimidate them into leaving the force on any significant scale. Today's RUC is a very different force, in terms of the characteristics of its members and of their strength of commitment, than the RIC that faced the IRA in 1919. Far from their numbers falling off, the RUC has had no trouble in filling its ranks or those of the RUCR; not only are both oversubscribed but they attract even more applicants (albeit from Protestants) as the violence increases.[35]

For the same reasons it is unlikely that ambushing police patrols will induce mass resignations. On the whole, these attacks have not succeeded in disrupting normal policing in most of Northern Ireland. However, it is also clear that in those areas where the IRA enjoys the greatest support, the RUC effectively ceased to function during the early 1970s (especially during the establishment of "no-go" areas in the Catholic ghettoes of Belfast and Londonderry) because the danger of attack was too great. Although well-publicized attempts were occasionally made to maintain a police presence, these were often no more than token gestures. For example, a police officer would deliver a traffic citation to a house in a staunch IRA area, but to do so would require a full army escort. During this time the IRA was able to establish itself as an alternative police force, one that also "tried" and then "punished" offenders.

Killings in Northern Ireland 1969–1981 *47*

The situation has undoubtedly improved in recent years and the police can now enter the former "no-go" areas on their own to investigate incidents, carry out inquiries, and make arrests more or less freely. Nevertheless, the continuing danger of attack still prevents a full return to performing police duties in a normal manner. For example, instead of responding immediately to reports of crimes the police often delay while the report is double-checked. This is because of the very real possibility that the report is a hoax or that the crime has been staged to lure a patrol into an ambush. Moreover, the IRA continues to operate as alternative local guardians of law and order.

The IRA policy of attacking on-duty officers has obviously not inhibited police operations to the extent that the IRA would undoubtedly prefer. Nor does it seem likely that it will have any greater success in the future. The RUC today is probably a stronger, more self-confident, and more effective force than at any time since 1969; the contrast with the RIC in 1920 could hardly be greater. The IRA, on the other hand, although undoubtedly not defeated, no longer enjoys the same freedom of action that it once did. Where the IRA attacks have succeeded is in a more significant area—the manner in which the police carry out their duties. The IRA has brought about through its attacks a certain style of policing that is more favorable to the IRA's interests and objectives. Current British government policy on security, presumably unintentionally, may reinforce this.

What the IRA has achieved, even if only temporarily, is the destruction of the hopes of the Hunt Committee that the RUC could lose its paramilitary role and the trappings that went with it and become instead a force that was indistinguishable from any in Britain in what it did and in how it did it. (Ironically, in the intervening years the British police have moved in a paramilitary direction.) The Committee believed that such a force could shake off the odium that attached to the old RUC in Catholic eyes and attract the support and assistance of both sides of the sectarian divide in its work. By concentrating on enforcing the law, rather than maintaining order, the RUC would be regarded as serving all groups impartially.

Whether this could have been achieved in any case, in the absence of any changes in the political framework is debatable, especially as the degree of community control introduced by the reforms was very limited.[36] However, any chances of success that the new policy might have had were effectively nullified by the escalation of violence after 1970. The revival of the conflict had a range of consequences, within and without Northern Ireland, but the immediate impact of the attacks on the police was to remove them from day-to-day contact with the Catholic community in many areas, the very people with whom they most needed to develop links. Also, the defensive measures adopted by the police in response to these attacks revived the outward appearance of a paramilitary force long before the change in government policy restored its internal security role.

The present policy of restoring the "primacy of the police" may very well exacerbate relations between the RUC and the Catholic community; these relations had been improving in the mid-70s, partly because of the RUC's firm handling of Protestants.[37] One aspect of the policy—the drive to bring increasing numbers of IRA members before the courts on criminal charges—led in 1977–1979 to accusations that RUC interrogators were using excessive force to induce confessions.[38] Involvement in duties such as riot control brings the ever-present danger that policemen will kill civilians in circumstances where there is considerable controversy about the legitimacy of their actions. In the closing months of 1982, RUC patrols in Armagh killed six unarmed Catholic civilians (five were members of PIRA/INLA). This led to claims by Catholic politicians (denied by the government) that the RUC was operating special units with a "shoot-to-kill" policy. In the atmosphere induced by such events the IRA finds it easier to justify the killings of police officers as acts of reprisal or of community defense. There is a danger of the wheel turning full circle to the events of 1969 that finally discredited the old RUC with the Catholic community.

Conclusions

This analysis of the circumstances of fatal attacks by republicans on the police and UDR in Northern Ireland has demonstrated that a failure to distinguish between these two groups in any discussion of the present violence can be misleading. The IRA clearly treats the two groups differently, and although other factors, such as residential or deployment differences, may be involved, the most likely explanation is that it does so because this policy furthers its objectives more effectively than any feasible alternative. Operations against the local security forces had a relatively low priority until recently but those that did occur were apparently tailored to the threats posed by the respective forces and to the impact that their deaths might have on the Protestant community and on furthering the aims of the IRA.

The overriding objective of the IRA is to bring about a complete withdrawal of the British from Northern Ireland and from any further involvement in its affairs. Despite considerable evidence to the contrary, the IRA apparently believes that the Protestants will then acquiesce in the absorption of Northern Ireland into an all-Ireland republic. (However, to facilitate the inevitable, the IRA now insists that before leaving the British government should disarm the RUC and UDR, while the IRA will retain its weapons.) Thus in a sense the operations against the local security forces may be seen as strategically defensive, albeit tactically offensive. Attacks on these groups cannot contribute directly to the IRA's prime objective but they have an important secondary role in enhancing the IRA's security.

The main threat to any terrorist or guerrilla movement operating like the IRA is intelligence. It is extremely unlikely that the IRA will be defeated in a conventional military fashion as it goes to great lengths to avoid combat except under the most favorable conditions for itself. The IRA can be defeated, however, if the security forces know enough about its personnel, equipment, and operations and are able to act on that information. In a situation such as pertains in Northern Ireland at present, where the emphasis is on removing the insurgents from action through due process of law, even though the procedures are emergency ones, the quality of information needs to be higher than in certain other contemporary struggles where the pro-government forces prefer to simply murder suspected opponents.

Thus in order to remain in being with sufficient strength and freedom of movement to realize its main aim, the IRA must reduce to a minimum the flow of intelligence to the security forces.

Put simply, the latter can acquire intelligence directly, through their own activities, or indirectly from citizens. In order to disrupt the former, the IRA must inhibit the movement of the security forces, particularly within the areas in which the IRA is organized. In order to disrupt the latter, the IRA must also drive a wedge between the Catholic community and the security forces, widen the physical and social distance between them. The attacks on the UDR appear to be directed at achieving the first objective, those on the RUC at both. As discussed above, these are probably not the only motives for killing the members of the police and the UDR—revenge also plays a part—but it seems likely that they are the most important.

Notes

1. E.g., Cynthia Enloe, *Ethnic Soldiers*. Harmondsworth: Penguin Books Ltd., 1980.

2. The two groups responsible for nearly all the killings discussed here are the Provisional IRA and the Irish National Liberation Army; the Official IRA declared a ceasefire in 1972. Although in most cases a specific killing can be reliably attributed to PIRA or INLA this is not always possible with the sources used here. For that reason, and given the similarities between the groups, the generic label IRA will be used here.

3. E.g., Tom Bowden, *The Breakdown of Public Security*. London: Sage Publications Ltd., 1977; Cynthia Enloe, "Police and Military in Ulster: Peacekeeping or Peace-subverting Forces?" *J. of Peace Research*. 15(3), 243–258, 1978.

4. Report of the Advisory Committee on the Police in Northern Ireland. Belfast: HMSO. 1969. Cmnd 535.

5. Arthur Hezlet, *The "B" Specials*. London: Tom Stacey Ltd., 1972.

6. Ironically, the first policeman to be killed in the present outbreak was shot by Protestant rioters demonstrating against the report.

7. E.g., *Hibernia*, September 5, 1974; *Hibernia*, December 3, 1976; *Fortnight*, February 6, 1976.

8. Cf. J. Bowyer Bell, *The Secret Army*. London: Anthony Blond Ltd., 1970; Bowden, op. cit.

9. In their entries in the Belfast Street Directory they gave their occupations as Inspector but they were bank inspectors.

Killings in Northern Ireland 1969–1981 51

10. E.g., Paul Wilkinson, *Terrorism and the Liberal State*. London: MacMillan, 1977.

11. Russell Murray, "Political Violence in Northern Ireland 1969–1977," in F. W. Boal and J. N. H. Douglas, eds., *Integration and Division: Geographic Perspectives on the Northern Ireland Problem*. London: Academic Press, 1982.

12. Alan O'Day, "Northern Ireland, Terrorism, and the British State," in Y. Alexander, D. Carlton, and P. Wilkinson, eds., *Terrorism: Theory and Practice*. Boulder: Westview Press, 1978.

13. E.g., *Hibernia,* January 16, 1976; J. K. Mitchell, "Social Violence in Northern Ireland," *Geog. Rev.,* 69(2), 179–201, 1979.

14. Mitchell, op. cit.

15. J. N. H. Douglas, "Northern Ireland: Spatial Frameworks and Community Relations," in Boal and Douglas, eds., op. cit.

16. For many years, and especially since Ireland and the U. K. joined the Common Market which gives different subsidies for the same produce in the two countries, there has also been a flourishing conventional smuggling industry across the border in both directions. There are reports that PIRA is involved in the smuggling of livestock as a source of funds.

17. The system of wards was taken from P. A. Compton, *Northern Ireland: A Census Atlas*. Dublin: Gill and MacMillan, 1978.

18. David Barzilay, *The British Army in Ulster. Vol. 4*. Belfast: Century Books, 1981.

19. O'Day, op. cit.; Mitchell, op. cit.

20. E. Moxon-Browne, "The Water and the Fish: Public Opinion and the Provisional IRA in Northern Ireland," *Terrorism,* 5(1–2), 41–72, 1981.

21. Compton, op. cit.

22. Compton, op. cit.; the Belfast wards have been counted separately and added to the total for Northern Ireland.

23. E.g., *Observer,* November 15, 1981; *Observer,* July 6, 1980.

24. Charles Townshend, *The British Campaign in Ireland 1919–1921*. Oxford: Oxford University Press, 1975.

25. Bowden, op. cit.

26. Townshend, op. cit.; Bowden, op. cit.; Bowyer Bell, op. cit.

27. The best exposition of this is Frank Burton, *The Politics of Legitimacy*. London: Routledge and Kegan Paul, 1978.

28. Tim Pat Coogan, *The I.R.A.* London: Fontana (second edition), p. 551, 1980.

29. Coogan, op. cit., p. 58.

30. Sean MacStiofain, *Revolutionary in Ireland.* Westmead: Saxon House, 1974.

31. MacStiofain, op. cit. This view was recently accepted by the British government when they issued medals to police officers for service in the present conflict. Although soldiers are eligible for a campaign medal if they have served in Northern Ireland since August 1969 the qualifying date for the police was set as 1971.

32. Barzilay, op. cit., p. 16.

33. *Observer,* January 11, 1981; *Daily Telegraph,* September 10, 1982.

34. *The Times,* December 4, 1982.

35. *Sunday Times Magazine,* November 28, 1982.

36. G. H. Boehringer, "Beyond Hunt: a Police Policy for Northern Ireland of the Future." *Social Studies,* 2(4), 399–414, 1973.

37. A survey in Northern Ireland in 1978 found that 73 percent of Catholics agreed with the statement: "The RUC is doing its job well." Moxon-Browne, op. cit.

38. Peter Taylor, *Beating the Terrorists?* Harmondsworth: Penguin Books Ltd., 1980.

Part III
The Impact of
Terrorism on the
Community

[9]

MEDICO-LEGAL SOCIETY

A MEETING of the Society was held at the Royal Society of Medicine on Thursday, 13 March 1975. The President, Dr. Julius Grant, was in the chair.

VIOLENCE AND ITS EFFECTS ON THE COMMUNITY

R A Hall, Esq, OBE, ARIC
Head of the Explosives Section of the Department of Industrial and Forensic Science, Belfast.

The lecture was accompanied by many vivid and informative slides which we are unable to reproduce. The excellence of Mr. Hall's paper is such that it can be fully understood without illustrations.—ED.

THE CHAIRMAN: Ladies and gentlemen, our subject this evening is "Violence and its effects on the Community" and our lecturer is Mr. R. A. Hall. As he is Head of the Explosives Section and as he comes from Belfast, he could hardly have better qualifications for this particular subject.

Mr. Hall has recently been honoured with the OBE which is a hallmark of his status and ability. I am sure that we shall have a very interesting evening. (*Applause*)

MR. R. A. HALL: Mr. President, ladies and gentlemen: first let me say that I consider it an honour to be invited to address your distinguished Society. I must, however, say also that it is with regret that the subject I am called upon to discuss is one which has caused so much grief and devastation to the community of which I am a part, and which has also caused much grief in Great Britain.

It has been estimated that during the past 5,000 years of recorded history there have been 14,553 wars and only 292 years of peace. It appears that man's desire for peace has proved a dream rather than a reality. Civil violence—as distinct from conflict between different nations—is a phenomenon which is naively considered to occur in other countries less stable than our own but it has many causative factors and current experience shows this view to be obsolete. When it does occur it comes to the majority of people as a shock since they consider their own modern society has overcome it and that it is immoral, ineffective and unnecessary.

Because of the dramatic and world-wide increase in civil violence which has taken place during the past ten years, a vast literature has built up in an attempt to understand the root causes of violence and, if possible, to alleviate or remove them. In many cases groups who indulge in terrorism are opposed to established authority and, because of lack of popular support, are frustrated in the normal channels of democracy. In these circumstances terrorism offers an outlet for their frustration and may even account for the basic violent philosophy of some of the more militant groups.

I would not claim that this brief introduction would account for the unprecedented terrorist campaign which has been waged in Northern Ireland

90

during the past five years. Nor is it within the scope of this address to try to explain a situation which is incomprehensible to most persons who are not of Irish descent and, indeed, even beyond the understanding of many in Northern Ireland. Rather it is my intention to show some of the terrorist tactics which have been used in Northern Ireland, the effects which the campaign has had on the community and, because forensic science is my subject, the role of the forensic science laboratory during a terrorist campaign.

I should explain that, because my particular interest is with terrorist explosives and devices, I will concentrate my remarks on these rather than on the use of firearms.

While I realize that cold figures convey little of the intensity of a situation, I would like to set the scene with some statistics. Northern Ireland has an area of approximately 5,500 square miles and a population of 1¼ million. Since 1969 there have been approximately 4,500 explosions, a similar number of devices have been neutralised, almost 5,000 incendiary devices have been counted, a large but unknown number of people have been injured and over 1,100 people have been killed. If the violence were to cease immediately, the total bill to settle claims for injury and damage is anticipated to be in the order of £160 million—£140 million of this for damage and £20 million for personal injury.

Of the 1,100 deaths, 270 have been soldiers or members of the Ulster Defence Regiment, 60 have been police and 780 have been civilians. It is scant comfort that of the 400 people who have died in explosions 60 or so have been terrorists who were blown up while manufacturing or planting their explosive devices.

There are two basic ways in which terrorism can operate—overtly, through the medium of street violence, or, covertly, in isolated hit-and-run type attacks. Street violence can take the form of simple hooliganism and vandalism of the type now too often exhibited by football fans and, although much damage can be caused, this manifestation of teenage aggression can hardly be classed as terrorism. On the other hand, protest demonstrations often contain amongst the ranks of sincere objectors active terrorists who seek to ferment hatred and, if possible, violence. Many countries have suffered the effects of the riots which have developed in this way and it is only because of skilful police handling and inept terrorist leadership that more serious confrontations have not occurred in Great Britain.

Northern Ireland was less fortunate in this respect and, as the whole world knows, street violence was a feature of the IRA terrorist campaign for several years. (*Slide*) Early contact in a riot is usually physical and this leads rapidly (*slide*) through stone throwing and petrol bombing to shooting. Of these the petrol bomb is probably the most potentially damaging—at least to property. Consisting of a bottle (*slide*) filled with petrol and fitted with a cloth wick which is ignited (*slide*) just before throwing, this weapon can have a devastating effect (*slide*). Produced in large numbers for a proposed (*slide*) riot they can be used against (*slide*) any type of target (*slide*) and many Northern Ireland premises were burnt to the ground before the lesson to board up windows or fit wire-mesh grilles was learnt (*slide*). Probably the most serious effect of these riots in a country supposedly notorious for its drinking habits was the number of bars attacked. These provide an easily identifiable target for the rioter intent on damaging the property of an opposing faction and certainly in Northern Ireland the clientele of a large percentage of bars will predictably belong to one of the many political groups. Usually running alongside overt terrorism are more insidious forms of attack. Of these, intended only to cause damage to property, the most potentially effective weapon in the terrorists' armoury is the incendiary device. The value of these devices lies in the fact that they can cause infinitely more damage than the equivalent explosive device. That terrorists were quick to appreciate this was shown at an early stage in our troubles, as the present state of civil violence has become colloquially known.

Large numbers of devices—often 40 or 50, or more—were distributed in shops and stores in the hour or so before closing and left to function after the staff and customers had gone home. It is fortunate that there was a high failure rate in these early devices otherwise considerably more damage would have been caused. (*Slide*) Cigarette packets or other inconspicuous packages as the container, a simple timing system based on acid corroding the rubber of a contraceptive sheath or a watch and battery system and an incendiary composition of weedkiller and sugar (*slide*) are all that is necessary for an effective device. An improvement to this system is (*slide*) obtained if some readily inflammable material is included in the device to extend the burning time and to enhance the incendiary effect. Firelighters, lighter fuel capsules and the use of waxed cardboard containers are a few of the ways this has been achieved. It is also fortunate that the full potential of these devices has not been developed otherwise the serious fires which, for example, destroyed a whole block of shops in Armagh (*slides*)—(and in this instance over £4,000,000 worth of damage was caused by four incendiary devices)— and a covered market in Belfast (*slide*) (in this case two incendiary devices set this blaze going) would have been repeated many times over.

Despite the high potential of the incendiary device, it is the bomb for which the terrorist is best known. Undoubtedly an explosion causes considerable property damage but the reason for its popularity is probably the terror which the sudden noise and shock produces along with the instant destruction. In its essence a bomb (*slide*) consists of a charge of explosive and a method for its initiation, preferably when the terrorist is safely away from the area in which it has been planted. It is usual, particularly in the early stages of a campaign to find suitcases, shopping bags and the like packed with explosive and left at targets often late at night when no one is about. A telephone call to a news agency or to the police ensures that casualties are kept to a minimum, if this is desired. As confidence grows, the attacks are more frequently carried out in daylight and, eventually, the device is brazenly carried into the target building and planted in full view of the staff. Any opposition is quelled by an armed bodyguard. This mode of attack not only ensures maximum damage but also creates more terror during evacuation and enables hoax calls to cause maximum disruption of normal business.

It is inevitable that a large proportion of devices laid are removed by courageous staff to a place where less damage is likely, or are neutralised by bomb disposal experts. This introduces a new facet into the campaign since

92

the terrorist, frustrated in his objectives, attempts to prevent casual interference and the attentions of the bomb disposal officer by the inclusion of
anti-handle components in his devices (*slide*).

This device was one of the first of the anti-handle devices encountered and
the first model of this cost the life of a bomb disposal officer. There is a
micro-switch in the base and one situated under where the lid would be, so
that any attempt to move the device or to screw the lid off results in its
initiation. (*Slide*) A variation is this device which apparently is an ordinary
shopping bag. Internally it contains a complex circuit, with wires placed
along the zip so that there is no interference with the device and within a
given time it will explode and at least claim the target building.

This increased sophistication has cost the lives of not a few of bomb
disposal officers and also not a few incautious civilians. Fortunately, they are
time-consuming to manufacture and wasteful of volunteer 'planters' so that
their use is limited.

So far as the size of bombs is concerned, the only constraint is that imposed
by the amount that can be transported. The constraint of availability of
explosive is removed because of the wide variety of agricultural and
industrial chemicals which can readily be converted into explosives. This
availability, combined with the necessity of creating larger and more
impressive explosions, inevitably leads to the 'car bomb', (*slide*) in which
massive loads of explosive can be transported to their target (*slide*) in an
apparently innocent vehicle and left to explode. Not only do (*slide*) the
normal (*slide*) business premises (*slide*) suffer from the attacks but even
heavily guarded police stations and Army barracks have suffered damage.
(*Slide*) This slide is of a police station in Nurne, Northern Ireland. It was a
slide that was taken just before a car bomb was driven into the archway
which you could see in the previous slide. (*Slide*) Alternatively, this is—or
was—a leading hotel in the centre of Belfast which was taken over as an
Army HQ unit and once again a bomb was parked just outside the fencing
to cause that damage.

So far I have been discussing the situation in which adequate warning is
given of impending explosions. It is when the terrorist ceases to care about
the safety of the public or even actively conspires to cause casualties either
to the public or to security forces that a campaign really becomes vicious.
I have already mentioned the way in which anti-handling devices can be used
in an attempt to prevent interference, but they can also be used deliberately
to cause casualties. Inadequate warnings of bomb locations may also be
given or inadequate time allowed for evacuation. The civilian casualties
thus caused can then be blamed on police incompetence and a propaganda
point scored for the terrorist. (*Slide*) In this situation a car was parked in one
of the main streets in Belfast. A warning was given for a street adjacent to
that in which the car was parked. The evacuation of the public was into the
street in which the bomb eventually exploded; nine people died and 356 were
admitted to hospital with injuries. Whether this was an accidental act or
whether this was deliberately planned is something that we shall never be
able to find out. (*Slide*) Another such incident occurred in a restaurant in the
centre of Belfast on a crowded Saturday afternoon. A warning was given
to the police one minute before the bomb exploded and it was given as a

general warning and not indicating a particular location. Two young girls tragically lost their lives and 146 were admitted to hospital, some with very serious injuries.

On the other hand, the attack may be entirely anti-personnel in nature and nail (*slide*) bombs, claymore mines (*slides*) and even improvised hand (*slide*) grenades used to produce a lethal effect by projecting a hail of shrapnel into the target area. The smaller devices may be thrown at the target but the larger ones are generally camouflaged as apparently innocent objects or containers and left at the target to explode. In this context, bars once again become a prime target for the terrorist and (*slide*) beer kegs, gas cylinders and fire extinguishers all provide inconspicuous containers and lethal shrapnel.

More selective attacks can be carried out by booby-trapping the prospective victims' cars and a number of police have died in incidents of this type. It takes only a few seconds to insert a simple crush (*slide*) switch under a wheel of the target vehicle and to push the attached explosive charge under the driver's area. (*Slide*) Once the car moves, the terminals are crushed together and (*slide*) the electrical circuit completed, firing the explosive charge. The occupants of both of these cars lost their lives as the result of these callous attacks.

It is not even necessary for the terrorist to expose himself to the danger of planting a booby trap as was amply demonstrated during the Black September letter bombing campaign of 1972. The IRA were not slow to appreciate the value of this (*slide*) weapon and in 1973 the first of their 100 or so letter and package bombs was posted. (*Slide*) It is fortunate that more people have not been killed by these devices since the effect of one which (*slide*) functions correctly is extremely severe. (*Slide*) In addition, the psychological effect of large numbers of bombs in circulation through the postal services causes serious panic.

It will have been obvious from what I have described that the community as a whole has suffered considerably during the five years or so of violence. Probably the most significant effect was the population movement which occurred with people from the two religious persuasions moving from mixed areas to safe areas of predominantly their own faith. This has resulted in a loss of contact between the two groups and, therefore, a reduced understanding of the other side's fears and problems.

The bombings and incendiarism themselves have had their effects in altering the pattern of shopping and leisure activities. Town and city centres which have been ravaged by a recent car bomb suffer a considerable reduction in trade as the shoppers seek more secure shopping areas. Similarly, bars in areas where terrorist bombings are prevalent lose their customers to bars sited well inside safe territory. It would, however, be true to say that after a time a large proportion of the population come to a stoic acceptance of the bombing and simply return to as normal a pattern of life as is possible.

In this situation, it is the counter measures which have been adopted in an attempt to control or defeat the terrorism which offers the greatest interference. Long traffic delays, because of security forces' random road blocks, cause considerable disruption in commuter traffic, as (*slide*) do the rows of 6″ high tarmac ramps put across the roads outside police and Army establishments to prevent the rapid retreat of a terrorist after a hit-and-run attack.

Individual searching of (*slide*) shoppers entering department stores or business premises or queues (*slide*) of people being searched before being allowed to enter fenced-off segments (*slide*) of a city are almost beyond the understanding of the outsider and certainly the sight of a native of Belfast forgetfully walking up to the doors of a store in London with his hands in the air offering himself for a body search is enough to surprise even the most impassive Londoner.

Another inconvenience is the restrictions which have been put on (*slide*) parking in most towns and cities so that car bombs can be easily recognised. To this end, unattended parking is prohibited so that even a simple trip to a shop requires the assistance of a friend to sit in the car. Failure to comply with these regulations carries the financial penalty of a £50 fine or the more effective penalty of having your vehicle treated as a potential car bomb and explosively disrupted.

So far as the Forensic Science Laboratory is concerned, the most striking effect of the last five years has understandably been in the (*slide*) amount of case work submitted for examination. This has increased dramatically and most of the extra work has gone to the explosives and firearm sections. Running a close second to this in terms of noticeability is the external appearance of the laboratories (*slide*). Bombed in our premises in 1970, we were fortunate in having new premises almost complete but, far from the landscaped open plan situation envisaged, we have now a veritable fortress with triple fencing, barbed wire, closed circuit TV and patrolling security guards.

The forensic scientist employed in an explosives section in some respects is akin to his colleagues engaged in the more traditional areas of work. He has the requirement to search for contact traces by examining the hands and clothing of a suspected person for explosive residues or to examine the mechanical cuts in the wiring of an explosive device and to compare these with the pliers found in the possession of the suspect so that a court can decide his innocence or guilt. He must also investigate explosive incidents with a view to establishing the true course of events.

One interesting case in this respect arose when a car travelling through the seaside town of Newcastle, Co. Down, exploded. Two policemen who were close by ran to the scene and found (*slide*) the car in two parts, the rear one containing the badly shattered body of one person and the front one the undamaged body of a female passenger. (*Slide*) Struggling out of the remains of the driver's area, was a male person, dazed and shocked, but apparently uninjured. Subsequent hospital examination showed this person's left ear drum to be perforated, his left lung to be damaged and the hair on the left and rear of his head to be singed. When questioned he claimed to have been innocently walking along the footpath when a car which was passing exploded and the next thing he claimed to know was that he was struggling from under the car wreckage. It was not difficult to establish that the explosion had occurred in the back seat of the (*slide*) car and that it was the result of the initiation of 5 lbs. or so of commercial blasting explosive. That the deceased from the rear of the car had been closely associated with the charge when it exploded was evident (*slide*) from his condition and that the deceased female had been in the front seat, more remote from the blast and protected to some extent from its effects by (*slide*) the seat was evident from hers. The question was: Who was in the driver's seat and, if it were the suspect, how did he survive the explosion when his two companions perished?

By the extent of the burning to his head and to the rear shoulder of his coat it was possible to position the suspect to within 10′ of the explosion, even allowing for channelling of the fireball through the car windows, and by the position of the singeing it was also possible to locate the explosion that occurred to his rear left. The fact that the singeing was present only on the shoulders and not on the back of the coat or on his trousers indicated these parts to have been shielded and the sharp edge of this damage indicated that the shielding object had been close to his back coupled with the extensive contamination of the front of the jacket and trousers with cotton flock from the top of the front car seats clearly put the suspect in the driver's seat at the time of explosion and was in complete agreement with the medical evidence of the ruptured left ear drum and damaged left lung.

As to the second part of the question, the female deceased died from lung damage due to the shock wave of the explosion and, since this type of injury is very dependent on the bulk of the subject and his attitude with respect to the shock wave, it was concluded that the suspect survived by a combination of his much greater bulk, his attitude when the explosion occurred and some shielding by the rear seat passenger. In this instance, the suspect was convicted of the charges preferred and sentenced to a lengthy prison sentence.

It is essential that the cause of an explosion, when it does occur, is ascertained without delay. Even during a terrorist campaign. innocent industrial accidents do occur and (*slide*) the dust or gas explosion must be recognised for what it is and not ascribed to terrorist activity. Alternatively, in a situation so highly charged with emotion, it is vital that the true authorship of an explosive incident is determined so that rumour and conjecture can be quelled. This is all the more important when, because of a mistake in timing or an accident during transportation, an explosion causes heavy civilian casualties amongst the terrorists' sympathisers. In these circumstances it is often the practice for the terrorist group responsible to try to pass off the explosion as the work of a rival group or even of the security forces and, by so doing, derive some benefit from the accident by putting themselves forward as protectors.

In one incident a land-rover carrying five television engineers to a remote TV mast in a mountainous area was wrecked by an explosion on the side of the trench. (*Slide*) The slaying of these five innocent civilians produced a widespread (*slide*) outcry from the community at large and (*slide*) this drew a rapid denial from the terrorist group suspected of having caused the outrage. Indeed, the denial went so far as to suggest that the explosion occurred within the vehicle and that, therefore, the five men were transporting the device to the mast in order to cause damage and subsequently to blame them.

It was a relatively simple task to determine that (*slide*) the charge had been buried in the ditch at the side of the track and activated by a fishing line trip wire (*slide*) tied across the track from a marker post to a clothes peg switch in the device. Furthermore, it became clear that the device was intended to blow up an Army patrol which used the track daily to check the security of the mast. By a quirk of fate, that morning the maintenance vehicle had arrived a short time before the Army. Despite this evidence, it is still believed in some sections of the community that the BBC vehicle was carying the device and even in Liam de Poar's book *Divided Ulster* it is claimed that no evidence was ever found to deny this allegation.

In addition to quelling rumour and conjecture, examinations in these circumstances may pave the way for a civil claim for damages since the family of a terrorist has little cause to expect financial compensation.

This is further demonstrated by an explosion which rocked a small (*slide*) engineering concern several months ago. The explosion had occurred in the hallway (*slide*) during tea break and at first (*slide*) it was thought that no serious injury had been caused, the workers having been in the canteen. A staff check, however, showed that one member of staff was missing and a clearance of part of the rubble revealed his badly (*slide*) mutilated body in the hall. Since the area surrounding the factory and, indeed, all of the workers could be considered extremely hostile to Crown forces, it was at first thought that the deceased had been involved in bomb manufacture at the time of his death. A careful scene examination showed the explosion to have been caused by probably not more than 5 lbs. of commercial explosive packed into an early brand of portable radio. This then elicited the information that the deceased had found a radio on the front steps of the factory that morning, had brought it into the hallway and left it on the hall table. It then became clear that what had happened was that a booby-trapped radio had been left outside the factory for an uncertain target. The deceased, on his way out of his office for his tea break, espied the radio which he had left on the hall table and being curious lifted it and attempted to turn it on with the inevitable results.

A great deal of intelligence information is obtained from such investigations and it is of great importance that security forces should be well informed on the degree of competence of the terrorist. It is essential that a bomb disposal officer has as much information as possible about the devices upon which he will have to operate. It is also necessary in a situation like that at present pertaining where two factions of the IRA are engaged in a bitter feud to know just who is bombing whom. For this reason, the Forensic Science Laboratory is the repository for all of the devices and information recovered from terrorist sources.

Finally, a careful check of the materials being used in the preparation of improvised explosives enables urgent controls to be introduced for their restriction. It is of little value exercising close scrutiny of commercial blasting explosives when hundreds of thousands of tons of agricultural ammonium nitrate are available in barns throughout the country. In fact, such restrictions may well be counter productive since a terrorist who has been satisfied with 5 or 10 lbs. bombs and whose supply is suddenly cut off is forced to search for alternative explosives. He then finds virtually unlimited supplies of chemicals in industry and in agriculture which he can convert to explosive with little difficulty. Hence the incautious use of controls can even be responsible for exacerbating a terrorist campaign.

I mention this final cautionary note with the benefit of hindsight since it was only after the illegal use of commercial explosive was restricted in Northern Ireland that the rapid escalation in bomb size took place.

I thank you for your indulgence. (*Applause*)

DISCUSSION

THE CHAIRMAN: Ladies and gentlemen, it would be wrong to say that we have had an enjoyable talk. The scenes of devastation and human suffering which have been shown on the screen leave us with a feeling of sympathy for those who suffer, but it has been an extremely interesting lecture. Mr. Hall has told his story as a scientist should, giving us the effects and without sensation. We have been privileged to hear it, because the pictures we have seen are not readily available to everybody.

Mr. Hall, I know, will be glad to answer questions and you are at liberty to put them.

MR. WILLCOX: May I join you, Mr. President, in thanking Mr. Hall for the lucid talk that he has given. May I raise two questions on the possibility of the prevention and detection of these bombing outrages which have occurred during the last six years in Northern Ireland.

On the question of detection, is it possible to find any means of detecting the presence of explosives in the way in which it has been possible to train dogs to detect the presence of drugs? I gather from the last remarks made by Mr. Hall that it is difficult to stop terrorists obtaining possession of materials which can be used to explode bombs. In the newspapers today we have seen letters saying that it may be that terrorists would be able to obtain plutonium to explode nuclear devices. Does Mr. Hall think that this is a possibility in the future?

MR. HALL: To answer your first question, yes, dogs can be and are used in the detection of explosives. The difficulty of using a dog is that it tires rapidly, its attention cannot be kept on the subject for long periods and, therefore, it has a short working span.

A considerable number of instrumental methods have been applied to the detection of explosives—some of them successfully—but once again they suffer from the difficulty that, particularly in improvised explosives, there is little of a detectable nature. When one is dealing with military or commercial explosives one is dealing with nitro-glycerine and compounds of that type, but in improvised explosives one can, for example, be dealing with a mixture of sodium chlorate and sugar which no instrument that I know is going to detect readily. So partly yes and partly no.

With regard to your second question, there is no secret that terrorists' plans for the construction of an atomic device have been recovered, not in Europe but in America. So the simple answer to that is yes, terrorists already know how to manufacture an atomic device and one occasion has already arisen where a device based on the scatter of radioactivity has been attempted. Apparently in the Los Angeles area plans for the scattering of radioactive waste into the Los Angeles Bowl were detected several years ago—not exactly an atomic device, but the same effects.

MR. LOADER: Can you tell us, Mr. Hall, how often in your experience a shopkeeper may blow up or burn his own shop in order to get compensation?

MR. HALL: We have been able to identify a number of occasions on which this has happened, but in relation to the overall level of activity, not often. It is easy for a person of limited intelligence to manufacture himself an incendiary device and plant it in his own premises but I do not believe that this happens to any great extent.

MR. LEONARD CAPLAN: I have the misfortune to be one of the Appeal Tribunal which sits sometimes for a week at a time in Long Kesh in regard to the detention orders that are made and one cannot be in Long Kesh without realizing that there are opportunities there for what might be called a 'university of terrorism'. I am particularly interested to know to what extent new devices are being planned and are coming into operation and to what extent anybody can say that they derive from the concentration of persons of skill in these matters, which there is in Long Kesh, with the opportunities that they have for getting out the information to those who are free to use them.

98

MR. HALL: I have little doubt, as I am sure you are aware, that a very considerable amount of energy is spent in Long Kesh in training and in the production of plans of new devices. Obviously, I am not in a position to answer your question fully, but I have evidence that in a large number of cases the devices which we are encountering have originated in the internment camp at Long Kesh.

MR. IAN HOLDEN: Mr. Hall, have you had any devices that have been initiated by radio?

MR. HALL: Indeed, yes. I did not go into the variations in design of devices, but some extremely sophisticated radio-controlled devices have been encountered. It is an easy enough task to obtain the radio control system for a model aircraft or a model boat and to arrange this so that it will trigger an explosion.

It is, however, equally obvious to the military forces that this has been attempted and they can safely stand at a distance and initiate their devices themselves. The sophistication has come in by way of trying to prevent either accidental initiation by random radio signals or by deliberate interference by the security forces. In this respect complex logic-boards have appeared between the radio receivers and the explosive charge, so that effectively one requires to know the key to operate the logic-board.

MR. WARE: Are all the explosive devices that you come across home-made or are some imported from external sympathizing powers?

MR. HALL: As you know, the famous or infamous incident of the Gloria was an example of material which was coming in from a supporting power, but the only weapon which is in common terrorist use which is imported from outside, apart from Ireland, is the Soviet RPG 7 rocket-assisted missile. That is the only explosive weapon that has been recovered of that type.

DR. BLACK: To change the emphasis slightly, has it been the practice for the organization of medical care for the injured to be provided in the hospitals or actually at the site? I was thinking particularly of, fortunately, a not very devastating explosion that took place in the North of England not long ago in a City centre store at the rush hour, closing time, and those of us who were doctors in the area at the time were in contact, because there was a possibility of organizing medical care at the scene rather than waiting until the casualties were moved into hospital. Has there been any particular emphasis in the way that has been planned in Ireland?

MR. HALL: You have hit on a gap in my knowledge. I really cannot answer your question.

DR. JANET THURSTON: Most of the devices that you have described seem to be of the sort that come upon the comunity unexpectedly, where nobody could be expected to know anything about it but is it the case that a member of the public may sometimes have information which would be helpful in detecting and preventing these explosions and if so, what is the general attitude of the public? Are they anxious to co-operate? Are they frightened to do so? Or have you any comments about how the public behave when they have information?

MR. HALL: There are two separate aspects. The terrorists frequently—particularly in Northern Ireland but I believe internationally as well—put themselves forward as protectors of the people, protecting the people from the forces of an authority, and in that respect, if the people accept that (which undoubtedly some of them do), those people will not pass on any information at all.

On the other hand, there will be large sections of the community who would be willing to pass information if there was a way in which they could do it without attracting attention to themselves.

In Northern Ireland we instituted a system of robot phones, where people could dial a particular number and leave a recorded message. Before the introduction of these robot phones the amount of information coming in was low. After they were introduced there was an enormous increase in the amount of information. It was heartening for those of us who get an inside look at the situation to realize that so many of the people of the community, regardless of their background, were still worried enough to ring up and report that such-and-such a thing was happening in their own street and that if the security forces were to come along they could apprehend some criminals.

THE CHAIRMAN: Would anybody like to speak on the psychology of terrorism?

MR. LEONARD CAPLAN: I wonder if I might, from experience, accept the invitation in this sense. I have been particularly perturbed at the prospects for the future, bearing in mind that so many very young people are engaged either in actual terrorist activities or in the assistance of terrorist activities. I am thinking in particular of the age group of about 11 to 15. At the age of 15 they graduate to the terrorism, but at 11 to 15 it seems that there are many young people who are being introduced to terrorism as assistants, look-outs and so on. It seems to me that one is going to have a legacy for many years in Northern Ireland from all that has happened.

The other thing that I found very interesting from the psychological aspect—or it may even be that it is not so much psychological as political—but one could not help noticing that the age of the Republican terrorists who were detained seemed on the whole to be much less than the age of the Protestant terrorists who were detained. They seemed to be of a different type; they seemed to have a different economic background, and in general one would find that a Protestant terrorist might be likely to be in the age group of, say, 25 to 40, whereas an IRA terrorist seemed generally to be something like 15 to 30.

THE CHAIRMAN: Do you have any comment on that?

MR. HALL: Only that I agree with you entirely. I am not at all sure of the reason for this, but I have noticed it myself. I deal more with people who are being charged with offences than with people who are being detained, but even there the same thing is noticeable. I cannot explain it.

A MEMBER: Can you say anything about protective clothing? There was a time when waistcoats and various things were issued to the Army; this seems to have died out. Is it that it just does not work or that it is impracticable?

MR. HALL: All military and police vehicles have a coating of 'macrolon', I believe it is called, and a lot of personnel wear flak-jackets; but you must remember that these are only protection against shrapnel from things like nail-bombs and grenades or a low velocity weapon; it does not protect against high velocity rifle bullets—and so many of the terrorists' firearms are of high velocity that a lot of people are discarding these protections.

A MEMBER: One gets terribly dismayed when one sees pictures in the Press of youngsters stoning soldiers who have gone to help with some explosion or other unpleasant incident. Can the Northern Irish Government or the education authorities and other sections do anything to control this and get them away from the attitude that 'it is fun to go out and beat up these soldiers'?

MR. HALL: The short answer to it is, 'Yes, it is possible', but it is perhaps five years too late. Unfortunately, our terrorist situation has developed through a feeling of one section being an under-dog and that children who move about and stone police and soldiers were helping in trying to achieve some just settlement for themselves. Then, when you get to the stage when you want to try and stop there, I think you run into great difficulties. So I think yes, it can be done and should be done, but probably it is five years too late.

MR. CHALMERS: This seems most depressing. Presumably, the only possibility is a political solution because it seems from the way you say it that terrorists are always going to be a jump ahead.

MR. HALL: If you are asking me if I believe that there is such a thing as a military solution, I feel that I must say yes, there is such a thing as a military solution even in Northern Ireland, but a military solution would be unacceptable to the British image throughout the world. Yes, I think that a political solution is the only answer.

100

THE CHAIRMAN: When you said 'a jump ahead' did you mean in the technicalities of bomb production?

MR. CHALMERS: I thought they seemed to be ahead in the element of surprise.

THE CHAIRMAN: Would you agree with that? Because my own feeling is—and I may be wrong—that the developments in bomb production have merely been in matters of activation; the ingredients and the principles on which the bombs are based are the same as we were using in 1940 when we thought that the Germans were coming. I made up a number of bombs like that. Thank goodness they were never required. Is that not a fact?

MR. HALL: Yes, it is up to a point. I believe that the terrorists in Northern Ireland have been responsible for discovering (if you like) at least two new explosives.

THE CHAIRMAN: Is that so?

MR. HALL: Yes. In fact we did not know about it and we would not even accept that they were explosives until we tried them out.

DR. PAUL KNAPMAN: Glyceryl trinitrate is a drug which is used for the treatment of angina. Is it possible to make a bomb out of such small quantities? Is it easily obtainable?

MR. HALL: No. I believe that the amounts used in therapeutic preparations are milli-grammes; it would be impracticable to manufacture a bomb in such a manner. Anyway, there are so many far more readily available materials that one could get.

MR. WAINSCOAT: This is really a comment on what Mr. Caplan said. I was a student in Trinity College about 25 years ago and there were students there from Southern Ireland, Northern Ireland and from England. Many of the Northern Ireland students said that, apart from any other question of getting good jobs in Northern Ireland, they did not want to go back to the atmosphere of hatred and bitterness in which they had been brought up.

THE CHAIRMAN: Perhaps there is an element of optimism in that thought, which appears to be the last one, since nobody else is anxious to speak.

This not an enjoyable subject, but it was a very interesting one, both in the presenta-tion of the paper and also in the questions. We are greatly indebted to you, Mr. Hall. You have gone to a great deal of trouble and you have come a long way. I hope you feel that the questions have justified it. Thank you very much indeed and we will show you our appreciation. (*Applause*)

MR. HALL: Thank you very much.

[10]

Psychological Genocide: The Children of Northern Ireland

RONA M.
FIELDS

Violence and social prejudice are not unknown in any society. Indeed, the history of every ethnic and national group is filled with incidents of threatened annihilation, reprieve, victory and defeat. For some groups, like the Jews, such traumatic events have occurred in almost every country in the world and at least once every hundred years. For other groups, there have been national enmities which have periodically exploded in warfare and changes in territorial boundaries. Still other groups, like the Armenians, lost in a single five year period of this century, half their population as the result of a deliberate campaign by the Ottoman Turks to destroy the entire people.[1] In still other societies, there is a long history of suffering under racist laws and systems. The condition of the American Indian, the Mexican-American and Black and Puerto Rican populations in the U.S. are products of a racist and colonial ethos.[2] These produce violent flare-ups, a kind of psycho-pathology as well as severe disruptions of basic social institutions for these groups. The American Indian was subjected to genocide[3] when, during the nineteenth and early twentieth century, whole tribes were massacred and the few survivors were subjected to death marches and other severe privations. The Mexican-American was deprived of citizenship and land rights; often too, became the target for explosions of sadistic frenzy by Anglo settlers. In all of these cases there has been damage to the survivors reaching into many generations beyond the generation which ex-

perienced the outrage. Many times the damage of attempted total destruction is compounded by the social status occupied by the group
after the attempted extermination has actually ceased.

In order to remediate the damage to some groups, various social, educational and psychological programs are attempted despite the lack of
empirical evaluations which could provide some sort of diagnostic profile to make remediation more likely and more efficient. Even if it were
not for purposes of designing "crash programs and services" which
more often assuage the guilt of the oppressor than provide aid to the
afflicted, there is a need to understand the view of the present held by
members of these groups in relation to their past.

The effects as well as the probable direction of a condition of rapid
political change are most readily reflected in the personality dynamics,
behaviors and attitudes of the children within that milieu. The destruction of the psychological integrity of a population is also first evidenced
in these dimensions. It is evidenced in the meanings attributed to the
events and the meaning of their own lives articulated by the children of
that population.

There are serious problems with comparing the effects on children
of various kinds of social and political conflict. One problem is that research carried out on the population utilizes different methods and is
differently interpreted from research carried out at another time and
place on another population group. Thus while the work of Coles[4] on
black and white children undergoing the crisis of racial integration in
the U.S. rural south provides many insights into the personality dynamics, attitudes and kinds of destruction wrought by these conflicts, it
is not directly comparable, for example, with the work done by Anna
Freud[5] with the young refugee-victims of the Nazi concentration camps.
Too often it is the case that even those researching the effects of war
and ongoing violence on children of the same geographic place, are doing nothing empirical, nothing longitudinal and systematic, and not
utilizing a broad common methodological base to permit comparability
of their findings. Research on the effects of the five years of violence in
the lives of children growing up in Northern Ireland is a case in point of
this kind of contradiction and confusion. It is also exemplary of another,
broader issue in the arena of social research, one described by William
Ryan as "blaming the victim."[6] (The kind of circumstance in which the
victim being studied is perceived as the source of his own misfortunes
because of either ineptness, or reaction in that circumstance.) In this
fashion, the poor are attributed to a "culture of poverty"[7] and the Jewish victims of the Nazi Holocaust are presented as "partners with the
Nazis in their own extermination."[8] Sophisticated scientists have become so wary of implying causal relationships to events on the one hand

PSYCHOLOGICAL GENOCIDE　　　　　　　　　**203**

and equally chary of appearing "political" and "subjective" that even those causal relationships which are directly traceable become transformed into "products of social history."[9]

Yet if one is to examine the nature of the human struggle for survival and the mechanisms both constructive and pathological initiated and developed through that struggle, then it is necessary to empirically and longitudinally examine the developmental processes of many individuals during the period of crisis. And in order to relate the individual and social processes, these must be viewed within the context of the political events. This is not to suggest that political events occur devoid of individual and social group interaction with political forces, but rather that the unit of study must encompass the interaction and the reaction. Since the political events predisposing a violent recourse are usually well underway before the child is of an age to comprehend them, we may suppose that these events are acting on the child long before there is any possibility of his/her interaction on them. Thus, a generation or several generations are processed into a scheme of reacting and coping psychologically, socially, and politically. By studying the children of a society it becomes possible to predict the probable social and political schemata which will emerge from that society within the next twenty years.

Motivation, or, as Arnold defines it, "mode of operation," is a fairly constant personality function. It is also a direct application of an individual's unique interpretation of reality in combination with his/her value system and self appraisal. Thus, one is "moved towards" action by the appraisal of something as a "good" for action.[10] By analyzing the motivations of children as they proceed through the developmental process from primary school age through early adolescence a pattern emerges on which to predict the probable attitudes, beliefs and behaviors of the child as adult. If, in addition to assessing motivation, we can gain insight into the growing persons' development of moral judgment/political socialization, then we have a sense of where the political direction of a society is oriented. And from these analyses there is evidence of the survival or demise of an entire people. For if the young see no "good" for action other than their own destruction, or see their future as inevitably and invariably beyond their own scope to effect and influence, then we might assume along with them their demise.

Through substituting opinion for lack of empirical evidence, many authorities even after examining the victims of on-going violence, suggest that such effects as are evidenced are short-term, and may even be beneficial to the balance of psychic energy somehow. Others, from equal lack of empirical strength argue that the escalation of violent behaviors in children foredooms them to permanent criminality.

204   RONA M. FIELDS

Events in Northern Ireland over the past five years have set the stage
for the airing of all of these contradictory claims in describing the current status of the children of that place.

One of the first systematic studies of the children of Belfast, was
conducted by Dr. Morris Fraser, a child psychiatrist affiliated with the
Royal Victoria Hospital in Belfast. Dr. Fraser correlated the 1969 riots
with the effects on mental health and found that there had been significant detrimental effects on both adults and children. In a series of articles and then in a book on the children, Dr. Fraser described these effects in terms of the kinds of clinical cases referred and treated, as well
as in case studies and anecdotal materials. He found that although in
some cases these effects were similar to those incurred in a condition of
full-scale war, their origins made them more debilitating than such a
context might have been

> . . . it might be expected that the effects on mental health would
> have been more deleterious than those of a war and results seem
> to bear this out. Riots in contrast to wars, do not seem to benefit
> any kind of psychiatric illness; in no area or group was there a sig-
> nificant decline in morbidity. Neurotics, in fact, seemed to deteri-
> orate. Stress is an ambiguous word but it seems justifiable here to
> conclude that stress productive of psychiatric morbidity appears
> to be maximal in areas under threat of upheaval or attack, rather
> than in those areas where there is direct combat or direct risk to
> life. . . . During the riot months there was a highly significant in-
> crease in the prescription rate for tranquilizers in the areas already
> involved.[11]

After appraising the clinical effects on children, Fraser said:

> It is not surprising in this situation that lots of children develop
> problems . . . they cry, they cannot eat, they wet their beds. And
> for some, the symptoms continue long after the rioting is over.[12]

In December of 1971, Dr. Joe Cosgrove, a General Practitioner, expressed his impressions of the young people who were supporters of
the IRA:

> . . . the young boys who were on the IRA and supported it had
> the need for an ideal, the need to seek the bubble reputation even
> in the common mouth. He believed that many were quite uncriti-
> cal as to the nature of their ideal. . . . German nationalism pre-
> sented to and uncritically adopted by Hitler Youth was a case in
> point. He often was undeveloped in play and lacking in concern
> for people which he thought could explain some of the savage
> shootings they hear about. He would believe that when these
> boys passed twenty their better emotions matured and they
> would suffer intense remorse for these acts. . . .[13]

PSYCHOLOGICAL GENOCIDE   **205**

But another psychiatrist, Dr. Lyons, has repeatedly suggested that violence has not only had no debilitating effect on the population but has actually had a tonic effect on the children.

> Children in Northern Ireland will turn into another "generation of bigots." A Belfast Psychiatrist said, Dr. H. A. Lyons, a consultant psychiatrist of a lay hospital in West Belfast, said "These children seem to quite enjoy the excitement of the present troubles but they are being taught a disrespect for law and order, and that violence pays off." He said also that the troubles in Northern Ireland could be reducing mental illness. . . . "By and large the children in troubled areas were not psychologically disturbed by violence in the short term." (*Boston Globe*, September 28, 1972).[14]

As for the effects on adults, Dr. P. O. O'Malley, a psychiatrist at the Mater Hospital, Belfast (a hospital with a mainly Catholic, working-class population) found that actual cases of attempted suicide had increased 73% during the troubles and that this statistic might be a better measure for the effects than the data on death by diagnosed suicide on which Dr. Lyons based some of his conclusions.[15]

In another kind of study, a sociologist working under the auspices of a government agency in Northern Ireland, found that the influence of history studies on the civic education of secondary school boys had a negative correlation with a propensity toward violence. Of course, his study, administered through the schools, was a questionnaire survey in which the boys reported their own "violent propensities." But he did find that Protestant youths expressed positive feelings toward the government more homogeneously than did Catholic youth. For the Protestant youths, aged 11-15, there was less difference relating to social class origins than there was for Catholic youths. If there is a correlation between attitudes expressed on a survey questionnaire and actual behaviors, then Russell is suggesting that Catholic working-class boys find violence a more appropriate behavior because they have not studied history as well as their Protestant and Catholic middle-class peers!

Social psychologist Neilsen of Norway has also studied the situation in Northern Ireland (particularly Belfast) from the perspective of the Frustration-Aggression hypothesis and concluded that the children had developed new moral norms. These norms included successful operation in groups to avoid detection.[16]

Journalists, in pursuit of a "story line" have not been at all reluctant to develop their superficial observations of the children into a profound diagnosis. If they cannot find a group of children throwing rocks at a military patrol, they are not above paying the children to do so in order to get a newsphoto.

There are several problems common to all of the aforementioned studies. First, none of them utilize empirical instruments validated on samples of populations in many different societies. In other words, there is no way to compare their data, except in the qualitative clinical sense, with the varieties of normal behaviors evidenced by children in the U.S., England, France or Mexico, for instance. There are no base lines for the behaviors since each study is a self-contained time sample or a series of case histories. While authorities in Northern Ireland have been very eager to promote studies and surveys which will indicate the short term nature of the effects of the "troubles" or suggest new curricula for schools and community relations groups, nowhere in the literature is there an attempt to come to grips with probable long-term effects of a childhood characterized by on-going bloodshed and destruction. There seems to be a fondness for pointing to the continuity of a history of segregation and prejudice;[17] a lack of focus for political socialization outside the family;[18] an ethos of tribalism; and the conviction that unemployment and poverty are the simple corollaries of violence.[19] (Thus, violence exists everywhere else in the world, too.) Longitudinal, cross-cultural empirical research can explore the nature, extent and probable long-term effects which also provides the means for effectively breaking the vicious cycle perpetuated through the experience of one generation onto the life circumstances of the next.

Prior to 1969, the 1935 sectarian riots in Belfast had left sufficient effect on their parents to provide the nexus of the pathologies which erupted in the behaviors of adults during the summer of 1969. Once again, these studies have, by removing the subjects from the historical-political context made incomprehensible the behaviors of the subjects. Thus, in the process, it is forgotten that the 1969 riots culminated a five-year non-violent civil protest movement which had been repeatedly violently attacked, not by children, but by middle-aged adults, many of whom wore the uniforms of the established forces of law and order. Not only are there ongoing complications to the socialization process of these children, but there are these cumulative effects as well. It is not a matter simply of segregated schooling, periodic rioting, paramilitary organizations seducing the allegiance of the young, anti-authoritarianism, nor even a perversity of the Irish cultural milieu. But without the basis of empirical, longitudinal study, such events, their context and effects become blurred and blunted into oblivion. What remains is the newsphoto of the angry adolescent throwing rocks and petrol bombs.

METHODOLOGY

This study was initiated by me in December, 1971. At this time the level of violence had reached a new peak. There were often as many as fifteen bombings in a single day, and the process of interning adult

PSYCHOLOGICAL GENOCIDE 207

males out of the Catholic section of the community was underway for four months. "No-go" areas had been established in the working-class Catholic districts of Belfast, often with the aid of the barbed wire and brick wall "peace-lines" established by the British army. The government of Northern Ireland was directed through the Stormont, a provincial government, with a predominantly Protestant, Unionist majority. Republicanism, the ideology of a united, independent Ireland, was still outlawed as a political party. One fairly new (1970) political party attempted to represent the Catholic minority, the Social Democrat and Labour Party (SDLP) but because of actions taken against the Catholic population, the SDLP were, at that time, taking an abstentionist position with regard to governmental participation. The primary target population for this study were the children of Belfast (pop. 407,000) where there had been the longest history of periodic sectarian violence and the greatest proximity of housing estates between the two groups. The program of testing children age six through fifteen was carried on at four-to-six month intervals, having included in each time sample equal numbers of Protestant and Catholic boys and girls, all residing in working class housing estates. In addition, two other groups were to be examined for purposes of establishing cultural norms. A group from Dublin (pop. 537,448) composed of ten working class Protestant and 12 Catholic (boys and girls) was examined in December, 1971. Another group of children from the Bogside and Creggan Estates of Derry were tested in summer of 1972. These were children who had either been themselves present at the January, 1972, Civil Rights March which had erupted into the massacre of fourteen participants; or who had relatives killed or injured that day. Otherwise, the children in this study are Belfast residents. Because of rapid population shifts in that city, it was impossible to plan a longitudinal study which would encompass the identical sample in each subsequent visit. However, many of the children in the Catholic sample were re-tested at intervals ranging up to three years after the first sampling.

The nature of the testing environment was a very unorthodox one since testing was done in schools and homes which were often, at that very moment, racked by sounds of a not-too-distant explosion; or intruded upon by armed patrols; and in one instance, a rubber bullet shot by an armed patrol, which landed in the hallway just outside the testing room. Because of this, often casette-taped test responses were inaudible for scoring. Also, there were problems with tapes having been magnetized in their transport from Northern Ireland back to the U.S. sometimes by way of a third or fourth stop-over en route. Thus, the total number of complete test protocols (no repeats) under consideration in this study are one hundred fifty-two. Of these 75 are from Protestant and 77 from Catholic children in Belfast. "Completed protocols" in-

208   RONA M. FIELDS

cluded those which had both the Thematic Apperception Test and the
Tapp-Kohlberg questions of Legal Socialization.[20] In addition to the
tests themselves, there were extensive interviews with the teachers
and/or school principals of most of the children and with the parents of
those children who were examined at home. This was done in order to
ascertain that the sample included children whose lives were immediately
affected by the violence as well as those who were not. Unfortunately,
this differentiation did not apply subsequent to December, 1971, although we continued to do extensive interviews with these adults in the
child's life anyway. More often, these sessions became a time to ex-
change information, suggestions, and appraisals about the child, rather
than gathering information to further distinguish parts of the sample.

   The TAT is a well-established projective test used to assess personality dynamics for clinical diagnosis, but also used more recently in large-
scale studies of social and cultural variables in personality dynamics.[21]
It has also been used to study political awareness;[22] and through Story
Sequence Analysis, it has been used to predict success in academia and
in clinical treatment.[23] Ten cards were used and until winter, 1974, the
same ten cards had been repeatedly used. However, at that time, it was
decided to change stimulus cards partly because the pictures had become fairly well known amongst the children in at least one of the
sample communities, and because so doing might further indicate
whether, as Arnold asserts, the particular stimulus cards are relatively
unimportant since it is the stories and their sequencing which provides
the raw data for analysis.[24]

   The TAPP questions consist of a series of 7 questions regarding rules
and laws which have been standardized on a sample of children from
many different countries. They had been used and reported on in studies of the development of moral judgment, legal socialization and political awareness.[25] I added an eighth question, "if you could change any
rule, which rule would you change?"

FINDINGS

   The first analysis of findings on the 1971 samples indicated a greater
difference between the children of Belfast and the children of Dublin
than between the Protestant and Catholic children of either city. The
sample was relatively small, 24 children from Belfast and 22 from
Dublin; 24 Catholic and 22 Protestant. This finding is of particular interest since the social conditions of the Catholic working class area at
that time, would seem to have been dramatically different from Protestant areas in Belfast. These differences evidenced themselves more
on the TAPP questions than on the TAT stories. However, the TAT

PSYCHOLOGICAL GENOCIDE 209

stories from Belfast were quite different from those of Dublin insofar as content was concerned. This occurred in two different directions. First, the length and fantasy content of the stories dropped off sharply after age nine, for the Belfast sample. This was not true of the Dublin group. The other differences had to do with the levels of pessimism and fatalism in the Belfast samples. Although there was no statistically significant difference in the dimension of activity/passivity-positive/negative, between the two groups, this might be attributable to the fact that the sample was small and that which would appear as a trend, would not (unless it was consistent for each individual in the sample) be evidenced as significantly different. For both groups the degree of fatalism evidenced in the stories might reflect the relative powerlessness of the child in the Irish society, which is very dominated by the authority of the adults. (See samples in the appendix.) The Belfast children age six through eight were totally unable to conceive of happy endings for their stories. Since there were only eight children out of the sample in this age category for each city, the trend remains statistically insignificant while clinically very suggestive. The older children in the Belfast sample also exhibited some of the same obsession with death and destruction, but this was not as consistent in their stories as it had been for the younger children. If the stories are analyzed by score per story per child, we do begin to obtain significant results for the younger sample, but for the 1971 sample of older Belfast children in contrast with their Dublin age-mates this does not reach significance. (See Table I)

As a group, the people in the stories told by Belfast children have little or no control over their own fates. They may choose to run away from "troubles" but the troubles pursue them. Their story characters have incomprehensible drives for destruction and the children in their stories are quite helpless to contravert them.

The differences between the Protestant and Catholic children of Belfast were only evidenced in the sources of expected malevolence. The Catholic children attributed it to a "malevolent fate" and the Protestant children saw it as coming from "those close to you." In contrast to the Dublin sample, the Belfast sample saw soldiering and warfare as an undesirable occupation. They also tended to focus their stories more on interpersonal relations, which then disrupted could be amended by the guilty party making amends.

In responding to the TAPP questions, there were further differences between the Belfast sample and the norms established through the other studies. (See Table II) These did not vary much throughout the three years of study. The Dublin sample tended to follow the general pattern of viewing rules and laws as prohibitive (ages 6-9) to seeing them as prescriptive (ages 9-14) and finally, some of the fourteen-year-olds were able to see them as the product of rational considerations in regulating behavior between people. In both cities the children tended not to see any differences between rules and laws. In response to the final question, "If you could change any rule, what rule would you change?" there was a sharp division between Belfast Protestant and Catholic children in 1971. Of the twelve Catholic children, eight responded that they would change "the Special Powers Act" or "the law about Internment." Seven of the Protestant children answered "the rules of all the bombing and killing."

Amongst the youngest children tested, those aged six and seven, there was some confusion about the word "rules." They were accustomed to a "law of the rule" whereby if one displeases a teacher, he or she gets hit with the "rule."

There were some differences in answers to other of the questions on the TAPP scale between the two groups of Belfast children. These differences were consistent until January, 1973, when, among the older Protestant boys (age 11-14) there were some shifts which have persisted through the January, 1974, test periods. This was in response to the third question, "What is a law?" Besides not seeing any difference between a "rule" and a "law," the Protestant children saw "the law" as being one or another authority figure such as the Queen or a policeman or "the government." They personified it. The Catholic children viewed rules and laws as anonymous prohibitive forces. This was further evidenced when they responded to the question "why should people follow rules." To this question they responded in terms of the negative and punitive consequences of not following rules. In this, the Protestant and Catholic Belfast children were alike and they diverged from the prescriptive nature of responses by middle-school aged children in the standardization sample.

None of the children in either Belfast or Dublin saw much possibility of rules being changed—at least not by themselves, either now or when they grow up. If rules are to be changed at all, it will be done by people "at the top" who are "in command" and they don't feel themselves likely prospects for that role.

The second field trip was carried out during June, July, and August of 1972. There were several changes in the political and social context by that time. Stormont, as a provincial seat of government, had been dissolved in March, 1972, following fast on the heels of "Bloody Sunday," the consequent demonstrations throughout Ireland, and the lesser known but politically even more significant parliamentary decision that the military be brought out from under the direction of the RUC, and that should go into effect *retroactively!* That decision came after a weekend emergency meeting of the House of Commons, the last weekend in February. William Whitelaw, a leader of the Conservative Party with some reputation for mediating disputes with creative solutions,

PSYCHOLOGICAL GENOCIDE 211

was named Minister of State for Norhtern Ireland Affairs in the Home Office (Whitehall) and Direct Rule from that office was established. This did not negate Parliamentary representation from Northern Ireland to Westminster, but it did eliminate the executive and legislative functions of the provincial government. The bombing campaign of the IRA was stepped up and a new organization emerged on the paramilitary scene—the Ulster Defence Association. This is an umbrella group for many of the Loyalist (Protestant) paramilitary and community organizations. They established No-Go areas in their enclaves and whether through that organization or apart from it, a campaign of assassinations had commenced. During the period of testing this sample several additional major events occurred. First in order was an IRA-British Army cease fire which lasted approximately two weeks. (The Official IRA had declared a cease fire in April of that year following a retaliation bombing of the Paratroopers headquarters at Aldershot in England.)

One Friday in mid-July, the center of Belfast was racked by a series of explosions which left nine people dead and many others seriously injured. The explosions were claimed by the Provisional IRA. (They claimed also to have given adequate warning but that the communication had been deliberately delayed by the British Army command.) Next, there was a confrontation between the UDA, massed in strength, and the British Army, who had demanded the removal of street barricades in their territory. The UDA with full uniform and equipment marched to a showdown. They won. Finally, in the midst of that period, the end of July, Operation Motorman was effected by the British army which, with twenty-three thousand troops and heavy equipment, smashed the barricades of the no-go areas and commenced heavy and constant patrols in the Catholic estates. They set up headquarters in the schools and when the fall term commenced did not relinquish these posts. Internment activities were stepped up. Into this scene of extreme and intense on-going violence, then, testing was carried on in Derry and Belfast. Twenty-six Catholic children were tested in Derry and another 26 were tested in Belfast (again, half were Protestant and half were catholic). The findings were as follows:

> The Derry children ranged in age from six through fourteen. As a group, they gave much longer stories which had more complexities and fantasy, than did the Belfast group. In comparison with the Belfast group examined within the same months, the Derry children told stories which were considerably more active in their imports and, for at least ten of the children, the majority of their stories carried the import, "If something bad happens take action against it, even if you can't win." These ten were in the age group of ten through fourteen. The younger children were less pessimistic and fatalistic than had been the Belfast sample, but

not significantly so. They were, however, obsessed with stories in
which someone gets shot; or stories about a place at which someone had been killed. Four of the younger children in that sample
were siblings whose fathers were, at that time, interned and who
had been one of the fourteen men tortured with the hooding
treatment. There had been considerable publicity about those
cases, and their mother, who visited her husband regularly, was
extremely depressed. These children told stories about orphans
and about a mythical Ireland. There were no particular changes in
the Belfast Protestant sample from the 1971 group, although different children were tested this time. There were more sectarian
themes in their stories, but again, nothing significantly different
from the previous six months. The Catholic children tested in Belfast during this period lived in Lower Falls and Ballymurphy, two
of the areas most heavily affected by constant military activity.
The differences in this group were greater. Even though the older
children in this group had longer stories than had been gotten
the previous time, the stories were characterized even more strongly by helplessness, death and destruction. (See Table III)

THE INTERVAL OF POWER SHARING

Winter of 1973 was marked by the increase of sectarian assassinations
which continued unsolved despite massive troop deployments. Several
of the killings were proven to have been the work not of sectarian gangs,
but rather of military personnel in unmarked cars and plain-clothes
emulating the weapons and dress of one or another extremist group.[26]
The strategy of "divide and conquer" was further evidenced in attempts
to maintain factional warfare between the two IRA organizations as
well. A study done that winter on intimidation out of homes in religi-
ously mixed areas indicated that the army was the major source for intimidation of Catholics, but this study was suppressed "lest the information further inflame the minority group," said the Director of Community Relations.[27]

In early spring, the new plan for a Power-Sharing Provincial government was announced in a White Paper. The Diplock Commission Report
and the Emergency Measures Provision which replaced older legislation
providing for internment without trial, proved by January 1, 1973, that
internment, now called "detention," could be extended to members of
the population who had previously been less vulnerable—women and
Loyalists (Protestants).

On January 1, 1973, the first woman was interned and in the months
that followed seven more joined her in the women's prison at Armaugh.
Attendance fell rapidly at the Finistion School, a primary school in

PSYCHOLOGICAL GENOCIDE 213

Old Park at which soldiers were garrisoned. Population fluctuations at St. Colman's School across the road reflected the doubling up of families as those who had been living in mixed or exposed areas, pressed back into this small Catholic enclave to stay with relatives. The first UDA scandal had surfaced. A former British Army non-com who had drilled and organized the Old Park contingent and then the larger UDA group defected and took his family off to England where he told his story to a team of reporters and the friction amongst the leadership of the UDA became public knowledge. By the time the White Paper was issued, four thousand people had been arrested, held and subjected to various degrees of ill-treatment, interrogation and torture. A total of fifty-two children were tested in Belfast in 1973. The testing times were during January, June, July, and December. Of this group, half of them again were Protestant and half of them were catholic, 26 girls and 26 boys. Twelve of the Catholic children tested in addition to this group (not included in the overall tallies) had been examined previously. Five boys had been examined originally in December, 1971, a month after they had been lifted and held in jail for the first time. By the time of the second testing, they had each experienced "lifting" and interrogation another five to eleven times each. Still another boy, age fourteen, who had been in the summer, 1972, Belfast sample, had died of injuries inflicted on him during a beating by soldiers. One twelve-year-old girl, examined in summer of 1972, had been lifted several times but not put through interrogation when she was recognized as a girl. It was clear from the interviews that several of the Protestant boys, age twelve through fourteen, who were tested at this time were members of Tartan gangs; several of the Catholic boys alluded to their membership in the IRA, although none of the children were ever asked about memberships. There were new problems and opportunities in gathering the sample in 1973. In some areas and among some persons concerned with youth, that which was already known about by research facilitated access to children living in areas not previously included, although they were working-class areas. In other cases, the political opinions expressed in vague allusions verbally and in writing by the Director of the Community Relations Commission and some of his associates, closed off access to previous samples in the Protestant community. Also, in July of 1973, my efforts were severely hampered by my own having been detained in Crumlin Road Jail, Belfast, whence I had gone to examine some prisoners at their solicitors' request. Although eventually, there was a letter of apology sent me by the Home Office, and despite being illegally detained and put through some of the ill-treatment experienced by others so detained, strangely enough, for the local populace, the onus was on me, rather than on those who had detained me. Even though, in 1973, Loyalists (Protestants) were beginning to be detained

214   RONA M. FIELDS

and the reaction in that segment of the community was similar to the
reaction of the Catholic community: i.e., "our lads are being framed . . .
they're not guilty . . . the army is stepping out of bounds . . . they're
out to demoralize us . . ." there is a distinct ambivalence about persons
who have been imprisoned and finally released. They are heroes to
those with whom they have little or no contact (and are simply a name),
and those with whom they are in close contact become frightened lest
they be assumed "guilty by virtue of association"—even while proclaiming that those who are thus detailed are not guilty! This ambivalence and concern is very prominent in the themes of the stories given
by the twelve adolescents who had themselves experienced this treatment. It crops up in the other protocols too, but not as consistently.
The striking characteristic of the TAT stories given in 1973 is the almost total negativism. That is, whether negative action or negative
passive, almost all of the children examined in both groups were giving
stories the imports of which suggested that bad things happen and that
one must either acquiesce to them or unsuccessfully fight them. (See
Table IV)

By the end of 1973, the new Northern Ireland Assembly and executive were sworn in amidst threats and demonstrations by both the UDA
and the Provisional IRA. Both groups felt disaffected and alienated.

BACK TO DIRECT RULE

Some of the children in the 1974 sample of 50 children were examined during January, others during July and the last group was examined
during December. Not included in the totals, but worth mentioning
separately, were four middle-class Catholic children examined first in
August, and then in December of 1974, in Belfast. Three girls, age 7, 9,
and 11 are sisters. Their father is a prominent lawyer, a graduate of
Queens University. Their mother is a teacher. The children spent their
earlier years living in an area not only predominantly Protestant, but
surrounded by Paisleyites. They presently reside in the most affluent
area in Belfast, again predominantly Protestant, but also having some
mixture of the more affluent (albeit few) Catholic families. The area is
quite cut off, however, from the kinds of organizations and grass roots
institutions which provide a sense of community and security for their
working class co-religionists. The voting pattern of their district indicated that its inhabitants were invested in maintaining this compromise
form of government rather than Direct Rule. These are the people who
voted either Alliance Party or Official Unionist Party. When the Ulster
Workers Council called its massive strike in May of 1974, demanding an
end to Power Sharing with the minority and a return to Protestant

PSYCHOLOGICAL GENOCIDE 215

hegemony in Northern Ireland politics, the resulting chaos and violence rocked the security of this part of Belfast to a greater degree than had anything else since the start of the troubles. The three girls tested demonstrated this insecurity in their stories. They did exhibit a greater amount of fantasy and vocabulary than did their working class peers, and they were quite well motivated (by SSA scoring criteria) with Motivation Index Scores of 115, 123, and 118 as of August. In December, their scores remained approximately the same, but they focussed on problems in human relationships and adversity almost entirely, whereas their earlier stories were concerned with right and wrong and achievement. There were few other children tested during the three years of sampling, who scored as highly on Motivation Index, and few of those who were repeat tested who scored as highly the second time as they did the first time. (See Table V)

Again, some of the 1974 sample included children who had been examined in previous visits. However, there were only five of these repeats. One of the boys examined in January, 1974, was shot in May and hospitalized during June and July whereupon he was sentenced to Borstal. Many of the others had exceeded the upper age limits of the study, even though these had been stretched to fifteen years of age in order to accommodate the repeats in 1973. However, the 1974 sample did include children who had been repeatedly lifted and interrogated, shot, beaten and crippled, orphaned and involved in Jr. UDA or IRA organizations. The trend which was so strong and obvious in the 1973 sample is again evidenced in the 1974 group. Both groups of children, Protestants and Catholics, evidenced a strong concern in their stories for law and order. Neither felt that there was any system of justice "out there" for them and that because wrongs went unchallenged and the world was chaotic, they had each to act as investigator, judge and executioner. In short, they expressed a vigilante thesis in combination with a view that any action undertaken in the name of freedom and justice for their group was intrinsically just. Achievement themes centered about overcoming pain and/or successfully overcoming respect for life and property in order to carry out an action for "the cause." By 1974, another frequently recurring theme was "emigrating"—leaving the place, and often too leaving the people to "tear each other apart, and getting oneself out."

As for rules and laws, the December, 1974, sample of children, both Protestant and Catholic, age ten and over, wanted to have changed the "law of internment." Both groups of children in ages six through eleven continued the earlier pattern of telling stories about being afraid, about death and destruction, about overwhelming events. Whenever they described a child in their stories, the child was depicted as helpless in a world which offers no alternatives and the frustration of hope. In 1971, this kind of story telling was common amongst the children age six through eight or nine, but by 1974, these same children were eleven and twelve years old and their age contemporaries reflected the continuity of this view of life into the pre-adolescent years. Meanwhile, children of six had no remembered experience of a time in which there was no violence. (See Table VI)

CONCLUSIONS

While the data of such extensive empirical testing are rich in hypotheses for additional study and replication research both in Northern Ireland and in other places in which minority populations are split off from their co-religionists or co-ethnics by partition boundaries and other such internationally created artificial boundaries, there are two kinds of immediate conclusions suggested by this data. The first regards the immediate and long-term effects on individuals growing up in a condition of ongoing violence and social prejudice. The second relates to the nexus of the probable survival of the group, the political future of that society, and the social implications of the attitudes, opinions and beliefs as well as the modes of operation developed by its population. A footnote to both of these kinds of conclusions derives from the relatively less extensive but suggestive data on the middle class and non-nuclear (Derry and Dublin samples) segments of the population.

As for the individual children, most of the conclusions by local mental health authorities attempt to segregate the effects into immediate and long-term and suggest that the immediate effects may be either dramatically pathological or equally free of pathology[28] (depending on which personality theory the author embraces). They seem to ignore the unity of yesterday with today and tomorrow. The TAT stories and TAPP-Kohlberg questions indicated the incorporation of models of operation with their attendant belief systems and perceptions into the personality dynamics of the Protestant and Catholic and the working class generation of the coming decade. As such we can examine the reflections and outcome of the violence and social prejudice which has characterized the past decade of Northern Ireland history.

The responses of the children of Belfast to the questions, as well as their stories, indicated, in 1971, their disaffection from the socio-political events of which they were unwitting victims. The level of paranoia reflected in the imports of these stories was higher for the younger children in the sample. The major difference between Protestant and Catholic children in that sample was one of the sources of malevolence. This might be explained in the context of the different value systems of the two religious groups: i.e., the Protestant ethic suggests that evil is a

PSYCHOLOGICAL GENOCIDE 217

personal production that that the individual who is unsuccessful is so because he or she is not blessed. Thus, the evil comes from those persons "near you." This feeling might also be explicable from the feelings of being encircled and surrounded which were expressed by many of the adults in these areas. They believed that there was some kind of organized conspiracy to isolate the Protestant enclaves from each other by the interjection of Catholic housing schemes. The reaction against the civil rights movement was also predicated on the encroachment of Catholics into the job market, thus disadvantaging the previously advantaged. In addition there is the carry over of the old propaganda line through Paisleyism, of the Church of Rome subverting their independence and freedom through the contemporary ecumenical movement. All of these themes play some part in the very consistent views of the children that they are being attacked by those near them. The Catholic children seeing themselves victimized by a "malevolent fate" are expressing both the theological position of human impotence and divine intervention and the very real perception of a minority community's powerlessness. Both groups of children themselves, members of minority groups which are the targets of strong prejudice, and both groups—the entire sample of Northern Ireland children—must indeed be examined from the perspective of disadvantaged minority groups. In the words of a Protestant RUC man, interviewed in December, 1971, at the scene of a pub bombing ". . . they know that if they can upset the social life of the community, they can win . . . because there are more of them than there are of us in the country . . . more Catholic Nationalists . . . we're just a minority up here . . . we've got to stop them before they bring about so much disruption that we get forced off the map entirely. . . ." He was referring to the presumed bombers—the IRA.

It is clear from their responses to the legal socialization questions that these children are developing in a perceived milieu of authoritarianism and hierarchial ordering. They feel no prospect of potential political efficacy. Furthermore, it is clear from their stories that this authoritarian regime carries the implication that power is the property of the strongest and that strength is engendered through the possession of the biggest weapon.

In 1971 and early 1972, the Protestant children age eight through fourteen, feeling themselves helpless to deal with adversity would refer to their elders, according to the TAT imports. However, even during that period, they were aware of the likelihood that their elders could not successfully overcome the adversity either. Their imports during 1973 and 1974 contained almost no indications that such problems should even be taken to authority figures for solution. By 1973, they along with their Catholic counterparts became obsessed with a passion for personally attempting to right the wrongs they experienced, and to

218   RONA M. FIELDS

do so meant injuring, killing or destroying other people and places. This pattern may be a product of the fact that the eight year olds who in 1971 were obsessed with death and destruction, feeling helpless and afraid, were, by 1974, amongst the older segment of the sample and had grown into adolescence with the conviction that death and destruction and being afraid were constants and as such less meaningful (commonplace). Or, this pattern may have readily developed from the escalation of violence and lawlessness often times personally experienced when having been quite innocent, they were lifted and beaten by soldiers, attacked by older members of the extremist groups for minor infractions of discipline, or experienced first hand the death or crippling of a close relative or friend. It is worth noting here that girls were no less inclined to violent solutions than were boys, and that they were less often personally the direct recipients of beatings by authorities, but they were not by any means beyond the possibility of receiving violent punishment from groups within their communities for infractions of their norms.

The longitudinal implications of the erosion of story imports which could be classified as positive/active, into a statistically significant negativistic mode of operation seems to illustrate the theoretical psychodynamic described and demonstrated in the researches of William James,[29] Karen Horney,[30] Kurt Lewin[31] and Gordon Allport.[32] When they described the emotion and experience of fear and the effect of it, they point out that, there are basically two ways to deal with a fearsome condition—that which one perceives as fearsome—one is to run away and the other is to take action against the feared object, creature, situation or person—violent, angry action. In order to take the latter course, the fear must mobilize into anger and the anger itself must locate an object. That object then becomes the target of hatred. For children who are at the first stage of development of moral judgment, as are the majority of the children in this study, the anger is likely to focus on the symbol quality of the target and hatred thus becomes directed at the "symbol value" of a person rather than at an individual as such, or a place as such. Thus the form taken by the fear-into-hatred-into-violent expression cycle about which so much research in social psychology has focused, becomes the rough road map of the psychohistory of childhood in Northern Ireland.

The society itself provides the symbols by virtue of which any given individual can be a non-person for the other. The combined circumstances of an authoritarian socio-political context with an historic attitude of prejudice provides a child-rearing atmosphere of conformity values, a submissive "uncritical attitude toward idealized authorities of the in-group; a tendency to condemn, reject and punish people who violate conventional values."[33]

PSYCHOLOGICAL GENOCIDE 219

Add to this the experience of belonging to a minority group which is the target of strong prejudice—a situation which is common to both the Protestant and Catholic populations—and the self-influence of that pressure becomes a determinant in developing self-protective schemata and expectations of violence and disaster.

Out of this three year interval sampling of two hundred children, what might one predict about the future of Northern Ireland? If the United Nations Convention on Genocide were to be applied to the circumstances of Northern Ireland, we would note that the inhabitants of that place are being destroyed both physically and psychologically through the conditions of life which have made of the children targets for each others' fears. The "mental harm" being inflicted on "members of that group" has seriously decreased the probable survival of the group. Emmigration has reached the level of a thousand monthly.[34] As of January, 1975, over fourteen hundred lives have been lost; over five thousand persons put through interrogation and internment; uncounted thousands crippled by bullets and explosions; and a generation of children who believe that there is no "objective" justice "out there," but that each of them must act to right the wrongs. As the population accustoms itself to the increasingly stringent measures of law enforcement applied to it, the room for divergent thinking, for non-conformity, dwindles. Authoritarianism if further entrenched with the ubiquitous military presence and frustration of attempts to participate in government. Bettelheim noted that there was a distinct tendency for concengration camp inmates to identify with their guards.[35] The guards in Northern Ireland are military, the children identify with militarism –not necessarily with the British army itself, but with their "own army."

There are various voluntary agencies setting up playschemes for the children of Northern Ireland. Psychiatrists and psychologists are engaging in more extensive clinical practice with children than they have ever before in Northern Ireland. However, the published theories and conclusions of most of the indigenous professionals betrays a kind of piecemeal wishful-thinking. There is no solution to the effects on children of on-going violence and political repression within that context. Once the military and political contest is resolved, there remains the need for massive efforts at rehabilitation. Without that, the children of Northern Ireland—those who survive physically, those who do not emigrate—will be militaristic automatons, incapable of participating in their own destiny.

Rona M. Fields is Associate Professor of Sociology, Clark University. Her training and research have included work as a Psychologist (clinical and social), as a consultant and organizer (resource person) for com-

220 RONA M. FIELDS

munity and ethnic militant groups, and she is author of A Society on the Run: A Psychology of Northern Ireland *and* Psychological Genocide: A Cast Study of the Irish People. *She is currently in Portugal studying the effects of the revolution on children there.*

TABLE I
Percentage of Death-Destruction Endings in Stories—1971

Age Group:	6–8.11		9–14	
Religion	*Protestant*	*Catholic*	*Protestant*	*Catholic*
Belfast	76%	83%	59%	62%
Dublin	47%	44%	50%	53%

TABLE II
Response Percentages on Questions Relating to Political Socialization: Comparison with U.S. Sample

	Educational Groups							
	Primary (6–10)				*Middle School (11–14)*			
LEVELS: Categories	DUB	TK	BEL 71-72	BEL 73-74	DUB	TK	BEL 71-72	BEL 73-74
	What would happen if there were no rules?							
I: violence/crime	55	50	89	95	50	57	85	90
II: personal desires not principles	20	15	–	–	25	20	–	–
II: anarchy/disorder/ chaos	30	25	11	5	60	57	15	10
II: impossible to imagine	–	–	–	–	10	7	5	5
III: man as self-regulatory (nothing would happen)	–	–	–	–	–	–	–	–
	What is a rule?							
I: prohibitive	76	60	92	98	36	30	80	90
II: prescriptive	17	20	7	–	40	40	12	10
II: enforcement	–	–	1	–	24	10	12	5
III: beneficial/rational	–	15	–	–	15	27	–	–
	What is a law?							
I: prohibitive	78	60	92	92	90	43	90	96
II: prescriptive	20	20	–	–	10	43	12	5
II: enforcement	–	10	–	–	10	23	8	–
III: beneficial/rational	–	–	–	–	5	13	–	–

(continued)

PSYCHOLOGICAL GENOCIDE   221

TABLE II (continued)

LEVELS: Categories	Primary (6–10)				Middle School (11–14)			
	DUB	TK	BEL 71-72	BEL 73-74	DUB	TK	BEL 71-72	BEL 73-74
Why should people follow rules?								
I: avoid negative consequences	53	50	60	82	25	13	50	90
I: authority	15	5	27	20	30	–	25	15
II: personal conformity	30	35	6	–	41	13	14	5
II: social conformity	–	10	13	5	10	53	12	3
III: rational/beneficial/ utilitarian	–	5	–	–	–	27	4	–
III: principled	–	–	–	–	–	–	–	–
Why do you follow rules?								
I: avoid negative consequences	65	60	94	96	26	47	89	90
I: authority	28	10	12	5	60	10	10	12
II: personal conformity	15	20	–	–	15	40	10	–
II: social conformity	–	–	–	–	10	40	10	5
III: rational/beneficial/ utilitarian	–	–	–	–	5	7	2	–
III: principled	–	–	–	–	–	–	–	–
Can rules be changed?								
I: no	40	20	98	98	46	–	64	70
II & III: yes	60	70	2	–	54	100	36	30
Are there times when it might be right to break a rule?								
I: no, unqualified	80	55	95	95	20	7	70	80
I: yes, unspecified	–	25	–	–	10	–	–	10
II: morality of circumstances	20	20	5	5	60	73	25	10
III: morality of rule	–	–	–	–	10	17	30	–

NOTE: all questions except "Can rules be changed?" and "Are there times when it might be right to break a rule?" are multiple coded; therefore, percentages may total over 100 per cent. Where answers were idiosyncratic or uncodable, the categories were omitted from the table. Level number indicates increasing cognitive maturity. (adapted from Tapp and Kohlberg, 1971, p. 76)

TK = Tapp and Kohlberg   BEL - Belfast sample   DUB = Dublin

222   RONA M. FIELDS

TABLE III
Derry and Belfast, 1972

| Age | Derry | | | | Belfast | | | | | | | |
| | | | | | Catholic | | | | Protestant | | | |
	N	M.I.	N/A%	N/P%	N	M.I.	N/A%	N/P%	N	M.I.	N/A%	N/P%
6-9.11	16	82	34	10	8	67	30	32	7	74	25	30
10-14	10	80	30	16	5	80	45	36	6	92	32	12
Totals	26	81			13	72			13	82		

KEY: M.F. = Motivation Index Scores Average (Mean)
N/A% = Percentage of Imports of Negative Active Type (10 imports per child)
N/P% = Percentage of Imports of Negative Passive Type (10 imports per child)

TABLE IV
TAT Imports—Belfast 1973

	N	M.I.	Pos/Act%	Pos/Pass%	Neg/Act%	Neg/Pass%
Protestant	13	74	3%	15%	60%	12%
Catholic	13	70	2%	6%	46%	46%

N = 26

TABLE V
M.I. Scores (Averages) Belfast

| | Working Class | | | | Middle Class | | Repeat Tested | | |
	Prot.	N	Cath.	N	Cath.	N	Prot.	Cath.	N
1971	85	12	80	12	–	–	–	–	–
1972	82	13	72	13	–	–	–	68	6
1973	74	26	70	26	–	–	–	64	12
1974	72	24	69	26	–	4	–	66	5
Totals		75		77		4			23

PSYCHOLOGICAL GENOCIDE 223

REFERENCES

1. *Commentary*. September, 1966: Marjorie Housemann, "The Unremembered Genocide," pp. 55-61. Also. C. F. Arnold Rose, *The Negro in America* (or) Stokely Carmichael, "Power and Racism." *N.Y. Review of Books*, September 22, 1966.

2. Joan Moore, "Colonialism: The Case of the Mexican-Americans," *Social Problems*, 17, Spring, 1970. For definition of genocide see U.N. Article II, adopted December 9, 1948. Article II, **CONVENT ON THE PREVEN-TION AND PUNISHMENT OF THE CRIME OF GENOCIDE: Adopted December 9, 1943.
"In the present Convention genocide means any of the following acts committed with intent to destroy, in whole or in part, a national, ethnical, racial or religious group, as such:
(a) Killing members of the group;
(b) Causing serious bodily or mental harm to members of the group;
(c) Deliberately inflicting on the group conditions of life calculated to bring about its physical destruction in whole or in part;
(d) Imposing measures intended to prevent births within the group;
(e) Forcibly transferring children of the group to another group."

3. For American Indian Genocide, cf. F. C. Battey's Introduction in *Our Red Brothers*, by Lothaum: University of Nebraska Press, 1970, (or) Vinie Deloria, *Custer Died for Your Sins*, MacMillan Company, 1969.

4. Robert Coles, *Children of Crisis: A Study of Courage and Fear*, Atlantic Monthly Press Book, 1964. Bruno Bettleheim, *The Informed Heart: Autonomy in a Mass Age*, The Free Press of Glencoe. Bruno Bettleheim, and Morris Janowitz, *Social Change and Prejudice*, The Free Press of Glencoe, 1964.

5. Anna Freud and D. Burlingame, *Infants Without Families*, N.Y. International Universities Press, 1944. or. *War and Children*, Medical War Books, New York. 1943.

6. William Ryan. *Blaming the Victim*.

7. Oscar Lewis, *Children of Sanchez*.

8. C. Fackenheim, "Jewish Faith and the Holocaust: A Fragment," *Commentary*, August. 1968.

9. Report of National Advisory Commission on Civil Disorders which described the origins of Race Riots as rooted in the social history of "White Racism" and failed to explore either its ideological basis, origins or impacts.

10. Magda Arnold. *Story Sequence Analysis*, 1962, Columbia University Press.

11. Morris Fraser. "The Cost of Contention." *British Journal of Psychiatry*, (March, 1971), pp. 18-19.

12. Morris Fraser quoted in *Newsweek*. September 16, 1971.

13. Dr. Joe Cosgrave quoted in *Belfast Telegraph*, December 20, 1971.

14. Dr. H. A. Lyons, "Psychiatric Sequelae of the Belfast Riots," *British Journal of Psychiatry* (March 1971).

15. Dr. P. O. O'Malley. "Attempted Suicide Before and After the Communal Violence in Belfast; August. 1969." *Journal of Irish Medical Association*, Vol. 56, No. 5.

16. B. Nielsen, Monograph published by Institute of Social Psychology, Bergen Norway. 1971. *Intergroup Conflict and Violence*.

17. Rex Cathcart, "To Build Anew." *The Northern Teacher*, Winter, 1973.

18. John Malone. "Schools and Community Relations," *The Northern Teacher*, Winter 1973.

19. John M. Bill, "Environmental Stress and Educational Outcomes," *The Northern Teacher*, Winter 1973.

20. Tapp and Kohlberg, *Journal of Social Issues*, December, 1971.

21. Triandis and Triandis, "The Making of Nations", *Psychology Today*, 1968.

22. Sanford, Nevitt and Knutson. Jeanne (Josey-Bass, 1972).

23. Magda Arnold, *Story Sequence Analysis*, Columbia University, 1962.

24. *Op. cit.*

224   RONA M. FIELDS

25. June Tapp and L. Kohlberg, "Developing Senses of Law and Legal Justice,"
     Journal of Social Issues, Vol. 27, No. 2.
26. M. Dillon, D. Lehane, *Political Murders in Northern Ireland,* Penguin, Ltd.
     1973.
27. Geoffrey Morris, "Intimidation Out of Housing," 1973, Unpublished report.
28. H. A. Lyons, *op. cit.,* Morris Fraser, *op. cit.*
29. William James, *Principles of Psychology,* Dover Press, 1950.
30. Karen Horney, *The Neurotic Personality of Our Time,* Norton, New York,
     1937; *Neurosis and Human Growth,* New York, Norton, 1950.
31. Kurt Lewin, *Resolving Social Conflicts,* Harper and Brothers, New York;
     Field Theory in Social Science, Harper and Brothers, 1951; *A Dynamic
     Theory of Personality,* McGraw Hill, New York, 1935.
32. Gordon Allport.
33. Marie Jahoda, *Race Relations and Mental Health,* 1969, UNESCO, p. 23.
34. An article datelined Belfast, December 27, 1974 (*The Plain Dealer,* Cleveland,
     Ohio) was entitled "Ulster is Suffering Brain Drain." Various authorities in
     Northern Ireland, commenting on the fact that every month about 1,000
     people in Northern Ireland emigrate, said, "We're losing some of our best
     people . . . an estimated on in three of youngsters leaving school." The rate
     of emigration has steadily increased since 1969 and is expected to top 12,000
     for 1974. This does not include large numbers of people from Northern Ire-
     land who move to England, Scotland, Wales and the Irish Republic since
     they are not considered immigrants in these places and do not pass through
     any sort of passport-control. According to the immigration applications to
     Australia, New Zealand, Canada and the United States, the people pulling out
     are engineers, doctors, lawyers, businessmen, teachers and skilled workers.
     They are not replaced by new residents in the province.
35. Bruno Bettelheim, *Truants from Life.*

[11]

Area Variations of Violence in Northern Ireland*

JAMES A. SCHELLENBERG

Indiana State University

SOCIOLOGICAL FOCUS

Vol. 10 No. 1

January, 1977

A marked pattern of area-to-area differences in violence is described for Northern Ireland during 1969-74. Violence, measured by death rates, is especially high in the two largest cities and in the southwestern area. Two variables which together account for most of the area variation in violence are population density and proportion Roman Catholic. These findings underline the relative importance of group mobilization for political challenge as a basis of recent Ulster violence.

Recent theories of collective violence have frequently emphasized a background of economic hardship, or at least of relative deprivation. Work by Davies (1971) and Gurr (1970) is illustrative of this direction of attention. On the other hand, some scholars have questioned this approach. Charles Tilly, for example, has argued that group mobilization in political conflict is much more closely associated with collective violence than is economic hardship (Snyder and Tilly, 1972; Tilly et al., 1975).

One approach toward testing theories of collective violence has been to compare violence rates of areas associated with different background characteristics. The work of Spilerman (1970; 1971) on causes of racial disturbances in the United States is probably the most extensive example, and his findings provide little support for theories of economic hardship or relative deprivation.

Although a variety of scholars have engaged in research on recent violence in Northern Ireland (for a review, see Schellenberg, forthcoming), there has been little attention to systematic study of area differences in violence there. Some preliminary evidence has been cited by Birrell (1972) in support of a relative deprivation interpretation. Further evidence will be examined in the present article.

BASIC QUESTIONS

It is common in Northern Ireland to hear areas identified as having "little trouble" or "a lot of trouble." Journalistic evidence seems to support such a designation of areas, but such evidence is limited in explaining why we should expect such variation.

*Material for this article was collected by the author while on sabbatical leave in Ireland during 1974 and 1975. The author wishes to acknowledge especially the help of the following institutions with which he was associated while carrying out this work: The New University of Ulster, Coleraine, Northern Ireland; University College, Cork, Republic of Ireland; and Western Michigan University, Kalamazoo, Michigan.

The first and most basic question of the present research is whether we can document with clear statistical evidence important area differences in violence for Northern Ireland.

The second basic question follows naturally: To the extent to which there are important area differences in violence, are they closely associated with certain background conditions?

In searching for possible background conditions, attention will be directed toward three sets of factors, which might be roughly characterized as (a) ecological-demographic, (b) socio-economic, and (c) socio-demographic. Although formal hypotheses were not drawn up to guide the research, there were some general expectations for each of these areas.

Among ecological-demographic factors, it was expected that violence might be associated with areas with greater population. In such areas, it might be predicted, social control would be likely to be less effective in regulating intergroup conflicts. Where population growth is more rapid, there might be added factors of social change which might heighten conflict. Furthermore, location relative to Belfast (generally viewed as the center of violence) or to the border with the Republic of Ireland might be additional ecological factors. Generally, then, it might be predicted that violence would be higher in areas with higher population density, closer to the border with the Republic, closer to Belfast, and in areas which are less rural and/or more metropolitan.

Among socio-economic factors, it might be generally expected that violence would be directly associated with indicators of economic hardship in an area. Two measures relevant here which could be obtained from census materials were per capita housing space and rates of unemployment. It was generally expected that violence would be higher in areas with more crowded housing and/or greater rates of unemployment.

Two variables of population composition were considered. Since violence in Northern Ireland is especially associated with activities of young men, it was expected that the proportion of young men in the total population might be a possible predictor. Finally, given the focus upon religious background factor, it was generally expected that violence would be higher in areas with a greater proportion of Roman Catholics.

METHODS

OBTAINING INDICES OF VIOLENCE

Death has been sufficiently common in the political turmoil of Northern Ireland since 1968 to provide a fairly clear index of violence. A case-by-case analysis was made of all 1,152 deaths resulting from the security situation in Northern Ireland during the years of 1969 through 1974. On the basis of information reported in the press or information obtained personally from officials of security agencies, all but 20 of these deaths could be identified by area. Population figures given by the 1971 census (Census, 1971) were than used to calculate area death rates. Rates are expressed as the mean annual deaths from political violence during the years 1969-

74 per 100,000 population. These death rates will be used as our indices of violence for different areas of Northern Ireland.

AREAS

The main geographical units historically recognized in Northern Ireland are six counties (Antrim, Armagh, Down, Fermangh, Londonderry, and Tyrone) and two "county boroughs" or major cities (Belfast and Deffy).[1] Death rates were calculated for these major divisions and also for smaller subdivisions. The smaller subdivisions were 34 areas, including the urban county boroughs of Belfast and Derry, the urban district of Newtownabbey, and the 31 rural districts (plus any town located within a rural district) which were in use as divisions at the time of the 1971 census.

BACKGROUND VARIABLES

Eleven area characteristics were selected for analysis as potential independent variables to explain area differences in violence: (1) total population, as given by the 1971 census; (2) population gain, 1966-71, expressed as a proportion of total population; (3) population density, expressed as number of persons per hectare of land area; (4) border distance, expressed as the number of areas it would be necessary to cross to travel by land from the Republic; (5) Belfast distance, expressed as the number of areas it would be necessary to enter in traveling by land from Belfast; (6) rural, indicated by the absence (or presence) of a city of 5,000 or more within the district; (7) metropolitan, indicated by the presence (or absence) of an urban district with a population of 50,000 or more; (8) housing space, indicated by the number of rooms per capita in all occupied private dwellings; (9) unemployment, indicated by the number of unemployed economically active males as a proportion of all males of age 15 or more; (10) adult males, indicated by the number of males of age 15 or more as a proportion of total population; (11) proportion Catholic, indicated by the percentage of the total population who gave their religion as Roman Catholic.

Variables 1, 2, 3, 8, 9, 10 and 11 were derived from the 1971 census (Census, 1971). Variable 1 is simply the raw figure given for the area (plus those of any municipal boroughs or urban districts which may be contained in it). Variables 2, 3, 8, 9, 10 and 11 are all proportions combining two different sets of census figures, as specified above for each.

Variables 6 and 7 were not directly derived from census figures, though they were still based on census data. Areas were placed in a rural category for variable 6 (and given a score of "1") if they had no city of 5,000 population; otherwise they were left out of this category (and scored "0"). Likewise, areas were called metropolitan (and given a score of "1") if they were urban areas with 50,000 or more in population; all other areas were left out of this category (and scored "0"). Likewise, areas were called metropolitan (and given a score of "1") if they were urban areas with 50,000 or more in population; all other areas were left out of this status (and given a score of "0"). A total of 13 areas were thus identified as rural and three were considered metropolitan (Belfast, Derry, and Newtownabbey).

Variables 4 and 5 were not obtained from census data but were instead simply derived from inspection of a map of Northern Ireland.

The first seven variables were all selected as indicative of demographic or geographic factors which might have an important influence upon the level of violence. Variables 8 through 11 were selected with more explicit consideration of social factors than the previous variables. Variables 8 and 9 were primarily economic. Since housing and unemployment were among the significant points of protest in the civil rights campaign of the late 1960s, it was considered important to include them as possible predictors of violence. In addition, they are taken to measure relative poverty, which might by itself be considered conducive to violence. Variable 10, adult males, was selected in recognition of the predominant association of violence with activities of men. Finally, variable 11 measures the relative proportion of Roman Catholics in the area. On its face it is simply a religious measure, but persons familiar with the sectarian politics of Northern Ireland will recognize it as also a measure of the underlying political orientation of an area—at least so far as Unionist support or opposition is concerned.[2]

Although all of these variables were measured for conditions as they existed in 1971, all described conditions antedated 1969. For this reason they may be considered as an interrelated set of independent variables representing conditions which may have affected the degree of violence during the years 1969-74.

To study the association of the eleven independent variables with area variations in death rates, zero-order coefficients of Pearsonian correlation were first inspected. Partial correlations were then obtained to discover the unique correlation of each of these variables after controlling for correlations with the other ten. Coefficients of multiple correlation were then obtained, first for the first seven variables (representing primarily demographic and geographic conditions), then for the last four variables (representing the more clearly social conditions), and then for all eleven variables combined.

Finally, an effort was made to discover whether most of the total variation in area violence rates could be accounted for by two or three particular variables. If so, the problem became that of identifying which particular variables would together have the strongest predictive power.

RESULTS

Table 1 gives death rates for main (county) divisions of Northern Ireland. Violence rates are especially high in the two leading cities (Belfast and Derry). The rates are generally higher in the south and west (Armagh, Tyrone, Fermanagh) than in the northern and eastern parts (Antrim, Down, and Londonderry).

Death rates were also calculated for smaller subdivisions. Figure 1 shows the general pattern of variation in death rates for these subdivisions. There is a marked contrast between the relatively high violence of Belfast, Derry, and border areas of the southwest, in comparison to the relatively low violence of most of the northern eastern sections.

Table 2 gives the basic results of the correlational and multiple regression analysis. The first column of Table 2 gives the zero-order coefficients of correlation of each of the eleven independent variables with violence rates. The second column

VIOLENCE IN NORTHERN IRELAND   73

Table 1

DEATH RATES BY MAJOR SUBDIVISIONS OF NORTHERN IRELAND

	Mean Annual Deaths per 100,000 population 1969 - 74
Belfast	27.5
Derry	34.5
County Antrim	3.3
County Armagh	12.9
County Down	3.1
County Fermanagh	10.4
County Londonderry	4.1
County Tyrone	10.8

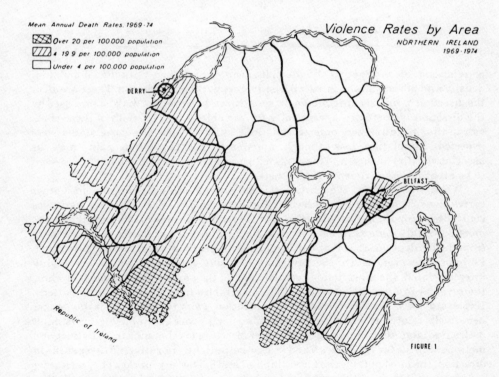

Mean Annual Death Rates. 1969-74

Over 20 per 100,000 population

4 - 19.9 per 100,000 population

Under 4 per 100,000 population

Violence Rates by Area
NORTHERN IRELAND
1969-1974

FIGURE 1

presents partial correlations, obtained to discover the unique correlation of each of the background variables after controlling for the other ten.

As can be seen in Table 2, a number of variables show substantial zero-order correlations with levels of violence. Indeed, most of them would be statistically significant at conventional standards (p = .05 when r = .338, two-tailed test). The

Table 2

ASSOCIATIONS BETWEEN SELECTED CHARACTERISTICS OF AREAS AND LEVEL OF VIOLENCE

	Measures of Association with Political Death Rates		
	Correlation Coefficient (zero-order)	Partial Correlation (10th order)	Coefficients of Multiple R
1. Total Population	.34	.09	
2. Population Growth	-.49	.13	
3. Population Density	.59	.38	Variables
4. Border Distance	-.37	-.40	1-7 .815
5. Belfast Distance	.29	-.20	
6. Rural	-.03	-.03	Variables
7. Metropolitan	.51	-.03	1-11 .903
8. Housing Space	-.47	.35	
9. Unemployment	.68	.33	
10. Adult Males	-.36	.08	Variables
11. Proportion Catholic	.61	.48	8-11 .729

correlations of violence with unemployment, proportion Catholic, population density and metropolitan status (all positive) are particularly strong. These are all in the direction of initial expectations. In some cases, however, we may be surprised by the direction of coefficients, especially for variables 2 and 10. Both of these show substantial negative zero-order correlations, although positive correlations were expected. Population loss, though apparently not population gain, may be associated with violence, and the areas with a greater proportion of adult males seem to be areas of lesser violence than others.

When we compare the partial correlations of Table 2 with the first-order correlations, a number of interesting findings appear. With all other variables controlled, proportion Catholic (variable 11) retains a value of .48, apparently the most powerful single variable. The next highest partial correlation is for distance from the border (variable 4) at -.40, slightly stronger than its zero-order correlation. Perhaps, however, given the problems of using indicators which are highly intercorrelated, the most notable contribution of the partial correlations is to show the reversal in direction of no less than 5 variables from their zero-order pattern. Expressed as a partial correlation, population gain (variable 2) is no longer negatively related to violence; neither is housing space (variable 8), nor is adult males (variable 10). Changing in the other direction are distance from Belfast and metropolitan status (variables 5 and 7), now both slightly negative. Of these shifts in direction, the most notable are for variables 7 and 8. The very marked (.51) zero-order correlation of violence with metropolitan status essentially disappears once all other variables are controlled. Even more dramatic is the change for housing space. Once the associated variables are controlled, housing space is positively correlated with violence—apparently indicating that crowded housing is not *per se* a condition conducive to violence.

It is of course questionable to read very much into these partial correlations, given problems of multicolinearity with the rest of the set of highly intercorrelated independent variables. To allow the reader to examine some of the complex interrelationships of the independent variables, Table 3 presents the full matrix of intercorrelations of these variables.

Table 3. Zero—order Correlations Among Independent Variables

Variable Names	1	2	3	4	5	6	7	8	9	10	11
1. Total Population	1.00										
2. Population Growth	-.18	1.00									
3. Population Density	.72	-.33	1.00								
4. Border Distance	.39	.40	.27	1.00							
5. Belfast Distance	-.47	-.36	-.14	-.76	1.00						
6. Rural	-.32	-.13	-.26	-.27	.22	1.00					
7. Metropolitan	.59	-.19	.92	.32	-.15	-.24	1.00				
8. Housing Space	.18	.35	-.04	.64	-.65	-.06	-.02	1.00			
9. Unemployment	-.06	-.48	.18	-.58	.57	.17	.14	-.77	1.00		
10. Adult Males	-.44	-.21	-.49	-.28	.25	.34	-.45	.17	-.29	1.00	
11. Proportion Catholic	-.23	-.41	-.00	-.69	.64	.12	-.02	-.82	-.81	-.13	1.00
Mean	46.246.703	0.049	5.381	2.412	4.559	0.383	0.088	1.324	0.084	0.339	0.357
Standard Deviation	65.860.688	0.068	14.645	1.234	1.862	0.493	0.288	0.141	0.035	0.018	0.167

The right-hand portions of Table 2 show coefficients of multiple regression for combined sets of variables. The first seven variables (primarily demographic and geographic) combine to produce a multiple R of .815, and the last four (primarily social and economic) combine for an R of .729. All eleven variables together give a multiple R of .903, thus accounting for slightly over 80 percent of the variance in area-by-area death rates.

Further regression analysis sought to discover small sets of variables which would account for most of the area-to-area variation in deaths. The two variables which together clearly made the simplest and best prediction were variables 3 and 11, population density and proportion Catholic. Just these two variables produced a multiple R of .851, thus explaining over 72 percent of the variation of the dependent variable. The beta weights of these two variables when combined as a single pair were .61 for proportion Catholic and .60 for population density. (With all 11 variables included in the equation, the corresponding beta weights for these two were .51 and .66 respectively.)[3]

DISCUSSION

One of the most widely used approaches to explain variations of violence, especially political violence within nations, is through the use of social psychological conceptions of frustration-aggression or (as a special application of this approach) relative deprivation (Gurr, 1970; Davies, 1971). The most significant attempt to apply this approach to recent events in Northern Ireland is by Birrell (1972), who uses the concept of relative deprivation to interpret both the emergence of radical political action and variations in the relative intensity of violence. Birrell points to correlations between socio-economic conditions and area variations as part of his interpretation of patterns of violence. However, he uses only simple zero-order correlations to indicate this relationship. In our analysis of area differences in the previous section, socio-economic indicators did appear at first to be strongly related to the amount of violence. Among zero-order correlations, the unemployment rate was most strongly associated with amount of violence (.68), and the measure of housing space showed a substantial negative (-.47) correlation. That Catholics tend to live in areas of higher unemployment and more crowded housing (corresponding correlations with percent Catholic are .81 and -.83 for unemployment and per capita housing space respectively) can be seen as illustrating the socio-economic foundations of their grievances. However, in our more probing analyses of partial correlations and multiple regression, the socio-economic factors receded in importance. With all other variables taken into account (in the partial correlations) each of the socio-economic indicators showed only modest associations with violence, and the direction of the correlation with housing was actually reversed. In the multiple regression analysis, neither of these two were among the two variables which together could best explain the variation in violence from area to area.

Although relative deprivation may be an important ingredient in some aspects of violence in Northern Ireland, our evidence would suggest that other approaches may be more useful for understanding the area differences we have demonstrated. The two variables in our analysis which we found most predictive of area-to-area differences in violence were population density and proportion Roman Catholic. Although it is not at once obvious why these two factors would together be the best pair of predictors, some further examination of these variables may give us important clues to understanding the violence in Northern Ireland.

Areas which are most compactly settled may have a number of advantages for promoting communal violence. Here the communication of resentments would generally be quicker and the opportunities for crowd action greater. Opportunities for organized paramilitary groups are also greater in more populated areas, and targets of violence are more conveniently available there, whether one is seeking to attack official institutions or a rival population group. Such actions can be planned and carried out on a small scale in densely populated areas without a high probability of apprehension. This is especially true when official agencies of law enforcement are unable to function normally. Furthermore, the normal social inhibitions against violence might be expected to be more relaxed under the relatively more anonymous conditions of high population density. For a combination of such reasons, we may expect a more sustained level of violence in densely populated areas. This of course assumes the presence of both deep-seated political alienation and a traditionally sanctioned recourse to political violence—and both of these factors are present in Northern Ireland.

The interpretation of proportion Catholic as a major predictor of violence is less straight-forward. Several different possibilities suggest themselves. One is that the intensity of conflict is positively related to the degree of equality of the two main communal groups. Where the proportion of Catholics is higher, this numerical equality would be generally best approached. Another possibility would be to consider the size of the Catholic population as a rough index of alienation from Unionist institutions. Thus, wherever the proportion of Catholics is high (regardless of the degree of equality with Protestants), there would also be the greatest issue of the legitimacy of those institutions. Finally, the proportion Catholic might be seen also as an index of the ease with which subversive operations might be organized. To the degree that the organized challenge to authority has come from the Catholic side (i.e., the I.R.A.), it can manifest itself most effectively in predominantly Catholic neighborhoods. Our present evidence does not allow us to weigh the relative merits of these interpretations, but all of them are likely to have some validity.

At first glance there appears to be a very strong parallel between our findings and those reported by Spilerman (1970, 1971) in his analysis of American racial disturbances in the 1960s. Spilerman reports that the variable that best predicted the city-to-city variation in the amount of violence was simply the absolute size of the Negro population. The obvious parallel in our results is the importance we found for the relative size of the Catholic population. Since he studied only urban areas, Spilerman would not be expected to have a factor parallel to population density in this study. However, two important contrasts between our results and those of Spilerman should also be noted. In the first place, our results emphasize the relative size of the Catholic population rather than its absolute size. After noting the general similarity to Spilerman's findings, we tried absolute size of the Catholic population in place of our measure of relative size, but the effectiveness in predicting the patterns of violence was then slightly reduced. In the second place, our patterns of area-to-area variation in violence were more marked than those in the cities studied by Spilerman. We were therefore able to find more factors strongly associated to area differences in violence even though we applied only a crude linear regression model.

Whatever the particular interpretations which may be made of our findings, their general import is to suggest a stronger role for specifically political factors than for those of socio-economic deprivation. The ability to mobilize and sustain a collective challenge to official authority (along with the resultant higher level of official security operations) may be the common feature of those areas of Northern Ireland most makred by violence. This line of interpretation is generally harmonious with that of Tilly (Snyder and Tilly, 1972; Tilly et al., 1975) who found European patterns of collective violence more easily interpreted in terms of the mobilization of power-seeking groups than in terms of indices of economic hardship.

FOOTNOTES

1. To avoid confusion we will consistently use the official name of "Londonderry" to apply to the county unit and the more locally popular (and more Irish) term of "Derry" to apply to the city itself.

2. Electoral statistics were unfortunately not available for the areas used, since the census areas did not coincide with those used for either Stormont (Northern Ireland) or Westminister (United Kingdom) elections.

3. The beta weights for all variables included in Table 2 (in order of listings) in the equation producing the multiple R of .903 were .08, .10, .66, -.37, -.17, -.02, -.03, .32, .35, .07, and .51 respectively.

REFERENCES

Birrell, Derek
    1972 "Relative deprivation as a factor in conflict in Northern Ireland." Sociological Review 20:313-343.
Census
    1971 County Reports for Northern Ireland. Belfast: Her Majesty's Stationery Office.
Davies, James E.
    1971 When Men Revolt—And Why. New York: Free Press.
Gurr, Ted Robert
    1970 Why Men Rebel. Princeton, New Jersey: Princeton University Press.
Schellenberg, James A.
  Forth- "Violence in Northern Ireland, 1969-
  Coming 1975." International Journal of Group Tensions.

Snyder, David, and Charles Tilly
    1972 "Hardship and collective violence in France, 1830 to 1960." American Sociological Review 37:520-532.
Spilerman, Seymour
    1970 "The causes of racial disturbances: A comparison of alternative explanations." American Sociological Review 35:627-649.
    1971 "The cases of racial disturbances: Tests of an explanation." American Sociological Review 36:427-442.
Tilly, Charles, Louise Tilly, and Richard Tilly
    1975 The Rebellious Century: 1830-1930. Cambridge, Mass.: Harvard University Press.

[12]

Terroristic Murder in Northern Ireland: Who Is Killed and Why?

Robert M. Pockrass

Law Enforcement Program
Mankato State University
Mankato, Minnesota

Abstract   Terrorism can be characterized as planned acts of violence, directed at civilians and carried out for the purpose of obtaining a political goal. This paper shows the changing patterns of terrorist murders in Northern Ireland for the period 1969 through 1984. The author proposes a model of motivation which will help to explain terroristic murders. In addition, terroristic violence has changed in its focus with members of the security forces becoming the prime target in the late 1970s and 1980s.

For approximately fifteen years, the sectarian conflict in Northern Ireland has never been far from the headlines of the newspapers. Frequently portrayed as a Protestant–Catholic struggle, a sort of modern day Thirty Years' War, the Northern Ireland problem is far more complex. There is, to be sure, religious bigotry—a great deal of it—as there is also a very long history of conflict based on cultural and ethnic differences, political economics, colonialism, and Irish nationalism. The subject has been covered at length by many writers, and will not be dealt with on the following pages.

The purpose of this article is to examine the violence, in particular the killings, in terms of what types of people became

Terrorism. Volume 9, Number 4
0149–0389/86/379–00$03.00/0

victims, and why they became victims. It is the thesis of this article that terrorism is not charcterized by random acts of violence but rather that the seemingly random acts are in fact planned out and have an underlying motivation. In plain language, this article could be subtitled "Who Gets It and Why."

A climate glorifying violence, and attitudes which revel in the past acts of killing of heroes and martyrs is an underlying truth about Ireland. It may be that many other societies glorify violence in terms of wars long past, but both Catholic and Protestant Irish men and women seem to take special relish in remembering and perpetuating old fights and old hates. In poetry and song, the past is celebrated, and the attitudes of the present and future generations are hardened.

It is not just that modern Ireland was born in blood, nor that Ulster, in effect, seceded from the rest of Ireland that is unusual. Even the fact that Ulster, or Northern Ireland as a political entity, has had 63 turbulent years of riots and border raids is also not particularly unusual in this century. Compared to the strife in some countries, for example, Zaire, Nigeria, or Colombia, Northern Ireland has been almost a peaceable kingdom. What is unique about Northern Ireland is not the level of violence, but the cultural expectations that violence past, present, and future was and is inevitable and even desirable.

In poetry, the "Greens" (Catholic, Republicans) have remembered and invoked the blood of the past in works such as "Farewell, O'Patrick Sarsfield,"[1] "Tone's Grave,"[2] and "Kevin Barry."[3] Although with a lesser known literary tradition, the "Oranges" (Protestants, Loyalists) too have celebrated in verse their heroes and events in poems such as "The Boyne Water"[4] and "An Ulsterman."[5] Often the same events became the subject of very different literary interpretations. For example, the siege of Londonderry, a famous Protestant victory in 1690, is remembered very differently by Catholic and Protestant, or if one prefers, in Republican and Loyalist verse. For the former:

> "But, for you, Londonderry, may plague invite and slay,
>   Your people, May ruin desolate you stone by stone,

Terroristic Murder in Northern Ireland   *343*

> Through you many a gallant youth his coffins lies today
>   With winds for mourners alone![6]

and for the Orange side:

> ". . . For blood did flow in crimson streams,
> On many a Winter's night.
>   They knew the lord was on their side,
> To help them in the fight."[7]

Unfortunately modern day Ulster is not all poetry and rhetoric; it is also poeple, our contemporaries, who are bleeding and dying. Let a few statistics serve as illustrations.

From the start of the most recent "troubles," 1969 through 1983, there were 29,853 shooting incidents, 11,336 bombings (exploded or defused), and 1,478 incendiaries.[8] During this time, there were 2,346 fatalities, 1,647 (70.2 percent) of them civilians, and 699 (29.8 percent) from the security forces, namely, the Royal Ulster Constabulary (RUC), Royal Ulster Constabulary Reserve (RUCR), British Army and Ulster Defense Regiment (UDR). As O'Malley states,[9] if the United States had suffered a calamity similar to Northern Ireland, but proportionate to its population, there would have been 345,000 dead and over 2.55 million injured.

In 1983, Republican terrorists carried out 54 incidents of murder, 286 attempted murders, and 178 explosions. Loyalists committed 7 murders, 13 attempted murders, and 6 explosions. This disparity of violence is caused by the fact that the Republicans consider themselves to be fighting a war of national liberation. Their attitude leads them to attempt to keep up the pressure against the security forces in particular. It is a formula which worked in the past, namely the 1919–1922 war against the "Black and Tans." The Loyalists are at this point more reactive in nature, primrily retaliating against Catholics, because of attacks on Protestant civilians, Ulster politicians, or the security forces. To keep the violence in perspective, however, an Ulster man or woman in 1983 was still 2.8 times as likely to be killed in a traffic accident as by terrorists.[10]

Violence was no stranger to Northern Ireland in the period from 1922 to 1968. There were sectarian riots in Belfast in the 1920s and 1930s, a Republican-sponsored border campaign in the 1920s and against in the 1950s, and sporadic bombings, shootings, and raids, mainly by the Irish Republican Army throughout that 46-year period. It was after Protestant mob violence directed against the largely Catholic Civil Rights Marchers in 1969 that sectarian conflict became epidemic in proportions.

Before attempting to look at and describe patterns of violence, a model based on motivation will be developed. Adlerian-oriented psychologists[11] have developed a motivational basis for explaining the actions of individuals or groups. These motives may be called attention, power, or revenge. It has been previously theorized that these three motives may be of use to the police in dealing with hostage and barricade situations[12] and that profiles of hostage-takers based on motivation are useful during the process of negotiation. A simple explanation is that when terrorists take hostages, they may have one or a combination of motives which caused them to commit their act. For example, seizing an embassy as Palestinians did in the wake of the Camp David Accords served as a means of publicizing the grievances of the Palestinians and their anger over Sadat's perceived betrayal of them.[13] That was attention. Seizing an airliner and attempting to bargain the lives of the passengers for the release of prisoners of Kuwaiti prisons as happened in December 1984[14] is an example of a power motivation. In other words, hostages were taken in order to attempt to force a government into an unwilling act. Revenge is the hardest motivation to describe. A hostage and barricade situation which occurs as a prelude to the murder of the hostage may serve as an example. Revenge may be carried out against an individual in order to make him pay for his alleged misdeeds or it may really be aimed at the larger society. The death, by bombing, of Lord Mountbatten is an act of revenge against Britain more than against him personally. Killing one of the last of Britain's great heroes from the Second World War can be seen as an act of vengeance against the collectivity which revered him.

It is also important to note that acts of terrorism where atten-

Terroristic Murder in Northern Ireland 345

tion is the motivation may have one of several publics to influence through the attendant publicity. There may be uncommitted neutrals in the society, foreign governments and populations, the enemy including their civilian supporters, and members of the terrorist group itself. The latter often need a lift to their morale that only a successful terrorist action can bring.*

The author believes that the motivational model has utility for explaining terrorist activities and targets. Rather than discounting terrorist attacks as crazy or senseless, police and government analysts must realize that the target is usually chosen with some goal in mind. The long-term goals of terrorists have been frequently discussed and reported upon: a Basque homeland, a Palestinian state, a United Ireland, or the destruction of the materialistic capitalist state of West Germany. It is when one looks at the actions carried out by terrorists toward the achievement of their ultimate end, that one must start to ask what the terrorists hoped to achieve by a particular assassination, kidnapping, bombing, or facility attack. Analysis of terrorist incidents may be able to more clearly delineate the combination of motivations underlying them, but there may be a discernible primary motive. Only future research can prove this hypothesis. In the ensuing pages, the author will discuss categories of political violence which have occurred in Northern Ireland. Possible motivations will be considered during these discussions.

Basically, incidents of political violence seem to fall into one of four broad categories. These are called sectarian violence, intra- or inter-organizational violence, terroristic violence directed at selected noncombatants and terroristic violence directed toward security force personnel.

The first category is sectarian violence. Sectarian violence is exactly what the words simply, as it involves the pitting of Protestants against Catholics or vice versa. Sectarian violence has had a relatively long past in Northern Ireland, especially in the

---

* At present, externally oriented publicity does not seem to be the major motivation of Republican terrorists. But a need to raise internal organizational morale may partly explain the reasons for the London parks bombings of 1982. See note 46 for further comments.

cities of Belfast and Londonderry. In 1969, sectarian violence broke out as Protestant mobs attacked predominantly Catholic civil rights marchers at Toome, Antrim, Maghera, Dungiven, Burntollet Bridge, and Londonderry.[15] Rioting spread as Catholics fought back in Londonderry's Bogside and went on the offensive in Belfast. Devlin[16] tells of how word was sent from the Bogside to West Belfast urging Catholics to cause disorders in order to force a withdrawal of Royal Ulster Constabulary personnel from Londonderry. The former RUC Commander in West Belfast[17] told the author how he had walked alone to receive a petition from a large crowd of West Belfast residents. Mob violence such as the above-mentioned riots in West Belfast seems to have had a power motivation, namely to force the RUC to reallocate resources away from Londonderry. As it was, in Londonderry, 450 RUC men were being overwhelmed by 14,000 rioters from both sides.[18]

Other forms of sectarian violence also seemed to have a power motive. Sectarian groups or mobs often burned out recalcitrant Catholic or Protestant householders who found themselves residing in or alongside neighborhoods dominated by the other religious faction. A recent Irish-made film, *Cal,* illustrated attempts by Orangemen first to intimidate then to burn out a Catholic worker from their neighborhood.[19] In Belfast, in the spring of 1984, Protestant terrorists carried out a bombing in an attempt to force the move of a Catholic family. It resulted in two deaths, one being the woman of the house, a Catholic. The other fatality was one of the RUC constables, a Protestant, who had responded to the call.[20]

The shift in the nature of sectarian violence away from mob action to attacks on individuals meant a higher degree in lethality and the emergence of true terrorism. In 1969 and 1970, the years dominated by riots, Northern Ireland experienced only 25 civilian deaths, while by 1972 there were 321 such deaths.[21] In the years since, although civilian deaths have almost continually declined, there has been a deliberate callousness and cruelty which is difficult to contemplate. Civilians are murdered for reasons of political strategy without regard to their involvement in the "Troubles." The Provisional Irish Repub-

Terroristic Murder in Northern Ireland 347

lican Army (PIRA) has attempts to constructively push back the border, especially in South Armagh. This has been accomplished by the murder of Protestant farmers or their eldest sons, who normally inherit the farms. The killings are then followed up by ensuring that the farms will be sold to Catholics who are IRA sympathizers.[22] This redrawing of the border by murder obviously gives the South Armagh IRA Action Service Units more room to hide and move in.

There has been an occasional series of murders which seem to be motivated by nothing more than hatred and a desire to kill. The infamous Shankhill Butchers, a Protestant gang, is an example. Finally, some murders, often involving plural victims, seem to have revenge as their motivation. Although the desire to shock, to terrify, and to intimidate is an obvious underlying factor in their occurrence, revenge seems to be the paramount motivation. The tit-for-tat murders of the Miami Show Band and the Kings Mills Massacre in South Armagh suggest revenge in the latter outrage.

The second category is concerned with inter- and intra-organizational violence. It is well known that the Protestant paramilitary organizations, the Ulster Freedom Fighters (UFF), Ulster Volunteer Force (UVF), etc. war on the Provisional Irish Republican Army (PIRA), or Irish National Liberation Army (INLA). Less well known is the fact that the Official and Provisional Wings of the Irish Republican Army struggled for supremacy on the streets of West Belfast in the mid 1970s.[23] Their feuding was partly ideological, and partly material in that they fought for control of the rackets in the Catholic ghettos of Belfast and Londonderry. Since 1977, there has been relative peace between the Republican factions, but there are housing estates or sections of the cities which are considered Provo country or INLA territory today.[24] The Protestant UDA and UVF have waged similar conflicts.

Violence has been carried out within the organizations in order to discipline members and to get revenge against police informers. The informer or "tout" has long been a fixture in the Irish revolutionary scene. The Special Branch of the colonial police, the Royal Irish Constabulary successfully penetrated nineteenth- and early twentieth-century Irish nationalist groups with informers. However, the IRA led by Michael Collins destroyed the government's intelligence services in 1919–1921 in part by successfully planting its own informers in the RIC and by killing those who were suspected or working for the police.[25] Today, the Northern Irish police, the RUC, use informants. Army Colonel Robin Evelegh advocated a wider and more effective development of informants by giving terrorists amnesty for past crimes, and by relocating them away from Northern Ireland complete with new identities.[26] The RUC and the Northern Ireland Department of Public Prosecution have done exactly that. The use of informants, who later turn states evidence at trial, has resulted in the arrests of many "Green" and "Orange" terrorist operatives. The effectiveness of the use of "supergrasses," as the informant-witnesses are called, was covered on the American television news program *60 Minutes*.[27]

In response to the "supergrasses" and the danger from informants, the PIRA and INLA have shot, bombed, and kidnapped suspected "touts." One recent example occurred in Belfast on April 12, 1984, when a Catholic was shot to death in his kitchen by two masked gunmen.[28] The Irish National Liberation Army claimed responsibility, justifying the killings by claiming that the man, recently released from prison, was in fact a "tout."[29] It is important to note, however, that IRA or INLA killings are sometimes "justified" by calling the victim who was killed for other reasons, an informer. The car-bomb murder of a Catholic farmer near Newry was such a case.[30]

The third category of terroristic violence relates to that which is directed at public officials and prominent persons. Northern Ireland's most prominent establishment figure, the Secretary of State, has so far escaped attack. So, too, has the Rev. Ian Paisley, M.P., Protestant Ulster's most extreme and vocal spokesperson. Not so lucky was Bernadette Devlin McAliskey, the best known Catholic spokesperson, who was wounded along with her husband in a UDA assassination attempt. An IRA gunman shot and killed the Reverend Robert Bradford, official Unionist M.P., in November 1981, while he was meeting constituents in a Commu-

Terroristic Murder in Northern Ireland   *349*

nity Center. Targets have also included lesser politicians, journalists, and businessmen. Gerry Adams, leader of the Provisional Sinn Fein, the Provos' political arm, narrowly escaped death in March 1984. The Irish National Liberation Army reached out to London to kill Conservative Party M.P. Airey Neave by car bomb, and to shoot *Guinness Book of Records* publisher Ross McWhirter. INLA also claimed responsibility for killing the World War II hero and relative of the Royal family, Lord Louis Mountbatten.

These and other attacks seem to stem from all three motives, power, attention, and revenge. In their book, *Target Terrorism,* Kobetz and Cooper[31] discuss the rationale of assassination. Among other things, the successful killing of a political figure removes him from his sphere of influence—a power motivation. This was certainly the case with Neave, a political confident of Prime Minister Thatcher. A successful assassination, or even a near miss, may serve to intimidate those near to the targeted figure, or those in similar positions. Again, power is the motive. Certainly, the recent bombing at the Conservative Party Convention in Brighton. England. must have had an inhibiting effect on the activities of Mrs. Thatcher and other politicians. Obviously, spectacular killings such as Mountbatten's, the Brighton bombing, or the car bombing of Airey Neave as he left the House of Commons underground parking garage, receive tremendous publicity. All viewers of television or newspaper readers, be they friend, neutral, or foe, cannot but be impressed by IRA skills. Finally, as stated earlier, there were strong elements of revenge against Britain as a whole in the Mountbatten murder. There were likely strong elements of revenge in the fatal shooting of McWhirter, an outspoken opponent of the IRA. His anti-IRA words were avenged by IRA bullets.

In Northern Ireland, members of the judicial and correctional systems seem to have been targeted. Prison guards were frequently killed at home, or while off-duty.[32] Mainly, the Republican groups have been responsible for these killings. In some cases, the dead guards were accused of inhumanities against Republican prisoners. If these accusations can be believed, it is suggested that a revenge motivation was present. The intimidation of the guards in the performance of their duties would also be a by-product of these killings; hence, a power motivation is also present.

Almost totally unpublicized outside of Ulster, there has also been a series of bombings of the cars of prison guards. These have tended to occur at night when the cars were parked by the residences of the guards and thus so far no casualties have occurred.[33] It seems that these bombings are being carried out by Loyalist gangs in an attempt to force changes in policy within H.M. prisons in the Belfast area.

Judges, particularly Catholics, have been attacked. It seems that these people are being targeted because of their being symbols of British justice. Catholic judges, of course, are seen as traitors to the cause of the Irish nation by the PIRA and INLA. One recent case involved the attempted murder of a Catholic Resident Magistrate named Travers. Resident Magistrates, or R.M.s, are lower-court judges in Ulster. It seems that R. M. Travers was the judge before whom Gerry Adams had appeared on the day of Adams's near assassination by the UDA. Traver's death may therefore have been a revenge killing, assuming that the Provos felt that Travers was somehow in on the UDA attempt against Adams. In any case, Travers, his wife, and 22-year-old daughter, Mary, were ambushed by gunmen as they walked home from mass. The R.M., shot six times, survived; Mary Travers, shot once, did not.

The fourth category is concerned with attacks against the security forces, the Royal Ulster Constabulary, the Royal Ulster Constabulary Reserve, the British Army, and the Ulster Defense Regiment. These attacks have been primarily, but not exclusively, the province of the "Greens." Since 1976, attacks against the security forces have become the dominant form of political violence in Northern Ireland.

Guerrilla style or terrorist attacks against the police are not common in all countries. Terrorists, typically, prefer to attack non-combatants, and prefer to carry out activities which will gain them maximum publicity at minimum risk. That has generally been the case in Western Europe, Germany, the Netherlands, Italy, and even in Israel and the Middle East. The Irish, however, have a tradition of attacking the security forces. The Irish nationalists in

Terroristic Murder in Northern Ireland 351

the War of Liberation in 1919–1922 fought a hit-and-run conflict against the British Army, the Royal Irish Constabulary (RIC), and particularly against the mercenary paramilitaries, the Black and Tans and the Auxiliaries. Monuments all over the Republic of Ireland commemmorate small skirmishes or ambushes with the "Tans" or other forces of the Crown. Similarly in the Civil War which followed the Treaty of December 1921, pro-treaty forces battled their old comrades in arms, the anti-treaty people. The civil war was also notable for attacks by the anti-treaty forces against the new Free State security forces. One of these ambushes took the life of General Michael Collins, the hero of the 1919–1921 conflict.

It is part of contemporary terrorist theory to advocate attacks on the police and the army. Carlos Marighella advocated the killing of the Chiefs of Police and of the Army in his "Minimanual of the Urban Guerrilla."[34] He further advocated attacks through snipings, ambushes, and bombings against the police. These attacks would make the police nervous and prone to overreact, thus further alienating the populace. Revolutionary terrorists around the world, the Tupamaros in Uruguay, the Red Brigades in Italy, the Baadar-Meinhof gang in West Germany, the Basque ETA in Spain, and the Provisional Irish Republican Army, have all followed Marighella's tenets. As was previously stated, the Republicans consider themselves to be fighting a war of national liberation. Their past history and contemporary theory suggest that the security forces should be targeted. Indeed such attacks give symbolic credence to the word "army" in the organizational names Irish Republican Army and Irish National Liberation Army. These are undoubtedly political dividends to be reaped from these attacks. One would be, for example, a reinforcement of the idea prevalent among Irish Americans, (who give much monetary support to the IRA) that the conflict is over Britain's last Irish colony, and that it would end with "Brits Out!"

From 1971 to 1982, the total deaths were as follows: RUC—112, RUCR—58, Army—394, UDR—127. In 1983, the RUC lost nine officers, the RUCR lost nine, the Army had five killed and UDR ten.[35] The figures for a single year, such as 1983, do not indicate the true picture of violence, however. These fatality figures are amazingly low, when one looks at the volume of attacks which are carried out against the security forces. In 1983, there were 155 shooting attacks, 159 attacks with explosives, and 623 gasoline bomb attacks directed against 2,228 members of the forces who were attacked while on duty.[36] Since the mid-1970s, the percentage of civilian fatalities as a part of the total has dropped. From 1972 to 1977, 74 percent of the fatalities from terrorist activity were civilians. In the period of 1978 to 1983, the civilians percentage dropped to 56 percent. Put differently, the fatality totals have fallen dramatically since the savage years of 1972–1976. But while the total deaths have been reduced, the percentage of those killed who came from the police or the military increased from roughly one out of four, to one out of two.

Statistics can never tell the story in human terms. What terrorism and political murder means in those terms is the face of a widowed bride at her constable husband's funeral—a quiet young Scot on a train, telling of the loss of 13 of his fellows during their regimental tour in Londenderry—the long list of 26 or 28 names on a memorial plaque in the Newry RUC station. In addition to the killings, thousands of security force personnel have been wounded. The Royal Victoria Hospital in West Belfast is claimed to have the best emergency room for gunshot victims in the world.[37]

The RUC tries to protect its personnel in the field by using armored vehicles and providing 22-lb. flak jackets for the officers to wear. The Army and UDR are similarly garbed.

Even so, the RUC are targets for snipers, RPG-7[38] attacks, gasoline bomb attacks, and perhaps worst of all, culvert bombs. The latter are virtually impossible to defend against as the bombs, often weighing 500–1000 lbs., are placed in advance, and set off by remote control. On the same day, August 27, 1979, that INLA killed Lord Mountbatten, the IRA struck at Warrenpoint in Northern Ireland. Two remote-control bombs killed eighteen British soldiers in a truck convoy, wounding several others. In early May 1984, in a three-day period, three separate culvert bombs destroyed three armored police vehicles in the Armagh-Newry area of Ulster, killing four officers and wounding three others.[39]

Public disorders, usually Green-fomented, frequently combine gasoline bombing and sniping. Gallon jugs or "sweets-jars" of gasoline are used to set the armored Land-Rovers or "Hotspurs" alight. When the vehicle engines stall due to oxygen deprivation, more "sweets-jars" are thrown against them, thus forcing the occupants to evacuate. A soldier was burned to death in such an incident in Londonderry in April 1984.[40]

In addition to attacks, police and soldiers are exposed to a constant and infinite variety of booby traps. Apparently abandoned weapons, ammo clips, cars, traffic cones, packages, even posters on walls[41] have been used to kill or maim the unwary.

Royal Ulster Constabulary facilities themselves have been attacked by gunfire, RPG-7s, and ingenious homemade mortars. In several instances, IRA technicians made multiple-barreled mortars which were hidden inside high-bodied heavy trucks. Trucks were parked near RUC stations, and the mortars fired off at one or two second intervals by timers.[42]

Nor are security personnel safe when they go off duty. Young soldiers have been set up for murder by girls they had picked up; pubs frequented by off-duty British soldiers have been bombed; and the private cars of soldiers and RUC men have been boobytrapped and bombed. During the May 1984 international fishing tournament in Enniskillen, a bomb planted in their car killed two British soldiers who were fishing contestants, and injured a dozen bystanders.[43] UDR men, in particular, are vulnerable to attack, as they are part-time soldiers who hold down regular jobs during the week. Members of the Ulster Defense Regiment have been killed as they have worked at their jobs as postal workers, school-bus drivers, or delivery men.

Regular RUC officers are all given special training with respect to personal security, and elaborate steps are taken to disguise their occupations from even their neighbors. Stress is placed on constables and their families because of the ever-present threat of attack. Constables told the author of how they reacted to the sound of an unexpected knock at the door, or to a strange car pulling up in front of the house at night.[44]

The IRA obviously looks upon members of the security forces as prime targets. They have taken a sizable toll of RUC and military personnel in their attempt to reunify Ireland by force. That the toll is not higher is due to the training and experience of the Constabulary, the Army, and the UDR. Morale in the RUC remains high, and there is no lack of recruits. From the standpoint of the IRA, every dead police officer is a small victory, and every IRA man killed in return is another martyr for Ireland. Either way, the terrorists get publicity from their attacks on the security forces. It is suggested that publicity is the chief motivation behind attacks of whatever kind on or off duty. It is a classic example of "propaganda of the deed."[45]

The IRA and INLA have carried their murderous violence outside the borders of Northern Ireland to Eire, Belgium, West Germany, and, most of all, to Britain. All have been the scene of bombings and assassinations. In turn, the Protestant Red Hand Commando has planted bombs in Dublin, presumably in retaliation against IRA bombings in the North. Since the early 1970s, the IRA has attempted periodically to bring their war home to the British people. In a few cases, such as Airey Neave, McWhirter, or the 1984 Brighton hotel bombing, there have been specific, highly personalized targets. In these cases, we may assume that a motivation, probably one of power, underlay the attempt. Most of the attacks in Britain have been bombings. The Hyde Park and Regents Park bombings in the summer of 1982, and the Harrod's Department Store Christmas bombing in 1983, were highly publicized incidents. In the two former cases, it has been speculated that these so-called senseless crimes were intended at least in part to raise the morale of IRA men back in Ulster.[46] In the Harrod's case, the IRA leadership disowned responsibility, blaming the bombing on renegades from the IRA. This is believed to be disinformation, deliberately put out by the IRA because of the extremely negative foreign (especially American) reaction to the Harrod's attack.[47] One well-placed RUC member stated that no actions were carried out by the PIRA or INLA without prior sanction from their leadership.[48]

To conclude, a definite change in the pattern of violence can be noted. Sectarian violence, meaning attacks on civilians of

Terroristic Murder in Northern Ireland 355

one religious faction or another, has decreased since the mid-1970s. Largely a thing of the past are large indiscriminately placed bombs. These bombs, used by both factions, were prevalent in 1972 and 1973, and were responsible for causing many deaths and injuries. For example, on March 1, 1972, 43 people were injured in an explosion in Londonderry; in Belfast on March 4, two girls were killed and 130 injured in the bombing of a busy restaurant; March 6 saw 52 people being injured in a Belfast theater bombing, and on March 20, six people, including two constables, were killed and 146 others injured in a downtown Belfast street bombing. A car bomb placed by the IRA in front of the Europa Hotel in Belfast on March 22 injured another 70 people, and on the same day, a 100-lb. bomb injured two boys in Enniskillen.[49] That was one month's total in what was the worst year for sectarian violence and killing.

As random sectarian violence has declined, attacks against the Royal Ulster Constabulary and the other security forces have increased. These attacks have also been characterized by increasing levels of sophistication. Crude bombs have been replaced by bombs fired by remote control or by timers. Street fighting tactics have been perfected by the "Greens," as they have learned to blend snipers in with the gasoline bomb and rock throwers. The terrorists, both Republican and Loyalist, have become more selective in their choice of targets as has been previously indicated. It is hypothesized, but as yet unproven, that the selectivity of targets is related to a motivation on the part of the terrorists. That means that in many cases people are killed because the killers wanted publicity, wanted to force some issue or change of policy (the hunger strikers certainly had a power as well as an attention motive), or desired revenge. Unfortunately, too few terrorist decision-makers are captured for analysts to be able to more closely determine motivation.

Irish Republican terrorists, unlike their less sophisticated Loyalist counterparts, are masters at the propaganda of the deed. They are skilled in playing to the media, and have frequently found sympathetic coverage in the Irish Republic, in the United States, and even in Britain.

Publicity or attention, however, is no guarantor of success. If Britain withdrew from Ireland in 1921, it was largely because Britain people and government tired of the cost of ruling Ireland. Similarly, other contemporary terrorists, especially those with nationalist or irredentist aspirations, have found that publicity, however satisfying, does not bring attainment of the major goal. The South Moluccans, the Palestinians, the Basques, or the Croatians are all peoples who have been on the world stage of terrorist theater. All of these groups have received world attention but are probably no nearer to the achievement of their goals today than they were 10–15 years ago.

The IRA leadership believes that the way to victory is through a war of attrition. Only when the British are worn down psychologically as well as literally, perhaps only the former, will they contemplate cutting the ties with Ulster. The French won the battles in Algeria, as the United States won them in Viet Nam, yet both countries lost the wars due to psychological weariness. The IRA may hope to achieve a similar psychological victory by attacking the security forces through a constant series of small harassments. That is, of course, the place where the analogy breaks down. Namely, the RUC and UDR are composed of Northern Irishmen, mainly Protestant, not Englishmen or Scots. The RUC and UDR, although the IRA sees them as members of the British Crown forces, are themselves composed of long-time residents of Ireland, with their own feelings of national or ethnic solidarity.

Attacks carried out against the RUC and UDR have a power motivation in that these organizations are presumably forced to react in a number of ways, any of which bring benefit to the Provos or INLA. First, the security forces may overreact or retaliate, thus further alienating Irishmen and Britisher alike. Or, almost as good from the Provos' viewpoint, since the RUC and the army are well disciplined and have generally declined to retaliate, the Protestant terror groups, the UVF, UFF, and UDA, may decide to seek revenge.[50]

Second, the will of RUC and UDR members themselves may be weakened. The police organizations themselves will become weaker, losing both new recruits and veterans alike. Like the

Terroristic Murder in Northern Ireland 357

"Wild Geese" of the seventeenth century, or the RIC men of the twentieth, the current membership of the security forces might go seek their fortunes elsewhere or accept the inevitable and capitulate.

From the standpoint of this goal to weaken security force resolution, one may suggest that even more ingenious and lethal means of attack will be developed. A desirable goal for the "Green" terror groups is a demonstration of the ability of the IRA to hit their opponents. The attempted destruction of fortified police stations or several "Warrenpoints" is more than likely to occur.

With respect to combatting terrorism, an analysis of terrorist violence is important. Using motivational or other models to help explain the nature of the attacks may serve as a tool for intelligence. Combined with more conventional intelligence, the analysis may become a predictive tool. If the security forces can begin to more accurately predict categories of people who will become targets, then they can more readily begin to preempt attacks against them. It is the hope and intention of the author that a first step toward the development of a new intelligence tool and a predictor of terrorist murder has been taken.

Notes

1. Kathleen Hoagland. *1000 Years of Irish Poetry* (Old Greenwich, Connecticut: Devin/Adair Co. 6th ed., 1981), pp. 168–170.

2. Ibid., pp. 481–482.

3. Ibid., pp. 751–752.

4. Ibid., pp. 240–250.

5. Ibid., pp. 630–631.

6. Ibid., "O'Patrick Sarsfield," p. 169.

7. "Derry's Walls" taken from Jill and Leon Uris, *Ireland: A Terrible Beauty* (London: Corgie Books, 1977), p. 180.

8. The Royal Ulster Constabulary, *Chief Constable's Report, 1983* (Belfast: 1984), p. 47.

9. Padraig O'Malley, *The Uncivil Wars: Ireland Today* (Boston: Houghton Mifflin Co., 1983), p. 11.

10. *Chief Constable's Report, 1983,* p. 48.

11. Harold Mosak and Rudolf Dreikurs, "Adlerian Psycho-

therapy," In Raymond Corsin, ed. *Current Psychotherapics* (Itaska, Illinois: F. E. Peacock, Pub. 1983).

12. Robert Pockrass and William Lewinski, *Profiling for Effective Negotiation Strategies in Hostage Situations*. Paper presented at Academy of Criminal Justice Sciences, Louisville, Kentucky, San Antonio, Texas, March 25, 1982.

13. Brian Jenkins, *Embassies Under Siege* (Santa Monica, CA: Rand Corporation, Jan. 1981), p. 34.

14. "Tehran Hijacking: A Story that Requires a Faith in Miracles," *Minneapolis Tribune*, December 16, 1984.

15. Northern Ireland Civil Rights Association, *We Shall Overcome: The History of the Struggle for Civil Rights in No. Ireland 1968–1978*. (Belfast: NICRA, 1978), p. 17.

16. Bernadette Devlin, *The Price of My Soul* (London: Pan Books, 1969).

17. Interview with Assistant Chief Constable David, April 22, 1984. Belfast. (The names of RUC officers other than that of the Chief Constable have been changed to protect them from being identified and possibly attacked.)

18. Interview with Chief Inspector Stanley, Operational Training Unit. Belfast, April 17, 1984.

19. Bernard MacLaverty, *Cal*, Engima Productions. Ireland. Distributed in the U.S. by Warner Brothers, 1984.

20. RUC Incident Log, April 11, 1984. RUC HQ Belfast.

21. *Chief Constable's Report, 1983*, Table 6.

22. Interviews with Chief Inspector Wheeler, and others at J Division, April 1984.

23. Alfred McClunge Lee, *Terrorism in Northern Ireland* (New York: General Hall Inc.), pp. 160–161.

24. Interviews with Superintendent Donnelly and others, N Division. April 1984.

25. Tom Bowden, *Breakdown of Public Security* (London: Sage, 1977).

26. Robin Evelegh, *Peace Keeping In a Democratic Society: The Lessons of Northern Ireland* (London: Hurst, 1978).

27. *60 Minutes*, CBS Television. December 18, 1983.

28. RUC Incident Log April 12, 1984, RUC HQ Belfast.

29. Belfast *Telegraph*, April 13, 1984.

30. BBC Television News. April 28, 1984.

31. Richard Kobetz and H. H. A. Cooper, *Target Terrorism* (Gaithersburg, Maryland: International Assn. of Chiefs of Police, 1978).

Terroristic Murder in Northern Ireland 359

32. William Hart, "Waging Peace in Northern Ireland," *Police,* May 1980, p. 24.

33. Interview with Inspector O'Brien, CID. Belfast.

34. Carlos Marighella, *Minimanual of the Urban Guerrilla* (São Paulo, Brazil, 1969). This monograph has been reprinted in a number of books and has been found among documents taken from terrorists all over the world.

35. *Chief Constable's Report, 1983.* Table 6.

36. Ibid., Table 5.

37. Interview with Superintendent McClellen, April 16, 1984.

38. Soviet-made antitank rockets.

39. News Reports, BBC-Belfast, RTE-Dublin, Week of May 1–8, 1984.

40. RUC Incident Log, April 22, 1984, RUC HQ Belfast.

41. Technical Services Unit, Lisnasharragh RUC, Belfast, April 13, 1984.

42. Interviews with Inspector Vickers, RUC HQ Belfast, April 13, 1984, and visit to Woodbourne RUC, Belfast.

43. BBC-Belfast Television News, RTE-Dublin TV news.

44. Interview with ACC David, April 29, 1984. Belfast.

45. Walter Laqueur, *Terrorism* (Boston: Little Brown & Co., 1977).

46. Interview, Chief Inspector Castle. British Police Staff College, August 1982. Bramshill, England.

47. Interviews, Criminal Investigation Division, RUC HQ Belfast.

48. Interview, Superintendent O'Brien, RUC HQ Belfast, April 15, 1984.

49. Edward F. Mickolus, *Transnational terrorism: A Chronology of Events, 1968–1979* (Westport Connecticut: Greenwood Press, 1980), pp. 302–307.

50. O'Malley, *The Uncivil Wars,* pp. 289–290.

[13]

BRIT. J. CRIMINOL. Vol. 23 No. 4 OCTOBER 1983

CRIMINAL STATISTICS AND STATISTICS ON SECURITY IN NORTHERN IRELAND

ROBERT J. SPJUT (*Canterbury*)*

THE Northern Ireland Office and the Royal Ulster Constabulary have published a vast amount of data on " terrorism " in the province. The former publishes quarterly and semi-annual *Statistics on Security* and, in ministerial replies to questions in the House of Commons and the Report of the Committee chaired by Lord Gardiner, it has supplied considerable information on terrorism. The Reports of the Chief Constable of the Royal Ulster Constabulary (hereafter called Chief Constable's Reports) since 1969 contain statistics on criminal offences and " public order ", including terrorism. No effort has been made to explain what data have been published or will and will not be published in the future.

This article describes the information which has been published by the two above sources, both in the periodically published *Statistics on Security* and Chief Constable's reports and in replies to questions in the House of Commons. The article also indicates what data governments have refused to publish. Finally, it examines, in the light of available information, the criteria which are probably used for classification of statistics on terrorism and crime. The article does not examine the problems of hidden crime nor does it analyse the causes of terrorism or crime in the province.

Terrorism and Criminal Offences

Although " terrorism " is now part of the everyday vocabulary of the press and media, the law provides it with a particular meaning in the United Kingdom. The term is used in the Northern Ireland (Emergency Provisions) Act, 1978, which provides " emergency " legislation in the province, and the Prevention of Terrorism (Temporary Provisions) Act 1976, which applies to the whole of the country. It means: " the use of violence for political ends and includes any use of violence for the purpose of putting the public or any section of the public in fear ". Acts of terrorism may, or may not, amount to a specific offence, but there is no independent crime of " terrorism ". The above definition of terrorism forms part of a complex of legal rules, the consequences of which include the exercise of extraordinary powers of arrest, detention, interrogation and exclusion.

The classification of statistics on terrorism only partly reflects the quite distinct category of " terrorism " in law. Table 1 presents an overview of statistical data on terrorism and related criminality in Northern Ireland

* Faculty of Social Sciences, Darwin College, University of Kent at Canterbury.

The writer is indebted to the Northern Ireland Office, Royal Ulster Constabulary, Director of Public Prosecutions for Northern Ireland and Attorney-General for information which has been used to confirm inferences drawn in the text of the article. He is grateful also for their permission to use this information and to acknowledge the source. Professors Kevin Boyle and Claire Palley and Dr. Paddy Hillyard made invaluable comments on an earlier draft of this article, though the errors and opinions are the responsibility of the author.

CRIMINAL STATISTICS ON SECURITY IN NORTHERN IRELAND

TABLE I

Summary of Statistical Information Published on Terrorism in Northern Ireland

| | Areas for which Data are Provided | | |
	Northern Ireland	Police Division	Belfast, Londonderry and Other
ATTACKS ON PERSONS			
Deaths	1968–*	–	–
Victims			
Security forces	1968–*	1970–76	1973–76
Civilians	1968–*	–	1973–76
Terrorists	1970–75, 1977	–	–
Age	1970–78**	–	–
Sex	1970–78**	–	–
Parties responsible			
Age	1975, 1978–80	–	–
Security forces	1970–78	–	–
Terrorists	1979–81	–	–
Unlawful killings			
Murders	1969–78	1969–75**	–
Manslaughters	1969–78	–	–
Shootings			
Punishment shootings	1973–80	1973–75	1973–77
Punishment shootings—victims' sex	–	1973–75	–
All shootings	1970–*	–	1973–76
Assassinations	1968–80*	–	1973–76
Injuries	1968–*	–	–
Intimidation	1968–	–	–
Armed robberies	1970–	–	–
ATTACKS ON PROPERTY			
Explosions	1970–*	–	1973–76
Defused bombs	1970–*	–	–
Rocket attacks	–	–	1973–75
Mortar attacks	–	–	1973–75
Malicious fires	1970–*	–	–
Hijackings	–	1979–	–

Notes: 1. Sources are listed in Appendix 1.
    2. * denotes figures are published on quarterly basis.
    3. ** denotes that a comment upon the figures is included in Appendix 1.
    4. Figures published for Northern Ireland are for the province as a whole; for police divisions the figures are published for each division. A list of these divisions is provided in Appendix 2. Figures are also aggregated into three areas: Belfast, Londonderry and other.

since 1969. " Attacks on persons " are classified as deaths connected with the security situation and unlawful killings connected with the security situation. Not all deaths so connected are unlawful killings (*e.g.*, a terrorist kills himself while preparing a bomb) and not all unlawful killings are connected with the security situation; hence two distinct categories are required. Figures for such headings as deaths indicate in a crude way terrorism in the province.

Another feature of classifications arises from the nature of armed combat in a modern, urban guerilla insurgency, especially the use of bombings and assassinations. The data published in the *Statistics on Security* and Chief Constable's reports include shootings and assassinations and divide victims according to civilian or security-force status. Similarly, attacks on property

ROBERT J. SPJUT

are classified as " explosions " and " defused bombs ", rather than according to such criminal offences as " causing explosion " or " placing explosives " respectively. The reason, this writer suggests, is that compilers of statistics and those Members of Parliament who solicit them perceive shootings and explosions as the two most significant indicators of armed combat, both among the various factions and between the Republican paramilitary groups and the security forces. Deaths, rather than homicides, are also a crude, aggregate indicator of armed insurgency, especially the deaths of members of the security forces.

Table 1 indicates that many of the data published concern deaths and unlawful killings connected with terrorism. In view of its generally perceived significance as an indicator of terrorism, this article will concentrate upon the available data concerning such categories.

Deaths and Unlawful Killings

The classification of deaths in Northern Ireland involves a double judgment by compilers in the N.I.O and R.U.C. First, there is a determination that there is some connection between the event and the security situation; if so, then it is accordingly classified. Second, there is an assessment that such deaths are unlawful killings connected with the security situation in Northern Ireland.

We will later examine in detail the problem of classifying unlawful killings as connected or unconnected with terrorism, but for the moment concern ourselves with the classification of deaths. The *Chief Constable's Report 1970* briefly describes the circumstances of every violent death in the province, whether or not it was connected with the security situation, and was the last such report to do so. Presumably, the dramatic rise in deaths in 1971 and following years precluded similar detailed explanation of all the deaths. There were seven non-criminal deaths connected with the security situation: four people were killed while engaged in attacks on the security forces, two while planting explosives and another during an Orange procession. The classification of this last death would indicate that the compilers of statistics adopt a wide view of what is related to the security situation and do not focus narrowly on acts of terrorism.

On the other hand, since 1969 there have been four deaths of persons who were in police custody. Three of these persons were held in detention under " ordinary " powers, one on drugs charges, another for disorderly behaviour and the third for drunkenness. (H.C. Deb., Vol. 978, col. *383*, (February 8, 1980)). The fourth, Brian Maguire, was detained under emergency powers at Castlereagh barracks, where he hanged himself. An examination of the figures for 1978, the year of Maguire's death, reveals that there were 71 unlawful killings and 10 other deaths connected with the security situation; all 10 other deaths are due to measures taken by the security forces during anti-terrorist operations. Though Maguire was in custody under emergency powers, his death is not classified as connected with the security situation. An inference might be that the compilers of the

CRIMINAL STATISTICS ON SECURITY IN NORTHERN IRELAND

TABLE 2

Unlawful killings and other deaths connected with security situation in Nortern Ireland 1969–1980

	1969	1970	1971	1972	1973	1974	1975	1976	1977	1978	1979	1980
Unlawful killings connected with security situation[1]	9	15	121	366	202	196	224	257	94	71	109	NA
Other deaths connected with security situation	4	10	53	102	48	20	23	40	18	10	4	NA
Totals[2]	13	25	174	468	250	216	247	297	112	81	113	76

Notes: (1) Figures for "unlawful killings" 1969–78 published at H.C. Deb., Vol. 969, cols. 223–224 (June 27, 1979).
(2) Figures are published in *Statistics on Security* and *Chief Constable's Report 1960*.

ROBERT J. SPJUT

statistics look to whether the victim was, at the time of his or her death, concerned in the civil disturbances.

This criterion also appears to apply to the classification of unlawful killings as connected with the security situation. Table 3 presents the available data for 1969–80. There is no separate *legal* category of murder or manslaughter " connected with the security situation ". Under the Northern Ireland (Emergency Provisions) Act 1978, murder and man-slaughter are " scheduled offences " which means that these offences are tried by a judge sitting without a jury, though the Attorney General may by certification de-schedule murder or manslaughter. (Appendix 3 provides a list of scheduled offences.) As offences are not necessarily cleared in the year in which they are committed, a person may be charged in years after the offence. As a result, certification by the Attorney-General will occur after murders and manslaughters have been classified as such and categorised as connected or unconnected with the security situation. The Chief Constable's reports for the years 1970–72, prior to the original Northern Ireland (Emergency Provisions) Act 1973 coming into force, classified murders as connected with the security situation. The *statistical* classification of unlawful killings as " unconnected " or " connected with the security situation " is not affected by the Attorney General's certification procedure, being governed solely by the criteria adopted by the N.I.O. and R.U.C. compilers of statistics.

The Chief Constable's reports for 1970 and 1971 include summary accounts of the circumstances of murders which were classified as having no connection with the security situation. It is difficult to draw inferences from the very brief descriptions contained in the reports, but some tentative observations are offered. In one case in 1970 and another in 1971, the perpetrator successfully pleaded not guilty by reason of insanity; in two other incidents in 1970 and three in 1971 the victims were women. Of one murder in 1970, of a 69-year-old woman, the Report (p. 34) says, " No political or sectarian motives were involved ". The implication is that the compilers of the statistics examined the circumstances surrounding the death of this woman to see if there was evidence from which they might infer that the perpetrators were, in some way, motivated by political or sectarian reasons. If there is no such evidence, then the killing is classified as not connected with the security situation.

Obviously, the task of classifying unlawful killings as " political or sectarian " or " normal " is not easy and on at least two occasions ministers have indicated their appreciation of this. Merlyn Rees, while Secretary of State for Northern Ireland (hereafter called Northern Ireland Secretary), went so far as to say that the motives of murderers could not be assessed so as to determine whether they were " politically motivated ". (H.C. Deb., 899, col. *835* (November 12, 1975); see also H.C. Deb., Vol. 877, col. 1802 (July 25, 1975)). Nevertheless, in so far as the *Statistics on Security* include unlawful killings in the category of " deaths connected with the security situation ", it would appear that the N.I.O. regularly assesses the political and sectarian motivation of killers. The text of the Chief Constable's reports

CRIMINAL STATISTICS ON SECURITY IN NORTHERN IRELAND

TABLE 3

Unlawful killings in Northern Ireland 1969–1980

(First figure refers to all unlawful killings and figure in brackets to murders only)

	1969	1970	1971	1972	1973	1974	1975	1976	1977	1978	1979	1980
Unlawful killings unconnected with security situation	4(4)	5(5)	23(6)	27(12)	13(5)	17(9)	23(14)	34(23)	27(23)	14(12)	27(20)	NA(19)
Unlawful killings connected with security situation	9(1)	15(9)	121(117)	366(364)	202(195)	196(194)	224(224)	257(257)	94(93)	71(70)	109(108)	NA(66)
Totals	13(5)	20(14)	144(123)	393(376)	215(200)	213(205)	247(238)	291(280)	121(116)	85(82)	136(128)	93(85)

Notes: (1) Figures for unlawful killings unconnected with the security situation 1969–78 are published at H.C. Deb, Vol 969, cols. *223–234* (June 27, 1979).

(2) Figures for murder and manslaughters unconnected with the security for 1979 are published in *Chief Constable's Report 1979*, p. 5.

(3) Figures for murders unconnected with security situation in 1970–79 are published in *Chief Constable's Reports*: 1970 (p. 33), 1971 (p. 30), 1972 p. 29), 1973 (p. 3), 1974 and 1975 (1975, ch. 1, p. 1), 1976 (p. 2), 1977 (p. 1), 1978 (p. 18) and 1979 (p. 5). Figures for murders unconnected with the security situation for 1974–78 are also published at H.C. Deb, Vol. 967, col. *310* (May 25, 1979). *The Chief Constable's Reports 1974,* 1977 and 1978 report 11, 15 and 11 murders respectively for each year, whereas the N.I.O reports 9, 23 and 12 respectively. The figures in the Tables are these published by the N.I.O.

(4) Figures for murders connected with the security situation for 1970 are published in the *Chief Constable's Report 1970* (p. 33), for 1972 in the Report 1972 (p. 29), for 1974–75 at H.C. Deb, Vol. 908, col. *470–471* (March 3, 1976) and for 1976 at H.C. Deb, Vol. 925, cols. *664–665* February 8. 1977.)

(5) Figures for murders and manslaughters connected with the security situation are calculated by deducting those reported as unconnected from the total of such offences reported in the "Indictable Offences known and cleared" in Chief Constable's reports 1969–80. The totals in the table are taken from these tables in the Chief Constable's reports 1969–80. The calculation for 1970 is nine murders connected with the security situation whereas the *Chief Constable's Report 1970* p. 33) reports 11 such murders.

(6) Figures for 1980 are calculated from murders perpetrated by paramilitary factions reported in *Chief Constable's Report 1980*, Appendix 4, Table 1, Figures supplied by the Northern Ireland Office are nine unconnected murders for 1980.

ROBERT J. SPJUT

suggests that, if there is evidence which points to reasons which are not political or sectarian or if there is no evidence from which to infer such motives, then the killing is not classified as connected with the security situation.

Political and Sectarian Murders

Two points in Table 3 stand out even upon superficial examination. First, there seems to have been a remarkable increase since 1969 in murders unconnected with the security situation. An explanation of this development lies outside the scope of this article. Second, a high proportion of the unlawful killings connected with the security situation are classified as murders. This point warrants consideration here.

The legal definition of murder in Northern Ireland is substantially similar to that in England and Wales. A killing is a murder only if the prosecution can prove beyond a reasonable doubt that the act which resulted in death was " aimed at someone " and the accused must have known there was a serious risk of death or grievous bodily harm to the victim. It is not enough that an individual takes a risk and recklessly exposes others to loss of life or serious harm; he must actually appreciate such risks before he can be liable for murder. This definition is the basis for classification of unlawful killings into murder and manslaughter.

Although neither the law nor the criminal statistics divide unlawful killings into assassinations and other homicides, the distinction will usefully illustrate the problem of classifying all " political and sectarian " killings as murders. For the years 1976–80 the *Statistics on Security* include separate figures for " sectarian and interfactional *assassinations* "—not to be confused with " political and sectarian " *killings*. The terms " sectarian and inter-factional " were never defined and it was not until 1979 that a Member of Parliament asked for clarification. Still, the Northern Ireland Secretary's reply did not offer much in the way of clarity and added " intra-factional " to the above two terms (H.C. Deb., Vol. 961, col. *163*, (January 24, 1979)). For the rest of that year the separate figures were entitled " sectarian, inter-factional and intra-factional ", but since then these separate figures are no longer provided. The implications of the separate figures are that data on killings are divided into " subversive " on one hand and " sectarian, inter-factional and intra-factional "; on the other they are also divided into " assassinations " and other killings. It is the combination of the two categories that results in what appears to be a single classification of " sectarian, inter-factional and intra-factional assassinations ".

The adjectives " sectarian, inter-factional and intra-factional " suggest that N.I.O. and R.U.C. compilers of statistics assess these motives for killings as apart from " subversive "; the evidence indicates otherwise. The *Chief Constable's Report 1974* explains the deaths of civilians:

Gunshot wounds	112
Explosions	28
Assaults	4
Total civilians killed	144

364

CRIMINAL STATISTICS ON SECURITY IN NORTHERN IRELAND

Of the 112 civilians who died by gunshot wounds, the following classification is possible:

Killed by security forces in anti-terrorist operations	13
Primary targets of terrorist attacks	92
Not primary targets of terrorist attacks	7
Total civilians killed by gunshot wounds	112

There are 93, 94 and 95 reported sectarian assassinations for that year, the first figure provided by the R.U.C. and the two latter by the N.I.O. (see Table 4). One possible inference is that the implicit division between " subversive " and " sectarian, inter-factional and intra-factional " turns on whether the victim is a civilian or member of the security forces. The other implicit classification, " assassination ", depends upon whether the victim was the primary target of a shooting.

Further support for the writer's inferences may be found in the *Chief Constable's Report 1979* which reports 33 " civilian assassinations ", though it does not use the term " sectarian ". Interestingly the *Statistics on Security* also reports 33 " sectarian and inter-factional assassinations " for that year. Both the R.U.C. and N.I.O. statistics include the killings of nine prison officers by the Provisional Irish Republican Army (hereafter PIRA) though such were part of its campaign against the security establishment. An authoritative source informed the writer that the killings were included in the R.U.C. figures for " civilian " assassinations because the officers were civilians. The N.I.O. explained to the writer that the officers were included in the figures for " sectarian and inter-factional assassinations " because they were civilians. It would appear that the controlling criterion is not sectarian or subversive motives, but the fact that a civilian is a primary target for a shooting.

Now, if the above inferences are correct, it is possible to divide the unlawful killing of civilians into assassinations and other killings. The figures for " assassinations " in Table 4 are those for " sectarian, inter-factional and intra-factional " provided by the N.I.O. As they are victims of acts clearly " aimed at someone " and intended to kill them, they are likely to be classified among the murders in the criminal statistics published in the Chief Constable's Report and by the N.I.O. The remaining figures, with few exceptions, refer to deaths due to explosions and assaults and present difficulties for compilers of statistics.

In particular, deaths caused by explosions cannot be *ipso facto* classified as murderers because the persons concerned in the incident may desire only to cause damage to property and not to harm anyone; this is arguably the case where a warning is given. In one case, *R.* v. *McFeely*, two armed robbers entered a public bar, stole the contents of the till and, upon leaving, told the people that there was a bomb " behind the counter " and that they had 10 minutes to get out. The police arrived, searched the bar but did not find the bomb. About one and one-half hours later, while a police officer was examining a footprint, the bomb exploded, killing the police

ROBERT J. SPJUT

TABLE 4

Political and sectarian killings of civilians in Northern Ireland 1969–79

	1969	1970	1971	1972	1973	1974	1975	1976	1977	1978	1979
Civilian assassinations	1	4	6	121	87	94	143	121	42	33	27
Other unlawful civilian killings	8	9	56	99	36	52	50	84	9	7	NA
Total unlawful killing of civilians	9	13	62	220	123	146	193	205	51	40	NA

Notes: 1. Sources for 1969–75 are H.C. Deb, Vol. 903, cols. *81–82* (January 12, 1976); for 1976–79 the *Statistics on Security.*

2. The figures for 1972, 1974 and 1975 are 122, 95 and 144 respectively in the *Statistics on Security.*

3. The category " civilian assassinations " is explained in the text. The figures are derived from " sectarian, inter-factional and intra-factional assassinations " in the above sources.

4. The figures for " other unlawful civilian killings " are calculated by deducting " civilian assassinations " from the total unlawful killing of civilians.

366

CRIMINAL STATISTICS ON SECURITY IN NORTHERN IRELAND

officer. McFeely, who drove the second escape car, was charged with murder, but the Lord Chief Justice, who tried the case, concluded that serious personal injury was not probable because a clear and specific warning had been given to the occupants of the bar; they were likely to escape. He further found that McFeely was not likely to have contemplated that any such injury was probable.

In another case, *R.* v. *Louden*, the accused drove a van containing a bomb between 50 and 100 pounds in weight into a loading-bay of a Belfast city centre premises and then ran off. A warning was sounded over the tannoy system to the persons in the premises to evacuate, but shortly afterwards another message was given that the bomb was in another building. The bomb exploded seven minutes later, killing a person in the room above the loading bay. The judge who tried Louden said that *McFeely* was different in that a few people in a small country pub could get clear of the premises, whereas only a few people were aware of the bomb in a large city premises. The risk of tragedy is greater in such circumstances, especially where there is pressure " to get the wheels of business turning again ". Louden was convicted of murder.

If one examines the high proportion of killings classified as murder in the criminal statistics, it will be apparent that those who compile them do not attempt a refined assessment of the various factors, for example, the clarity and sufficiency of the warning. If anything, the statistics suggest that nearly all such killings are classified as murders. Although the outcome of a criminal trial is hardly a measure by which to assess the accuracy of criminal statistics, the figures in Appendix 3 suggest that manslaughter figures more significantly than indicated by the statistics. No firm conclusions may be drawn, but there is good reason to suggest that the criminal statistics present an incidence of murder higher than may, strictly speaking, be warranted.

The point made by this writer should not be confused with the position recently adopted by the Northern Ireland Secretary. In replies to questions in the House of Commons in 1976 and 1977, ministers provided figures for the number of murders connected with the security situation in 1974–76. Since 1979, it would appear that this Government has changed its policy and, while data on " unlawful killings " connected with the security situation are provided, the Northern Ireland Secretary has declined to provide separate figures for murder and manslaughter because the figures are not categorised until shortly before proceedings are initiated in court. (H.C. Deb., Vol. 969, cols. *223–224*, (June 27, 1979); Vol. 983, col. *270* (April 24, 1980)). The position adopted by this writer is that certain killings, notably assassinations, can be categorised as murders, whereas bombings, in view of the law relating to " intent ", cannot be easily classified. The N.I.O. and the R.U.C. ought not to abandon the distinction nor apply a criterion which appears to ignore such relevant factors as the clarity and sufficiency of the warning that an explosion is about to occur.

Responsible Parties and Victims

Although the present conflict in Northern Ireland includes an insurgency,

ROBERT J. SPJUT

spearheaded by the P.I.R.A., against the government, there is also inter-communal guerilla warfare; an understanding of the conflict requires some effort to classify the above deaths and unlawful killings according to those responsible and the victims' involvement in terrorism. One writer, Michael McKeown (1973, p. 8), has attempted such a classification, based principally upon his own knowledge of the killings in the province, and the figures in Table 5 summarise his findings.

TABLE 5

Category of victims and force responsible
for deaths in Northern Ireland, October 1968–August 1973

Force responsible	Category of Victims				
	Security forces	Combatants		Total	Non-combatants
		Republicans	Loyalists		
Security forces	4	48	6	58	93
Republican	264	64	5	333	138
Loyalist	6	5	5	16	177
Total	274	117	16	407	408

Neither the N.I.O. nor the R.U.C. has published a similar account and it seems unlikely that they will. In 1974, Merlyn Rees, then Northern Ireland Secretary, replied to a written question that Loyalists were responsible for the " murders " of two soldiers. (H.C. Deb., Vol. 872, col. *386* (April 29, 1974)). Since then successive governments have declined to publish data that attribute responsibility for killings to either named paramilitary bodies or generally to Loyalist and Republican organisations. (H.C. Deb., Vol. 902, col. *797* (December 19, 1975); Vol. 935, col. *201* (July 13, 1977); Vol. 944, col. *92* (February 13, 1978); Vol. 982, col. *504* (April 14, 1980); Vol. 983, col. *270* (April 24, 1980); Vol. 4, col. *45* (May 5, 1981)). The R.U.C., on the other hand, published in the 1980 and 1981 Chief Constable's reports figures that attribute responsibility for murders and attempted murders to Loyalists and Republicans. A reliable source informed the writer that these figures are not available for the years before 1979. The N.I.O. has not made available what should be regarded as data essential to an informed public opinion on the conflict: the number of deaths attributed to the security forces, Loyalists and Republicans.

There are only limited data on the victims of killings in the province. There are no published data on the sex or age of victims. A Northern Ireland Minister, in reply to an oral question in 1975, supplied figures for the numbers of Catholic and Protestant victims of sectarian murders (H.C. Deb., Vol. 877, col. *1802* (July 25, 1975)), but ministers have since then declined to publish these data on grounds that such a breakdown is contrary to the public interest. (H.C. Deb., Vol. 903, col. *82* (January 12, 1976); Vol. 919, col. *444* (November 15, 1976); Vol. 919, cols. *939–40* (November 22, 1976)). The Chief Constable's reports do not classify data on unlawful killings according to the victims' religious affiliation, though they do for victims of intimidation.

CRIMINAL STATISTICS ON SECURITY IN NORTHERN IRELAND

The N.I.O. has published figures for the number of persons killed by the security forces during anti-terrorist operations in the province. These are included in Table 6. If one of two assumptions is valid then it is possible to categorise deaths according to responsible parties: security forces, terrorists and other. The first assumption is that none of the killings of civilians by the security forces during anti-terrorist operations has been classified by the R.U.C. as either murder or manslaughter. This writer was able to obtain information from an authoritative source that the figures for " Indictable offences known and cleared " in the 1973, 1974 and 1979 Chief Constable's reports each include one killing by members of the security forces. On the basis of this information the writer asked the Director of Public Prosecutions in Northern Ireland for a list of all killings by the security forces which had resulted in criminal proceedings, but this was refused on grounds that publication was contrary to the public interest. The writer also requested this information from the Attorney-General, but did not even receive an acknowledgement of the request. Finally, the writer asked the R.U.C. for the number of killings by the security forces which had been categorised in their tables as " Indictable offences known and cleared ", but this request was refused on the grounds that it is not Force policy to " enter into any dialogue or correspondence in relation to the published statistics, nor, as an operational Force, are we able to divert staff to do research to enable us to answer queries ". While we know that at least three such killings are classified as either murder or manslaughter, we cannot ascertain how many are so categorised.

The other assumption is that the figures for killings by the security forces during anti-terrorist operations do not include killings which are classified

TABLE 6

Lawful and unlawful deaths connected with the security situation and caused by security forces and terrorists in Northern Ireland 1970–79

Party responsible	1970	1971	1972	1973	1974	1975	1976	1977	1978	1979
Security forces										
Lawful	5	42	65	30	12	6	13	7	10	NA
Unlawful	—	—	2	1	1	—	—	—	—	1
Total	5	42	67	31	13	6	13	7	10	NA
Terrorists										
Lawful	5	11	37	18	8	17	27	11	0	NA
Unlawful	15	121	364	201	195	224	257	94	71	108
Total 3	20	132	401	219	203	241	284	105	71	NA

Notes: 1. Figures for total killings by security forces published at H.C. Deb., Vol. 968, col. 525 June 19, 1979). To these figures the writer has added two for 1972 on the assumption that the killings of Michael Naan and Andrew Murray are not included in the published figures.

2. Figures for unlawful killings by the security forces are based on the writer's hypotheses confirmed by an authoritative source which requested that it should not be acknowledged.

3. Figures for unlawful killings by civilians are calculated by deducting the known unlawful killings by security forces from the total unlawful killings connected with the security forces from the total unlawful killings connected with the security situation in Table 3.

4. Figures for lawful killings by civilians are calculated by deducting lawful killings by the security forces from " other deaths connected with the security situation " in Table 2.

ROBERT J. SPJUT

as unlawful by the R.U.C. The murders of Andrew Murray and Michael Naan in October 1972 were initially reported by the press and police as sectarian killings in view of their brutal nature, though later it was learned that soldiers had in fact killed both (Dillon and Lehane, 1973, p. 139; Deutsch and Magowan, 1974, Vol. 2, p. 231). As a result two soldiers were convicted of murder. The writer asked the N.I.O. whether the killing of Murray had been classified along with other killings of civilians by the security forces, but they replied that this information was unavailable. There is no information available to determine the validity of this second assumption.

Both the R.U.C. and N.I.O. classify data for deaths and injuries into civilians and security forces and the latter is sub-divided into " Army/ U.D.R." and " R.U.C./R.U.C. ' R ' ", The Chief Constables's reports provide separate figures for the Army, U.D.R. (Ulster Defence Regiment), R.U.C. and R.U.C. ' R ' (Royal Ulster Constabulary " Reserve "). As already noted, no breakdown is provided for religious affiliation of the victims of deaths and injuries. There are, however, limited data on deaths of " terrorists ": the Statistics on Violence in the Gardiner Report provides figures for 1971 to November 1974 and the Chief Constable's reports for 1973, 1974, 1975 and 1977 supply figures for those years. The available data are presented in Table 7.

The figures for " terrorists " in Table 7 must be read with considerable caution. On one hand, the figures for 1971 include Seamus Cusak and Desmond Beattie, shot in Londonderry on July 8, 1971 in circumstances alleged by the army to show that both men were committing offences; but the fact that compensation was later awarded to their relatives suggests that these allegations could not be proved. The figures for 1972 include all 13 persons killed by the security forces on January 30, 1972, popularly known as " Bloody Sunday ". The Widgery Tribunal which examined the events of January 30, 1972 concluded that two of the 13 deceased may have handled a firearm prior to their deaths (paras. 76, 82), and that there was no evidence that the other eleven were concerned in a terrorist-type offence. Compensation was awarded to the relatives of all 13 victims. The N.I.O., which admits the categorisation of these 15 deaths as " terrorists ", explained to the writer that these were " in error ". The writer also asked the N.I.O. how many other persons in respect of whose deaths compensation had been paid had been categorised as " terrorists " in the Statistics on Violence. The N.I.O. replied that this information is unavailable. The writer has been able to ascertain from a reliable source that similar errors have not been made in respect of the figures contained in the R.U.C. reports.

On the other hand, the *Chief Constable's Report 1977* explains that six of the " terrorists " were justifiably shot by the security forces and four others died during a premature explosion. In all, seven persons were shot by the security forces that year, and the one victim whose death is excluded from the categorisation of " terrorist " was found to have been wholly unconcerned in terrorism. Although no definite inference can be drawn, it appears that the criterion for categorising a death as that of a " terrorist "

CRIMINAL STATISTICS ON SECURITY IN NORTHERN IRELAND

TABLE 7

Victims of deaths connected with security situation in Northern Ireland

	1971	1972	1973	1974	1975	1976	1977	1978	1979	1980	1981
Security Forces											
RUC/RUC "R"	11	17	13	15	11	23	14	10	14	9	21
Army/UDR	48	129	66	35	20	29	29	21	48	16	23
Total	59	146	79	50	31	52	43	31	62	25	44
Civilians											
Terrorists	48	50	43/55	22	20	—	10	—	—	—	—
Non-combatants	67	272	128/116	144	196	—	59	—	—	—	—
Total	115	322	171	166	216	245	69	50	51	50	57

Notes: 1. Sources for security forces and total civilians is *Statistics on Security*.

2. Source for "terrorists" 1971–73 is Statistics on Violence, Gardiner Report.

3. Sources for "terrorists" 1973–75, 1977 are *Chief Constable's Reports 1973–1977*.

4. The *Chief Constable's Report 1973* reports 55 terrorists killed, whereas the Gardiner Report reports 43. The calculations for non-combatants are accordingly affected.

ROBERT J. SPJUT

TABLE 8

Deaths of terrorists compared with deaths other than unlawful killings of civilians connected with security situation 1971–1977

	Civilian deaths by security forces	Civilian deaths other than by security forces or unlawful killing	Total civilian deaths other than unlawful killing	Terrorists
1971	42	11	53	48[1]
1972	66	36	102	80[1]
1973	31	17	48	43^1/55[2]
1974	13	7	20	22[3]
1975	6	17	23	20[4]
1976	13	27	40	NA
1977	7	11	18	10[5]

Notes: (1) Gardiner Report, Statistics on Violence, Appendix B.
     (2) *Chief Constable's Report 1973*, p. 1.
     (3) *Chief Constable's Report 1974*, p. 1.
     (4) *Chief Constable's Report 1975*, p. 1.
     (5) *Chief Constable's Report 1977*, p. 1.
     (6) NA = not available.

depends upon whether the victim at the time was in some way concerned in a terrorist-type offence. If this is so, the approach adopted by the R.U.C. is similar to that of the Northern Ireland Secretary, who declines to publish figures on the number of terrorists killed but supplies separate figures on persons killed while committing a terrorist-type offence. (H.C. Deb., Vol. 903, col. *86* (January 12, 1976); Vol. 982, col. *504* (April 14, 1980)). The figures for " terrorists " in the Statistics on Violence and Chief Constable's reports do not refer to all combatants—members of paramilitary bodies— but to those killed by the security forces or themselves while committing an offence (see Table 8). If this is correct, then the division in Table 7, adopted with modifications from the Statistics on Violence, is misleading because it suggests that " civilians " are unconcerned with terrorism. A more accurate statement is quite simply that no division of " civilians " into combatants and non-combatants is possible on the basis of information surrounding the circumstances of deaths of civilians.

The information contained in Tables 6 and 7 may be combined in order to indicate the extent to which terrorists and the security forces are responsible for the deaths of civilians and security forces. These data are supplied in Table 9. They provide, at least, a general and crude picture of the extent to which terrorism is directed against the security forces and civilians in the province. Table 9 rests upon the same assumptions as Table 6, namely that none of the killings by the security forces have been classified by the R.U.C. as indictable offences or those which have been are excluded from the category of killings by the security forces during anti-terrorist operations. Additionally, Table 9 assumes that there have been two killings of members of the security forces by other security forces. This assumption is incompatible with the figures published in Table 5 but is here made because these are the only published official figures. Although there is no information available to test these assumptions, Tables 6 and 7 provide a

CRIMINAL STATISTICS ON SECURITY IN NORTHERN IRELAND

TABLE 9

Responsibility for killing civilians and the security forces in Northern Ireland 1971–78

Party Responsible Victim	1971	1972	1973	1974	1975	1976	1977	1978
Security forces								
Security forces	—	—	—	2	—	—	—	—
Civilians	42	67	31	13	6	13	7	10
Total	42	67	31	15	6	13	7	10
Terrorists								
Security forces	59	146	79	48	31	52	43	31
Civilians	73	255	140	153	210	232	62	40
Total	132	401	219	201	241	284	105	71

1. Figures for killings of security forces by security forces reported at H.C. Deb., Vol. 870, cols. 1340–50 March 21, 1974).
2. See text for discussion of sources.

generally accurate picture of killings connected with the security situation. If they are considered together with Table 4 it is possible to identify deaths resulting from certain features of the present conflict: attacks on the security forces, civilian assassinations, explosions and related incidents, and anti-terrorist operations of the security forces.

Locality

A prerequisite to a basic understanding of the present conflict is knowledge of the breakdown of residential areas into predominant support for one or another faction. The security forces use maps of the province which are coloured orange and green to denote support for Loyalist and Republican factions respectively. What would be useful is some breakdown of the data on deaths and killings according to the police divisions, as this might indicate how patterns of insurgency and inter-communal conflict have emerged and persisted in particular areas.

Unfortunately, only limited information along these lines has so far been published by the N.I.O. The Northern Ireland Secretary, in reply to a question in the House of Commons in 1976, designated certain police divisions as areas where policing is not normal, but this list has not since been updated. Table 1 shows that very few data on deaths and killings, let alone other incidents, have been provided for police divisions. This is not to suggest that the N.I.O. has refused to publish these data; rather Members of Parliament have not asked for it.

Conclusions

The writer's study of the available data on terrorism in the province has led him to two general conclusions. While some breakdown of the data can be attempted, and has been in this article, only a very general picture of terrorism can be constructed. This writer has suggested that attribution of responsibility for incidents, at least along the lines adopted in the Chief Constable's reports 1980–1981, is essential if observers of the conflict are to learn which factions are involved in particular patterns of activity.

ROBERT J. SPJUT

Further, there should be categorisation of victims, at least by age, sex and religious affiliation. Finally, these data ought to be divided into police divisions, enabling students of the present troubles to understand patterns of insurrection and inter-communal strife in particular areas. Such data would not provide detailed or comprehensive information about the troubles, only a basis upon which observers might conduct a further inquiry. The present policies preclude observers from securing even this rudimentary knowledge of the conflict.

Secondly, certain of the reported statistics ought to be read with considerable scepticism as to their true meaning. We have seen that the reported figures for " murder " in the Chief Constable's reports may include a number of deaths caused by explosions that are, strictly speaking, manslaughters. More importantly, the category " sectarian, inter-factional and intra-factional assassination " does not, as it appears, refer to a motive but to the civilian victim and would more accurately be termed " civilian assassination ", as it was in the *Chief Constable's Report 1979*. The category " terrorist " in the Statistics on Violence in the Gardiner Report is misleading not only in view of the erroneous categorisation of particular deaths, but because the criteria would appear to be limited to persons believed to have been in the act of preparing or committing a terrorist-type offence when they were killed: Even the general category of " deaths connected with the security situation " is not altogether certain and may refer to a narrower category of persons who died while participating, in some way, in the civil disturbances. Obviously compiling statistics on the security situation in Northern Ireland is not an easy task, but those published ought not to appear to represent some phenomena which they clearly do not.

REFERENCES

DEUTSCH, R. and MAGOWAN, V. (1974). *Northern Ireland 1968–73, A Chronology of Events*. Belfast: Blackstaff Press.

DILLON, M. and LEHANE, D. (1973). *Political Murder in Northern Ireland*. Harmondsworth: Penguin Books.

McKEOWN, M. (1973). The Northern Ireland Death Toll. *Hibernia*, **37,** no. 14, September 7–20.

Hibernia (1974). " 86 Deaths: 7 Soldiers Charged ". **38,** no. 19, August 30– September 12.

Hibernia (1974). " British Army Before the Courts ". **38,** no. 23, November 23– December 7.

Hibernia (1975). " No Lull in the Killings ". **39,** no. 10, May 16–29.

ROYAL ULSTER CONSTABULARY (1970–1981). *Chief Constable's Reports, 1970–1981*. Belfast: H.M.S.O.

GARDINER, LORD. (1975). Report of a Committee to consider, in the context of civil liberties and human rights, measures to deal with terrorism in Northern Ireland. London: Cmnd. 5847. H.M.S.O.

CRIMINAL STATISTICS ON SECURITY IN NORTHERN IRELAND

Statistics on Security, semi-annual returns 1977–82, published in H.C. Deb., Vol.
915, cols. *646–50* (July 23, 1976); Vol. 936 cols. *525–32* (July 28, 1977);
Vol. 943, cols. *237–42* (February 1, 1978); Vol. 955, cols. *419–24* (August 2,
1978); Vol. 963, cols. 165–69, (February 20, 1979); Vol. 973, cols. *325–31*
(November 9, 1979); Vol. 978, cols. *605–14* (February 12, 1980); Vol. 990,
cols. *167–80* (August 6, 1980); Vol. 997, cols. *315–20* (January 26, 1981);
Vol. 9, cols. *527–32* (July 9, 1981); Vol. 17, cols. *421–24* (February 11, 1982);
Vol. 28, cols. 798–802 (July 30, 1982).

Social Trends (1980). *10*, Central Statistical Office. Ed. J. Thompson.

Social Trends (1981–1982). *11–13*, Central Statistical Office. Ed. D. Ramprhash.

WIDGERY, LORD. (1972). Report of a Tribunal appointed to inquire into the
events on Sunday, January 30, 1972, which led to loss of life in connection
with the procession in Londonderry that day. London: H.M.S.O. H.C. 220.

APPENDIX 1

Sources and Notes on Table 1

1. Deaths connected	CC, SS, ST.
2. Victims—security forces	CC, SS, ST for NI; H.C. Deb., Vol. 902, cols. *791–794* (December 19, 1975) and Vol. 927, cols. *73–74* (February 28, 1977) for PD; H.C. Deb., Vol. 916–2, cols. *755–58* (August 3, 1976) and Vol. 929, cols. *269–70* (April 1, 1977) for BLO.
3. Victims—civilian	CC, SS, ST for NI; Deb., Vol. 916–2, cols. *755–758* (August 3, 1976) and Vol. 929, cols. *269–70* (April 1, 1977) for BLO.
4. Victims—terrorists	GR, Appendix 4 for 1971–73 and CC for 1973–75, 1977.
5. Victims—age	H.C. Deb., Vol. 968, col. *525* (June 19, 1979). Data are only for persons killed by the security forces.
6. Victims—sex	As item 5.
7. Parties responsible—age	ST 1980, 1981, 1982.
8. Parties responsible— security forces	H.C. Deb. 968, col. *525* (June 19, 1979).
9. Parties responsible— factions	CC 1980, 1981
10. Murders connected	H.C. Deb., Vol. 908, col. *470* (March 3, 1976); Vol. 925, cols. 664–665 (February 8, 1977); Vol. 967, col. *310* (May 25, 1979). See H.C. Deb., Vol. 904, cols. *537–8*, February 3, 1976 provides breakdown for PD for aggregate period October 5, 1968 to January 29, 1976.
11. Manslaughters connected	H.C. Deb., Vol. 969, cols. *223–224* (June 27, 1979).

ROBERT J. SPJUT

APPENDIX 1—*cont.*

12. Punishment shootings—total	See Appendix 4 for NI. For PD see H.C. Deb., Vol. 903, cols. *81–82* (January 12, 1976). For BLO see H.C. Deb., Vol. 951, cols. *527–528* (June 13, 1978).
13. Punishment shootings—victim's sex	H.C. Deb., Vol. 903, cols. *81–82* (January 12, 1976).
14. All shootings	CC, SS, ST; H.C. Deb., Vol. 916–2, cols. *949–58* (August 3, 1976) and Vol. 929, cols. *269–70* (April 1, 1977) for BLO.
15. Assassinations	CC, SS; same as item 14 for BLO.
16. Injuries	CC, SS, ST.
17. Intimidation	CC.
18. Armed robberies	CC, SS, H.C. Deb., Vol. 985, col. *364* (May 22, 1980). See Appendix 4.
19. Explosions	CC, SS, ST for NI; for BLO see H.C. Deb., Vol. *916–2*, cols. *949–58* (August 3, 1976) and Vol. 929, cols. *869–70* (April 1, 1977).
20. Neutralised bombs	CC, SS, ST.
21. Rocket attacks	H.C. Deb., Vol. 915, col. *216* (July 14, 1976).
22. Mortar attacks	Same as item 21.
23. Malicious fires	CC, SS, ST.
24. Hijackings	H.C. Deb., Vol. 984, col. *542* (May 14, 1980); CC 1979–81.

Abbreviations: CC = Chief Constable's Reports, Royal Ulster Constabulary.
GR = Gardiner Report.
SS = Statistics on Security.
ST = *Social Trends.*

CRIMINAL STATISTICS ON SECURITY IN NORTHERN IRELAND

APPENDIX 2

Divisions of the Royal Ulster Constabulary and Areas for which Statistical Information is Published

Belfast

*A (Central Belfast)
*B (West Belfast)
*C (West Belfast)
*D (North Belfast)
 E (East Belfast)
*F (South Belfast)

Londonderry

*N (Part of Londonderry
     and part of Tyrone)
 O (part of Londonderry
     and part of Antrim)

Other

*H (South Armagh and South Down)
 J (North Armagh and West Down)
 K (West Armagh and South East Tyrone)
 L (South West Tyrone)
 M (part of Tyrone and part of Fermanagh)
 P (North Antrim)
 R (South Antrim and part of Tyrone)

Notes: 1. *indicates areas in which policing was not normal in 1976. No similar designation has been requested or published since 1976.
      2. Sources: Chief Constable's Reports, H.C. Deb., Vol. 913, col. *420* June 20, 1976).

ROBERT J. SPJUT

APPENDIX 3

Persons convicted at Belfast City Commission 1976–81

Offence	1976	1977	1978	1979	1980	1981
Offences against the person						
Murder	55	73	45	59	23	34
Attempted murder	23	37	30	16	7	18
Conspiracy to murder	2	1	5	4	6	6
Manslaughter	12	21	11	27	8	14
Wounding with intent to do grievous bodily harm	12	25	12	38	23	14
Causing grievous bodily harm	8	11	11	13	13	8
Assault occasioning actual bodily harm	8	9	8	10	16.	3
Intimidation	2	6	7	3	—	—
Aggravated burglary	21	35	10	6	8	—
Robbery	238	177	167	197	197	174
Kidnapping and false imprisonment	10	5	19	19	11	5
Explosives offences						
Causing explosion	38	97	46	39	24	16
Placing explosives	14	2	—	—	1	3
Possessing explosives with intent	46	53	27	36	17	9
Explosive offences	1	24	27	16	9	5
Petrol bomb offences	17	23	10	3	11	34
Firearms offences						
Possessing firearm with intent	91	71	24	53	21	18
Possessing firearm	118	6	28	3	—	—
Carrying a firearm with intent	18	20	16	8	13	11
Other major firearms offences	62	109	19	82	62	84
Minor firearms offences	15	31	55	19	—	2
Offences against property						
Hi-jacking	25	56	76	37	52	18
Arson	41	66	56	43	39	46
Malicious damage	12	13	7	2	—	—
Criminal damage	—	—	—	—	—	12
Public order offences						
Riot	1	—	—	—	—	—
Assisting offenders and escape						
Escape offences	16	16	4	6	1	1
Assisting offenders	8	1	5	14	3	4
Withholding information	—	—	7	10	9	5
Prescribed organisations offences						
Membership of illegal organisation	31	66	87	93	35	12
Contributing to resources of a proscribed organisation	—	—	—	—	1	1
Soliciting support for a proscribed organisation	—	—	—	—	1	1
Unlawful collection of information	15	7	28	7	4	2
Illegal training	3	—	—	1	—	2
Possessing prohibited articles	—	1	8	2	1	—
Totals	963	1,101	872	869	621	557

Notes: 1. Source is the semi-annual returns of the *Statistics on Security* published by the Northern Ireland Office.

2. The offence classifications are based on those used by the Crown and Peace Office in their annual return.

3. Some jury trials are included in cases where the Attorney General certified out of the scheduled mode of trial, i.e. non-terrorist serious offences.

4. Where a person has been convicted of more than one offence only the most serious or that which received the longest sentence is recorded in the statistics.

5. The tables relate to persons convicted at the Belfast Crown Court. This covers all scheduled offences tried on indictment.

CRIMINAL STATISTICS ON SECURITY IN NORTHERN IRELAND

APPENDIX 4

Armed robberies in Northern Ireland 1971–1980

	1971	1972	1973	1974	1975	1976	1977	1978	1979	1980
Chief Constable's Report	438	1,795	1,215	1,231	1,324	889	676	380	446	414
Statistics on Security	437	1,931	1,215	1,231	1,201	813	591	439	434	912
Reply to questions in House of Commons	489	1,931	1,317	1,353	1,324	889	676	493	504	—

Notes: 1. Sources for armed robberies in Chief Constable's reports are 1971 (p. 34), 1973 (p. 4), 1974 (p. 4), 1975 (p. 5), 1976 (p. 4), 1977 (p. 4), 1979 (p. 63), 1980 (p. 52).
2. Figures for Statistics on Security are reported in the returns commencing January 1981 and published at H.C. Deb, Vol. 997, cols. 315–316 (January 26, 1981).
3. Source for reply to question in House of Commons is H.C. Deb, Vol. 985, col. 364, (May 22, 1980).
4. The following discrepancies are inexplicable: Chief Constable's Reports 1972, 1978 and 1979. Statistics on Security for 1975, 1976, 1977, 1978 and 1979 and the reply for 1971, 1973, 1974, 1978 and 1979.

379

ROBERT J. SPJUT

APPENDIX 5

Punishment shootings 1973-1980

1973	74
1974	127
1975	187
1976	88
1977	32
1978	67
1979	76
1980	77

Sources: (1) 1973–75: H.C. Deb., Vol. 903, cols. 81–82 (January 12, 1976); Vol. 951, cols. 527–2
June 13, 1978).

(2) 1976–77: H.C. Deb., Vol. 951, cols. 527 (June 13, 1978).

(3) 1978–80: H.C. Deb., Vol. 997, col. 312 (January 26, 1981).

Part IV
Responses
to
Terrorism

The Question of Individual and Public Rights

[14]

JUDGING WITHOUT CONSENSUS

The Diplock Courts in Northern Ireland

CHARLES CARLTON
North Carolina State University

This article examines nonjury trials for political/terrorist offenses in Northern Ireland. It traces the origins of the current troubles; the breakdown of the jury system; the work of the royal commission, chaired by Lord Justice Diplock; and the establishment of courts, known as Diplock Courts, in which a single judge tries cases using modified rules of evidence and lowered standards for the admission of confessions. Finally, the article evaluates the work of the Diplock Courts, and suggests their wider relevance to future policy-making. In doing so, it touches upon a fundamental role of governing through courts—the maintenance of the ability to govern, particularly in a society that has neither political nor judicial consensus.

I t would be hard to think of a court system operating within the Anglo-American tradition that has faced a more acute crisis in the last decade than that of Northern Ireland, when called upon to handle political crimes.[1] Since the start of the troubles in 1969, over 2000 people have died, and ten times as many have been wounded, including police, prison officers, judges and juries.

Basically, Northern Ireland lacks political consensus (Rose 1971, 1976). The Catholic third of its population feel little loyalty to the province, refusing to accept its links with the United Kingdom, its political system, queen or parliament. In return the

AUTHOR'S NOTE: *I would like to thank the members of the judiciary, bar, and public who talked to me about the Diplock Courts during a trip to Northern Ireland in July 1980. For understandable reasons our conversations were off the record.*

LAW & POLICY QUARTERLY, Vol. 3 No. 2, April 1981 225-242
© 1981 Sage Publications, Inc.

226 | LAW AND POLICY QUARTERLY | April 1981

Protestant majority regard Catholics as potential, if not actual traitors, who must be excluded from place and power.

This lack of consensus has affected the province's courts. For the first three years of trouble they failed to deal with political crimes fairly, or effectively. Judges and juries, prisoners, police, prosecutors, and defense attorneys could not agree on the proper roles, rules, and purposes of courts. Eventually, as the courts became less effective, and the internal security situation got worse, Ulster's government (commonly known as Stormont), resorted to the internment of political suspects without trial.

For the United Kingdom government, which has ultimate responsibility for the province, this lack of judicial consensus has posed several problems of public policy, that have involved trying to balance the preservation of law and order with the protection of democratic rights and due process. Public policy options, such as the withdrawal of British troops, the creation of an independent Ulster, a pan-Irish confederation, the redrawing of the borders between Northern and Southern Ireland, and the forceable repatriation of minorities, have been dealt with elsewhere (Carlton 1977).

This article will discuss judicial options. It will examine the British government's efforts to handle political crisis through the creation of special courts, known as Diplock Courts, in which a single judge hears cases without a jury, using modified rules of evidence, and lowered standards for the admission of confessions. The emphasis of this paper will be empirical. It will trace the origins of the Diplock Courts, describe their procedures, evaluate their performance, see how well they have served consumer needs, and finally, suggest how they may be relevant to future policy-making. In doing so, this article will touch on an important aspect of governing through courts. In assessing how courts *create* law (a much studied aspect of the American legal tradition that is virtually absent from the British), we may forget that their function in *maintaining* law is far more common and significant. For centuries political philosophers have recognized that the maintenance of law is a fundamental purpose of government. Without it life soon becomes nasty, brutish, and short.

BACKGROUND

Trying to judge without consensus is as old as England's colonization of Ireland. In 1803, for example, the great Irish patriot, Robert Emmett, told the judge at his treason trial, "I have done my duty, and no doubt the court will do their's."[2] After the division of Ireland in 1922, and the establishment of a separate province in the North, this problem received a new twist. In Northern Ireland, London set up a court system, modeled on the English one, with a Supreme Court, Court of Appeals, Queen's Bench, assize, county and magistrates' courts, and the right to appeal to the House of Lords, the United Kingdom's Supreme Court (*Ulster Year Book,* 1978/1979). But this did nothing to placate the minority's demands for civil rights, or end religious discrimination (McLean, 1972). For one thing, Ulster became, as its first Prime Minister, Lord Craigavon boasted, a Protestant state for a Protestant people, in which the majority unionist party monopolized political power.

The province's judiciary was very politicized. Unlike the rest of the United Kingdom, many judges were retired Attorneys General or unionist politicians. As recently as 1976 Protestants held 68 out of 74 senior court appointments. The laws they enforced could be Draconian. The 1922 Special Powers Act allowed the Minister of Home Affairs to intern people and ban organizations at will (Northern Ireland, 1922).

Lacking a written constitution, bill of rights, or strong tradition of judicial review, United Kingdom courts have been loath to remedy administrative abuses. As early as 1922, in the O'Hanlon case, Northern Ireland's High Court refused to interfere with the arrest and internment of a prosperous hotelier on conspiracy charges, saying the facts of the case were not their concern (1922, 56 *ILTR,* 170). As recently as 1967, the House of Lords refused (McEldowney v. Forde, 1972), to overturn the Minister of Home Affair's closing of a republican club in Derry, even though the record clearly showed it was not a threat to public order. They accepted the firmly established constitutional principle that courts cannot reverse a minister unless he has acted in bad faith.

228 / LAW AND POLICY QUARTERLY / April 1981

Thus it is no surprise that Father Dennis Faul, one of the Northern Ireland Civil Rights Association's legal experts, concluded in 1969, "Our people are afraid of the Courts: they believe the judicial system as it operates in the blatantly sectarian conditions of life here is loaded against them" (Irish Times, Dec. 2, 1969).

In McEldowney v. Forde the law lords were not merely reflecting the traditional reluctance of British courts to govern through judicial intervention, but the unwillingness of the executive in London to intervene in Northern Ireland's internal affairs. In both houses of parliament the speaker refused to entertain questions about the province, thus preventing an effective means of remedying administrative abuses. In the Home Office, the large ministry responsible for a host of matters, the department that handled Ulster had only six civil servants, who had a number of additional duties, including the prevention of importation of rabid dogs! In fact, most British policy makers cared little, and knew less about Northern Ireland. All they remembered was that since Elizabeth I executed the Earl of Essex in 1601, Ireland had been, to use the phrase of another of its distinguished casualties, Gladstone, the graveyard of British politicians. Thus in early 1969, Home Secretary James Callaghan declared that Britain "on no account wanted to get sucked into the Irish bog" (Callaghan, 1973).

But within a few weeks it was.

Following months of civil rights demonstrations that culminated in two days of rioting in Derry and Belfast, on August 14 Prime Minister Wilson ordered British troops to patrol Northern Ireland. Although Catholics initially welcomed the soldiers, by the end of the year a complex urban guerrilla war had developed between the army and Royal Ulster Constabulary (R.U.C.) on one side, and the Official and Provisional wings of the Irish Republican Army (I.R.A.) on the other, with Protestant paramilitary groups, such as the Ulster Defense Association (U.D.A.) fighting both. The war became so serious that two years later Stormont invoked the 1922 Special Powers Act to intern suspected terrorists without trial.

In the late fifties and early sixties internment had effectively curbed the I.R.A.'s rural offensive. But in August 1971 it was a disaster. New, younger and more radical leaders replaced those arrested, often on the basis of intelligence a decade out of date. Police and army methods of interrogation—which can only be described as torture—inflamed Catholic sentiment. In the four months before internment began eight people were killed; in the four months after 114 died (Sunday Times, 1972: 269).

Legal challenges to the emergency provisions by groups of lawyers, such as the Association for Legal Justice, got nowhere. In R. v. Flynn and Leonnard in 1972, a magistrate ruled that common law permitted an army officer to impose a curfew to maintain the peace.

Even when the courts limited the security force's powers, as in R. v. JP's for . . . Londonderry, and re McElduff, by finding they had used the wrong arrest procedures and ordered some internees paid damages, their judgments did not result in a single prisoner being freed. The semijudicial form of review Stormont introduced in September 1972, by asking Mr. Justice Brown to examine the Minister of Home Affairs' internment orders, was equally ineffective. By mid-December out of 1567 internees, only 20 had been released on the judge's recommendation, compared to 914 at the minister's initiative.

Other administrative procedures the government initiated did little to protect civil rights: The powers of the Ombudsman to review administrative actions were extremely limited, while police review boards could—or would—not curb R.U.C. misconduct (National Council on Civil Liberties, 1975; *Ulster, Year Book,* 1978/1979: 22). In spite of the introduction of mandatory six-month sentences for riotous behavior, the R.U.C. continued to favor Protestants by charging them with the lesser offense of disorderly conduct.[3] Trial by jury, which Blackstone (1830: 379) had boasted was "the glory of English law," failed to safeguard civil rights. Selected from lists of property tax payers, which excluded renters and public housing tenants, predominantly Protestant juries frequently acquitted defendants of their own

230 | LAW AND POLICY QUARTERLY | April 1981

religion. For instance, they let off a man found with a gun in his
car, three men who were seen to throw weapons from theirs,
several hijackers in whose U.D.A. headquarters stolen goods
were found (House of Common Debates [H.C.D.] 855, 381-382),
and two policemen charged with beating up a prisoner.[4] By May
of 1971 jury bias had become so blatant that 100 members of
Northern Ireland's bar (a body not known for its concern for civil
rights) signed a public letter of protest.

The most damning critique of the courts came from two
academics, Tom Hadden and Paddy Hillyard, whose *Justice in
Northern Ireland: A Study in Social Confidence* (1973) statistically demonstrated a pattern of discrimination. In political
cases, magistrates denied bail to 79% of Catholics and 54% of
Protestants, as did the Belfast City Commission in 73% and 46%
of the cases respectively, as compared to denial rates of 50% and
53% in criminal cases. The bias of juries, who acquitted 15% of
Protestants and only 5% of Catholics, would have been even more
marked had not judges directed the acquital for lack of evidence
of the latter three times more often than for the former.

THE DEVELOPMENT OF THE DIPLOCK COURTS

Following the disaster of internment, Prime Minister Heath
dissolved Stormont in March 1972, and appointed Secretary of
State William Whitelaw to rule Northern Ireland directly from
London. Recognizing that the province's courts were unable to
deal with the increased level of violence, in September, Heath
appointed a royal commission, chaired by Lord Justice Diplock,
to consider new legal procedures. As a stop-gap measure, the
government issued the Detention of Terrorists Order in November which permitted the holding of suspected terrorists on an
administrative court order.

After three months of hectic work, the Diplock Committee
published its report on December 20, 1972. It was based on three
politically palatable premises. If the first, that the judiciary and
courts in Northern Ireland have "in general held the respect and

the trust of all except the extremists," were true then one wonders why a commission to investigate them was necessary. Similar doubts were raised about the second assumption: that there was a deliberate campaign to thwart the process of justice through the systematic murder and intimidation of witnesses and juries. Later interviews with lawyers confirm that this was in fact the case, and that the report did not cite names and addresses to prevent further retribution. Third, the report argued that current procedures must be changed to conform with the European Convention of Human Rights, which the United Kingdom had just accepted on joining the Common Market (Rauch, 1973; Council of Europe, 1976). In retrospect this seems to be an exceptionally farsighted approach, since it avoided a whole series of appeals to the European Courts. At the time, however, it was taken on the advice of the R.U.C.'s lawyers. Having found no satisfactory precedents for handling terrorist suspects in English law, they turned to the European magisterial tradition.

The Diplock report made seven main recommendations:

(1) the army and police should be allowed to hold suspects for up to four hours without charge, and for as long as 28 days on remand;
(2) setting bail should be transferred from magistrates, who were susceptible to intimidation, to high court judges;
(3) a single high or county court judge sitting without a jury should try political offenses;
(4) the burden of proof in firearms and explosives cases should be shifted from the prosecution to the defense;
(5) written affidavits should be accepted from murdered witnesses;
(6) the standard for the admission of confessions should be lowered from that mandated by the English "judges' rules" to those required by article 3 of the European Convention;
(7) the abolition of the 1922 Special Powers Act and capital punishment in Northern Ireland.[5]

Reactions to these recommendations were predictable. Bernadette Devlin damned them. The Ulster Vanguard Movement hailed them as "totally acceptable to loyalists" because they "would help to get rid of the I.R.A. cancer in society." (New York

232 / LAW AND POLICY QUARTERLY / April 1981

Times, Dec. 21, 1972: 43). Ian Paisley welcomed the report. John Hume, leader of the Social Democratic Labor Party, called it "a complete reversal of the Judicial process." (London Times, Dec. 21, 1972: 2, 13). Editorials in the London *Times* and *Economist* favored it, while in the *Criminal Law Review,* Professor William Twining (1973) called it a hastily written, poorly researched, panicky response to a crisis.

The morning the Diplock report was published the British government accepted its recommendations, introducing the Northern Ireland (Emergency Provisions) Bill into parliament the following spring to put them into effect. At the opening debate in the Commons, on the bill's second reading on April 17, 1973, William Whitelaw declared the government was "firmly committed to the restoration of law in Northern Ireland," and "will continue to bring suspected persons before the courts whenever possible" (H.C.D., 855, 277). Bernadette Devlin attacked the bill, demanding statistics to support its assumptions about the intimidation of jurors and witnesses. When Stanley McMaster (a Unionist from Protestant East Belfast), started to give them, Devlin walked out, missing McMaster's claim that "the terrorists seek to hide behind the laws of evidence." Gerry Fitt of the Social Democratic Labor Party said he "vehemently opposed" the bill. Ian Paisley equivocated. Although pleased with its law-and-order provisions, he resented the implication that Protestant juries could possibly be biased. Toward the end of the debate, discussion centered on the symbolically crucial issue of juries. Charles Fletcher-Cook, one of the few English back-benchers to speak, went to the heart of the matter with his observation that "a very homogenous community is needed to support a jury system." The bill easily passed its second reading, eventually becoming law on August 8, 1973 (H.C.D., 856, 1025-1146; 860, 1490).

AN EVALUATION

Naturally any evaluation of the Diplock courts depends on one's perception. Those adamantly opposed to Ulster's links with the United Kingdom have continued to criticize the courts. For instance, Father Edward Daly, Bishop of Derry, told U.S. Representative Joshua Eilberg that Diplock procedures were "intolerable." The congressman agreed, voicing a deep faith in the jury system that was not, it turned out, profound enough to dissuade him from pleading guilty without trial to federal bribery charges four months later (U.S.A., 1978, 193, 202). At the other end of the political spectrum, hardline Tories have criticized the 1973 Act as being soft on the gunmen (Times, correspondence, June 14-17, 1974). More disturbing were the findings of a survey taken in Belfast after the Diplock courts had been in operation for a year. Only 63% of Protestants, and 79% of Catholics were aware of the abolition of jury trials. Of them, 27% and 88% respectively, believed a person did not get a fair trial in the province. On the other hand, 55% of Catholics, as compared to 5% of Protestants, thought that Diplock procedures were an improvement on internment (Boyle, 1975: 144-150).

The effectiveness of the Diplock courts in achieving the public policy goals of the British government—which is one of the main consumers of their services, as well as their architect—may best be assessed in the context of the wider objectives of the United Kingdom's Ulster policies. Prime Minister Wilson stated them clearly in the Downing Street Declaration which he issued on August 19, 1967, a week after he first sent troops to Derry and Belfast. Her Majesty's government promised not to withdraw the army until "law and order has been restored," and, secondly, to guarantee all the provinces' citizens "their equal rights and protection under the law" (Carlton, 1977: 133).

Since the institution of the Diplock court, the internal security situation in Ulster has improved. Killings fell from 482 in 1972 to 238 in 1976. Violence has become internalized (like that in American inner cities), with paramilitary groups fighting each other and not the British army, whose casualties have dropped from 102 to 10, much to the relief of the government which has had to deal with an English "bring the boys home" campaign. Diplock courts have been able to convict and incarcerate a growing number of political offenders. For instance, between

234 | LAW AND POLICY QUARTERLY | April 1981

1972 and 1977 murder convictions rose from 9 to 77, woundings from 142 to 499, and robbery from 791 to 1836.[6] By July, 1975, the government felt that things had improved so much that they could afford to end detention by Christmas, and on December 5 released the last of 1981 prisoners held without trial since August 1971. While it is impossible to assess what effect the Diplock Courts have had compared to other factors, such as improved army and police intelligence and training, increased public spending, political initiatives, and simple war weariness, it does seem that they have made a significant contribution to the restoration of an acceptable level of law and order.[7]

In some regards the Diplock Courts have done little to promote the government's second objective of "equal justice under the law." There have been complaints about the slowness of its proceedings. A. W. Logan, a lawyer experienced in representing Diplock defendants, charged in a letter published in the London *Times* in September 1978, that it took an average of fourteen months for a case to reach trial, and that the police were stalling as a substitute for internment whenever a defendant was remanded in custody. With unusual speed the Law Officers' Department wrote back two days later denying the charges: during 1971, 211 defendants had been granted bail and 307 denied it, with the period between arrest and trial averaging only nine months.

Since their establishment, Diplock Courts have convicted with increasing frequency, laying themselves open to charges that they have become rubber stamps for the prosecution. Between 1973 and 1979 the proportion of acquittals has fallen from 15% to 6%, while those pleading guilty has risen from 59% to 75%. The official explanation that these high rates are the result of the excellent cases that the prosecution presents would be easier to accept if the acquittal rate for members of the security forces was equally low, and secondly, if so many civilian convictions were not based almost entirely on confession given during the 28-day arrest period, and accepted under the 1973 Act's relaxed standards.

Because the army's main concern is gathering intelligence to fight a guerrilla war, in contrast to the R.U.C.'s of obtaining evidence to use in court to secure a conviction, suspects were still ill treated during interrogation (Amnesty International, 1978; Kitson, 1971; Lowry, 1977, 1978). Notwithstanding the extensive recommendations of the Parker (1972) and Bennett (1979) commissions, abuses will probably continue so long as long as the pressures of waging a guerrilla campaign remain.

On the positive side, Diplock Courts have ended the gross sectarian bias of juries. In their first six months of sitting, judges acquitted 5% of Protestant defendants, as compared to 12% of Catholics. The proportion of Protestants pleading guilty rose from 31% to 70%, mainly because they could no longer count on a friendly jury. Over the past six years these rates have remained cosntant (Boyle, 1975, 1979). They have been confirmed by an analysis of the 31 Diplock cases in the law reports—admittedly by no means a representative sample. In them, 9 Catholics were convicted and 8 acquitted, as compared to 4 and 5 Protestants, respectively. On appeal, Protestants were far more successful, winning 5 out of 7 cases, while both Catholic appellants lost. The bias of those figures is surprising, since the army, which is less interested in getting usable evidence, tends to initiate cases against Catholics, while the R.U.C., which finds I.R.A. strongholds too dangerous to patrol, usually starts them against Protestants.

In sentencing, Diplock judges have shown no marked sectarian bias, except toward defendants (invariably Catholics) who refused to recognize the court. On the recommendation of the Hunt (1969) and MacDermott (1972) commissions, the government transferred prosecutions from the R.U.C. to a public prosecutor modeled on Scottish lines, ending the practice of bringing more serious charges against Catholics than Protestants for similar acts.

Trying cases without juries and using lowered standards of evidence presented judges with problems for which there was little guidance. In R. v. MacNaughton (1978), a case involving an army sergeant charged with shooting a prisoner while attempting to escape following a bomb explosion in the I.R.A. stronghold of South Armagh, Lord Chief Justice Lowry confessed, "A case like

236 / LAW AND POLICY QUARTERLY / April 1981

this raises an unusual situation for which there is little precedent."
In R. v. Fitzpatrick (1976), the court of criminal appeals had to
search Canadian, Tasmanian, Queensland, and New York codes.

In applying the 1973 act, judges have tended to ameliorate
parliament's intentions. While the Diplock report envisaged that
they would rarely grant bail, in fact they did so in 41% of the cases.
At the same time, the number of those absconding decreased
(Times, October 30, 1978; Boyle, 1975: 107-109). After seeming to
accept the act's provisions on the burden of proof in explosives or
firearms cases in R. v. Laghlin (1975), the court of appeals
softened them in R. v. Lavery (1977), and R. v. Derry (1977).
Similarly, after accepting a confession made following several
hours of interrogation in R. v. Tohill (1974), six months later in
R. v. Killie (1974), the court of criminal appeals refused to allow
another confession likewise given because they were not "satisfied
beyond a reasonable doubt of the guilt of the accused."[8] Lord
Chief Justice Lowry took this point further in R. v. Hetherington
(1974), when he ruled that the court must be convinced "not on a
pure balance of probabilities," but "beyond a reasonable doubt"
that a confession had not been extracted by the three prohibitions
of the European Convention: torture, inhumane or degrading
treatment.

Two years later, in R. v. McCormick (1976), Mr. Justice
McGonigal defined those prohibitions in a more stringent fashion
than the European Court used. In their first six months, Diplock
courts accepted ignorance as a defense in 9 out of 24 firearms or
explosives cases involving Catholics and 3 out of 15 involving
Protestants. This practice, which ran contrary to the hard-nosed
intention of the framers of the 1973 Act, was most common when
one of the accused admitted knowledge to take the rap for the
others. The court did not take full advantage of the act's relaxed
standards for the admission of hearsay evidence. In summary,
trained in the traditions of the law, Diplock judges have shown a
marked distaste for eroding its protections more than absolutely
necessary, especially with the improvement of the internal
security situation after 1974.

External review of the Diplock courts tend to support the
conclusion that they were doing a reasonably good job under the

circumstances. As the Gardiner Committee, chaired by a distinguished and unusually liberal jurist, concluded in 1975, "There has been wide agreement among those who gave evidence before us, and who were best qualified to judge that the new system has worked fairly and well." In a recent article, Kevin Boyle, Tom Hadden, and Paddy Hillyard, three leading legal scholars, concurred (Boyle, 1979). Because parliament first passed the 1973 Act as a temporary measure, with a year's life, it has renewed the act annually, passing amending legislation in 1975 and 1978. The debates on renewal and amending acts would suggest that the 1973 statute has been widely accepted, discussion in the House of Commons having become the occasion for a review of the government's Ulster policies as a whole.

Diplock Courts have gained a degree of acceptance among Ulster's minority community. There is something reassuring about the reappearance of the familiar symbols of justice, the bewigged lawyers, ermine-robed judges, and oak-panelled court rooms (Edelman, 1971). Because the rates of legal aid, which pay for the defense of the overwhelming majority of those tried in Diplock Courts, are generous, defendants have been able to retain some of the best members of the province's criminal bar. Since barristers may be hired to prosecute a case one day, and defend another the next, (unlike public prosecutors or defenders in the U.S.) they have not become identified with a particular side, which may explain why terrorists have not tried to kill them. Similarly the lack of assassination attempts against judges (as compared, say, to Italy), and the growing willingness of I.R.A. defendants to plead guilty, and thus recognize the court's legitimacy, would suggest that minority opposition to it has waned.

In one regard, however, this has not been so. When the United Kingdom insisted on treating all prisoners convicted after 1976 as regular felons, many I.R.A. men objected, arguing that since they had been tried by special courts they were entitled to special treatment. At Long Kesh, 300 of them staged a "dirty protest," refusing to wear prison clothes, follow prison routines or rules, or use prison facilities, employing their cell walls and floor rather than Her Majesty's toilets (Washington Post, March 16, 1979;

238 | LAW AND POLITICS QUARTERLY | April 1981

New York Times, May 22, 1978; New Statesman, September 30, 1977). Because this protest has not had the effects that its sponsors hoped, the I.R.A. turned its attentions to prison officers, murdering 17 of them by the end of 1979.

PUBLIC POLICY IMPLICATIONS

Northern Ireland is a subject about which there is little scholarly agreement. Its troubles are far from solution, their religious basis making them seem more appropriate to the seventeenth than the twentieth century. Therefore any conclusions about the public policy implications of the Diplock Courts must be highly tentative and limited.

By ensuring, as Mr. Justice Jones put it, "that nonjury trials should be conducted on lines as near as possibly approximating jury trials," the British government has tried to deviate from the normal legal forms as little as it can. It has attempted to isolate areas that lack judicial consensus from those that retain it. It spite of the troubles, Northern Ireland's court system has been able to function in nonpolitical areas in a remarkably normal fashion. Cases are heard and appealed. Many of those who oppose the crown's links with the United Kingdom use the queen's courts to sue the army and police for damages, demonstrating a willingness to work within the system that goes beyond mere hope of financial compensation. In the last few years Northern Ireland's nonpolitical court system has been reformed to bring it in line with English practice, and jury lists have been opened up to all voters, with—presumably nonsectarian—computers selecting people for service (MacDermott, 1972; Lord Chancellor's Department, 1977). In summary, the prevention of the erosion of public support for the entire court system has been crucial in maintaining an ability to govern. One of the first stages of the loss of British control over Southern Ireland after the Easter Rising of 1916, and half a dozen years before the formal concession of independence, was the establishment of an independent court system which rapidly supplanted the crown's.

The policy of isolating controversial judicial matters, while reenforcing acceptable ones, might well be transferred to the formation of political or internal security policy. Rather than trying to devise a viable provincial government for the whole of Ulster, London could concentrate on establishing workable county councils, at which level sectarian differences are not as intense; effective models for such controversial ideas as power-sharing already exist in English local government. Instead of being one police force, the R.U.C. could be divided into a special branch that would investigate political crimes, leaving the main body to deal with ordinary offences, such as drunk driving or automobile thefts by joyriding children, which both communities agree must be curbed.

Yet the British government has become complacent with its success. It has reverted to the inertia that has characterized so much of its policies towards Ireland over the past seven centuries. However, the best time to introduce reforms to Ulster is when its inhabitants are not violently demanding them. For example, the Attorney General could exercise his discretionary powers under the 1978 Emergency Provisions Act to transfer cases from the Diplock Courts to jury trial. On their own initiative Diplock judges might further stiffen the requirements for the admission of confessions. The 28-day arrest period could be shortened by administrative action. And if these reforms did not work they could be quickly and quietly reversed. In other words, by focusing on those areas that have agreement, and by carefully and actively building on them, those responsible for forming public policy in Northern Ireland may be able to do much to alleviate the intractable problems of both judging and governing without consensus.

NOTES

1. I have accepted Joel Grossman's definition (1976) of a "political" crime or trial as one where the chief motive of the prosecution and/or defense is political. I fully recognize that the intent and result of such crimes may usually be abject terror.

2. Which it did, hanging Emmett a few days later.

3. Mandatory sentences are virtually unknown in English law. All 109 of those charged under the Criminal Justice (Temporary Provisions) Act, 1970, were convicted.

4. It is a sad reflection on the judiciary that the most acceptable commission report on Northern Ireland was chaired by a retired general, best known for leading the first successful Everest expedition (Hunt, 1969).

5. The report also made several recommendations concerning juvenile offenders, which were passed into law by the Northern Ireland (Young Persons) Act of July 1973.

6. Most of these offenses were essentially political, particularly murders, of which Ireland had the world's lowest rate before the "troubles."

7. Public spending rose by 47% in real terms between 1967 and 1977 as compared to 14% for the rest of the U.K. (Fortnight, November, 1979: 7).

8. Nonetheless the judge found Tohill not guilty because witnesses failed to substantiate his confession.

CASES

R. v. DERRY (1977) N.I. 164
R. v. FITZPATRICK (1976) N.I. 20-34
R. v. HETHERINGTON (1974) N.I. 164-202
R. v. KILLIE (1974) N.I. 164-202
R. v. LAGHLIN (1975) N.I.L.Q.
R. v. LAVERY (1977) N.I. 148-155
R. v. MacNAUGHTON (1978) N.I. 110-110
R. v. McCORMICK (1976) N.I. 104-202
McELDOWNEY v. FORDE (1972) 3 WLR 179
R. v. TOHILL (1974) N.I.L.Q. 353

REFERENCES

Amnesty International (1978) Report on . . . Mission to Northern Ireland. London.
BENNETT, H. H. (1979) Committee of Inquiry into Police Interrogation Procedures in Northern Ireland. London: Her Majesty's Stationery Office, Cmnd. 7497.
BLACKSTONE, W. (1830) Commentaries on the Laws of England. London.
BOYLE, K., R. HADDEN, and P. HILLYARD (1979) "Emergency powers: ten years on." Fortnight 174: 6-8.
——— (1975) Law and the State: The Case of Northern Ireland. London: Robertson.
CALLAGHAN, J. (1973) A House Divided: The Dilemma of Northern Ireland. London: Collins.
CARLTON, C. (1977) Bigotry and Blood. Chicago: Nelson Hall.
Council of Europe—European Commission on Human Rights (1976) Ireland Against the United Kingdom.

DIPLOCK, Lord (1972) Report of the Commission to Consider Legal Procedures to Deal With Terrorist Activities in Northern Ireland. London: Her Majesty's Stationery Office, Cmnd. 5185.

EDELMAN, M. (1971) Politics as Symbolic Action. New York: Academic Press.

GARDINER, G. E. (1975) Report of a Committee to Consider in the Context of Civil Liberties and Human Rights Measures to Deal With Terrorism in Northern Ireland. London: Her Majesty's Stationery Office, Cmnd. 5847.

GROSSMAN, J. (1976) "Political justice in the democratic state." Polity 8: 358-388.

HAYDEN, T. and P. Hillyard (1973) Justice in Northern Ireland: A Study in Social Confidence. London: Cobbet Trust.

HUNT, J. (1969) Police in Northern Ireland. Belfast: Her Majesty's Stationery Office, Cmnd. 535.

International Committee of Jurists Review (1972) Northern Ireland—A New Preventative Procedure. December, 68-74.

KITSON, R. (1971) Low-Intensity Operations. London: Faber.

Lord Chancellor's Department (1977) Courts in Northern Ireland—The Future Pattern. London: Her Majesty's Stationery Office, Cmdn. 6892.

LOWRY, D. R. and R. SPJUT (1978) "European convention and human rights in Northern Ireland." Case Western Reserve J. of Int. Law 10: 251-297.

——— (1977) "Terrorism and human rights: counter-insurgency and necessity at common law." Notre Dame Lawyer 53: 49-89.

MacDERMOTT, J. C. (1972) "The decline for the rule of law." Northern Ireland Legal Q. 22: 474-495.

McLEAN, J.A.L. (1972) "Some developments in Northern Ireland since 1921." Northern Ireland Legal Q. 23: 82-90.

National Council for Civil Liberties (1975) The Royal Ulster Constabulary: A Report on the Complaints Procedures. London.

[NILQ] (n.d.) "Annual survey of the law of Northern Ireland.

Northern Ireland (1922) The Public General Acts of 1922. Belfast: Her Majesty's Stationary Office.

PARKER, Lord (1972) Report of the Committee of the Privy Consellors Appointed to Consider Procedures for the Interrogation of Persons Suspected of Terrorism. London: Her Majesty's Stationery Office, Cmnd. 4901.

RAUCH, E. (1973) "The compatibility of the Detention of Terrorists Order (Northern Ireland) with the European Convention for the Protection of Human Rights." New York Univ. J. of Int. Law and Politics: 61.

ROSE, R. (1976) Northern Ireland: Time of Choice. Washington, DC: American Institute for Public Policy Research.

——— (1971) Governing Without Consensus: An Irish Perspective. Boston: Beacon.

TWINING, C. L. (1973) "Emergency powers and criminal process: the Diplock Report." Criminal Law Rev.: 406-417.

Ulster Year Book (n.d.) Biannually since 1926. Belfast.

U.S.R. [United States House of Representatives] (1978) Committee on the Judiciary, "Northern Ireland, a role for the United States?" December 1978.

242 / LAW AND POLICY QUARTERLY / April 1981

CHARLES CARLTON has a B.A. from the University of Wales and a Ph.D. from UCLA. He is the author of *The Court of Orphans* (Leicester: Leicester University Press, 1974) and *Bigotry and Blood* (Chicago: Nelson Hall, 1977), and is currently an Associate Professor of History at North Carolina State University.

[15]

Public Security and Individual Freedom: The Dilemma of Northern Ireland

Thomas P. Foley†

Northern Ireland has been the scene of recurring and often horrifying violence since 1969, as terrorist groups have clashed with each other, with the British Army, and with the Royal Ulster Constabulary (R.U.C.). The situation has been a difficult one for both the people and the legal system of Northern Ireland: faced with the problem of highly dedicated terrorists, the British government has had to confront directly the tension between its duty to protect public security and its concomitant obligation to safeguard individual freedom. This Article focuses on the British government's most recent legislative response to this tension, the Emergency Provisions Act (EPA),[1] and appraises its success in accommodating the competing demands of public safety and private liberty.

The EPA cannot be assessed without some understanding of the historical background of the current situation and of the different sources of the violence wracking Northern Ireland. Section I of the Article is intended to provide this information in capsule form. Section II explains the operation of the EPA, with particular attention to its breadth and to its potentially counterproductive effects. The standards for the admissibility of confessions to crimes covered by the EPA and the lack of procedures for the independent investigation and evaluation of complaints against the security forces are analyzed in detail in Sections III and IV, respectively. In Section V, the Article concludes with recommendations for legal reform that would establish a better balance between the need for public security and the need for legal protection against excessive or unnecessary intrusions on individual freedom.

I. Origin and Nature of the Present Conflict

British control of all of Ireland was consolidated in the sixteenth cen-

---

† J.D. Yale University, 1982.

1. Northern Ireland (Emergency Provisions) Act, 1978, ch. 5. The first version of the EPA was enacted in 1973. *See* Northern Ireland (Emergency Provisions) Act, 1973, ch. 53. Unless otherwise indicated, all citations in this Article are to the 1978 EPA.

Northern Ireland

tury,[2] and maintained for hundreds of years thereafter despite repeated
insurrections by Irish desirous of breaking the link that had been established by force of arms.[3] The Government of Ireland Act, passed by
the British Parliament in 1920,[4] formally partitioned northern and
southern Ireland by establishing separate parliaments of limited powers
for each.[5] The northern entity, composed of six counties within the
province of Ulster, became Northern Ireland, and has remained contin-
uously within the British domain.[6] Under the terms of the Anglo-Irish
Treaty of 1921,[7] the southern entity, composed of the remaining
twenty-six counties of Ireland, became in 1922 the Irish Free State.[8]
Today it is the Republic of Ireland, which is completely independent of
Great Britain.[9]

The demographic fact that helped shape the creation of Northern
Ireland and that remains basic to the situation is that approximately
65% of the population are Protestants,[10] the descendants of seventeenth-century Scottish and English colonists,[11] whose religion[12] and
history differ from those of the Catholic minority. The Republic of
Ireland, on the other hand, has a predominantly Catholic population,[13]
and a constitution that until recently conferred on the Catholic church
a special role in national affairs,[14] and that still outlaws divorce.[15]

---

2. *See* Hayes-McCoy, *The Tudor Conquest (1534-1603)*, in THE COURSE OF IRISH HIS-
TORY 174 (T. Moody & F. Martin eds. 1967).
3. Concise histories of Ireland include R. EDWARDS, AN ATLAS OF IRISH HISTORY
(1973); J. BECKETT, A SHORT HISTORY OF IRELAND (1973); THE COURSE OF IRISH HISTORY
(T. Moody & F. Martin eds. 1967); T. MOODY, THE ULSTER QUESTION: 1603-1973 (1974); L.
DE PAOR, DIVIDED ULSTER (1973).
4. *See* McCartney, *From Parnell to Pearse (1891-1921)*, in THE COURSE OF IRISH HIS-
TORY, *supra* note 3, at 294, 311-12.
5. Government of Ireland Act, 1920, 10 & 11 Geo. 5, ch. 67; *see* R. HULL, THE IRISH
TRIANGLE, CONFLICT IN NORTHERN IRELAND 34 (1976).
6. R. HULL, *supra* note 5, at 19-20.
7. *See* Treaty, Dec. 6, 1921, Great Britain-Ireland, 26 L.N.T.S. 10.
8. *See* Irish Free State (Agreement) Act, 1922, 12 Geo. 5, ch. 4.
9. *See* R. HULL, *supra* note 5, at 19-21. Great Britain formally recognized this independence with the passage of the Ireland Act of 1949. Ireland Act, 1949, 12, 13 & 14 Geo. 6, ch.
41.
10. IRELAND, A CHRONOLOGY AND FACT BOOK 143 (W. Griffin ed. and compiler 1973)
[hereinafter FACT BOOK].
11. *See* Clarke, *The Colonisation of Ulster and the Rebellion of 1641 (1603-1660)*, in THE
COURSE OF IRISH HISTORY, *supra* note 3, at 189.
12. It should be noted that Protestantism in Northern Ireland is not monolithic; it embraces many separate sects. *See* FACT BOOK, *supra* note 10, at 143.
13. Data collected in 1961 indicated that about 90% of the population was Catholic. *Id.*
This figure may actually understate the percentage of Catholics, for intermarriage during the
last generation is widely thought to have pushed the Catholic percentage over 95%. *See*
Perry, *These Irish Eyes Aren't Smiling on a Paddy's Day Parade*, Wall St. J., Mar. 15, 1983, at
26, col. 3.
14. BUNREACHT NA HÉIREANN (Constitution of Ireland), arts. 44.2, .3 (repealed 1972).
15. *Id.* art. 41.3(2).

The Yale Journal of World Public Order   Vol. 8:284, 1982

Great Britain partitioned Ireland ostensibly to guarantee that the Protestants in the North would be ensured political power in their own state
despite the existence of the overwhelming Catholic majority in the
South.[16] The demographic consequence of this partition, however, was
to create a Catholic minority in Northern Ireland that itself has been
without political power. This demographic and political dilemma—
whether the Protestants in the North should be a minority as compared
with the Catholics throughout Ireland, or whether the Catholics in the
North should be a minority as compared with the Protestants there—
heretofore has proven insoluble.

While the conflict in Northern Ireland is often described as one pitting the Protestant majority against the Catholic minority, this strictly
religious characterization obscures the true nature of the conflict. The
term "Protestant" describes that part of the population which traces its
lineage to the seventeenth-century colonists, and which is largely Protestant, while the term "Catholic" describes the native Irish, who have
been predominantly Catholic since the fifth century. To the extent that
these sectarian labels imply that the conflict is a "religious war," that
Protestants are attacked because they attend a Protestant church, and
that Catholics are attacked because they attend a Catholic one, they are
misleading. Rather, the conflict should be understood as one between
the Unionists, or Loyalists, who wish to maintain the state of union
with Great Britain as a link to their heritage, and the Nationalists, or
the more militant Republicans, who wish to reinstitute an undivided
Ireland as a link to their heritage. Two related issues—the preservation
of historical and cultural ties, whether to Great Britain or to Ireland,
and the fact that political power may depend on which ties are preserved—have inspired the violence, not religious beliefs per se.[17] The
historical division between Unionist and Nationalist, and therefore be-

---

16. *See* R. HULL, *supra* note 5, at 55-56.
17. As described by The Times of London,

[t]here are two communities in Northern Ireland, different in their origins, nursing different historical myths, possessing distinguishable cultures, having different songs and
heroes, and wearing different denominations of the same religion. Religion is the clearest badge of these differences. But the conflict is not *about* religion. It is about the self-
assertion of two distinct communities, one of which is dominant in the public affairs of
the province.

The Times (London), Aug. 30, 1969, at 7, col. 1 (editorial) (emphasis in the original)
     This is not to suggest that "sectarian" murders—ones committed against an individual
known to be of a certain religion—do not occur. The important point is that the victims in
such murders are likely to have been chosen because it is assumed that they also oppose the
political aspirations of their assassins. Politics in most cases has primacy over religion, although the religious element plays some role, and the religious labels often are used for the
sake of convenience. Some Unionist factions, however, do stress the "evils" of Catholicism
See P. MARRIAN, PAISLEY: MAN OF WRATH (1973).

Northern Ireland

tween Protestant and Catholic, rendered even more acute by years of discrimination against the minority, has made Northern Ireland fertile ground for violence and civil unrest.

The Unionist Party, closely connected through much of its existence to the often violently anti-Catholic Orange Order,[18] governed Northern Ireland without interruption until 1972,[19] when the imposition of direct rule from Westminster effectively suspended parliamentary government within Northern Ireland.[20] It is now admitted that during this period discrimination against the Catholic minority was widespread in housing, employment, and the administration of justice.[21]

Progress toward equality of opportunity in housing[22] and employment[23] has been made, but true economic equality between majority and minority has not yet been realized.[24] The burdens of inequality have been complicated by the fact that Northern Ireland generally is much poorer than the rest of the United Kingdom.[25] Attempts to remedy inequalities have been handicapped during the last decade by economic decline, as continuing violence and the problems in the British and world economies have combined to deter new industry from locating in Northern Ireland and to persuade some existing firms to close or

18. W. FLACKES, NORTHERN IRELAND. A POLITICAL DIRECTORY, 1968-1979, at 103 (1980).
19. T. MOODY, *supra* note 3, at 32, 48.
20. Northern Ireland (Temporary Provisions) Act, 1972, ch. 22 (authorization of direct rule); *see generally* THE SUNDAY TIMES INSIGHT TEAM, ULSTER 280-310 (1972).
21. *See* THE SUNDAY TIMES INSIGHT TEAM, *supra* note 20, at 27-55 (general discussion of discrimination); FAIR EMPLOYMENT AGENCY FOR NORTHERN IRELAND, AN INDUSTRIAL AND OCCUPATIONAL PROFILE OF THE TWO SECTIONS OF THE POPULATION IN NORTHERN IRELAND (1978) (general discussion of employment discrimination); R. MILLER, OCCUPATIONAL MOBILITY OF PROTESTANTS AND ROMAN CATHOLICS IN NORTHERN IRELAND (1979) (structural discrimination in occupational patterns); K. BOYLE, T. HADDEN & P. HILLYARD, LAW AND STATE: THE CASE OF NORTHERN IRELAND, chs. 2, 7, 9 (1975) (discrimination in the administration of justice).
22. Public housing is now being awarded on the basis of objective criteria, which has reduced significantly concern about discriminatory awards. Housing remains a serious problem, however, as 14.1% of the housing stock is classified as unfit for human habitation, compared with 4.6% for England and Wales. Rowthorn, *Northern Ireland: an economy in crisis*, 5 CAMBRIDGE J. ECON. 1, at 15 (1981).
23. The Fair Employment Agency, which was established to monitor public and private employment practices, now requires the recipients of government contracts to hold Equal Opportunity Certificates, which the agency may revoke upon findings of non-compliance with their terms. *See* FAIR EMPLOYMENT AGENCY FOR NORTHERN IRELAND, SIXTH REPORT AND SETTLEMENT OF ACCOUNTS 4-5, 10-12 (1982).
24. Rowthorn, *supra* note 22, at 8-10, 18-22. This study found that "[m]any people continue to live in real poverty and deprivation—especially Catholics, who remain lower paid, more poorly housed, and more prone to unemployment than Protestants." *Id.* at 15.
25. The standard of living in Northern Ireland was substantially lower than that of the United Kingdom generally until the late 1960's. Although important gains have been made since then, average earnings remain lower, and unemployment higher than in the United Kingdom as a whole. *Id.* at 14-16.

The Yale Journal of World Public Order   Vol. 8:284, 1982

relocate.[26]

Catholic suspicions about fairness in the administration of justice still run deep.[27] The foundations for these fears are embedded deeply in Irish history.[28] In Northern Ireland, the Unionists maintained their control from 1922 to 1972 with the help of the Special Powers Act,[29] a sweeping measure that gave authorities extraordinary powers of search and seizure, internment, and censorship.[30] The Act was supplemented by additional regulations and statutes which prohibited, for example, membership in proscribed organizations[31] and the display of certain flags and emblems.[32] The Unionists used the legislation to stifle dissent in the minority community,[33] which was not protected by a written system of constitutional rights,[34] and which lacked the political power to

---

26. *Id.* at 16-18. It has been estimated that the conflict has destroyed or prevented the creation of 25,000 manufacturing jobs in Northern Ireland. *Id.* at 18. Unemployment in Northern Ireland is now running at about 24% of the work force. Irish Times, Jan. 5, 1983, at 9, col. 1.

27. The basis for these suspicions, embodied in an expression heard often in the poorer Catholic communities that "there's one justice for 'them,' and another for 'us,' has been thoroughly documented in K. BOYLE, T. HADDEN & P. HILLYARD, *supra* note 21, at chs. 7, 9.

28. For example, in the eighteenth century the all-Protestant parliament of Ireland enacted a comprehensive set of anti-Catholic measures which forbade Catholics from holding any government office, from entering the legal profession, and from holding commissions in the army and navy. See Wall, *The Age of the Penal Laws (1691-1778)*, in THE COURSE OF IRISH HISTORY, *supra* note 3, at 217.

29. Civil Authorities (Special Powers) Act (Northern Ireland), 1922, N. Ir. Pub. Gen. Acts, 12 & 13 Geo. 5, ch. 5, *repealed by* the Northern Ireland (Emergency Provisions) Act, 1973, ch. 53, § 31(2).

30. *See* Bishop, *Law in the Control of Terrorism and Insurrection: The British Laboratory Experience*, 42 L. & CONTEMP. PROBS. 140, 157-58 (1978).

31. Bishop, *supra* note 30, at 159.

32. Flags and Emblems (Display) Act (Northern Ireland), 1954, N. Ir. Pub. Gen. Acts, 2 & 3 Eliz. 2, ch. 10.

33. The history of the special power laws in Northern Ireland, as well as the Catholic perception of their effect, was offered in 1978 by Gerry Fitt, M.P. for West Belfast:

As anyone in Northern Ireland knows, emergency provisions legislation of this description was first placed on the statute book in the Northern Ireland House of Commons in 1922. It was known as the Special Powers Act. From 1922 until 1929 it was renewed every twelve months by the Parliament in Northern Ireland. In 1929 the Government said that the Act should become a permanent part of Northern Ireland legislation. Therefore, it was not of necessity debated every year in the Northern Ireland House of Commons.

Throughout those years certain sections and provisions of the Special Powers Act were used against individuals in Northern Ireland. That did not stop the violence, it increased it. Every year, at Easter, whenever there was a Royal visit or if there seemed to be a heightening of tension between Republican and Loyalist communities, the Act was brought into being, and though people were not charged, they were interned.

Looking back, we now see that such legislation as this is no guarantee that there will be a diminution of violence.

959 PARL. DEB., H.C. (5th ser.) 1544 (1978) (statement of G. Fitt, M.P. for West Belfast)

34. Rose, *On the Priorities of Citizenship in the Deep South and Northern Ireland*, 38 J. POL. 247, 275-76 (1976).

Northern Ireland

defend itself.

The Special Powers Act was justified on the ground that it was necessary to combat a highly feared secret organization, the Irish Republican
Army (I.R.A.).[35] Ironically, however, during the period from 1922 to
1968, the I.R.A. was largely inactive as a military unit in Northern Ireland.[36] Nonetheless, official state visits by British dignitaries and British national holidays were marked by systematic arrests and temporary
detention of suspected I.R.A. members.[37]

The current wave of violence began in 1968, when civil rights marchers protesting housing discrimination were attacked by Protestant mobs
and by members of a new disbanded all-Unionist reserve police force.[38]
The violence, which has continued with only brief respites,[39] has
sprung from several sources[40] and has claimed thousands of victims
from both sides.[41] On the side of the Republicans, two groups have
been especially active. The best known is the Provisional I.R.A.,[42]

---

35. *See* Bishop, *supra* note 30, at 157.

36. For example, its one northern "campaign," conducted by the I.R.A. from 1956 to
1962, resulted in the deaths of eighteen persons, the majority of them members of the I.R.A.
See J. BELL, THE SECRET ARMY, 321-97 (1972).

37. *See supra* note 33.

38. *See* THE SUNDAY TIMES INSIGHT TEAM, *supra* note 20, at chs. 1-4; DISTURBANCES
IN NORTHERN IRELAND: REPORT OF THE COMMISSION APPOINTED BY THE GOVERNOR OF
NORTHERN IRELAND, N. IR. CMD. No. 532 (1969) (Lord Cameron, Chairman) [hereinafter
CAMERON REPORT].

39. Almost 2,300 people have been killed, and over 25,000 seriously injured, in politically related violence since 1969. During the same period, over 12,000 bombs and incendiary devices have been exploded in Northern Ireland, and 29,429 shooting incidents have
been reported. The violence peaked in 1972, the year after internment without trial was
introduced, and the first year of direct rule from Westminster, with almost twice as many
violent incidents as any of the next succeeding four years. ROYAL ULSTER CONSTABULARY,
CHIEF CONSTABLE'S ANNUAL REPORT 1982, at 48 (table 6) (1983). Violence declined
sharply in 1980. *Id.* It escalated again in 1981, however, when 101 people were killed (44
members of the security forces, and 57 civilians, some terrorists), 578 bombs were exploded,
and 1,142 shooting incidents took place. *Id.*

40. It has been estimated that of 2,250 politically related fatalities classified as of June,
1982, 53.2% were caused by Republican terrorist organizations, 27% by Loyalist organizations, 11.2% by security forces, and 8.2% by undetermined agents. McKeown, *Numbering the
Dead: A Register of Northern Ireland's Casualties*, IN DUBLIN, Dec. 16, 1982, at 20, 22.

41. Of the fatalities, 56.9% were civilians, 29.2% were members of the security forces,
11.5% were members of terrorist groups, and 2.4% could not be classified. *Id.* Of the 1,885
dead who were natives of Northern Ireland, 1,016 were Catholic and 839 were Protestant.
Id. Given that over half the fatalaties have been caused by Republican groups, the conclusion seems inescapable that a substantial number of Catholics have died at the hands of
their co-religionists.

42. It is important to distinguish the Provisional I.R.A. from the Official I.R.A.—"Official" because a majority of the delegates at a 1970 I.R.A. congress voted to support its position. It maintained a distinct military presence until 1972, when it declared a unilateral
cease-fire on the ground that a majority of the population of Northern Ireland favored union
with the United Kingdom. Its policy, first announced in 1970, has been to work for full
minority rights within the United Kingdom, but also to support a decentralized government

The Yale Journal of World Public Order   Vol. 8:284, 1982

which has directed an assassination campaign against representatives of the British Army, the R.U.C., the Ulster Defence Regiment (U.D.R.—a kind of National Guard composed of volunteers from Northern Ireland), and their respective reserves.[43] The Provisional I.R.A. also has killed politicians, judges, prison employees, and members of other terrorist groups, as well as hundreds of unintended victims.[44] A second group, the Irish National Liberation Army (I.N.L.A.) is the military wing of the Irish Republican Socialist Party.[45] It too wages a military battle, sometimes with terrifying success,[46] but its membership is apparently less numerous than that of the Provisional I.R.A.[47]

Loyalist terrorist activity seems motivated by fears of a possible union with the Republic of Ireland and by anger at what is perceived to be violence directed against the Protestant and Loyalist majority community. This activity has been aimed primarily at Catholics, through intimidation of families living in mixed areas and attacks on Catholic pubs and individuals.[48] Just as different Republic factions have engaged in internecine strife, Loyalist groups occasionally have attacked each other, although their differences appear to concern territorial control and racketeering more than differences in political and military strategy.[49]

There are two major Loyalist terrorist organizations. The Ulster Volunteer Force (U.V.F.) originated in the early twentieth century in response to the "threat" posed by an independent Ireland, but then largely disappeared after the partition of Ireland.[50] A group claiming its name and heritage emerged violently in the 1960s, and was declared illegal in 1966.[51] This proscription was lifted briefly in 1974, when the

---

in Northern Ireland which, it believes, would lead eventually to union with the Irish Republic. *See* W. FLACKES, *supra* note 18, at 111-20.

43. *See* T. COOGAN, THE I.R.A. 461-81 (1980).

44. *Id. See also supra* notes 39-41.

45. W. FLACKES, *supra* note 18, at 72.

46. The group claimed responsibility for the March, 1979 assassination of Airey Neave. M.P., Conservative Shadow Secretary for Northern Ireland and close friend of Prime Minister Thatcher. *Id.* It also claimed responsibility for a December, 1982 pub explosion which left 16 people dead and 29 seriously injured. Wash. Post, Dec. 8, 1982, at A28, col. 3.

47. W. FLACKES, *supra* note 18, at 72.

48. *See* K. BOYLE, T. HADDEN & P. HILLYARD, TEN YEARS ON IN NORTHERN IRELAND, 21-22 (1980) [hereinafter TEN YEARS ON]. It is easily, but not necessarily correctly, argued that Loyalist terrorists are more "sectarian" than their more "political" Republican counterparts. This apparent distinction is probably a function of the nature of the conflict. Republican terrorists can pick "political" targets who are symbols of the political and economic status quo, while Loyalist targets are more obviously "sectarian." *Id.*

49. *Id.*

50. M. DILLON & D. LEHANE, POLITICAL MURDER IN NORTHERN IRELAND 28 (1973)

51. *Id.* at 28-35.

Northern Ireland

U.V.F. undertook a short-lived political action campaign.[52] It soon reverted to terrorism, however, and was banned again under the terms of the EPA.[53]

The second, and much larger, Loyalist organization, is the Ulster Defence Association (U.D.A.). Founded in 1971 to coordinate opposition to the I.R.A. among various Protestant groups,[54] it has recruited large numbers of working class Protestants from all over Northern Ireland.[55] Its initial purpose was to demonstrate the strength of opposition in Northern Ireland to a united island, and to that end it organized impressive and disciplined public military maneuvers.[56] It changed its position in 1977 and campaigned politically for the creation of a Northern Ireland independent of Great Britain and the Irish Republic.[57] In 1981, however, during a hunger strike by Republican prisoners, the U.D.A. abandoned the approach and returned to its Loyalist position.[58] While the U.D.A. has never been proscribed, it has played a major role in the intimidation of Catholics, and few doubt that some of its members have been involved in assassination and bombing.[59]

The final actors in this military drama are the government forces, which include some 30,000 members of the British Army and the R.U.C.,[60] and who patrol a country of 1.5 million inhabitants.[61] These troops are ostensibly assisted in their efforts to maintain order by the existence of emergency legislation, the scope and effects of which this Article is intended to analyze.

II. The EPA: Protection of Public Security at the Expense of Individual Freedom

Adopted in 1973 following the recommendation of a British government commission chaired by Lord Diplock,[62] the EPA has remained

52. W. FLACKES, *supra* note 18, at 147.
53. *Id.*
54. *Id.* at 138-39.
55. *Id.* at 138.
56. *Id.* at 139.
57. *Id.* at 140-41.
58. Interview with Andrew Tyrie, Chief of Staff, U.D.A., in Belfast, Northern Ireland (Oct. 20, 1981).
59. TEN YEARS ON, *supra* note 48, at 20.
60. As of July, 1979, 13,000 regular soldiers and almost 12,000 police and reservists were deployed in Northern Ireland. 969 PARL. DEB., H.C. (5th ser.) 934-35 (1979), (statement of Humphrey Atkins, Secretary of State for Northern Ireland). By December 1980, the total had climbed to 31,500. TEN YEARS ON, *supra* note 48, at 25.
61. NORTHERN IRELAND INFORMATION SERVICE, FACTS AT YOUR FINGERTIPS 4 (1981).
62. *See* REPORT OF THE COMMISSION TO CONSIDER LEGAL PROCEDURES TO DEAL WITH TERRORIST ACTIVITIES IN NORTHERN IRELAND, CMD. 5, No. 5185 (1972) (Lord Diplock, Chairman) [hereinafter DIPLOCK REPORT]. The EPA contained a provision repealing the

The Yale Journal of World Public Order   Vol. 8:284, 1982

fundamentally unaltered since its enactment. A government committee, chaired by Lord Gardiner and appointed in 1974 to assess the anti-
terrorist measures in the context of human rights and civil liberties,
recommended some important changes,[63] but essentially the EPA was
left intact. Sixteen semi-annual reviews of the EPA undertaken by the
British Parliament have resulted in only one major change: the power
of internment, which originally could be invoked at the discretion of
the Secretary of State, can now be invoked only with parliamentary
approval.[64] At each review, the British government has recommended
continuation of the EPA,[65] and Parliament has appeared willing to accept this recommendation virtually automatically.[66] A small but vocal
minority (about 20 of the approximately 670 members of Parliament)
has consistently criticized the invasions of individual freedom permitted under the EPA,[67] but it received no widespread support, at least
during the first fourteen renewal debates.[68]

While the application of the EPA is confined to Northern Ireland,[69]
its scope within the province is far-reaching. The Act applies primarily
to "scheduled offenses,"[70] which generally constitute "terrorist" crimes
such as arson, kidnapping, use of explosives, and hijacking.[71] It established special police and judicial procedures to be used in the investiga-

---

Special Powers Act. EPA, 1973, ch. 53, § 31(2). It should be understood as the latest version
of the emergency laws that have been in effect in Northern Ireland since its establishment.
See supra notes 29-33 and accompanying text.

63. *See* REPORT OF A COMMITTEE TO CONSIDER, IN THE CONTEXT OF CIVIL LIBERTIES
AND HUMAN RIGHTS, MEASURES TO DEAL WITH TERRORISTS IN NORTHERN IRELAND, CMD.
5, No. 5847 (1975) (Lord Gardiner, Chairman) [hereinafter GARDINER REPORT]. The Gardiner Report's criticisms of the internment program were instrumental in persuading the
government to abandon internment in favor of the trial of suspected terrorists in special
courts. *See id.* at para. 148, at 43; *infra* note 105 and accompanying text. The Report also
recommended that Parliament reaffirm judicial discretion to exclude the admission into evidence of statements made under questionable circumstances. GARDINER REPORT, *supra*,
para. 50, at 17. The recommendation was not adopted. *See infra* notes 181-85 and accompanying text.

64. Northern Ireland (Emergency Provisions) Act 1978 (Continuance) Order, 1980
STAT. INST., No. 1049.

65. *See, e.g.,* 959 PARL. DEB., H.C. (5th ser.) 1499-1500 (1978) (statement of Roy Mason,
Secretary of State for Northern Ireland); 969 PARL. DEB., H.C. (5th ser.) 931-35 (1979)
(statement of Humphrey Atkins, Secretary of State for Northern Ireland).

66. *See, e.g.,* 969 PARL. DEB., H.C. (5th ser.) 925-1066 (1979) (parliamentary debate on
continuation of the EPA); 959 PARL. DEB., H.C. (5th ser.) 1499-1586 (1978) (same).

67. *See, e.g.,* 959 PARL. DEB., H.C. (5th ser.) 1539 (1978) (statement of Tom Litterick,
M.P. for Birmingham); 969 PARL. DEB., H.C. (5th ser.) 944 (1979) (statement of Brynmor
John M.P. for Pontypridd).

68. *See infra* notes 81-82 and accompanying text.

69. EPA § 36(2).

70. *Id.* § 30, sched. 4.

71. *Id.*

Northern Ireland

tion and trial of scheduled offenses.[72] It permits arrest and search without warrant of those suspected of "committing, having committed, or being about to commit" offenses covered by the EPA,[73] and makes it illegal for those witnessing or having knowledge of terrorist incidents to refuse to cooperate with the authorities.[74] Persons suspected of being terrorists may be arrested without warrant and detained for up to seventy-two hours.[75] Moreover, its extraordinary powers are not limited to scheduled offenses: British troops are permitted to arrest and detain temporarily without charge or warrant any individual suspected of any crime.[76] The EPA also creates new categories of crimes, such as wearing hoods in public,[77] and retains many features of earlier emergency laws.[78] Given this scope, the conclusion that the EPA has touched the lives of many thousands of people in Northern Ireland is inescapable.

British government officials have acknowledged the wide sweep of the EPA as well as its intrusive character. Merlyn Rees, a former Secretary of State for Northern Ireland, described its scope as follows:

—all terrorist type offenses to be categorized as "scheduled offenses";
—trials of scheduled offenses to be by a senior judge, sitting alone [no right to a jury trial], but with more than usual rights of appeal;
—bail in scheduled cases to be given only by the High Court (rather than by a magistrate) and then only if stringent precautions were made;
—the arrest without warrant and detention by the police for up to 72 hours of any person suspected of being a terrorist . . .;
—the arrest and detention of a suspect [for any offense] for up to four hours by members of the Army;
—wide powers of search and seizure by members of the security forces;
—reversal of the normal onus of proof in relation to offenses of possession of arms and explosives;

---

72. *See, e.g., id.* § 2 (special conditions for bail); *id.* § 6 (special courts for trial of scheduled offenses); *id.* § 7 (no jury trials of scheduled offenses).

73. *Id.* §§ 13, 14.

74. Section 18 of the EPA provides that "any member of Her Majesty's forces on duty or any constable may stop and question any person for the purpose of ascertaining" the person's identity and movements "and what he knows concerning any recent explosion or other incident . . . ." Failure to stop or refusal to answer to the best of one's "knowledge or ability" can result in six months in prison or £100 fine, or both. *Id.* § 18.

75. *Id.* § 13. Other anti-terrorist legislation permits the detention of suspected terrorists for periods up to seven days. Prevention of Terrorism (Temporary Provisions) Act, 1976, ch. 8, § 12(2).

76. *Id.* § 14(1).

77. *Id.* § 26.

78. For example, section 21 of the EPA prohibits membership in proscribed organizations. *Id.* § 21. This offense is analogous to one defined under regulations issued pursuant to the Special Powers Act. *See supra* note 31 and accompanying text. Both the Provisional I.R.A. and the U.V.F. are proscribed. EPA § 21, sched. 2.

—a fresh system of detention by the executive.[79]

Acknowledging the severity of the measure at the time of its enactment, then Secretary of State William Whitelaw declared that "[t]he Bill contains some features unpalatable to a democratic society. Her Majesty's government does not disguise the fact that it imposes serious limitations on the traditional liberty of the subject."[80]

The bipartisan consensus that had supported automatic continuation of the EPA broke down in 1981, when the British Labour Party supported a motion introduced in Parliament that called for a broad investigation of the operation of the Act.[81] In analyzing the emergence of opposition to the EPA, it may be noted that the Act has generated two distinct but related concerns: (1) that the EPA must be scrutinized because it contemplates intolerable violations of individual rights; and (2) that the EPA, when considered instrumentally, must be judged a failure because its counterproductive effects—the possible swelling of terrorist ranks, and the erosion of respect for law and order—fuel the very crisis that the EPA was intended to quell.[82]

Regarding the first concern, while it is undeniable that the right to live is the most basic human right, and that the right to live without fear of death or grievous bodily injury is almost equally central, it seems undeniable that the government's responsibility to protect individual freedom has been seriously compromised under the emergency regime. Military forces are virtually omnipresent.[83] Almost 300,000 warrantless home searches were authorized between 1971 and June, 1978.[84] These home searches occurred at an average rate of about ninety per day.[85] Between 1972 and 1978 more than 25,000 persons were arrested and detained for periods ranging from four hours to

---

79. Rees. *Terror in Ireland—and Britain's Response*, in BRITISH PERSPECTIVES ON TERRORISM 83, 84 (P. Wilkinson ed. 1981).

80. PEACE PEOPLE, THE CASE FOR THE REPLACEMENT OF THE EMERGENCY PROVISION ACT BY NORMAL JUDICIAL PROCESS 3 (n.d.) (quoting William Whitelaw) (on file with *The Yale Journal of World Public Order*).

81. *See* 7 PARL. DEB., H.C. (6th ser.) 1032-46 (1981). The motion was defeated by a vote of 279 to 213. *Id* at 1046.

82. J. Don Concannon, M.P. and former Minister of State for Northern Ireland, articulated these concerns as follows:

[w]hile we fully accept the need to protect the community against terrorism, we are deeply concerned about the erosion of basic civil liberties. The continued and unreviewed emergency powers as they stand may impede the possibilities of a peaceful settlement.

Id. at 1040.

83. *See supra* note 60 and accompanying text.

84. PEACE PEOPLE, TIME FOR A CHANGE 8 (1980) (parliamentary submission) (on file with *The Yale Journal of World Public Order*) [hereinafter TIME FOR A CHANGE].

85. *Id.*

Northern Ireland

seven days.[86] Of those detained between September, 1977 and August,
1978, only about 35% were ultimately charged with an offense.[87] In the
first ten months of 1980, 3,868 persons were arrested by the police and
army under the EPA.[88] A mere 8.6% of those arrested were eventually
prosecuted,[89] compared with an 80 to 90% average for those arrested in
England and Wales.[90]

Important as this immediate concern for human rights may be, it can
be argued that the second concern—that the EPA produces longterm
counterproductive effects—is even more fundamental. If the EPA creates resentment, drives people into the terrorist groups, and undermines basic respect for the rule of law across Northern Ireland, it may
be exacerbating the violence it was designed to combat and making it
even more difficult to achieve a definitive resolution of the situation
that would guarantee public security and basic individual freedom.

With respect to the relationship between the EPA and the recruitment of terrorists, it seems plausible that the incursions into homes
through search and seizure and the arrest and detention of persons
without warrant or charge may encourage the involvement of young
people in the violence. It should be noted that the current violence is
largely the product of young people who have grown up since the beginning of the most recent period of terror. Two-thirds of those serving
prison terms longer than four years were under fifteen years of age
when the current emergency began; one-third were under nine.[91]
Northern Ireland, which formerly had the lowest per capita prison population in Western Europe, now has the highest and youngest.[92] More-

86. TIME FOR A CHANGE, *supra* note 84, at 9.

87. *See* REPORT OF THE COMMITTEE OF INQUIRY INTO POLICE INTERROGATION PROCE-
DURES IN NORTHERN IRELAND app. l, at 141, CMD. 5, No. 7497 (1979) (His Honor H.G.
Bennett, Chairman) [hereinafter BENNETT REPORT].

88. 945 PARL. DEB., H.C. (5th ser.) 271, 605-06 (1980) (response of Humphrey Atkins,
Secretary of State, to written parliamentary question no. 49).

89. *Id.* Given that so few of those detained under the EPA are ever charged with an
offense, concern has arisen that the provisions of the EPA are not being used to investigate
terrorist incidents, but rather to compile information about individuals and even entire communities. One recent survey found that 72% of a geographically and socioeconomically diverse sample of arrestees were not questioned about their involvement in specific incidents
at all. *See* D. WALSH, ARREST AND INTERROGATION: NORTHERN IRELAND 1981 (1981) (on
file with *The Yale Journal of World Public Order*).

90. *See* ROYAL COMMISSION ON CRIMINAL PROCEDURE, REPORT, CMD. 5, No. 8092,
para. 3.17, at 43, para. 4.43, at 83 (1981).

91. NORTHERN IRELAND OFFICE, THE CORRYMEELA CONFERENCE (OCTOBER 1979) ON
PRISONS IN NORTHERN IRELAND, 1980 ONWARDS, WITH SPECIAL REFERENCE TO THE
LONG-TERM PRISONER 13 (Chart 3) (1979) (government paper submitted to the conference)
(on file with *The Yale Journal of World Public Order*).

92. THE PEACE PEOPLE, THE H-BLOCK PROTEST, HUNGER STRIKES AND EMERGENCY
LAW 7 (1980) (on file with *The Yale Journal of World Public Order*).

The Yale Journal of World Public Order   Vol. 8:284, 1982

over, one study of the backgrounds of terrorists has concluded that most I.R.A. operations are carried out by recent recruits whose backgrounds make them representative members of the working class Catholic communities in which they live.[93] In short, many of the terrorists at work are typical members of a younger generation that has grown up with violence and with the extreme measures taken to curtail it.

While the history and traditions of the Catholic communities in Northern Ireland ensure substantial resentment of British security forces and justice,[94] the process by which this general resentment is translated in individual cases into active support of a terrorist group is not clear. Perhaps the internment of a relative without trial or the destruction of property during a pre-dawn house search, or harassment on a local street might be sufficient to push a Catholic youth into membership in the youth wing of the Provisional I.R.A. But even given this uncertainty, the potential effects of the searches permitted under the EPA on terrorist recruitment is enormous. If only 2% of the 600 families whose homes were searched each week between 1970 and 1978 produced terrorist volunteers, the Provisional I.R.A. could have afforded a complete turnover every year in its corps of 500 active duty volunteers.[95]

The second pernicious effect of the EPA is that it may be undermining the respect for law and order necessary for a peaceful long-term solution to the crisis. This danger was recognized nine years ago in the Gardiner Report, which noted that the basic strategy of the terrorists was to provoke governmental reactions that would destroy the popular support that the government would otherwise enjoy.[96] It also noted that short-time measures might restore order, but that long-term solutions required popular support.[97] Unfortunately, these warnings do not appear to have been heeded, as the government, at least since the pas-

---

93. Boyle, Hadden & Hillyard, *Emergency Powers: Ten Years On*, FORTNIGHT, Jan. 1980, at 3, 4. The authors based their conclusions on their systematic review of the record in cases adjudicated by the courts of Northern Ireland in 1975 and 1979. *See also* TIME FOR CHANGE, *supra* note 84, at 9-10.

94. *See supra* notes 27-34 and accompanying text.

95. A secret paper of the British Ministry of Defence estimated that the Provisional I.R.A. had 500 "activist" members. MINISTRY OF DEFENCE, NORTHERN IRELAND FUTURE TERRORIST TRENDS, at G-1 (Dec. 15, 1978) (on file with *The Yale Journal of World Public Order*). A copy of the report was diverted and made public. The numerical strength of terrorist groups is, for obvious reasons, difficult to estimate accurately.

96. GARDINER REPORT, *supra* note 63, para. 17, at 7. For a discussion of this strategy generally, see R. CLUTTERBUCK, LIVING WITH TERRORISM 17 (1975); P. WILKINSON, TERRORISM AND THE LIBERAL STATE 66 (1977).

97. GARDINER REPORT, *supra* note 63, para. 19, at 7.

Northern Ireland

sage of the EPA, has focused almost exclusively on imposing repressive measures, and not on building a long-term consensus.

Even accepting the primacy of the EPA's short-term goal—the suppression of violence—the EPA must be adjudged a failure, because violence continues to wrack Northern Ireland.[98] Because the Act has failed to stop the terror, the population has lost confidence and has grown angry at the legal system, which has deprived individuals of basic civil liberties without offering any compensating increase in personal security. While the issue is not susceptible to quantitative analysis—for obvious reasons the participants are unwilling to speak— it seems plausible that as this loss of confidence and anger grow, the net effect of the EPA may be to produce more violence, not less.

The loss of respect for law is a dangerous development in any country, but especially so in Northern Ireland, where history guarantees a long and deep popular memory of civil strife.[99] Decision-makers should assess carefully whether measures implemented for short-term gains are outweighed by less tangible but more dangerous long-term consequences. While some form of emergency law will probably continue in Northern Ireland, further reliance on the deprivation of liberty demonstrates that the government itself is not fully committed to the rule of law as the appropriate vehicle to preserve public order. Thus, so long as the current crisis lasts, the daily impact of emergency law must be tempered by respect for the equitable administration of justice.

III. Admissibility Standards

A detailed analysis of the admissibility standards created under the EPA suggests strongly that the EPA should be reformed to make inadmissible as evidence statements obtained from persons interrogated under suspicious circumstances.

Section 8 of the EPA provides that any statement made by the accused during the investigation of a scheduled offense is admissible unless the accused can present "prima facie evidence" that he or she was "subjected to torture, inhuman or degrading treatment" for the purpose of inducing a statement.[100] This new standard represents a substantial

---

98. *See supra* notes 193-96 and accompanying text.
99. DIPLOCK REPORT, *supra* note 62, para. 13, at 9.
100. Section 8 of the EPA (formerly section 6) provides that:
(1) In any criminal proceedings for a scheduled offence, or two or more offences which are or include scheduled offences, a statement made by the accused may be given in evidence by the prosecution in so far as—
    (a) it is relevant to any matter in issue in the proceedings; and
    (b) it is not excluded by the court in pursuance of subsection (2) below.

The Yale Journal of World Public Order   Vol. 8:284, 1982

erosion of the traditional common law principle of voluntariness, under which a statement was admissible only if offered freely.[101] The new standard is also dangerously vague, because it leaves uncertain how much abuse constitutes "inhuman or degrading treatment."[102] This issue is of more than academic concern. Permitting the security forces to mistreat prisoners to the point of "torture, inhuman or degrading treatment" has ensured that this provision of the EPA would generate enormous tension and controversy.[103] Finally, reflecting the standard's vagueness, the courts of Northern Ireland have proven incapable of interpreting it in a coherent fashion.[104] These factors make a powerful argument that the standard should be fundamentally changed.

A. *The Controversy*

Since 1975 the anti-terrorist strategy of the British government has been to eschew internment, in which detainees were held up to four years without charge or trial, in favor of the pursuit of convictions in the courts.[105] Those accused of terrorist offenses have been tried by special non-jury "Diplock Courts" created by the EPA in 1973.[106] The

---

(2) If, in any such proceedings where the prosecution proposes to give in evidence a statement made by the accused, prima facie evidence is adduced that the accused was subjected to *torture or to inhuman or degrading treatment* in order to induce him to make the statement, the court shall, unless the prosecution satisfies it that the statement was not so obtained—
   (a) exclude the statement, or
   (b) if the statement has been received in evidence, either—
      (i) continue the trial disregarding the statement; or
      (ii) direct that the trial shall be restarted before a differently constituted court (before which the statement in question shall be inadmissible).
(3) This section does not apply to a summary trial.
EPA § 8 (emphasis added).
   101. *See infra* notes 136-37 and accompanying text.
   102. *See infra* notes 186-88 and accompanying text.
   103. *See infra* notes 116-27 and accompanying text.
   104. *See infra* notes 168-79 and accompanying text.
   105. Internment, which had been the official strategy since 1971, proved counterproductive. *See* K. BOYLE, T. HADDEN & P. HILLYARD, *supra* note 21, at 55-77. In the four months following its implementation in 1971, the number of murders increased twelvefold over the number committed in the preceding four months. SUNDAY TIMES INSIGHT TEAM, *supra* note 20, at 269. The Gardiner Report severely criticized the internment strategy. GARDINER REPORT, *supra* note 63, para. 148, at 43. Its criticisms helped persuade the government to change strategy. TEN YEARS ON, *supra* note 48, at 24.
   Nearly 2,000 people, including only 107 Protestants, were interned without trial for varying periods of time between August, 1971 and December, 1975. N.Y. Times, Dec. 6, 1975, at 1, col. 1, at 6, col. 2. The power of internment is still on the books, EPA § 12, sched. 1, but it can be invoked only with parliamentary approval. *See supra* note 64 and accompanying text. It has not been used since 1975. TEN YEARS ON, *supra* note 48, at 24. The government continues to retain and to use its significant powers of temporary detention. EPA §§ 11, 14; *see supra* notes 75, 86 and accompanying text.
   106. The courts are known by the name of the chairman of the commission that recom-

Northern Ireland

hope of the government has been that the return to the rule of law—
symbolized by the end of internment—would alleviate the deep-seated
mistrust of the legal system prevalent in the Catholic community.[107]
The basic problem with this hope has been that the emergency regime
of the EPA, despite the suspension of internment, cannot be viewed as
normal law.[108]

In particular, section 8, by removing the common law test of voluntariness in the admissibility of confessions, has caused major changes in
traditional police and legal procedure. At the police level, a shift has
occurred from pre-arrest acquisition of independent evidence to post-
arrest interrogation as the primary tool of gathering evidence.[109] At the
trial level, a shift has occurred from the jury's determination of the
accused's guilt or innocence to judicial rulings on the admissibility of
the accused's confession[110]—rulings that, given the reliance on confessions, are practically dispositive of the question of guilt or innocence.

During 1976 and 1977, the two years after internment was abandoned, 3,147 persons were charged with scheduled offenses under the
EPA.[111] A conviction was obtained in 94% of these cases, a figure not in
itself alarming.[112] However, between 70 and 90% of these convictions
were based wholly or mainly on admissions made to the police and
held admissible by the courts under section 8.[113] At the same time, the
number of complaints of ill treatment during interrogation increased
from 180 in 1975 to 384 in 1976,[114] and almost 1100 for 1977 and 1978
combined.[115]

---

mended their establishment. *See* DIPLOCK REPORT, *supra* note 62, at paras. 35-41, at 17-19.
Among their special features are the lack of jury trial, EPA § 7, and the reversal of the
burden of proof in bail proceedings and trials of possession offenses. EPA §§ 2, 9. For a
general discussion of the operation of Diplock Courts, see TEN YEARS ON, *supra* note 48, at
57-88.

107. *See* TEN YEARS ON, *supra* note 48, at 102.

108. *See supra* notes 69-80 and accompanying text.

109. Grier, *The Admissibility of Confessions Under the Northern Ireland (Emergency Provisions) Act*, 31 N. IR. L.Q. 205, 208 (1980).

110. *Id.*

111. AMNESTY INTERNATIONAL, REPORT OF AN AMNESTY INTERNATIONAL MISSION TO
NORTHERN IRELAND 2 (1978) (AI Index EUR 45/01/78) (reporting data supplied by the
R.U.C.).

112. Sunday Times (London), Oct. 23, 1977, at 3, col. 1 (reporting research of the Law
Department, Queen's University, Belfast).

113. *Id.* Research on the evidence used against defendants in Diplock trials between
January and April, 1979 indicates that in 56% of the cases a statement from the defendant
was the only evidence, in 30% of the cases the evidence consisted of the defendant's statement and other evidence, in 6% of the cases no statement was made, and in 6% of the cases
the nature of the evidence could not be determined. TEN YEARS ON, *supra* note 48, at 44.

114. TEN YEARS ON, *supra* note 48, at 39.

115. TIME FOR A CHANGE, *supra* note 84, at 17.

The Yale Journal of World Public Order   Vol. 8:284, 1982

The opening of special police interrogation centers at Castlereagh and Gough Army Barracks was accompanied by large increases in the number of complaints of ill treatment during interrogation made against the police.[116] Such complaints were made by the Northern Ireland Civil Rights Association, by representatives of the mainly Catholic Social Democratic and Labour Party,[117] by the Catholic Church,[118] and by solicitors defending alleged terrorists in the Diplock Courts.[119] The Ulster Defence Association and the Loyalist-oriented Ulster Civil Liberties Advice Center also complained,[120] which indicates that the perception of ill treatment was not confined to the Catholic community. The wave of complaints received widespread publicity through two national television documentaries.[121] Finally, after the Police Surgeons Association began to speak out,[122] and Amnesty International issued a damning report about the situation,[123] the government appointed a Committee of Inquiry into Police Interrogation Procedures in Northern Ireland—the Bennett Committee.[124]

The Bennett Committee was not empowered to investigate individual complaints, as could Amnesty International,[125] but nevertheless in its March 1979 report it found that there were cases "in which injuries, whatever their precise cause, were not self-inflicted and were sustained in police custody."[126] The Committee's report contained sixty-four findings and recommendations designed to improve the supervision of interrogation and to eliminate the possibility of further abuses.[127] These recommendations included installing closed-circuit T.V. in all interview rooms,[128] limiting the length of interviews and the number of

---

116. TEN YEARS ON, *supra* note 48, at 39; *see generally* P. TAYLOR, BEATING THE TERRORISTS? INTERROGATION IN GOUGH AND CASTLEREAGH ch. 7 (treatment at Castlereagh) & ch. 12 (treatment at Gough).

117. *See* AMNESTY INTERNATIONAL, *supra* note 111, at 3 (complaints of Northern Ireland Civil Rights Association and Social Democratic and Labour Party).

118. *Id.* (statements of Tomas O'Fiach, Archbishop of Armagh).

119. *Id.* at 3-4 (solicitors' letter of complaint to Secretary of State).

120. *Id.* at 3 (dossier compiled by Ulster Defence Association), 4 (videotape produced by Advice Center).

121. *See* P. TAYLOR, *supra* note 116, at 163-64 (March 1977 BBC broadcast of interview alleging mistreatment) & at 221-22 (October 1977 Thames Television Company broadcast of "Inhuman and Degrading Treatment").

122. *Id.* at 261. Doctors working at the Crumlin Road Jail examined the medical records of forty-four prisoners and found twenty-eight to have significant physical injuries. *Id.*

123. AMNESTY INTERNATIONAL, *supra* note 111.

124. *See* BENNETT REPORT, *supra* note 87.

125. *Id.* para. 2, at 1.

126. *Id.* para. 163, at 55.

127. *Id.* para. 404, at 135-40.

128. *Id.* para. 404(36), at 138.

Northern Ireland

interviewers,[129] promulgating a formal code of conduct for interviewers,[130] and granting an absolute right of access to a solicitor after a
person had been detained forty-eight hours in custody.[131] The government has formally accepted most of these recommendations,[132] though
questions have been raised as to whether that commitment has been
honored fully in practice.[133] But even accepting that improvements
were made as a result of the Bennett Committee report, the basic difficulties created by the section 8 legal standard remain.

B. *Legal Debate: Standards Old and New*

The Diplock Commission, whose recommendations guided the draft-
ing of the EPA,[134] believed that the then prevailing common law standard regarding the admissibility of confessions so favored the
defendant in Northern Ireland that in the struggle against terrorism the
authorities were being forced to rely on the detention of suspected terrorists and not on their trial in courts of law.[135] The necessary implication of the Commission's judgment was that to foster a return to the
rule of law symbolized by judicial trials, it was necessary to suspend an
important legal protection—the principle of voluntariness in the admissibility of confessions.

The principle of voluntariness, operative throughout the United
Kingdom before the enactment of the EPA, was deeply established in
the common law.[136] It is well summarized in an official R.U.C. manual
that describes the law of evidence outside the context of the EPA: "The

---

129. *Id.* para. 404(24), at 137.
130. *Id.* para. 404(25), at 137.
131. *Id.* para. 404(45), at 138-39.
132. NORTHERN IRELAND OFFICE, ACTION TO BE TAKEN ON THE RECOMMENDATIONS
OF THE COMMITTEE OF INQUIRY INTO POLICE INTERROGATION PROCEDURE IN NORTHERN
IRELAND (n.d.) (on file with *The Yale Journal of World Public Order*).
133. *See* Walsh, *Arrest and Interrogation,* in THE ADMINISTRATION OF JUSTICE IN
NORTHERN IRELAND 6 (proceedings of conference held in Belfast, June 13, 1981) (on file
with *The Yale Journal of World Public Order*). Walsh found that recommendations regarding the permitted number of detectives involved in interrogation and the right of access to
solicitors were often ignored. *Id.* at 7.
134. *See supra* note 62 and accompanying text.
135. DIPLOCK REPORT, *supra* note 62, para. 87, at 31.
136. *See* Ibrahim v. Rex, [1914-15] All E.R. 874. The case involved the appeal of a
soldier who had been convicted of murder; the issue of the admissibility of the defendant's
confession was raised because he had confessed when asked by his commanding officer why
he had committed the crime. After reviewing the development of the common law doctrine
on admissibility, Lord Sumner concluded that

[i]t has long been established as a positive rule of English criminal law that no statement by an accused is admissible in evidence against him unless it is shown by the
prosecution to have been a voluntary statement, in the sense that it has not been obtained from him either by fear of prejudice or hope of advantage exercised or held out
by a person in authority.

The Yale Journal of World Public Order   Vol. 8:284, 1982

accepted test of voluntariness is in these terms:—The confession must not have been induced by threat of prejudice or detriment or hope of advantage of a temporal character held out by a person in authority, or by oppression."[137] The Diplock Commission recommended that the law be changed so that in trials of scheduled offenses confessions obtained in violation of the principle might still be admissible.[138] Its proposed substitute rule, derived from Article 3 of the European Convention for the Protection of Human Rights and Fundamental Freedoms,[139] was to make statements admissible unless "torture or . . . inhuman or degrading treatment" was used to induce them.[140] This suggestion, adopted in what is now section 8 of the EPA,[141] represented a sharp and obvious departure from the principle of voluntariness.

1. *Non-physical Force Atmosphere—Flaws in the Diplock Commission's Approach to Interrogation*

The Diplock Commission clearly foresaw that the new admissibility standard would permit interrogators to use psychological pressure to induce confessions. It stated that the proposed standard would permit the creation of a psychological atmosphere in which the person being

---

Id. at 877.

This venerable doctrine still plays an important role in British criminal law. *See* Director of Public Prosecutions v. Ping Lin, [1975] 3 All E.R. 175 (House of Lords). In this case a drug possession conviction was upheld after a finding that any hint of inducement in the questioning of the defendant had been overcome by three specific refusals by the police to make a deal. The language of the opinion laid out the principle of voluntariness in virtually the same language as had been used in the *Ibrahim* case of some sixty years before. *Id.* at 175.

The voluntariness test has also been accepted by the courts of Northern Ireland in deciding cases outside the context of the EPA. *See* Regina v. Corr, 1968 N. Ir. L.R. 193 (C.C.A.). The court found admissible statements made by the defendant after questioning by the police. Although the appellant made no allegations of oppressive, harsh, or misleading interrogation, the court noted in dicta that even "vigorous cross-examination" might have been enough to render the admission involuntary.

The effect of a vigorous cross-examination or . . . of a series 'of searching interrogatories' on one who is not free to get away from his questioner may, in certain circumstances, be to arouse hope of release or fear of further detention or other prejudicial result in the mind of the suspect according to whether or not he makes answers or keeps silent. But it also acts more directly by subjecting the person questioned to a degree of pressure which saps his will and makes him talk. We think such pressure may well . . . suffice to make statements obtained by it inadmissible in point of law.

Id. at 211.

137. K. MASTERSON, EVIDENCE IN CRIMINAL CASES 21 (1978).
138. DIPLOCK REPORT, *supra* note 62, para. 89, at 32.
139. *See* European Convention for the Protection of Human Rights and Fundamental Liberties, art. 3, 213 U.N.T.S. 221; DIPLOCK REPORT, *supra* note 62, para. 90, at 32. Article 3 is not an admissibility standard per se; rather, it flatly prohibits the use of "torture, inhuman or degrading treatment."
140. DIPLOCK REPORT, *supra* note 62, para. 89, at 32.
141. *See supra* note 139.

Northern Ireland

questioned would be more willing to speak, and, furthermore, that in creating this atmosphere the use of "promises of favours" and "indications of [unfavorable] consequences" to induce statements was allowed.[142] The common law standard excluding statements made in "hope of advantage" or under "threat of detriment" thus was clearly rejected. The Commission believed that modern techniques of interrogation, which seek to create in the suspect the desire to confide in the questioner, do "not involve cruel or degrading treatment."[143] The actual or threatened use of violence, however, was to continue to render a confession inadmissible.[144]

At the Castlereagh and Gough interrogation centers, both of which have been designed to intensify the prisoner's sense of isolation and thereby create the "psychological atmosphere" foreseen by the Diplock Commission,[145] suspects are kept isolated for up to seven days.[146] They suffer severe stress and fatigue.[147] The future appears grim—they may believe they will be beaten or will receive long prison sentences—and they are kept awake long hours and probably find it difficult to sleep in a strange and frightening environment.[148] Each day relaxed interrogation teams start the questioning anew, alternately menacing or befriending the disoriented suspect.[149] Evidence indicates that these techniques succeed relatively quickly, as "even the strongest wills" weaken due to isolation, stress, fatigue, and uncertainty.[150]

Psychological pressure theoretically may be sufficient to produce confessions, but in the atmosphere sanctioned by the Diplock Commission it was perhaps inevitable that the psychological approach would be mixed with or give way to violence. As has been seen, evidence from numerous and diverse sources suggests that violent interrogation has occurred frequently.[151]

---

142. DIPLOCK REPORT, *supra* note 62, para. 89, at 32.

143. *Id.* para. 84, at 30.

144. *Id.* para. 91, at 32. The Commission's attitude toward violence may be inferred from the following:

> [w]e do not think that . . . the police . . . should be discouraged from creating by *means which do not involve physical violence, the threat of it, or any other inhuman or degrading treatment*, a situation in which a guilty man is more likely than he otherwise would have been . . . to speak . . . .

Id. (emphasis added).

145. *See* TEN YEARS ON, *supra* note 48, at 45.

146. *Id.* at 45-46.

147. *Id.* at 46.

148. *Id.*

149. *Id.*

150. *Id.* at 45.

151. *See supra* notes 116-22 and accompanying text.

2. *"Torture, Inhuman or Degrading Treatment"—Flaws in the Diplock Standard*

The second major problem with the section 8 admissibility standard is that it is fundamentally ambiguous in two critical respects. First, an important inconsistency separates the Diplock Commission's intended interpretation of "torture, inhuman or degrading treatment" and the interpretation of that standard by the European Commission on Human Rights, to whose decisions, given the origins of the standard,[152] the courts of Northern Ireland inevitably have looked for guidance. Second, it is unclear to what extent the section 8 standard preserves the common law tradition of judicial discretion in ruling on the admissibility of confessions. These two ambiguities have combined to produce enormous and dangerous confusion.

The European Commission offered a thorough interpretation of the "torture, inhuman or degrading treatment" standard in its opinion in the 1969 *Greek Case (Denmark v. Greece)*.[153] The case involved a complaint by four countries brought against Greece over its suspension of certain constitutional rights afforded its citizens, as well as its alleged torture of political prisoners. In sustaining some of the allegations of the complaint the Commission rendered the following definitions:

> Inhuman treatment: at least such treatment as deliberately causes severe suffering, mental or physical, which in the particular situation is unjustifiable.[154]

> Torture: often used to describe inhuman treatment, which has a purpose, such as the obtaining of information, or confession, or the infliction of punishment, and it is generally an aggravated form of inhuman treatment.[155]

> Non-physical torture: the infliction of mental suffering by creating a state of anguish and stress by means other than bodily assault.[156]

> Degrading treatment: treatment or punishment of an individual may be said to be degrading if it grossly humiliates him before others or drives him to act against his will or conscience.[157]

The Commission's majority opinion stated that a distinction must be drawn between acts prohibited by Article 3 and "a certain roughness of treatment [that] may take the form of slaps or blows of the hand on the

---

152. *See supra* note 139 and accompanying text.
153. 1969 [THE GREEK CASE] Y.B. EUR. CONV. ON HUMAN RIGHTS 1 (Eur. Comm'n on Human Rights). The case was a consolidation of applications by Denmark, Norway, Sweden, and the Netherlands.
154. *Id.* at 186.
155. *Id.*
156. *Id.* at 461.
157. *Id.* at 186.

Northern Ireland

head or face."[158]

An illustration of the Commission's view of this distinction may be found in the case of *X against the United Kingdom*,[159] a routine criminal case in which the applicant claimed to have been attacked by a police dog and assaulted twice while handcuffed.[160] While the Commission rejected the applicant's version of the facts, it concluded in dicta that even on its face the application did "not disclose a treatment so serious as to amount to inhuman or degrading treatment within the meaning of Art. 3 of the Convention."[161] Thus, it is clear that the interpretation by the European Commission tolerates physical mistreatment not permissible under the voluntariness principle—a possibility that the Diplock Commission apparently did not foresee.[162]

Two decisions on admissibility, handed down immediately before and after the enactment of the EPA, illustrate well the nature of the change that the implementation of the standard of the European Convention was intended to effect. Shortly before the EPA established the new admissibility standard, the Lord Chief Justice of Northern Ireland held in *Regina v. Flynn*[163] that confessions obtained at the Holywood Army Barracks were inadmissible because the Barracks was "a set-up officially organized and operated to gain information . . . from persons who would otherwise have been less willing to give it."[164] The Diplock Report specifically criticized this decision,[165] and the Lord Chief Justice accommodated that criticism in an opinion delivered shortly after the new standard took effect. In construing the new standard, he found in *Regina v. Corey*[166] that "[t]here is no need now to satisfy the judge that a statement is voluntary in the sometimes technical sense which that word has acquired in relation to criminal trials."[167]

---

158. *Id.* at 501. Ironically, the Commission used these exact definitions in rendering its opinion in the 1971 case of Ireland v. United Kingdom, which involved a number of complaints of ill-treatment during interrogations at the Holywood Army Barracks between August and December 1971. Ireland v. United Kingdom, 1978 E.C.H.R. 377, No. 5310/71 (judgement of Jan. 18, 1978). At the time of the complaint the Special Powers Act, the predecessor of the EPA, was still in effect. *See supra* notes 29-32 and accompanying text.

159. 1971 Y.B. Eur. Conv. on Human Rights 250 (Eur. Comm'n on Human Rights).

160. *Id.* at 252.

161. *Id.* at 276.

162. *See supra* note 144 and accompanying text.

163. (Belfast City Comm'n, May 23, 1972) (ruling by Lowry, L.C.J.), *digested in* 23 N. Ir. L.Q. 343 (1972).

164. Note, *Admissibility of Confessions and the Common Law in Times of Emergency*, 24 N. Ir. L.Q. 199, 202 (1974) (quoting Regina v. Flynn (Belfast City Comm'n, May 23, 1972)).

165. Diplock Report, *supra* note 62, para. 83, at 30.

166. Note, 1979 N. Ir. 49 (Belfast City Comm'n, Dec. 6, 1973) (ruling by Lowry, L.C.J.), *digested in* 25 N. Ir. L.Q. 180 (1974).

167. 1979 N. Ir. 50.

The Yale Journal of World Public Order   Vol. 8:284, 1982

Despite this apparent initial clarity, later cases have revealed that the courts of Northern Ireland are deeply troubled by the departure from the common law, and are finding the new standard difficult to interpret. One leading case on section 8 which betrays this difficulty in *Regina v. McCormick*,[168] which concerned the admissibility of statements made by five defendants charged with offenses ranging from murder to membership in a proscribed organization.[169] After noting that the European Convention cases permit " 'a certain roughness of treatment,' " the Lord Justice (the trial court judge) wrote that decisions under article 3 appear to contemplate the use of physical violence not permitted under the common law standard.[170] He further argued that if the Diplock standard were interpreted in the same way as article 3,[171] it must be read to permit the use of "a moderate degree of physical maltreatment for the purpose of inducing a statement."[172] Put differently, the court appeared to hold that a statement would be held admissible unless "torture, inhuman or degrading treatment" in the sense described by the European Commission was used for the purpose of inducing it.[173]

Shifting directions, however, the opinion then examined the power of judicial discretion, which, it maintained, provided non-statutory control over the means by which statements are obtained.[174] It invoked language from *Regina v. Corey*,[175] the earlier case interpreting the section 8 standard, to the effect that judges were still permitted to exclude statements if their admission " 'would not be in the interests of justice.' "[176] Seizing on this "interests of justice" rationale, the opinion excluded some of the statements at issue in *McCormick* because in its view they had been induced by physical violence.[177]

---

168. 1977 N. Ir. 105.
169. *Id.*
170. *Id.* at 110.
171. On this issue, the court asserted that
    the terms torture or inhuman or degrading conduct in section 6 of the 1973 Act are taken from Article 3 and Parliament in using these words was accepting as guidelines the standards laid down in the European Convention on Human Rights and incorporating these in the domestic legislation.
Id. at 109.
172. *Id.* at 111.
173. *Id.*
174. *Id.*
175. *See supra* notes 166-67 and accompanying text.
176. 1977 N. Ir. at 112 (quoting Regina v. Corey (Belfast City Comm'n, Dec. 6, 1973)). Judicial discretion permits the court to exclude statements which satisfy the strict legal tests of admissibility, but which the court concludes could not be admitted without "operat[ing] unfairly against a defendant." Collis v. Gunn, [1964] 1 Q.B. 495, 501. Like the principle of voluntariness, which section 8 explicitly abandoned, it is deeply embedded in the common law. *See* GARDINER REPORT, *supra* note 63, para. 47, at 16.
177. 1977 N. Ir. at 112. In a later case, *Regina v. O'Halloran*, the Lord Chief Justice

Northern Ireland

In short, the opinion is contradictory. After apparently endorsing the view that "it is open to an interviewer to use a moderate degree of physical maltreatment for the purpose of inducing a statement,"[178] the opinion excluded statements precisely on the ground that violence had been used to obtain them. The rationale of the opinion was further obscured by language in the conclusion to the effect that the discretionary power "should not be exercised so as to defeat the will of Parliament as expressed" in section 8.[179]

The second basic ambiguity in the interpretation of section 8 is, however, precisely that the will of Parliament with respect to the judicial power of discretion is impossible to determine. The Diplock Commission clearly intended that its proposed standard would suspend the common law principle of voluntariness, and would remove from judges the discretionary power to depart from the standard even should the "interests of justice" require it.[180] It seemed neither to anticipate the use of physical violence in interrogation, nor to be aware that the case law under article 3 permitted such conduct.[181]

The Gardiner Committee, the only Parliamentary body to review the EPA, conceded that reading the Diplock Report might lead one to believe that by enacting the EPA, Parliament had intended that judges no longer have discretion over admissibility in trials of scheduled offenses.[182] It rejected this view, however, and argued that Parliamentary withdrawal of such well-established judicial power could only be made in "clear terms,"[183] which the EPA failed to do. The Gardiner Report favored an express statutory affirmation that judicial discretion was unimpaired, and recommended a provision to that effect to Parliament.[184] Such language has not been inserted, however.

In short, the language which the Gardiner Committee maintained was necessary to remove the power of discretion has not been inserted in the EPA. Nor has the language it suggested that would affirm ex-

appeared to deny the permissibility of any degree of physical violence. 1979 N. Ir. 45 (C.A.). In dicta, he expressed doubt that even under the section 8 standard a court should ever admit statements once violence had been shown to have occurred during the interrogation. *Id.* at 47.

178.   1977 N. Ir. at 111.
179.   *Id.* at 114.
180.   The Diplock Report asserted that "the current technical rules, practice and judicial discretion as to the admissibility of confessions ought to be suspended for the duration of the emergency in respect of Scheduled Offences." DIPLOCK REPORT, *supra* note 62, para. 89, at 32.
181.   *See supra* notes 153-61 and accompanying text.
182.   GARDINER REPORT, *supra* note 63, para. 48, at 16-17.
183.   *Id.* at 17.
184.   *Id.* para. 50, at 17.

The Yale Journal of World Public Order   Vol. 8:284, 1982

plicitly the power of discretion. While Parliament has not resolved the matter, some courts in Northern Ireland have concluded that their discretionary power still survives.[185]

It seems fair to draw at least two conclusions from this confusion. First, the section 8 standard is inherently ambiguous in two fundamental respects. First, the approach of the Diplock Commission and that of the European Commission differ with respect to the permissibility of the use of physical violence. This tension has not been resolved, and the courts of Northern Ireland have been left with the difficult task of reconciling the Diplock approach, which did not contemplate the use of physical violence,[186] and the European Commission approach, which has found "slaps or blows of the hand on the head or face not unacceptable."[187] In addition, it is not clear whether in trying to reconcile these two approaches, the courts of Northern Ireland may invoke their common law discretionary powers, although some have continued to do so.[188]

The second conclusion to be drawn is that it seems likely that the confusion over the "torture, inhuman or degrading treatment" standard has contributed to the use of violence during interrogations. One study of post-*McCormick* cases has concluded that "the possible exclusion of statements did not act as an effective control of police malpractice."[189] The authors of the study asserted that the inherent ambiguity of section 8 as revealed in judicial application may have persuaded some interrogators that physical ill treatment was permissible.[190] Although section 8 and the admissibility of confessions were, strictly speaking, outside its mandate,[191] the Bennett Committee noted that "the uncertainty, despite the standards upheld and applied by the courts, about what is permissible and what is not, short of the use of physical violence or ill treatment, may tempt police officers to see how far they can go and what they can get away with."[192] It is clearly questionable whether the Commission's confidence that the application of

---

185. An evidence manual written by an R.U.C. investigator has concluded that the judicial power of discretion survived the enactment of the EPA. *See* K. MASTERSON, *supra* note 137, at 25-26. Grier has concluded, rather safely, that "a precise analysis of the scope of the judicial discretion in the context of section 8 is not yet feasible." Grier, *supra* note 109, at 224.

186. *See supra* notes 143-44 and accompanying text.

187. *See supra* notes 153-58 and accompanying text.

188. *See supra* notes 176-77 and accompanying text.

189. TEN YEARS ON, *supra* note 48, at 48.

190. *Id.*

191. BENNETT REPORT, *supra* note 87, para. 3, at 2.

192. *Id.* para. 84, at 31.

Northern Ireland

the standard would prevent the use of physical violence was justified.
It is unquestionable that its general apprehension of the problems
likely to be caused by the standard was justified.

C. *Defense of the New Standard: A Rebuttal*

A defense of the new standard of admissibility would probably focus
on its ostensible efficacy. Concern that the standard may encourage
psychological or even physical violence is misplaced, it could be argued, because such violence can be justified in the name of community
safety. Confessions are crucial, given the present situation, because
witnesses are reluctant to testify out of fear of the terrorists or out of
general disrespect for the system of justice. Confessions are difficult to
obtain with traditional means of interrogation, however, because dedicated terrorists are not likely to "crack" as would ordinary criminals.
In short, such a defense would squarely pose an alternative: a choice
must be made between violence in interrogation and violence in the
streets, and the former is to be preferred.

This defense is vulnerable to several attacks. In the first place, it can
be argued that questions of efficacy are simply irrelevant. The techniques contemplated under section 8 are *a priori* unacceptable. The
psychological damage inflicted by the non-physical abuse may be just
as significant as that inflicted by more physical forms of persuasion.
The physical violence that is the inevitable product of the new standard
would never be tolerated as punishment for persons already proven
guilty. Accordingly, it cannot be accepted as an appropriate instrument
for use in the determination of guilt.

Even should the efficacy argument be accepted in principle, it can be
defeated on its own terms. The new admissibility standard has not, as
far as can be ascertained, contributed to a decline in the level of violence. While the overall level of violence fell sharply in the last four
months of 1976,[193] this decline was in all likelihood due to the emergence of the Peace People, a non-sectarian peace group which inspired
broad-based marches calling for an end to the conflict.[194] There was,

---

193. The indices for the measurement of terrorist activity showed declines of 30% to 60%
during the last four months of 1976 as compared with the same period for 1975. ROYAL
ULSTER CONSTABULARY, CHIEF CONSTABLE'S ANNUAL REPORT FOR 1977, at 72-73 (tables
1-5) (1978). Nonetheless, terrorist activity, as measured by the number of politically related
murders, ran at high levels in 1976, the first full year of the new emphasis on conviction in
courts of law. The data show the year to have been the third worst since the outbreak of the
violence in 1969. *See* ROYAL ULSTER CONSTABULARY, CHIEF CONSTABLE'S ANNUAL RE-
PORT 1982, at 48 (table 3) (1983).
194. *See* N.Y. Times, Sept. 5, 1976, at 15, col. 1; *id.*, Oct. 24, 1976, at 18, col. 1; *id.*, Nov.
28, at 17, col. 1.

The Yale Journal of World Public Order   Vol. 8:284, 1982

however, no evidence that the interrogation practices tolerated under section 8 were effective in decreasing the number of terrorist crimes,[195] whatever their success in producing individual confessions.[196] In fact, terrorist acts measured in number of deaths by violence and number of terrorist incidents actually increased in 1976, the full first year in which the new approach was employed. It is plausible that the interrogation controversy increased opposition to government policies and added new recruits to terrorist rolls, at least on the Republican side.

A second flaw in the efficacy argument is that it fails to take account of data indicating that only a relatively small number of those interrogated under the new standard have been charged with a crime. For the period between September, 1977 and August, 1978, only 37% of those interrogated at Castlereagh and 24% of those interrogated at Gough and Strand Road, Londonderry were ultimately charged.[197] During the first ten months of 1980, only 8.6% of all those arrested under the EPA were ever charged.[198] These figures admit of only two conclusions: either large numbers of innocent people have been subjected to prolonged interrogation, or prolonged interrogation failed in most cases to produce a confession from those who had something to confess.

Equally damaging to the efficacy defense of section 8 is the finding by Boyle, Hadden and Hillyard that "the majority of those who did make a confession did so relatively quickly."[199] Fifty percent of all those covered in their survey who chose to make a statement did so within the first three hours of interrogation, and a further 25% within the next three hours.[200] Prolonged interrogation, stress, fatigue, and mental and physical harassment do not appear to have been important factors in inducing most confessions. Perhaps the extended interrogations could be justified if it could be shown that the last 25% of the confessions, those which were not forthcoming until after the initial six hours of interrogation, came from hardened men and women of violence. The very fact that the government has never produced any data which support this conclusion is suggestive; if evidence showing that

195. Despite the substantial decline at the end of the year, 297 politically related fatalities occurred in 1976, as compared with 247 in 1975. ROYAL ULSTER CONSTABULARY. CHIEF CONSTABLE'S ANNUAL REPORT FOR 1979, at 59 (table 6) (1980). Similarly, 3,339 terrorist incidents were reported in 1976, as compared with 2,496 in 1975. *Id.*

196. Charges were brought against 708 terrorist suspects in 1976, more than double the number for 1975. P. TAYLOR, *supra* note 116, at 80.

197. BENNETT REPORT, *supra* note 87, app. 1, at 141.

198. *See supra* note 89 and accompanying text.

199. TEN YEARS ON, *supra* note 48, at 44-45.

200. *Id.* at 45.

Northern Ireland

those who confessed after prolonged interrogation tended to be those most responsible for the violence, one must assume that it would have been given wide publicity during the long period of criticism of the security forces for their interrogation practices.[201]

Whatever success section 8 may be claimed to have had in inducing true confessions must be balanced against the significant danger that it may also induce false confessions. The underlying rationale of the voluntariness principle was to guard against this danger, as well as to discourage improper police practices.[202] Although no clear proof of a false confession has been found, substantial doubts about the validity of confessions have been raised in a significant number of cases.[203] One R.U.C. detective, a member of an interrogation team, has estimated that 2% of all those convicted were innocent.[204] That would suggest that between 1976 and 1977 over 50 innocent people were convicted.[205]

The last and most damaging argument to be made against those who would justify section 8 on grounds of efficacy is that it contributes to the perceived substantive unfairness in the legal system.[206] Police interrogation practices as condoned by section 8 are certain to arouse popular anger, and further diminish prospects for popular cooperation with security forces. The Diplock Commission warned that "the reputation of Courts of Justice would be sullied if they countenanced convictions on evidence obtained by methods which flout universally accepted standards of behavior."[207] Ironically, however, section 8 is contributing to precisely that result.

IV.   Police Complaint Procedures

So long as extraordinary powers are conferred on the security forces by statutes such as the EPA, it is essential that the exercise of these powers be tempered by the establishment in Northern Ireland of procedures for the independent investigation and evaluation of allegations of police misconduct. The need for such procedures is made even more pressing by the longstanding tradition of discrimination against the Catholic minority in the administration of justice.[208] Therefore, it must

---

201. *See supra* notes 116-24 and accompanying text.
202. R. Cross, Evidence 446-47 (2d ed. 1963).
203. Ten Years On, *supra* note 48, at 46.
204. P. Taylor, *supra* note 116, at 339.
205. *Id.*
206. *See supra* notes 27-28 and accompanying text.
207. Diplock Report, *supra* note 62, para. 89, at 32.
208. *See supra* notes 27-33 and accompanying text.

The Yale Journal of World Public Order   Vol. 8:284, 1982

be regarded as a critical failing of the legal system in Northern Ireland that such procedures are virtually nonexistent.

The call for the establishment of procedures for the independent investigation of complaints was sounded almost as soon as the current cycle of violence began in Northern Ireland in 1969. The Cameron Report, which studied the rioting of that year, recommended the abandonment of the longstanding policy that only the Chief Constable institute disciplinary courts of inquiry,[209] and that independent procedures be established.[210] These recommendations were not adopted, however, and despite further calls for the institution of such procedures,[211] and the implementation of some superficial reforms,[212] the need remains as pressing as ever.[213]

In 1970, the parliament of Northern Ireland significantly overhauled the administration of the R.U.C. by the passage of the Police Act (Northern Ireland),[214] which removed the constabulary from the direct control of the Minister of the Interior of Northern Ireland.[215] The act made the constabulary responsible to the Police Authority,[216] a public body appointed by the Governor of Northern Ireland[217] and to be composed of diverse community representatives.[218] Part of the Police Authority's mandate was, and remains, to keep itself "informed as to the manner in which complaints from the public against members of the police force are dealt with by the Chief Constable."[219] As part of its

---

209. *See* Constabulary (Ireland) Act, 6 & 7 Will. 4, ch. 12, § 24.
210. CAMERON REPORT, *supra* note 38, at para. 230.
211. *See* GARDINER REPORT, *supra* note 63, para. 97, at 32.
212. *See infra* notes 222-28 and accompanying text.
213. This issue also has received substantial attention throughout the United Kingdom as a whole. *See* REPORT OF A WORKING PARTY APPOINTED BY THE HOME SECRETARY ON THE ESTABLISHMENT OF AN INDEPENDENT ELEMENT IN THE INVESTIGATION OF COMPLAINTS AGAINST THE POLICE, CMD. 5, No. 8193 (1981) (Lord Plowden, Chairman) (rejecting the establishment of independent investigations in favor of reliance on investigation by officers from other forces); REPORT OF AN INQUIRY INTO THE BRIXTON DISORDERS, CMD. 5, No. 8422 (1981) (Lord Scarman, Chairman) (concluding after analysis of the causes of the Brixton race riots that independent evaluation of complaints is appropriate).
214. 1970 N. Ir. Pub. Gen. Acts, ch. 9.
215. *Id.* § 1.
216. *Id.*
217. *Id.* § 1(3), sched. 1, §§ 1-9. After the imposition of direct rule from Westminster, control over the Police Authority was vested in the Secretary of State for Northern Ireland.
218. *Id.* This reform was instituted at the recommendation of the Hunt Committee, which had been appointed in the wake of the 1969 rioting to analyze the structure of the police force. *See* REPORT OF THE ADVISORY COMMITTEE ON POLICE IN NORTHERN IRELAND, N. IR. CMD., No. 535, at 3 (1969) (J. Hunt, Chairman) [hereinafter HUNT REPORT]. The committee found that the police were too directly responsible to elected officials in a political system in which victory virtually was guaranteed to the members of a single party. *Id.* paras. 84-85, at 21-22.
219. 1970 N. Ir. Pub. Gen. Acts, ch. 9, § 12(1). The wording of the statute speaks of the

Northern Ireland

general power to keep itself informed, the Authority can request reports on complaints and investigations,[220] and in cases that affect "the
public interest," can require the Chief Constable to convene a tribunal
of inquiry.[221]

The issue of police complaint procedures has received extensive attention in Northern Ireland since the publication of the Cameron Report. In addition to proposing the establishment of the Police
Authority, the Hunt Commission recommended that complaints be investigated by police officers from counties different from those of the
officers being investigated,[222] and the Black Report, which reviewed the
problem once more in 1974, found that this reform had been implemented.[223] In the meantime, the Gardiner Report had called for the
establishment of independent procedures,[224] but this proposal was rejected by the Black Report, which instead endorsed the establishment
of a Police Complaint Board.[225] Finally, the Bennett Report of 1979
recommended further limited reforms, including a policy that in cases
that have aroused "public disquiet," every effort be made to use investigating officers from other police forces in the United Kingdom.[226]

Despite all this attention to the problem, the basic structure remains
the same. As the Black Report endorsed as a fundamental principle,[227]
and as the Bennett Report accepted for what it claimed was the lack of
a better alternative,[228] operational control over the investigation of
complaints remains in the hands of the police. While four separate
procedures for the investigation of complaints have been established,
none can be called independent in any meaningful sense. Thus, the
complaint procedures remain inadequate, and the public perception of
the legal system suffers as a result.

A. *Criminal Prosecution by the Director of Public Prosecutions*

Under regulations issued pursuant to the 1970 Police Authority Act,
the Chief Constable is the disciplinary authority for all ranks up to and

"Inspector General," but regulations issued since its enactment have replaced that phrase
with the phrase "Chief Constable." BENNETT REPORT, *supra* note 87, para. 284, at 96.
   220. 1970 N. Ir. Pub. Gen. Acts, ch. 9, § 15(2).
   221. *Id.* § 13.
   222. HUNT REPORT, *supra* note 218, para. 133, at 32.
   223. REPORT OF THE WORKING PARTY FOR NORTHERN IRELAND, CMD. 5, No. 6475
(1975) (Sir Harold Black, Chairman) [hereinafter BLACK REPORT].
   224. GARDINER REPORT, *supra* note 63, para. 98, at 32.
   225. BLACK REPORT, *supra* note 223, para. 53, at 16. This reform was instituted in 1977.
See infra notes 259-71 and accompanying text.
   226. BENNETT REPORT, *supra* note 87, para. 357, at 118.
   227. BLACK REPORT, *supra* note 223, para. 22(i), at 8.
   228. *Id.* para. 356, at 117-18.

including Chief Superintendent, while the Police Authority is given responsibility for the higher ranks.[229] The authority for the lower ranks has been delegated to a Senior Deputy Chief Constable, who evaluates the complaint in the first instance and then assigns a member of the Complaints and Discipline branch of the R.U.C. to investigate it.[230] After the investigator's report has been reviewed, the Chief Constable must send it to the Director of Public Prosecutions (D.P.P.) unless he is "satisfied that no criminal offence has been committed."[231]

Under Article 5 of the Prosecution of Offences Order,[232] the decision to press any criminal charge, including the indictment of a police officer, is entirely the responsibility of the D.P.P., whose discretion in this regard is subject only to his accountability to the Attorney General of the United Kingdom.[233] The inherent weakness of this putative independence is apparent, however, in that the Order establishes no power of investigation, and, in fact, the D.P.P. has no staff for investigation.[234] Any further information required by the D.P.P. must be requested from the Chief Constable.[235] Thus, the prosecution decision is only nominally an independent one; the D.P.P.'s dependence on the R.U.C. for the investigation of any complaint against members of the R.U.C. is absolute.

B. *R.U.C. Disciplinary Procedures*

The role of the D.P.P. in the evaluation of complaints against the police is to determine whether the senior police officer's report contains sufficient evidence upon which to initiate criminal proceedings against the accused policeman.[236] A variety of factors, including the credibility of potential witnesses, the admissibility of evidence, and the presence of competing demands on limited staff may influence the D.P.P.'s decision.[237] None of these factors may necessarily address the issue of whether an assault or some other behavior warranting disciplinary ac-

---

229. R.U.C. (Complaints) Regulations, 1977 STAT. R. & O.N. IR., No. 235; R.U.C. (Discipline and Disciplinary Appeals) Regulations, 1977 STAT. R. & O.N. IR., No. 236.
230. BENNETT REPORT, *supra* note 87, para. 285, at 97.
231. 1970 N. Ir. Pub. Gen. Acts, ch. 9, § 13(5). Pursuant to powers conferred by the Prosecution of Offences Order, the D.P.P. has required the Chief Constable to send it any allegation of criminal conduct made against a police officer. Prosecution of Offences (Northern Ireland) Order, 1972 STAT. INST., No. 538, art. 6(3)(b); *see* BENNETT REPORT, *supra* note 87, para. 286, at 97.
232. Prosecution of Offences (Northern Ireland) Order, *supra* note 231, art. 5.
233. *Id.*
234. BENNETT REPORT, *supra* note 87, para. 288, at 98.
235. *Id.*
236. P. TAYLOR, *supra* note 116, at 57.
237. *Id.*

Northern Ireland

tion has occurred. Nonetheless, the R.U.C. has consistently interpreted British double jeopardy rules to require that if the D.P.P. has considered and rejected criminal charges against a constable or police officer, internal disciplinary action is automatically precluded. The result of this interpretation has been substantially to undercut whatever role the R.U.C. internal disciplinary procedure might play in the investigation of complaints against the police.

The literal wording of the double jeopardy rule would not appear to require that a decision not to prosecute rule out internal disciplinary proceedings. According to the Police Order of 1977, "where a member of the police force has been acquitted or convicted of a criminal offence he shall not be liable to be charged with any offence against discipline which is in substance the same as the offence of which he has been acquitted or convicted."[238] As the Bennett Report pointed out, however, "[a]cquitted means, of course, acquitted by a court, but, in the application of the 'double jeopardy' rule, 'acquitted' has also been taken to refer in some degree to decisions by the Director of Public Prosecutions that there should be no prosecution."[239] It also noted that the R.U.C. approach to the double jeopardy rule has been more absolute than was intended.[240] Nonetheless, the R.U.C. disciplinary machinery, which could play an important role in controlling misconduct that falls below the level of an indictable offense but that is still counterproductive or unbecoming, will not investigate a case in which the D.P.P. has declined to prosecute.

C. *Tribunals of Inquiry*

A third procedure for the evaluation of complaints against the police is that the Police Authority can require the establishment of a tribunal of inquiry.[241] In cases in which the complaint "relates to a matter affecting or appearing to affect the public interest,"[242] the Police Authority can require the Chief Constable to refer the complaint to a tribunal consisting of a lawyer appointed by the Lord Chief Justice of Northern Ireland and two police officers appointed by the Authority itself.[243]

---

238. Police (Northern Ireland) Order, 1977 STAT. INST.. No. 53, art. 14.
239. BENNETT REPORT, *supra* note 87, para. 364, at 120.
240. *Id.* para. 365, at 121. This policy has continued despite the issuance in 1977 of a Home Office circular that warned specifically against an overly broad application of the double jeopardy rule in the context of police disciplinary procedures. *Id.*
241. Police (Northern Ireland) Act, 1970, ch. 9, § 13(2).
242. *Id.*
243. *Id.* § 13(3). These officers may be affiliated with any police force in the United Kingdom. *Id.*

315

The Yale Journal of World Public Order   Vol. 8:284, 1982

Although the tribunal option would appear to offer some promise of independent investigation, as of 1979 it had been invoked only once since the Police Authority was established in 1970.[244] The number of complaints has remained relatively constant; in 1972, 2,617 complaints were filed, and in 1979, 2,183 were filed.[245] To discharge its statutory mandate to keep itself informed of complaints against the police, the Police Authority during this period relied exclusively on the reports it received from the R.U.C. It had considered the tribunal option only twice before the first and only establishment of a tribunal of inquiry, which was appointed in 1979 to consider the case of James Rafferty.[246]

The facts and aftermath of the Rafferty case suggest that any hope that the tribunal of inquiry might be able to exercise independent investigatory power is misplaced. After his arrest on November 11, 1976, Rafferty, who had no prior criminal record, was interrogated for three days.[247] Upon his release he was examined by two doctors, one a police surgeon, who found him to be suffering severe bruises and a spinal laceration, and who recommended urgent hospital treatment.[248] Rafferty was hospitalized for four days after his release, during which time the extent of his injuries was confirmed by two more doctors, one a Fellow of the Royal College of Surgeons.[249] No criminal charge was ever brought against him.

Although the matter was raised by one of its own members almost immediately after the incident, for two years the Police Authority refused repeated requests to initiate a tribunal of inquiry.[250] During that period the investigations undertaken by the R.U.C. and by the D.P.P. both came to naught.[251] Finally, in October, 1978, the Police Authority agreed that a tribunal should hear the case, and in the spring of 1979, the tribunal was appointed.[252] The tribunal began to hear testimony in December, 1980.[253] After medical testimony corroborated the severity of his injuries, Rafferty himself testified. Certain cross examination of

---

244. BENNETT REPORT, *supra* note 84, para. 392, at 130. During the same period, almost 20,000 formal complaints were filed against the police, including 1,382 alleging an assault during interrogation, during the period from 1976 to 1978. *Id.* app. II, at 142 (data supplied by the R.U.C.).
245. NORTHERN IRELAND CIVIL RIGHTS ASSOCIATION, THE RAFFERTY FILE 13 (1980) (copy on file with *The Yale Journal of World Public Order*) [hereinafter RAFFERTY FILE].
246. P. TAYLOR, *supra* note 116, at 105.
247. *Id.* at 88.
248. *Id.* at 96.
249. *Id.* Rafferty was also found to be suffering from some degree of amnesia. *Id.* at 97.
250. *Id.* at 97-105.
251. *Id.*
252. *Id.* at 105.
253. RAFFERTY FILE, *supra* note 245, at 7.

Northern Ireland

Rafferty by counsel for the police witnesses was ruled improper, whereupon counsel and the police witnesses refused to participate further in
the proceedings.[254] Following this action, the tribunal sought and obtained subpoenas that required the police witnesses to testify.[255] Six of
the witnesses appealed this decision, and nine days later Lord Justice
Gibson quashed the subpoenas,[256] ruling that the tribunal was not exercising a judicial function and therefore could not avail itself of the
subpoena power of the courts.[257] This decision effectively ended the
inquiry, for the police witnesses indicated that, at the advice of counsel,
they would not participate further in the inquiry unless legally compelled to do so.[258] Thus, the Police Authority's first and heretofore
only tribunal of inquiry, held four years after the occurrence of the
incident it was to investigate, broke up after two days of testimony.
Any confidence that the community might have had in its institutional
capacity to conduct independent investigations was perhaps permanently destroyed.

D.   *The Police Complaints Board*

   The fourth procedure for the evaluation of complaints lies with the
Police Complaints Board, which consists of at least six members,[259]
none of whom may be affiliated with a police force.[260] According to
the Black Report, which endorsed the establishment of the Board,[261]
the rationale underlying its creation was to introduce "some form of
independent scrutiny" into the investigation of complaints made
against the R.U.C. but which are not referred to the D.P.P.[262] The
Board was intended neither to make its own investigations,[263] nor to
usurp the position of the D.P.P.;[264] rather, by receiving copies of complaints and investigation reports,[265] it was to consult with and make
recommendations to the Chief Constable about possible internal disci-

254.   *Id.*
255.   *See In re* Sterritt, 1980 N. Ir. 234, 234.
256.   *Id.*
257.   *Id.*
258.   *Id.* at 235. Lord Justice Gibson called the result "singularly unfortunate," but held
that the law left him no room for a different decision. *Id.* at 240.
259.   Police (Northern Ireland) Order, *supra* note 238, art. 3(1).
260.   *Id.* art. 3(2).
261.   BLACK REPORT, *supra* note 223, para. 53, at 15-16.
262.   *Id.* para. 16, at 6-7; *see supra* notes 229-31 and accompanying text.
263.   BLACK REPORT, *supra* note 223, para. 22(i), at 8.
264.   *Id.* para. 22(ii), at 8.
265.   Police (Northern Ireland), Order, *supra* note 238, art. 5.

plinary procedures.[266] The Board is not sent copies of complaints that the Chief Constable forwards to the D.P.P. until after the question of criminal proceedings has been settled.[267]

The fundamental problem with this structure is that because virtually all complaints made against the police allege some criminal conduct,[268] they are therefore sent first to the D.P.P.[269] Thus, the Board is not involved in the evaluation of any complaint that alleges criminal conduct; either the D.P.P. presses criminal charges, which eliminates any role for the Board, or the D.P.P. does not, which, given the peculiar interpretation of the double jeopardy rule in Northern Ireland, has the same effect.[270]

In short, the Police Complaint Board's power is confined to whatever role it might play with the Chief Constable concerning the appropriateness of internal disciplinary proceedings in those rare cases in which criminal behavior is not alleged in the complaint at issue. Even this limited power has not been used effectively,[271] and if it were, it is the possible criminal behavior of members of the R.U.C., not minor disciplinary infractions, with which the public is most concerned. Thus, it is most unlikely that the Board will ever play an important role in the investigation of complaints against the police.

E. *The Need for Independent Investigations*

No procedure for the independent investigation of complaints against the police yet exists in Northern Ireland. Criminal prosecution by the D.P.P., the tribunals of inquiry, and the Police Complaint Board are all thoroughly dependent on the cooperation of the R.U.C. The constabulary's internal disciplinary powers, even should they be exercised in good faith, are seriously handicapped by the interpretation of the double jeopardy rule. Until this failing is remedied, public confi-

---

266. *Id.* art. 6. As a power of last resort the Board can compel the Chief Constable to initiate a disciplinary hearing. *Id.* art. 6(2).
267. *Id.* art. 8(1).
268. *See* BENNETT REPORT, *supra* note 87, para. 329, at 110.
269. *Id.*; *see supra* notes 229-31 and accompanying text.
270. *See supra* notes 236-40 and accompanying text. In a special report to the Secretary of State, the Board itself expressed the view that the extent of the restriction on its scope caused by the double jeopardy rule was not fully appreciated by its members at the time of their appointment, and that the rule "constitutes a serious curtailment" of the effectiveness of their role. BENNETT REPORT, *supra* note 87, para. 397, at 132.
271. The Bennett Report noted that as of March, 1979, the Board had not exercised any of its powers. *Id.* para. 398, at 132. In June, 1981, an independent investigatory group found that the Police Complaint Board and the tribunals of inquiry, whose weakness had been betrayed in the Rafferty case, were "equally ineffective." THE ADMINISTRATION OF JUSTICE IN NORTHERN IRELAND, *supra* note 133, at 4.

Northern Ireland

dence in the legal system, so important to the achievement of a peaceful solution to the conflict, will remain seriously diminished.

Two factors guarantee that even if the R.U.C. changed its interpretation of the double jeopardy rule to permit departmental investigations despite a decision not to prosecute, independent investigations would still be required. The first, not unique to Northern Ireland, is the inherent difficulty in asking members of the police force to investigate their colleagues. Members of the R.U.C., like policemen everywhere, share a spirit of loyalty and are anxious not to harm a fellow officer performing a difficult job. This spirit of corporate unity, no doubt made even more intense by the deaths of 173 members of the police at the hands of terrorists between 1969 and 1982,[272] inevitably penetrates and weakens the independence and objectivity of police investigations.

The second factor arguing in favor of the need to establish independent complaint procedures is a legal one which concerns the possibility of conflict of interest. In cases in which the complaint stems from police conduct during an interrogation, the complainant may have been charged with a criminal offense on the basis of his or her admission. A vigorous investigation of the complaint may have the effect of rendering inadmissible the confession made by the criminal defendant *qua* complainant. In light of this circumstance, the Bennett Commission found that the "investigation of a complaint will consciously or unconsciously be influenced by the wish to support the Crown case against the complainant."[273] A vigorous investigation of a complaint may be viewed not only as a slap against fellow officers, but also as an actual reward for criminal defendants. Thus, a conflict of interest inevitably is presented to the prosecutor who directs the investigation of the complaint and to the police who perform the actual investigation itself.

So long as no independent investigation of complaints against the police exists in Northern Ireland, the perception of discrimination in the administration of justice, already so deeply rooted in the Catholic community,[274] is bound to continue. Thus, one important goal of the last decade of British policy in Northern Ireland—public acceptance of the R.U.C. as "civilian, impartial, and accountable"[275]—is bound to fail. The data show that only fourteen prosecutions were pressed against police officers in the years 1976 through 1979, and not a single

272. ROYAL ULSTER CONSTABULARY, CHIEF CONSTABLE'S ANNUAL REPORT 1982, at 48 (table 6) (1983).
273. BENNETT REPORT, *supra* note 87, para. 352, at 117.
274. *See supra* notes 27-33 and accompanying text.
275. HUNT REPORT, *supra* note 218, para. 176; *see* AMNESTY INTERNATIONAL, *supra* note 111, at 1-2.

conviction was obtained.[276] Despite the wave of negative publicity that preceded the appointment of the Bennett Committee, at the time its report was issued not a single police officer had been convicted of a crime arising out of a maltreatment claim.[277] The Standing Advisory Committee on Human Rights has repeatedly urged that "justice must not only be done, it must be seen to be done."[278] Given the present state of the procedures for the investigation of complaints against the police, it is hardly surprising that many people neither see justice being done, nor believe that it is being done at all.

V. Ameliorating the Situation: An Agenda for Reform

Incremental reforms can be implemented that would help convince the public that a system offering substantive and procedural fairness can be built in Northern Ireland. Indeed, the very implementation of reforms in the admissibility standard and in the procedures for the investigation of complaints made against the police would send a clear signal that the authorities themselves are determined to govern within reasonable limits prescribed by law, and without resort to "emergency" powers that invite arbitrary and capricious misuse. No reform can be expected to eradicate overnight centuries of hatred and mistrust. Sensible and feasible measures are available, however, that could begin the process of building confidence in the rule of law that is the surest weapon against those who would resort to violent and extra-legal means to achieve their objectives.

A. *Interrogation Practices and the Admissibility Standard of Section 8*

The fact that the admissibility standard of section 8 of the EPA is derived from the European Convention on Human Rights does not justify ignoring the manifold problems it has created. Decisions under the Convention appear to condone the use of physical violence in interrogations by the police, and the standard's imprecision has made impossible the coherent judicial interpretation of its requirements. Reforms must be implemented to resolve both these difficulties.

---

276. P. TAYLOR, *supra* note 116, at 58.
277. BENNETT REPORT, *supra* note 87, para. 157, at 52. During this period 19 officers were prosecuted. Of these, 16 were acquitted outright, in one case the prosecution declined to continue after trial had begun, and 2 convictions were reversed on appeal. *Id.*
278. *See* STANDING ADVISORY COMMITTEE ON HUMAN RIGHTS, FIFTH REPORT (1980) (on file with *The Yale Journal of World Public Order*). The committee was created by the Northern Ireland Constitution Act, 1973, ch. 36, § 20.

Northern Ireland

1. *Physical Violence in Interrogation Is Counterproductive and Should Be Specifically Proscribed*

The use of physical violence in interrogation is counterproductive in at least two ways: (1) as the Diplock Commission recognized, it may prevent the development of any rapport between the person questioned and the questioners; and (2) it only exacerbates the atmosphere of community distrust that permeates Northern Ireland. An explicit and absolute ban on its use might make possible more effective interrogation and certainly would improve community relations.

To make such a ban meaningful, the message must be clearly conveyed to all concerned that not only will evidence that has been obtained by the use or threat of violence be excluded from the courts, but that members of the police force who violate the proscription will be punished. The promulgation of a code of permissible interrogation practices would constitute a useful first step in the communication of such a message.[279] In addition, the establishment of independent procedures for the evaluation of complaints made against the police would deter further abuse and assure the public that the problem is taken seriously by the authorities.

2. *The Admissibility Standard of Section 8 Should Be Abolished and the Common Law Test of Voluntariness Restored*

The practical operation of section 8 has created serious problems that have not been offset by any compensating increase in public safety. This fact should be recognized, and the standard abolished. The voluntariness test should be restored, together with a re-affirmation of the power of judicial discretion to exclude admissions of dubious probative value or ones made under questionable circumstances. Other provisions of the EPA have provided the security forces sufficient powers of investigation and detention such that this counterproductive and unfair standard can be safely abandoned.

B. *The Investigation of Complaints Against the Police*

The clear lack of any power of independent investigation in the hands of the D.P.P., the Police Authority, or the Police Complaints Board and the regular acquittals in the few prosecutions of members of the police preclude the development within the Catholic community of any feeling of confidence in the fairness or impartiality of the R.U.C.

---

279. *See* BENNETT REPORT, *supra* note 87, paras. 180-83, at 63-64. Professors Boyle, Hadden, and Hillyard have drafted such a code that could serve as a model on which to base the regulation of interrogation practices. TEN YEARS ON, *supra* note 48, at 110-13.

321

The Yale Journal of World Public Order   Vol. 8:284, 1982

That confidence is especially important in a society in which the police are, and have been for decades, vested with special emergency powers of unreviewable discretion that permit the detention of suspects for days without charge. A thoroughgoing reform of the procedures for the investigation of complaints against the police is essential in a community in which distrust between members of a minority community on the one hand, and members of the security forces and the majority community on the other, is rampant.

1. *The Rule Against Double Jeopardy Must Be Construed Literally*

A decision by the D.P.P. not to prosecute should not result in the absolution of those accused of disciplinary offenses that do not rise to the level of criminal behavior. The use of internal disciplinary machinery should not be confused with the public prosecution of a criminal offense. Misconduct which is less than criminal still may merit disciplinary sanction, and the R.U.C.'s interpretation of the double jeopardy rule should be changed to take cognizance of this fact.

2. *Complaints Must Be Investigated by Persons Institutionally Independent from Those Persons Being Investigated*

Systems for the investigation of complaints made against the police generally involve four steps—the receipt of the complaint, the investigation of the complaint, the determination whether to initiate proceedings, be they disciplinary or judicial, and the ultimate resolution of the complaint. Independence can be established at any or all of these steps.[280] It can be ensured by establishing a special police unit to investigate complaints, or by creating an oversight position in the form of an ombudsman.

A special police unit established solely to investigate complaints against the police should be designed to take account of the need to protect police morale as well as the need for the thorough and independent investigation of complaints. As a full-time body, the unit would be able to develop expertise in the investigation of complaints.

---

280. The author has surveyed elsewhere possible methods for the creation of such independence. *See* T. FOLEY, COMPLAINTS AGAINST THE POLICE (1980) (mimeo) (copy on file with *The Yale Journal of World Public Order*). *See also* Note, *The Administration of Complaints by Civilians Against the Police*, 77 HARV. L. REV. 499 (1964); Grant, *Complaints Against the Police—the North-American Experience*, 23 CRIM. L. REV. 338 (1976) (independence in the determination and resolution of charges); Hudson, *Police Review Boards and Police Accountability*, 36 LAW & CONTEMP. PROBS. 515 (1971) (survey of complaints procedures with emphasis on police cooperation); Lenzi, *Reviewing Civilian Complaints of Police Misconduct*, 48 TEMPLE L.Q. 89 (1974) (analysis of alleged systematic violations of constitutional rights by members of the Philadelphia Police Department, with suggestions for more effective complaint procedures).

Northern Ireland

Its independence from other branches of the police and the freedom of
its members from ordinary police work should serve to insulate it to a
substantial degree from the pressures typically created by the investigation of fellow officers. This independence should serve to impress the
public with the seriousness with which the police examine allegations
of wrongdoing, although public perception in Northern Ireland will depend ultimately on the achievement of demonstrably fair results. That
such a unit can successfully identify and investigate problems within
the ranks of police has been demonstrated elsewhere.[281]

A second alternative to the present system would be the creation of
an ombudsman, a Public Complaints Commissioner, who would have
the authority to scrutinize all investigations of complaints within a certain period after the receipt of the complaint by the police.[282] A staff of
civilian investigators would assist the ombudsman, who would possess
full subpoena power, the right of access to police records, and the
power to order public hearings on the basis of either the staff or police
investigations.

A combination of the two approaches—the creation of both special
investigation unit and an ombudsman—would be an ideal solution to
the complaint problem in Northern Ireland. Under this plan, a special
investigation unit would answer to the Chief Constable, but its actions
would be monitored by an ombudsman.[283] The ombudsman would
play several roles—he or she could receive complaints independently of
the police, serve as a conciliator in cases calling for informal resolution,
monitor ongoing investigations, and conduct investigations when the
circumstances require. Providing the ombudsman with an independent
staff empowered to compel testimony and the production of documents
by the police would eliminate the problems encountered heretofore by

---

281. *See Get the cops*, ECONOMIST. May 28, 1977, at 71 (successful investigations of corruption in the Hong Kong police); *Sins of the fathers*, ECONOMIST. June 25, 1977, at 23
(efforts of Scotland Yard special investigating team to uncover police corruption). The resignations from the constabulary of the corrupt officers identified by the Scotland Yard team
are reported to have increased public confidence in the police and heightened departmental
morale. *Id.*

282. For general discussions of the ombudsman concept, see Gellhorn, *The Norwegian
Ombudsman*, 18 STAN. L. REV. 293 (1966); Gellhorn, *Finland's Official Watchmen*, 114 U.
PA. L. REV. 327 (1966); Gellhorn, *Settling Disagreements with Officials in Japan*, 79 HARV. L.
REV. 685 (1966). A police complaints ombudsman was established in Toronto in July, 1981.
Civilians Are Watching the Watchmen, MACLEANS, Aug. 24, 1981, at 54. The possible estab-
lishment of such a position has received extensive attention in Australia. *See* AUSTRALIAN
LAW REFORM COMMISSION, REPORT NO. 1: COMPLAINTS AGAINST THE POLICE (1979);
AUSTRALIAN LAW REFORM COMMISSION, REPORT NO. 9: COMPLAINTS AGAINST THE PO-
LICE (Supplementary Report 1980).

283. This approach is under review by the Australian Law Reform Commission. *See*
AUSTRALIAN LAW REFORM COMMISSION, REPORT NO. 1, *supra* note 282, paras. 65-79, at 17-
21.

The Yale Journal of World Public Order   Vol. 8:284, 1982

the Police Authority and the Police Complaints Board. Public hearings ordered under the ombudsman's powers would have real authority, in contrast to the tribunals of inquiry, and would be likely to produce full police cooperation. Although this approach would not institutionalize a completely independent investigation process, it would accommodate the demands of investigative competence and objectivity, police morale, and public confidence.

No procedure for the investigation of complaints against the police can operate effectively without police cooperation. Moreover, a police force cannot function effectively without the consent and support of the community it serves. The Chief Constable has, therefore, two mutually reinforcing interests—the enforcement of respect for the law among the constabulary and the encouragement of community support and respect for the rule of law, which is critical to effective law enforcement. Criminal activity, whether committed by police or terrorists, undermines respect for law if left unpunished. The public's revulsion at acts of violence is the natural ally of the police, but the lack of an independent procedure for the investigation of complaints deprives the constabulary of the support which could be so important in the struggle for peace in Northern Ireland.

Legal institutions and protections will not themselves eradicate the generations of mistrust in Northern Ireland. But as the public's patience with the terrorism committed in its name wears thin, desire for the rule of law undoubtedly will grow stronger. This popular desire for fair and effective law enforcement will not materialize, however, unless a legal system is established in which justice not only is done, but is seen to be done. In Northern Ireland, where memories are understandably long, reforms of the kind suggested in this Article must be implemented if this critical goal is to be achieved.

[16]

TERRORISM AND HUMAN RIGHTS:
COUNTER-INSURGENCY AND NECESSITY AT COMMON LAW

*David R. Lowry**

I. Introduction

Emergency powers have existed in Northern Ireland from the beginning of the state in 1920.[1] Northern Ireland came into being as a result of the partition of Ireland by the British Parliament, whereby the six north-eastern counties of Ireland remained an integral part of the United Kingdom.[2] Following partition, one-third of the population of Northern Ireland were Catholics who were predominately Nationalist or Republican in ideology.[3] As a consequence, partition was viewed as a huge gerrymander and a denial of self-determination of the enclosed Nationalist minority.[4] Civil unrest has been a recurring feature in Northern Ireland[5] and government has been conducted by the dominant group (Protestant), without consensus, since 1920.[6]

For the purposes of this article it is significant to note that elements of the minority have, from time to time, resorted to force of arms in pursuit of an irredentist political philosophy.[7] Because of the state's monopoly of force, the

---

* Associate Professor, University of Toledo, College of Law. LL.B. (1969) Queen's University, Belfast; LL.M. (1970) New York University; LL.M. (1973) Columbia University, A.C.I.S., Barrister and Solicitor, Nova Scotia, Canada.

1 The fifth statute enacted by the fledgling Northern Irish Parliament (Stormont) was a particularly wide and odious emergency powers statute. Civil Authorities (Special Powers) Act, 1922, 12 & 13 Geo. 5, c.5 (N.I.) *as amended by* 23 & 24 Geo. 5, c.12 (N.I.) (1932). For an analysis of the early operation of this statute see, National Council for Civil Liberties, The Special Powers Acts of Northern Ireland (1936). For an assessment of the operation of the act between 1944 and 1954 see Edwards, *Special Powers in Northern Ireland* Crim. L. Rev. 7 (1956). For a brief assessment of the role of the act in exacerbating the current conflict see K. Boyle, T. Hadden & P. Hillyard, Law and State: The Case of Northern Ireland 6-36 (1975) (hereinafter cited as *Law and State*).

2 The partition was created by a statute of the British Parliament, Government of Ireland Act, 1920, 10 & 11 Geo. 5, c.67. For a lucid account of the partition of Ireland see N. Mansergh, The Irish Question 1840-1921 (3d ed. 1975) and N. Mansergh, The Government of Northern Ireland (1936). An excellent succinct account of the constitutional history of Northern Ireland is now available: T. W. Moody, The Ulster Question 1603-1973 (1974). An admirably eclectic survey of constitutional law and history is found in Palley, *The Evolution, Disintegration and Possible Reconstruction of the Northern Ireland Constitution,* 1 Anglo-American L. Rev. 368 (1972).

3 Several works chronicle the fate of the Catholic minority in the new state of Northern Ireland. In particular, see F. Lyon, Ireland Since the Famine (1971); L. de Paor, Divided Ulster (1970); M. Farrell, Northern Ireland: The Orange State (1976). For a Marxian view of partition in an historical perspective, see T. Jackson, Ireland Her Own (1947).

4 For an explanation of this viewpoint, *see, e.g.,* S. MacStiofain, Memoirs of a Revolutionary (1975). From 1970-1973 Mr. MacStiofain was Chief-of-Staff and founder of the newly formed Provisional I.R.A.

5 A short description of civil unrest since 1920 is found in A. Boyd, Holy War In Belfast (2d ed. 1970). For an analysis of the much used internment power under the Special Powers Act, see J. McGuffin, Internment (1973).

6 On the precise nature of the devolved government in Northern Ireland, see R. Rose, Government Without Consensus (1971); D. Barrett & C. Carter, The Northern Ireland Problem: A Study in Group Relations (1962).

7 For a critical exposition of nationalist thinking see E. McCann, War and an Irish Town (1974). For the role of the I.R.A., see J. Bell, The Secret Army (1970) and T. Coogan, The I.R.A. (1970).

activities of the militant irredentists have been confined to guerilla campaigns. And, since 1971,[8] the Irish Republican Army (I.R.A.) has embarked upon a protracted guerilla campaign which has emphasized a shift from rural to urban guerilla warfare or urban terrorism.[9] Such terrorism constitutes a shift from *direct* terror to *indirect* terror in that its primary objective is to demonstrate that the state cannot protect its citizens, cannot enforce the rule of law and is, consequently, ungovernable.[10] Indirect forms of terror have led to new attritional policies of counter-terror (counter-insurgency) whereby the military and the police seek primarily to "contain" terror prior to its gradual elimination.[11] However, new systems of terrorism and counter-insurgency do not operate in a legal vacuum. The primary objective of this article is to examine the legal framework under which the continuing Northern Irish urban guerilla warfare and counter-insurgency tactics operate. Secondly, the recently developed and applied theories of counter-insurgency will be identified and analyzed. Finally, some conclusions will be drawn from the Northern Irish experience regarding, on the one hand, civil liberties and human rights and, on the other hand, legal controls over military behavior in a contemporary emergency situation.

II. Counter-Insurgency: The Legal Framework

During war or insurrection there is a manifest need for strong and effective government. Even liberal democratic systems of government reserve the right to concentrate power in the hands of the executive during an emergency or crisis.[12] Historically society responded to war and similar crises by declaring martial law by which the executive exercised the right to use force against force within the realm in order to suppress disorder.[13] Under early English law, the monarch

---

8   For the origin of the present I.R.A. campaign, see C. O'BRIEN, STATES OF IRELAND (1972); Sunday Times Insight Team, *Northern Ireland* (1972); and R. DEUTSCH & V. MAGOWAN, NORTHERN IRELAND 1968-1973: A CHRONOLOGY OF EVENTS, vol. I 1968-71 (1973).

9   For an interesting comparative analysis see J. BELL, ON REVOLT: STRATEGIES OF NATIONAL LIBERATION (1976).

10   For a fuller explanation of direct and indirect forms of terrorism, *see* E. HYAMS, TERRORISTS AND TERRORISM ch. 1 (1974).

11   Modern theories of counter-terror or counter-insurgency are found in J. McCUEN, THE ART OF COUNTER-REVOLUTIONARY WAR (1966); R. THOMPSON, DEFEATING COMMUNIST INSURGENCY (1966); F. KITSON, LOW INTENSITY OPERATIONS: SUBVERSION, INSURGENCY, PEACEKEEPING (1971) (hereinafter cited as *Kitson*). The latter work is of particular importance in the context of the present Irish crisis and has influenced military theory, strategy and response to the I.R.A. campaign. For an informative critical evaluation of Kitson's theories, see J. KELLY, GENESIS OF REVOLUTION (1976). Mr. Kelly was, until recently, head of Irish Army Intelligence for Northern Ireland.

12   One commentator has observed that war requires "totalitarian" government (K. WHEARE, FEDERAL GOVERNMENT 187 (4th ed. 1963)), while another has used the descriptive term "constitutional dictatorship" (C. Rossiter, *Constitutional Dictatorship* at 4-5 (1948)).

13   There are various definitions of martial law but the most appealing is that of the Duke of Wellington: "Martial law is neither more nor less than the will of the General who commands the army. In fact, martial law means no law at all." HANSARD, col. 880 (1851). However, in this instance the Duke of Wellington was referring to the relationship of the military to alien enemies when abroad. Martial law also encompasses the right of the executive to suspend or supersede municipal law in order to suppress internal civil disorder. On the various meanings attributed to the term "martial law" see R. HEUSTON, ESSAYS IN CONSTITUTIONAL LAW 150-53 (2d ed. 1964); I. BROWNLIE, THE LAW RELATING TO PUBLIC ORDER 124-25 (1968). Perhaps the most extensive study of martial law is to be found in C. FAIRMAN, THE LAW OF MARTIAL RULE (2d ed. 1943) and C. FAIRMAN, THE LAW OF MARTIAL RULE AND THE NATIONAL EMERGENCY, 55 HARV. L. REV. 1253 (1941-42). Note that some American commentators use the term "martial rule" in preference to "martial law."

sometimes issued commissions to try subjects under martial law in peacetime.[14] This practice was curtailed by the *Petition of Right* in 1628,[15] and thereafter the Crown was prevented from using military courts rather than ordinary courts of law in times of peace.[16] With the exception of an unused and short-lived statutory imposition of martial law in 1914,[17] the executive has not resorted to martial law in Britain (as opposed to Ireland and the Colonies)[18] since the eighteenth century.[19] However, it is clear that the prerogative power to declare martial law in war was not extinguished by the *Petition of Right* and is now vested in the executive.[20] Additionally, some commentators take the view that the common law confers a duty upon the executive to use whatever force is necessary to suppress civil disorder.[21]

The justification for martial law is found in the doctrine of necessity.[22] Once the courts have been satisfied that war exists,[23] they will not further scrutinize military actions or related executive acts *durante bello*.[24] One jurist has noted that: "Martial law arises from the State necessity, and is justified at the common law by necessity, and by necessity alone. . . ."[25] A major difficulty lies in the fact that, as martial law has rarely been used in Britain, there is a paucity of direct judicial and legislative authority prescribing the parameters of extremely wide and unfettered executive powers.[26] But it is clear that the courts do not regard martial law as "law"[27] and that military tribunals are not courts but advisory committees carrying out the orders of the military commander.[28] This policy of judicial abnegation ceases when war terminates, at which time the military authorities may be held liable *ex post facto* for actions in excess of the powers conferred.[29]

14　F. MAITLAND, THE CONSTITUTIONAL HISTORY OF ENGLAND 266-67 (1908), who asserts that this questionable practice of permitting martial law to exist in peacetime alongside regular courts was never subject to judicial review because "[t]he judges of the courts of common law were very distinctly the king's servants."

15　[1628] 3 Car. I, c. 1.

16　For an illuminating historical analysis of martial law see Holdsworth, *Martial Law Historically Considered*, 18 LAW Q. REV. 117 (1902).

17　Defense of the Realm Act (No. 2), 1914, 4 & 5 Geo.5 c.63. *See also* Bowman, *Martial Law and the English Constitution*, 15 MICH. L. REV. 93 (1916).

18　*See also* K. Roberts-Wray, COMMONWEALTH AND COLONIAL LAW 642-43 (1966).

19　"[M]artial law has never been attempted to be exercised [since the Petition of Right] in the realm of England by virtue of the prerogative." per Lord Cockburn C.J. in R v. Nelson & Brand, F. Cockburn Sp. Rep. (1867). For a contrary interpretation, see Pollock, *What Is Martial Law?*, 18 LAW Q. REV. 152, 155 (1902).

20　Egan v. Macready [1921], 1 IR. 265.

21　MAITLAND, *supra* note 14, at 267; HEUSTON, *supra* note 13, at 152.

22　For a lucid examination of the necessity doctrine see D. KEIR & F. LAWSON, CASES IN CONSTITUTIONAL LAW 434-40 (4th ed. 1954).

23　The courts have expressly reserved the right to review whether the crisis calls for a sufficient use of military power to justify a state of war, R(Garde) v. Strickland, [1921] 2 I.R. 317.

24　KEIR & LAWSON, *supra* note 22, at 435-36.

25　Dodd, *The Case of Marais*, 18 LAW Q. REV. 143, 145 (1902).

26　Much of the case law and legislation judicially considered relates to colonial unrest or disturbances in Ireland. *See also* KEIR & LAWSON, *supra* note 22, at 432.

27　Re Clifford and O'Sullivan, [1921] 2 A.C. 570.

28　R v. Allen, [1921] I.R. 241. Similarly the U.S. Supreme Court has ruled that it has no power to review the proceedings of a military commission, the commission not being part of the judicial system, Ex parte Vallandigham, 68 U.S. (1 Wall.) 243 (1863).

29　Higgins v. Willis, [1921] 2 I.R. 386. Usually an Act of Idemnity is passed to retrospectively protect people who have acted in good faith. *See, e.g.,* Indemnity Act, 1920, 10 & 11 Geo. 5 c. 48.

Thus, while direct precedent is scarce,[30] martial law allows for uncontrolled use of exceptional measures. The courts regard martial law as non-justiciable *durante bello* and refuse to balance the potentially tyrannical nature of unfettered military power against the rights and privileges of the citizen.[31] Furthermore, in this century British courts have retreated from the traditional safeguard established in the *Wolfe Tone Case*,[32] namely that civilians could not be tried by courts-martial while the ordinary courts were still open.[33]

The modern reality of the sweeping nature of common law war powers makes martial law superfluous.[34] By prerogative,[35] common law[36] and, more

---

30 It would be wrong, however, to deduce that British history is free from violent protest and insurrection. One recent study analyzed such events between 1485 and 1976 and found that there had been 209 uprisings and insurrections. N. Pennick, *British Disaffection* (1976) (unpublished). For a short review of this study see *Peace News* (London), Feb. 11, 1977, at 12.

31 After analyzing the relevant case law KEIR & LAWSON, *supra* note 22, at 437, make the startling observation:

> On the one hand, the citizen should not be subject to acts of tyranny at the hands of one who cannot be made responsible: on the other hand every argument against allowing the courts to interfere with the course of military operations weighs equally heavily against submitting every one of the commander-in-chief's acts to be judged by a common jury. These are matters for experts. . . .

This reflects the view in R v. Allen, *supra* note 28 (Malony, C. J.), in which the Court refused to review a death sentence imposed by the British military commander in Ireland:

> It is the sacred duty of this court to protect the lives and liberties of all His Majesty's subjects, and to see that no one suffers loss of life or liberty save under the laws of the country; but when subjects of the King rise in armed insurrection and the conflict is still raging, it is no less our duty not to interfere with the officers of the Crown in taking such steps as they deem necessary to quell the insurrection . . . [this court] . . . cannot, *durante bello*, control the military authorities, or question any sentence imposed in the exercise of martial law. . . . It seems competent, if war exists, for the military authorities to use special military Court machinery, and to impose any sentence, even death, without being disabled. . . . When peace is restored, acts in excess of what necessity requires . . . may require the protection of indemnifying legislation.

2 I.R. 241 at 264, 272.

32 27 State Tr. 759 (1798). For an interesting comment on this ruling see HEUSTON, *supra* note 13, at 36-38. *The Wolfe Tone* ruling was later reiterated in The Joint Opinion of the Law Officers of the Crown (Sir J. Campbell and Sir R. Rolfe), Re: Power of the Governor of Canada to proclaim Martial Law (1838), *reprinted in* KEIR & LAWSON, *supra* note 22, at 445-46.

33 Ex parte Marais, [1902] A.C. 109 (P.C.) later applied in R v. Allen, [1921] 2 I.R. 241 (1921) and R. (Childers) v. Adjutant-General, [1923] I.R. 5. An interesting contrast with *Marais* is provided by the U.S. Supreme Court in Ex parte Milligan, 71 U.S. (4 Wall.) 2, 121-22 (1866) (Chase, C.J.), which relied upon British Constitutional practice prior to *Marais* and applied the *Wolfe Tone* ruling. The court formulated a markedly different test from *Marais*, namely: "The necessity must be actual and present: the invasion real, such as effectually closes the courts and deposes the civil administration." *Id.* at 127. The test in *Milligan* was later modified in Moyer v. Peabody, 212 U.S. 78 (1909) regarding a Governor's liability, but was reaffirmed in Sterling v. Constantin, 287 U.S. 378 (1932). *See also* Duncan v. Kahanamoku, 327 U.S. 304, 326 et seq. (1946) (concurring) (Murphy, J.). For a critique of *Milligan*, see Fairman, *The Law of Martial Rule and the National Emergency*, 55 HARV. L. REV. 1253 (1942). On the use of martial law in Hawaii during World War II, see Farrell, *Civil Functions of the Military and Implications of Martial Law*, 22 U. KAN. CITY L. REV. 157 (1954) and Frank, *ex parte Milligan v. The Five Companies: Martial Law in Hawaii*, 44 COL. L. REV. 639 (1944). For an excellent discussion of martial law in America in an historical perspective see F. WIENER, CIVILIANS UNDER MILITARY JUSTICE (1967).

34 This view is shared by some leading contemporary British constitutional lawyers. *See, e.g.,* I. BROWNLIE, *supra* note 13, at 125 and S. DE SMITH, CONSTITUTIONAL AND ADMINISTRATIVE LAW 518 (2d ed. 1973).

35 Thus, e.g., the actual declaration of war is a prerogative power as are the powers to intern and deport enemy aliens; R v. Bottrill, ex parte Kuechenmeister, [1947] K.B. 41; R v. Vine Street Police Station Superintendent, ex parte Liebmann, [1916] 1 K.B. 268; R v. Commandant of Knockaloe Camp, ex parte Forman, [1917] 117 L.T. 627. *See also* Garner, *Treatment of Enemy Aliens*, 12 A.J.I.L. 27 (1918). On the seizure of property by prerogative

usually, statutory emergency powers,[37] the executive possesses broad power to suspend civil liberties, deny access to judicial review,[38] and curtail parliamentary scrutiny of executive action[39] while concentrating control into its own hands. In fact, short of a nuclear war,[40] it is difficult to envisage the future use of martial law in Britain, since virtually identical "emergency powers" are readily available. Moreover, emergency powers of a statutory nature do not carry the stigma of martial law nor entail the likelihood of close international political and judicial scrutiny[41] and opprobrium.[42]

Appellate rulings arising out of the operation of emergency powers during World War I provide the basis for determining the limits upon executive power. The case law of this period of particular doctrinal importance reveals, on the one hand, judicial abnegation regarding the protection of civil liberty and, on the other hand, a cautiously responsive and protective judicial attitude toward the

---

power, see Attorney-General v. De Keyser's Royal Hotel Ltd., [1920] A.C. 508; Burmah Oil Co. Ltd., v. Lord Advocate, [1965] A.C. 75; and The Broadmayne, P. 64 (1916). On the right of angary, see Commercial and Estates Co. of Egypt v. the Board of Trade, [1925] 1 K.B. 271. On the residual nature of prerogative power, see A. DICEY, INTRODUCTION TO THE STUDY OF THE CONSTITUTION 430 *et seq.* (10th ed. 1965).

36   For example, the right of the Crown to enter private property and construct defense works to repel an invasion *see* The Case of the King's Prerogative in Saltpetre, 12 Co.Rep. 12 (1606). *See also* S.9., Emergency Powers (Defense) Act, 1939, 2 & 3 Geo. 6, c.62. For common law doctrine of the duty to suppress disorder, see the charge to the grand jury in the Bristol Riots Case, 3 State Tr. N.S. 1; 5 C & P 261 (1832) (Tindal, C. J.); R v. The Inhabitants of Wigan, 1 Wm.Bl. 47 (1749); REPORT OF COMMITTEE ON FEATHERSTONE RIOTS, PARL. PAPERS C.7234 (1893-94). For a brief resume of law relating to the use of the military in aid of the Civil Powers, see 2 MANUAL OF MILITARY LAW, S.V. (1951).

37   Emergency legislation, as enacted in this century, has usually delegated wide law-making powers to the Executive, see The Defense of the Realm (Consolidation) Act, 1914, 4 & 5 Geo.5, c.8; Defense of the Realm (Amendment) Act, 1915 5 Geo.5, c.34; Emergency Powers Act, 1920, 10 & 11 Geo.5, c.48; Emergency Powers (Defense) Act, 1939, 2 & 3 Geo. 6, c.62; Emergency Powers (Defense) Act, 1940, 3 & 4 Geo.6, c.20; Emergency Powers (Defense) (No. 2) Act, 1940, 3 & 4 Geo.6, c.45; Emergency Powers Act, 1964, c.38.

38   Although it should be noted that, following a discernible policy of judicial abnegation in emergency situations, the courts will refuse to question the *ultra vires* nature of the exercise of executive action in the absence of *mala fides*. *See* McEldowney v. Forde, [1971] A.C. 632; [1969] 3 W.L.R. 179 (H.L.). For the limits of judicial review of civil liberties in an emergency, see the landmark case Liversidge v. Anderson, [1942] A.C. 206 (H.L.). *See also* Greene v. Secretary of State for Home Affairs, [1942] A.C. 284 and, more recently, Employment Sec. v. ASLEF, (No. 2), [1972] 2 Q.B. 455. On the doctrine *Salus Populi Suprema Lex,* see Lowry, *Internment: Detention Without Trial in Northern Ireland,* 5 HUMAN RIGHTS 261 (1976).

39   In constitutional theory the Executive is answerable to Parliament even on matters of national security. In reality, however, Cabinet Ministers usually refuse to answer to Parliament on the grounds of national security. For a study of parliamentary questioning concerning internment under wartime emergency conditions and the use of the national security rationale, see Cotter, *Emergency Detention in Wartime: The British Experience,* 6 STAN. L. REV. 238 (1954). However, parliamentary review of delegated legislation in normal times is hardly noticeable or, in the view of DE SMITH, *supra* note 34, such review "tends to be perfunctory" at 333.

40   For an interesting American analysis of the role of law in a modern nuclear war setting, see Cavers, *Legal Planning Against the Risk of Atomic War,* 55 COL. L. REV. 127 (1955). *See also* R. RANKIN & W. DALLMAYR, FREEDOM AND EMERGENCY POWERS IN THE COLD WAR 55-81 (1964).

41   On the international justiciability of emergency legislation under Article 15 of the European Convention of Human Rights, see Lawless v. Ireland, [1958] 2 Y.B. EUR. CONV. ON HUMAN RIGHTS 308 (Eur. Comm. on Human Rights) and [1961] 4 Y.B. EUR. CONV. ON HUMAN RIGHTS 438. For an account of this ruling see A. ROBERTSON, HUMAN RIGHTS IN EUROPE 51-3, 111-14 & 212-21 (2d ed. 1977).

42   For an assessment of the significance of international public opinion and the role of international prestige in the enforcement of human rights see Bilder, *Rethinking International Human Rights: Some Basic Questions,* WISC. L. REV. 171, 193 *et seq.* (1969).

protection of property rights from arbitrary executive action under the guise of prerogative power.

Pursuant to wide powers conferred by the emergency legislation enacted for World War I, the Home Secretary (a cabinet officer) sought to authorize, by delegation legislation, extra-judicial preventive detention by executive action.[43] The use of this internment power was quickly challenged in a case which was to become a constitutional *cause celebre* and a leading authority confirming un-limited executive power in an emergency. In *R. v. Halliday, ex parte Zadig*,[44] certain internment provisions of the Defense of the Realm (Consolidation) Act[45] were challenged. Section 1(1) of the Act conferred power upon the executive during the duration of the War (World War I) "to issue regulations for securing the public safety and the defense of the realm" and Regulation 14B,[46] made in purported exercise of this power, empowered the Home Secretary to intern persons posing a threat to national security.

Under this Regulation the Home Secretary ordered the detention of one Zadig, who was a naturalized British subject of German birth. Zadig, having un-successfully argued before the Advisory Committee, applied for a writ of *habeas corpus* on the ground that Regulation 14B was *ultra vires* the Defense of the Realm (Consolidation) Act of 1914. The Court of Appeal unanimously dis-missed his appeal on the basis that the regulation impugned was authorized by the express language of the Act, which was precise, clear, and free from am-biguity. Zadig appealed to the House of Lords.

The challenged Regulation had been passed as passions became inflamed with the escalation of World War I,[47] and the *Halliday* case demonstrates that the House of Lords was similarly subject to such feelings. The Lord Chancellor, Lord Finlay, delivered the majority judgment and affirmed the Court of Ap-peal.[48] Having noted that Parliament had power to pass the Act, Lord Finlay then examined the construction of the Act and dealt with the six main arguments of the appellants, which may be summarized: (1) that some limitation must be put upon the general words of the statute; (2) that there was no provision for imprisonment without trial; (3) that the provisions made by the Defense of the Realm Act 1914, for the trial of British subjects by a civil court with a jury strengthened the contention of the appellant; (4) that general words in a statute could not take away the vested rights of the subject or alter the fundamental law of the constitution; (5) that the statute was in its nature penal and must be strictly

---

43   A brief note on the World War I legislation is found in H. Bellot, Leading Cases in Constitutional Law 126-29 (7th ed. 1934).
44   [1917] A.C. 260.
45   [1914] 5 Geo.5, c.8.
46   Defense of the Realm Consolidated Regulations, Reg. No. 14B, stated, *inter alia*:
     Where on the recommendation of a competent naval or military authority or of one of the advisory committees hereinafter mentioned it appears to the Secretary of State that for securing the public safety or the defense of the realm it is expedient in view of the hostile origin or associations of any person that he shall be subjected to such obligations and restrictions as are hereinafter mentioned, the Secretary of State may by order require that person . . . to be interned in such place as may be specified in the order.
47   *See* Garner, *Treatment of Enemy Aliens*, 12 Am. J. Int'l L. 27 (1918), for the legisla-tive history of Regulation 14B.
48   Lords Dunedin, Atkinson and Wrenbury delivered separate concurring opinions.

construed; (6) that a construction that is repugnant to the constitutional traditions could not be adopted. Counsel for the appellant had also argued historically, recalling various interferences with *habeas corpus* in times of danger and questioned why historical precedent had not been followed.

Lord Finlay rejected all of the appellant's arguments. On the argument that untrammelled emergency powers could result in the use of the death penalty without judicial review, Lord Finlay responded:

> It appears to me to be a sufficient answer to this argument that it may be necessary in time of great public danger to entrust great powers to his Majesty in Council, and that Parliament may do so feeling certain that such powers will be reasonably exercised.[49]

Thus, the *purpose* of the legislation, in the opinion of Lord Finlay, overrode the principles of construction and the requirement of meaningful judicial review in emergency situations.[50] The majority opinions show that the House of Lords was prepared to assume that Parliament had intended to devolve to the executive complete and unfettered discretion to implement whatever measures the executive might deem to be necessary for defense. The real or actual necessity for the measures thus chosen was not justiciable as the majority would not inquire into the executive definition of the threat to "public safety." Thus the majority saw the emergency powers possessed by the executive as analogous to the Crown Prerogative insofar as the only safeguard against abuse in the absence of *mala fides*[51] is parliamentary scrutiny. Similarly, the majority took the view that the power conferred by the words of the statute was "subjective" to the Home Secretary and incapable of objective judicial oversight.[52]

Lord Shaw delivered a lengthy and, in parts, obscure dissent.[53] His Lordship thought that the detention of "[persons] . . . of hostile origins and associations" was vague in the extreme[54] and took up counsel's point regarding unscrutinized summary execution by asking the question ". . . why, on the same principle and in the exercise power [of internment], may he not be shot out of hand?"[55] And on the constructive or implied repeal of constitutional guarantees of *habeas corpus* Lord Shaw concluded his dissent by restating the hitherto generally accepted

---

49   *See* note 44 *supra*, at 268-69.
50   The statute was passed at a time of supreme national danger, which still exists. The danger of espionage and of damage by secret agents to ships, railways, munition works, bridges, etc. had to be guarded against. The restraint imposed may be a necessary measure of precaution, and in the interests of the whole nation it may be regarded as expedient that such an order should be made in suitable cases. This appears to me to be the meaning of the statute. *Id.* at 269.
51   However, the difficulty in showing *mala fides* was illustrated in a case concerning Regulation No. 2 of the 1914 Act. In Sheffield Conservative and Unionist Club Limited v. Brighten, 32 T.L.R. 598, 85 L.J.K.B. 1669 (1916), the premises of a club were taken by the executive acting under powers conferred in Regulation No. 2. It was held that the purpose for which they were taken, even if only indirectly necessary for defense, was *intra vires* the Regulation. It had been argued that the military authorities had acted so unreasonably that they could not have acted in good faith, but Avory held that unless the court could say that the action of the authorities was so unreasonable as to be obviously not *bona fide*, the opinion of the military would be conclusive.
52   *See* Lord Finlay, *supra* note 44, at 269 and Lord Atkinson at 271-2.
53   *Id.* at 276 *et seq.*
54   *Id.* at 292.
55   *Id.* at 291.

principles of statutory construction that constitutional safeguards must be expressly, rather than impliedly, repealed by a statute.[56] Lord Shaw took the view that, notwithstanding the breadth of the emergency powers granted by the legislature to the executive, it was incumbent upon the courts to strictly scrutinize the enabling statute prior to declaring delegated legislation to be *intra vires*. But only Lord Shaw, dissenting, thought that the fundamental issue of abuse of executive abrogation of civil liberty in an emergency was a justiciable issue. Thus a majority of the House of Lords abstained from examining the subjective exercise of discretion by the Minister of Home Affairs when detaining people without trial as a preventive measure during an emergency.

The outbreak of hostilities in 1939 caused the issue of internment to again provide the House of Lords with an opportunity to circumscribe emergency powers and yet again the court abrogated its duty to judicially scrutinize executive action. The source of the power to intern during World War II in Britain was the Emergency Powers (Defense) Act of 1939[57] which provided the Executive in the person of the Home Secretary with, *inter alia,* wide powers of internment.[58] Pursuant to these powers the executive passed Regulation 18B which gave the power to intern suspects "[I]f the Secretary of State has reasonable cause to believe any person to be of hostile origins or associations."[59] That the scope of this power to intern is very wide is obvious from the draftsman's use of "reasonable cause to believe" rather than the World War I term "satisfied."[60] The precise nature of the powers conferred and the courts' willingness to scrutinize executive acts of internment were quickly brought before the House of Lords in the landmark civil liberties ruling of *Liversidge v. Anderson*.[61]

In this case a detention order was made by the Home Secretary against Liversidge (alias Perlzweig) on the ground that he had reasonable cause to believe that Liversidge was a person of hostile associations, and that it was therefore necessary to exercise control over him. Liversidge was accordingly detained

---

56 In the latest edition of Maxwell on the Interpretation of Statutes, I find the law exactly as I view it stated thus: "Repeal by implication is not favored. A sufficient Act ought not to be held to be repealed by implications without some strong reason. It is a reasonable presumption that the legislature did not intend to keep really contradictory enactments in the statute book, or, on the other hand, to effect so important a measure as the repeal of a law without expressing an intention to do so. Such an interpretation, therefore, is not to be adopted unless it be inevitable. Any reasonable construction which offers an escape from it is more likely to be in consonance with the real intention." [1917] A.C. 260 at 268.

The construction I have ventured to propose appears to me to be not unreasonable, but to square with every familiar and accustomed canon. I think that the judgment of the Courts below is erroneous, and is fraught with grave legal and constitutional danger. In my opinion the appeals should be allowed, the regulation challenged should be declared *ultra vires,* and the appellant should be set at liberty. [1917] A.C. 260 at 305.

57 [1939] 2 & 3 Geo.6, c.62.

58 "[Defense Regulations] . . . for the detention of persons whose detention appears to the Secretary of State to be expedient in the interests of the public safety or the defense of the realm." *Id.* at S. 1(2)(9).

59 S.R. & O., 1939, No. 1681, Regulation 18B, ¶ 1. For a discussion of the origin of Regulation 18B, see COTTER, *supra* note 39, at 239-42.

60 *See also* C. K. ALLEN, LAW AND ORDERS 412-26 app. ˈ(3d ed. 1964).

61 [1942] A.C. 206. *See also* Heuston, *Liversidge v. Anderson in Retrospect,* 86 LAW Q. REV. 33 (1970); Heuston, *Liversidge v. Anderson: Two Footnotes,* 87 LAW Q. REV. 161 (1972).

in Brixton Prison, and the next year he sought a writ against the Home Secretary, containing a declaration that his detention was unlawful and claiming damages for false imprisonment. The Home Secretary did not make any affidavit showing why, or on what information, he had reached his decision, but merely produced the order purporting to be made under Regulation 18B. The action proceeded on a claim for particulars of defense: there was no suggestion that the Home Secretary had not acted in good faith; and the House of Lords, with Lord Atkin dissenting, held that the order was valid and the Home Secretary's answer sufficient.

The Lord Chancellor, Lord Maugham took the view that internment under the Regulations was a matter for executive discretion and that the Home Secretary was not acting judicially. Moreover, Lord Maugham recognized that a decision to intern must necessarily be based upon confidential information but that the Home Secretary was answerable to Parliament in this regard and not to the courts.[62] His Lordship noted that Parliamentary scrutiny was envisaged by the Regulation as the Home Secretary had to give a monthly report to Parliament[63] and the internee's only redress was seen to be recourse to the Home Secretary's Advisory Board.[64] In Lord Maugham's view the words "reasonable cause to believe" meant that the Home Secretary should personally consider each case and the only requirement placed upon him by law was that he must act in good faith.[65] Lord Maugham's opinion, and the concurring opinions,[66] emphasize the fact that the powers conferred upon the executive were emergency executive powers at a time of great national peril and were necessary on grounds of national security. Thus the majority abrogated their duty to scrutinize executive acts on the grounds of *Salus Populi Suprema Lex.*[67]

Lord Atkin, in a famous and spirited dissent, was far more conscious of the fundamental constitutional issue of civil liberty and refused to see the issue solely as one of technical construction.[68] Rejecting the majority's view that the words must be construed subjectively, Lord Atkin emphasized that the words "if he has reasonable cause to believe" did not mean "if he *thinks* he has reasonable cause to believe" and that consequently the words had an objective meaning giving rise to a justiciable issue.[69] Lord Atkin scathingly characterized the majority view

---

62   [1942] A.C. at 218.
63   But the Home Secretary could avoid particularized parliamentary questioning on the grounds of "national security." *See* COTTER, *supra* note 39.
64   "It seems to me that, if any . . . appeal had been thought proper, it would have been to a special tribunal with power to inquire privately into all the reasons for the Secretary's action, but without any obligation to communicate them to the person detained." [1942] A.C. at 222.
65   *Id.* at 219.
66   Lords MacMillan, Romer and Wright issued separate opinions concurring with Lord Maugham, L.C.
67   *See also* R v. Home Secretary ex parte Lees, [1941] 1 K.B. 72.
68   In this country, amid the clash of arms, the laws are not silent. They may be changed, but they speak the same language in war as in peace. It has always been one of the pillars of freedom, one of the principles of liberty for which on recent authority we are now fighting, that the judges are no respecters of persons and stand between the subject and any attempted encroachments on his liberty by the executive, alert to see that any coercive action is justified in law. In this case I have listened to arguments which might have been addressed acceptably to the Court of King's Bench in the time of Charles I. [1942] A.C. at 244.
69   *Id.*

and respondents' arguments as analogous to a children's fantasy.[70]

However, Lord Atkin joined the majority in a subsequent case in which the House of Lords dismissed an appeal on an application for *habeas corpus* arising out of the same Regulation,[71] and the *Liversidge* ruling became the authoritative decision regarding justiciability of executive actions affecting individual liberty during an emergency.[72] The recent House of Lords ruling in *McEldowney v. Forde*[73] has reaffirmed *Liversidge* by holding that when individual liberty is curtailed by executive action under emergency legislation, the executive is immune from subsequent judicially imposed accountability in the absence of *mala fides*.

The House of Lords, as court of last resort, has demonstrated a consistent policy of judicial abnegation in failing to define the limits of executive discretion under statutory emergency powers and has ensured that executive incursions into the field of civil liberties remain non-justiciable in the absence of *mala fides*. By failing to afford the citizen a forum or redress against arbitrary use of unfettered executive powers the courts have blocked one important avenue of legitimate protest.

However, while the doctrinal cases reveal extreme reluctance on the part of the courts to scrutinize emergency executive actions in the area of individual rights or civil liberties, one field of constitutional rights benefitted from an assertive and protective judicial posture, namely the rights to private property. The courts adopted an activist stance in circumscribing executive emergency activities in the areas of taxation and acquisition of property.

This activist stance in proprietarian matters is illustrated by controversial emergency legislation enacted during World War I which empowered the executive to requisition ships.[74] Pursuant to this power, the executive passed a regulation directing a shipping company to continue plying its trade but, henceforth,

---

70   I know of only one authority which might justify the suggested method of construction: " 'When I use a word,' Humpty Dumpty said in rather a scornful tone, 'it means what I choose it to mean, neither more nor less.' 'The question is,' said Alice, 'whether you can make words mean so many different things.' 'The question is,' said Humpty Dumpty, 'which is to be master—that's all.' " ("Through the Looking Glass," c.vi.) After all this long discussion the question is whether the words 'If a man has' can mean 'If a man thinks he has.' I am of opinion that they cannot, and that the case should be decided accordingly. *Id.* at 245.

71   Greene v. Home Secretary, [1942] A.C. 284. In this case the Home Secretary filed an affidavit setting out some particulars and stating that he had acted upon information obtained from responsible and experienced persons. Here Lord Atkin held this affidavit to be a sufficient answer and refused to inquire further into the necessity or justification of the appellant's internment.

72   *See, e.g.,* Budd v. Anderson, [1943] 1 K.B. 642. However, *Liversidge* received a mixed reception from contemporary legal commentators. *See, e.g.,* C. K. ALLEN, *supra* note 60: D. KEIR & F. LAWSON, *supra* note 22, at 262-64. Perhaps because of the controversy surrounding the *Liversidge* ruling the House of Lords, sitting as the Judicial Committee of the Privy Council on an appeal from Ceylon, was at pains to point out that *Liversidge* applied *only* to judicial review of executive acts in emergency conditions; Nakkuda Ali v. Jayaratne, [1951] A.C. 66.

73   *See* note 38 *supra.* For an assessment of the contribution of this judicial posture to the escalation of the Northern Irish conflict, see T. HADDEN & P. HILLYARD, JUSTICE IN NORTHERN IRELAND: A STUDY IN SOCIAL CONFIDENCE 8-20 (1973). In Northern Ireland judicial abnegation regarding emergency powers has had the effect of tacitly reinforcing a repressive *status quo* while concomitantly closing the last outlet for legitimate protest. It was only after the *McEldowney* ruling that street protest and civil rights demonstrations grew in size and number.

74   Defense of the Realm (Consolidated) Regulations, Regulation 39B.

to do so on behalf of the government which was to be credited with all earnings which accrued. In *China Mutual Steam Navigation Co. Ltd. v. MacLay*,[75] the shipping company credited its own account with the profits, claiming that the government was not entitled to the earnings since the empowering regulation was *ultra vires,* being tantamount to taxation without the clear authority of Parliament. Although declaring the impugned regulation to be *intra vires,*[76] it was nevertheless held by Bailhache, J. that the executive directive which ordered the shippers to continue running the company *was,* in fact, *ultra vires.*[77] The learned judge took the view that power to requisition ships, while valid in itself, did not include the power to requisition the services of the owners. Bailhache, J. concluded by indicating that the owners should be subjected to "negotiations" rather than "command."[78]

While *China Mutual* was not appealed beyond the trial stage, the Court of Appeal was soon presented with the opportunity to establish the parameters of the constitutionality of executive taxing powers during an emergency. In *Attorney-General v. Wilts. United Dairies Ltd.,*[79] the Court of Appeal examined the broad emergency powers of executive control over food supplies.

Pursuant to legislative enactment, the executive was empowered to, *inter alia:*

> make orders regulating or giving directions with respect to the production, manufacture, treatment, use, consumption, transport, storage, distribution, supply, sale or purchase of, or other dealing in or measures to be taken in relation to any article . . . when it appears to him necessary or expedient to make such order for the purpose of encouraging or maintaining the food supply of the country.[80]

Under the purported exercise of this power, the executive, in the person of the Food Controller, sought to secure a levy of two pennies per gallon on milk prior to the grant of a license to any dairy. The Court of Appeal held that the tax was improper since the legislation did not expressly provide for executive taxing authority.[81] In the opinion of Lord Justice Atkin:

> [If] an officer of the executive seeks to justify a charge upon a subject made for the use of the Crown . . . he must show in clear terms, that Parliament has authorized the particular charge.[82]

The court asserted that, notwithstanding the condition of war, the executive could not exclusively determine necessity, and, when such a measure eroded fundamental liberty under the Bill of Rights[83] the executive's case would be strictly scrutinized and must be permitted in "clear terms."

---

75   [1918] 1 K.B. 33.
76   *Id.* at 39.
77   *See also* dicta in Lipton Ltd. v. Ford, [1917] 2 K.B. 647 at 655.
78   *See* [1918] 1 K.B. at 41.
79   37 L.T.R. 884 (1921).
80   New Ministries and Secretaries Act, 6 & 7 Geo. 5, c.68, §§ 3 & 4; Defense of the Realm (Consolidated) Regulations, Regulation 2F.
81   *See* 37 L.T.R. at 885 (Scrutton, L.J.).
82   *Id.* at 886.
83   1 Will. & Mar. Sess.2, c.2 (1688).

This "clear terms" principle was also applied at this time by the Court of Appeal to restrain the executive from controlling the rights of landlords in *Chester v. Bateson*.[84] In this case the executive had sought to curtail the use of ejectment proceedings by landlords against munitions workers unless prior ministerial consent had been obtained.[85] The landlord maintained that the impugned regulation encroached upon the *Magna Carta* in that it deprived the landlord of his right of access to the courts.[86] It was held that such an encroachment could only be by "direct enactment"[87] which seemed to be a reformulation of the clear terms principle, albeit in more restrictive terms.

Inevitably the limits of executive power in regard to property rights came before the House of Lords and in *Attorney-General v. De Keyser's Royal Hotel Ltd.*,[88] the court did not hesitate to balance executive necessity against fundamental liberty. In *De Keyser* the War Office informed the hoteliers that the Army Council intended to take possession of their hotel, stipulating that *ex gratia* compensation would be paid but would be "strictly limited to the actual monetary loss sustained."[89] The Crown denied liability for full compensation by virtue of prerogative right and emergency enabling legislation, which provided:

> Any such regulation may provide for the suspension of any restrictions on the acquisition or user of land or the exercise of the power of making by-laws, or any other power under the Defense Acts, 1842 to 1875, or the Military Land Acts, 1891 to 1903.[90]

The House of Lords held that the executive could not rely on the prerogative to justify requisition since statutory powers had superceded executive prerogative and, consequently, the prerogative was abated to the extent that the statute was operative.[91] Since the prerogative power had been limited by statute, it fell to the court to determine whether it was for the executive or for the courts to divine if, in fact, the statute "directly dealt" with the same subject matter. In *De Keyser* the court opted for justiciability,[92] notwithstanding its earlier but recent decision against justiciability of other fundamental rights in *Halliday*. Property rights were thus placed in a relatively advantageous position when set against individual rights.

In defining the limits of emergency executive power and discretion, the court forsook the opportunity to rearticulate the long-established constitutional principles enshrined in the *Magna Carta*, Petition of Right, and Bill of Rights, which protected citizens from the state acquisition of property without compensation.[93] Instead, the court relied upon a perceived "national sentiment" that

---

84 [1920] 1 K.B. 829.
85 Defense of the Realm (Consolidation) Act, 1914, 5 Geo. 5, c.8, § 1(1), Regulation 2A(2).
86 25 Edw.I, 1927, c.29.
87 *See* [1920] 1 K.B. at 833.
88 [1920] A.C. 509. *See also* Central Control Board (Liquor Traffic) v. Cannon Brewery Co. Ltd., [1919] A.C. 744.
89 [1920] A.C. at 510.
90 *See* note 85, *supra* at § 1(2).
91 *See* [1920] A.C. at 561.
92 *Id.* at 559.
93 For a commentary on the historical significance of these constitutional provisions, *see* F. MAITLAND, *supra* note 14.

". . . it was equitable that burdens borne for the good of the nation" should be evenly distributed.[94] This activist stance resulted in the court departing from constitutional principles while establishing a new constitutional doctrine which Lord Sumner chose to call a presumption of interpretation:

> The presumption must be, both that the executive action was taken under powers by which it can be justified, rather than beyond all powers whatever, and that the available powers have been exercised so as to prevent and not so as to cause avoidable injury to the subject.[95]

Although the grant of power had been extremely wide on its face the discretion of the executive in war was only unfettered insofar as the powers executed the protective function of "public security and the defense of the realm" and, significantly, the court limited the general words to the specific means provided *and* necessary to achieve those ends.[96]

In *De Keyser* the general empowering words "for the suspension of any restrictions" were narrowly construed so as "not to cause avoidable injury to the subject." The power to acquire was deemed to be independent of the question of payment and is completed and exhausted prior to the time at which the obligation to pay arose. Accordingly, this narrow construction meant that the obligation to pay compensation was not a "restriction" within the meaning of the Act and could not, therefore, be suspended by the executive.[97] In this result *De Keyser* upheld the constitutional tradition of protecting private property from expropriation. More significantly, the House of Lords formulated the *De Keyser Doctrine*: that the courts, in the face of unfettered executive discretion via emergency powers, reserve the right to scrutinize executive acts to ensure that they are in fact necessary, and will limit the general words of an emergency statute to the specific means provided *and* necessary for the task. Thus, the *De Keyser Doctrine* established the justiciability of executive necessity in an emergency.

The *De Keyser Doctrine* may be distinguished from the *Halliday-Liversidge-McEldowney* approach in that *De Keyser* and the other emergency property rights cases dealt only with property rights and interests as opposed to internment of suspects. Jurisprudentially, the key difference is found in the opposing approaches to the *ultra vires* doctrine. In *De Keyser* the House of Lords unequivocally declared executive necessity in an emergency to be justiciable whereas in *Halliday* such an approach was rejected when it was deemed that ". . . no tribunal . . . can be imagined less appropriate than a Court of Law" to examine executive necessity.[98] Indeed, the *De Keyser* doctrine follows the spirit of the dissent in *Halliday* in which Lord Shaw declared that "fundamental rights [are] . . . exempt from infringement by delegated power unless Parliament has expressed itself with unmistakable clarity."[99] Thus while judicial activism has ensured justiciability of property rights in emergencies, civil liberties have suffered

---

94 *See* [1920] A.C. at 553.
95 *Id.* at 559.
96 *Id.* at 529-30 (Lord Dunedin).
97 *Id.* at 558.
98 See [1917] A.C. at 269 (Lord Finlay, L.C.).
99 *See generally* [1917], A.C. 260.

at the hands of a clearly discernible policy of judicial abnegation perpetuating
the problem aptly characterized by Neumann:

> The state of siege, martial law, emergency powers—these merely indicate
> that reasons of state may actually annihilate civil liberties altogether. Com-
> mon to these institutions in most countries is the fact that the discretionary
> power of those who declare an emergency cannot be challenged. It is they
> who determine whether an emergency exists and what measures are deemed
> necessary to cope with it.[100]

The importance of the doctrine of necessity in the Northern Irish context is
readily apparent when it is recalled that the fifth statute enacted by the fledgling
Northern Irish Parliament (Stormont) was the notorious Special Powers Act of
1922[101] which remained in force for 50 years until it was replaced by modified,
yet equally repressive, British emergency legislation.[102]

In recent years the British experience in Northern Ireland has inevitably
placed heavy reliance upon emergency executive powers to deal with the newer
and more complex problem of the urban guerilla. Because of these changes in
the social context, it is necessary to examine the judicial attitude to the terrorist
phenomenon in the light of the above doctrines. In fact only three cases are, for
our purposes, of doctrinal significance as they indicate a sub-category of the concept of necessity, namely the doctrine of *operation necessity*.

In *R. v. Allen*[103] the Court of King's Bench Division of Ireland confronted
the issue of the justiciability of extremely repressive military action during a
period of martial law in Ireland. Although *Allen* has been regarded as a definitive analysis of military and executive powers during martial law, the pleadings
of the military and the reasoning of Chief Justice Molony offer highly persuasive
authority concerning the parameters of executive discretion in dealing with
urban guerillas. In *Allen* the court declined jurisdiction to intervene so as to
prevent a military court from executing a person found in possession of arms.
The military argued, *inter alia*, that the court did not have jurisdiction and that
the exercise of martial law powers, *durante bello,* was not justiciable.[104] The key
issue in *Allen* was characterized by Chief Justice Molony to be: "What are the
powers of the Executive Government in dealing with armed insurrection?"[105]
although the court was also prepared to examine whether, in fact, a state of war
existed justifying martial law.

After carefully reviewing the history of insurrection from the fourteenth
century, Molony noted that the traditional approach had been to use severe
repressive measures, including the suspension of *habeas corpus,* and to protect the
military and executive from judicial review *post durante bello* by the vehicle of
Indemnity Acts. The Chief Justice observed that none of these Acts had contemplated either courts-martial or death sentences. However, Molony distinguished all prior armed insurrections on the factual basis that the then extant

---

100   Neumann, *The Concept of Political Freedom,* 53 Col. L. Rev. 901, 917 (1953).
101   *See* note 1 *supra.*
102   Northern Ireland (Emergency Provisions) Act, 1973, c.53.
103   [1921] 2 I.R. 241.
104   *Id.*
105   *Id.* at 244.

insurrection consisted "exclusively of warfare of a guerilla character."[106] It was noted that guerillas did not wear uniforms and often were ". . . posing as peaceful citizens."[107] As long as guerilla warfare of this type continued, the Chief Justice was of the opinion that ". . . the Government is entitled and, indeed, bound to repel force by force, and thereby put down the insurrection and restore public order."[108] Moreover, precedents which had emphasized the justiciability of martial law powers "while the ordinary courts were still open" were distinguished: "[It] may, however, be doubted whether they contemplated such a system of guerilla warfare as now described."[109] The military derived both its "sole justification and authority" from the existence of rebellion and also ". . . the duty of doing *whatever may be necessary* to quell it, and to restore peace and order."[110] The death sentence for possession of arms was, in the opinion of the military and of the court, ". . . absolutely essential."[111] The court, therefore, accepted that which in modern parlance would be termed an argument of "operational necessity." In essence guerilla warfare was deemed to create a broader and more repressive category of necessity, namely operational necessity, emanating from the military commander and beyond the oversight of both due process of law and judicial review at an appellate level.

But if, in a guerilla war, the military can execute citizens via courts-martial on the basis of operational necessity, a further issue remains as to other legal or justiciable checks and balances or constraints placed upon the military during an emergency, such as the current Northern Irish emergency, in which the military and the executive are acting not under martial law but under sweeping and repressive emergency legislation. Two further cases are of relevance in this regard: *R. v. Smith*[112] and *Attorney-General for Northern Ireland's Reference (No. 1 of 1975).*[113]

In *Smith* a soldier ordered a civilian to produce equipment promptly as guerillas were known to be in the neighborhood. The civilian behaved in a dilatory fashion and when the accused soldier reported this fact to his superior officer, he was ordered to shoot the civilian if his dilatory demeanor did not change. The soldier, noting the further delay of the civilian, shot and killed the civilian and was later charged with murder. The soldier pleaded in defense that he was following superior orders. In this case it was admitted that the killing was deliberate and intentional and, therefore, the only issue for the court was whether or not the defense of obedience to orders made the killing justifiable homicide or murder. In acquitting the soldier of the charge the court declared that a soldier is not culpable if he, subjectively, believes he is obeying the commands of a superior and the order given is not "manifestly illegal" so that he ought to have known it to be unlawful.[114] These twofold subjective and objective criteria enabled the court to sidestep the more thorny issue presented by the defense,

---

106   *Id.* at 268.
107   *Id.*
108   *Id.* at 252.
109   *Id.* at 270.
110   *Id.* at 271.
111   *Id.* at 272.
112   17 Cape of Good Hope Sup. Ct. Rep. 561 (1900).
113   [1976] 3 W.L.R. 235 (H.L.).
114   *See* 17 Cape of Good Hope Sup. Ct. Rep. at 563.

namely that in a period of guerilla warfare when guerillas were thought to be proximate ". . . the order was not altogether an unreasonable or unnecessary one."[115] While the court said that "there is a good deal to be said in favor" of this defense contention,[116] it seems clear from the facts and the context of the case that the circumstances of guerilla warfare could well have determined the issue of lawfulness of the order had the question been reached. The problem remains, however, of determining, after the *Smith* ruling, just what, if any, superior orders are of a type as to be clearly illegal.

This dilemma has been posed by a leading constitutional text:

> There is really no satisfactory authority on the point. On the one hand, the citizen should not be subject to acts of tyranny at the hands of one who cannot be made responsible: on the other hand, every argument against allowing the courts to interfere with the course of military operations weighs equally heavily against submitting every one of the Commander-in-Chief's acts to be judged by a common jury. These are matters for experts.[117]

Clearly the balancing of such "acts of tyranny" against operational necessity should speak strongly in favor of justiciability so as to provide impartial scrutiny. The impartiality of experts, presumably those trained in military expertise, is, it is submitted, highly questionable and, *prima facie* unlikely to provide the high degree of skepticism which would be appropriate in a liberal democratic system. Indeed the recent anti-guerilla operations in, for example, Vietnam and Northern Ireland, have sometimes revealed military experts to be deficient in matters of judgment involving the balancing of liberty against operational necessity.

The concept of operational necessity was recently before the House of Lords in *Attorney-General for Northern Ireland's Reference*.[118] In this case a British soldier shot and killed an unarmed civilian whom, it was alleged, he honestly though mistakenly suspected of being a member of the I.R.A. The soldier had apparently ordered the deceased to halt and when he did not do so, he killed him. A judge, sitting without a jury, acquitted the soldier on the grounds that he had had no conscious intent to kill and that the killing was justifiable homicide. Perhaps in response to the great public outcry generated by this verdict, the Attorney General for Northern Ireland took the unusual step of appealing by way of a Reference via the Northern Irish Court of Appeal to the House of Lords. In the House of Lords the decision turned upon the jurisdictional point of whether the court could entertain the reference application and it was decided that jurisdiction would be assumed.[119] However, it was further reasoned that the issue of criminal liability of the honest but mistaken belief of the soldier in killing the suspect was so framed that it did not raise a point of law but rather a question of fact and, as such, the court declined to review the matter.[120]

The second question as to the nature of the killing was, therefore, not

---

115 *Id.* at 564.
116 *Id.*
117 D. KEIR & F. LAWSON, CASES IN CONSTITUTIONAL LAW 437 (4th ed. 1954).
118 *See* [1976] 3 W.L.R. 235.
119 For jurisdictional reasoning see *Id.* at 238-41 (Lord Diplock).
120 *Id.* at 248 & 256-57.

reached.[121] Although the House of Lords continued its policy of judicial abnega-tion, it is clear from the *obiter* in the reasoning that the conditions of guerilla warfare weighed heavily in the minds of the judges. According to Lord Diplock the question of the guilt of the soldier would depend upon the circumstances in which the accused made his decision to use force and the amount of time avail-able for such a decision.[122] Lord Diplock then hypothesized that an escaping suspect could be attempting to join a band of armed terrorists who "might be lurking in the neighborhood" and, consequently, as the time for the decision to shoot was short "even a reasonable man could only act intuitively."[123] Thus, he continued, a court would have to balance "risk against risk" with the caveat that "the calm analytical atmosphere of a court-room" with the "benefit of hindsight" might be inappropriate if it was not recalled that the soldier's decision was made "but in the brief second or two" and "under all of the stresses to which he was exposed."[124]

Lord Diplock concurred with the finding of fact by the trial judge that the soldier "may have acted intuitively or instinctively without foreseeing the likely consequences of his act [beyond preventing escape]."[125] In the circumstances the soldier had no choice as to the degree of force because shooting the suspect was the only means of preventing his escape. Consequently, arguments regarding the degree of force in self-defense were inapplicable.[126]

At trial the judge found that the soldier had fired because he believed that the man who was seeking to escape *might* be a terrorist.[127] The reasonableness of the action would depend upon the circumstances and the trial judge took the view that mere failure to halt would not, *per se*, be sufficient grounds for using a rifle.[128] Clearly all courts in this case took the view implicitly that the circum-stances extant in Northern Ireland are most unusual in that the possible proximity of armed guerillas mitigated the harshness of the soldier's actions:

> [I]t would be open to the jury to take the view that it would not be unreason-able to assess the kind of harm to be averted by preventing the accused's escape as even graver—the killing or wounding of members of the patrol by terrorists in ambush, and the effect of this success by members of the Provisional I.R.A. in encouraging the continuance of armed insurrection and all the misery and destruction of life and property that terrorist activity in Northern Ireland has entailed.[129]

---

121 The Attorney-General indicated that it was his hope that this reference would lead to some general guidance being given as to the use of force. I regret that I do not see that that is possible, particularly as we are asked to give our opinion on the particular circumstances stated in the reference which may not be repeated. *Id.* at 257 (Viscount Dilhorne).

122 [A]re we satisfied that no reasonable man (a) with knowledge of such facts as were known to the accused or reasonably believed by him to exist, (b) in the circum-stances of the time available to him for reflection, (c) could be of the opinion that the prevention of the risk of harm to which others might be exposed if the suspect were allowed to escape justified exposing the suspect to the risk of harm to him that might result from the kind of force that the accused contemplated using? *Id.* at 246 (Lord Diplock).

123 *Id.* at 247.
124 *Id.*
125 *Id.* at 248.
126 *Id.*
127 *Id.* at 244, 255-56.
128 *Id.* at 255-56.
129 *Id.* at 247 (Lord Diplock).

A major difficulty presented by such reasoning is that, as the I.R.A. does not wear uniform, almost any citizen *might* be a member. Moreover, the proximity of terrorist activities as a major circumstance to be considered would, in the case of Northern Ireland, include vast geographic areas, some of which have a high population density. In other words, the reasonableness criteria of remote and unsubstantiated suspicion of terrorist involvement coupled with the geographic proximity of hostile areas put almost one-third of the population at risk and are an inadequate restraint upon the conduct of the armed forces against the unarmed civilian population. The result of the decision in this case and the *dicta* of the House of Lords are that killing unarmed civilians erroneously suspected of being guerillas may be justifiable homicide. This serves to show both the strains placed on the notion of emergency executive powers by the concept of operational necessity, and the failure of even modern courts to attempt to circumscribe the military or the executive during an emergency.

Thus the unwillingness of the courts to define the parameters of executive power over civil liberty in emergency situations, coupled with the inability to establish criteria other than operational necessity for military action in emergencies, necessitates a close scrutiny of military theory, if not tactics, currently applied to urban guerilla warfare. To what extent does this counter-insurgency theory, which provides the theoretical underpinning of the doctrine of operational necessity, respect or diminish civil liberties? Should the failure of the courts to advance criteria for the protection of liberty in emergencies and their reluctance to examine military and executive encroachment of fundamental personal rights be a major cause for concern?

III. Theories of Counter-Insurgency and the Common Law

During the last thirty years, since the end of World War II, the world has witnessed the growth and development of terrorism or guerilla warfare by revolutionary groups in various jurisdictions. A common feature is that the revolutionaries have often been indigenous, irregular soldiers utilizing stealth to attack civilian and military targets *within* the State, as opposed to fighting an openly declared interstate war as envisaged by the Geneva Convention.[130] This type of revolutionary warfare relies heavily upon assassination, bombing, intimidation and significant support from sections of the population.[131] Consequently, the task of the military and the police in suppressing and containing guerilla warfare is extremely difficult for several reasons, not the least of which is that most standing armies have been trained and equipped to deal with external threats by other states, i.e., conventional warfare. This fact, when coupled with the inherent problem of fighting an indigenous enemy which is immediately reabsorbed into the population, makes counter-insurgency action a demanding task. In recent years new theories, strategies, and technology have been developed and utilized

---

130   For an interesting analysis of the limits of the Geneva Conventions, the position of urban guerillas and the doctrine of necessity, see T. Taylor, Nuremberg and Vietnam: An American Tragedy (1970).

131   An informative discussion of the modern terrorist phenomenon is found in: R. Clutterbuck, Guerillas and Terrorists (1977).

by most nations faced with "internal subversion" in the form of guerilla warfare with varying degrees of success and failure.[132]

Inevitably, the role of military theory is of crucial importance in determining both the attitude and the response of the State to internal subversion in that it accounts for any shifts in the concept of operational necessity. It is facile to examine the particular strategies and technology employed by the military in guerilla situations without first examining the theoretical premises upon which such strategies and tactics are based. In this connection a close examination of military theory and its implications for legal theory in Northern Ireland is particularly appropriate as, not only is the United Kingdom a liberal democracy, but also a modern civilized industrial state. Therefore, by looking closely at the evolution and development of socio-legal and theoretical norms in Northern Ireland during the current emergency, it may be possible to examine the fundamental implications for law and legal systems presented by the current theories of counter-insurgency.

This section will attempt briefly to outline the current guerilla theories and the counter-insurgency theory as developed and used in Northern Ireland. By outlining and elucidating the two opposing strategies, it is possible to obtain a deeper understanding of the changing role of law and legal systems in emergency situations short of martial law and to facilitate meaningful criticism of the justifications advanced for extreme measures.

The British military interest in guerilla warfare and counter-insurgency tactics emanates from the British experience in Ireland during the period from 1919 to 1921. During that time, the British army together with the police constituted over 80,000 men, and yet they were unable to maintain law and order during martial law. In particular, the urban environment became increasingly difficult to control in terms of security and for all other political purposes. It is now known that the guerillas during this phase (the I.R.A.) never numbered more than 3,000, of whom very few could be considered to be activists.[133] Nevertheless it was clear to British planners and strategists that, despite the government's overwhelming superiority, the guerillas had effectively made Ireland impossible to govern. The British withdrawal from the south of Ireland in 1921 constituted a victory for the guerillas because they had achieved their objective in demonstrating that the colonial power was unable to *effectively* govern.[134]

This lesson was not lost on British military theorists, who between 1921 and the Second World War developed techniques for countering guerilla activities (insurgencies). As a result, various amendments were made to Field Service Regulations by the outbreak of the Second World War.[135] By 1940, for example,

---

132 On the role of science, innovation and technology, see C. ACKROYD, K. MARGOLIS, J. ROSENHEAD, & T. SHALLICE, THE TECHNOLOGY OF POLITICAL CONTROL 151-286 (1977).

133 R. TABER, THE WAR OF THE FLEA: GUERILLA WARFARE THEORY AND PRACTICE 110 (1965).

134 The shift in emphasis in guerilla tactics from *direct* confrontation in the classical sense to indirect terror, the aim of which is to demonstrate the failure of a government to govern effectively, is a crucial change in the tactics of terrorism. Most contemporary guerilla groups cannot hope to win a direct confrontation and, therefore, concentrate on demonstrating the ineffectiveness of government. If successful this achieves, *inter alia*, a diminution of public social confidence in law and deleteriously affects social solidarity within the state. For an examination of indirect terror, see E. HYAMS, TERRORISTS AND TERRORISM 9, 10-11 (1975).

135 On the historical evolution of British theory see J. KELLY, THE GENESIS OF REVOLUTION 43-44 (1976).

the British army had established a Special Operations Executive under which agents were placed behind enemy lines and the training of these agents was based upon the lessons learned from Ireland in 1921.[136] British military publications of that date emphasized the need for a friendly population which was deemed to be necessary to protect both the identity and the operations of guerillas. Other publications outlined the technique and strategy of assassinations and the use of explosives.[137]

The use of guerillas in German-Occupied Europe is generally regarded to have been a success, but immediately after the cessation of hostilities in 1945, Britain itself, as a colonial power, was faced with a growing number of guerilla movements against British interests throughout the world. Most notable among these was the outbreak of guerilla violence in Palestine immediately after the Second World War and the outbreak of guerilla hostilities in Malaya and Kenya during the early 1950's.

These revolutionary situations enabled the British to develop further strategies for countering guerilla activity.[138] By the 1960's military strategists had begun to look for a theory which would explain both the role of the army in the counter-revolutionary situation and the role of guerilla. Three military theoreticians have played predominant roles in the development of contemporary military theory. In particular, the writings of Lieutenant Colonel John J. McCuen (U.S. Army) in his book *The Art of Counter-Revolutionary War*[139] and the British theorist Sir Robert Thompson paved the way for the current contemporary theoretical model of Brigadier Frank Kitson which was propagated in his influential book *Low Intensity Operations*.[140]

McCuen divides revolutionary war into four phases: (1) the period of organization (subversion); (2) the period of terrorism (and to a certain extent small-scale guerilla warfare); (3) the period of guerilla warfare; (4) finally, the period of mobile warfare.[141]

It is clear that McCuen bases his propositions upon the fact that revolutionaries have to start from virtually nothing. Essentially, McCuen's view is atheoretical and seems to regard guerillas as a modern form of "mindless gangster" operating without a cause or socio-political motivation. If guerillas are viewed as merely power-hungry individuals, then McCuen's theoretical model has a high degree of validity. If, on the other hand, guerillas have a clearly discernible political reason and motivation for taking up arms within a state, then McCuen's four-stage model is suspect. In the Irish context its validity is doubtful because of

---

136   *Id.*

137   *Id.*

138   Moreover, all of the development in strategy and tactics by military planners in Palestine, Kenya and other colonies has been wholly based upon the insight derived from the British experience in Ireland in 1921, in that it is essential to recognize that guerillas cannot function without the support of a sympathetic or friendly population. The British colonial wars, in countries such as Aden, Malaya, Kenya, Cyprus, Palestine and Ireland have contributed to the steady development of military technique and tactics; sometimes based upon ad hoc considerations which were seen to be necessary in the particular circumstances and at other times based upon new developments in theory and politics.

139   (1965) [hereinafter cited as McCuen].

140   (1971) [hereinafter cited as Kitson]. After writing this book (and serving in Northern Ireland), Kitson was promoted and put in command of the British Infantry Training School.

141   *See* McCuen, *supra* note 139, *passim.*

the strong irredentist reaction of the minority population to the partitioning of Ireland which excluded the six northeastern counties from independence.

Perhaps the McCuen model was unduly influenced by the events in Cuba during the Castro rebellion. It was because of the success of the Castro guerillas that the so-called "Foco theory" of guerilla warfare gained acceptance.[142] According to this theory, it is not necessary to organize the population as a prelude to revolt. Foco theorists claim that a small group operating from a remote area could act as a focus of discontent in the country as a whole.[143] This theory runs essentially counter to the theory of Mao Tse-tung in that Mao laid emphasis on the fact that a population must be highly organized before a resort to arms.[144] When set against Mao's theory of guerilla warfare and Lenin's concept of objective and subjective revolutionary criteria,[145] the Foco theory in its pure form appears more akin to anarchism than a socialist or communist revolutionary theory. Moreover, neither the Foco theory nor McCuen's analysis emphasize or understand the fact that most forms of successful guerilla warfare have been predicated upon the common factor of existing discontent among the population in general, making the guerillas' cause socially and politically acceptable to the populace. It is clear that McCuen regarded his role as merely that of a tactician in the military sense and divorced himself from questions of social context when preparing his analysis. Thus McCuen's models, so carefully drawn in military terms, must be used with extreme caution in the context of urban guerilla warfare in a modern society.

142 For a full explanation and analysis of the "foco theory," see G. FAIRBAIRN, REVOLUTIONARY GUERILLA WARFARE: THE COUNTRYSIDE VERSION (1974).
143 For the failure of this theory as used by Che Guevara in Bolivia, see *Id*. at 270-78.
144 *Id*. at 98-114.
145 V. LENIN, THE WAR AND THE SECOND INTERNATIONAL 13 (International Publishers ed. 1932):

> For a Marxist there is no doubt that a revolution is impossible without a revolutionary situation; furthermore we know that not every revolutionary situation leads to revolution. What are, generally speaking the characteristics of a revolutionary situation? We can hardly be mistaken when we indicate the following three outstanding signs: (1) it is impossible for the ruling class to maintain their power unchanged; for there is a crisis "higher up," taking one form or another; there is a crisis in the policy of the ruling class; as a result there appears a crack through which the dissatisfaction and the revolt of the oppressed classes burst forth. If a revolution is to take place it is usually insufficient that "one does not wish down below," but it is necessary that "one is incapable up above" to continue in the old way; (2) the wants and sufferings of the oppressed classes become more acute than usual; (3) in consequence of the above causes, there is a considerable increase in the activity of the masses who in "peace time" allow themselves to be robbed without protest, but in stormy times are drawn both by the circumstances of the crisis and *by the "higher-ups" themselves* into independent historic action.
>
> Without these objective changes, which are independent not only of the will of separate groups and parties but even of separate classes, a revolution as a rule is impossible. The co-existence of all these objective changes is called a revolutionary situation. (Emphasis supplied.)

And, after analyzing the failure of prior Russian and German revolutions, he concluded:

> [B]ecause a revolution emerges not out of every revolutionary situation, but out of such situations where, to the above-mentioned objective changes, subjective ones are added, namely the ability of the revolutionary *classes* to carry out revolutionary mass actions *strong* enough to break (or to undermine) the old government, it being the rule that never, not even in a period of crises, does a government "fall" of itself without being "helped to fall." (Emphasis supplied.)

Id. at 13-14. *See also*, GUERILLA WARFARE AND MARXISM (W. Pomeroy ed. 1969).

The current British theories of counter-insurgency are largely to be found in the writings of Sir Robert Thompson[146] and Brigadier Frank Kitson. The Thompson-Kitson approach emphasizes military intelligence as the key to any military theory dealing with guerilla warfare. The approach clearly assumes that guerillas cannot function effectively without the support of a friendly population and the resulting counter-insurgency theory and tactics revolve around breaking the relationship between the guerilla and the friendly population. Thompson establishes five basic principles which must be followed and within which all government measures must fall.[147] Thompson's first principle is that the government must have a clear political aim. He argues that civil courts must be allowed to function during a period of emergencies, but emphasizes that emergency laws can be passed to enable counter-insurgency to proceed while the civil courts are open.[148] He envisages the normal judicial process being amended and changed through changes in laws of procedure and evidence so that a government can pass very tough repressive laws. The only limitation on governmental discretion, which Thompson refers to as a "golden rule," should be that each new law must be fairly and firmly applied.[149] It is clear that by fair application of repressive emergency laws Thompson envisages that emergency powers should be applied equally to all the population. Within his concept of emergency laws Thompson lists, *inter alia,* laws imposing curfews, mandatory death penalties for carrying arms, life imprisonment for providing supplies to terrorists, restricted residence, detention without trial for suspected terrorist supporters, and judicially sanctioned preventive detention by use of "a tribunal presided over by a judge which advises the government."[150] In other words, Thompson's first principle is that the government must have a political aim and objective and must not shrink from passing repressive emergency laws which must be applied equally to all inhabitants—a principle which may be termed the "equality of repression" principle.

The second principle offered by Thompson is that the government must function in accordance with the law, albeit draconian law. Thompson explicitly regards governments as recipients of harsh measures as well as the repository of them.[151] He argues that it is not only morally wrong for a government to be above the law but that it creates practical difficulties which will present insuperable problems. The third principle is that the government must have an overall plan.[152] By this Thompson means that the plan must cover not just military-security measures but also political, social, economic, administrative, police and other matters which may have a bearing on insurgency. Implicit in this point is that the military should be involved to an intimate degree in civilian government

---

146 R. THOMPSON, DEFEATING COMMUNIST INSURGENCY; THE LESSONS OF MALAYA AND VIETNAM (1966). Thompson is the author of several books on insurgency and is a leading international strategist. He was recently a Presidential Advisor to President Nixon on the Vietnam war, a rare distinction for a retired British officer.
147 *Id.* at 50.
148 *Id.* at 50-52.
149 *Id.* at 53.
150 *Id.*
151 *Id.* at 53-54.
152 *Id.* at 55.

and political strategy—a concept of "total strategy."[153] The fourth principle is that the government must give priority to defeating political subversion as opposed to merely defeating political guerillas.[154] It is in this context that Thompson makes the insight that all governmental operations should be designed to break the contact between the guerilla unit and subversive political organizations. In this way Thompson believes that guerillas can be cut off from their sources of supply.[155] The fifth principle envisaged by Thompson is that, in the guerilla phase of insurgency, a government must secure its base area. Such a view entails the virtual surrender of large remoter areas of the country and its population to the guerillas in the initial stages of counter-insurgency operations.[156]

Although Thompson's theories are vague on some points it is clear that, because of his success in defeating communist insurgency in Malaya, his tactics and strategy have been held in high regard by British and American theorists. The problem is, however, that Thompson pays little regard to the causes of unrest other than by enunciating a principle that the government must not be corrupt. Thus the social-economic or political causes of unrest are not deeply examined and merely relegated to a position whereby a government must pay attention to some of the more apparent effects without imposing the obligation of analyzing in any depth the *real* or underlying causes of unrest. Thus Thompson can be faulted for being apolitical and non-theoretical in his approach to defeating insurgency.[157]

Kitson's book, *Low Intensity Operations,* was written in 1971 after Kitson had been able to study closely the operations of the British army in Northern Ireland.[158] The book is important, therefore, because it emphasizes the role of counter-insurgency measures in the context of the modern urban guerilla. Much of the writing which had been used hitherto in counter-insurgency theory by military planners and strategists had been in response to Mao Tse-tung's theory of rural guerilla warfare, whereas Kitson's book establishes various insights into breaking the relationship between the guerillas and the friendly population in an

---

153 For a full explanation of the total strategy concept, see C. BARNETT, STRATEGY AND SOCIETY (1974). The total strategy concept would appear to be difficult to publicly achieve in a democratic state in which the separation of powers doctrine is operative.

154 *See* THOMPSON, *supra* note 146, at 55-57.

155 A disturbing feature of the Thompson-Kitson approach and, indeed, all modern military theorists, is the blurring of the distinction between lawful protest, civil disobedience and subversion (including treason). *See* KITSON, *supra* note 140, at 82-83. Subversion is never defined but is described as including lawful protest. The military panacea is close surveillance of protest groups as they are described as a form of incipient terrorists in a preliminary (subversive) state. *See* KITSON, *supra* at ch. 2, ch. 5. Given this basic failure to define subversion and to distinguish it from lawful protest, the recent revelations in the United States regarding sustained and illegal surveillance of political groups is comprehensible, albeit reprehensible. *See* C. PERKUS, COINTELPRO: THE FBI's SECRET WAR ON POLITICAL FREEDOM (1975). It is, however, deeply significant that no British or American military theorist has felt the necessity or obligation to define "subversion," a term which is freely used in delimiting the concept of surveillance and counter-insurgency theory and practice.

156 *See* THOMPSON, *supra* note 146, at 57-58.

157 Of course Thompson was primarily concerned with defeating communist insurgency and not with other forms of urban guerilla violence which have come to the fore since his book was written.

158 Kitson undertook the writing of his book after he had commanded a brigade in Belfast for a year. Kitson also had actively participated in counter-insurgency operations in Kenya in the 1950's. *See also* F. KITSON, BUNCH OF FIVE (1977). Kitson can be fairly described as the most highly qualified counter-insurgency theorist in the British Army.

urban environment and as such is worthy of close scrutiny.[159]

Like Thompson, Kitson emphasizes the overriding importance of intelligence gathering in dealing with guerilla unrest. While the Kitson approach is as politically unsophisticated as Thompson's, it does place emphasis on the fact that a joint military civilian command is necessary at the very highest level of government and he sees the army's role under three headings: first, advisory to the extent of deciding between defensive and offensive roles; second, the army may contribute towards organizing the population; and third, the collection of "background information" which the army can then develop into what is termed "contact information."[160] This third aspect, the collecting of background information, is crucial to the Kitson thesis. Basically it entails the collection and evaluation of what is termed "low level intelligence."[161] By this is meant intelligence information which will not of itself be of very great importance but which, when collated and taken together, may form the basis for further inquiry. Kitson explicitly envisages intelligence organizations working together to collect information through informers, agents, and the interrogation of prisoners but does not preclude other "special operations" which may be necessary in the situation.[162]

Briefly stated, Kitson's theory is that there are two separate functions involved in countering guerilla activities. The military commander must first of all establish an intelligence organization capable of producing background information or low level intelligence which is then fed to operational commanders who develop this information into "contact information" so that guerillas can be militarily engaged. The key to Kitson's theory, however, lies in its implementation. The intelligence network is not viewed as being separate from the counter-insurgency force itself. Rather, the collection of data is in fact conducted by the commanders in the field who also have the responsibility for establishing and maintaining contact with the guerillas. It is this unified command structure which has been tested in Northern Ireland.[163]

Kitson is intriguingly vague in his explanation of how intelligence is in fact gathered. He lays emphasis on the capture of prisoners who are then "persuaded" to talk and, if possible, converted into informers.[164] But, as Kitson points out, the principal problem in fighting guerillas lies in establishing contact with them and the process of developing low level intelligence information into contact information he describes as "the basic tactical function of counter-insurgency operations."[165] To develop background information, Kitson emphasizes that part of

---

159   KITSON, *supra* note 140, at 85-89.
160   *Id.* at ch. 6.
161   *Id.* at 103-107.
162   *Id.* at 122-26, 191-96.
163   However, implicit in this new devolved or delegated military structure is the belief that commanders in the field be permitted to act speedily and on their own initiative. Thus, "operational necessity" decisions are delegated to low-ranking officers in the field which may help to explain the continuing patterns of brutality on a widespread basis in Northern Ireland.
164   KITSON, *supra* note 140, at 119-22.
165   *Id.* at 99. While envisaging that the developing of background information into contact information falls upon normal military units he notes that special skills are required for exploiting the characteristics of captured insurgents, and it is clear from the language used by Kitson that he sees a role for Special Forces, such as the Special Air Service (SAS) or Rangers. Moreover Kitson's training leads him to deduce that a special operations unit attached to normal infantry units might involve an elaborate operation of building up pseudo-gangs out of captured insurgents who are, in some way, persuaded to work the counter-insurgency forces.

the approach is to regain a measure of control over the population and subsequently to develop low level information into the type of information necessary for making contact with armed groups.[166]

Kitson points out that four facets of counter-insurgency tactics might be used either singly or together. In this connection he envisages the concentration into villages of those people lying in scattered and remote areas of the countryside. This is reminiscent of both the concentration camp concept or, to use the modern euphemism, the strategic hamlet.[167] He also advocates a government role in psychological warfare by the dissemination of information which is carefully controlled and tailored to meet the military-security situation.[168] Another facet is the development of a census by which basic data can be collected from all the population, both hostile and non-hostile,[169] and Kitson favors the use of identity cards for each individual to implement this. But it is clear from Kitson's examples that he envisages the use of very detailed and basic information about the target group, such as the financial stability of inhabitants of the community, and any immediate change in their circumstances, so as to be able to identify even minor changes in the social relationships within a community which may indicate the presence of outside income or resources.

Interestingly, in one of his examples, Kitson notes that after a degree of background information has in fact been gathered it may be necessary to utilize what he terms "shock treatment"[170] whereby, having established a change in financial circumstances of a particular inhabitant of a community, the military commander may then decide "to interrogate four of the people who, from his investigations, seem *least* likely to be supporting [the communists]."[171] Thus Kitson proposes the arrest of innocent people with a view to interrogation merely to establish low level intelligence. Moreover, within this scenario the army is seen as persuading each of the four innocent people to help to gather and corroborate information of this type. As he points out "in fact no one need know that any information has been given,"[172] and envisages the army as prosecuting a

---

(There is some evidence that this approach was used in Algeria, Kenya, Cyprus and, more recently, in the United States.) *See* M. OPPENHEIM, THE URBAN GUERILLA at 62 (1970).

166 KITSON, *supra* note 140, at 106.

167 *Id.* at 107.

168 *Id.* On the role of the press in Northern Ireland see E. McCANN, THE BRITISH PRESS IN NORTHERN IRELAND (1972); J. McGUFFIN, INTERNMENT ch. 15 (1973). On self-censorship of the press see S. WINCHESTER, IN HOLY TERROR (1975). Fisk, *British Clamp on Northern Ireland Propaganda,* Irish Times (Dublin) Mar. 25, 1975, at 6, col. 5; O'Clery, *Psychological Warfare Training Given to 262 Civil Servants,* Irish Times (Dublin), Oct. 28, 1976, at 5, col. 1; McHardy, *Black Propaganda Stopped,* Manchester Guardian Weekly, Mar. 6, 1977, at 5, col. 4; Blundy, *The Army's Secret War in Northern Ireland,* Sunday Times (London), Mar. 13, 1977, at 6, col. 3. This overt and covert abuse of freedom of expression has played a significant role in ensuring a lack of informed, skeptical public scrutiny of events in Northern Ireland. As noted above, judicial review *durante bello* is absent because of the policy of judicial abnegation and, therefore, the normal checks and balances of public opinion in a democracy skeptical of executive use and abuse of power is of special importance. The manipulation of the media advocated by Kitson, and the distortion of information which has recently been admitted to have been practiced for the past five years in Northern Ireland are a serious breach of the principle of freedom of expression.

169 KITSON, *supra* note 140. It should be noted that at common law, there is no established right to privacy.

170 *Id.* at 109.

171 *Id.* at 110.

172 *Id.*

case against the innocent individuals so that a small fine is exacted for the offense for which they had ostensibly been arrested. In this way intelligence information is consolidated. The moral and legal questions regarding the interrogation and punishment of innocent people apparently do not concern the author.[173]

Other forms of interrogation are also noted by Kitson in that he proposes informal talks with captured guerillas so as to persuade them to talk but also less informal talks with captured insurgents.[174] In a later example Kitson does not explain how captured insurgents are to be persuaded to talk and to help the military authorities. However, it is clear, if only by omission, that "unusual" measures are contemplated.[175]

Kitson does not differentiate between rural and urban terrorists. Rather, he asserts that the "important weakness" of both groups is that the actions of guerillas must be related to a particular purpose which in turn involves: (1) building up some degree of support among the population; and (2) at the same time causing the population to act in accordance with the program designed to achieve the aims of those running the political subversion campaign.[176] There must, therefore, be a point of contact between the guerillas and the political leaders controlling the subversive organization.

Kitson's scenario for gathering and developing low level intelligence into contact information is thought to be applicable in both rural and urban settings because of this central weakness in guerilla strategy. Thus, he envisages that when sufficient degrees of low level intelligence information have been gathered and a degree of background information on the target community collated, then various techniques can be used to develop such information.[177] For example, special operations can then be directed towards target groups and road blocks and checking of vehicles or searching of buildings can be conducted on a large scale.[178] But, as Kitson is quick to point out, this system for developing background information can only work if there is a good deal of information to develop. That is to say it is not as important that such information is *reliable* but

---

173 On the theory of telishing, that is, the punishment of innocent people, see Rawls, *Two Concepts of Rules,* [1955] PHILOSOPHICAL REV. 3; and H. HART, PUNISHMENT AND RESPONSIBILITY 11 *et seq.* (1968).

174 KITSON, *supra* note 140, at 119.

175 *Id.* at 122. Two British investigations have acknowledged the ill-treatment of suspected I.R.A. terrorists in Northern Ireland. *See* Report of the Enquiry into Allegations Against the Security Forces of Physical Brutality in Northern Ireland Arising out of Events on the 9th August 1971, CMND. 4823 (1972) and Report of the Committee of Privy Counsellors Appointed to Consider Authorized Procedures for the Interrogation of Persons Suspected of Terrorism, CMND. 4901 (1972). *See* Lowry, *Ill-Treatment, Brutality and Torture: Some Thoughts upon the Treatment of Irish Political Prisoners,* 22 DE PAUL L. REV. 553 (1973). Recently the European Commission of Human Rights made a finding of torture against the British in Northern Ireland and the matter has now been referred for adjudication to the European Court of Human Rights. *See* Report of the European Commission of Human Rights: Ireland v. United Kingdom, Application No. 5310/71 (1976).

176 KITSON, *supra* note 140, at 127.

177 For the past three years low-level intelligence, that is, information gathered against suspects, terrorists and citizens at large, has been stored on a central computer facility at the British Army Headquarters, to which military patrols have immediate radio access. It must be emphasized that such accumulated, and often irrelevant, trivia is insufficient to form probable cause for a search or arrest warrant at common law. On the computerization process, see Fisk, *Army's computer has data on half of population in Ulster,* The Times (London), Dec. 5, 1974, at 1, col. 7; and ACKROYD *et al., supra* note 132, at 41-42.

178 KITSON, *supra* note 140, at 130.

that there is a sufficient quantum of it so as to develop a full community profile.[179]

Kitson is also far more subtle in his approach to the political aspects of counter-insurgency matters than previous theorists. He sees conditional concessions in a political sense being given by the government to moderate or passive supporters of the subversive organization. Such concessions are to have the effect of separating the more moderate supporters of protest from the hard core of subversives.[180] Essentially, Kitson would not shrink from co-opting such moderates into the government. Thus, Kitson sees a role in splitting the moderate support from the hard core support so as to effectively utilize a political manipulative "carrot and stick" campaign whereby reforms are conceded to the moderates while at the same time hard core dissent is repressed in counter-insurgency fashion.[181]

According to Thompson's first principle the government under attack must be seen to be fair and at least not corrupt, whereas Kitson develops the "total strategy" concept whereby concessions are made to elements of the insurgent group in such a way that moderate support is alienated from the insurgents.

A major question arises as to the role of the legal system in such an arrangement. Thompson explicitly argues that law should play a vital role in that, by statute, emergency laws can be simplified so as to insure that tough repressive laws are applied equally among the population. Clearly Thompson does not envisage due process in any accepted sense of the term, but rather a manipulation of the substantive law and procedural changes so that the appearance of fair and evenhanded justice is maintained while severe repression is implemented. Kitson, on the other hand, regards the role of law in a more sophisticated light in that he sees two possible uses for the law. On the one hand, law can be "just another weapon in the government's arsenal" and in such a case the law provides little more than a "propaganda cover" for the disposal of unwanted members of the public.[182] However, for this to happen the legal system must be discreetly tied into the system of government, and the judiciary, in effect, must be controlled by the supreme military-civilian command.

Kitson's second alternative is that the law should remain impartial and administer the laws of the country without any direction from the government.[183] Moreover, Kitson, like Thompson, admits that such a government can introduce

---

179 However, it is clear that the military concept of relevance differs from the legal; for example, Fisk, *supra* note 177, notes that the Army computer stores such information as the color of furnishings in the homes of people they regard as political activists.

180 KITSON, *supra* note 140, at 82.

181 *Id.* at 87:

> Although with an eye to world opinion and to the need to retain the allegiance of the people, no more force than is necessary for containing the situation should be used, conditions can be made reasonably uncomfortable for the population as a whole, in order to provide an incentive for a return to normal life and to act as a deterrent towards a resumption of the campaign.

Thus "necessary" force would here encompass the notion of deterrence which was expressed somewhat more concretely by a serving Army officer: "You know when we were in Ballymurphy [a Belfast Catholic ghetto], we had the people really fed up with us, terrified really. I understand what the refugees must feel like in Vietnam . . . after every shooting incident we would order 1,500 house searches—1,500!" Quoted in C. ACKROYD *et al., supra* note 132, at 38.

182 *Id.* at 69.

183 *Id.*

very repressive legislation to deal with subversion which the law and the legal
system can administer. But he questions the resulting situation because there is
a danger that the legal system and its law officers might not recognize any difference between the forces of the government and that of the enemy. As a consequence, any violation of the law from whatever quarter would be treated in
the same way.[184] Notwithstanding this problem Kitson prefers the second alternative, because he deems it to be both morally right and also expedient because
it will help to maintain the allegiance of the population. Kitson does, however,
recognize that the second alternative may impose unacceptable delays upon the
efficiency of military operations and thus such a system might prove to be "unworkable."[185]

Thus, both Thompson and Kitson regard law and the legal system merely
as weapons in the armory of the government, and view the legal system and its
law officers in a highly manipulative light. In the Northern Ireland context, the
manipulation of law has followed the method advocated by Thompson in that
the judicial system has been drastically affected by both substantive provisions
passed so as to legitimate, *ex post facto,* repressive emergency powers,[186] and by
procedural or systematic alterations which have, for example, abolished jury
trials, imposed reverse onus upon the accused regarding the admissibility of
coerced confessions, and allowed for detention without trial for prolonged
periods.[187]

Moreover, the judiciary has been overtly tied into the system of repression
by the use of judicial inquiries into torture and murder by the security forces.
In such a way, Lord Parker, the former Lord Chief Justice of England, and Lord
Widgery, the Lord Chief Justice of England, have both been used by the vehicle
of judicial inquiries to legitimate both the torture of suspected subversives[188] and
the killing of unarmed and peaceful protesters.[189] It seems clear that this use of
the judiciary to legitimate repressive actions falls within Kitson's first alternative
for the legal system, but the government has been careful to maintain the facade
of Kitson's second alternative.

It is also apparent that within the Thompson-Kitson theory the concept of

---

184   While Kitson does not evince an awareness of the concept of the rule of law in the
classical sense, it is clear from his distaste for laws equally applied that the Diceyan concept
has not been seriously considered. *See also* A. DICEY, AN INTRODUCTION TO THE STUDY OF THE
LAW AND THE CONSTITUTION (10th ed. 1959).

185   KITSON, *supra* note 140, at 69.

186   In R v. Londonderry Justices, ex parte Hume, [1972] N.I. 91, the Northern Irish
Court of Appeal declared British Army action under the Special Powers Act to be *ultra vires*
and hence unconstitutional. In a matter of hours, the Northern Ireland Act, 1972, c.10, was
passed by the British Parliament retrospectively validating all such unconstitutional acts by
the security forces. *See also* Lowry, *Internment: Detention Without Trial in Northern Ireland,*
5 HUMAN RIGHTS 261, 290-91 (1976).

187   Northern Ireland (Emergency Provisions) Act, 1973, c.53, §§ 5, 6 & 7; these measures
were originally proposed in Report of the Commission to Consider Legal Procedures to Deal
with Terrorist Activities in Northern Ireland, CMND. 5185 (1972) [hereinafter cited as the
Diplock Report]. The Diplock Commission relied exclusively on the submissions of the security forces and accepted the rationale of "operational necessity." *See Diplock Report,* ¶ 6.

188   *See* note 175 *supra.*

189   Report of the Tribunal Appointed to Inquire into the Events on Sunday 30th January
1972, H.L. 10 H.C. 220 (1972) [the Widgery Report]. For an excellent critique of this inquiry and its findings see S. DASH, JUSTICE DENIED: A CHALLENGE TO LORD WIDGERY'S
REPORT ON BLOODY SUNDAY (1972).

strategic hamlets or protected areas is central to the development of background information. The rationale for this is given as protection of the population from the insurgents, but there is the rather obvious additional advantage of preventing the potentially hostile population from providing succor to the enemy.[190] Thus the concept of protected zone or strategic hamlet of necessity requires a restriction upon freedom of mobility or freedom of movement of the population as a whole and the target group in particular. Clearly such a diminution in the freedom of movement is more easily obtained in a system of society which does not possess a written constitution guaranteeing freedom of movement.[191] The strategic hamlet concept thus implies the use of force against citizens who have not been proved, nor even suspected, of perpetrating an illegal act.

Crucial to Kitson's thesis is the use of psychological warfare by the government. It seems clear that psychological warfare not only encompasses the use of favorable positive propaganda but also the use of "black propaganda." This form of propaganda involves the manipulation of the media to such an extent that false information is in fact disseminated.[192] In some jurisdictions this will prove to be difficult without constitutional change as the media are often protected by constitutional guarantees ensuring freedom of the press. In Northern Ireland, however, without the benefit of formal guarantees of freedom of expression, it is a relatively simple matter to manipulate the media and curtail freedom of expression. The role of psychological warfare has increased in importance with the changing role of urban guerilla warfare in recent years from direct terrorism to indirect terrorism. This change poses new problems because the latter seeks to demonstrate to the populace that the state cannot govern in order to undermine the social confidence in authority and in law.[193] This indirect form of terrorism relies upon the use of free and unfettered media which are at liberty to report the successes (and failures) of the insurgent group. Seen in this light, it becomes paramount that the government should be able to manipulate the media to such an extent as to curtail the impact of the success of terrorism upon the psyche of the populace. This should prevent the population at large from either panicking or giving support to what may be perceived as a successful insurgent force.[194] The use of propaganda weapons such as this inevitably entails

---

190   KITSON, *supra* note 140, at 107.
191   This has been achieved in Belfast by blocking access to urban ghettoes and restricting access and egress, after dark, to two routes controlled by Army checkpoints. Intimidation of minorities within ghettoes has forced massive shifts in population in Northern Ireland and, while this has not been perpetrated by the security forces, little action has been taken by the military to prevent the concentration of people into ghettoes. On intimidation by officially tolerated Protestant para-military groups, see Holland, *The Newtownabbey Exodus*, Hibernia (Dublin), Aug. 20, 1976, at 8, col. 1.
192   *See* note 168 *supra*.
193   On the significance of social confidence in law, see T. HADDEN & P. HILLYARD, JUSTICE IN NORTHERN IRELAND (1973). On the sociological concept of social solidarity, see E. DURKHEIM, THE DIVISION OF LABOR IN SOCIETY, (3d ed. Simpson trans. 1964).
194   The most spectacular being the "Bloody Friday" bombing campaign by the IRA in which the IRA, in accordance with its usual practice, gave three warnings to the police that bombs were about to go off in several locations in Belfast. For some inexplicable reason the military security authorities did not heed these warnings causing great loss of life and injury among the civilian population. The government then indicated that no warnings had in fact been given. The revulsion felt in most countries and, more importantly, by the civilian population, was very great indeed and it was not until Parliament reconvened and questions were asked some days later that it became apparent that warnings had in fact been given but had

both the curtailing of the freedom of the press and risking innocent lives so as to achieve a military objective.[195] None of these manifestations of psychological warfare are new and the important point for legal purposes is to clearly understand that a free press is antithetical to the maintenance of modern counter-insurgency tactics and strategy.[196] The implications of psychological warfare in an urban environment are great indeed and the recent revelations regarding the training of civil servants as well as military personnel in psychological warfare technique do not augur well for the future of freedom of the press.[197]

The key stage in Kitson's thesis emerges when a high degree of low level intelligence information is collected to form background information. At some point in the procedure, according to the Kitson scenario, innocent people—those citizens acknowledged and known to be innocent—will be arrested without reasonable and probable cause and interrogated. Moreover, by the use of the holding charge such people will be interrogated, held incommunicado, and ultimately convicted of a minor offense. The problem here is that this technique is a clear and unequivocal manipulation of the legal system and judicial process. Assuming that Kitson's theory is accurate, it is at least questionable for military theoreticians to openly advocate subversion of both judicial process and civil liberties by the vehicle of holding charges.

By the vehicle of the Emergency Provisions Act of 1973, the British army in Northern Ireland was empowered to arrest innocent people and hold them incommunicado for up to four hours.[198] In this way not only was low level intelligence to be gathered under the guise of proving identity, but also background low level information against third parties could be sifted and checked by interrogation. "Screening" has been employed against whole sections of the community.[199] The problem with screening, however, is that whatever the intent of the security forces, it necessarily entails the dragnet arrest and detention of large numbers of innocent people without probable cause.[200] The drawback from the military point of view is that, perhaps inevitably, many of the people so arrested

---

not been heeded by the security forces and thus the population put at considerable risk. For a full explanation of this event and the news management involved see KELLY, *supra* note 11, at 78-82. The reaction to the bombings enabled the British Army to remove the barricades around Catholic ghettoes and occupy Catholic neighborhoods with no resistance. It has also been recently revealed that these bombings ended secret peace negotiations which were taking place, see *Bloody Friday Bombs Ruined MacBride Moves—O'Connell,* Irish Times (Dublin), Feb. 12, 1977, at 1, col. 1. Why the British Army psychological warfare unit should use this situation to effectively terminate peace negotiations has yet to be explained.

195 Similarly, the British military fraternization and support for counter gangs of vigilantes such as the UDA (Ulster Defense Association) and the UWC (Ulster Workers Council) have similarly placed suspected terrorists at risk. *See* BLUNDY, *supra* note 168; R. FISK, THE POINT OF NO RETURN: THE STRIKE WHICH BROKE THE BRITISH IN ULSTER (1975).

196 Recent research into the role of war correspondence would seem to support the view that the military in a war situation can quite easily control the dissemination of information without censorship due to the disadvantageous position of the war correspondent and the pressure for instant "copy" placed upon him by his superiors. *See* P. KNIGHTLEY, THE FIRST CASUALTY: THE WAR CORRESPONDENT AS HERO, PROPAGANDIST AND MYTH MAKER FROM THE CRIMEA TO VIETNAM (1975).

197 *See* O'CLERY, *supra* note 168.

198 *See* note 187, *supra* at s.12(1).

199 BOYLE, HADDEN & HILLYARD, *supra* note 1, at 43-45.

200 Screening of communities must be examined in the light of the British Army practice of dragnet street and block searches, for example in 1974 a total of 71,914 house searches took place, C. ACKROYD *et al., supra* note 132, at 38.

will become alienated from the forces of law and order and be unappreciative of the circumstances of their arrest and confinement. Moreover, if, as in the case of the Northern Irish unrest, many people so detained are harshly treated during detention, the screening policy runs the grave risk of being entirely counter-productive. In this way whole communities have become alienated from the forces of law and order.[201]

The Kitson scenario relates to what is termed "containment" in military parlance.[202] Hostile areas are sealed off and house raids, block searches, and screening methods are conducted. Ostensibly, these are executed in a search for fugitives but they really serve to gather low level intelligence data. However, while this may contain a hostile community it does not necessarily bring terrorists into the open. The problem then becomes one of translating background information into contact information.

It is at this juncture that the most controversial aspect of counter-insurgency operations comes to the fore, as guerillas must be flushed out into the open. This was attempted in Northern Ireland by staging various military operations, the most famous being the so-called "Bloody Sunday" shootings in Londonderry.[203] It was on this occasion that thirteen civil rights demonstrators were murdered during an anti-internment protest demonstration in Londonderry. According to Kitson's strategy, it would appear that these people were killed so as to make the I.R.A. break their cover and fight in the open. The purpose of the military strategy was to force the guerilla army to fight in the open and thus be subjected to superior fire power of the security forces who had staged the event and were fully prepared for it. It was the I.R.A., however, which scored a great propaganda victory by exposing the British army counter-insurgency tactics of killing innocent protestors while at the same time refusing to be provoked into the open.[204]

The events in Northern Ireland have revealed that the security forces use various methods, including torture and brutality, to persuade terrorists and suspected terrorists to give information. It would be a mistake to regard interrogation of suspected terrorists in this situation as merely following the classic pattern of brutality as used in Chile or Brazil.[205] It is true that in many instances suspected terrorists have been routinely tortured upon capture, in some cases for information, and in other cases by way of reprisal.[206] However, the significance of sensory deprivation techniques used in Northern Ireland seems to base its validity on the speed rationale.[207] In other words captured guerilla suspects have

---

201 Normal policing is still impossible in many urban Catholic areas. In many areas the police will not patrol without Army protection and will not patrol after dark in very many more. *See* McKeown, *R.U.C. In Search of a Role,* Hibernia (Dublin), Nov. 28, 1975, at 8, col. 2 and Ryder, *Ulsterization: Plans are Speeded up for Troops to Hand Over to Police and U.D.R.,* Sunday Times (London), Apr. 25, 1976, at 3, col. 5.

202 KITSON, *supra* note 140, at 110.

203 *See* note 189 *supra.*

204 *See also* KELLY, *supra* note 11, at 28-31; WINCHESTER, *supra* note 168 *passim.*

205 For a world survey see AMNESTY INTERNATIONAL, REPORT ON TORTURE (1973).

206 AMNESTY INTERNATIONAL, REPORT OF AN ENQUIRY INTO ALLEGATIONS OF ILL-TREATMENT IN NORTHERN IRELAND (1972) and Lowry, *Draconian Powers: The New British Approach to Pre-Trial Detention of Suspected Terrorists,* COLUM. HUMAN RIGHTS L. REV. (forthcoming).

207 According to a British inquiry, speed made brutality and torture operationally necessary. *See* note 175 *supra. See also* KELLY, *supra* note 11, at 35.

been subjected to sensory deprivation techniques which quickly break down the will of the suspect. These techniques were originally developed by the Soviet KGB and are now in use by the intelligence service of the British army.[208] This is separate and distinct from routine brutality in the sense that it requires special training for interrogators who use scientific techniques to shut off stimuli to the brain by the use of hooding and white noise. It must be conducted with some care so as not to induce insanity prior to the acquisition of information.[209]

The recent European Commission on Human Rights findings in the *Ireland v. United Kingdom* case in Strassburg have confirmed that Britain has used these techniques in the past on suspected terrorists and others.[210] While Kitson does not specify that sensory deprivation techniques should be used, it is clear from his experience in Kenya, Northern Ireland, and elsewhere that he was aware of its use by the British army in such situations.[211]

Kitson's theory is necessarily premised on methods which will speedily obtain either cooperation or information from suspected terrorists, and it is clear that in many situations nothing less than sensory deprivation and brutality may suffice. Thus, the acceptance of counter-insurgency theory as enunciated by Thompson and Kitson involves the use of torture by the authorities as an operational necessity unless it is assumed that every captured terrorist will be cooperative and, further, be speedily cooperative.[212]

The mistake made by some analysts in the past has been to view torture in relative isolation.[213] Clearly, under the Thompson-Kitson theory torture becomes an integral part of the counter-insurgency strategy of the military and is inevitable once the political decision has been taken to adopt the counter-insurgency program.[214] As such, the legal system will be manipulated into either (a) accepting torture or (b) failing to recognize its use, or (c) investigating in an *ad hoc* manner particular cases of torture *without* reference to its role in military theory and strategy. All three alternatives have been utilized at various times in Northern Ireland and the net result has been to regard instances of torture as merely regrettable and isolated episodes resulting from the exigencies of a particular stressful situation or the narrow facts of a particular case. However, in the light of modern counter-insurgency theory, it can now be appreciated that torture and brutality are an ongoing component of prevailing military theory and tactics. The legal system, by merely awarding *ex post facto* civil damages[215] has

---

208   J. McGuffin, The Guinea Pigs (1974). On sensory deprivation, see generally W. Sargent, The Battle for the Mind (1957).

209   The pre-planning and special training of torturers were admitted by the second British inquiry, per Lord Gardiner minority report, *supra* note 175, at ¶ 6, p. 12. According to Amnesty International, the British continue to train approximately 240 soldiers per year in these newer techniques of interrogation. The Leveller (London), Dec. 1976, at 4-5.

210   *See* note 175 *supra.*

211   *See* note 175 *supra,* majority reports, ¶ 10 at 2-3.

212   Judge Conaghan in Moore v. Ministry of Defense, Armagh County Court, (Feb. 10, 1972) noted the "primitive circumstances" of arrest procedures and that they were "preconceived." This preconceived [brutality] was described as ". . . deliberate, unlawful and harsh." *See also* Lowry, *supra* note 186, at 281-83. The *Moore* case was a civil suit for damages for assault during detention and wrongful arrest.

213   *See* Twining, *Emergency Powers and Criminal Process: The Diplock Report,* [1973] Crim. L. Rev. 406.

214   On the precipitate use of counter-insurgency tactics in Northern Ireland see Lowry, *supra* note 186, at 265-68.

been found to be weak and unable to prevent torture because of its failure to view torture in its theoretical context.

After this stage of the operations is complete and guerillas have presumably come out into the open and been killed or captured and persuaded to cooperate, the Kitson model then considers the continued acquisition of background information which can be obtained by car and block searches and this is the current posture of the British army in Northern Ireland. The difficulty here is the clear derogation of the notion of "reasonable cause" and resulting ongoing breach of human rights. The random selection of cars and houses for search does not constitute reasonable cause and would not justify a search warrant under normal criminal process. Nevertheless, this seems to be the avenue envisaged by Kitson for keeping intelligence gathering at an optimum level.

The legal implication of the use of community groups, however, is somewhat difficult to assess as Kitson does not specify exactly how community groups could be used except to say that they should be set up "when plausible reasons" exist[216] and may be used to get to know the leadership of a community and the existing relationship within the community of prominent people in general. How and by whom are the "plausible reasons" created? In other words, special forces or the military in general could be used to create pretexts or to increase the level of security activities so that community groups would be invited to study a particular problem seemingly generated by the civil unrest.[217] Thus, if incidents reached a level in a community approaching a high degree of discomfort in Kitson's scenario, it would be appropriate for the community leaders to gather and channel grievances towards the military who would be kindly disposed to receive them. However, in doing so the military would in fact be acquiring information on the potential or emerging political and social leaders in the community and would be categorizing people for future surveillance and interrogation.[218]

The problem here is that community-based social workers, priests, and others who have been used once in such a manner by the military authorities might be reluctant to allow themselves to be used in a subsequent matter. This might entail the further alienation of the military from the community workers and could lead to yet more entrenched alienation from the community as a whole. The morality of such a deception is yet another consideration.

VI. CONCLUSIONS

There are at least two readily identifiable alternative theories protective of human rights when society is faced with violent unrest in the form of urban guerilla activities. Initially, it is always open to society to identify and ameliorate the political *causes* of civil unrest. This recognizes that the people involved in

---

215 Subsequent to the *Moore* ruling *supra* note 212, over 978 damage suits have been initiated, less than one-third of which have been settled in agreed out of court terms. Apparently the British government prefers to settle out of court in all cases and no cases have been tried after the *Moore* decision. The Leveller (London), December 1976 at 4-5.

216 KITSON, *supra* note 140, at 129.

217 For an assessment of the use of assassination by the British army *see* M. DILLON & D. LEHANE, POLITICAL MURDER IN NORTHERN IRELAND at 292 *et seq.* (1973).

218 For past practice of the British Army in this regard see Sunday Times Insight Team (Ulster) (1972) at 236-43.

political violence or terrorism are not necessarily gangsters or merely unthinking individuals. In other words, a political approach necessitates the realization that there may be socio-economic or irredentist causes of unrest and such a political perspective presupposes that the problem of urban guerilla warfare is essentially political in nature and capable of political solution.

In the case of Northern Ireland, this theory would entail recognition of the problem presented—the denial of self-determination to one-third of the population—as one capable of political solution, albeit that radical means may be needed to achieve that end.[219] Nevertheless, it must be realized that often the causes of unrest are capable of amelioration or solution by non-revolutionary and non-violent means. This is not to say that governments will not regard guerilla campaigns by their very nature as antithetical to democratic process but rather to recognize that guerillas are not necessarily thugs and gangsters but rather an unpleasant symptom of a societal wrongs.[220]

Such societal wrongs are generally economic or political and permeate society to the extent that, in the case of Northern Ireland, a major section of the population labor under a deep and continuing sense of injustice against the established rule.[221] Thus when the civil rights campaign commenced in Northern Ireland in 1967-68 the immediate symptoms of unrest were the civil rights campaign for one man one vote and similar egalitarian reforms. The government was unable to respond to these needs, perceiving such reform to be counter to the interests of the state as a whole, and this resulted inevitably in intransigence by the majority and violence on the part of the deprived minority.[222] This in no way justifies the use of violence by the guerillas,[223] but merely goes to explain that the cause was in many respects political in origin.

In a narrow sense, Kitson recognizes that political causes play a part when he seeks to drive a wedge between the moderates supporting a just cause and the hard core who seek to use that cause to obtain a further goal. Thus, according to Kitson, the I.R.A. and hard core nationalists must be separated from the moderate or the middle class civil rights activists. This separation could be accomplished, in theory, by acceding to the demands of the civil rights movement without the state being necessarily threatened.[224] In some senses this may be true,

---

219 A British withdrawal is feasible if safeguards for the Northern Protestants are included in such a concept. Moreover, the British achieved a withdrawal in similar circumstances in Kenya in the 1950's after safeguarding the interests of the white minority. Similarly France faced such a problem in Algeria. A phased withdrawal with economic inducements for the Northern Protestants could ensure a minimal quantum of violence. Of course, the British army might have to enforce such a plan against the wishes of "hard core" Protestant extremists.
220 The rebirth of the I.R.A. in 1970 in the form of the Provisional I.R.A. is based on the reluctance of dominant Protestant politicians to reform society. *See* O'BRIEN, *supra* note 8, at 205; Sunday Times Insight Team, *supra* note 218 *passim,* and LOWRY *supra* note 186, at 261-75.
221 For a useful historical analysis see FARRELL, *supra* note 3 *passim,* and G. BELL, THE PROTESTANTS OF ULSTER (1976) which analyzes the nature and extent of Protestant privilege and its ideology and provides useful insights into the extent of entrenched patterns of discrimination against Catholics. *See also* Lowry, *Religious Discrimination in Northern Ireland,* J. INTERNAT. L. & POLITICS (forthcoming).
222 For an analysis of the early civil rights struggle see LOWRY, *supra* note 186, at 261-75.
223 On the justification of political violence see N. CHOMSKY, FOR REASONS OF STATE (1973); T. HONDERICH, THREE ESSAYS ON POLITICAL VIOLENCE (1976).
224 Such an attempt was made by the vehicle of the Sunningdale Agreement which was accepted by the Catholic middle class and moderate opinion but was rejected by the I.R.A.

but it becomes increasingly difficult for a government to accede to, for example, effective affirmative action programs in the field of employment discrimination since to do so would effectively undermine the rationale for the state of Northern Ireland and the hegemony of the Northern Protestants.[225] The state of Northern Ireland was in part created to preserve a protected enclave of Protestant privilege for a minority of Irishmen who are Protestant. Thus, to provide for equal access to employment for Roman Catholics would be to sever the unique relationship between the Protestant working class and the Protestant elite[226] which has sought to entrench its power in Northern Ireland through discrimination in various fields including employment. The whole *raison d'etre* of the state was to seek to secure and entrench a privileged position for the Irish Protestant minority in a particular area of Ireland where it happened to be the majority.[227]

Thus, if ameliorative reforms were implemented encompassing affirmative action or positive discrimination in favor of Catholics in Northern Ireland in the area of employment, it would be tantamount to attack the underlying justification for the state. This seems to be one of the major dilemmas plaguing British policy makers since the recent civil rights unrest commenced in Northern Ireland. While the first alternative to counter-insurgency theory is always to seek a reformative solution, it must be recognized that reforms and compromise solutions of this sort can only be obtained at a price, and this price may be unacceptable to the ruling government.

The unique problem presented by Northern Ireland, or any other colonial power in an alien country, is that the issue of self-determination cannot be faced without alienating a significant proportion of the population who depend on the colonial power for their privileged position. However, common ground must be found between the privileged group of Protestants occupying power as the dominant group in Northern Ireland and the disaffected nationalist minority who support both the I.R.A. and the more acceptable nationalist counsensual political parties supportive of irredentist ideology.

A second alternative which is always open to a government to utilize in a time of guerilla warfare or political violence is the due process model as envisioned by Packer.[228] Packer creates two models—the crime control model and the due process model.[229] While it is inappropriate to regard the Kitson approach as in any way analogous to Packer's crime control model, the due process model has been used by Britain in countering its only major threat presented by urban guerillas prior to the advent of the I.R.A.

In 1970 a group of anarchists in Britain known as the "Angry Brigade" embarked upon a series of sporadic bomb attacks upon the homes of prominent

---

as falling short of self-determination. Paradoxically the Sunningdale Agreement was wrecked by militant Protestants who thought too much had been conceded. *See* Ireland (Tripartite Conference) 866 H.C. Debs, col. 28, December 10, 1973, and for an explanation of the Protestant General Strike which led to its demise, see FISK, *supra* note 195.

225 *See also* LOWRY, *supra* note 221.
226 BELL, *supra* note 221. This is the recurrent theme in Bell's analysis of the creation and use of Protestant power in Northern Ireland.
227 FARRELL, *supra* note 3 *passim.*
228 Packer, *Two Models of the Criminal Process*, 113 U. PA. L. REV. 1 (1964).
229 *Id.* at 8-16.

people and various other symbolic targets.[230] At first the authorities were completely baffled by the appearance of this anarchist phenomenon about which little was known. However, as has been detailed in a recent study, the Special Branch of Scotland Yard quickly adapted itself to closely monitor and study the publications of anarchist groups and keep anarchists under general surveillance without violating their civil rights. This method ultimately paid dividends in that the violent anarchist group was arrested and convicted by normal process of law. The problem here is that it was necessary to devote considerable resources to effect continued surveillance of a relatively small group of anarchists. Nevertheless, it is clear that the due process model can in fact work if sufficient resources are allocated to the task in the form of continued surveillance and intelligent use of criminal charges such as conspiracy so that preventive measures can be taken without putting society at risk.[231] Thus, it may be argued that the only barrier to successful use of conspiracy charges and due process of law is the financial cost involved, which is admittedly high, in maintaining a highly organized police surveillance team and forensic squad necessary to gather and evaluate evidence against subversive groups.

However, the fact is that the due process model has never been seriously tried in Northern Ireland as emergency powers have in fact been in operation since the state came into being. This is unfortunate since the due process model has the built-in advantage of not provoking a backlash to repressive measures which almost inevitably emanates from counter-insurgency theory. There is no diminution of respect for law and social confidence in the legal system, and the rule of law is preserved. The due process model does not run the risk of the state losing control of counter gangs and vigilante groups such as the Ulster Defense Association (UDA).[232]

The other attribute which the due process model possesses, in contrast to the counter-insurgency approach of Kitson, is that while Kitson visualizes reforms as splitting moderates from the hard core insurgents in a manipulative "carrot and stick" fashion, Kitson does not fully comprehend that the "carrot" may become rapidly irrelevant due to the bitterness which the "stick" engenders in the target group. This certainly seems to be the case in the Northern Irish urban ghettos. Thus, if Kitson's theory is either misapplied or merely mistimed, the consequences are highly significant in that the reforms needed to divide the guerillas from their popular support will, in some instances, be viewed as a sign of weakness without the concomitant benefit of alienating the moderates from the extremists.[233]

Of special interest to lawyers, of course, is that the due process model pre-

---

230 For a full account of this episode, see G. CARR, THE ANGRY BRIGADE (1975).
231 The conspiracy offense in British law is wide and vague in the extreme and is about to undergo reform. On reform proposals see *The Law Commission Report on Conspiracy and Criminal Law Reform*, No. 76 (1976); on the scope of conspiracy see R. HAZELL, CONSPIRACY AND CIVIL LIBERTIES (1974); G. ROBERTSON, WHOSE CONSPIRACY? (1974) and J. SMITH & B. HOGAN, CRIMINAL LAW at 175-90 (3d ed. 1973).
232 The apparent powerlessness of the state to control Protestant para-military groups has been shown by FISK, *supra* note 195.
233 The prorogation of the devolved Stormont Parliament in 1972 has thus been widely held to be a "defeat" for the British and the Protestants by the I.R.A. rather than a political gambit or concession.

serves the integrity of legal institutions and law officers. If the due process model is maintained and seen to work, then social confidence in the law and in the legal system is fostered, whereas the use and manipulation of the legal system and its offices under the Kitson model run the grave risk of the public perceiving law and the legal system to be merely additional instruments of arbitrary repression. This problem of public perception has been particularly troublesome in Northern Ireland in that the transition from the civil rights campaign to guerilla warfare has been linked by some observers to the decline in social confidence in law and legal institutions.[234] If legal institutions are not seen to behave impartially but instead are viewed merely as an arm of repression, then it becomes almost inevitable that dissidents will turn to violence to achieve political objectives.

One further problem with counter-insurgency theory as opposed to the due process model is that it is essentially a theory of containment rather than military victory. Thus, the forces of law and order are seen to be merely containing the guerillas, rather than vigorously pursuing the instigators of violence.[235] This has a deleterious effect on the morale of the soldiers and of that portion of the civilian population which is supportive of the forces of law and order. Sometimes, as in Northern Ireland, this leads to the growth of counter-revolutionary terrorist organizations,[236] some of which may be beyond the control of the forces of law and order.[237]

Thus, counter-insurgency theory, by placing the integrity of the legal system in jeopardy, also runs the grave risk of permitting vigilantes to usurp the policing function. This would not be so under a due process model in which the forces of law and order would be perceived as an impartial arm of the state and the judiciary would be kept separate from the state. Moreover, since the target group in the counter-insurgency theory is the so-called hostile population, it would seem that the repressive powers envisaged by counter-insurgency theory would not be applied equally but rather only to the target community. In the case of Northern Ireland this means that the Protestant majority are not subjected to the full panoply of military powers of repression as are the Catholic community, which is comprised of both dissident groups and their moderate supporters.[238]

The further and most important problem presented by counter-insurgency theory is the danger to civil liberty which is implicit in the use of emergency powers. These powers, when allied to modern counter-insurgency theory, negate any notion of the "right to be left alone" because of the reliance on dragnet arrests and the demise of reasonable cause. Moreover, largely unscrutinized and wholly repressive powers once enjoyed may not be easily discontinued.[239] This "slippery slope" argument is of particular relevance to Northern Ireland when it

---

234 *See* T. HADDEN & P. HILLYARD, *supra* note 73, at 8-26.
235 It was just such a claim which contributed to the recent Protestant General Strike in Northern Ireland, *see* McHardy, *Loyalists 11-day Loser*, Manchester Guardian Weekly, May 22, 1977 at 5, col. 3.
236 Nelson, *Ulster: Gunmen in Politics*, New Society, May 1, 1975 at 255.
237 *Behind the Assassinations*, Hibernia, Oct. 25, 1974 at 4, col. 2.
238 *See* LAW AND STATE, *supra* note 1, at 78-151.
239 Already there is some evidence to suggest that some specific wide repressive powers may be unwarranted but, nevertheless, remain law. *See* Price, *Less and Less Temporary*, Hibernia, Dec. 12, 1975 at 11, col. 1.

is recalled that emergency powers have been in force continually since the origin
of the state.

If nothing else the Northern Irish experience has demonstrated certain
weaknesses in the operation of the European Convention on Human Rights.[240]
Although many of the enumerated rights are vague and drafted on a high level
of generality, when taken together the Convention may fairly be said to reflect
the minimum standards necessary to preserve the rule of law and due process
from arbitrary abuse by the executive in a democratic state.[241] However, in an
emergency, the executive can derogate from the constraints of the Convention[242]
and the judicially imposed standard of executive abuse, "the margin of appreciation" test,[243] is exceedingly wide and vague. This permits executive evasion of
the European Convention in emergencies.[244] But the use of the European Convention would at least assure judicial scrutiny of executive action in emergency,
whereas British common law does not.[245]

Clearly the Northern Irish experience indicates the overriding need to devise
a system in which executive action affecting human rights is justiciable. This is
not to say that the judiciary should scrutinize any and all activities, but to emphasize the necessity for adequate controls on executive power and discretion.
The *ultra vires* doctrine, as interpreted by British courts in emergency situations,
has been an inadequate check upon the potential for arbitrary use and abuse of
executive power.

A preferable criterion is to be found in the American "clear and present
danger" test[246] which has the advantage of ensuring that, at some point, the
executive is put into a position in which it must justify its assumption of wide
executive power. Moreover, a clear and present danger doctrine could dispense
with the somewhat odious distinction between individual rights and property
rights in emergencies under British common law. Such a test could also con-

240   *Convention for the Protection of Human Rights and Fundamental Freedoms,* Rome
(1950), Cmnd. 2894 (1950); 156 Brit. & Foreign State Papers 915; I. Brownlie, Basic
Documents on Human Rights (1971).
241   For a full explanation, *see* A. Robertson, Human Rights in Europe (2d ed. 1977).
242   *Supra* note 240, at Article XV, but note that Article III provides an absolute right not
to be tortured and nations may not derogate from this provision. However, due process can be
suspended.
243   Lawless v. Ireland, Application No. 332/57, 4 Y.B. Eur. Conv. on Human Rights
438. "Apprehended" emergencies are included in this criterion, see Denmark, Norway, Sweden
and Netherlands v. Greece, Application No. 3321/67, 12 Y.B. Eur. Conv. on Human Rights.
See also Robertson, *supra* note 241, at 39-41 & 111-12.
244   The breadth of this criteria was shown clearly in Robertson, *supra* note 241, at 134.
      The concept behind this doctrine is that Article 15 has to be read in the context of
      the rather special subject matter with which it deals: the responsibilities of a Govern-
      ment for maintaining law and order in times of war or public emergency threatening
      the life of the nation. The concept of the margin of appreciation is that a Govern-
      ment's discharge of these responsibilities is essentially a delicate problem of appre-
      ciating complex factors and of balancing conflicting considerations of the public
      interest; and that, once the Commission or the Court is satisfied that the Govern-
      ment's appreciation is at least on the margin of the powers conferred by Article 15,
      then the interest which the public itself has in effective Government and in the
      maintenance of order justifies and requires a decision in favor of the legality of the
      Government's appreciation.
245   Unlike most international tribunals the European Commission and Court will receive
individual applications, per Article 25. *See also* Robertson, *supra* note 241, at 149-53.
246   Yates v. United States, 354 U.S. 298 (1957); Dennis v. United States, 341 U.S. 494
(1951); Abrams v. United States, 250 U.S. 616 (1919); Chafee, *Thirty-Five Years with
Freedom of Speech,* 1 Kan. L. Rev. 1 (1952).

tribute to the judicial definition of limitations on the use of dragnet arrest, search, interrogation and detention without trial favored by contemporary counter-insurgency theorists. A justiciable clear and present danger doctrine must, in the light of the Northern Irish experience, constitute a minimal criterion for balancing human rights against the necessity doctrine in an emergency.[247]

The prevailing policy of judicial abnegation may be thought to preserve judicial neutrality during upheaval, but it is suggested that judicial abnegation is socially dangerous, since the consequence of this policy is to deny a useful and desirable forum for impartial scrutiny and barriers to abuse of power. Thus, judicial abnegation may have the social effect of channeling protest and dissent towards violence.

The doctrine of necessity at common law has never been adequately defined but is, functionally, protective of the executive in emergencies. However, it does not follow that non-justiciable necessity does not have an identifiable content. By focusing on current military theory it is possible to discern a clear but unlimited content in the form of operational necessity. In *R. v. Allen*[248] military trial and execution were justified, and legally upheld, on the specific ground of operational necessity. Similarly, the denial of due process in Northern Ireland seems to be firmly based on operational necessity in the *Diplock Report*[249] which foreshadowed the Emergency Provisions (Northern Ireland) Act 1973.[250] Brutality and torture of suspects have been accepted by a Judicial Inquiry explicitly on the grounds of operational necessity.[251] And the silence of the *Gardiner Report*[252] on "screening" or acquisition of low-level intelligence involving dragnet arrests of wholly innocent nonsuspects at least tacitly accepts the justification of operational necessity.

A close scrutiny of Kitson's work makes it possible to deduce that operational necessity in the urban guerilla context is less a factor of the exigencies of combat and more a predetermined theory with a discernible form and content. Significantly, Kitson's theory includes telishing,[253] that is, the deliberate punishment of innocent people, which is the clearest denial of due process imaginable as well as the negation of all commonly accepted notions of human rights. Furthermore, the *Widgery Inquiry*[254] into the shooting of unarmed demonstrators, and the House of Lords' ruling in the *Attorney-General's Reference*[255] case, in no way inhibit the summary execution of either suspects or innocents mistaken for suspects.

---

247 On the doctrine *Salus Populii Suprema Lex* see LOWRY, *supra* note 186, at 314-22.
248 *See* note 193 *supra*.
249 *See* note 187 *supra*. It is clear that the Diplock Report merely reflects the advice of the security forces as the Inquiry did not receive any other evidence, *see further* LAW AND STATE, *supra* note 1, at 39-41.
250 *See* note 187 *supra*.
251 *See* note 187 *supra*.
252 *Report of a Committee to Consider, in the Context of Civil Liberties and Human Rights, Measures to Deal with Terrorism in Northern Ireland,* Cmnd. 5847 (1975). On the Gardiner Report in general, see LOWRY, *supra* note 186, at 308-14. For the tacit acceptance of screening, see *Security: The Missing Chapter,* Fortnight Rev. (Belfast) No. 98, Feb. 1975 at 5, col. 1.
253 *See* note 173 *supra*.
254 *See* note 189 *supra*.
255 *See* note 113 *supra*.

The current policy in Northern Ireland is to criminalize political violence.[256] Suspected guerillas are now held for up to seven days incommunicado and often coerced into signing confessions.[257] They are then tried without a jury and with a reverse onus placed upon an accused regarding the admissibility of the confession. Since, as a practical matter, it is impossible for an accused to show that he was tortured, he is convicted as a common criminal and usually sentenced to a long term of imprisonment. In this highly structured manner, society is able to dispose of *both* urban guerillas and political sympathizers or dissidents while publicly proclaiming that there are no political prisoners, merely convicted criminals. The continuing prison unrest and hunger strikes to obtain political prison status may be viewed, therefore, as a post-sentence effort to achieve internationally recognized minimum standards of treatment and a furtherance of the struggle for human rights.[258] That society should structure its legal system in this way may be seen as a considered attempt to criminalize politically violent and non-violent dissenters so as to, within the Kitson scenario, split moderates from the "hard core" who have been elaborately processed and labelled as criminal deviants rather than political offenders. This too may be seen as a further use and abuse of the legal system by the executive and, in the long term, may irreparably harm social confidence in law and the legal system.

A major mistake, although an understandable error in a fluid situation, is to adopt an approach common to many civil libertarians and proponents of human rights in adopting an *ad hoc* view of terrorism and human rights. Many libertarians, although responsive to the last revelation or the latest atrocity, have not placed such incidents into a broader theoretical perspective. It is suggested that more can be learned by placing specific incidents and patterns of terror and counter-terror into a theoretical justificatory framework so as to measure and adequately balance the overall impact of counter-insurgency repression on civil liberties and human rights. In this way the principled efforts of successive Irish governments to expose and constrain the use of torture and discrimination before the European Court of Human Rights may be placed in their proper legal and societal perspective. The non-justiciable nature of the doctrines of necessity and operational necessity may be shown to give the executive carte blanche to ignore and abrogate human rights. As events have escalated and patterns of unscrutinized repression become refined and entrenched in Northern Ireland, there is the manifest danger that human dignity and life itself may be placed in even greater jeopardy.

Perhaps the only approach now open to proponents of human rights is to adopt an idea from the military theorists, that of "total strategy."[259] Just as to the military total strategy means the unification of military, legal, and political structures and ideology, libertarians must adopt a "total strategy" for the propa-

---

256   RYDER, *supra* note 201.
257   For an analysis of current pre-trial detention law and practice, see Lowry, *supra* note 206.
258   On the treatment of Irish political prisoners in British jails, see Logan, *Treatment of Irish Prisoners Convicted of Terrorist Offenses*, 73 LAW GUARDIAN GAZETTE 980 (1976). For a first person account of prison brutality, *see* H. FEENEY, IN CARE OF HER MAJESTY'S PRISONS (1976).
259   *See* note 153 *supra*.

gation and preservation of human rights. Such a "total strategy" must be predicated upon a fuller understanding of the ideology of terror and counter-insurgency and should endeavor to enunciate a critical theory of executive power in an emergency so as to maximize liberty in a crisis. It is suggested that this is the major lesson to be learned from nine years of terror and counter-terror in Northern Ireland.

JOURNAL OF LAW & SOCIETY
VOLUME 9, NUMBER 1, SUMMER 1982

Defending the Terrorists: Queen's Counsel before the Courts of Northern Ireland

BIRTHE JORGENSEN*

Criminalization, normalization and Ulsterization, the three prongs of the British Government's approach to the "troubles" in Northern Ireland, have required the maintenance of a structure of criminal courts to provide one of the demarcations between Northern Ireland and a situation of civil war and martial law. Though criminal courts have continually existed in Northern Ireland, the challenges to their authority both of those appearing before these courts and by the state's own preference in using internment and detention without trial to avoid their jurisdiction destroyed their symbolic function between 1970 and 1972. The British Government in a quest to halt the crumbling of yet another of the pillars of British liberal democracy, established in 1972 a commission to consider legal procedures to deal with terrorist activities in Northern Ireland, chaired by Lord Diplock.[1] *The Northern Ireland (Emergency Provisions) Act* 1973, which was derived from the commission's report, introduced an amputated shadow of the British due process model in Northern Ireland, where the amputation was intended to permit the more effective dealing "with terrorist organisations by bringing to book, otherwise than by internment by the Executive, individuals involved in terrorist activities."

Three fundamental requisites for maintaining an adversarial criminal court are counsel to stand between the subject and the Crown, representing the best interests of the accused, counsel to present the state's case against the accused, and finally an independent judiciary to determine whether the accused did the acts complained of, and whether these acts were in contravention of that state's laws. Platitudinous as this sounds, these requisites cannot be taken for granted in situations of civil strife. On the contrary, challenges to the state by armed force and the state's response have frequently undermined the existence of all three in several jurisdictions.[2]

The struggle for political legitimacy in Northern Ireland by all participants has taken place, since the breakdown of the myth of the ballot box, on the streets and to a lesser extent in the courts. This study was the product of my interest in the participants involved in the court legitimation process. The underlying questions can be summarized as follows: Who defended the terrorists? Who prosecuted them? Was there a distinction between the two groups? What motivated these counsel? How did they

*Centre of Criminology, University of Toronto.

view the accused, their work and the caricatured system which had developed over the course of some of their careers? What personal or career effects rebounded from the legitimization struggle within the courts?

THE ROAD TO DIPLOCK

For those unfamiliar with the so-called Diplock courts of Northern Ireland, a short historical description follows.[3] The most recent round of the nationalist/unionist struggle challenging the legitimacy of the existence of Northern Ireland state as six counties separate from the Republic of Ireland and in union, as a province, with Great Britain, began from a widespread largely Catholic civil rights movement in Northern Ireland in 1968. A Unionist backlash of proportions unanticipated by the British Government or the civil rights movement, and aided by the partisan actions of the Royal Ulster Constabulary and the B-Special militia, prompted the British Government to place British army units in Northern Ireland, initially as a peace-keeping force. Their subsequent lack of impartiality escalated what was then a crisis of legitimacy in the political arena, into a more broadly based public support for the armed struggle of the previously defunct Irish Republican Army.[4] The Northern Ireland community, polarized as it already was, experienced an extreme fissure, so extensive that the police and security forces completely lost control of large segments of the urban areas, and were, as one of many consequences, unable to investigate atrocities as they occurred. Internment without trial was introduced in August 1971 to detain those who were suspected of participating in terrorist activities but about whom no evidence proving guilt beyond a reasonable doubt for the purposes of judicial prosecution was obtainable. Internment resulted in a deepening of the fissure. Not only were persons interned who were above suspicion in the eyes of their fellow citizens, but also, all but one of those interned was Catholic.[5] Yet the commission of atrocities within the community was certainly not their sole prerogative.

Throughout this period criminal courts continued to conduct trials, often with the presence of a jury. Enormous skepticism greeted these trials, both from the general public and as the research revealed, from the lawyers and the judges, on two counts. First, the number of perverse jury verdicts of not guilty and the number of dismissals for lack of prosecution where witnesses were intimidated from appearing, severely undermined the proceedings. Second, their concrete existence threw into sharp contrast the quasi-legal, *sub rosa* justice of internment without trial, where a lack of evidence resulted in the same consequences for the individual (deprivation of liberty) as would conviction. The pillar was crumbling. In 1972 the Diplock Commission was convened.[6]

The resultant legislation created what was known as the Diplock courts, where those offences likely to be committed by terrorist offenders were to be tried in courts presided over by a judge sitting alone. In no case, could trial by jury be elected. Additionally, the standard for admissibility of confessions was lowered from that of the common law which specified that confessions obtained through fear or favour are inadmissible, to one which permitted the admission of all statements obtained unless coerced as a result of inhuman or degrading treatment.[7]

Key advantages for the criminalization, normalization, Ulsterization policy were secured through these recommendations. Now convictions could be obtained in what *appeared* to be courts of law through what *appeared* to be voluntary confessions, thus securing the semblance of legitimacy (although internment without trial was continued until 1975 in parallel with the court system).

Some form of actual courts were retained, an apparent victory for civil libertarians, but it should be noted that, as with other civil libertarian victories, the retention of any court structure has a two-edged effect. While securing some form of trial, the actual structure of a trial bars the raising of legally irrelevant political issues from the courtroom. Thus, in Northern Ireland, the continuation of this amputated court structure, retaining as it did all the legal propositions as to what is relevant, essentially barred the possibility of a trial raising the larger unionist/republican political issues. The newly created Diplock courts further restricted the use of the courts as a political arena.

The British common law tradition has always held in abhorrence the notion that political issues, even public policy issues, be raised in court. These matters are best left, it has been held, particularly in times of emergency, to legislators or state civil servants.[8] Where convictions are based on confessions whose admissibility may be the only legally relevant consideration, the perimeters as to what issues may be raised at a criminal trial in Northern Ireland are even more closely drawn. Factors such as the accused's motivation, or his philosophical beliefs are considered irrelevant when determining guilt or innocence. If these ideas are raised it will be during sentencing and then serve only to increase the sentence incrementally rather than as mitigation. These notions of legal legitimacy are strongly echoed by legal philosophers who have addressed the question of political trials, and, most importantly, are reinforced in the legal training and shared beliefs of the legal profession.[9]

Diplock raised and dismissed concerns about public confidence in the judiciary and legal profession of Northern Ireland. Despite existing evidence that large segments of the population had no confidence in the courts, the judiciary, or the officers of those courts, Diplock stated that:

> The judiciary has nevertheless managed to maintain a reputation for impartiality which rises above the divisive conflict which has effected so many other functions of government in the province, and the courts of law and the procedures that they use have in general held the respect and trust of all except the extremists of both factions. We regard it as of paramount importance that the criminal courts of law and judges

and resident magistrates who preside in them should continue to retain that respect and trust throughout the emergency and after the emergency has come to an end.[10]

Given this proposition, no new personnel were introduced into the Diplock courts. The same barristers, solicitors and judges served the new courts as had served and continued to serve the ordinary criminal courts, and in some cases, the commissions examining internment orders. Those same barristers who had been trained to and felt comfortable with barring political considerations from trials or internment hearings carried on what they saw as their work. In this way, they were party to the process of keeping politics out of the courtroom, and so legitimizing the new courts.

THE SAMPLE

Northern Ireland has a divided profession, like Great Britain or the Republic of Ireland and certain states in Australia. For those unfamiliar with this distinction, it essentially rests on the notion that solicitors interview clients, prepare witness statements and cases and marshall arguments, giving legal advice. Barristers, or counsel, provide in court advocacy, instructed by solicitors but untainted or unaffected by client contact. In Northern Ireland barristers appear in all scheduled cases in Diplock courts, both as prosecutors and defense counsel. Indeed, any barrister except those appointed Senior Crown Counsel or on staff with the Department of Public Prosecutions can appear in either capacity in the courts.

The Northern Ireland bar had 212 barristers in 1980, 24 of whom were Queen's Counsel. In order to address the desired questions and, additionally, in order to attempt to gain a pre-Diplock/post-Diplock comparison, it was determined to attempt to interview all Queen's Counsel of the Bar of Northern Ireland. It was further hoped that by interviewing all counsel using this simple criteria, impartiality would be maintained and so perceived by the barristers.[11]

Access to any lawyers, because of the demands placed on their time by their work and their professional suspicion of outsiders is difficult at any time in any situation. In Northern Ireland, these difficulties are compounded by the inaccessibility of the one Inn of Court, the strain of security surrounding barristers and the almost universal suspicion of outsiders. In the result, it was possible to interview eleven counsel, which was a representative sample.

Demographically those interviewed were male, between their mid-thirties and mid-fifties. The majority were Protestant. Almost all had been educated either at Queen's University, Belfast or Trinity College, Dublin, and had gone directly from their studies to the Bar and into practice. Although several were also called to the Bar in the Republic of Ireland and in England, their practices were in Northern Ireland.

Several of those interviewed had close relatives who were solicitors or barristers and a number had fathers who had been police officers or civil servants at some time in Northern Ireland. Not only was this sample strongly entrenched in the professional class of Northern Ireland, but seven of those interviewed served the profession voluntarily as Benchers or in another official capacity. These counsel, then, formed an integral part of what might loosely be described as the Northern Ireland ruling class.

In Northern Ireland a group of barristers and solicitors formed the Association for Legal Justice which set out initially in the early 1970s to encourage the use of legal processes to deal with allegations against the security forces. As well as bringing civil and criminal proceedings against the security forces and encouraging the use of the courts to challenge inequities, this group at one point suggested members of the Bar boycott the hearings of the Internment Commission at Long Kesh (the internment camp) in order to put pressure on the Government to end the internment system.[12]

> There was an opposing faction which argued that there was no practical alternative to the Commissioner's hearings and that it was the duty of lawyers to represent their clients to the best of their ability, whatever the system. The meeting broke up without any decision being reached, as did a second meeting the following Friday . . . Many of those opposed to the system believe that it is the incredibly high level of fees paid to those who do agree to take part which ensures that the system can be maintained at all.[13]

The subjects interviewed for this study were those who were doing their duty and earning fees without complaint.[14] None of those interviewed felt that it was ever necessary or would be useful for members of the Bar to boycott the Diplock courts.

The two key points which all counsel wished to emphasize in their interviews were, first, that they viewed themselves as doing their duty in difficult circumstances and second, that they were professionals working in a highly competitive business.

A HIGHLY COMPETITIVE BUSINESS

In the early 1970s the outbreak of the civil unrest created an increased volume of courtroom and internment commission work, requiring new judicial appointments and more Queen's Counsel for appearances on the more severe charges. Most of the Queen's Counsel interviewed for this study "took silk" (became Queen's Counsel) at this point. Previously the mean length of time between admittance to the Bar and "taking silk" had been fifteen years, serving as junior counsel. The "troubles" shortened the periods between taking the call, taking silk and appointments to the Bench.

In the past eleven years there has been a four-fold increase in the number of barristers on the rolls in Northern Ireland. By comparison, where Northern Ireland's 212 barristers serve a population of one-and-a-half million people, 130 barristers serve a population of three million in the

Republic of Ireland. The barristers interviewed in this study were very aware of the growing numbers at the Bar. They particularly emphasized that if the "troubles" were to come to an end, there would be "a very small pie left to feed so many". They were concerned that not only might young barristers not survive, but with so many more Queen's Counsel being appointed, they might find themselves without sufficient work.

Ten of the eleven spent the major portion of their time engaged in criminal work, six doing both defense and prosecutorial work and four engaged almost solely in prosecutorial work. All had experience in both capacities. All stated that the proportion of their time devoted to criminal work had greatly increased over the previous ten years, to the almost complete exclusion of their civil practices. They were no longer thought of by solicitors as available for civil litigation. The loss of the civil litigation was a matter of concern to all of them, since it was both more lucrative and more readily monopolized by those whose exclusive work it was. They predicted that much of this work would also dry up with the end of the "troubles".

The interchangeability of roles was unproblematic for the subjects. Preference was regarded as a matter of "how a man was made", but the sort of work they did and what capacity they appeared in was a matter of the work they were asked to appear in. This, in turn, was the result of reputation and previous accomplishments and in their view, was out of their hands.

In short, they were the epitome of the legal "hired gun" or "mouthpiece", appearing as asked and providing a service which was necessary. They did not generate work and they would not turn it away if asked.

A MATTER OF DUTY

None of the barristers with whom I spoke felt that their careers had been adversely effected by the current civil unrest. On the contrary, several stated that since the "troubles" work of all sorts had greatly increased and their opportunities to gain confidence and professional and financial success had considerably improved over their predecessors.

None thought that their reputation in the legal profession in Northern Ireland had been effected by the clientele which they represented. None thought that clients sought barristers who were politically sympathetic or that a barrister's political beliefs would dictate the nature of the cases he was asked to represent. None thought that the religious denomination of a barrister would alter the course of his career or the nature of the cases which he was asked to represent. Although several stated that solicitors might be sought by clients on the basis of religion and political sympathies, and that in turn, solicitors might employ barristers using the same criteria, all explained that they themselves were evidence to the contrary of this proposition.

120

No regulation or statutory provision in Northern Ireland did or ever had led to hesitation through fear of personal consequences on the part of a barrister in accepting a brief, according to these counsel.[15]

All those interviewed expressed their satisfaction at having sufficient input into recent commissions of inquiry and resulting legislative amendments in Northern Ireland. Although the Bar Council had never made a joint brief to any Commission (seen as an impossibility because of the range of political views inside the bar) apparently opinions had always been solicited and freely circulated in the Bar library thereby reaching commissioners and civil servants without difficulty.

Perhaps for this reason, none of those interviewed expressed disapproval of the Diplock courts in their present form or the security measures taken in the province as a whole. "The best system possible in the circumstances" was the refrain. Several barristers provided pre-Diplock court anecdotes from their own experiences which for them confirmed the necessity of the introduction of the Diplock courts. As one barrister put it:

> The problem is that whatever is done is always right for one side or the other. You may not like it, but it may be necessary. It will be a good thing for law and order.

None of those interviewed felt that the introduction of the Diplock courts in Northern Ireland had altered their view of the administration of justice in Northern Ireland. Their opinions as to the importance of the rule of law and the maintenance of an open administration of justice had not been altered in any way by the "troubles" or the legislated criminal management of them.

As to the personal consequences of their work, those interviewed expressed the opinion that the pressure and stress of their work was similar to their counterparts in England. Although they pointed to the volume of work they took on, particularly the number of trial days, and their responsibilities to do the best job possible in their role either as prosecutorial or defence counsel and to the discomfiture of working and appearing in old, highly secure courtrooms without adequate facilities for their comfort, they nevertheless did not think that pressure or stress was increased for them because of the nature of their work.

With one exception, they did not think their lives had been threatened *as a result of their work*, although they were at the time all under threats.[16] Although many took precautionary measures to avoid the potential fulfillment of these threats, the threats themselves related to their status politically or militarily and not their role in court. As one counsel jocularly put it, "We just keep our backs turned and hope they (defendants, their relatives or their supporters) don't notice us. All they see is the back of the wig and gown. After all, we are only doing our job." The accused and the para-militaries were to see them as only a working part of the overall court apparatus and not directly responsible for the subsequent sentences and treatment.

Some of those interviewed gave accounts of clients whom they had been unwilling to represent or to prosecute because of the view which personal acquaintances outside of the profession would hold of that work. Key to the accounts was the notion that a decision based on such considerations was an aberration. Where decisions viewed unfavourably in the community were seen to result from their work, comments had been made at social gatherings. Though the comments were dismissed, their isolating effects on the barristers was apparent.

No consensus existed as to which career patterns were most effective to achieve judicial appointment. Those interviewed suggested that neither fear of threats nor disapproval of the Diplock courts would lead them to refrain from accepting a judicial appointment.

In terms of actually doing their work, all stated that their view of their work and the zeal with which they undertook it was unaltered if the accused was a police officer or a member of the military. Only offences which would be treated as scheduled offenses were appearing in the Diplock courts, in their opinion.[17] None thought that the motivation for an offence on the part of a client would in any way alter their management of the case. The accused paramilitary affiliations only interfered with their work, in the sense that the organization might over-rule their advice to the client, for instance, during the period of the I.R.A.'s policy of refusal to recognize the courts. But, in their view, it did not alter their presentation. The courtroom was not a political forum. None felt that their duty to the court and to their client had ever been in conflict.

Consensus was expressed that "statement fights" (dispute over admissibility of confessions, contested on the basis that they were obtained by inhuman or degrading treatment or torture) were the most difficult matters in which barristers appeared. Some suggested that it was the boredom and tedium which made these matters difficult. Others suggested that the monolithic and routine front presented by police and security personnel made the challenges difficult. Whatever their views, a circulating notion at the time of the interviews was that the paramilitaries had established a new policy to contest all confessions. This led to enormous sensitivity on the part of some barristers engaged in defense work, since other barristers cast innuendos that defense counsel were assisting the paramilitaries by pursuing these "frivolous" challenges.

LEGITIMIZING THE LEGITIMATORS

A strong sense of duty in a highly competitive business: this is the summarized view which these counsel held of themselves and their work. After all, they were remunerated by legal aid resulting in a lower income than their counterparts in private civil practice. They worked in dreadful surroundings and their clients were not the nicest sorts of people. The demands were tremendous and like any other dedicated professional, they could only do their best. As a body, they were no different, nor viewed themselves as any different from traditional lawyers in any other country, in any other court. Surely, their objectivity and professional distance would be admired anywhere.

An outsider may have grave difficulties with the above, given the "troubles" in Northern Ireland. Foremost is that very lack of political content in the trials in Northern Ireland. Once the larger political policy of criminalization has been adopted and the form and outer perimeters of the court's work have been determined, those perimeters go unchallenged. Within those perimeters, duty can be done, justice can be upheld, all behaviour can be modified to and examined in the light of this larger decision. These counsel, having had a hand in the establishment of the arena, can balk at the restrictive walls, plead overwork, insecurity, distaste and good intentions because the larger political decisions now appear removed from their hands. Indeed, they can criticize, minimalize and marginalize those who attempt to bring the political arena into the court as actually undermining the principles on which the court is based.

If one accepts that those appearing before these courts are there because they are murderers, thugs and thieves ("a criminal is a criminal is a criminal") there can be no need for hesitation in withdrawing their protections. But if, in light of our knowledge as to who the terrorists are and our insight into the nature of the circumstances which brings them before the courts, one sees them as political offenders engaged in political struggle, as do relatively large segments of the Northern Ireland public, the antiseptic, apolitical forum of these trials takes on a surreal nature.[18] In a society made ungovernable by conflict, selecting such a symbol of consensus as a court of law whose rules are expected to reflect a consensus decision as to relevancy and justice, can only further mark the fissure between dominant and subordinate groups. These courts ensure that the conflict in Northern Ireland is framed so as to deflect attention from the larger political questions while stifling the political questions pertinent to those brought before them.

These barristers formed a powerful segment of the status quo of Northern Ireland. As in many situations of economic depression, war or civil unrest, some segments of the population prosper, and these subjects financially prospered. The divided profession coupled with the difficulties (largely financial) of gaining access to the profession, assists in creating a large socio-economic gap between barristers, their clients and even their solicitor colleagues. High incomes in combination with social standing have assisted in providing shelter from the largely working-class strife. The similar pursuits and respect of family and fellow workers serve to further protect and reinforce barristers in their work. These barristers were satisfactorily paid, professionally challenged, independent, self-employed business people, confirmed in their work by their apparent success. In the most

123

cynical of all views, they had absolutely no stake in the "troubles" *ever* coming to an end.

Perhaps it would be asking too much that they should take a hand in ending the "troubles." However, given their social standing, their knowledge, and their actual political impact, let alone their *potential* political impact, this then is another grave difficulty.

A third difficulty which has most certainly arisen in other jurisdictions, is the willingness of these barristers to marginalize and ostracize those lawyers who do not hold their same view of the function of the courts and the place of political trials or unpopular clients or of themselves, within these courts. In many jurisdictions, lawyers representing unpopular clients and causes themselves become the subject of, if not open attack, then ostracism by their fellow members of the profession. German lawyers representing members of Baader-Meinhoff, Italian lawyers representing members of the Red Brigades, Israeli lawyers representing members of the Palestinian Liberation Army, Counsel for the American Civil Liberties Association representing neo-Nazis, Canadian lawyers representing members of the Front de Liberation du Québec: all of these and many more in many other jurisdictions have found themselves not only under attack from the public, but also under attack from their brethren at the Bar.[19] That lawyers resort to available legal procedures in the defense of their clients may come to be viewed as an abuse of these procedures and protections.

The next step in the chain of reasoning dictates that the procedures themselves be altered to disallow these procedures, now considered "abuses".[20] The casting of innuendo on counsel for engaging in statement fights, which have become the only defense where 96% of convictions are based on confessions obtained in what are known to be extraordinary detention conditions, points in such a direction. Similarly, the willingness of these counsel to state that solicitors take cases out of political sympathy and religious preference shows that same willingness to exclude those others who doubtless see themselves as equally doing their duty.

These then are those who defend and prosecute the terrorists. They are by no means the only barristers in Northern Ireland, but they form the most powerful segment of the Bar. Their views of themselves and their work demonstrates how a professional group adapts to what for many others would be an insupportable, intolerable situation. Through their views they are able to legitimate their work and their place in a not fully legitimate circumstances.

The study also teaches a good deal about how Northern Ireland continues "intractable."

NOTES AND REFERENCES

[1] Report of the Commission to consider legal procedures to deal with terrorist activities in Northern Ireland, (1972; Cmnd. 4594; Lord Diplock).

[2] See *infra* n. 19.

[3] It is impossible to do justice to the complexities of the history of the Northern Ireland State in the short space available here. Readers are referred to the following works for more detailed accounts of the relevant history: The Sunday Times Insight Team, *Ulster* (1972), T. Hadden and P. Hillyard, *Justice in Northern Ireland: A Study in Social Confidence*; (1973) H. Kelly *How Stormont Fell* (1972); K. Boyle, T. Hadden and P. Hillyard, *Law and State: The Case of Northern Ireland* (1975); P. Bew, P. Gibbon, and H. Patterson, *The State in Northern Ireland* (1979); and O'Dowd, "Shaping and Re-Shaping the Orange State" in L. O'Dowd, B. Rolston and M. Tomlinson, *Northern Ireland: Between Civil Rights and Civil War* (1980); K. Boyle, T. Hadden and P. Hillyard, *Ten Years on in Northern Ireland* (1980) 24.

[4] The Sunday Times Insight Team, *Ulster* contains a full account of these events and charts the re-birth of the IRA.

[5] K. Boyle, T. Hadden and P. Hillyard *Law and State: the Case of Northern Ireland* (1975) 55–77, The Sunday Times Insight Team *op. cit*, pp. 260–276. As Boyle, Hadden and Hillyard remark; "The continuing use of internment by the Army in the case of most Republic suspects while Loyalist suspects were for the most part dealt with by the police and the courts confirmed the feelings in the Catholic community that internment and the military security systems that went with it were discriminatory and unacceptable" K. Boyle, T. Hadden and P. Hillyard, *Ten Years on in Northern Ireland* (1980) 24.

[6] For a more detailed analysis of the Diplock courts see Boyle, Hadden and Hillyard (1980) *op. cit* Chap 6.

[7] Now Northern Ireland (Emergency Provisions) Act 1978, s.8. In *R.* v. *McGrath* (C.A.(N.I.)), unreported, (13 June, 1980) the Court of Appeal further lowered the standard of admissibility by ruling that not only must the effect of the treatment be inhuman and degrading, but it must be intentionally inflicted torture.

[8] For example see *Fort Frances Pulp and Power Co.* v. *Manitoba Free Press Co.* [1923] A.C. 695 and *Co-operative Committee on Japanese Canadians* v. *Attorney General for Canada* [1947] A.C. 87.

[9] O. Kirchheimer, *Political Justice* (1961) chap. 6,.

[10] *Op. cit.* par. 13, p. 8. As to public confidence, see Miller, "The Orange Judiciary" (1976) 40 *Hibernia Review* 6, and T. Hadden and P. Hillyard *op. cit.* n. 3.

[11] It was not possible to interview members of the judiciary.

[12] K. Boyle, T. Hadden and P. Hillyard, *Law and State: The Case of Northern Ireland* (1975) 130–136.

[13] Hadden, "Long Kesh Lawyers" *Fortnight* 18 October 1975, 5.

[14] By 1980, per diem fees were high, reported to yield incomes of between £60,000 and £80,000 per annum for these subjects.

[15] Throughout its history, Northern Ireland had had statutory interference with solicitor/client privilege (for example, under the *Civil Authorities (Special Powers) Act* 1922–1972, Regulation 13(1) and the *Northern Ireland (Emergency Provisions) Act* 1973, Schedule 1, section 17) and even with counsel's ability to represent accused (for example, on remands, under *The Remand (Temporary Provisions) (Northern Ireland) Order* 1978 S.I. 1585 (N.I.24)). No mention of these restrictions were raised by counsel.

[16] The first hunger-strike (subsequently terminated without fatalities) was in progress during the fieldwork period. Many prominent Ulster citizens received threats that retaliation against themselves and their families would be exacted if any strikers died.

[17] In the Republic of Ireland there have been allegations made by the Irish Civil Liberties Union that non-terrorist offenders have been brought before martial law courts.

[18] See K. Boyle, T. Hadden and P. Hillyard, *Ten Years on in Northern Ireland* (1980) Table 3:2, 23, as to the lack of previous criminal records of the accused.

[19] Regarding German lawyers, see J. Becker, *Hitler's Children* (1977) and J. Friedlander, *Terrorism Vol. 1* (1980) 285. Regarding Italian lawyers, see Armstrong, "Lawyer commits suicide while being arrested" *Guardian* 21 April 1980, 8. Regarding Israeli lawyers, see Morris, "Devil's Advocate" *Guardian* 6 May, 1980, 8. Regarding the American Civil Liberties Union, see Goldberger, "The Right to Counsel in Political Cases: The Bar's Failure" (1979) 43 *Law and Contemporary Problems* 321. Regarding Canadian lawyers, see R. Haggart, *Rumours of War* (1971) Appendix E.

[20] Corves, "Terrorism and Criminal Justice Operations in the Federal Republic of German" in *Terrorism and Criminal Justice* (1978; ed. R. D. Crelinstein).

Official and Public
Reaction to Terrorism

[18]

Terrorism, Volume 10. pp. 113–124
Printed in the UK. All rights reserved.

0149-0389/87 $3.00 + .00
Copyright © 1987 Crane, Russak & Company

Public Support for Emergency (Anti-Terrorist) Legislation in Northern Ireland: A Preliminary Analysis

JOHN E. FINN

Department of Government
Wesleyan University
Middletown, Connecticut 06457

Abstract *Anti-terrorist legislation in the United Kingdom is premised upon the assumption that the existence of special criminal procedures for terrorist offenses will not affect how citizens evaluate the legitimacy of the legal process and of legal institutions more generally. I examine the implications and question the plausibility of that assumption in this article. For my analysis, I shall rely upon public opinion data concerning the extent to which Roman Catholics and Protestants support the emergency legislation and special courts in Northern Ireland. My findings suggest, contrary to the assumptions upon which the emergency legislation is predicated, that certain aspects of the emergency legislation have seriously eroded public confidence in the administration of criminal justice in Northern Ireland. This finding has considerable significance for societies that hope to control political terrorism by relying upon modified versions of the rule of law.*

I. Introduction

Anti-terrorist legislation in Great Britain and Northern Ireland proceeds on the assumption that political terrorism imposes highly unusual strains on ordinary criminal processes, strains so severe that they warrant the existence of special legislation to govern terrorist offenses. There are two such statutes currently in force in the United Kingdom —the Northern Ireland (Emergency Provisions) Act 1978, applicable only in Ulster, and the Prevention of Terrorism Act 1976, which applies both in Northern Ireland and in Great Britain.

Although the assumption that terrorism imposes severe strains on the criminal processes seems warranted,[1] these statutes also proceed upon yet another, perhaps more fundamental and certainly more contestable set of premises. They assume, for example, that it is possible to control (if not to eradicate) political terrorism through legal measures that, while not ordinary, at least approximate normal legal processes. In this respect, British anti-terrorist policy, as is true in most European democracies, is predicated upon the conviction that liberal societies are limited in how they can respond to terrorism, and that at least some of those constraints derive from their commitment to liberal values and the rule of law.[2]

Ultimately, of course, those values and our commitment to them depend upon public support for their authority. Indeed, the legitimacy of liberal institutions, including courts, and hence the ability of those institutions to govern, is in large measure a function of public confidence in them.[3] And insofar as we commonly associate courts and judges with our commitment to the rule of law, an essential element in the classical conception of the liberal state, public confidence in judicial institutions may be an especially acute measure of regime legitimacy and public alienation in liberal democracies. Public confidence in judicial institutions, then, is no less important than public confidence in any liberal institution.

British anti-terrorist statutes reflect that awareness: Anti-terrorist legislation in Northern Ireland is premised upon the explicit and publicly stated assumption that the existence of special criminal procedures for terrorist offenses will not negatively affect how citizens evaluate the legitimacy of the legal process and legal institutions more generally. The Diplock Committee stressed just this point, observing that

> We regard it as of paramount importance that the criminal courts of law and judges and resident magistrates who preside in them should continue to retain [the] respect and trust [of the public] throughout the emergency and after the emergency has come to an end. If anything were done which weakened it, it might take generations to rebuild, for in Northern Ireland memories are long.[4]

This led the Committee to acknowledge that "any derogation from ordinary procedures . . . which interfered too radically with accepted common law values" might undermine public respect for and trust in the ordinary courts.[5] Coupled with this caution was an assumption that "the maintenance of an entirely separate procedure for the administrative detention of terrorists would not affect public attitudes to the ordinary courts."[6]

It is the plausibility of this latter assumption that I shall explore here. There is, of course, little doubt that public dissatisfaction with the emergency legislation is widespread in Ulster. But how widespread? Is dissatisfaction with the emergency processes limited simply to the Roman Catholic minority, or is it shared by elements of the Protestant majority as well? To what extent is that dissatisfaction based on informed appraisals of the system? And finally, as I suggested before, to what extent, if any, has public dissatisfaction with the emergency system affected public confidence in the administration of justice in Northern Ireland more generally? Before I address these questions, I first review the major provisions of Northern Irish anti-terrorist legislation and the tragic history that makes such legislation necessary.

II. Northern Ireland: A Legal History of Anti-Terrorist Legislation

A. *The Emergency Provisions Act*

Upon its creation by the British government in 1921, Northern Ireland was in a state of incipient civil war. Its boundaries and the loyalties of one-third of its population, perhaps half in the border counties, were uncertain. Indeed, Ulster's second city, Londonderry, was predominantly Catholic and republican. Even more troubling, the Irish Republican Army immediately commenced guerrilla operations against the fledgling state. Protestant leaders feared a Catholic uprising, and not without reason, for sectarian violence was so widespread that almost 300 people were killed between 1920 and 1922. In the latter year alone, "232 people were killed (including two Unionist MPs), nearly 1,000 were wounded, and more than £3 million worth of property was destroyed."[7]

It is hardly surprising that Northern authorities thought it necessary to pass emergency legislation in such circumstances. Given the sad history of violence in the thirty-two counties, it would have been more surprising had Northern Irish authorities *not* resorted to emergency measures. One constitutional lawyer described the resulting legislation, the Special Powers Act (SPA), as a "desperate measure taken to deal with a desperate situation."[8] But desperate measures have a way of enduring beyond the life of the situations that give rise to them. As originally drafted, the Special Powers Act was a temporary statute, its duration limited to one year. Stormont, the Northern parliament, annually renewed the Act through 1928, and in 1933 Stormont finally made the Act permanent.

The SPA was an extremely harsh measure. Included in its provisions, for instance, was the power to intern suspected terrorists indefinitely without trial. Section 1 of the Act granted the Minister of Home Affairs authority to "take all such steps and issue all such orders as may be necessary for preserving the peace and maintaining order." Under section 2(4), also an extremely broad provision, an individual could be guilty of a criminal offense even if the action was not proscribed by a specific regulation:

> If any person does any act of such a nature as to be calculated to be prejudicial to the preservation of the peace or maintenance of order . . . and not specifically provided for in the regulations, he shall be deemed to be guilty of an offense against the regulations.

There is little doubt that the Special Powers Act was directed almost solely at the Roman Catholic minority and that it was often used by Protestant authorities, along with gerrymandering and discrimination in the provision of public welfare, to suppress legitimate political dissent.[9] As a consequence, repeal of the Act was a major goal of the Northern Irish civil rights movement in the late 1960s and early 1970s. Partly to appease civil rights activists, one of Westminster's first objectives upon resuming direct control of the province in 1971 was to enact "more acceptable" emergency legislation.[10] Two years later, in 1973, the government appointed Lord Chief Justice Diplock to chair a committee to consider

> What arrangements for the administration of justice in Northern Ireland could be made in order to deal more effectively with terrorist organizations. . . .[11]

As the Committee's charter makes clear, Lord Diplock proceeded on the assumption that the Northern Irish judicial system had been unable to cope effectively with political terrorism in the province. It is not difficult to identify the areas that had given rise to concern. First, the Committee concluded that "technical" common law rules on the admissibility of confessions had "resulted in a substantial number of cases based on confessions obtained during prolonged interrogation [being] lost or withdrawn."[12] A second concern was the very real possibility that paramilitary organizations, such as the IRA or UVF, would try to intimidate prospective witnesses and jurors. Finally, the Diplock Committee feared the possibility of sectarian bias on the part of jurors: As I indicate later, the prosecution's power to "stand by" Catholic jurors had led to allegations of "perverse acquittals" in a number of cases involving Loyalist defendants.

Most of Lord Diplock's recommendations were incorporated in the SPA's successor, the Northern Ireland (Emergency Provisions) Act 1973. Subsequently amended and reorganized in 1978, the Emergency Provisions Act restructures the entire criminal process, from arrest and detention to sentencing and appeal. Its influence reaches from the powers of the security forces to stop and question ordinary citizens suspected of no offense to the trial and conviction of terrorists in special, juryless courts.

In general, it is fair to say that the EPA embodies two primary strategies. The first involves shifting burdens of proof from the state to the defendant. For example, in the English common law the state bears the initial burden of proving that a defendant's confession was voluntary. Under the Emergency Provisions Act, the confession is admissible unless the defendant first establishes a *prima facie* case that it was obtained through torture, inhuman, or degrading treatment.[13] Partly as a result of this relaxed rule, in most cases the only significant evidence of a defendant's guilt is a confession. One study concluded that in 86 percent of the cases, the defendant made a statement while in custody.[14] Only in 30 percent of those cases was the confession supported by additional forensic or identification evidence. The Act works similar changes in the burden of proof with regard to offenses involving possession of firearms and explosives. At the common law, the state bears the burden of proving both the physical presence of the firearm and the defendant's knowledge of it. Under the Emergency Act, however, the prosecutor need only show the first element. The burden then shifts to the defendant to show that he had no knowledge of the article or control over it.[15]

The second strategy, and the more important one for our purposes, shifts control of the criminal process away from judges and toward the executive. Provisions for internment, for example, are almost exclusively executive in nature and do not admit of judicial review.[16] Additional sections of the Act severely circumscribe judicial control over the pretrial proceedings. Provisions regarding a defendant's release on bail, for instance, limit judicial discretion in the pretrial process by providing that bail may be granted only by a High Court judge and then only upon satisfaction of a number of other conditions. Similarly, under the common law, a magistrate can dismiss unwarranted prosecutions at the remand hearing; under the emergency legislation, the magistrate cannot so much as compel the state to show probable cause until trial. As one commentator has noted of the pretrial proceedings, "it would not be unreasonable to claim that, from the point of view of the defendant, all the proceedings . . . have been bureaucratic rather than judicial."[17]

The same logic can be found in the four arrest and detention provisions of the Emergency Provisions Act. Some of these, such as section 18, concern the power of the security forces to stop and question any citizen. Others, such as section 14, relate to the power of the police and military to arrest and detain those individuals. Some sections permit detention only for "terrorist-related" offenses; others apply even to offenses against the ordinary criminal law. Some limit detention to four hours, while others authorize detention for as long as three days. All four provisions, however, permit security forces to question citizens under procedures considerably less protective of individual rights than the ordinary criminal law of Northern Ireland.

An example of this is the omission of a requirement of reasonableness of suspicion in the four arrest and detention provisions. The effect of this omission is to leave the security forces, who report to the executive, with unlimited and judicially unreviewable power to arrest and detain individuals. True, there is nothing in the legislation that formally precludes a judicial challenge through a writ of habeas corpus, but in practice there is no way in which such a petition could succeed. The lack of a requirement of reasonableness of suspicion to arrest deprives a court of any ground upon which to challenge its legality—the arresting officer need only state that he suspected the individual of having committed an offense. Since the suspicion need not be reasonable, the charge could be dismissed only upon a showing of bad faith.

A recent case, although it originated under the Prevention of Terrorism Act, demonstrates the difficulties that a typical petition will face. On May 27, 1980, the Royal Ulster Constabulary arrested the defendant, Lynch, under one of the arrest provisions of the

Emergency Powers Act.[18] Three days later, the RUC released him from custody without charge. On June 2, the police rearrested the defendant, this time under one of the arrest provisions of the Prevention of Terrorism Act. Lynch applied *ex parte* the same day to a high court judge for a writ of habeas corpus. The court refused to issue the writ on grounds that what must be communicated to the suspect at the time of his arrest is the "true ground" of the arrest, which means informing the suspect of the offense of which he is suspected.[19] Since the suspicion need not have been reasonable, there was no way in which the court could have determined whether the charge was supported by probable cause.

The most extreme example of the shift from judicial discretion to executive control over the criminal process is the practice of internment without trial, which has a long history in Northern Ireland. Indeed, before 1975 internment was the government's foremost weapon in its efforts to control terrorism; in one form or another, internment has been a more or less constant feature of the Northern Irish security system since the state's creation in 1921. The process is most complicated in its most recent form.[20] The first stage in internment proceedings is the making of an "interim custody" order by the Secretary of State for Northern Ireland or one of his deputies. The order need not set forth in detail the allegations against an individual; and, since no criminal charges are required, it will rarely do so. An interim order authorizes detention for twenty-eight days, but if the Chief Constable of the RUC refers the case to a Commissioner—a process I describe more fully later—the suspect may be detained until the Commissioner decides his case.

After the Secretary issues an interim order, there is a hearing before a "judicially qualified" Commissioner, appointed by the Secretary. The term "judicially qualified" means that the Commissioner has either held judicial office in the United Kingdom or has been a barrister or solicitor of ten years' standing. The Commissioner is required to hold a formal, but private, hearing in the presence of the suspect and his counsel. At the hearing, the suspect is first provided with a formal statement of the allegations against him. But the utility of even this minimal requirement is questionable: The allegations are not formal charges and are usually set forth in vague and cryptic language that hints at much but discloses little.

The final stage in the internment process is review by the Commissioner not less than twelve months after the issuance of the detention order, and then every six months. Reviews are limited to the question of whether the internee's continued detention is necessary for the public safety. In addition, the Secretary of State, who issues the original order and appoints the Commissioner, may order the release of an internee at any time.

The Secretary's power to intervene at any point during the proceedings demonstrates the essentially non-judicial nature of the internment process: An order to intern is *not* a judicial decision.[21] It is instead an executive order that is for all practical purposes immune from judicial supervision or review. Hence, the Gardiner Committee observed that the power to intern without trial is a

> decision by government to deprive individuals of their liberty without trial and without the normal safeguards which the law provides for the protection of the accused. It is an executive and not a judicial process. It is not known to the common law. . . .[22]

The provisions in the EPA that govern internment proceedings are, therefore, the most dramatic embodiment of one of the primary strategies of the emergency legislation, that of shifting power from the judiciary to the executive. Moreover, the internment provisions are the most radical departure (with the possible exception of suspension of jury trials) from those "accepted common law values" that Diplock thought so essential to the maintenance of public confidence in legal institutions.

B. Trial in the Diplock Courts

Despite its comprehensive nature, the Emergency Provisions Act has attracted the attention of scholars and critics largely because of provisions that establish special, juryless tribunals for the trial of terrorist offenses, tribunals first proposed by Lord Chief Justice Diplock and for whom they are named. Sections 6 and 7 of the Act create the special courts, in which a single high court judge hears cases involving "scheduled offenses" under relaxed rules of evidence. (Less serious offenses may be heard by a county court judge.)

As we saw, the legislation that creates the Diplock courts and defines their jurisdiction severely limits the discretion that judges normally enjoy in the criminal process. Hence, the Diplock courts are only the most obvious of the EPA's provisions—they are hardly the most important or troublesome. Nevertheless, the symbolic significance of the Diplock courts is considerable. An overwhelming majority of both Catholics and Protestants in Ulster are aware that jury trials have been suspended for certain terrorist-related offenses. A 1974 study, for example, found that 63 percent of Protestants and 79 percent of Roman Catholics knew that jury trials had been suspended.[23]

The British government justified suspension by suggesting the possibility that terrorists would intimidate both witnesses and jurors. The Diplock Committee also feared the possibility of "perverse" verdicts that might result from a jury's sectarian bias, although Lord Diplock conceded that, "It is fair to say that we have not had our attention drawn to complaints of convictions that were plainly perverse and complaints of acquittals which were plainly perverse are rare."[24] Nonetheless, my interviews with solicitors and barristers in Northern Ireland suggest that the fear of perverse verdicts, at least in 1973, was well-founded.[25]

The Committee's fear of perverse convictions should be understood as a fear that Protestants would unfairly convict Catholics or (less likely in Ulster) that Catholics would unfairly convict Protestants. In fact, prior to the 1973 emergency legislation, juries were composed almost exclusively of Protestants, in part because prosecutors could excuse, or "stand by" Catholic jurors on grounds that they were more likely than Protestants to be biased or subject to intimidation.[26]

Put in this way, the government could justify the suspension of trial by jury as a measure designed to protect not only witnesses and jurors, but also the rights of the accused, most of whom were Catholic. But magistrates always have the discretion to set aside perverse or improper verdicts, verdicts in which the weight of the evidence is insufficient to support the conviction. Moreover, the sensible solution to the problem of biased juries is not to suspend them, but rather to restrict the prosecution's right to "stand by" prospective jurors to those cases in which he can show cause—to cases, in other words, where he can articulate a reason, other than a juror's religious affiliation, to show a danger of bias.

All of this at least hints that concern over perverse convictions was not really what lay behind the decision to suspend juries. More probable was the fear of perverse *acquittals*, of cases in which Protestant juries would unfairly acquit Loyalists. In fact, after jury trials were suspended. the percentage of Protestant defendants who pled guilty rose considerably. "presumably because they could no longer count on a friendly jury."[27]

III. Public Confidence in the Emergency Legislation

In sum. the British government justified the emergency legislation in general. and suspension of trial by jury in particular. as measures designed to restore public confidence in the capacity of Northern Irish courts to deal with political terrorism both effectively and fairly. Coupled with this was an assumption that the "maintenance of an entirely separate procedure for the administrative detention of terrorists would not affect public attitudes to the ordinary courts."[29]

But do citizens in Northern Ireland support the special courts? A recent survey by the *Belfast Telegraph*. a nonaligned newspaper, clearly demonstrates the extent to which one must distinguish between Catholics and Protestants in answering that question. The *Telegraph*'s survey found that 57 percent of Catholics believe that "in the main the legal system in Northern Ireland dispenses justice" unfairly or very unfairly.[30] Only 9 percent of the Protestants agreed. Likewise. Edward P. Moxon-Browne has recently argued that Roman Catholic dissatisfaction with Northern Irish justice is widespread and that it significantly contributes to Catholic alienation from the state.[31]

Some commentators, however. such as Charles Carleton. have argued instead that the "Diplock Courts have gained a degree of acceptance among Ulster's minority community."[32] Carleton based his conclusion on the relative infrequency of assassination attempts against Diplock judges and the growing tendency of IRA defendants to plead guilty "and thus recognize the court's legitimacy."[33]

Carleton's reasoning is unpersuasive. My interviews with barristers and solicitors in Belfast indicate that Republican defendants are more likely to plead guilty than to contest the courts' jurisdiction. as they did in the early years of the courts' existence. because they hope to secure more lenient sentences in return for their pleas. Pleading thus becomes an exercise in organizational survival for the IRA. and should not be taken as a measure of the court's legitimacy. Boyle et al. agree, suggesting that.

> the sharp decline in the number of refusals to recognize . . . appears to be due largely to the fact that defendants . . . are being instructed by their respective paramilitary organizations to recognize the court and to attempt to obtain either an acquittal or a less severe sentence. . . .[34]

Others have concluded that public dissatisfaction with the special courts and emergency legislation is considerable. In a 1974 study. for example. Boyle, Hadden, and

Table I
Knowledge of Changes

	Protestant		Catholic	
	No.	%	No.	%
Respondents who knew of suspension of jury trials	74	63	45	79

Source: Boyle. Hadden. and Hillyard. *Law and State: The Case of Northern Ireland* (London: Martin Robertson. 1975), p. 145.

Hillyard interviewed 180 persons, selected on a quota basis to reflect class, sex, age, and religious divisions in Belfast. As Table I indicates, the respondents demonstrated that they knew of the changes made in the province's criminal processes. Sixty-three percent of the Protestants and 79 percent of the Catholics, for example, knew that jury trials had been suspended for certain terrorist-related offenses. Catholics and Protestants differed considerably, however, in their support for those changes. As Table II indicates, 47 percent of the Protestants objected to internment without trial, whereas 95 percent of Catholics objected to internment.

The importance of this latter finding should not be underestimated. Table III demonstrates that 59 percent of the Protestant respondents and 93 percent of the Catholics reported the practice of internment without trial decreased their confidence that defendants received fair trials in Northern Ireland's ordinary courts. The implications of this finding are of tremendous significance, for it challenges the very presuppositions—that the existence of special procedures for terrorists will not negatively affect public confidence in the ordinary courts—upon which British attempts to control terrorism in Ulster are predicated.

In his 1975 review of the emergency legislation, commissioned by the British government, Lord Gardiner recommended that the power to intern be withdrawn.[35] The policy was subsequently discontinued but remained statutorily intact. In 1980, the Standing Committee on Human Rights in the United Kingdom also urged that the power be withdrawn, arguing that

> the power to detain without trial persons suspected of being terrorists has always been an anathema to the rule of law and a serious obstacle to claims that human rights in Northern Ireland were as fully protected as they ought to be.[36]

Parliament finally permitted section 12, the provision authorizing internment, to lapse on July 22, 1980, but it may be renewed by the Secretary of State without parliamentary approval by virtue of sections 33(3)(c) and 32(3)(b).

Has the government's decision to let the internment power lapse restored public confidence in the administration of the emergency criminal process or in the administration of justice more generally? A study conducted in 1982 by Norman Shannon, a Belfast solicitor, suggests that the decision may have had some effect. Shannon interviewed 132 people randomly selected in Belfast and Londonderry. Using the same questions, I interviewed an additional 36 people, also selected randomly, in late July 1982—23 in Belfast, and 13 in Londonderry.

The Shannon survey is of particular interest because it fails to confirm the 1974 findings. Only 24 percent of the Protestants and just 6 percent of the Catholics in Shannon's survey believed that a fair trial was possible in the emergency courts (Table IV). But whereas in Boyle's survey 59 percent of the Protestants and 93 percent of the

Table II
Opposition to Internment

	Protestant		Catholic	
	No.	%	No.	%
Total opposed	56	47	54	95

Source: Boyle, Hadden, and Hillyard, *Law and State: The Case of Northern Ireland* (London: Martin Robertson, 1975), p. 145.

Table III
Confidence in Ordinary Courts

	Protestant		Catholic	
	No.	%	No.	%
Increased confidence	17	14	1	2
Decreased confidence	70	59	53	93
No change	10	9	3	5
No opinion	21	18	0	0

Source: Boyle, Hadden, and Hillyard, *Law and State: The Case of Northern Ireland* (London: Martin Robertson, 1975), p. 147.

Catholics stated that the practice of internment without trial had decreased their confidence in ordinary courts (Table III), in Shannon's survey only 20 percent of the Protestants and 33 percent of the Catholics reported a lack of confidence in them (Table V). My data approximated Shannon's findings.

These figures represent a considerable decrease from those reported by Boyle et al. almost ten years earlier. One explanation for the change might be the mere passage of time. When Boyle undertook his survey, the emergency legislation was fresh and the contours of its eventual implementation and application were uncertain. But over the past decade, greater familiarity with the emergency legislation, although it apparently has done little to increase public confidence in the emergency courts themselves, may have reassured the public that the process does not affect the quality of British justice in ordinary courts.

This explanation, however, ignores the importance of internment. A near majority of Protestants and almost all of the Catholics in the 1974 study reported that it was the practice of internment that had decreased their confidence in the ordinary courts. The British government has not used internment since 1975, and the statutory provisions that authorize it have been in abeyance since 1980. If internment is the key to the 1974 study, it should come as no surprise that public confidence in the ordinary courts would increase once internment had been phased out.

IV. Policy Implications and Conclusions

What little data we have concerning the extent to which the public in Northern Ireland supports the emergency legislation confirms Moxon-Browne's argument that dissatisfaction among the Roman Catholic community is considerable. Moreover, there is every

Table IV
Fairness of Trials in Emergency Courts

	Protestants		Catholics	
	No.	%	No.	%
Fair trial is possible	11	24	3	6
Fair trial is not possible	21	47	48	85
No opinion	9	20	5	9

Source: Interviews conducted by Mr. Norman Shannon in Belfast, Northern Ireland (July 1982). These figures do not include my interviews or those respondents who did not include their religious preference.

Table V
Decreased Confidence in Ordinary Courts

	Protestants		Catholics	
	No.	%	No.	%
Increased confidence	0	0	1	2.5
Decreased confidence	9	20	18	48
No change	18	40	15	27
No opinion	18	40	12	22

Source: Interviews conducted by Mr. Norman Shannon in Belfast, Northern Ireland (July 1982). These figures do not include my interviews. At the time I spoke with Shannon, he had no plans to conduct a more sophisticated study.

indication that the dissatisfaction extends to at least some elements of the Protestant majority as well.

Perhaps more intriguing are indications that the public in Northern Ireland can distinguish between what are in effect two different legal systems for two different sets of defendants. In the 1974 survey, a majority of Protestants and Catholics alike reported that their negative evaluations of internment had decreased their confidence in ordinary courts. The 1982 survey, taken after internment had been discontinued, failed to find the same degree of decreased confidence in the ordinary courts, thus implying that the public's lack of confidence in the fairness of emergency criminal processes need not extend to the administration of justice in Nothern Ireland's ordinary courts. This latter finding is of considerable importance for any society that hopes to control terrorism by relying upon modified versions of the rule of law, for it suggests that the existence of special procedures for certain classes of defendants need not necessarily endanger the legitimacy of legal institutions more generally.

But there are clear limits to that policy. When emergency legislation departs too radically from "accepted common law values," as Lord Diplock acknowledged, it threatens public confidence even in the ordinary criminal processes. As we saw, British anti-terrorist legislation seeks to shift control over the criminal process from judges to the Northern Irish executive. The surveys reviewed here clearly suggest that internment without trial, the most extreme example of that shift, is too radical a departure from those common law values. Indeed, it is misleading and inaccurate to call internment a form of judicial process at all. Nevertheless, its use in Ulster has had severe consequences for Northern Ireland's judiciary and for public confidence in the administration of justice in ordinary courts.

Finally, professional students of Northern Ireland may find it curious that I have not discussed "supergrasses," another highly controversial aspect of British anti-terrorist policy. A "supergrass" is an informant, usually himself suspected of terrorist activities. In the supergrass system, large numbers of defendants are prosecuted in the Diplock courts, often solely on the strength of the informant's testimony. In the first three supergrass cases, 80 percent of those tried were ultimately found guilty, most without any corroborative evidence.[37]

In December 1985, for example, 27 defendants were convicted on the testimony of Harry Kirkpatrick, a former member of the Irish National Liberation Army.[38] The common law requires of judges that they warn juries of the unreliability of such "accomplice" evidence, especially when it is uncorroborated. But the Diplock courts sit without juries, so "the danger warning has been ritualistically given by the judge to himself."[39]

A survey completed in 1984 found that 72 percent of Catholic respondents disapproved or strongly disapproved of the supergrass system, whereas only 21 percent of Protestant respondents expressed disapproval.[40] The precise extent to which the supergrass system may have eroded public confidence in the administration of criminal justice more generally is, of course, unclear. But the opinion of most observers is that it has had a negative effect. Jennings and Greer argue that the issuance of "ritualistic warnings," "has attracted much criticism from legal quarters and has exposed the legal process to public ridicule."[41] Similarly, Moxon-Browne concludes that "the system of supergrasses has tended to discredit the judicial system and is partly to blame for the alienation of the Catholic community from it."[42]

Notes

1. See notes 10–12 below and accompanying text.

2. See, for example, the assertion by Merlyn Rees, former Secretary of State for Northern Ireland, that "The powers which have evolved . . . represent a determination by successive British governments that such legislation will depart as little as possible . . . from the traditions of British justice." "Terror in Ireland—and Britain's Response," in Paul Wilkinson, ed., *British Perspectives on Terrorism*. (London: George Allen and Unwin, 1981), p. 85.

3. But cf. William A. Gamson, *Power and Discontent*. (Homewood, Ill.: Dorsey Press, 1968), chap. 3.

4. Diplock, *Report of the Commission to Consider Legal Procedures to Deal with Terrorist Activities in Northern Ireland*. Cmnd. 5185 (London: HMSO, 1972) para 13. (Hereafter *Diplock Report*.)

5. Kevin Boyle, Thomas Hadden, and Paddy Hillyard, *Law and State: The Case of Northern Ireland* (London: Martin Robertson, 1975), p. 143. (Hereafter Boyle, *Law and State*.)

6. Ibid., at 144.

7. Paul Arthur, *Political Realities: The Government and Politics of Northern Ireland* (Burnt Mill: Longman Group, Ltd., 1980), pp. 25–26.

8. As quoted in John Magee, *Crisis and Conflict* (London: Routledge & Kegan Paul, 1975), p. 77.

9. Cameron, *Disturbances in Northern Ireland: Report of a Commission Appointed by the Governor of Northern Ireland*. Cmnd. 532 (Belfast: HMSO, 1969), paras. 228–30.

10. Ibid., at 151.

11. *Diplock Report*, supra note 4.

12. Kevin Boyle, Thomas Hadden, and Paddy Hillyard, *Ten Years On in Northern Ireland: The Legal Control of Political Violence* (Nottingham: Russell Press, 1980), p. 57 (Hereafter Boyle, *Ten Years On*.)

13. The *Diplock Report* borrowed this terminology from the European Convention on Human Rights. See Desmond S. Greer, "The Admissibility of Confessions Under the Northern Ireland (Emergency Provisions) Act," 31 N.I.L.Q. 205, 232–233 (1980).

14. Boyle, *Ten Years On*, p. 44.

15. There is some precedent for the shift in the burden of proof. Under section 24 of the Metropolitan Courts Act 1839, repealed in 1977, a person found in possession of stolen goods could be convicted unless he could account for his possession.

16. See notes 20–22 below and accompanying text.

17. Boyle, *Ten Years On*, p. 69.

18. Ex Parte Lynch, [1980] N. Ir. 126 (Q.B. Div.).

19. Ibid.

20. An excellent description of the process can be found in Boyle, *Law and State*, pp. 58–74. See also David R. Lowry, "Internment: Detention Without Trial in Northern Ireland," *Human Rights* 5:261 (1976); John McGuffin, *Internment* (Tralee: Anvil Press, 1973).

21. Boyle, *Law and State*, p. 61.

22. Lord Gardiner. *Report of a Committee to Consider. in the Context of Civil Liberties and Human Rights. Measures to Deal with Terrorism in Northern Ireland.* Comnd. 5847 (London: HMSO. 1975).

23. Boyle, *Law and State.* p. 145.

24. *Diplock Report.* paras. 35–38.

25. Many of the solicitors and barristers I interviewed in Northern Ireland predicated their cooperation on my promise that I not disclose their identities.

26. Boyle, *Ten Years On.* pp. 40–41.

27. Ibid.

28. As quoted in Charles Carleton. "Judging Without Consensus." *Law and Policy Quarterly* 3:225, 237 (1981) (Hereafter Carleton. *Judging Without Consensus*); see also Boyle. *Ten Years On.* p. 86.

29. Ibid.

30. *Belfast Telegraph.* February 6, 1985. p. 7.

31. Edward P. Moxon-Browne. "Alienation: The Case of Catholics in Northern Ireland." Paper delivered at the 1985 Annual Meeting of the American Political Science Association, New Orleans. August 29–September 1, 1985, pp. 7–9 (Hereafter Moxon-Browne. *Alienation.*)

32. Carleton. *Judging Without Consensus.* p. 237.

33. Ibid.

34. Boyle, *Ten Years On.* p. 75.

35. Ibid.

36. Standing Advisory Committee on Human Rights. Annual Report for 1979–1980. House of Commons Paper. 143. p. 6. The Standing Committee was established by the Northern Ireland Constitution Act. ch. 36. section 20.

37. Tony Jennings and Stephen Greer. "Final Verdict on the Supergrass System." *Fortnight: An Independent Review for Northern Ireland* 232 (January 27. 1986). 8–9. See also Steven C. Greer. "Supergrasses and the Legal System in Britain and Northern Ireland." *Intl. L. Q.* 102:198 (1986); T. Gifford. *The Use of Accomplice Evidence in Northern Ireland* (Nottingham: Russell Press, 1984).

38. Ibid.

39. Ibid.

40. *Fortnight: An Independent Review for Northern Ireland* (November 1984).

41. Tony Jennings and Stephen Greer. op. cit.

42. Moxon-Browne. *Alienation.* p. 8.

[19]

Irish Terrorism Investigations

"In spite of FBI successes, Irish nationals and sympathetic U.S. citizens continue to attempt to obtain weapons and money in the United States in violation of existing Federal laws."

By
J.L. STONE, JR., M.P.A.
Supervisory Intelligence Research Specialist
Terrorist Research and Analytical Center
Federal Bureau of Investigation
Washington, DC

Within the parameters of the FBI's overall law enforcement mission, Irish terrorism investigations are addressed through a twofold approach—prevention and reaction. In this regard, FBI field divisions are prepared to assume either a preventive or reactive stance as the situation dictates. Given a choice, the obvious preference would be to prevent terrorist activity. Lawful intelligence gathering techniques, such as use of informants, undercover operations, and court-ordered electronic surveillance, are instrumental tools in this effort. Also of benefit are good working relationships with intelligence and law enforcement agencies at all levels, both in the United States and internationally.

The second approach involves traditional law enforcement activity after U.S. statutes have been violated. Principal emphasis here is on stabilizing the situation, if necessary, and on arresting the perpetrators with the ultimate goal of prosecution and incarceration. Successes in terrorism investigations have resulted in a precipitous decline in the number of total incidents in the United States over the past several years.

The FBI has adopted a strategy of viewing terrorists, including Irish, to be individuals involved in criminal enterprises. This allows for investigations predicated on criminal activity rather than on political or ideological motivations. With this emphasis, there is less concern with why this activity is being employed than with the fact that crimes are being committed. Irish terrorism investigations involve identification of subjects and group leaders, development of associations, and tracing of financial and support structures. The focus is on the total network and the object is to gather evidence for eventual prosecution.

As a result of this aggressive investigative effort, the FBI has been successful in a number of Irish terrorism investigations by obtaining indictments and convictions. Additional investigations are ongoing, which should lead to future legal action.

These investigations are focused on three principal areas of activity: (1) Involvement in weapons procurement in the United States and illegal transport of these weapons to Northern Ireland or the Republic of Ireland, (2) fundraising efforts in the United States with illegal transfer of this funding to Northern Ireland to directly support Irish terrorist elements operating there, and (3) identifying Irish terrorists who are in the United States illegally.

Irish terrorism matters are investigated under specific guidelines relating

Mr. Stone

to international terrorism investigations. Criminal activity is investigated under the Attorney General's Guidelines for General Crimes, Racketeering Enterprises, and Domestic Security/Terrorism Investigations (1983). Electronic surveillances in criminal matters are generally pursued under the provisions of Title III of the Omnibus Crime Control and Safe Streets Act of 1968. These matters are also investigated under the Attorney General's Foreign Counterintelligence Guidelines (1983). Electronic surveillances are generally conducted according to the Foreign Intelligence Surveillance Act of 1978 (FISA) and are authorized by a specially constituted Federal court. While the primary purpose of these intercepts is the collection of intelligence data bearing on the national security, clear provisions are made for the use of evidentiary material in criminal prosecutions (see *United States* v. *Megahey*, 553 F. Supp. 1180 (E.D.N.Y. 1982), affirmed, 729 F.2d 1444 (2d Cir. 1983). Recent court decisions indicate that surveillances under FISA will continue to be valuable in both preventing and reacting to terrorist activity.

In all such matters, protection of individual and group first amendment constitutional rights is of paramount concern. For example, no case is initiated solely on the basis of membership in an organization or the donation of money to the organization or cause. In many instances, donors believe that this money is going for charitable causes (e.g., aid to support families of imprisoned Irish soldiers). Barring specific articulable facts which indicate that a group or individual's activities (collecting funds, weapons procurement, etc.) are criminal in nature, such as aiding and abetting Irish terrorist elements, there is no basis for pursuing an investigation.

Major Irish Groups Active In The United States

Investigations have shown that Irish group activity in the United States, in support of the Irish Republican Movement, centers around three principal elements: The Irish Republican Army or Provisional Irish Republican Army (PIRA) as it is often referred to, the Irish National Liberation Army (INLA), and the Irish Northern Aid Committee/Northern Irish Aid (NORAID). One other group with possible sympathizers in the United States, the Ulster Volunteer Force (UVF), is a "loyalist" and antimovement element.

PIRA

PIRA is a militant Marxist organization composed primarily of residents of Northern Ireland and/or the Republic of Ireland who are committed to achieving British withdrawal from Northern Ireland and the establishment of a united 32-county democratic socialist republic in Ireland. It is an extremely violent group, having committed numerous terrorist acts against the British military, Irish civilians, and those they perceive as upholders of British rule in Northern Ireland. One such act resulted in the death of a U.S. citizen in the December 1983, bombing of Harrod's Department Store in London. PIRA is extremely well-armed and well-organized. Investigation of PIRA activities in the United States has centered on individuals who are operatives or supporters of this organization involved in the acquisition of weapons or funds to procure them.

> ### *"Investigations have shown that Irish group activity in the United States...centers around three principal elements: The Irish Republican Army or...the Irish National Liberation Army...and the Irish Northern Aid Committee...."*

INLA

INLA is essentially a Marxist-Leninist oriented group also dedicated to the formation of a united 32-county democratic socialist republic in Ireland. It subscribes to violence as a means of ousting the British from Ulster and overthrowing the Government of the Republic of Ireland. It is the military wing of the Irish Republican Socialist Party. Although activities often parallel actions of PIRA, there is no formal alliance between the two organizations.

NORAID

NORAID is the main Irish fundraising organization in the United States and purports to raise funds to support families of imprisoned PIRA and Republican Movement members. It was founded in 1970 by Michael Flannery and two Irish Republican Movement veterans of the 1919-1921 period. In January 1982, a U.S. court ruled that NORAID must comply with provisions of the Foreign Agents Registration Act (1938) and register as an agent of PIRA. FBI investigations have centered on individuals suspected of being couriers of funds to PIRA or actively aiding and abetting any Irish terrorist organization. NORAID is headquartered in New York City with chapters located throughout the United States.

UVF

On the other side of the spectrum, the UVF is a "loyalist" paramilitary organization which represents a working class response to what is viewed as a threat to Protestantism posed by Irish Republican terrorism and Roman Catholicism. The UVF was formed in 1966 by Protestant extremists opposed to improved relations between Northern Ireland and the Republic of Ireland. It took its name from the original UVF, which was established by Sir Edward Carson in 1912 to resist the need for Ulster to participate in Irish Home Rule.

UVF sympathizers in the United States are involved, albeit sporadically, in rather low-level attempts to obtain weapons which would be used by UVF members in Northern Ireland against Republican elements. The UVF is largely sectarian and anti-Catholic in its motivation. In the United States, the UVF has been generally inactive. As an example of the UVF's participation in the problems of Northern Ireland, during the summer of 1984 in Belfast, the UVF was involved in an unsuccessful assassination attempt on Gerry Adams, leader of the Sein Finn, formerly the Provisional Sein Finn, the political wing of PIRA. There have been instances where weapons recovered in Northern Ireland, which have been attributed to the UVF, have been traced to the United States. Analysis indicates these weapons possibly originated in the midwestern United States. To date, there has been no prosecution of UVF operatives here.

Summary Of Significant Activity In The United States

The following highlights significant Irish terrorist activity in the United States and the FBI's investigative response.

1981 - 1982

—On September 30, 1981, William Joseph Quinn was arrested by the FBI in San Francisco, CA, and charged with violation of Title 18, USC, Section 3184 (fugitive from a foreign country). Quinn had been sought by British authorities for the 1975 murder of a constable in London and conspiracy to cause explosions.

In October 1983, in U.S. District Court, Northern District of California, the presiding judge rendered a decision that Quinn should be released from custody. The judge made this ruling based on his interpretation that the extradition treaty between the United States and Great Britain did not cover what the judge defined as a "political murder," for which Quinn was being held. The U.S. Government immediately filed an appeal before the Ninth Circuit Court of Appeals, contesting the judge's decision and requesting that the decision be stayed pending further appellate proceedings. This appeal was subsequently granted and Quinn was not released from custody.

In February 1986, the Ninth Circuit Court of Appeals ruled that Quinn should be extradited to Great Britain. In July 1986, Quinn's attorneys appealed this decision to the U.S. Supreme Court. In October 1986, the Supreme Court denied to hear the appeal and Quinn was ordered extradited to Great Britain. Quinn was subsequently transported to London, England, formally charged and remanded to prison.

—From June 1981, through June 1982, the FBI initiated investigations against Gabriel Megahey and Andrew Duggan. Megahey had been identified as the leader of a PIRA cell in the United States with sole responsibility being the acquisition of weapons for PIRA. Duggan, a suspected PIRA member, was alleged to be involved in purchasing highly sophisticated electronic equipment for PIRA. Stemming from investigative information obtained and an undercover operation, Megahey and Duggan were arrested on June 21, 1982. Arrested concurrently were Megahey's associates, Eamon and Colm Meehan. These individuals were arrested as a result of a seizure of weapons at the Port of Newark on May 28, 1982. In May 1983, Megahey, Duggan, and Eamon and Colm Meehan were found guilty of violations of the National Firearms Act.

—Resulting from another undercover operation directed by the FBI, two NLA members, Colm Murphy and Vincent Toner, were arrested on July 21, 1982, for Federal firearms violations. The undercover operation was directed against INLA's efforts to procure weapons in the United States. During July 1983, both Murphy and Toner were convicted.

1983 - 1984

—Joseph P.T. Doherty was arrested in June 1983, in New York City as an illegal alien (Title 18, USC, Section 3184). Doherty, a member of PIRA's infamous "M-60" Gang, had escaped from a Belfast, Northern Ireland, prison in September 1982, while awaiting trial for the murder of a British army officer. He was subsequently convicted and sentenced in absentia to life imprisonment. Information regarding Doherty's whereabouts in the United States was obtained from an FBI source. On December 13, 1984, the U.S. District Court for the Southern District of New York ruled that Doherty could not be extradited from the United States to answer charges in Ireland for the murder of a British army officer, as the offense was political in nature and not extraditable under the U.S.-Britain extradition treaty. He is presently being held without bond at Metropolitan Correction Center, New York, pending deportation and new extradition proceedings, based upon amendments to the U.S.-Britain extradition treaty which were adopted during June 1985.

—On May 17, 1984, Joseph Cahill and James Noel Drumm were arrested in New York City for entering the United States illegally (Title 8, USC, Section 1326). Cahill is considered the "godfather" of PIRA who has been extensively involved in weapons procurement on behalf of PIRA. Drumm has been described as the "money man" for PIRA and is known to be involved in the financing of weapons procurement activity. Cahill, following trial in New York, was deported to Dublin, Ireland, on July 2, 1984. Drumm agreed to voluntary deportation, which occurred May 18, 1984, the day after the arrest.

At the time of the arrest, both Cahill and Drumm had in their possession documentation which indicated they had entered the United States illegally on March 11, 1984, at New York City. For 2 months they were involved in numerous fundraising events.

—On July 27, 1984, Robert Emmett Hunter was arrested in Los Angeles, CA, for fraud and misuse of visas, permits, and other entry documents (Title 18, USC, Section 1546). Hunter is associated with PIRA and had previously been imprisoned on charges resulting from a bombing and possessing a firearm. A search of Hunter's residence revealed four blank birth certificates and additional documents relating to his illegal residency in the United States. On November 30, 1984, criminal charges against Hunter were dropped so that deportation proceedings could be undertaken.

—On September 29, 1984, a cache of firearms, ammunition, and explosives, totaling approximately 7 tons, was seized by Irish Federal Police on board the fishing trawler "Marita Ann" as it was heading for the port of Dingle on the southwest coast of Ireland. Five individuals, identified as Martin Ferris,

John Crawley, Gavin Mortimer, John McCarthy, and trawler owner Michael Brown, all PIRA members, were arrested. Subsequent information indicated that the cache had been offloaded earlier from the trawler "Valhalla" off the west coast of Ireland.

On October 16, 1984, the "Valhalla" was located by the United States Customs Service (USCS) in Boston, MA. Interviews by the FBI and USCS of a "Valhalla" crew member clearly identified this vessel as the "mothership" involved in the PIRA weapons shipment. The "Valhalla" was allegedly loaded with weapons on September 13 to 14, 1984, at Gloucester, MA, and then sailed to the Irish Sea for offloading onto the "Marita Ann."

One of the five individuals arrested, John Crawley, was allegedly involved in PIRA activities in the United States. Crawley and six other individuals were indicted in April 1986, for violation of the Arms Export Control Act, Title 22, USC, Section 2778, the Export Administration Act, Title 50, USC, Section 2410, and various sections of Titles 18 and 26 USC. During May 1987, three of the individuals pled guilty to various counts of the indictment. These and the others are awaiting further legal proceedings in Boston, MA.

1985 - 1986

—The continuing investigation surrounding the seizure of weapons at the Port of Newark on May 28, 1982, (*Megahey*, supra) determined that some of the weapons for this shipment were purchased by an individual using the name Robert Power.

A subsequent fingerprint analysis was done comparing the fingerprints of an individual named Liam Ryan of New York City with those developed from the

Weapons seized during "Marita Ann" case.

Federal firearms registration form in the Megahey weapons shipment case. A match of the fingerprints determined that Ryan was the individual who purchased these weapons using the name of Robert Power.

Ryan returned to the United States from Ireland on April 14, 1985, and was arrested on April 24, 1985, in New York City for violation of Title 18, USC, Section 1001 (making false, fraudulent, and fictitious statements), stemming from his weapons purchase in the above case. On September 18, 1985, Ryan pled guilty to one count of Title 18, USC, Section 1001 in the U.S. District Court, Eastern District of New York.

—Another investigation identified an individual named Sean Gerard Mackin, an individual considered to be an INLA member in the United States.

As part of the ongoing investigation, Mackin was arrested on July 16, 1985, by Immigration and Naturalization Service (INS) and FBI Agents for violation of Title 8, USC, Section 1252 (overstay of B-2 visa). Mackin was released on $15,000 bond on July 19, 1985, and is presently awaiting an INS hearing.

—Investigation by the Los Angeles FBI Office from February 1985, until June 1986, indicated that the INLA was using William Wallace Norton and his wife Eleanor Elias Norton to procure weapons in the United States. Norton, a

"This allows for investigations predicated on criminal activity rather than on political or ideological motivations...."

retired screenwriter for Walt Disney Productions, moved from Los Angeles, CA, to an area near Dundalk, Republic of Ireland, during March 1986. On June 5, 1986, the ship carrying Norton's vehicle arrived in Rotterdam and the vehicle, still in the shipment container, was off loaded and transported to LeHavre, France.

On June 11, 1986, at LeHavre, France, French authorities, based on information provided by the FBI, searched the vehicle and found 2 machine guns, 12 AR-15 rifles, 24 handguns, a rifle scope, silencers, and approximately 2,200 rounds of ammunition. Norton, his wife, and three Irish nationals, Sean Hughes (aka Anthony James Mackenzie), James Joseph McLaughlin, and Suzanne May, were arrested by French authorities and charged with arms trafficking when they attempted to take possession of the vehicle.

The Nortons are currently being held in France, without bond, on weapons conspiracy charges. On June 18, 1986, a U.S. arrest warrant was issued for Norton and a complaint filed in Los Angeles, CA, charging Norton with one count of violating Title 22, USC, Section, 227 B (C) (Willfully Exporting U.S. munitions without a valid license or written approval of the U.S. Department of State). Norton was also charged with violating Title 18, USC, Section, 922(E) (Knowingly Delivering a Vehicle Containing Firearms and Ammunition to a Common Carrier for Transportation in Foreign Commerce). Prosecution in this case is pending, but will be delayed until the Nortons stand trial in France.

—In March 1985, an undercover FBI Special Agent (UCSA) was placed in contact with an individual named Jackie McDonald. McDonald in turn introduced the UCSA to Noel B. Murphy, an Irish citizen living in Boston, MA. During discussions between Murphy and the UCSA, Murphy expressed interest in purchasing automatic rifles for shipment to the PIRA. Negotiations between Murphy and the UCSA culminated with an agreement for Murphy to purchase 100 M-16 rifles at $500 each, 1 Redeye surface-to-air missile at $10,000, 5,000 rounds of .223 caliber ammunition, and two ammunition clips for each weapon. The total package price was to be $60,000.

On May 15, 1986, the UCSA met with Murphy and Cairan Hughes, an Irish citizen who was responsible for getting the weapons shipped to Ireland, to finalize the deal. On May 20, 1986, the UCSA met with Murphy, Hughes, and five individuals subsequently identified as Roy Paul Willey, John Fitzgerald, James Boyle, Steven MacDonald, and Michael P. McLaughlin in a Bedford, MA, hotel. The UCSA, Murphy, and Hughes left the hotel and went to Hanscom Airfield to inspect the weapons. The other five subjects and two other UCSAs remained in the hotel room waiting for Murphy and Hughes to return. Upon arriving at the airfield, Murphy and Hughes were arrested. Simultaneously, the five subjects in the hotel room were arrested, and Jackie MacDonald was arrested at his place of employment.

On June 4, 1986, Federal grand jury indictments were returned charging all eight subjects with Conspiracy to Violate the Arms Export Control Act, Title 18, USC, Section 371, Conspiracy to Violate Federal Firearms Laws, Title 18, USC, Section 922 (A) (4), and Title 25, USC, Section 5861 (D). Murphy and Hughes were also indicted for dealing in firearms and ammunition without a license and being an alien in possession of a firearm.

On October 2, 1986, McLaughlin pled guilty to one count of conspiring to violate the Arms Export Control Act. On October 7, 1986, Jackie McDonald and Roy Willey pled guilty to the same charge. On October 8, 1986, John Fitzgerald, James Boyle, and Stephen McDonald pled guilty to the conspiracy charge under Title 18, USC, Section 371. On October 23, 1986, in U.S. District court, Boston, MA, a jury returned guilty verdicts against Noel Murphy and Cairan Hughes on all charges except the indictment for being an alien in possession of a firearm.

Conclusion

The FBI, through cooperation with other U.S. Government agencies and foreign police services, has enjoyed significant accomplishments against individuals procuring weapons and funds in the United States for use by Irish terrorist organizations. These successes, obtained by using both preventive and reactive investigative techniques, have produced a substantial decline in arms procurement activities in the United States by Irish nationals.

In spite of FBI successes, Irish nationals and sympathetic U.S. citizens continue to attempt to obtain weapons and money in the United States in violation of existing Federal laws. Consequently, the FBI will continue its investigative efforts into the activities of Irish terrorist organizations operating in the United States.

FBI

Intelligence and Psychological Warfare Operations in Northern Ireland

By DAVID A. CHARTERS

The author is Canadian. At present, he is a research student in the Department of War Studies, King's College, University of London.

Between the end of World War I and the outbreak of the "troubles" in Northern Ireland in 1969, the British Army had been involved in numerous counter-insurgency campaigns. Indeed, probably no army has entered a conflict with such a wealth of relevant experience as the British Army did in Ulster. It is not unreasonable to suggest that by 1969 the Army had developed a proven counter-insurgency doctrine based on the experience of those campaigns.

But it has been difficult to apply this doctrine in Ulster, owing to its unique status as a province of the United Kingdom while being part of geographical Ireland. The purpose of this study is to discuss the intelligence and psychological warfare aspects of counter-insurgency, showing how and why the Army could not easily apply its doctrine in Northern Ireland. The sources for this study are predominantly unofficial publications, but some are regarded as classic works by recognised experts, and without turning to official sources they provide a clear understanding of the issues.

Terrorist insurgency is a violent process of social reorganisation, involving the premeditated use of criminal techniques by a clandestine organisation to restructure society in accordance with its strategic aims, by creating a "rival state" within that society. Using an on-going process of psychologically selective violence to immobilise and isolate the population, this "parallel government" attempts to expand its control of the population by infiltration and subversion of public institutions and organisations until such time as it can successfully challenge the legal government's power to rule, or at least force it to change policy or grant concessions.

The security forces, therefore, must give priority to defeating the clandestine subversive organisation. And since "the problem of defeating the enemy consists very largely of finding him, it is easy to recognise the paramount importance of good information".[1] Intelligence thus becomes the most important task, and the security forces must concentrate on identification and elimination of members of the subversive organisation. Under normal circumstances this task would be the responsibility of the police Special Branch, but the

22

Army may be required to protect and strengthen the Special Branch.[2] This was the case in Ulster.

There were good reasons for this. First, the Royal Ulster Constabulary (RUC) was politically suspect in the eyes of most Catholics because, in spite of efforts to make it otherwise, the force was almost completely Protestant. The Chief Constable was directly responsible to the Northern Ireland Prime Minister, a situation which gave the impression, reinforced by the RUC's handling of civil rights demonstrations, that it was simply an arm of Protestant domination. As a result, the RUC were not welcome in Catholic areas, and in some places had ceased to function at all.[3]

Secondly, the RUC were understrength and demoralised. The 3,000-man limit imposed by the Northern Ireland Act of 1922 had been lifted in 1963, but as late as spring 1969 plans were to expand the force to only 3,200 by 1975. Thus the RUC were vastly outnumbered in the widespread riots of August 1969 and were unable to contain them. By the time the Army was deployed in Ulster in August, the RUC was a force under considerable strain.

Further blows were to follow. In October Stormont adopted the recommendations of the *Hunt Commission Report*: the B-Specials were disbanded, and the RUC disarmed and made responsible to the courts, in accordance with practice in the rest of the United Kingdom. Though the new establishment was set at 5,000, recruitment fell from 1970–73; in the face of a hostile population with a "frontier mentality", morale was very low. In 1974 the force was still 1,000 below strength, and was suffering casualties at a rate much higher proportionately than the civilian population. Its composition remained largely Protestant—terrorist intimidation ensured that it would remain so—and thus it was still suspect in Catholic eyes. No policeman would dare to patrol in a Catholic area without an Army escort.[4]

Thirdly, the police intelligence organisation was suffering from neglect.

> Financial constraints and lack of foresight led, in Ulster, to insufficient attention being paid to the activities of the Special Branch and other intelligence-gathering agencies. These agencies were insufficient in size to cope with the situation once the conflict started and it is an unfortunate fact that any terrorist organisation can expand at a faster rate than the agencies responsible for providing information on them.[5]

The RUC's files were out of date, and their intelligence network in the Catholic areas badly neglected.

The Army's role

Thus, the Army has largely taken over the intelligence role, a task for which it was not suited initially, being a "foreign" force, unfamiliar with the area, the people, and the sources of information. Aided by the Special Branch, the Army had to rebuild the intelligence apparatus from scratch in a hostile and deteriorating environment. Its contribution to the "intelligence war" has included the following:[6]

1. Army Intelligence Corps personnel seconded to the RUC Special Branch;

2. close Army/RUC cooperation, maintained by joint operations centres;

3. local censuses to build up a street-by-street register of the population, and a card index of known or suspected terrorists, their families, friends, habits—the index is cross-referenced to reports and intelligence summaries so that a complete dossier, including photographs, can be put together for any person;

4. constant mobile and foot patrols, which allow troops to familiarise themselves with their area and to pick up background information;

5. snap searches, particularly vehicle check points established at short notice;

6. joint Army/RUC patrols, and a special Army/RUC murder investigation squad to deal with sectarian killings;

7. covert operations—specially trained plainclothes patrols; use of the Special Air Service Regiment (SAS) in South Armagh; and use of infiltration, captured documents, informers and defectors to gain information;

8. interrogation techniques.

These methods are designed to destroy the subversive organisation by increasing the flow of information to the security forces, by immobilising or eliminating members of the organisation, and by denying them arms, explosives, refuge, recruits, and intelligence. This in turn will break the organisation's hold on the population and will prevent expansion of the "rival state".

Three problem areas have arisen in the Army's intelligence operations. First, after Direct Rule was imposed in March 1972 and William Whitelaw, the new Secretary of State for Northern Ireland, launched his political initiatives, the Government ordered the Army to adopt low-profiled patrolling in the Catholic areas of Belfast and Londonderry. Street patrols were reduced; some areas were patrolled only at night, and then not at all; the Army stopped "hot pursuit" of terrorists and put strict limitations on making arrests and conducting searches. At the same time, the Government began to phase out internment. These decisions immediately endangered the Army's intelligence network, carefully constructed over nearly three years to link intelligence centres to the community. Reduced patrolling led to a loss of overt and background intelligence; the ending of "hot pursuit" took the pressure off the terrorists, allowing them to regroup—some released internees went right back into the IRA; new recruits joined the IRA and remained unknown to the security forces when the conflict intensified, because there were no records on them; and in what had become known as "Free Derry" the IRA succeeded in establishing a "rival state" in defiance of the Government. Intelligence did not begin to flow again until after Operation Motorman in August.[7]

The second problem concerns the Army's covert operations. These had mixed results in the early stages because the terrorist organisation grew faster than the intelligence network. They became more important in 1972 when the Army adopted its low profile, but as overt intelligence operations virtually ceased, covert operations became increasingly hazardous: in October 1972, one of these, the "Four Square Laundry", was blown by the IRA. Further problems surround the use of the SAS. Until January 1976, the Army and the Ministry of Defence consistently denied that the SAS had been operating in Ulster. The regiment's popular image of "highly professional men pursuing enemies of the state by highly uncivilised means" meant that there were grave implications in using the force within the confines of the United Kingdom. The propaganda risks are great: the IRA has accused the Army of using "assassination squads", and incidents such as the border crossing in May 1976 and the kidnapping of Captain Nairac in May 1977 bring unnecessary publicity to the regiment's activities, which rely on secrecy for effect. Moreover, owing to a misunderstanding of its role, the SAS was misused at first, its special skills wasted because ordinary infantry commanders did not know how to make best use of them.[8]

Interrogation

Finally, there is the question of interrogation techniques. On 9 August 1971, 342 persons were arrested and interned. Twelve of these were subjected to "interrogation in-depth", the techniques of which caused a public outcry, both in Britain and in Ireland. Two committees investigated allegations of brutality and the interrogation methods themselves, and after March 1972 the security forces stopped using interrogation in-depth. But the issue remained a political football, and in 1976 the European Commission on Human Rights condemned such methods as torture.[9]

Two problems emerge here: first the public image of interrogation; and secondly, the applicability of such methods in the Ulster situation. Cyril Cunningham, formerly Senior Psychologist for PoW Intelligence at MoD, makes some interesting observations on the public image of interrogation. He feels it is a widely held impression that,

by definition interrogation consists of close and hostile questioning with the sole object of extracting information from a suspect or prisoner, if necessary by force.[10]

He goes on to say that such attitudes, beloved of novelists and film directors, have created a series of myths,

which endow interrogators, . . . with superhuman powers and para-psychological insight in order to account for their apparently exceptional knowledge of their victims' activities and psychological weaknesses.[11]

These myths, of course, reveal an appalling ignorance on the part of the informed public, not to mention governments themselves, of the nature and purposes of interrogation, and they go a long way to explain the public reaction to the mere mention of the word. Though in the short run the popular image had some useful effects, in the long run making an issue of it destroyed interrogation as a useful weapon.

The second problem is more complex. Cunningham argues that since 1917, interrogation has been declining in use as a means of obtaining useful military information. Instead, it is used as it has been used since ancient times—to extract confessions, thereby providing a

political weapon, and to select, induct, and control informers, secret agents, and stoolpigeons. For such purposes, interrogation of the type which holds the public fascination is rather too primitive. If used at all in a really efficient system, its role is merely to cover other methods, to throw the victim off his guard, thereby making it easier to employ indirect and clandestine methods. The hallmark of the expert interrogator is the ability to manipulate the prisoner's social situation, to manoeuvre the victim into a position of stress, tension, or even ostracism, so as to increase pressure and stimulate conversation. The Chinese Communists used such group dynamics with devastating effect in Korea, and it was in response to this experience that the British Army developed its techniques. The Army trained its soldiers to resist this kind of interrogation if taken as PoW, but they also used these methods to obtain information, in Cyprus, Aden, and eventually, Northern Ireland.[12] This, of course, raises the central question—were these methods appropriate to the situation?

From a purely intelligence point of view, the answer is yes—they were effective in obtaining information which could not have been acquired by any other means, and which probably saved many lives. The methods worked directly and indirectly. Those interrogated in-depth gave information on 700 members of the Provisional and Official IRA, including the identification of those responsible for 85 incidents hitherto unsolved, and made possible the discovery of a large quantity of arms, ammunition and explosives—more than had ever been previously located.[13] Indirectly, publicity played an unique, if short-lived, role. The IRA had so frightened themselves with their own propaganda about torture (enhanced, no doubt, by the public hue and cry) that for a while soldiers found it almost impossible to prevent arrested IRA members from telling all before they were handed over to the appropriate authorities. Unfortunately, this attitude changed when the security forces stopped using these methods; the IRA, realising what was happening, soft-pedalled their propaganda to their own members and introduced training in resistance to interrogation.[14]

Interrogation in-depth had revealed a great deal of information in a war where intelligence was at a premium. But success in counter-insurgency operations cannot be measured in purely military terms. The interrogation issue was a political setback for the security forces and a propaganda victory for the IRA. As such, however, it provides a useful vehicle to introduce the discussion of psychological warfare in Northern Ireland.

The definition of terrorist insurgency offered at the beginning of this article places no small emphasis on the psychological effect of the terrorism process—to immobilise and isolate the population. If the intelligence branch has the task of physically breaking the subversive organisation, then the role of the psychological warfare section is to break it psychologically, and to end the "climate of fear" in which the population lives by restoring their sense of security. To this end, the psychological warfare programme should be closely integrated with the other elements of the counter-insurgency campaign. A Director of Psychological Warfare should sit on the security committee, with easy access to the Director of Operations, and with a psyops staff to support him. The government's message, which must be the truth, should be spoken by one voice, directed at two targets: first, the insurgents, to sap their morale, to sow dissension, to encourage surrenders, and to put across the image of a firm, efficient, just, and generous government; secondly, the people themselves, loyal, uncommitted, and hostile, to ensure that the insurgents' objectives do not coincide with those of the people, and to convince the people that they stand to benefit from supporting the government.[15]

The offensive

The Army recognised that in counter-insurgency, "actions speak louder than words", and within a few months of its initial deployment in the province, the Army went on the psychological "offensive". Its efforts since autumn 1969 have included the following.[16]

1. A "hearts and minds" offensive beginning in November 1969—community projects; bisectarian youth clubs in Belfast; dances, hiking trips, sports facilities for young people; and a meals-on-wheels service for the elderly in Londonderry.

2. About the same time, the establishment of joint Army/RUC county security committees, to coordinate activities outside Belfast and Londonderry.

3. From October 1970, the Army used civil representatives (civil servants) in districts to coordinate civil-military efforts and to win over the population. The civil representatives acted as trouble-shooters, dealing with a wide range of problems, from youth and welfare work to damage claims following violence. With representatives from the Army, RUC, and local councils, they sat on coordinating committees which were open to all and would hear complaints and organise action.

4. The public relations programme was stepped up at Army HQ at the end of 1971, with the establishment of an information policy cell—a "PR think tank" which studied trends in reporting and tried to keep one step ahead in the propaganda war.

5. Operation Motorman, 31 July 1972—a classic security operation, perfectly timed to exploit a major IRA blunder (Bloody Friday, 21 July). The Army drove a wedge physically and psychologically between the IRA and the Catholic population, and re-established itself as the protector of the people.

6. A basic policy of openness with the Press, making every facility available to them, providing information, allowing them to come on patrols and operations, and encouraging individual soldiers to explain their job to the press—the Army recognised that on TV the private soldier is sometimes more credible than the GOC.

Problems

Even so, the security forces encountered major problems in the psychological warfare campaign, most of which were beyond the scope of the Army to deal with because they were political problems related directly to Ulster's status as part of the United Kingdom. The first problem was that until Direct Rule, there was no one voice speaking as the authority on Northern Ireland. Stormont and Westminster could disagree publicly on political and security issues, and there was not even unity of outlook within the ruling Unionist Party at Stormont. Thus for nearly three years, the Government's approach to psyops and countering propaganda failed in this crucial aspect. From 1972 onwards the problem was of a different nature: the Army, which was supposed to be neutral in the conflict between Catholic and Protestant, found itself fighting terrorism from both sides. So it was difficult for the security forces to put out a single, direct message drawing a clear distinction between "good" and "bad".

Secondly, complete freedom of the Press, any restriction of which would be politically unacceptable, left the Government and the security forces at the mercy of the media. Unfortunately, emotions run high in the Ulster situation, and the first story, or the most sensational story, out of any incident is the one most likely to be believed. The Army has always felt that the truth will out in the end to the satisfaction of all concerned, but this has not necessarily been the case. Thorough investigation of incidents takes time, and by the time a report appears, the damage already done may be irreparable. Internment, interrogation, and "Bloody Sunday" are classic examples of issues which were cleverly exploited by IRA propagandists before the government could respond in detail. It was not until this year that the Army changed the way it issued information to the Press—emphasising Army successes, and reporting incidents only when specifically requested to provide details.[17]

Thirdly, it has proved impossible to counter IRA propaganda internationally. Until recently, American politicians exploited the strongly Republican Irish lobby for their own domestic purposes. Furthermore, because it regards Ulster as an internal problem, the British Government refuses to discuss it at the United Nations, where damaging charges have gone unanswered.

Finally, during the first few years of the emergency, the Army's own psyops capabilities were limited. One officer remarked that, "It would take an advertising campaign of genius to sell the British Army in the Catholic ghettoes . . .",[18] but in 1970, the Army's entire psyops resources consisted of 30 men, half of whom were overseas and the remainder in England. As late as 1973 there was still a need for a high-ranking civilian to advise the security committee on public relations forward-planning to pre-empt hostile propaganda.[19]

British doctrine

The Army's counter-insurgency doctrine, evolved over 25 years of fighting insurgency in the Empire, was difficult to apply in Ulster because the doctrine was not designed for domestic use, that is, for a semi-peace-keeping role between two warring communities within the United Kingdom. The restrictions and harsh measures which had made a successful campaign possible in Malaya could not be applied readily in Britain, with its long traditions of individual liberty and freedom of the press. In Malaya, thousands of miles from home, operations beyond the jungle fringe could be conducted in almost complete secrecy; in Ulster, the daily movements of a patrol may be seen on TV that evening, in Belfast and in London. Moreover, because Northern Ireland is constitutionally part of the United Kingdom, the problem is a domestic one, and politicians in London are more inclined to intervene directly in the actual conduct of security policy and operations, the decision to order low-profile patrolling being a case in point. Thus, British counter-insurgency doctrine, while applicable from the point of view of general principles, required specific modification to take into account Ulster's unique position. Owing to police weakness, the Army had to adapt intelligence-gathering techniques which had been developed in less visible environments, where they were less open to question or criticism. It is obvious, however, that more thought should have been given to interrogation, which was an obvious target for press interest and IRA propaganda. And it is in the field of psychological warfare that the greatest weaknesses were revealed. Despite several decades of experience in fighting against "propaganda wars backed by force", both the British Government and the Army appear to have been unprepared to fight that kind of war in Ulster. The Army's psyops resources were insignificant at the outbreak of the war, so its efforts tended to be *ad hoc*. The British Government, for its part, showed a complete lack of understanding of the power (for good and evil) of propaganda. Apart from letting itself get trapped into propaganda disasters such as internment, the Government does not appear to have made a conscious effort to "sell" the British case either to the people of the province or to the rest of the United Kingdom. Nor was there, until 1972, an organised plan to counter IRA propaganda or to discourage bad journalism; until that time the IRA held the initiative in the propaganda war. It was weakness in this aspect of the campaign that posed the greatest threat to the intelligence side: the Government was unable to prevent certain methods from being compromised simply by virtue of their being called into question, either deliberately by IRA propagandists or unwittingly by merely inquisitive journalists. The Government and the security forces were continually on the defensive, forced to justify rather than to explain.

It is probably fair to say that, in the light of the current state of affairs in Northern Ireland, many of these problems have been overcome. The security situation, while far from stable, is vastly improved since 1972, owing in no small part to successful intelligence and psychological warfare operations. But it is not unreasonable to conclude that Northern Ireland's close proximity to Britain and its status as a province, the ambivalent position of the Army between the Catholic and Protestant communities, and the high visibility that ensued from this unique position, made intelligence and psychological warfare operations difficult in the first few years of the emergency, and forced the British Army to modify its counter-insurgency doctrine to fit the special requirements of Northern Ireland.

1 Frank Kitson, *Low Intensity Operations: Subversion, Insurgency, Peacekeeping* (London), 1971; repr. 1972, p. 95; see also Sir Robert Thompson, *Defeating Communist Insurgency. Experiences from Malaya and Vietnam* (London), 1966, p. 55.

2 All of the standard works on counter-insurgency devote a great deal of attention to intelligence. See Kitson, pp. 95–131; Thompson, pp. 55–57, 84–89; Richard Clutterbuck, *The Long, Long War: The Emergency in Malaya 1948–1960* (London), 1966, pp. 95–111, 122–31; Julian Paget, *Counter-insurgency Campaigning* (London), 1967, pp. 157–64; and Simon Hutchinson, "The police role in counter-insurgency operations", *RUSI Journal*, 114, December, 1969, pp. 56–61.

3 Richard Clutterbuck, *Protest and the Urban Guerrilla* (London), 1973, pp. 60–66, 70–93.

4 Ibid.; see also Tom Bowden, "Men in the middle—the UK Police", *Conflict Studies*, 68, February 1976, pp. 7–8, 17–18; and Rt Hon. James Callaghan, *A House Divided. The Dilemma of Northern Ireland* (London), 1973. The police suffered 368 casualties in the 1969 riots, and 522 between 1970 and August 1975, which means that nearly one policeman in four had been killed or wounded. Civilian casualties for the same periods amounted to 1 in 150. See Clutterbuck, *Protest and the Urban Guerrilla*, p. 88; and David Barzilay, *The British Army in Ulster* (Belfast), 1975, v. 2, p. 254.

5 Brigadier G. L. C. Cooper, "Some aspects of conflict in Ulster", *British Army Review*, 43, April 1973, p. 72.

6 "Ulster: politics and terrorism", *Conflict Studies*, 36, (June 1973), pp. 9–10; Brigadier W. F. K. Thompson, "Northern Ireland to 1973", *Brassey's Annual*, 1973, p. 77; Robert Moss, "The spreading Irish conflict, Part 2: the security of Ulster", *Conflict Studies*, 17, November 1971, p. 22; Barzilay, *British Army in Ulster*, v. 2, pp. 89, 91; Clutterbuck, *Protest and the Urban Guerrilla*, pp. 100–103; Colonel Norman L. Dodd, "The corporals' war: internal security operations in Northern Ireland", *Military Review*, 56, July 1976, pp. 62–63; Simon Winchester, "How the SAS moved in on the terrorists", *Guardian*, 11 December 1976, p. 11.

7 "Ulster: politics and terrorism", *Conflict Studies*, pp. 6, 10; Thompson, "Northern Ireland to 1973", *Brassey's Annual*, p. 76; Clutterbuck, *Protest and the Urban Guerrilla*, pp. 129–31.

8 Covert operations, by their very nature, must remain secret to be successful; sources on such operations, therefore, are sketchy at best. See "Ulster: politics and terrorism", *Conflict Studies*, pp. 6, 10; Barzilay, *British Army in Ulster*, v. 2, p. 91; Colonel M. A. J. Tugwell, "Revolutionary propaganda and the role of information services in counter-insurgency operations" *Canadian Defence Quarterly*, 3, Autumn, 1973, p. 29; Winchester, "How the SAS . . ." *Guardian*, p. 11; Derek Brown, "SAS men join army patrols", *Guardian*, 11 December 1976, p. 20. There have rarely been more than 60 SAS members in the province at any one time, but soldiers from other units, trained by the SAS, have served in Northern Ireland. Since the summer of 1976 the role of the SAS has been expanded beyond County Armagh. The Army has denied that Captain Nairac was a member of the SAS, but said that he has worked with them.

9 "Ill-treatment but not brutality", *Guardian*, 20 November 1971, p. 8—a summary of the evidence and findings of the Compton Tribunal; Stewart Tendler, "Ulster interrogation is condemned as torture", *The Times*, 3 September 1976, p. 4; staff reporter, "Techniques were changed after report", *The Times*, ibid.; the objectionable methods included the wall standing posture, hooding, noise, sleep deprivation, and diet. Twelve persons were subjected to these methods in August 1971, and two more in October, making a total of 14. The Compton Tribunal investigated allegations of brutality against the security forces, and the committee of Privy Councillors under Lord Parker studied interrogation techniques.

10 Cyril Cunningham, "International interrogation techniques", *RUSI Journal*, 117, September 1972, p. 31.

11 Ibid.

12 Ibid., pp. 32–33; Major Michael Banks, "The Army in Northern Ireland", *Brassey's Annual*, 1972, pp. 151–52. The latest instructions on interrogation procedures, including basic safeguards, were issued in 1965 and were revised after a report on interrogation methods used in Aden. Two changes were made—a requirement for daily medical inspection, and a decision that interrogation should not be carried out by Army personnel. In Ulster, the Army trained the RUC in interrogation. See Mr Roderic Bowen, QC, *Report, on procedures for the arrest,*

interrogation and detention of suspected terrorists in Aden, Comd. 3165 (London), November 1966; Francis Boyd and David Fairhall, "Lord Parker heads inquiry", *Guardian*, 20 November 1971, p. 7.

13 Clutterbuck, *Protest and the Urban Guerrilla*, p. 101.

14 Thompson, "Northern Ireland to 1973", *Brassey's Annual*, p. 77.

15 As with intelligence, the classical writers devote a great deal of attention to psychological warfare. See Chapter 8, "Information Services", in Thompson, *Defeating Communist Insurgency*, pp. 90–102; Kitson, *Low Intensity Operations*, pp. 77–79, 187–97; Paget, *Counter-insurgency Campaigning*, pp. 124, 148–50, 160, 173–74, 178; and Tugwell, "Revolutionary propaganda . . .", *Canadian Defence Quarterly*, pp. 32–34.

16 Banks, "The Army in Northern Ireland", *Brassey's Annual*, pp. 153–54; Clutterbuck, *Protest and the Urban Guerrilla*, p. 89; Cooper, "Some aspects of conflict . . .", *British Army Review*, p. 73; Lieutenant-Colonel P. W. Graham, "Low-level civil/military coordination, Belfast, 1970–73", *RUSI Journal*, 119, September, 1974, pp. 80–84; Lieutenant-Colonel H. C. Millman, "The watch on the Foyle", *The Infantryman*, 86, November 1970, pp. 21–23, 25–26; Captain T. A. Coutts-Britton, "Clausewitz on Ulster", *British Army Review*, 43, April 1973, p. 13; "Ulster: politics and terrorism", *Conflict Studies*, p. 7.

17 Banks, "The Army in Northern Ireland", *Brassey's Annual*, pp. 151–52, 154–55; Cooper, "Some aspects of conflict . . .", *British Army Review*, pp. 76–77; Chris Ryder, "Army plans to stress 'successes' ", *Sunday Times*, 27 February 1977 p. 2.

18 Banks, "The Army in Northern Ireland", *Brassey's Annual*, pp. 153–54.

19 According to Kitson, *Low Intensity Operations*, p. 188, the total psyops forces available to the three services in 1970 consisted of: 1 staff officer at MoD and 1 at each of three overseas HQs; 2 officers on strength at the Joint Warfare Establishment, who ran courses on psyops—those who attended the courses were earmarked as being suitable for employment in psyops should the need arise; a service team, consisting of 1 officer and 11 other ranks, deployed at that time in an undisclosed overseas location (not Ulster); and one reserve team being formed as part of an infantry battalion—if required for an operation it would have to be detached from the unit which would therefore lose all the benefit of having raised and trained the team. See also Thompson, "Northern Ireland to 1973", *Brassey's Annual*, p. 79.

Aside from the sources already quoted, the following provided useful background reading: Brigadier C. N. Barclay, "British Forces and internal security: past experience and the future", *Brassey's Annual*, 1973, pp. 81–95; J. Bowyer Bell, "Revolts against the Crown: the British response to imperial insurgency", *Parameters*, 4, 1974, pp. 31–46; General The Lord Bourne, "The direction of anti-guerrilla operations", *Brassey's Annual*, 1964, pp. 205–13; Lieutenant-Colonel R. L. Clutterbuck, "Bertrand Stewart Prize Essay, 1960", *Army Quarterly and Defence Journal*, 81, October 1960, pp. 161–80; Anthony Deane-Drummond, *Riot Control* (London), 1975; General Sir Richard Gale, "Old problem: new setting", *RUSI Journal*, 117, March 1972, pp. 43–46; and Julian Paget, *Last Post: Aden 1964–67* (London), 1969.

[21]

Extradition Law and Practice in the Crucible of Ulster, Ireland and Great Britain: A Metamorphosis?

by
Bruce Warner

INTRODUCTION

The cases of Gerard Tuite, Dominic McGlinchey, Seamus Shannon and, potentially, Evelyn Glenholmes, are milestones as regards Anglo-Irish relations in the difficult area of extradition between Eire and the two constitutent parts of the United Kingdom — Ulster and Great Britain. Some would say these cases represent a notable step forward in the application of the principle *aut dedere, aut judicare* (extradite or prosecute) to Irish Republican 'terrorists,' while others would insist that these same cases contain an odious reversal of Ireland's historical policy of granting asylum to Irish 'patriots.'

To understand and appreciate fully the significance of these decisions, it is initially necessary to outline the Irish and British positions on the extradition of fugitive political offenders. This paper then considers the practical application of these positions following the renewal of civil conflict after 1969. The effect of the 'flanking movement' contained in the extra-territorial legislation of 1976 is detailed while other suggested solutions to the extradition problem such as an all-Ireland Court are covered briefly. The period after 1981 is examined, particularly in relation to the aforementioned cases. Conclusions drawn from these cases along with the recent signing of the European Convention for the Suppression of Terrorism (ECST) by Ireland provide some signposts regarding the future direction of extradition among the three parties.

BACKGROUND PRE-1969

The Irish Republic occupies as peculiar a place in British political culture as does Ulster in its relationship to Eire. Ireland is a sovereign republic, yet its citizens enjoy the British franchise.[1] Ulster, according to Article 2 of the Irish Constitution, is an integral part of Eire, yet this is without practical effect due to the partition of 1921. This situation is characterized by the number of citizens of each state resident in the other. According to 1979 figures approximately 34,000 Irish citizens were usually resident in Ulster, and calculations based upon the 1971 census indicate 26,183 Ulstermen and 84,038 persons born in Great Britain were resident in Eire.[2] This interpermeability of populations suggests the historical ties in the triangular relationship better than any historical review.

The peculiarity of the relationship is also manifest in the rendition of fugitive offenders among the three. To speak of extradition, as it occurs between other sovereign, foreign states, is somewhat misleading since the return of fugitives between Eire and the U.K. occurs under a

Winter 1987

system of 'backing of warrants.' The system operates not by treaty but under reciprocal legislation and with validated warrants endorsed in Ireland as capable of enforcement in the U.K. and vice versa.[3] Although initiated when Ireland was a British colony, the practice was maintained after the Anglo-Irish Treaty (1921). It lasted until 1964 between Eire and Great Britain but broke down as early as 1929 between Eire and Ulster due to a decision of the Dublin High Court that there was no authority for such a practice.[4] Authorities in Northern Ireland reciprocated by refusing to endorse Irish warrants and from 1930-1965 there was no formal rendition between the two constituent parts of Ireland.[5] That the relationship between Eire and Great Britain worked more smoothly is illustrated by the 109 Irish warrants executed in Great Britain and 89 British warrants executed in Eire during 1957.[6] However, in 1964 the practice ended when decisions in the House of Lords stopped endorsement of Irish warrants in Britain, and an Irish Supreme Court ruled that the process of backing of warrants was repugnant to the Constitution.[7] Thus, in 1964, all three jurisdictions were potential havens from extradition.

Even while the original system was in place, it contained several points of departure from normal extradition procedure. With no judicial control, the accused was protected by none of the normal safeguards. Particularly significant to this study, was an absence of the 'political offence exception.' Nonetheless, these points did not prove the major barrier to the operation of the system possibly for two reasons. Firstly, within Ireland the system ceased operation within a decade of the founding of the Irish Republic while, secondly, the British authorities attempted to be circumspect in advancing warrants with political overtones, as evidenced in a 1923 Home Office circular urging restraint.[8] This demonstrates an acute awareness on the part of the British that rendition of fugitive political offenders, while legally feasible, could prove politically difficult.

British extradition law was codified in the 1870 Extradition Act, and the definition of the political offence developed from case law dating to the 1890s. In *Castioni* (1891), the court ruled that to benefit from the exception to extradition, the offence must not only be incidental to and part of political disturbances, but must also be in furtherance of the same. In *Meunier* (1894), the requirement that there be two parties vying for control of the state was added.[9] These two cases form the basis of the British approach, the 'political incidence' theory.[10] It concentrates on the offence and the context of the offence rather than on the offender and his motive, a distinction clearly made in the case of *Schtraks v. The Government of Israel* by Viscount Radcliffe:

> In my opinion the idea that lies behind the phrase 'offence of a political character' is that the fugitive is at odds with the State that applies for his extradition on some issue connected with the political control or government of the country.... There may, for instance, be all sorts of contending political organizations or

> forces in a country and members of them may commit
> all sorts of infractions of the criminal law in the belief
> that by so doing they will further their political ends:
> but if the central government stands apart and is con-
> cerned only to enforce the criminal law that has been
> violated by these contestants, I see no reason why
> fugitives should be protected by this country from its
> jurisdiction on the ground that they are political of-
> fenders.[11]

This is how British law stood in the mid-1960s when the Irish Republic formulated its own Extradition Act.

Faced with the breakdown of the old system, authorities on both sides of the Irish Sea worked out a new arrangement, known in the U.K. as the Backing of Warrants (Republic of Ireland) Act 1965, and in Eire as Part III of the Extradition Act, 1965. The terms of the Irish legislation were heavily influenced by the 1957 Council of Europe Multilateral Extradition Convention. Lacking the requirement of a *prima facie* case,[12] which the British use in dealing with other states, the Irish legislation differs significantly from British law. O'Higgins suggests that Irish insistence on dropping such items was due to a desire to harmonize the Anglo-Irish practice with the extradition procedures followed with other states.[13]

More significant, for the purpose of this paper, is the discrepancy in the statement of the 'political offence exception' contained in the two pieces of legislation. The British law refers to denial of surrender for an "offence of a political character" while the Irish act refers to "a political offence or an offence connected with a political offence."[14] Therefore, two pieces of legislation existed which intended to impose identical and reciprocal obligations and which, by their wording, might not. The two phrases do not, necessarily, define the same offence. Certainly in 1965, it was unclear whether the Irish courts would turn to British case law for a definition of political offences or, given the central role of the 1957 Convention, to European examples. In his commentary, written the year after the 1965 Act came into being, O'Higgins opined that, "... the Irish courts in interpreting this provision will not be able to rely upon Anglo-American decisions... . They will have nothing to guide them as to the meaning of 'political offence'."[15]

The wider interpretation given by the Irish courts in their developing case law from 1965 until 1970 prior to the onset of the latest manifestation of 'The Troubles' is best displayed in two cases. *Bourke v. the Attorney-General,* and *The State (Magee) v. O'Rourke* resulted in Supreme Court decisions and both contained a noteworthy dissent by Mr. Justice Fitzgerald, who later held the post of Chief Justice briefly in 1973-74. In the former case, the defendant assisted the escape and sheltering of a Soviet spy jailed in England. The Supreme Court ruled this offence was connected with a political offence, and stated that the 'connected offence' itself did not have to be political in character. Chief Justice O'Dalaigh argued that the connection must be "spelt out by the courts in the widest possible manner.''[16] In his dissent Justice Fitzgerald noted it was the spy's original offence which was political, not his offence of escape; therefore, Bourke's offence of assisting the escape could not be connected with a political offence. However, the majority of the court disagreed with Fitzgerald's view.

In the latter case extradition was requested for blatantly non-political crimes, but the appellant claimed he might be charged with political offences if returned. In support he produced affidavits concerning his role in a 1963 IRA raid on a British military barracks in Ulster, and the fact that he had been questioned about it by the Royal Ulster Constabulary (RUC). The Chief Justice gave the court's opinion that due to the appellant's virtual admission of complicity in the political offence of the raid, Magee had brought himself within the purview of S.50(2)(b) of the Irish Act. This limited application of the specialty rule in Anglo-Irish law disallows extradition if there are 'substantial grounds' for belief that, once returned, a fugitive will be tried for a connected offence or a political offence. In the early 1970s the Irish Supreme Court was evidently willing to impute bad faith to the prosecuting authorities of Ulster. This is explicit in Justice Fitzgerald's dissent with which Justice Teevan was in accord. They felt that Magee failed to produce the necessary 'substantial grounds' and were unwilling to speculate that the Ulster authorities might not adhere to the limited specialty rule.[17] Only two of the five judges of the Irish Supreme Court were willing to extend the benefit of the doubt to the judiciary in Northern Ireland.

While the British position regarding the political offence exception prior to 1970 can be characterized as 'political incidence' theory, the Irish position is less easily defined. Clearly Irish courts do not apply the British approach, but, as various commentators note, there have been too few published cases to determine the Irish position absolutely, beyond its tendency toward the more broadly defined European approach.[18]

As the Irish Supreme Court worked toward defining its position, the conflict in Ulster was coming to a head in 1969-70. Concomitantly, the British courts maintained their adherence to their stated position when faced by Irish extradition requests for two Irish gunmen. Patrick Dwyer was held in England after jumping bail on a charge of shooting at officers of the Garda Siochana. The gunfire allegedly came from a car transporting arms and came in an attempt to evade arrest. Dwyer claimed membership of a group splintered from the IRA. In his ruling granting extradition, Lord Parker stated he was not satisfied that shooting at police officers was a political offence.[19] It is probable, given the decisions in the cases of Bourke and Magee, that an Irish court would have decided otherwise.

Of equal import is the case of Patrick F. Keane accused in Eire of two bank robberies and the murder of a Garda during the commission of one robbery. He claimed membership of Saor Eire which had acknowledged it carried out several similar actions with the purpose of providing arms for comrades in Ulster.[20] Keane had been a member of the IRA until 1964, served time for an attack on the governing Fianna Fail party office in 1967, and was often questioned about other occurrences by the Garda. This information was given as background to his application for a writ of *habeas corpus* from the High Court, claiming he feared that if returned for a non-political offence he would be detained or tried for a political offence under S.2(2)(b). Again Chief Justice Lord Parker refused the application stating that Keane had failed to prove 'substantial grounds' for his claim.[21] This decision was upheld unanimously by the Law Lords to whom Keane was given leave to appeal because the matter rested on a point of law of general public import. In giving the decision of the Law Lords, Lord Pearson noted two affidavits from the Irish Attorney General stating Keane would only be tried on the offences cited in the warrant:

> assurances such as are contained in these two affidavits are properly admissible and can properly be taken into account under S.2(2)(b) of the Act, although, in view of the uncertainty of future developments and the possibility of new political situations and exigencies arising, they should not be regarded as conclusive.[22]

The Keane decision was completely opposite the highest Irish court's ruling in the Magee case. While the Irish Supreme Court apparently attributed actions of 'bad faith' to the courts in Northern Ireland, the highest British court was unwilling to do so in regard to courts in the Republic. A clearer division cannot be found.

'THE TROUBLES' REVISITED

The first British military fatality in the renewed conflict in Northern Ireland came in February 1971, quickly followed by the introduction of internment without trial by authorities in Belfast. In the context of the worsening situation, the RUC began to request the return, from Eire, of those who had committed offences in Ulster. Due to the lack of centralized collection of statistics and the inevitable discrepancy among sources, it is practically impossible to determine an exact figure for the number of returns sought by the Ulster authorities in these early years. In November 1972 Joint Minister of State for Northern Ireland David Howell claimed that extradition was sought from Eire in 31 cases during 1971.[23] A second source claims the same figure of 31 warrants for 'subversive activities,'[24] but a third, by far the most well-documented source, claims only 15 and lists the individuals by name and by the date the warrant was forward to Eire.[25] It must also be pointed out that there are instances of more than one request being forwarded for specific individuals. This should be taken into account when considering any claim concerning the number of unsuccessful extradition applications made by the RUC. A further point to note is the number of fugitives who, after a warrant was forwarded to Eire, were subsequently apprehended in Northern Ireland. A more detailed examination of these statistics is found in the final section of this paper.

These considerations are evident in the cases of two groups of Provisional IRA (PIRA) fugitives who escaped custody in Ulster in late 1971.

Of seven individuals who broke out of Belfast's Crumlin Road Jail on November 16, 1971 and whose extradition was requested, five were eventually recaptured in Ulster.[26] A further three who escaped on December 2, 1971 and whose return was requested on December 15, 1971 illustrate both points mentioned above. Martin Meehan was recaptured in Belfast in August 1972, and there was a second extradition request made for Anthony 'Dutch' Docherty in January 1972.

Other problems encountered as the requests multiplied, due to the violence in Ulster, are illustrated by two of the first applications before the Irish courts in 1971. Edward MacDonald, Thomas McNulty and Edward Hamill came before Monaghan District Court in September. The extradition warrant listed a charge of possession of explosives in County Tyrone in early 1971. The judge, who was the only Protestant district justice in Eire, held that there was insufficient evidence before the court to identify the three as those named in the warrant and he discharged them after commenting he was not satisfied with the *de jure* status of the requesting state, Northern Ireland.[27] A similar breakdown in the process occurred with the request for Sean Gallagher. He was detained in October on a warrant alleging murder of an RUC constable but released by Killybegs District Court. The court claimed, as in the previous case in a different court, insufficient identification evidence.[28] However, in answer to a parliamentary question in London, a government minister noted that a photograph, full description, details of tattoo marks, fingerprints and a witness were available. The Minister of State for the Foreign & Commonwealth Office outlined the British position on such decisions:

> ... the Executive has no power to interfere in the actions of the judiciary. For this reason, it would serve no useful purpose to raise officially with the Government of the Irish Republic decisions made by the courts of that country. On certain occasions, however, there have been puzzling features about such decisions in extradition cases, for example, refusal to accept apparently conclusive identification evidence, and we have asked the authorities of the Irish Republic to explain them.[29]

Through 1972 the situation remained static. While British Ministers claimed there were approximately 155 persons wanted by the RUC for questioning and known to be in Eire, according to figures released in Parliament, only sixteen requests for extradition were made to Eire throughout 1972.[30] In Eire itself the government clampdown on the IRA (Provisionals and Officials) was strengthened in May with the formation of the non-jury Special Criminal Court (SCC). It was to try 'scheduled offences' under the Offences Against the State Act 1939 and various arms and explosives offences. In October 1972 Irish Justice Minister O'Malley noted that the bulk of those convicted before the SCC were from north of the border.[31] Noteworthy as well was the apparent tightening of the Irish government's attitude towards extradition. Several of those released by the district courts in 1971 were rearrested in 1972, often at the instigation of the Irish authorities. In many of these cases the district courts then granted the extradition requests and those affected appealed to the High Court in Dublin.

This apparent tightening of attitude on the part of the Irish authorities, as distinct from the judiciary, may be attributable in part to the increase in violence in Eire directly linked to the conflict in Ulster. Furthermore, in 1972-73 the Republic itself was beginning to request the return, from Ulster, of fugitives involved in acts committed in Eire in the context of the overall conflict. In October 1972 seven Republicans detained in Curragh Camp in the Republic escaped from custody. Four of the group were from Ulster and on November 11, 1972 one, Thomas Corrigan, was recaptured there. He was extradited to Eire two days later by a court in Armagh and chose not to appeal the decision.[32]

In another case a Protestant gunman, Robert Taylor, was accused by Irish police of the murder of a couple in County Donegal on January 1, 1973. Ordered extradited by a court in Northern Ireland, he appealed. He claimed the benefit of the 'political offence exception' alleging that one of the victims was affiliated with the PIRA. This was not accepted in the Queen's Bench Divisional Court and a writ of *habeas corpus* was denied. The only evidence offered in support of Taylor's claim was his personal assertion and an affidavit which stated that he had received information that one of the victims was a Provisional. In dismissing the application Lord Chief Justice Lowry found the evidence "totally imprecise and lacking in detail" and further it was

> impossible to find any other judicial pronouncement which would support a definition of the phrase 'an offence of a political character' wide enough to assist the present applicant.[33]

Taylor was extradited to Eire in June, in an atmosphere of widespread Loyalist demonstrations orchestrated by the Ulster Defence Association (UDA) and threats of disruption and worse if Taylor were returned to Eire for trial. Ironically, the SCC acquitted the defendant after his extradition, ruling that there were irregularities in the only major piece of evidence against him, namely, his own confession.[34]

During this period the appeal procedure in the Republic was proving extremely lengthy. The three applications before the courts in December 1972 rose to ten by July 1973.[35] However the Irish government pressed the rules committee of the High Court to devise a speedier procedure so that cases would be heard by the High Court within three months of a lower court extradition order. By Novmber 1973 a total of eleven persons were appealing extradition orders[36] and the first High Court decision on these matters came in December. Anthony Francis Shields was charged with possessing ammunition in Belfast in 1971 and fled south while on bail. He admitted membership of an illegal organization and claimed the RUC had threatened him with charges over the attempted murder of several British soldiers. In quashing the extradition order, Justice Butler based his findings on Shields' evidence of IRA membership. He noted that it had not been challenged, adding he

could come to no other conclusion but that the offence
charged in this case was a political offence and that if
the plaintiff did have possession of the ammunition, it
was to be used in furtherance of IRA activities.[37]

This decision accepted that activities engaged in by the IRA would
be considered political by the second highest court in the Irish Republic.
The Shields ruling was soon buttressed by two more involving much
more serious charges. In both cases the High Court's opinion was given
by Mr. Justice Finlay who was to become Chief Justice in 1985. Sean
Gallagher was detained on the second warrant for his return. His alleged
murder of the RUC constable was deemed political based on previous
cases and Justice Finlay stated that if an offence was committed by someone seeking to change by force the government then that crime was a
political offence.[38] It is also worth noting the comments of Justice Finlay
in the case of James 'Seamus' O'Neill. He was accused of an RUC station bombing which killed two passersby and had been ordered extradited for the murder of one of them. On appeal, the murder was ruled
a political offence. In so ruling Mr. Justice Finlay stated,

> I am not entitled to have any regard to the fact that the
> admitted activities of the present applicant seemed to
> breach any concept of humanity or any civilized form of
> conduct.[39]

These two cases reinforced the position of the Irish courts that,
however serious the offence and whatever its effects on the victims, so long
as the applicants could prove a connection with the activities of the IRA,
their crimes would be ruled political offences. This was taken even further
in the ruling in the case of Roisin McLaughlin. The crime alleged was the
murder of three unarmed, off-duty British soldiers, lured into an ambush
in which the plaintiff took part. Following the district court decision to
allow extradition, there were rallies in Eire, similar to those in Ulster over
the Taylor case. Provisional Sinn Fein Vice-President Maire Drumm
issued the thinly-veiled threat that if McLaughlin were extradited to Northern Ireland, the conflict there could spread into the Republic.[40]
McLaughlin's appeal was heard in December 1974 and was remarkable in
that, unlike previous appeals, the appellant neither gave evidence nor admitted or denied commission of the offence. This removed the usual statement of motive before the court and a political link had to be built through
the evidence of others. McLaughlin's husband claimed the RUC had informed him they believed she was involved in the ambush in her role as a
PIRA intelligence officer. Mr. Justice Finlay ruled out any likelihood of a
personal motive of revenge or robbery due to the number of people involved in the ambush, the degree of organization, and the obvious intent to kill
all the soldiers involved. Echoing his previous findings he wrote,

> There could be no doubt that even murder, and even
> such a dastardly murder as that described ... in this case,
> if carried out by an organization which, by such
> methods, sought to overthrow the government of a
> country by force, was a political offence.[41]

The fullest expression of the Irish position concerning fugitive political offenders at that stage came in the case of a Catholic priest accused of handling explosives in Scotland. Michael Farrell characterizes the decision as remaining "for almost a decade ... the key pronouncement on the political offence exception in relation to the IRA and the Northern Troubles."[42]

In the case of Father Bartholemew Burns, as in the others, there was no doubt concerning his involvement in the offence charged. Two Irishmen convicted in Glasgow of the same explosives offence implicated the priest[43] and he himself admitted the offence in his appeal. Along with the appeal Father Burns was also reported to be attempting to challenge the constitutionality of the Extradition Act.[44] It is necessary to quote directly certain segments of Mr. Justice Finlay's upholding of the appeal for two reasons: to reinforce points made in previous rulings, and to facilitate a comparison with his decisions made over a decade later when he became Chief Justice of the Irish Supreme Court.

Justice Finlay noted that the only issue necessary for this determination was whether the safekeeping of explosives for the PIRA, which was engaged in the attempt to "overthrow and change the political structures of a country by the use of violence," was an offence connected with a political offence or was, in itself, a political offence.[45] Referring to the Castioni decision and the political incidence theory of the U.K., he stated,

> It seems again to me impossible to categorize the existing situation in Northern Ireland and Britain ... as being otherwise than a political disturbance part of and incidental to which is the keeping of explosives for the organization known as the IRA.[46]

This was the sole question on which Justice Finlay was required to rule by his own determination and he pronounced himself satisfied that the offence was political. However, Justice Finlay went a step further and stated his belief that the same conclusion would be reached by a common sense appraisal of what constituted a political offence.[47]

While the aforementioned cases primarily concerned offences alleged to have been committed in Northern Ireland, other requests from Great Britain for a number of individuals accused of involvement in bombings in England fared as poorly. The first concerned Patrick Joseph Gilhooley, accused of planting a bomb at Aldershot station. He was detained in Eire on an extradition warrant on leaving Portlaoise Prison on December 1, 1975 on completion of a sentence for IRA membership.[48] Extradition was granted by a lower court and appealed to the High Court.

In the interim, the case of Margaret McKearney occasioned a series of confused moves in London and Dublin but never reached the actual state of the forwarding of a warrant to Eire. She was the subject of an April 1975 arrest warrant in Hampshire and in September became the center of a burst of media speculation. The commander of the Scotland

Yard Bomb Squad claimed that an application for her extradition was likely, and the police issued an unusually detailed account of her alleged activities as a courier of arms and explosives, and her involvement in several shootings. Police sources were quoted as believing there was little chance of a successful extradition, but felt that the widespread publicity would neutralize her further usefulness to the Provisionals. On November 29th she was detained by the Irish Special Branch under the 1939 Act but was released within 48 hours due to a lack of evidence. Scotland Yard was then reported to have officially requested her detention pending the forwarding of an extradition warrant which was said to be with the Director of Public Prosecutions (DPP). However the application was never sent to Dublin and there was media speculation that the British were awaiting the outcome of the Gilhooley appeal, then before the High Court in Dublin.[49] This reticence, especially following British police claims in September, caused not a little uncertainty and anger in the Irish capital. The result was a report that "there is now widespread feeling in the Irish coalition Cabinet that the police in Britain do not possess enough evidence to support the charges they made against Miss McKearney in two press conferences."[50]

Whether or not this was the case, if the major reason for the delay was to await the outcome of Gilhooley's appeal the British were to be disappointed. In line with previous decisions, the High Court ruled the offence political, in spite of the 'disagreeable' nature of the offence according to Mr. Justice McMahon. Gilhooley's statement in court claiming IRA membership indicates why a court in Eire would have little difficulty in finding that his crimes were political offences. He states,

> The IRA is an organization, one of the aims and objectives of which is, by the use of armed force if necessary, to secure radical change in the continued government of that part of Ireland not yet reintegrated with the remainder.[51]

Finally there was the case of Brendan Swords linked to an IRA arsenal unearthed in London in April 1976.[52] Arrested in Eire in February 1977 on IRA membership charges he was acquitted in March. Soon after, Scotland Yard applied for his extradition charging involvement in a series of bombings. On appeal to the High Court his offences were, as usual, ruled political and he was rendered immune from extradition. The timing of the offences proved crucial. When a Bomb Squad officer appeared before the district court in July 1977, he stated the warrant was for conspiracy to cause explosions and that a series of sixteen incidents "obviously committed by the same team"[53] was under investigation. This particular offence was the only one under the new Criminal Law (Jurisdiction) Act which, if committed in Great Britain, could be tried by the courts in Eire. Unfortunately for the British police, the extraterritorial legislation was not retrospective and the offences were committed prior to the CL(J)A coming into force. Swords joined Gilhooley, McKearney and others as beneficiaries of the asylum Eire was granting Irish Republican bombers and gunmen through the actions of her courts.

While British authorities were singularly unsuccessful in securing the return of fugitives charged with offences committed in Great Britain, in contrast, the British courts continued to return fugitives accused of committing offences in Eire which were part of the Irish conflict. Space does not permit detailed examination though two distinctive reasons can be considered.

In the celebrated case of the Littlejohn brothers, wanted for armed robbery in Ireland, the brothers claimed the political offence exception stating that they had been working in the Republic for British Intelligence as agents provocateurs. The Ministry of Defence admitted contact with the pair but dismissed claims that offences committed in Ireland were at their behest. Following extradition proceedings held *in camera*, the two were returned to Eire in March 1973 and subsequently convicted by the SCC. One year later they escaped and Kenneth Littlejohn made it back to England. He was rearrested there in December 1974 and during these extradition proceedings the details of the secret 1973 proceedings were revealed. In the earlier court case the applicants claimed that the robbery was a political crime within S.2(2) of the 1965 Act due to their links with the IRA. This connection was not doubted by the court, nor was it disputed that the raid was to obtain funding for the IRA. However in 1973, Lord Widgery CJ referred to Viscount Radcliffe's dictum of 1962 regarding the court standing apart from the political issues. In summary he wrote,

> Thus one reaches the stage now on the weight of authority ... that an offence may be of a political character, either because the wrongdoer had some direct ulterior motive of a political kind when he committed the offence, or because the requesting state is anxious to obtain possession of the wrongdoer's person in order to punish him for his politics rather than for the simple criminal offence referred to in the extradition proceedings.[54]

Neither of these conditions pertained in 1973 so the brothers were extradited. The only new element injected into the proceedings in 1975 was Kenneth Littlejohn's claim that trial by the SCC after their initial extradition indicated their crime was a political offence under S.2(2)(b). Lord Widgery examined the establishment of the SCC under the 1939 Act and could find no acknowledgement that trial before this non-jury court meant the offence in question was necessarily political. Extradition was therefore granted. Had the brothers carried out their robbery in Ulster on behalf of the IRA it is likely that an Irish court would have refused their extradition to Ulster based on a reading of the same facts. The key difference is that in this hypothetical reverse situation it could be argued that the suspects were at odds with the government in Ulster and were engaged in an attempt to change it by obtaining funds for the IRA. By no means could the brothers be conceived of as attempting to overthrow the Irish government in the case, despite their acknowledged links to British Intelligence.

The second instance also involved an alleged link to British Intelligence and is noteworthy because it referred to an alleged abduction in

Eire, the first of several. William Poacher failed in an attempt before the High Court in Great Britain in December 1973 to stop his extradition to Eire. He claimed to fear for his life because of his participation in the suspected abduction of a senior PIRA member, Sean Collins, from Eire to Ulster. Lord Widgery stated that it was apparent the appellant had infiltrated the PIRA to act as an informant at the behest of the British security forces. The fact that he feared for his life as result was not grounds on which the court could act.[55] The abduction to which Poacher alluded occurred in January 1972 in Dundalk and also allegedly involved Kenneth Littlejohn. Collins' solicitor claimed that a man resembling Littlejohn abducted his client at gunpoint in the Republic on January 13, 1972 and drove him into Ulster where he was delivered into the custody of the British Army.[56]

If these claims were valid, this case marks a descent into illegality by elements of the security forces in Ulster, a move which can be traced to frustration over the lack of success in extradition from Eire. Other incidents have recently come to light which suggest that the alleged Collins kidnapping was not an isolated incident.[57]

Several points emerge from an examination of Anglo-Irish extradition practice in the period up to the mid-1970s and the enactment of the aforementioned extra-territorial legislation. First, and most compelling, is the difference in the interpretations of the political offence exception between the Irish and British courts. Courts in the U.K. maintained a strict adherence to the political incidence theory and the related idea that the fugitive must be at odds with the requesting state over some issue connected with the governance of the country. The Irish courts have followed a broader interpretation, though it is clear that the cases studied, in some instances, could also be defined as political under the British interpretation. Recalling Mr. Justice Finlay's words, they could also be considered political under any 'common sense' interpretation of the term and as several Irish judges maintained, this was the only issue before them for a judicial decision. The judges had no authority to comment upon the morality, or lack of morality in what were, in many cases, heinous crimes of murder and mutilation involving innocent civilian bystanders.

While the courts limited their attention to strictly legal determinations, it can in no way be said that the Irish authorities were 'soft' on the IRA. The IRA had been a proscribed organization in Eire well before being so designated in Ulster. Further, under the amended 1939 Act, the unsupported assertion by a police officer that he believed the defendant to be a member of the IRA provided all the evidence necessary for conviction in the Irish Republic on that charge. These are not the acts of a government lax in its concern with the IRA. Perhaps the position of the Irish coalition government in power in the mid-1970s is best summarized in the following statement of the Minister of Justice before the Dáil in April 1975:

> I feel that there is well nigh universal embarrassment in
> this country at the predicament in which our judges find
> themselves, being constrained as they are in ...

extradition applications to release persons accused of most serious crimes. This widespread embarrassment is compounded by the knowledge that the release of these fugitives is a matter of grave scandal in Northern Ireland where our fellow Irishmen have suffered so much in their persons and properties at the hands of these people.[58]

EXTRA-TERRITORIAL JURISDICTION — A FLANKING MOVEMENT

The deterioration in the security situation and the inability of the Ulster authorities to secure extradition of Republican gunmen occurred in the context of the changing political situation in Ulster and Eire. On 'Bloody Sunday' January 1972, the shootings by the Parachute Regiment in Londonderry crystallized anti-British feeling among large segments of the Nationalist minority hitherto unmoved by the situation. Two months later, in March, the Stormont government was suspended and direct rule from London was instituted. In Eire, the Garda arrested Provisionals, seized arms and on December 22, 1971, had its first serious confrontation with the PIRA when the arrest of three members in County Donegal occasioned serious riots.[59] At the 'Ard Fheis' of Provisional Sinn Fein in October 1973 Vice-President David O'Connell reiterated the threat that Dublin would not remain immune in the event of extradition of Republicans to Ulster.

It was in this atmosphere that representatives from London, Dublin and Belfast met at the Sunningdale Conference in December 1973. The main aim was to structure a power-sharing executive but conference members also discussed the idea of a common law-enforcement area to bypass the problems of extradition. Dublin's ideas had been put to the Northern Ireland Secretary, William Whitelaw, in November by Irish Foreign Minister Dr. Garrett Fitzgerald. The conference led to the formation of an eight-man[60] legal commission to examine various alternatives. All parties at Sunningdale had agreed,

> ... that persons committing crimes of violence, however motivated, in any part of Ireland should be brought to trial irrespective of the part of Ireland in which they are located.[61]

The Commission examined four alternatives: all-Ireland Court, extradition, extra-territorial jurisdiction, and mixed courts. The first was dispensed with as being too involved to deal quickly with the problem as the Commission was ordered.[62] The idea of amending extradition procedures by appending a list of scheduled offences for which the political offence exception could not be claimed was discussed but discarded as the Commissioners could not agree on the legal validity of extraditing those who, at present, enjoyed immunity contingent upon the exception. The concept of mixed courts containing judges from both jurisdictions was debated, however, it was found to provide no legal or procedural advantage over purely domestic courts for the purposes of extra-territorial jurisdiction.

Winter 1987

Both parties were able to agree upon the use of extra-territorial jurisdiction. Those opposed to extradition, the Irish jurists, favored it above all other methods, while the British jurists found it worthy of recommendation where extradition was unavailable. Further, the speed with which extra-territorial jurisdiction might be implemented was a matter of prime consideration for the Commission.

Two specific points were stressed by the Commissioners in choosing this method. First, its success depended upon measures designed to secure evidence and testimony and move it between jurisdictions. Second, it would only apply to a schedule of offences comprising crimes of violence, a list appended to the report.[63]

Even prior to the formation of the Commission, some crimes had fallen under extra-territorial jurisidiction. On December 20, 1973 the Irish government revived the dormant S.9 of the Offences Against the Person Act, 1861,[64] allowing the prosecution of an Irish citizen in Eire for the crime of murder committed in Ulster. The change was followed by a sweep of IRA suspects in Eire and the first official meeting of RUC and Garda chiefs to take place in years. However, the legislation was not retroactive and no cases were known to be prosecuted under its terms. Reportedly, an Irish government official remarked,

> The fact that this exceptional legal provision has never been invoked shows clearly that there has been no evidence available against anyone resident in the Republic during the past two years ... that is not the impression given recently by some spokesmen in London and Belfast.[65]

Yet, the Irish courts dealt promptly with Republicans guilty of crimes within Eire. From the May 1972 introduction of the SCC to February 1974, a total of 338 persons were convicted of 'IRA offences' primarily related to arms and explosives.[66]

The collapse of the power-sharing executive left the agreement on extra-territorial jurisdiction as the only matter of substance to survive from the Sunningdale talks. The two parliaments drafted implementing legislation, adding only the offence of causing explosions in Great Britain in response to the mainland bombing campaigns; this was achieved by amending the Explosive Substances Act, 1883.[67] Legislation passed smoothly through Westminster but not through the Dáil. The opposition Fianna Fail fought it as unconstitutional,[68] preferring the all-Ireland Court option. However, the Criminal Law (Jurisdiction) Act, 1976 passed with a small majority in March 1976 to become law on June 1, 1976, concurrent with the British Criminal Jurisdiction Act, 1975. Former Chief Justice, now President, O'Dalaigh referred the Act to the Supreme Court for a ruling on its constitutionality and it had been pronounced legal and valid.[69] Following its enactment, the PIRA retaliated with a threat against any "Free State civil servant, court official, solicitor, counsel, judge or police officer"[70] administering the law, breaking the precedent set by the original IRA, dating to 1963, of not considering members of the Irish security forces as legitimate targets. In making this threat the PIRA demonstrated the extent which it feared successful implementation of the Act. During the election campaign of 1977, Fianna Fail leader Jack Lynch hinted his party would scrap the law if elected:

> I have already said that I regard it as unworkable. We
> will look at it again. Our preference is for all-Ireland
> courts operating on both sides of the border.[71]

Fianna Fail won the election but left the CL(J)A in place. The legislation has thus far proved of limited use. As far as can be ascertained, there have been only a few cases in Eire and perhaps two in Ulster, undoubtedly due in part to the problems of obtaining evidence and witnesses just as the Commission predicted. As has been repeatedly noted, some 90% of terrorist-type convictions in Ulster are the result of suspects incriminating themselves during interrogation which can last up to seven days.[72] The RUC cannot interrogate suspects in Eire or even be present at their questioning by the Garda. Due to the insufficiency of forensic evidence in such cases confessions are often the key to conviction. Understandably, there is a wariness concerning police methods of interrogation. In Eire, Amnesty International, and in Ulster, both Amnesty and the European Commission on Human Rights, have discovered evidence of maltreatment of suspects by the police.[73] Given this, it is perhaps surprising that there have been any prosecutions at all under the legislation and it is worth examining them in closer detail to ascertain their special features.

Despite media speculation that a charge was likely against a gunman recovering in Dundalk after a border gunbattle, the first prosecution occurred in Ulster. Five men were charged with kidnapping British army intelligence officer Captain R. Nairac in Ulster and murdering him across the border in Eire in May 1977. On December 15, 1978 they were sentenced to terms ranging from three years to life on a variety of charges including abduction, murder, manslaughter and firearms offences.[74]

The case was noteworthy in that a Garda officer gave evidence in a Belfast court on the murder which was the only extra-territorial offence committed.[75] Yet both sides initially displayed some reticence. A sixth person, Liam Townson, was charged in Eire with the murder, convicted on November 8, 1977 and given a life sentence. While a British officer travelled to Dublin and gave evidence, Townson's defence team was denied access/use to statements taken from the other five in Ulster by the RUC.[76] When the trial began in Ulster in February 1978, it was temporarily adjourned because the Irish would not release certain exhibits from the Townson trial for evidence, claiming that the exhibits would be needed at some unspecified future date for Townson's appeal.[77] Despite these problems, the authorities won convictions in both trials.

As far as can be determined there has been only one other prosecution in Ulster under the Criminal Jurisdiction Act 1975. Former Stormont Speaker Sir Norman Stronge and his son were murdered in Northern Ireland on January 21, 1981 and Owen McCartan Smyth was

71

Dimensions of Irish Terrorism

charged in Northern Ireland with their deaths. However he was charged under the CJA with counselling and procuring the murder in Eire as he did not take part in the actual murder, which occurred in Ulster and thus was not extra-territorial. Two points of interest came out of the trial. First, court proceedings temporarily transferred to Dublin to enable Justice Hatton to hear evidence there, and Smyth was taken to that city under guard. Despite a separate hearing in Dublin's High Court, where he claimed a right to stay in Eire, he was returned to Ulster. Smyth further claimed he had not been offered the option of trial in Eire, but Justice Hamilton ruled this not to be the case and ordered his return to Ulster.[18] The second point worthy of comment actually caused the abandonment of the charges. Under S.6(3) of the CJA the initiation of extra-territorial proceedings must have the consent of the Attorney-General. The Northern Ireland court ruled that since such consent had not been obtained the charges were therefore null and void.[19] Seemingly, this is indicative of a basic ineptitude on the part of the prosecutors which can only be partially excused by their lack of familiarity due to the infrequency of cases under the CJA.

The situation south of the border presents more evidence from which one can draw tentative conclusions concerning the efficacy of the extra-territorial laws. Press speculation mounted in 1979 that Desmond O'Hare was to be tried under the CL(J)A for crimes committed in Ulster but such a line was not pursued, perhaps because he was jailed for nine years under the 1939 Act on November 11, 1979.[60] The first actual prosecution in Eire came in 1980 and concerned the murder of a former Ulster Defence Regiment (UDR) officer in Ulster. Three men were charged and, with the absence of confessions, the case hinged upon forensic evidence. It took the SCC just thirty minutes to acquit the suspects. Mr. Justice Hamilton explained the court's reasoning, citing the purely circumstantial character of the forensic evidence. It could not be proven beyond a reasonable doubt that mud and hay on the defendants' clothing, while matching that found at the crime scene, could have come only from the crime scene. Further, though firearms discharge residue on their clothes connected them to the firing of a gun, it did not necessarily connect them with the murder in question.[61] The court had no option but to acquit.

The next case in Eire produced a conviction but was overturned on appeal. Again, the crime was the murder of a former UDR officer and while it occurred this time in Eire, the accused's guilt or innocence hinged upon his gathering information about the victim in Ulster. The basis for conviction was a confession in an unsigned statement. The Court of Criminal Appeal quashed the conviction on July 28, 1981, ruling that although there was no breach of fair procedure while the statement was taken, the defendant had been held for twenty-two hours of almost continuous interrogation by that point. Mr. Justice Griffin gave the court's opinion that this went beyond the bounds of fairness. The confession should not have been admitted in evidence and without it there was insufficient evidence to convict.[62]

During the same period the Irish authorities lost another case under the CL(J)A. An RUC reservist was kidnapped in Eire and murdered in Ulster in an exact reversal of the circumstances of the Nairac case. The defendant's lawyer, Sean McBride, argued that his client had not been given the option of trial in the jurisdiction in which the crime was committed as offered in the extra-territorial law. Justice Hamilton agreed that this was correct; the court had failed to meet its statutory obligation and thus must disavow jurisdiction and dismiss the case. The defendant, Seamus Soroghan, was later convicted for firearms offences and sentenced to five years.[13] Ironically, the option that Soroghan was not offered amounts, in effect, to an invitation to extradition and is unlikely to be taken up by many of those charged under the CL(J)A. The error, however, indicates that an unfamiliarity with the provisions of the legislation was not confined to the authorities in Ulster.

Two further cases appear involving individuals from the same group who escaped from Crumlin Road Jail in June 1981. In the first instance, Michael Ryan had been awaiting trial for a 1979 murder and Robert Campbell was actually on trial when they escaped. Campbell was sentenced *in absentia* to life on a murder charge June 12, 1981. A total of twelve RUC personnel gave evidence concerning the escape and the ensuing gunbattle during the recapture in Eire. Ryan and Campbell pleaded not guilty to a charge of escaping lawful custody, attempted murder and firearms possession. Acquitted of the attempted murder charge they were convicted of escape and sentenced in December to ten years each.[14] In that month and in January 1982 a number of their fellow escapees were also apprehended in Eire. Four of them went on trial in Dublin on similar charges and were convicted and sentenced on Feburary 25, 1982.

These later cases illustrate the efficiency of the extra-territorial laws when used in trials requiring no civilian witnesses and with offences, such as escape, which are easily proved. A somewhat more complex case, and the first CL(J)A case to concern offences committed in Great Britain, concerned Gerard Tuite. He had been arrested originally in England but escaped Brixton Prison while on remand. He was charged with offences in relation to bombings in Great Britain in 1978-79. British police flew to Dublin to give evidence once he was rearrested.[16]

In the first trial Tuite was found guilty in July 1982 of possessing explosives in England. Mr. Justice Hamilton also proclaimed himself satisfied that Tuite had hired the automobiles used in two London car bombings. A second trial for conspiracy to cause explosions in Great Britain was deferred while the first conviction was appealed.[17] The appeal failed and Tuite was refused leave to go before the Irish Supreme Court. There were seven grounds for appeal including a claim that the SCC lacked jurisdiction to try extra-territorial cases. Irish legal commentators proclaimed the decision,

> an effective tightening up of the ... legislation that could pave the way to greater utilization of the law aimed at stopping fugitives gaining a safe haven from United Kingdom justice in the Irish Republic.[18]

73

The Tuite case indicated that the CL(J)A could and would be used to cover scheduled offences committed in Great Britain if the fugitive were apprehended in the Irish Republic. The Appeal Court ruling reinforced the legal standing of the legislation. However, the extra-territorial laws were not designed as a total replacement for extradition of fugitive political offenders. As the Law Enforcement Commission had emphasized the laws were an interim measure. Developments were to take place in the 1980s which would increase the likelihood that fugitive political offenders would face justice either through the extra-territorial laws or via extradition.

THE NEW ERA

By no means did all the terrorism flow in one direction in Ireland. Various Protestant Loyalist paramilitary groups, the UDA as well as the Ulster Volunteer Force (UVF) and the Ulster Freedom Fighters (UFF), claimed responsibility for a series of bombings in Eire through the mid-1970s.[89] Some of these bombers appeared before the Irish courts but the majority avoided detection. This led to an intriguing irony. On November 29, 1975, for example, a bombing at Dublin Airport, claimed by the UDA, killed one and injured several others. The Irish Foreign Ministry lodged an official complaint with the British Embassy alleging that the North was being used as a sanctuary for Loyalist terrorists.[90] Given recurrent claims in Ulster concerning the alleged immunity of PIRA bombers and gunmen in Eire, the irony in such an allegation was undoubtedly intentional. However, as with the previously mentioned Taylor case, the courts in Northern Ireland were prepared to extradite such individuals when presented with valid warrants.

Whatever the problems in the extra-territorial method, the Ulster authorities continued to make extradition applications to the Republic. In the 69 months from June 1976 to February 1982 there were a total of 141 warrants forwarded by the RUC with 34 of these, just under 25%, related to terrorist-type offences.[91] The extradition success rate, as before June 1, 1976, was non-existent, but by 1982 changes were occurring in judicial and political areas which would affect this situation. Providing the context for these changes were the public attitudes toward the situation in Ulster and Eire.

Using an ESRI Survey for Eire and the 1978 Northern Ireland Attitude Survey as the data base two facts of particular interest emerge.[92] Two Likert items produced the following results:

Question	Response		
	Northern Ireland		Eire
	Protestant	Catholic	
The Irish government should agree to extradition, that is, to agree to hand over to the authorities in Northern Ireland or Britain, people accused of politically motivated crimes in Northern Ireland or Britain.	98%	67%	46%

74

Conflict Quarterly

Question	Response		
	Northern Ireland		Eire
	Protestant	Catholic	
The Irish government is not doing its best to ensure that the IRA is unable to operate from the Republic's side of the Border.	91%	41%	45%

While the strength of Protestant feeling in Northern Ireland is unsurprising, the fact that 67% of their fellow citizens of Catholic background, the traditional IRA constituency, believe the Irish authorities should extradite is. It is also worth nothing that 46%, or just under half, of the Irish respondents were also in favor of this point, though the Irish government remained opposed, most commonly using the argument that a change in policy would conflict with the Constitution. This argument was based on Article 29.3 which stated that Ireland accepted the generally recognized principles of international law as ruling its conduct in international relations, further claiming that one of these principles was non-extradition of political offenders. This position was reaffirmed when Eire refused to sign the ECST. The Foreign Affairs Department's legal advisor stated,

> We have no alternative but to refuse because the generally recognized principles of international law do not allow a country to extradite someone wanted by another country for a political crime. For us the matter is closed unless these should change in the next five or ten years."

Less than decade later Ireland signed the ECST.

The first change came when Dublin signed the Agreement Concerning the Application of the ECST, henceforth referred to as the Dublin Agreement." Born of a meeting in December 1979 of the nine European Economic Community (EEC) Justice Ministers, the Dublin Agreement obligates non-signatories of the ECST, or those who have imposed reservations on the ECST, to submit for prosecution under their own law those whom they refuse to extradite. The necessary machinery for prosecution already existed between Eire and the U.K. in the form of the CL(J)A. The purpose of the Dublin Agreement was to act as an interim measure among the nine countries, preparatory to the full ratification, without reservation, of the ECST by all twenty members of the Council of Europe.

There was also increasing bipartisan support in Eire for the concept of the all-Ireland Court so beloved of Fianna Fail. When that party regained power in June 1977, it was given increased prominence. Foreign Minister O'Kennedy claimed,

> An all-Ireland court is the most effective way, because you have a representative court supervising the activities of the police force and army on both sides, and the

75

Winter 1987

> court is the guarantor that the army and police, on
> whatever side, will act within the terms of the law ... any
> citizen breaking the law is made amenable to the court,
> and any citizen has the right to go to the court in the
> event of infringement of the law by the institutions of
> the state.[95]

By 1981 the new Fine Gael-Labour coalition government was also
reported to be favoring the concept. The institutional arrangements
would provide three judges, one from each jurisdiction and the third
from the locus of the crime, to sit wherever the need arose. Interrogation
would be covered by a set of common rules enforced by the court and
prosecution would be conducted by an all-Ireland prosecutor. In an interview in November 1981 Taoiseach Fitzgerald stated,

> The fact is that the problem is an all-Ireland one. They
> step across the border; but far from being a problem of
> fugitive offenders down here who can't be got at, the
> more crucial problem is the no-go area in Northern
> Ireland, in South Armagh — from which criminals
> operate into the Republic, and through the Republic in-
> to Northern Ireland, coming in and out again.[96]

Fitzgerald went on to explain that there would have to be an institutional
umbrella, such as an Anglo-Irish Council, under which the court could
function. It is this feature that causes Ulster Loyalists to be unremittingly
opposed to any such arrangement for fear that it will impinge on their
sovereignty and will eventually lead to the absorption of the Six Counties
by the Twenty-Six. These fears are summarized in a pamphlet by the late
Edgar Graham, dedicated Ulster Unionist:

> By setting up all-Ireland courts the Irish Republic would
> be invoking Articles 2 and 3 of the Irish Constitution
> which asserts the right of the Irish Parliament to
> legislate for Northern Ireland. Those articles have
> always been deeply offensive to Unionists in Northern
> Ireland. But worse than that they have always given a
> legitimacy to the IRA who claim to be fulfilling the con-
> stitutional claim by fighting for re-unification.[97]

While such ideas were discussed in political circles, the Irish courts
continued to refuse to extradite those deemed political offenders. In
some cases the connection between the political cause and the alleged offence was extremely tenuous. In July 1978 Francis Heron successfully
resisted extradition on a warrant charging that he had caused grievous
bodily harm to a woman in County Tyrone, claiming the crime was the
result of a punishment beating ordered by the PIRA. The High Court
refused to sanction extradition and though counsel for the state labelled
the action "an unconventional form of political activity," the decision
was not appealed.[98]

Not all the RUC requests during the 1970s were refused on grounds
of the political offence exception, nor did these refusals necessarily

protect the accused from justice. While bearing in mind the above-mentioned strictures concerning statistics, some intriguing facts do emerge from a compilation of extradition requests for Republican fugitives in the period 1971-80.[99] Some eighty requests are listed with four pending for a total of 76 requests. Of these, eleven were withdrawn by the RUC (14.5%), and eighteen individuals were apprehended in the United Kingdom after their warrants had been sent to Eire (23.7%). Some of those individuals later detained in the U.K. may have been the beneficiaries of refusals to extradite by the Irish courts but the compilation does not reveal this. It does reveal that there were 45 refusals (59.2%) to extradite: 34 refused on the ground of the political offence exception (44.7%); nine refused on the grounds of there being no comparable offence in Eire (11.8%); and two granted writs of *habeas corpus* by the courts. This accounts for 74 cases. Of the two remaining, one individual was actually extradited and the other was in prison in Eire for offences committed in that country at the time of the request. Of those whose extradition was requested for terrorist-type offences almost 25% were subsequently apprehended in the U.K., weakening Loyalist assertions that all Republican bombers and gunmen were totally immune from prosecution due to the sanctuary they enjoyed in Eire.

In 1976 a lower Irish court agreed to what became the only extradition of an alleged political offender on record until the 1980s. Patrick Damien McCloskey was returned to face arson charges in Ulster, but it was not until 1981 that the Irish Supreme Court was again called upon to further delineate the Irish position. In 1971 the Supreme Court ruled on an IRA case in Magee v. O'Rourke, and in 1981 the case under consideration dealt with an offence which occurred ten years earlier. Mauric Hanlon, charged with handling stolen explosives in England, had been arrested there in January 1972, and then fled to Eire in March 1972 while on bail.[100] As indicated by the hiatus between the granting of bail in January and the fugitive's flight three months later, it seems unlikely that Hanlon was a professional Provisional bomber. Detained in Eire and ordered extradited by a district court, he appealed to the High Court which reserved judgement in April 1975. This judgement was not delivered until October 1980 when the Court held that the appellant should be denied relief on any and all of the three grounds he claimed: inordinate delay, no comparable offence, and/or commission of a political offence or an offence connected with a political offence. Hanlon then appealed to the Supreme Court.

By this point, Ireland's highest court had undergone personnel changes. The liberal interpretations of the political offence in the cases of Bourke and then Magee had appeared under Chief Justice Cearbhall O'Dalaigh, who retired in 1973 and was replaced by W. O'B. Fitzgerald in 1973-74. Fitzgerald, in turn, was replaced by Thomas O'Higgins who held the position until January 1985. The family background of Chief Justice O'Higgins was strongly anti-IRA and the Chief Justice himself had lost both a grandfather and an uncle to IRA assassins in the 1920s.[101] However, the Supreme Court of 1981 still had in its ranks two judges,

Walsh and Henchy, who had put the Irish position against extradition while serving on the Law Enforcement Commission. The court's character had altered significantly but not completely.

In its decision on the Hanlon case in October 1981 the Supreme Court held that the High Court had been correct in its original finding. Mr. Justice Henchy declared his acceptance of the High Court's reasoning by agreeing

> that there is no acceptable evidence to satisfy ... that any of the proceeds of (the accused's) criminal activities was used for the purposes of the IRA in such a way as to lend political colour to the offences.[102]

However, Mr. Justice Henchy went an important step further, and with the concurrence of Chief Justice O'Higgins and Mr. Justice Griffin, stated:

> even if it had been found as a fact that the explosive material mentioned in the charge ... had been intended for transmission to the IRA, it would not necessarily follow that the accused would be exempt from extradition on the ground that the offence charged is a political offence, or an offence connected with a political offence. There has been no decision of this court on such a point. It must be left open for an appropriate case.[103]

Mr. Justice Henchy also criticized the loophole provided by the idea of corresponding offences and called for the negotiation of new extradition arrangements designed to specify offences for which extradition would be granted. This is worth noting in light of the statistical analysis mentioned earlier.

The Hanlon decision signalled the changing nature of the political offence in Irish jurisprudence, leaving the door open for an 'appropriate case' to test the new parameters. Such a case came before the Supreme Court in Dublin in late 1982. During that year the climate of opinion in Eire regarding bombers and gunmen had grown increasingly hostile. In March the annual meeting of the Association of Sergeants and Inspectors of the Garda Siochana reflected this mood. The Association's General Secretary called for joint questioning of suspects to bolster the extra-territorial laws. He also supported the view of former Attorney-General Lord Robinson that the definition of a political offence should be reconsidered and added that the Irish government should initiate an international debate aimed at a more precise definition.

> Nowadays, so called political crimes very often involve murder or injury to completely innocent people... . How long can we allow the most vile criminals to live freely and openly in this country when we know, and in some cases they have publicly admitted, that they have committed all forms of crime including the murder of our colleagues in the North, the destruction of property and the killing and maiming of innocent civilians.[104]

Dominic McGlinchey seemed to fit just such a characterization. Interned in the early 1970s, he served time for arms possession in Ulster and formed part of an Active Service Unit (ASU) which terrorized south Londonderry through the mid-1970s. Arrested in Eire in September 1977 following a mail van robbery, he was sentenced for four years.[105] While in jail, a warrant was forwarded for his extradition, charging him with the murder of an elderly woman killed on March 28, 1977 in Northern Ireland when several gunmen sprayed her house with automatic weapons. Her only connection with the security forces was filial with a daughter in the RUC and a son in the RUC Reserve who was wounded in the attack.

Released from the original Irish sentence in January 1982, McGlinchey was immediately rearrested on the extradition warrant and ordered returned by a district court. He claimed the offence was political in an application for a writ of *habeas corpus* to the High Court. This claim was dismissed in May with Mr. Justice Gannon holding there was nothing in the appeal to connect the murder charged with a political offence.[106] McGlinchey then appealed to the Supreme Court. He dropped his claim under S.50(2)(a) that the crime was a political offence, although the crime had been acknowledged by the PIRA and McGlinchey himself claimed to have been on active service with the PIRA at the time. Instead he stated that, because he was wanted for other offences by the RUC he therefore fell under S.50(2)(b) and would be prosecuted or detained for a political offence in Ulster if he was returned for the non-political offence named in the warrant.

McGlinchey faced the same Supreme Court judges who had decided in Hanlon that the redefinition of the political offence awaited an appropriate case. Because the appellant had withdrawn his claim under S.50(2)(a) the court was not required to rule on whether the offence in question was itself political. Nevertheless Chief Justice O'Higgins, with the concurrence of the other justices, laid out what was obviously a departure from previous determinations concerning political offences. While stressing the fact that the victim was a civilian, the Chief Justice argued that civilian or not it would not necessarily follow that the offence could be categorized as political, even if the victim was killed or injured. He added,

> The judicial authorities on the scope of such offences
> have in many respects been rendered obsolete by the fact
> that modern terrorist violence ... is often the antithesis
> of what could reasonably be regarded as political, either
> in itself or in its connections.[108]

In discussing McGlinchey's claim under S.50(2)(b), Chief Justice O'Higgins developed the Irish position further. He used phrases such as "what could reasonably be regarded as political" and "the ordinary scope of political activity," alluding to a test of the political offence applied by a "reasonable man." He further spoke of the suffering caused by "self ordained arbiters" and argued that excusing offenders under the exception "is the very antithesis of the ordinances of Christianity and civilization and of the basic requirements of political activity."[109]

79

The executive was absolved of the necessity of making an immediate decision on whether or not to return McGlinchey as he had jumped bail prior to the Supreme Court decision. Legal commentators characterized the ruling as a landmark decision, but also noted that further case law would be required to confirm its status.[110] This was not long in coming but was not quite as straightforward as the authorities in the U.K. might have wished. Indeed developments from 1983-86 were strewn with basic technical errors, misjudgements and frequent recrimination on both sides of the border and the Irish Sea.

In May 1983 there were reports that Scotland Yard had identified John Downey as one of the perpetrators of the Hyde Park and Regent's Park bombings of 1982. Safely ensconced in Eire, Downey denied such action and there was no immediate attempt to extradite him perhaps because of insufficient evidence as in the McKearney incident.[111] In August, the Irish High Court granted a request for the return of Philip McMahon which was then appealed. He was one of a group which had escaped custody in Ulster back in March 1975. Jailed in Eire in October 1975 for a year term, the Ulster authorities were therefore aware of his location although they did not issue an extradition request until 1983 after the McGlinchey ruling.[112] The reasons became apparent in the Supreme Court appeal the following summer. In the interim, the High Court had ordered the extradition of Seamus Shannon (January 1984) with Attorney-General Peter Sutherland basing the state's argument on the McGlinchey ruling. The High Court judges agreed that the murders cited in the warrant were too 'heinous' to be reasonably described as political.[113] Both the Shannon and McMahon appeals came before the Supreme Court in the summer of 1984.

In the meantime, McGlinchey had been recaptured in Eire. His lawyers obtained an injunction to delay any handover to allow a challenge of the validity of the original extradition order but the Supreme Court over-ruled the challenge in an unprecedented Bank Holiday evening sitting. The panel hearing the argument was identical to that which granted the original extradition and the fugitive was placed in RUC custody at the border on March 18, 1984. In response to critics of the decision, Taoiseach Fitzgerald replied,

> It is a sad kind of nationalism that thinks that people
> against whom there are charges of murder, would not be
> proceeded against by the normal processes of the law
> and that murder could be a political offence.[114]

In the cases of McMahon and Shannon the Supreme Court produced decisions with contradictory results. The order for McMahon's extradition was quashed in June, however there were special circumstances invoived in the first, post-McGlinchey, ruling. Four of McMahon's fellow escapees had been apprehended in Eire in the year of the their escape (1975) and their extradition had been refused on the grounds of the political offence exception. McMahon argued that his escape was a political act taken to enable him to continue the struggle. In a unanimous decision the Supreme Court quashed the High Court order, basing the decision on the four previous cases.[115] Chief Justice O'Higgins explained that an order to extradite in the McMahon case

> would mean that contradictory declarations in relation to the same incident would have issued from our courts. If such occurred, respect for the administration of justice in our courts would surely suffer and the court's process would certainly have been abused.[116]

For the Irish Supreme Court, the McMahon decision can be categorized as a retreat. However, in the Shannon case the following month the judges circumscribed the political offence further. Following the McGlinchey ruling and expanding upon it, the judges were in total agreement on extradition but divided on the reasoning behind it. Two members of the Court, and its Chief Justice, were of like mind[117] agreeing that,

> the Provisional IRA have abjured normal political activity in favour of violence and terrorism, (and) the circumstances disclosed as to the murders in question here were so brutal, cowardly and callous that it would be a distortion of language if they were to be accorded the status of political offences or offences connected with political offences.[118]

It must be pointed out that while this opinion concentrated on the 'objective' circumstances, rather than the 'subjective' motivation of the offender, it went beyond the English political incidence theory which tended to avoid commentary on the morality of actions carried out incident to, or in furtherance of, a political disturbance. Mr. Justice Anthony Hederman, a former Fianna Fail Attorney-General, and defence counsel in the McLaughlin appeal, explicitly rejected the McGlinchey test of the 'reasonable man,' believing it 'could only create uncertainty' since political activities such as rebellion, assassination and other violent acts might be considered by many people to be unreasonable.[119] Hederman noted the PIRA was engaged in just such a political struggle and that acts done in furtherance of this could be seen as relative political offences. However, he drew a fine distinction in the Shannon case — because the offences charged to Shannon were claimed as 'reprisals' by the Provisionals, they could not be considered part of the armed struggle to remove the British from Ulster. More significantly, Justice Hederman stated that "the decisive criterion ... is whether the perpetrator acted with a political motive or for a political purpose."[120] Since Shannon denied involvement in the offence, his motive could not be determined and he was thus eligible for extradition. This 'subjective' test creates its own problems, as Farrell notes. It requires self-incrimination which would operate against the person if he was extradited and puts innocent persons at a decided disadvantage since they could not give evidence of motive for something they did not do.[121] Mr. Justice McCarthy rejected Hederman's approach and produced his own criterion for determining the political offence, combining both 'objective' and 'subjective' features such as motivation, circumstances of the offence, identity of the victims, and the proximity of each specific feature to the alleged political aim which was objectively determinable.[122] In Shannon's case McCarthy felt that the distance between the offence and the political purpose was sufficient to allow extradition. This approach is reminiscent of the Swiss proportionality or predominance theory,[123] and seems to combine the best features of both approaches, the one outlined in McGlinchey and supported by Chief Justice O'Higgins, and the other supported by Mr. Justice McCarthy.

Shannon had also challenged the constitutionality of Part III of the Irish Extradition Act but this challenge was denied by the court and he was returned in July 1984 to Ulster. In the meantime the Dublin High Court seemed to be backing away from the thinking of the Supreme Court, if only through negligence. Founder/member of the Scottish Republic Socialist Party, David Dinsmore, had been arrested in Eire in December 1983. Having fled Scotland while on bail on a letter-bomb charge, extradition of Dinsmore was granted by an Irish district court and he appealed. Incredibly, given the circumstances of his flight from Scotland, he was granted bail while awaiting his appeal in Eire and promptly decamped to Spain which had no extradition treaty with the U.K.[124] Such laxity did not encourage the belief of British authorities in the willingness of the Irish courts to return political terrorists. Nonetheless, in early September 1984, at a conference in London the DPP, the Attorney-General and the head of the Anti-Terrorist Squad (ATS) agreed to prepare papers for a series of extradition requests. The mistake in the Dinsmore case could not be taken as a deflection of the trend apparent in McGlinchey and Shannon.

In the challenge to the constitutionality of the 1965 Act in November 1984 Shannon's lawyers raised three substantive issues as well as a number of technical points. The substantive issues concerned the lack of necessity for a *prima facie* case under the backing of warrants system, the lack of a clause prohibiting return where the fugitive might be subjected to prejudice because of race, religion, nationality or political opinion, and that the interrogation, detention and trial of terrorist suspects in Ulster fell short of the minimum requirements of fair procedure in Eire.[125] In May 1984 High Court President, Mr. Justice Finlay, had rejected all three claims[126] and the Supreme Court held the same opinion. Both courts were, in effect, giving the Northern Ireland legal system what amounted to an explicit endorsement.

Contemporaneously, the British authorities attempted to secure the extradition of suspected PIRA bomber Evelyn Glenholmes, initiating a seventeen month catalogue of technical errors and misjudgements leavened by recrimination. In late October 1984 a magistrate in London issued warrants on the basis of information sworn under oath by an official of the DPP. They were taken to Dublin by an Inspector of the ATS, found to be faulty and returned to London and withdrawn. The errors were revealed by the DPP through a written reply in the House of Lords in March 1986 and consisted primarily of incomplete addresses of the criminal incidents named in the warrants.[127] On November 6, 1984 the same magistrate issued new warrants but these were again technically faulty as was subsequently revealed. The suspect vanished on November 8th and reports which broke in the British press on the 11th caused a storm of criticism.[128] British authorities took considerable pains to ensure that none of this criticism would be directed towards the Irish authorities and the British Attorney-General even issued a statement absolving them of either negligence or bureaucratic foot-dragging.[129]

During the sixteen months before Glenholmes was finally arrested, the Supreme Court continued to tighten the political offence exception under new leadership but the subordinate High Court seemed less eager to follow its lead. In January 1985 Chief Justice O'Higgins moved to the European Court and was replaced by former High Court President, Mr. Justice Finlay. In Finlay's first six months he and his fellow judges were faced with two more cases where the political offence exception was claimed in relation to alleged Republican activities.

John Patrick Quinn was wanted in England for passing stolen travellers' cheques and had been ordered extradited. In an appeal to the High Court, he submitted an affidavit that admitted the crime but claimed it was an attempt to raise funds for the Irish National Liberation Army (INLA) and was thus a political offence.[130] The High Court rejected this, stating that Quinn had not established sufficient connection between the crime and a political offence. He appealed to the Supreme Court which dismissed the appeal and ordered extradition in February 1985. In his judgement, the new Chief Justice went beyond the McGlinchey and Shannon decisions to what could be described as a 'new frontier' of the political offence in Irish jurisprudence. Quinn's affidavit said that the INLA, in which he claimed membership, aimed to create a Thirty-Two County Workers' Republic through armed action in Ulster, the Republic and elsewhere. Finlay declared that it must be assumed that the Dáil did not intend the Extradition Act to be interpreted in a manner which would offend the Constitution. Since achievement of the INLA objective would require the destruction of that Constitution by prohibited means, a member of the INLA could not escape extradition through the political offence exception.[131] The Chief Justice was supported by Justices Hederman and McCarthy in separate judgements. Seemingly, this decision removed INLA members from the scope of the political offence exception because they were inherently opposed to the Irish government. Such a decision approaches that made nearly one hundred years previous by British courts in the Meunier case when it was decided that anarchists could not avail themselves of the exception because they were the enemies of all governments. The decision also demonstrates a change in thinking by Chief Justice Finlay. In 1974 in the case of Father Burns, Finlay had said the crime of keeping explosives "for an organization attempting to overthrow the state by violence is ... an offence of a political character."[132] Just eleven years later, the Quinn decision seems to offer a virtual reversal of this position.

In June 1985 the High Court refused to order the extradition of

Claretan Gerard Maguire to England for a robbery he claimed to have
undertaken on behalf of the PIRA. Mr. Justice Egan, in obvious
reference to the Quinn decision, said he found nothing in Maguire's affidavit concerning the overthrow of the Constitution, therefore he was
not prepared to hold that PIRA offences could not be considered
political "until the Supreme Court tells me specifically."[133] The Supreme
Court overturned this decision and ordered extradition in July 1985 but
on the ground that there was not sufficient evidence to establish the robbery in question as an act of the PIRA. Mr. Justice Walsh did not comment on the question of whether or not PIRA offences would no longer
be considered political and thus avoided Egan's request for a specific
ruling.[134]

The aftermath of the Quinn extradition had produced some tension
between Dublin and London, mainly because of the errors on the part of
the British prosecuting authorities which led to his release following extradition. As a result of mistakes by both Scotland Yard and the DPP,
there were rumours that the British would abandon the charge for which
Quinn was extradited and pursue trial on another offence. This caused
the Irish Attorney-General John Rogers to phone his British counterpart
and indicate that the Irish authorities would condemn, unreservedly, any
such move. After the collapse of the case, Ireland lodged complaints with
London,[135] demonstrating the sensitivity in Eire where political risks
were being taken by the Executive in granting extradition orders, supported by the Supreme Court, only to see their efforts nullified by
rudimentary mistakes on the part of the British.

Such mistakes were again apparent in early 1986 in the Glenholmes
case though prior to this, in December 1985, the Dublin High Court
again showed its tendency toward retreat. A district court had ordered
the extradition of Brendan Burns, wanted in connection with the murder
of five British soldiers in 1981 in a landmine explosion. In December
1985 the High Court upheld his appeal and quashed the extradition
order, ruling that he had been held illegally and that the warrants were
faulty. Apparently an RUC Inspector had not been under oath when the
warrants were issued and thus they were null and void.[136] As with Quinn,
basic errors on the part of the requesting authorities had allowed the
fugitive to gain his freedom.

Incredibly a similar mistake features in the Glenholmes fiasco.
Glenholmes was arrested in Dublin on March 3, 1986 on the basis of nine
warrants issued in November 1984. However, during the proceedings on
March 21st the ATS Inspector who had delivered the warrants in both instances was forced to admit that when the warrants had been revised in
1984, the evidence contained had not been re-sworn in front of the
magistrate. Immediately, the defence counsel claimed this made them in-
valid pointing out that such warrants state they are issued as a result of
information sworn before the magistrate "on this day."[137] The
authorites were only able to gain a 24-hour adjournment and since they
were unable to produce any further clarification, the fugitive was released. A new, corrected, warrant was issued by Bow Street magistrates in

London on the day Glenholmes was released but a second Irish district justice would not accept that a telephone call informing Irish authorities of the existence of the warrant was sufficient reason to detain the suspect until the warrant arrived in Eire.[138] The new warrant reached Dublin on the 24th, two days after Glenholmes' release and her subsequent disappearance underground.

The catalogue of errors in both phases of the Glenholmes incident caused renewed criticism in Ireland. Irish Justice Minister, Alan Dukes, said that 'furious' was an accurate description of his government's reaction.[139] Again the British government was pushed into the position of explaining and rationalizing mistakes, while trying to defuse Dublin's anger. Northern Ireland Secretary, Douglas Hurd, maintained there was "no criticism of the cooperation we received from the Irish authorities," but added, "choosing my words with care, it would have been possible for the court to take a different decision."[140] Even such muted and implicit a criticism of the Irish courts is unhelpful in a situation which can only be characterized by terms such as delicate. The court in this instance was maintaining the letter of the law, if not the spirit as demonstrated in the Supreme Court decisions. After the errors in the cases of Burns and Quinn and the mistakes in the first Glenholmes warrants, it is nothing short of amazing that the second set would not have been checked more scrupulously for technical errors. In fact, one source reports that in November 1985 the Irish Attorney-General's office had requested just such a check.[141] Following the Glenholmes failure the British Attorney-General, Sir Michael Havers, instructed the DPP for both Great Britain and Northern Ireland to

> ensure personally that all outstanding warrants in respect of terrorist offences are checked at once for accuracy and sufficiency.[142]

That the current Irish government has demonstrated the political will to try to extradite Republican terrorists to the U.K. is clear. Indeed, in February 1986 Dublin finally signed the ECST removing the political offence from a list of crimes and legislation is expected soon to place this on the Irish statutes. Coupled with the changes in the political offence exception delineated by the Supreme Court, outlined above, and the extraterritorial legislation, this means the bomber and the gunman in Ireland face ever greater difficulties.

The difference between 1975 and 1985 is striking in terms of the attitudes of the Irish judiciary and executive. Eire was increasingly affected throughout the period by the spillover of violence from Ulster carried out by both Loyalist and Republican extremists. There was also a growing realization that the Provisionals were unlike the old IRA in both their tactics — for example, the targeting of civilians — and in their goals, opposing Dublin as well as Belfast and being more than slightly Marxist in orientation. The INLA just exacerbated this difference. The realization of these differences is reflected in the shift in judicial opinions during those ten years. In 1974 High Court Justice Finlay commented in the

Winter 1987

McLaughlin case that even such a "dastardly murder" as that committed by the appellant was to be considered political if committed by a group seeking to overthrow the government in Belfast by such means. In the O'Neill appeal of the same year, he shied away from commenting on activities which "seemed to breach any concept of humanity" and ruled they were political offences. Eleven years later the same judge, now a Supreme Court Chief Justice, signalled a complete reversal of his position in the Quinn decision, joined by all four Supreme Court Justices in his ruling.

Complacency on the part of observers would, however, be ill-advised. There is still much controversy in Eire surrounding the recent decisions of the higher courts. Furthermore it cannot be assumed that the political will to ensure extradition will always exist in Dublin. Following the Glenholmes incident the opposition leader, Charles Haughey, criticized both Dublin and London and stated his position on what he saw as a "catastrophic change" in extradition practices. He believed Glenholmes should not be returned if arrested and added:

> In view of the serious doubts I have about the fairness of the trial they would get in British courts, anybody accused of these crimes should be dealt with before our courts so that we know at least they would get a scrupulously fair trial.[143]

Haughey's doubts may be relieved by the fact that McGlinchey, on appeal, and Shannon were acquitted by Northern Ireland courts following their extradition.[144] As well, Northern Ireland Secretary Hurd has noted that of those who plead not guilty before the courts in Ulster, 50% are acquitted in jury trials, and a higher proportion, 53% are acquitted by the non-jury Diplock courts.[145] However it is unlikely that Fianna Fail will drop its opposition to extradition.

This makes it all the more necessary for the British authorities in both London and Belfast to encourage the recent shifts in opinion in Dublin. There must be a more careful attitude toward requests for extradition and the absolute assurance that human error is minimized in the issuing of new requests and in any prosecutions which may result. It is hoped that success in this field will improve the Ulster Unionists' acceptance of the Anglo-Irish accord agreed in November 1985. Advances such as this on the political front are much more likely to destroy the basis for terrorism than any movements in the criminal justice arena.

Endnotes

1. Representation of the People Act, 1949, c. 68, S. 1.

2. *Hansard,* 6th Series, vol. 6, col. 28, June 8, 1981, and vol. 52, col. 232, January 18, 1984.

3. Paul O'Higgins, "The Irish Extradition Act, 1965," *International and Comparative Law Quarterly,* vol. 15, no. 2 (April 1966), p. 370. Lists all statutory provisions for backing of warrants between England, Ireland, Scotland, Isle of Man and the Channel Islands. Warrants issued in the U.K. were endorsed by the Inspector-General of the Royal Irish Constabulary or his deputy and vice-versa.

4. O'Boyle and Rodgers v. Attorney-General O'Duffy, (1929) *Irish Reports,* p. 558. Counsel had argued that since Northern Ireland did not exist when the Petty Sessions (Ireland) Act 1851 came into effect there was no authority to extend it to the North and Meredith J. concurred. As has been since noted this was 'bad law' as the Irish government had made an order in 1924 which provided *inter alia* that provisions for execution of all U.K. warrants should also apply to warrants from Ulster. See also Michael Farrell, *Sheltering the Fugitive? The Extradition of Irish Political Offenders* (Cork and Dublin: The Mercier Press, 1985), p. 30, and Margaret McGrath, "Extradition: Another Irish Problem," *Northern Ireland Legal Quarterly,* vol. 34, no. 4 (Winter 1983), p. 295.

5. Informally, the RUC and the Garda engaged in what amounted to abduction until this was declared a 'contempt of court' in The State (Quinn) v. Ryan, (1965) *Irish Reports,* p. 70. See also Farrell, pp. 34-36, and 39; O'Higgins, *I&CLQ,* p. 370, fn. 15; O'Higgins, "Irish Extradition Law and Practice," *British Yearbook of International Law,* vol. 34 (1958), p. 294; Seamus Breathnach, *The Irish Police from Earliest Times to the Present Day* (Dublin: Anvil Books Ltd., 1974), p. 171; and Alexander McCall-Smith and Philip Magee, "The Anglo-Irish Law Enforcement Report in Historical and Political Context," *Criminal Law Review,* (1975), p. 205.

6. O'Higgins, *BYIL,* p. 305.

7. Metropolitan Police Commissioner v. Hammond, (1964) 2 *All England Reports,* p. 772; and The State (Quinn) v. Ryan, (1965) *Irish Reports,* p. 70.

8. Farrell, p. 29.

9. In re Castioni, (1891) 1 *Queen's Bench,* p. 149, and In re Meunier, (1894) 2 *Queen's Bench,* p. 415.

10. Christine Van den Wijngaert, *The Political Offence Exception to Extradition* (Deventer, Boston, Antwerp, London, Frankfurt: Kluwer, 1980), p. 111.

11. Schtraks v. The Government of Israel, (1962) 3 *All England Reports,* p. 540.

12. The British require a state requesting extradition to present enough evidence in the extradition hearing that could lead to commital for trial if the case were being tried by a British criminal court.

13. O'Higgins, *I&CLQ,* pp. 391-92.

14. S. 2(2) Backing of Warrants (Republic of Ireland) Act 1965, an identical phrase is employed in the Extradition Act 1870.

15. O'Higgins, *I&CLQ,* p. 382.

16. Bourke v. Attorney-General, (1972) *Irish Reports,* pp. 36-38.

17. The State (Magee) v. O'Rourke, (1971) *Irish Reports,* pp. 211 and 216.

18. Van den Wijngaert, pp. 119-20, and McGrath, *NILQ,* p. 303.

19. Re Dwyer, (1970) April 13 (unreported) DC, as cited in Ivor Stanbrook and Clive Stanbrook, *The Law and Practice of Extradition* (Chichester and London: Barry Rose Publishers Ltd., 1980), p. 111. See also *Guardian,* November 6, 1979, p. 5, and *Irish Press,* April 14, 1970, p. 3.

20. *New York Times,* December 6, 1970, p. 8.

21. R. v. Governor of Brixton Prison and another, ex parte Keane, (1970) 3 *All England Reports,* p. 745.

22. Keane v. Governor of Brixton Prison, (1971) 1 *All England Reports,* p. 1168.

Winter 1987

23. *Hansard*, 5th Series, vol. 847, col. 109, November 28, 1972. Of these, nine warrants were executed, eight more were refused, nine were outstanding, and five referred to persons who could not be located in Eire or were subsequently arrested in Northern Ireland.

24. Farrell, p. 57.

25. Cleaver, Fulton & Rankin (solicitors), *Submission on Admissibility — Council of Europe, European Commission on Human Rights — Application No. 9360/81, Edith Elliot and others Against Ireland* (Belfast, February 1982), Appendix 3.

26. *Ibid.*, p. 67 Those recaptured were: Thomas Maguire, Thomas Keane, Peter Hennessey, James Storey and Terence Clarke.

27. Patsy McArdle, *The Secret War* (Cork and Dublin: The Mercier Press Ltd., 1984), p. 32; and Farrell, p. 57. There was no photographic or fingerprint evidence and no police witnesses travelled from Ulster to aid identification. Just over a year later they were re-arrested and the district court granted extradition but on appeal to the High Court the offences were ruled political and extradition refused.

28. *Times*, December 6, 1976.

29. *Hansard*, 5th Series, vol. 846, cols. 240-241, November 17, 1972, and vol. 829, col. 957, January 24, 1972.

30. *Hansard*, 5th Series, vol. 836, vol. 179, May 4, 1972, statement of David Howell, Joint Minister of State for Northern Ireland, and vol. 848, col. 597, December 14, 1972.

31. *Times*, October 16, 1972, p. 12. From 1973-76 a total of 25% of those convicted in the SCC were from Ulster. See M. Robinson, "The Special Criminal Court: Almost 10 Years On," *Fortnight*, no. 175 (March 1980).

32. Farrell, p. 58, and *Times*, November 18, 1972, p. 14. In a much larger escape nineteen men fled from Portlaoise Prison on August 18, 1974 and at least two were recaptured in the U.K. — Martin McAllister seized in Ulster on September 13, 1974 and Sean Kinsella in Liverpool on July 10, 1975.

33. In re Taylor, (1973) *Northern Ireland Law Reports*, p. 164.

34. *Times*, September 21, 1973, p. 2.

35. *Hansard*, 5th Series, vol. 851, col. 40, February 19, 1973, and vol. 860, col. 1600, July 25, 1973.

36. *Sunday Times*, September 30, 1973, p. 8. The eleven individuals and the decisions rendered on requests for their extradition follow:

       Roisin McLaughlin — refused on grounds of political offence
    James 'Seamus' O'Neill — refused on grounds of political offence
   Marguerite 'Rita' O'Hare — refused on grounds of political offence
  Anthony 'Dutch' Docherty — refused on grounds of political offence
        Bernard Elliman — refused, granted habeas corpus
           Thomas Fox — refused, granted habeas corpus
       Peter Hennessey — arrested in Ulster
     Edward McDonald — refused on grounds of political offence
     Thomas McNulty — refused on grounds of political offence
       Michael Willis — refused on grounds of no comparable offence
      Anthony Shields — refused on grounds of political offence

Details from Cleaver, Fulton & Rankin, pp. 67-69.

37. *Irish Press*, December 5, 1973, as cited in Farrell, pp. 59-60.

38. Edgar Graham, *Ireland and Extradition, A Protection for Terrorists* (Belfast: European Human Rights Act, Ulster Unionist Party, September, 1982), p. 3.

39. *Times*, July 30, 1974, p. 2.

40. *Economist*, June 16, 1973, p. 34.

41. *Irish Press*, December 21, 1974, as cited in Farrell, p. 63.

42. Farrell, p. 60.

43. *Times*, May 5, 1973, p. 2.

44. *Economist*, June 16, 1973, p. 34.

45. Bartholemew Burns v. Attorney-General, (February 4, 1974) (unreported) as cited in Farrell, p. 60.

46. Farrell, p. 61.

47. *Ibid.,* pp. 12-62.

48. *Times,* December 3, 1975, p. 2.

49. *Times,* December 5, 1975, p. 2.

50. *Times,* December 16, 1975, p. 2.

51. *Times,* June 4, 1976, p. 5.

52. *Times,* April 23, 1976, p. 1. Swords was arrested along with eight others in Dublin in April 1983 but the SCC acquitted everyone of charges of IRA membership. *Keesing's Contemporary Archives,* 33482A.

53. *Times,* July 12, 1977, p. 2.

54. R. v. Governor of Winson Green Prison, Birmingham, ex parte Littlejohn, (1975) 3 *All England Reports,* pp. 211-12.

55. *Times,* December 22, 1973, p. 3.

56. *Times,* October 8, 1973, p. 2.

57. In 1976 Sean McKenna was allegedly abducted from Dundalk although an official Army Press statement says he "stumbled across" the border into a patrol. Even more conclusive evidence exists concerning the kidnap attempt on PIRA suspects Patrick McLoughlin and Seamus Grew on March 29, 1974. Grew's extradition had been requested in August 1973 on an attempted murder charge and refused. Three Ulster Protestants were arrested by the Garda on March 29, 1974 in possession of maps, details of Grew's movements and a plan indicating where to dump their victims in Ulster. The three initially pleaded not guilty to kidnap charges, but changed their plea on the lesser charge of conspiracy to assault. All received five years from the SCC. It has since been claimed that the plot was organized by Army Intelligence in Lurgan and one of the three has admitted this while refusing to identify the officers involved. See *New Statesman,* May 11, 1984, p. 12, and *Times,* June 15, 1974, p. 2. The DPP was considering allegations on two kidnappings by Army Intelligence officers in late 1984 as well. *Observer,* November 18, 1984, p. 6.

58. *Dail Debates,* cols. 450-51, April 24, 1975 as cited in McGrath, *NILQ,* p. 303.

59. *Keesing's Contemporary Archives,* 25108A.

60. Members were: Supreme Court Justice Walsh;
      Supreme Court Justice Henchy;
      T.A. Doyle, Esq., SC;
      D. Quigley, Esq.;
      Lord Chief Justice (Northern Ireland), Sir Robert Lowry;
      Lord Justice Scarman;
      Sir Kenneth Jones, Home Office Legal Advisor; and
      J.B.E. Hutton, Esq. QC, Senior Crown Counsel, Northern Ireland.

61. *Report of the Law Enforcement Commission* (Cmnd. 5627) (London: HMSO, 1974).

62. *Ibid.,* p. 3. "... if time had been a less important factor, the all-Ireland court method would call for a more careful and detailed examination."

63. *Ibid.,* p. 42. The Scheduled offences listed below along with comparable sentencing details in Ulster and Eire:

Offence	Maximum term Ulster	Maximum term Eire
Capital Murder (Eire retained death penalty for certain categories of murder into the 1980s)	Not applicable	Death
Murder	Life	Life
Arson	Life	Life
Kidnap and false imprisonment	Life	Life
Offences against the person a) wounding with intent to cause GBH	Life	Life
b) causing GBH	5 years	5 years

Winter 1987

Explosives

a) causing explosion likely to endanger life or property	Life	Life
b) attempting to cause an explosion likely to ... or possessing explosives with intent to ...	Life	Life
c) making or possessing explosives in suspicious circumstances	14 years	14 years

Robbery and Burglary

a) robbery	Life	Life
b) aggravated burglary	Life	Life

Firearms

a) possession with intent to endanger life or seriously damage property	Life	20 years
b) possession in suspicious circumstances	10 years	5 years
c) carrying with criminal intent	14 years	10 years
Hijacking of vehicles	15 years	15 years
Membership of illegal organizations	5 years	7 years
Inciting or inviting people to join illegal organizations	5 years	10 years

Taken from *Hansard*, 5th Series, vol. 918, cols. 473-74, November 1, 1976.

64. *Times*, March 7, 1985, p. 9, and January 3, 1974, p. 1.

65. *Times*, December 6, 1975, p. 2.

66. *Economist*, March 9, 1974, p. 47.

67. *Times*, December 9, 1974, p. 2; and Michael Hirst, "The Criminal Law Abroad," *Criminal Law Review*, (1982), pp. 503-04.

68. F.H.A. Micklewright, "Irish Criminal Law (Jurisdiction) Act," *New Law Journal*, August 26, 1976, p. 856.

69. In the matter of Article 26 of the Constitution and in the matter of the Criminal Law (Jurisdiction) Bill, 1975, (1977) *Irish Reports*, p. 129.

70. *Times*, June 2, 1976, p. 2.

71. *Times*, May 27, 1977, p. 2.

72. *Times*, February 8, 1981, p. 6; and *Daily Telegraph*, July 13, 1979, p. 8.

73. Farrell, p. 75 and 77.

74. *Daily Telegraph*, December 16, 1978, p. 3.

75. *Daily Telegraph*, July 13, 1976, p. 8.

76. *Times*, October 11, 1977, p. 4, and October 12, 1977, p. 4. See also *New Statesman*, October 21, 1977, p. 535.

77. *Times*, March 8, 1978, p. 2.

78. *Times*, May 18, 1982, p. 2.

79. McGrath, *NILQ*, p. 308, citing R. v. McCartan Smyth reported as R. v. Smyth, (1982) *Northern Ireland Law Reports*, p. 271.

80. *Daily Telegraph*, November 12, 1979, p. 2; and *Guardian*, November 30, 1979, p. 28.

81. *Times*, October 10, 1980, p. 6, and Graham, p. 11.

82. *Irish Times*, July 29, 1981, cited in Cleaver, Fulton & Rankin p. 77.

83. *Guardian*, July 21, 1981, p. 1.

84. *Times*, December 15, 1981, p. 2, and December 24, 1981, p. 2.

85. *Keesing's Contemporary Archives*, 31577A.

86. *Times*, March 8, 1982, p. 2, July 2, 1982, p. 3, and July 7, 1982, p. 2.

87. *Times*, July 14, 1982, p. 2.

88. *Guardian*, May 3, 1983, p. 2.

89. For a detailed survey see McArdle, Chapter 8 "Loyalist Attacks," pp. 57-60.

90. *Times,* December 4, 1975, p. 1.

91. *Hansard,* 6th Series, vol. 19, col. 296, March 8, 1982.

92. Cited in E. Moxon-Browne, "The Water and the Fish: Public Opinion and the Provisional IRA in Northern Ireland," *Terrorism,* vol. 5, nos. 1 and 2 (1981), p. 61.

93. *Times,* January 26, 1977, p. 2. The U.K. signed and ratified the ECST and implemented it by enacting the Suppression of Terrorism Act 1978.

94. *Bulletin of the European Communities,* vol. 12, no. 12 (1979), pp. 90-91.

95. Interviewed by BBC Northern Ireland Political Correspondent for Radio Ulster and interview printed in *The Listener,* September 15, 1977, p. 327.

96. *Sunday Times,* November 1, 1981, p. 16.

97. Graham, p. 13. He was former Chairman of the Ulster Young Unionist Council, honourary secretary of the Ulster Unionist Council, and was assassinated by the PIRA in December 1983.

98. Farrell, p. 93.

99. Cleaver, Fulton & Rankin, Appendix 3.

100. Hanlon v. Fleming, (1981) *Irish Reports,* p. 493.

101. Farrell, p. 94.

102. (1981) *Irish Reports,* p. 495.

103. *Ibid.*

104. *Times,* April 1, 1982, p. 2, and April 3, 1982, p. 7.

105. Details drawn from the following: *Times,* April 13, 1977, p. 2; *Observer,* July 17, 1983, p. 2; *Sunday Times,* October 16, 1983, p. 5; *Guardian,* March 12, 1986, p. 4; and Farrell, p. 96.

106. Farrell, p. 97, and McGrath, *NILQ,* p. 312, citing an unreported decision of the High Court.

107. McGlinchey v. Wren, (1982) *Irish Reports,* p. 154.

108. *Ibid.,* p. 159.

109. *Ibid.,* p. 160.

110. McGrath, *NILQ,* p. 314.

111. *Times,* May 27, 1983, p. 1, May 28, 1983, pp. 1 and 4, and May 31, 1983, p. 1.

112. Farrell, p. 100.

113. *Guardian,* January 28, 1984, p. 2. Owen McCartan Smyth had already been tried under the CJA for offences connected with this incident.

114. *Times,* March 19, 1984, p. 30.

115. *Guardian,* June 27, 1984, p. 4.

116. McMahon v. Governor of Mountjoy Prison and David Leahy, June 26, 1984 (unreported), cited in Farrell, p. 101.

117. Extradition cases can be heard by a three-man court as in McGlinchey but all subsequent decisions were heard by all five Supreme Court Justices.

118. Shannon v. Fanning, July 31, 1984 (unreported), cited in Farrell, p. 102.

119. *Ibid.*

120. *Ibid.*

121. Farrell, pp. 104-05.

122. Shannon v. Fanning, as cited in Farrell, p. 105.

123. For further explanation see Van der Wijngaert, pp. 126-32.

124. *Observer,* November 18, 1984, p. 6.

125. Shannon v. Ireland and the Attorney-General, S.C., November 16, 1984 (unreported), cited in Farrell, p. 111.

Winter 1987

126. Shannon v. Ireland and the Attorney-General, H.C., May 11, 1984 (unreported), cited in Farrell, p. 112.

127. Lord Glenarthur in the House of Lords, written reply, *Guardian*, March 27, 1986, p. 2.

128. For details of events and their chronological order see: *Sunday Times,* November 11, 1984, p. 1; *Times,* November 12, 1984, p. 1; *Guardian,* November 12, 1984, pp. 1 and 28; *Times,* November 13, 1984, p. 2; *Guardian,* November 13, 1984, p. 4, and November 21, 1984, p. 3; and *Sunday Times,* November 25, 1984, p. 4.

129. *Guardian*, November 12, 1984, pp. 1 and 28.

130. *Observer*, August 4, 1982, p. 3.

131. *Guardian*, March 1, 1985, p. 2; and Farrell, p. 118 citing Quinn v. Wren, S.C., February 28, 1985 (unreported).

132. Batholemew Burns v. Attorney-General, February 4, 1974 (unreported) cited in Farrell, p. 119.

133. Farrell, p. 120.

134. Farrell, p. 137 citing Maguire v. Keane, S.C., July 31, 1985, (unreported).

136. *Guardian*, February 16, 1984, p. 1; *Observer*, March 25, 1984, p. 2; and *Guardian*, December 14, 1985, p. 28, and March 25, 1986, p. 3.

137. *Guardian*, March 24, 1986, p. 3.

138. *Guardian*, March 25, 1986, p. 7.

139. *Guardian*, March 24, 1986, p. 1.

140. *Guardian*, March 25, 1986, p. 7.

141. *Observer*, March 30, 1986, p. 12.

142. *Guardian*, March 25, 1986, p. 7.

143. *Guardian*, March 25, 1986, p. 1.

144. *Guardian*, February 21, 1986, p. 4, and December 14, 1985, p. 28. Following acquittal McGlinchey was returned to Eire, tried on arms charges connected with his apprehension in Eire prior to extradition to Ulster, and jailed for ten years. See *Guardian*, March 12, 1986, p. 5.

145. *Hansard*, 6th Series, vol. 80, col. 1001, June 13, 1985.

[22]

CAPITAL PUNISHMENT AND TERRORIST MURDER: THE CONTINUING DEBATE

By Major K. O. Fox, M.A., R.A.E.C.

On 11 December 1975, the House of Commons, for the second time in 12 months, decisively rejected a motion calling for the restoration of the death penalty for terrorist murderers. As in the earlier campaign leading to the Murder (Abolition of the Death Penalty) Act, 1965, the arguments have turned on the well-worn issues of morality and expediency. Those who favour the restoration of the death penalty argue that it is the only suitable punishment which matches the gravity of the crime. Those who are opposed to the measure, on the other hand, condemn its retributive aspect and argue that it springs from a desire for revenge rather than a cool-headed appraisal of how best to meet and overcome the terrorist threat. Besides, they argue further, to restore the death penalty would be a retrograde step for a civilized and Christian society and is just as likely to be seen to set the official seal of approval on killing as it would be to deter potential killers.

Nevertheless, retribution, should not be dismissed lightly. There are those who are opposed to the taking of life by the state under any circumstances, but their position is scarcely tenable when not only individual citizens but the whole population of the state faces a terrorist threat to its security. Surely whatever immorality attaches to the hanging of terrorists is outweighed by the morality of preserving the peace for all citizens. By his methods the terrorist murderer may be said to forfeit his right to live and society should be allowed its revenge for indiscriminate killing and maiming.

Retribution by itself however is not enough, for the aim of the state is to suppress the terrorist movement not simply to punish terrorists for their acts. The question therefore is whether the punishment will assist in suppressing terrorism by acting as a deterrent. Since the terrorists appear to give a high priority to death in their activities, it may be inferred that their own deaths would be a real deterrent. Although the abolitionists argued that fear of the legal consequences had little effect since most murders were committed in a moment of passion, terrorist murders are planned in advance. Accordingly, ample time is available for the terrorists to contemplate fully the consequences of their actions and it is difficult to believe that any sane person would lightly disregard the consequence of his own death.

Sanity however is not the hallmark of terrorists and, as the medical evidence presented to the Royal Commission on Capital Punishment,

CAPITAL PUNISHMENT AND TERRORIST MURDER

1949–53, made clear, mentally-unbalanced persons with suicidal or exhibitionist tendencies may well derive encouragement from the thought of their own eventual death as the culminating point of their murderous activities. Again, terrorists who believe strongly in the ideals of their own cause are likely to accept the loss of their own life as a sacrifice in the promotion of that cause. They may even see in death a means of expiation for the crimes they have committed while their apparent martyrdom may serve as an inspiration rather than a deterrent not only to the remaining followers of the movement but also to those previously uncommitted. The deterrent argument, therefore, is no more conclusive than the moral argument.

Even if it were possible to be certain that the death penalty would act as a deterrent, there would still be difficulties in defining the legal charges against terrorist murderers. Should the capital charge be murder, the difficulty would arise of justifying hanging for political killing while continuing to exempt from capital punishment those guilty of ordinary murder. At the same time of course, the legal authorities would have the added difficulty of proving that a murder had been committed for political and not private reasons. And to add to the confusion on this point, some murders committed ostensibly for political reasons are in reality motivated by personal considerations. Clearly, if the crime with which the terrorists are to be charged is murder, it would appear more logical and more just to demand the restoration of the death penalty for all murders. Should the capital charge be treason however, the death penalty could be imposed for a variety of offences apart from murder, for treason encompasses a wide range of crimes against the state. In addition, no new legislation would be necessary for the Treason Act, 1814, is still in force and it carries the death penalty, though since the Chartist uprising in 1839 its only use has been against traitors in time of war.

To use the Treason Act, however, raises a further question of morality, for the assumption must be that the state is right and the rebels wrong, not just for the murders they commit but also for the cause which they pursue. History has shown that such a dogmatic assumption is difficult to sustain and at least some consideration should be given to the rebels' cause since no rebellion is completely without justification. All that can be said on this point with any degree of confidence is perhaps that the cause may be understandable, even in some aspects laudable, but the means used to prosecute it, if these include assassinations and bombings, are abhorrent and cannot be tolerated. It follows, therefore, that the task of government is to give due weight in its policy to the reasonable grievances underlying the rebellion while dealing firmly with rebels who act on the belief that their campaign for social justice must be fought with unjust means.

CAPITAL PUNISHMENT AND TERRORIST MURDER

This being the case, the Treason Act is unlikely to be helpful for it arraigns the terrorists and their cause and makes their cause their principal offence. Besides, to resurrect this Act (which originated in the Act of 1352) in order to deal with internal disorder would be an act of desperation on the part of the government since it belongs to a more violent age than the one in which we live, when public disorder was endemic and government insecure and when, in the absence of a regular police force, severe punishment was regarded as the best preventive of crime.

In fact, however, severe punishment had little effect on crime rates and tended, if anything, to increase the incidence of the more serious crimes since thieves, for instance, had nothing to lose but everything to gain from killing those they robbed in order to avoid being identified later. The irony of the situation in the eighteenth century was that although the death penalty was imposed for hundreds of offences, many of them trivial like defacing Westminster Bridge, being in the company of gypsies, and cutting down cherry trees, lawlessness was rife and public disorder an everyday feature of life, particularly in London and the manufacturing districts. It was the introduction of the regular police in the following century which contributed most to the marked decrease in the incidence of crime and by 1861 the death penalty had been removed for all crimes apart from murder, treason, piracy with violence, and the destruction of public arsenals and dockyards. The lesson which has been drawn from this historical development is that the best preventive of crime is not the severity of the punishment but the certainty of arrest.

Accordingly, those who oppose the restoration of the death penalty for terrorist murders have argued that the more effective and acceptable alternative is to set up a system of police and intelligence which will provide the certainty of arrest. If the terrorist threat is as grave as it is in Northern Ireland, the population itself could be involved in this system, being organized, for instance, into a hierarchy of family, street, and town cells, with the heads of households and other responsible persons acting as the leaders of their particular cell, and all being issued with identity cards. Such a drastic step however could be justified only by necessity and should not be adopted simply as an expedient. Naturally the certainty of arrest would have to be backed by the certainty of conviction, and one way of assisting in this is to remove from the persuasions or coercion of the terrorists members of the public liable for jury service by instituting trial without jury. This, of course, has already been done in Northern Ireland by the Emergency Provisions Act, 1973. A further method might be to hold terrorist trials in camera and this would serve to deny the terrorists the publicity which they receive on such occasions. The disadvantage of this however is that a

CAPITAL PUNISHMENT AND TERRORIST MURDER

move towards secrecy in the affairs of the state is likely to erode the open nature of our society. Again this is a measure which should be applied only as a matter of necessity and the government should use its judgement carefully in weighing up the advantages and disadvantages of introducing it.

Having arrested and convicted the terrorists however, there is still the difficulty of finding a suitable punishment for them. If hanging is not to be used, then the only feasible alternative is imprisonment. This, of course, offers the opportunity to release those wrongly convicted and to help terrorist prisoners to become decent members of society when they are released. On the other hand, if rehabilitation fails they are likely to return to their terrorist activities when they are released and their period of imprisonment may have soured them further, thereby deepening their bitterness towards the state. Imprisonment also presents the government with numerous difficulties of a moral and of a practical nature. Should terrorists be imprisoned with ordinary criminals in the existing prisons for instance, or should we build special prisons for them? If we choose the former course we may be accused of refusing to admit the slightest element of justice in the terrorists' cause, thus supplying them with ammunition for their propaganda. If we choose the latter course, we are likely to be condemned equally strongly for using the methods of tyrants and comparisons are likely to be drawn with other states which make a practice of incarcerating "prisoners of conscience." Again, imprisonment is no more likely to act as a deterrent than the death penalty, for the terrorist can always look forward to release under the terms of an amnesty or as the result of the victory of his cause. Of course, if we reject amnesties for terrorists, as the Home Secretary has done recently, this particular avenue will be closed to them, but this too raises difficulties. Can we be certain, for instance, that terrorists are beyond all possibility of redemption? Is life imprisonment really more acceptable morally than hanging? And will the policy of the government be served by removing one of the most useful measures it possesses in obtaining a political settlement with the terrorist leaders? Surely the quality needed by the government in dealing with the terrorist problem is flexibility, and what could be more inflexible and potentially self-defeating than for the government to tie itself to a measure which the terrorists are most unlikely to accept and which will therefore block every subsequent attempt to negotiate a settlement?

Here of course is the nub of the whole argument, for the principal question is whether capital punishment for terrorist murders will assist in suppressing terrorism, specifically in suppressing the I.R.A. The chances are that it will not, and may even prove more of an advantage to the I.R.A. than to Westminster. Indeed, it is significant that many

CAPITAL PUNISHMENT AND TERRORIST MURDER

police and Army officers with experience of counter-terrorist operations in Northern Ireland are convinced that the restoration of the death penalty will simply reverse the progress they have already made. The need therefore is not to introduce such a dubious expedient, which would have, in addition, far-reaching and damaging consequences unrelated to the prosecution of the government's effort in Northern Ireland, but to provide the R.U.C. and the Army with every facility necessary for the greater effectiveness of their operations. That the death penalty has been demanded in the Commons twice in the space of 12 months is the result of the extension of the I.R.A.'s activities to England, but it would be folly indeed to believe that these activities can be curtailed while the Ulster conflict continues. The vital theatre is in Northern Ireland itself, and it is on the success or failure of the government's action there that the security of English towns will rest.

Name Index